Essential Writings of Thorstein Veblen

This volume is the definitive collection of the writings of Thorstein Veblen (1857–1929). Among the most influential economists and social theorists of the twentieth century, Veblen pioneered the development of evolutionary and institutional economics. As acknowledged by several recent Nobel awards, these subfields are of immense contemporary importance, and Veblen's enduring contribution to their development gives his writings enhanced interest today.

The 38 selections in the volume include complete texts of all of Veblen's major articles and book reviews from 1882 to 1914, plus key chapters from his books *The Theory of the Leisure Class* (1899), *The Theory of Business Enterprise* (1904), and *The Instinct of Workmanship* (1914). These writings present a wide range of Veblen's most significant contributions, especially with respect to the philosophical and psychological foundations of economics, sociology, and other social sciences. The volume showcases Veblen's use of evolutionary ideas, particularly from Darwinism, an aspect of his work that retains a high degree of relevance and importance for researchers today, making a major contribution to our understanding of the role and importance of institutions and of technological change.

A thoroughly comprehensive volume, this is the only collection to present Veblen's writings in chronological order, so that their development can be correctly understood. The volume is edited by a leading sociologist and a prominent economist, who provide extensive introductory essays that include item-by-item commentaries that place each selection in its intellectual-historical context and in relation to subsequent developments in economics. It makes for a valuable source of reference both for students and researchers alike.

Charles Camic is John Evans Professor of Sociology at Northwestern University. Previously, he was Martindale-Bascom Professor of Sociology at the University of Wisconsin-Madison.

Geoffrey M. Hodgson is a Research Professor in Business Studies at the University of Hertfordshire. He is an academician of the Academy of Social Sciences and the author of over 120 academic journal articles and numerous books and is also Editor-in-Chief of the *Journal of Institutional Economics*.

Essential Writings of Thorstein Veblen

Edited by
Charles Camic and Geoffrey M. Hodgson

Routledge
Taylor & Francis Group

LONDON AND NEW YORK

First published 2011
by Routledge
2 Park Square, Milton Park, Abingdon, Oxon, OX14 4RN

Simultaneously published in the USA and Canada
by Routledge
711 Third Avenue, New York, NY 10017

Routledge is an imprint of the Taylor & Francis Group, an informa business

© 2011 selection and editorial matter: Charles Camic and Geoffrey M.
Hodgson.

Typeset in Times New Roman by CPI Antony Rowe,
Chippenham, Wiltshire

First issued in paperback 2013

British Library Cataloguing in Publication Data
A catalogue record for this book is available from the British Library

Library of Congress Cataloging in Publication Data
A catalog record for this book has been requested

ISBN 978-0-415-77790-2 (hbk)
ISBN 978-0-415-71871-4 (pbk)

Contents

General Introduction

In the canon of American economists and social thinkers, Thorstein Veblen has long occupied a position that is both commanding and controversial as a result of a series of writings that he authored in the closing years of the nineteenth century and the opening years of the twentieth century.

This volume contains the principal items from this oeuvre and presents them chronologically in four parts, with accompanying editorial essays that introduce each of the 38 selections. The following two-part essay offers a short introduction to Veblen's biography and to the general theoretical premises of his work as a whole.

1. Veblen's life and times

Thorstein Veblen was born in Manitowoc County, Wisconsin, on July 30, 1857 and died in Palo Alto, California, on August 3, 1929.[1] The years of his life coincided with momentous events and changes in American society. Veblen's seven decades spanned seventeen US presidencies (from James Buchanan to Herbert Hoover), and witnessed three presidential assassinations (Abraham Lincoln, James Garfield, William McKinley), three wars in which Americans fought (the Civil War, the Spanish–American War, and the First World War), and three major waves of European immigration (before the imposition of strict immigration quotas in the 1920s). The same period saw the abolition of slavery, the extension of voting rights to African American men and eventually to women, and the enactment of federal civil service reform.

No less significant for the astute analyst of modern economic life that Veblen was, his era also marked America's dramatic transformation from a rural,

---

1 The fullest available biography of Veblen is Dorfman (1934), which scholars of previous generations regarded as the definitive work on its subject. More recently, the writings of Bartley and Bartley (1999a, 2000), Edgell (2001), and other researchers have exposed Dorfman's interpretive biases as well as the numerous factual errors (of both omission and commission) in his account. While no modern work yet supercedes Dorfman's biography in scope, in this section we rely principally on recent studies that deal with more limited aspects of Veblen's life.

agricultural economy to an urban, industrial economy. Economic historians Jeremy Atack and Peter Passell (1994, pp. 457–58) describe this change as follows:

> Until the 1880s agriculture was the chief source of wealth in America. By 1890 the value of manufactures was three times that of agricultural products. Industrial concerns – labor unrest, monopoly power, pollution, and occupational hazards – increasingly occupied the public attention and dominated public policy. In ... 1860, American industrial output had lagged behind that of Britain and France and possibly Germany as well. By 1894, however, the United States produced more manufactures than any other country in the world, and on the eve of World War I America produced as much as its three nearest competitors – Britain, France, and Germany – combined. Within the course of a century America [jumped] from industrial outpost ... to industrial leader.

Thorstein Veblen's family of origin formed part of the American agricultural economy during the years when it was still a dominant force – and part of the storied American immigrant experience as well. In 1847, his father Thomas and his mother Kari emigrated from the mountainous Valdres region of south-central Norway to east-central Wisconsin, as early participants in the vigorous stream of mid-nineteenth-century Norwegian migration to America's upper Midwest. A carpenter by trade in his homeland, Thomas sought the greater opportunities for land ownership that the United States offered during this period, and he proved himself a great success in this regard. By the time of the birth of Thorstein – his fourth surviving child – in 1857, Thomas had already bought and sold (for a handsome profit) one 160-acre tract, and he and his growing family had moved to another Wisconsin farm property that they would soon expand to 200 acres.[2]

In 1865, the family relocated again, moving to an area of Norwegian settlement in southeastern Minnesota, where Thomas acquired a 290-acre farm that became the Veblens' permanent homestead. Here, in the years that followed, Thomas Veblen built a large farmhouse, cultivated the soil using the latest improvements in farm machinery, and – by dint of hard work and thrift – made the Veblens one of the wealthiest and most prominent families in their county. At the same time, he and his wife took a particular interest in the education of their children, another eight of whom arrived following the birth of Thorstein.

Thorstein Veblen's own formal education began before the age of five in a common school in Wisconsin, and he received – in the words of his older brother Andrew – "a bilingual training in speech, from the start," acquiring a Norwegian vernacular dialect at home and English both in school and from

---

2 We base this paragraph and the next on Larson (1995), Melton (2004), and Joranger (2007).

his older siblings.[3] After the family's move to Minnesota, his common school education continued until at age seventeen Thorstein joined Andrew and his sister Emily at Carleton College, a recently established nondenominational Christian institution in neighboring Northfield, Minnesota. Here Thorstein spent the next seven years, the first four in Carleton's "subcollegiate," or pre-paratory program, where he pursued the classical course of study, and the final three (1877–80) in the college proper, where he followed a fixed curriculum that required courses in geometry, trigonometry, calculus, surveying, chemistry, botany, physiology, astronomy, geology, and natural philosophy.[4] The authors of the texts that Veblen encountered in these courses included some of America's leading scientific researchers, as they were then in the process of presenting to their student-readers stronger or weaker versions of contemporary evolutionary doctrines.

From his period at Carleton dates Veblen's first systematic exposure to the sub-ject of political economy. This occurred though his coursework with John Bates Clark, who in later years would emerge as one of the pioneers of marginal utility theory (which later Veblen would sharply attack). During his years on the Carleton faculty, however, Clark was more a critic than a mainstream pro-ponent of economic theories of this type, and his teachings impressed Veblen deeply. Impressing Veblen in other ways at this time was his classmate Ellen Rolfe, niece of Carleton's president, daughter of a prosperous Iowa businessman (with extensive interests in grain elevators), and the woman who would even-tually become Veblen's first wife. In the meantime, however, he planned to pursue postgraduate studies; and, after teaching for a year at a Scandinavian academy in Madison, Wisconsin, Veblen embarked on the next stage of his education.

Prior to this era in US history, Americans seeking postgraduate training repaired to Europe, particularly to Germany. With the growth of the nation's economy in the final decades of the nineteenth century, however, came a fundamental transformation in American higher education and the emergence of programs of graduate study both at newly founded universities, of which Johns Hopkins in Baltimore was the first, and at long-established colleges, like Harvard and Yale, where courses of graduate study were grafted onto older arrangements for the education of undergraduate boys. At institutions of both types, younger cohorts of faculty members increasingly conceived of themselves as research-oriented scholars, dedicated to the intellectual advance of their specialized fields of knowledge production and to the training of future generations of academic researchers. Concomitantly, university admin-istrators proved increasingly willing to recognize and to support the develop-ment of many newer fields of knowledge, not only within the traditional boundaries of the natural sciences and the humanities, but also within the

---

3 Andrew Veblen made this comment in a letter to Joseph Dorfman, dated February 25, 1930. Andrew Veblen Papers, Minnesota State Historical Society.
4 On Veblen's education at Carleton, see Bartley and Bartley (2002) and Hilleman (2004).

upstart precincts of the social sciences, where separate departments and disciplines of political economy, psychology, anthropology, and sociology began to take root and to acquire differentiated identities. Onward from the time of his departure from the upper Midwest in 1881, Veblen's own intellectual career continually intertwined with this unfolding educational revolution.

Indeed, Veblen's first destination was Johns Hopkins University itself. Here, during the fall term of 1881, he took courses with philosophers George S. Morris and Charles S. Peirce, historian Herbert Baxter Adams, and economist Richard T. Ely—all of them dynamic young figures in their respective fields of scholarship—before relocating to Yale University in early 1882. At Yale, Veblen studied with philosopher (and university president) Noah Porter, under whom he completed a PhD in philosophy in 1884 with a dissertation on the German philosopher Immanuel Kant. While at Yale, Veblen also worked closely both with philosopher George T. Ladd, who was then finishing a pioneering treatise of physiological psychology, and with political economist (and outspoken public controversialist) William Graham Sumner, who propounded the social evolutionary theories of British philosopher Herbert Spencer and was, at this point, transitioning into the field of sociology.[5]

Veblen's time at Yale was followed by an interval of nearly seven years spent away from the academic world and residing with family members back in the Midwest.[6] During the first four years of this period, he lived mainly on his parents' farmstead in Minnesota, recovering slowly from a state of seriously debilitated health brought on in part by malaria, which he had contracted at Yale. In the spring of 1888, Veblen married Ellen Rolfe and then moved to the home of her parents in the town of Stacyville, Iowa. Throughout this entire period, he continued to read the contemporary scholarly literature voraciously, and in early 1889 began making inquiries about possible faculty positions at several Midwestern colleges. When none of these possibilities materialized, Veblen, who was likely aware of the rising demand in American colleges and universities for teachers of political economy, decided that he would return to graduate school to obtain a PhD in economics (which had been his minor field at Yale).[7]

With this aim in view, Veblen left in early 1891 to attend Cornell University (in Ithaca, New York), which had recently established a School of History and Political Science that included a large Department of Economics and also offered funds for graduate student fellowships. At Cornell, he studied with institutional historians Moses Coit Tyler and Herbert Tuttle but was principally a student of orthodox conservative economist J. Laurence Laughlin,[8]

---

5 On Veblen's education at Johns Hopkins and Yale, see Camic (2011).
6 For a thorough account of this period, see Bartley and Bartley (1999a).
7 Veblen thus joined many of the greatest economists – including Smith, Marx, Mill, Marshall, and latterly Keynes and Schumpeter – in having training in philosophy as well as economics.
8 On Veblen at Cornell, see Viano (2009) and Camic (2011).

who hereafter became a major figure in Veblen's academic career. When the University of Chicago opened its doors in 1892, Laughlin became the chairman of its new Department of Political Economy and was authorized to staff the department as he saw fit. A great admirer of Veblen's intellect, Laughlin brought Veblen with him to Chicago, and it was at the University of Chicago that Veblen remained until 1906. In these years, he slowly ascended the university's byzantine hierarchy of positions, serving, in turn, as Graduate Fellow (1892–93), Reader in Political Economy (1893–94), faculty Associate (1894–96), and faculty Instructor (1896–1900), before belatedly receiving the title of Assistant Professor (1900–06) (Laughlin 1916, pp. 7, 10). Throughout this period, Veblen also served as managing editor of the *Journal of Political Economy*, which Laughlin founded and edited.

Veblen's move to Chicago occurred at the start of a watershed decade in America's Gilded Age, and Chicago furnished a keen vantage point from which to view *fin de siècle* society. In regard to the nation at large in this period, Richard McCormick (1997, pp. 117–18) writes:

> Historians now regard the 1890s as a momentous turning point in American history. Within a single decade, immigration from southern and eastern Europe emerged as one of the greatest forces in the long history of the peopling of America. A new culture of leisure and consumption that would dominate twentieth-century life made its first ... appearance. The movement toward consolidation in business and industry took long strides toward permanently transforming the nation's economy. The political parties went through their most dramatic realignment since before the Civil War. And the United States burst onto the world stage. ... Many Americans living during the 1890s probably were at least dimly aware of these fateful developments, [and] most people experienced those years as a time of crisis.

With respect to the economy, the accelerating movement toward industrial consolidation proved especially forceful, and by the decade's end more than 1,800 smaller firms were swallowed up in the course of business mergers. Simultaneously, due to technological changes that made possible the mass production and mass distribution of manufactures and due as well to organizational changes that facilitated the integration of processes of mass production and distribution, "a new kind of firm – the modern business enterprise" – emerged and rose to prominence in the hands of "robber barons" who reaped vast profits from these new arrangements,[9] at the same time as they violently repressed the efforts of factory workers to organize, as vividly demonstrated by brutal crackdowns on the strike against the Carnegie Steel Company in Homestead, Pennsylvania, in 1892 and on the strike at the Pullman Railroad Company on the south side of Chicago in 1894.

9 Here we follow the account of Atack and Passell (1994, p. 472).

The years between 1893 and 1897 were marked also by the most serious economic depression that America had experienced up to this point in its history. Closing tens of thousands of businesses and hundreds of banks, the depression of the 1890s hit farmers and factory workers with special ferocity, leaving millions unemployed and spawning armies of vagabonds who roamed the countryside in search of food. The crisis was particularly widespread in Chicago, which had recently taken shape as America's first "industrial metropolis"[10] – and as a place where "wealth became the main criterion of social standing"[11] – and which provided a showcase of new forms of economic organization (in leading industries such as railroads and meat-processing) and of the complex social problems that accompanied these forms. In Chicago during the first year of the depression alone, 20 percent of the workforce stood jobless, while a contemporary observer reported: "the depression and panic of 1893–94 [are] nowhere else so severe as in Chicago, [which is undergoing] unprecedented extremes of poverty, unemployment, and unrest" (Ray Stannard Baker, as quoted by Painter 2008, p. 117).

At the newly opened University of Chicago, however, the vast philanthropic resources of Standard Oil tycoon John D. Rockefeller provided an effective shield against these economic torrents and allowed University President William Rainey Harper to proceed with plans to build a world-class university in the sciences, the humanities, and the social sciences. As a consequence of Harper's efforts, Veblen had as his colleagues, during his time at Chicago, not only a number of other important economists (in addition to Laughlin, Adolph Miller, and William Caldwell, and, in later years, former graduate students Wesley Mitchell and Herbert Davenport), but leading figures such as John Dewey in Philosophy and Psychology, W. I. Thomas and Frederick Starr in Sociology and Anthropology, and Jacques Loeb in Physiology – with all of whose work Veblen became deeply engaged. In this stimulating milieu, Veblen's own writings, which had been meager up to this point, began to pour forth, and his years at Chicago became the most productive of his career. In this period, Veblen wrote nine of the fourteen items in Part I of this volume and all fifteen items that make up Parts II and III. Among these writings are Veblen's first two books, *The Theory of the Leisure Class* (1899) and *The Theory of Business Enterprise* (1904), both classics in the literature of the social sciences.

Early on in these years of intense intellectual productivity, Veblen's first marriage broke apart, and in 1896 he asked his wife Ellen for a divorce.[12] His explanation to her was that he was in love with a graduate student in his

---

10 The comment is that of Cashman (1993, p. 40). More generally for Chicago in this period, we draw on Cronon (1991) and Miller (1996).

11 The remark is that of Bessie Louise Pierce, an early historian of Chicago, as quoted by Papke (1999, p. 1).

12 In this paragraph, we draw on Jorgensen and Jorgensen (1999), as supplemented by Bartley and Bartley (1999a, 1999b) and Eby (1999, 2001).

department, Sarah Hardy. Although (so far as scholars can determine) Hardy did not reciprocate Veblen's romantic affections and the relationship between the two remained platonic, Ellen immediately left Veblen and (apart from a brief reconciliation in 1906–07) lived separately from him for the next sixteen years, until in 1912 she finally consented to their divorce. Throughout this period, Ellen monitored Veblen's connections with other women, and on two documented occasions she used pieces of information in her possession to insinuate impropriety and damage his career. The first of these instances took place in Chicago in 1904 when Ellen communicated to President Harper – already adverse to Veblen because of his criticisms of contemporary economic institutions – rumors of marital infidelities, which led Harper to advise Veblen to seek employment elsewhere (or risk dismissal at any point). A second similar episode occurred subsequently at Stanford. By these actions, Ellen fomented Veblen's enduring reputation as an incorrigible womanizer, although modern historians generally agree that there is clear evidence of only one marital infidelity. Sometime in 1904–05, while separated from Ellen, Veblen (then in his upper forties) began what evolved into a continuing affair with Ann Bradley Bevans, twenty years his junior, daughter of a prominent Chicago educator, and soon-to-be-divorced mother of two – the woman who, after his divorce, became Veblen's second wife.

By that point, Veblen was long departed from the University of Chicago, from which he moved in 1906 to become an associate professor of economics at Stanford University, another of the country's newly established institutions of higher education (built, in this case, from the wealth of Southern Pacific Railway magnate Leland Stanford). Veblen found appealing Stanford's bucolic setting in the San Francisco Bay area of California, and the school's faculty included several scholars pertinent to his interests, among them economists Allyn Young and former Chicago student Harry A. Millis, as well as philosopher Henry Stuart (another former student). Veblen's friend Jacques Loeb and Veblen's former colleague (and student) Wesley Mitchell were then nearby at the University of California in Berkeley, and this fresh environment initially proved congenial to Veblen's work. While at Stanford, he wrote several major articles, including the first five of the seven selections in Part IV (the two remaining selections also were both begun in this period, although not completed until shortly afterwards). Within a few years of his arrival in Palo Alto, California, however, Veblen encountered opposition from Stanford President David Starr Jordan. Previously an admirer of Veblen's writings, Starr summarily forced Veblen's resignation from the university in 1909 after Ellen Veblen came forth with sordid information about his personal life (see Jorgensen and Jorgensen 1999).

Additional relocations punctuated the final decades of Veblen's life,[13] against the larger backdrop of America's continuing industrial expansion and

---

13 On Veblen's career during these years, we follow Bartley and Bartley (1999a,) and Jorgensen and Jorgensen (1999).

growing international role, as well as the activities of Progressive social reform movements – many of whose leaders revered Veblen's ideas, even as they failed to enlist his participation. Following his resignation from Stanford, Veblen held positions on the faculty of the University of Missouri's School of Commerce in the town of Columbia, Missouri (1911–18), on the research staff of one of the US government's World War I planning agencies (the Food Administration) in Washington, DC (1918), and on the editorial board of *The Dial*, a magazine that dealt with postwar economic reconstruction and which was situated in New York City (1918–19). Between 1919 and 1926, Veblen returned to teaching at the experimental New School for Social Research, which he helped to found, along with John Dewey, Wesley Mitchell, Charles Beard, and other leading New York intellectuals.

In this period, Veblen published six more books, *The Instinct of Workmanship* (1914), *Imperial Germany and the Industrial Revolution* (1915), *The Higher Learning in America* (1918), *The Vested Interests and the State of the Industrial Arts* (1919), *The Engineers and the Price System* (1921), and *Absentee Ownership and Business Enterprise in Recent Times* (1923). After the death of his second wife in 1920, Veblen increasingly assumed the task of surrogate parent to her daughters, and in this same period he witnessed as the circles of his own followers and appreciative dissenters continued to grow. In 1925 some 200 members of the American Economic Association signed a petition to install Veblen as the association's president on condition that he would deliver an acceptance speech, but Veblen declined the honor. In 1926, he left New York for his property near the Stanford campus, where he died at age 72 in 1929.

2. Foundations of Veblenian theory

In Veblen's writings, readers will find economic theory, socio-historical analysis, psychological and anthropological argument, radical political commentary, satire, and much else. For much of the past century, discussion of Veblen's work has tended to focus attention on his biting satirical attacks on the habits of the rich and powerful and on the intellectual gyrations of the academic apologists for the socially privileged.

Veblen's contribution was rich and multidimensional and his political and ideological stance is important. Veblen's greatest contribution, however, was in neither the ideological nor the political area. His political activity was highly limited, his contribution to political theory was slight, his excursions from theory into matters of economic policy are undeveloped and relatively unimpressive, and, despite his immense philosophical aptitude, he generally avoided the terrain of moral philosophy. Veblen was one of the greatest economists of the twentieth century. But compared to some others of this highest rank – including John Maynard Keynes, Gunnar Myrdal, and Friedrich Hayek – Veblen's legacy is much weaker in matters of policy, politics, or morality.

It is in other areas that Veblen's contribution is supreme. His theoretical critique strikes at the foundations of neoclassical economics. He undermines its fundamental assumption that individuals are rational utility-maximizers, and criticizes its orientation toward the analysis of equilibrium outcomes. Veblen develops an alternative perspective that is principally influenced by the pragmatist philosophy of Charles Sanders Peirce and others, the instinct-habit psychology of William James, and the evolutionary principles of Charles Darwin. Because of both the survival of the neoclassical paradigm today, and the proven and enduring value of these philosophical, psychological, and evolutionary insights, much of Veblen's theoretical and philosophical contributions remain as powerful and relevant in the twenty-first century as at the start of the twentieth.

The eclipse and return of Veblenian theory

Ironically, these aspects of Veblen's work were relatively neglected, even by his followers, for much of the twentieth century.[14] This is partly because of seismic shifts in the social sciences themselves. In the first quarter of the twentieth century the Anglophone social sciences were transformed by massive changes in their underlying philosophical, psychological, and theoretical assumptions (O'Donnell 1985, Degler 1991, Hodgson 2004).

In philosophy, pragmatism became unfashionable by the 1920s and positivist attitudes enjoyed a resurgence.[15] This closed down much discussion of ontological (or metaphysical) assumptions, in the mistaken belief that science could proceed on the basis of manifest empirical evidence alone.

In psychology, behaviorism displaced the earlier approaches of William James, William McDougall, and others. Behaviorists such as John B. Watson eschewed consciousness and intentionality as "unscientific" concepts because they could not be observed directly. By 1919 "what had been ... a sort of rebellious sideshow among the academic psychologists took on the dimensions of an intellectual revolution" (Kallen 1930, p. 497).

Furthermore, the project to apply Darwinian principles rigorously to social evolution was pushed off the agenda of the social sciences around the time of the First World War (Degler 1991, Hodgson 2004). Phrases such as "survival of the fittest" had been slogans for racists and nationalists, and many intellectuals supported eugenics. In reaction, a growing movement within the Anglophone intelligentsia rejected all links between biology and social thought. Evolutionary language of any kind became suspect. This was the "dark age" for evolutionism in the social sciences: "During this time evolutionism was severely criticized and came to be regarded as an outmoded

---

14 An important but relatively neglected exception is Daugert (1950).

15 The original positivism of Auguste Comte (1853) was enormously influential in the second half of the twentieth entury. Ernst Mach's version of positivism became popular in the 1890s. The "Vienna School" logical positivism became increasingly powerful in the interwar period. Positivism was the leading school in the philosophy of science until the 1950s, when it was met by the critiques of Quine (1953) and others.

approach that self-respecting scholars should no longer take seriously ... even the word 'evolution' came to be uttered at serious risk to one's intellectual reputation" (Sanderson 1990, p. 2). As Joseph Schumpeter (1934, p. 58) put it: "the evolutionary idea is now discredited in our field."

This drift of opinion profoundly affected American institutional economics. Veblen's notion that Darwinian ideas apply to economic evolution was abandoned by almost all leading institutionalists.[16] Veblen's student Wesley C. Mitchell (1936, p. xlix) eventually lost all confidence in both Darwinism and instinct-habit psychology as foundations for institutionalism: "The Darwinian viewpoint is due to be superseded in men's minds: the instinct-habit psychology will yield to some other conception of human nature." John R. Commons (1924, p. 376) insisted that Darwinism was inappropriate for the understanding of socio-economic evolution. Despite adopting the concept of habit in one major work, Commons (1934) also promoted an un-Veblenian notion of unexplained volition and made relatively little use of the psychologies of James or McDougall.

Clarence Ayres was one of the most influential American institutional economists after 1945. He inspired a whole generation of institutionalists, not only with his own insights but also with his interpretation of Veblen. Generally, his ideas were more in line with prominent movements in psychology and the social science from the 1920s to the 1960s. But Ayres's interpretations of Veblen are sometimes open to challenge, and on decisive issues the views of the two authors diverge (Jones 1986, Hodgson 2004).

For example, Ayres (1921a, 1921b) had been one of the earliest and most energetic critics of instinct-habit psychology. He also differed strikingly from Veblen in his assessment of Darwinism (Jones 1995). In his book on *Huxley*, Ayres (1932, p. 95) wrote that "since the opening of this century ... all of Darwin's 'particular views' have gone down wind: variation, survival of the fittest, natural selection, sexual selection, and all the rest. Darwin is very nearly, if not quite, as outmoded today as Lamarck." According to Ayres (1932, pp. 96–97), Darwin's *Descent of Man* "is quaint, an outmoded classic." And while he rejected the positivist label, Ayres's (1942, p. 343) philosophical approach shared with positivism an infeasible rejection of all "metaphysical" assumptions. Ayres also treated moral questions in about the same way that positivists treated factual questions; the positivist principle of empirical verification was extended to the realm of values (Webb 2002, p. 991). On these and other points Ayres diverged from Veblen, but these differences were swept under the carpet. Ayres's immense influence meant not only that American institutionalism took a new direction, but also it helped to create a legacy of misinterpretation of Veblen's ideas.

Because of broader movements in psychology and the social sciences, and like several other important social scientists of his time, Veblen's

---

16 An exception was Morris Copeland (1931). But he too embraced behaviorist psychology and Comtean positivism.

psychological emphasis on habit has been downplayed (Camic 1986). Furthermore, as social scientists were persuaded by theories of cultural determination in the interwar period, Veblen was wrongly interpreted in terms of a primary and perhaps exclusive emphasis on culture and institutions rather than a conception that also underlined individual agency (Hodgson 2004).

Given these misinterpretations, and a widespread rejection of some of the most fundamental philosophical, psychological, and evolutionary assumptions behind Veblen's work, it is perhaps surprising that his reputation endured throughout the twentieth century. But there has been a cost: the philosophical, psychological, and evolutionary character of his work has been downgraded. This volume attempts to help rehabilitate the true Veblen, by concentrating on his most fundamental ideas and removing some of the layers of subsequent misinterpretation.

The time is ripe for Veblen's rehabilitation. On by one, many of the underlying interwar shifts in the underlying presuppositions of social scientists were reversed in the second half of the twentieth century. In philosophy, Willard van Orman Quine (1953) showed that even positivism and empiricism depended on metaphysical assumptions. Some anthropologists began to acknowledge the biological roots of human nature (Degler 1991, pp. 218–21). By the 1960s the concept of instinct had reemerged in American psychology (Degler 1991, pp. 223–24) and behaviorist psychology came under attack (Chomsky 1959, Burt 1962).

After being eclipsed for much of the twentieth century, pragmatist philosophy has reemerged to become "if not the most influential, at least one of the fastest growing philosophical frameworks on the intellectual land-scape" (Hands 2001, p. 214). In psychology, after the hegemony of behavior-ism from the 1920s to the 1960s, Jamesian and other evolutionary approaches are now enjoying a renaissance in psychology (Degler 1991, Plotkin 1994, 1997). The key Veblenian concept of habit has also reemerged in modern psychology (Ouellette and Wood 1998, Wood *et al.* 2002, 2005, Wood and Neal, 2007).

As Darwinian ideas are making a comeback in contexts outside biology, again Veblen's ideas appear strikingly modern. While embracing Darwinism, Veblen emphatically discarded the idea that explanations of phenomena can or should be reduced exclusively to biological terms. Instead, Veblen (1899c, p. 251 [in this volume]) suggested a multiple-level selection theory, where in addition to the natural selection of individuals in terms of their fitness, there was a "natural selection of institutions" as well. Veblen used the concept of selection in a social context on numerous occasions. Veblen thus foreshadowed modern anthropological theories of "dual inheritance" where selection and informa-tion transmission operate at the cultural as well as the biological level (Boyd and Richerson 1985, Durham 1991, Richerson and Boyd 2004). Veblen was also one of several early theorists who generalized Darwinian principles to social evolution and inspired recent work in this area (Aldrich et al. 2008, Hodgson and Knudsen 2006, 2010).

Overall, Veblen's position is strikingly modern in the context of these and other developments in philosophy, psychology, sociology, anthropology, and economics. This rehabilitation of Veblen puts emphasis on the philosophical, psychological, and Darwinian foundations of his thought, and contrasts with former accounts where these aspects are marginalized.

Remaining sections in this part of the General Introduction are organized thematically. We start with some fundamental philosophical themes and move progressively toward psychological, theoretical, and policy issues. It is impossible to give a full outline of his work in the space available, so the following sections are intended to complement other existing accounts.

Veblen on positivism, ontological commitments, and causality

Veblen was a deeply philosophical writer. As Stanley Daugert (1950, p. 1) remarked: "Not until we understand Veblen's philosophy can we assess fully the extent of his contributions to our knowledge of economic processes." But his emphasis on causality and other "metaphysical" principles have been overlooked because the social sciences have been seduced by forms of positivism that denied the relevance of unobservables for science.

"Positivism" is a widely used word that has acquired several meanings. In its original Comtean sense, it meant the rejection of metaphysics and a view that science operates by the collection of evidence, with the goal of prediction rather than causal explanation (Comte 1853, Lenzer 1998). Most accounts of positivism stress its rejection of value judgments from science. Ayres and many other critics of "positivism" explicitly counter this rejection, while sharing with positivism its rejection of metaphysics.

We take the attempt to reject metaphysics first, and consider the question of value judgments in the following section. In contrast to Auguste Comte, Veblen believed that metaphysical (ontological) assumptions were unavoidable. He explicitly countered the positivist rejection of metaphysics and asserted the importance of causal explanation. He rejected the view that science could be founded on experience or experiment alone, without additional presuppositions that themselves cannot be grounded upon observation. Veblen (1900a, p. 226 [in this volume]) argued that the "ultimate term or ground of knowledge is always of a metaphysical character." For Veblen (1900a, pp. 233–34 [in this volume]), "a point of view must be chosen" and consequently the "endeavor to avoid all metaphysical premises fails here as everywhere." For Veblen, unlike the positivists, "metaphysical" was not a term of abuse. Veblen rightly held that some "metaphysical presuppositions" were necessary and unavoidable for science.[17]

---

17 See Veblen (1900a, pp. 226, 233 [in this volume]; 1904b, pp. 311, 314, 344; 1906a, p. 363 [in this volume]; 1914, pp. 260, 336). The consensus view among modern philosophers of science is that "metaphysical presuppositions" or ontological commitments are unavoidable. See Quine (1953), Kuhn (1970), Popper (1972), Caldwell (1982), and many others.

Also against Comte, Veblen asserted the need for science to impute causal relations. David Hume had rightly pointed out that no causal connection can itself be observed. The imputation of causal connections must always involve preconceptions by the analyst, and such imputations cannot be derived from experience or data alone. Hence, for Comte, any investigation into causes is biased and futile. Taking a contrary view, Veblen (1906a, p. 363 [in this volume]) appropriately identified the "preconception of causation" as necessary for "the actual work of scientific enquiry." As Veblen (1908d, p. 479 n. 2 [in this volume]) elaborated:

> Causal sequence ... is of course a matter of metaphysical imputation. It is not a fact of observation, and cannot be asserted of the facts of observation except as a trait imputed to them. It is so imputed, by scientists and others, as a matter of logical necessity, as a basis of systematic knowledge of the facts of observation.

Veblen (1914, p. 260) repeated, in a similar vein, again redolent of Hume: "The principle, or 'law,' of causation is a metaphysical postulate; in the sense that such a fact as causation is unproved and unprovable. No man has ever observed a case of causation." Veblen (1904b, p. 67) himself followed "a habit of apprehending and explaining facts in terms of material cause and effect." This involved a materialist ontology: "Its metaphysics is materialism and its point of view is that of causal sequence."

Aristotle identified four types of causality: the formal, material, efficient, and final. His broad notion of "cause" included considerations of the origin, nature, form, and material constitution of phenomena. In modern usage, causes refer more narrowly to factors leading to an effect. As Jochen Runde (1998, p. 154) put it: "a cause of an event [includes] anything that contributes, or makes a difference, to the realization of that event in one or more of its aspects." Within this narrower and more dynamic meaning of "cause," two of Aristotle's categories remain: efficient and final causality. Efficient causality is similar to the concept of causality in the modern natural sciences. "Efficient" here does not necessarily mean optimal or unwasteful: it simply means capable of having an effect. "Final" causality is teleological in character: it is directed towards a purpose or aim. Hence Aristotle promoted a causal pluralism, with a separation between "efficient" and "final" causes. Much later, René Descartes retained another similar division, with his dualistic separation of physical forces from the independent, volitional, and supposedly immaterial human soul.

Veblen also used the term "sufficient reason." This confusing term derives from the philosopher Gottfried Leibniz and has since carried many different meanings (some of which contradict one another) including: (i) every event has a cause, or (ii) every event has a reasonable and justifiable explanation, or (iii) God's reason lies behind events, or (iv) human reason is sufficient to explain events, or that (v) some events are the consequences of reason.[18] Voltaire in *Candide* satirized the second and third meanings. Veblen (1904b, p. 311, 1909c [Selection 36 in this volume]) rejected the view that human reason is sufficient to explain events. He saw "sufficient reason" as viable in the limited sense that some events are consequences of reason, but regarding this as partial and inadequate. Veblen also upheld that every event has a cause, but he never used the term "sufficient reason" to describe this proposition.

Like many modern philosophers, Veblen opposed causal dualism. He advocated a form of materialism where all causes are efficient in the Aristotelian sense. Reasons and intentions are causes, but they themselves are ultimately the outcome of material causes. For Veblen (1909c, p. 516 [in this volume]) "hedonistic economics" – which is based on the idea of utility maximization – is "confined to the ground of sufficient reason instead of proceeding on the ground of efficient cause." Veblen continues:

> The contrary is true of modern science, generally (except mathematics), particularly of such sciences as have to do with the phenomena of life and growth. ... The two methods of inference – from sufficient reason and from efficient cause – are out of touch with one another and there is no transition from one to the other; no method of converting the procedure or the results of the one into those of the other.

This passage is an important philosophical criticism of ontologies with two or more modes of causation, including (a) outcomes traceable ultimately to human intentions or reasons (Aristotle's "final cause") described here by Veblen as "sufficient reason," and (b) outcomes resulting from material forces (Aristotle's "efficient cause"). Veblen makes the important point that if there were multiple modes of causality, then how would one affect another? For instance, by what precise mechanism or linkage could ideas affect material circumstances? To deal with this problem one must assume either that material reality consists of ideas, or that ideas emerge from a material basis in the brain. Veblen took the latter position.

Others since have echoed Veblen's argument against separate types of cause and rejected a dualism of matter, on the one hand, and mind and reason, on the other. For example, Barry Hindess (1989, p. 150) asked pertinently: "If human action is subject to two distinct modes of determination, what happens when they conflict, when intentionality pushes one way and causality pushes another?" We do not and cannot know the answer, because to reach it would involve the reconciliation of irreconcilables. John Searle (1997, pp. xii–xiii) similarly remarked: "dualism ... seems a hopeless theory because, having

---

18 Bromley (2006) seems to associate "sufficient reason" with Aristotelian final causes. Despite his use of the term in his book's title and his close affinity with the original institutional economics, Bromley explores neither its ambiguities, its origins in Leibniz, nor the fact that Veblen rejected final causes on the grounds that they too are caused.

made a strict distinction between the mental and the physical, it cannot make the relation of the two intelligible." Mario Bunge (1980, p. 20) put it in a nutshell: "*Dualism is inconsistent with the ontology of science.*"[19] Veblen (1909c, p. 517 [in this volume]) underlines this point:

> The modern scheme of knowledge, on the whole, rests, for its definitive ground, on the relation of cause and effect; the relation of sufficient reason being admitted only provisionally and as a proximate factor in that analysis, always with the unambiguous reservation that the analysis must ultimately come to rest in terms of cause and effect.

While "sufficient reason enters very substantially into human conduct" and "this element of discriminating forethought … distinguishes human conduct from brute behavior," for Veblen, intentions and beliefs are all themselves caused and all require explanation. "Sufficient reason" is insufficient. This is not a trivial point, because much of social science in the twentieth century – including neoclassical economics, much of Marxian theory, the institutional economics of Commons (Hodgson 2003, 2004), most "new" institutional economics, and some approaches in sociology – has taken preferences, intentions, or beliefs as given.

While we remain on the question of causality, modern readers may misunderstand and overlook the intention behind Veblen's frequent use of the word "genetic." This word was widely used in methodological and scientific circles in the nineteenth century. It should not be confused with the modern biological term "gene," which was first introduced into biology in 1909 by the Danish botanist Wilhelm Johannsen. The German term *genetisch* also alludes to origins and is found in the in the eighteenth-century writings of Johann Herder and Friedrich Schiller.[20]

Accordingly, Veblen used the terms "genetic" and "genetic method" to denote matters of causal explanation.[21] Originally genetic (like genesis) referred to causal origin or determination. Veblen (1903h, p. 332 [in this volume]) described the "genetic" method as one that "deals with the forces and sequence of development and seeks to understand the outcome by finding how and why it has come about. The aim is to organize social phenomena into a theoretical structure in causal terms." Veblen (1908a, p. 412 [in this volume]) also wrote of "a genetic study" as "a study of economic institutions approached from the side of their origins."

---

19 See Bunge (1959), Salmon (1998), and Pearl (2000) for philosophical perspectives on causality.

20 Apparently, the word "genetic" in this same general (and not particularly biological) sense was introduced into English by Thomas Carlyle (Hayek 1988, p. 147).

21 The word "genetic" is found in Veblen (1898c, pp. 388–89; 1899b, p. 152 [in this volume]; 1899f, p. 279 [in this volume]; 1900a, pp. 235, 239, 241 [in this volume]; 1901b, pp. 315–19, 322 [in this volume]; 1903a, p. 301; 1903b, p. 327 [in this volume]; 1908a, p. 412 [in this volume]; 1908d, p. 482 [in this volume]; 1909c, pp. 518–20, 538, 542 [in this volume]; 1914, pp. 131, 159, 207, 218, 228, 326, and [in this volume] pp. 538, 542.

Although Veblen kept up to date with many developments in biology, it is clear that he was not referring to genes, and could not have done so before 1909. Instead he was arguing that general causal explanations, including of individual tastes and dispositions, were required, particularly to understand institutional change. As he made clear, Veblen (1909a, p. 509 [in this volume]) did not uphold that this explanation would be entirely in biological terms.[22]

Contrary to the positivists, Veblen emphasized the hidden causes behind observable events. Causal mechanisms may exist but they are not necessarily always operable or manifest. When Veblen (1899d, p. 192 [in this volume]) wrote that the "laws of nature are ... of the nature of a propensity," he foreshadowed a prominent view among modern philosophers of science (Bhaskar 1975, Harré and Madden 1975, Popper 1990). Central to most strands of modern realist philosophy is the distinction between the *potential* and the *actual*, between dispositions and effects, where in each case the former are more fundamental than the latter.[23] Science is about the discovery of causal laws or principles. Causes are not events; they are mechanisms that can, under specific conditions, give rise to specific events. Causes relate to potentialities; they are not necessarily realized in outcomes. This understanding of potentialities should be borne in mind when we consider the concepts of instinct and habit below.

Veblen on value judgments in science

Veblen used many ethically loaded words like "waste" and "sabotage." In *The Leisure Class* he used the extreme word "invidious" several times, but then claimed that "there is no intention to extol or depreciate, or to commend or deplore any of the phenomena which the word is used to characterise" (Veblen, 1899c, p. 34). Veblen may have been ironic, but there is no evidence that his irony masked a hidden belief that ideology and science are indistinguishable. Instead, Veblen was satirizing the many apologetic scientists of the Victorian era, who habitually invested their "scientific" work with claims that it endorsed the established order.

Contrary to some writers today – including some followers of Veblen – Veblen did not claim that judgments of value and judgments of fact *are the*

---

22   Veblen's acceptance of biological influences on behavior and his interest in racial types have led several authors to accuse him of "racism." Ayres (1952, p. 25) wrote of Veblen: "worst of all, perhaps, was his tentative addiction to racism. He was somehow persuaded that 'the dolicho-blond race' was possessed of certain peculiar propensities which shaped its culture – an idea which present-day anthropologists most decisively reject." But while Veblen's speculations concerning "the dolicho-blond race" are implausible in the light of modern research, they do not amount to racism. As Tilman (1992, p. 161) pointed out, such allegations of racism ignore the fact that Veblen never expressed animosity toward any race in his writings. No racial difference was ever seen by him as grounds for discrimination or repression. Furthermore, unlike many of his contemporary colleagues, Veblen (1934a) was critical of eugenics and wrote a satirical critique of that doctrine.

23   This distinction is traceable back to Aristotle (1956, pp. 227–28).

same thing. He might have accepted that value judgments are unavoidable in science. But that does not mean that judgments of fact and value can be conflated. The final passages of Veblen's (1899f [Selection 22 in this volume]) reply to John Cummings must be taken seriously. There Veblen calls for a "dispassionate" approach to inquiry in economics that focuses on matters of cause and effect. Veblen had strong opinions and clearly upheld many normative propositions. But he repeatedly argued that for the social scientist, analysis and explanation should have priority over moral pronouncements. In his response to Cummings, Veblen made clear his desire to disentangle factual and moral issues as much as possible. He urged economists and other scientists "to keep the cultural value and the moral content ... apart" (p. 279 [in this volume]). After provoking his readers of *The Leisure Class* with ethically loaded terms, Veblen declares that the foremost purpose of science is understanding and causal explanation of the existing and the possible. He repeatedly argued that analysis and explanation should have priority over moral pronouncements in social science.

Veblen took a similar stance in his 1901 critique of Gustav Schmoller. In a passage that is difficult to read as ironic, Veblen criticized Schmoller when he abandoned a "dispassionate analysis and exposition of the causal complex at work" and preoccupied himself instead with "the question of what ought to be and what modern society must do to be saved" (p. 317 [in this volume]). Veblen thought that Schmoller's "digression into homiletics and reformatory advice means that the argument is running into the sands just at the stage where science can least afford it" (p. 317 [in this volume]). Veblen criticized Schmoller for excessive concentration on what is "more desirable." For Veblen, such matters were "beside the point so far as regards a scientific explanation of the changes under discussion" (p. 318 [in this volume]). These are not simply casual asides by Veblen. His criticism of Schmoller for lacing science with normative opinions on "what ought to be and what modern society must do to be saved" and for proceeding in places "on grounds of taste and predilection, not on grounds of scientifically determinate cause and effect." persists for no less than eight pages in the original (Veblen 1901b, pp. 84–92).

Another example appears in Veblen's critique of John Bates Clark. Veblen (1908a, p. 415 [in this volume]) notes Clark's "uncompromising" statements in support of "the competitive system." Instead of countering Clark's normative statements directly, perhaps with some radical alternative, Veblen simply responds that they are "not economic theory." Keen to retain the boundaries between science and ideology, Veblen in a footnote questions "the scientific ranking of a botanist who should spend his energy in devising ways and means to neutralize the ecological variability of plants, or of a physiologist who conceived it the end of his scientific endeavors to rehabilitate the vermiform appendix or the pineal eye" (p. 415, n. 5).

In the same essay Veblen (1908a, p. 417 [in this volume]) criticizes Clark for elevating a normative "Order of Nature" or "Natural Law" over analysis of existing reality. Instead of "the actual run of material facts," we find "the facts so interpreted as to meet the needs of the taxonomist in point of taste, logical consistency, and sense of justice." Instead of scientific inquiry we have matters "of taste and predilection ... touching the matter of what ought to be."

Could the above statements be ironic attempts by Veblen to secure his scientific credentials among the academic establishment? To interpret his repeated insistences on the distinction between science and ideology in this way would amount to an unwarranted assault on his integrity and honesty.

Was he being ironic? The use of irony was characteristic of Veblen. But if we claim too recklessly that Veblen was ironic, then we end up treating nothing he wrote with due seriousness. We should take no statement immediately at face value. But there is no basis to assume that Veblen meant the opposite of what he actually and repeatedly wrote, including his criticisms of those who favor "homiletics and reformatory advice" over hard "analysis and exposition of the causal complex at work." If we dismiss these remarks, on the grounds of possible irony or whatever, then we are in danger of abandoning his legacy. We might end up imputing to Veblen a set of propositions that stem from our own imagination, without any possibility of corroboration in his texts.

Veblen did not treat facts and values as the same. All science is infused with judgments of value. But for Veblen this did not undermine the priority of analysis, at least as a precondition for policy. Veblen's own normative position is important and must be acknowledged, but his theoretical analysis is not the same thing. Any viable attempt to change the world is premised on a better understanding of how the existing world works.

Veblen's psychology: instincts and habits

Veblen adopted James's (1890) concepts of instinct and habit. Consider instinct first. Veblen (1914, p. 538 [in this volume]) saw instinct as an "innate propensity or predisposition." Veblen (1914, pp. 538–39 [in this volume]) clearly acknowledges that institutions are conditioned by both "the material environment and by the innate and persistent propensities of human nature" and for the latter "no better designation than the time-worn 'instinct' is available." Instinct "involves consciousness and adaptation to an end aimed at."

We should thus resist the temptation – to which many have succumbed in the era of behaviorist psychology – to dismiss the concept of instinct in Veblen's writings as archaic and anachronistic survival.[24] It is a concept that has enjoyed a substantial renewal in modern research, which no longer sustains the untenable dogma that unobservable dispositions have no place in scientific discourse.

---

24 In letters dated 1935 and 1966, Ayres recollected a conversation where Veblen allegedly admitted that he "never did" give an "exact definition" of instincts and attempts to "define instincts exactly" would be confounded (quoted in Tilman 1996, p. 106). But Veblen (1914, pp. 538–39 [in this volume]) did provide a workable definition. He also made it clear in these pages that he did not wish *arbitrarily* to "prescribe a definition" but "to indicate as closely as may be what sense is attached to the term." And "this definition of the concept does violence neither to colloquial usage nor to the usage ... in scientific discussion, particularly in discussion of the instinctive proclivities of mankind."

While Veblen retained the concept of instinct in his writing, later institutionalists abandoned it. Ayres (1921a, p. 561), in particular, described the "prolific and varied instinct literature" as "largely self-refuting." Ayres (1958, p. 25) later proclaimed: "the very notion of instincts is now scientifically obsolete." The influence of behaviorism was so strong that most other institutionalists followed Ayres's lead. Today we can read Veblen through different eyes.

For Veblen, human instinct is associated with intelligence. Veblen (1914, p. 540 [in this volume]) argued that "it is only by the prompting of instinct that reflection and deliberation come to be so employed." Veblen (1914, p. 553 n. 14 [in this volume]) recognized "that intellectual functions themselves take effect only on the initiative of the instinctive dispositions and under their surveillance." By adopting this view, the false "antithesis between instinct and intelligence will consequently fall away."

In this and many other respects he followed Charles Darwin (1871, vol. 1, p. 37) who rejected an "inverse ratio" between "instinct and intelligence."[25] This contradicts other influential social scientists. For example, Émile Durkheim (1984, pp. 262, 284) wrote in 1893 that: "It is indeed proven that intelligence and instinct always vary in inverse proportion to each other … the advance of consciousness is inversely proportional to that of the instinct." As the social sciences broke from biology in the interwar period, this false antithesis between intelligence and instinct became commonplace.

But in recent decades the contrary view of Darwin and Veblen has been reinstated. Psychologists Leda Cosmides and John Tooby (1994, p. 330) wrote of "reasoning instincts" and Henry Plotkin (1994, p. 165) has explained that: "Rationality and intelligence are extensions of instinct and can never be separated from it. … *Instinct is the mother of intelligence.*" As with Veblen, instinct is not the antithesis of reason, but one of its preconditions.

Veblen (1914, pp. 538, 544 [in this volume]) stated that instincts were "innate and persistent propensities" and "hereditary traits." But a few pages later, Veblen (p. 557) wrote that: "All instinctive behaviour is subject to development and hence to modification by habit." Several authors have seized on this latter sentence as evidence that by instinct Veblen did not mean fixed and inherited dispositions. Instead, he here seemed to suggest that an individual's instincts could be altered by an individual's development and environment. This would seem to contradict the earlier statement that instincts were "innate and persistent."

But the contradiction disappears when it is realized that in the first passage (p. 538) Veblen refers to "instinct" and in the latter (p. 557) he refers to "instinctive behavior." The instincts of an individual cannot be changed, but "instinctive behavior" can. Behavior promoted by instincts can be modified or repressed by countervailing habits or constraints. Our sexual instincts, for

---

25 Other statements that instinct and intelligence are complementary can be found in the writings of the heterodox British economist John Hobson (1914, p. 356) and the American sociologist Charles Horton Cooley (1922, p. 30).

example, are biologically inherited but can lead to a variety of behavioral forms, depending on cultural and other influences.[26]

Veblen retained both instinct and habit – nature and nurture – in his explanations of human behavior. Human deliberation and habits of thought are shaped by the social culture. Instincts help to spur emotions that drive many of our actions and deliberations. Veblen saw instincts as not only the basis of human purposes and preferences but also as the primary drives and prompts of intelligent deliberation and action. Inherited nature is necessary for nurture to function. Nature and nurture are not rivals but complements.

Veblen saw habits, like instincts, as essential for conscious deliberation. Habit is not opposed to reason but part of the act of deliberation itself. In turn, the habit-driven capacity to reason and reflect upon the situation could give rise to new behaviors and new habits. Habits and reason can interact with one another, in an ongoing process of adaptation to a changing environment. This capacity to form new habits, aided by both instincts and reason, has helped to enhance the fitness of the human species in the process of natural selection.

Veblen (1914, p. 557 [in this volume]) explained that

> the habitual acquirements of the race are handed on from one generation to the next, by tradition, training, education, or whatever general term may best designate that discipline of habituation by which the young acquire what the old have learned.

Veblen saw conventions, customs, and institutions as repositories of social knowledge. Institutional adaptations and behavioral norms were stored in individual habits and could be passed on by education or imitation to succeeding generations.

Veblen (1914, p. 565 [in this volume]) also emphasized that habits were the mechanisms through which the individual was able to perceive and understand the world: "All facts of observation are necessarily seen in the light of the observer's habits of thought." In other words, habits of thought are essential to cognition. Habits are acquired through socialization and provide a mechanism by which institutional norms and conventions are pressed upon the individual.

Veblen thus emphasized the *double weight of the past* on human deliberation and decision making. First, the natural selection of instincts over hundreds of thousands of years has provided humans with a set of basic dispositions, albeit with substantial "variations of individuality" (Veblen 1914, p. 544 [in this volume]) from person to person. The newborn infant enters the world with

---

26 Mitchell (1914, 1936) was one of the first of a long list of writer who have seized upon this apparent ambiguity, arguing that by instinct Veblen did not or should not really mean "innate and persistent ... hereditary traits" but malleable individual dispositions molded by the environment. Such thinking became popular with those who tried to turn Veblen into a behaviorist. But this reading has no clear support in Veblen's texts.

these fixed and inherited propensities. But, second, this world is one of specific customs and institutions into which the child must be socialized. The individual learns to adapt to these circumstances, and through repeated action acquires culturally specific habits of thought and behavior. These customs and institutions have also evolved through time; they are the weight of the past at the social level. Instinct reflects the phylogenetic evolution of the human population.[27] Habituation is the mechanism through which the weight of social institutions can make its mark on the ontogenetic development of each individual.

In Veblen's writings, the term "habit" suggests a propensity or disposition, not behavior as such. Veblen often coupled the words "habit and propensity" or "propensities and habits" together. Veblen (1898c, p. 153 [in this volume]) thus wrote of "a coherent structure of propensities and habits which seeks realization and expression in an unfolding activity." Here habit is tied in with other propensities and "seeks realization," suggesting that habit itself is a disposition rather than behavior. Even more clearly, Veblen (1898d, p. 159 [in this volume]) remarked that "man mentally digests the content of habits under whose guidance he acts, and appreciates the trend of these habits and propensities." Here habits are not actions, but the dispositions that guide them.[28]

Veblen's usage was consistent with the pragmatist philosophers and instinct psychologists, who saw habit as an acquired proclivity or capacity, which may or may not be actually expressed in current behavior (Hodgson 2004, pp. 169–70). Repeated behavior is important in establishing a habit. But habit and behavior are not the same. If we acquire a habit we do not necessarily use it all the time. It is a propensity to behave in a particular way in a particular class of situations.[29]

Many thinkers have difficulty accepting the idea of habit as a disposition. They prefer to define habit as behavior. A source of the problem is a reluctance to remove reason and belief from the exclusive driving seat of human action.

---

27 Phylogeny is the evolution of a whole population, typically involving natural selection. Ontogeny is the lifetime development of a single individual.
28 Ault and Ekelund (1988, p. 442) criticize Veblen for neglecting that habits "are themselves the product of past adaptations driven by economic calculations." This "mind first" criticism overlooks the fact that "economic calculations" themselves rely on habits (and instincts). The outcomes of decision and reason may sometimes give rise to habits, but contrary to Ault and Ekelund, habits are always required for decision and reason, and habits themselves do not necessarily rely on deliberation.
29 Lawson (2003, p. 333) interprets Veblen differently, "as using the term habit to indicate certain (repeated) forms of action" but does not give any textual evidence to support this interpretation. In contrast, the passages from Veblen quoted above suggest a view of habits as propensities or dispositions. Furthermore, Veblen was immersed in a pragmatist milieu where a dispositional interpretation of habits was preeminent. Lawson (2003, p. 48) also argues that discursive reflection and habits "require, and causally condition, each other. Although everything in the social world turns on human practice, no feature of social life warrants explanatory/analytical priority." This symmetrical treatment of deliberation and habit is wrong. Reason always requires habit to begin to operate. But the reverse is not always the case, because although sometimes decisions lead to habits, we often form habits as the result of nondiscursive impulses such as instincts. Furthermore, habits precede reason in our evolutionary past: we are descended from organisms that had no developed capacity to reason.

The "mind-first" conception of action pervades social science. If habits affect behavior then it is wrongly feared that reason and belief will be dethroned. The concern is that volition would be replaced by mechanism. However, from a pragmatist perspective, reasons and beliefs themselves depend upon habits of thought. Habits act as filters of experience and the foundations of intuition and interpretation. Habit is the grounding of both reflective and nonreflective behavior. But this does not make belief, reason, or will any less important or real.[30]

Leading pragmatists emphasized the priority of habit over belief and reason. Charles Sanders Peirce (1878, p. 294) declared that the "essence of belief is the establishment of habit." Josiah Royce (1969, vol. 2, p. 663) announced in his 1902 presidential address to the American Psychological Association: "The organization of our intelligent conduct is necessarily a matter of habit, not of instantaneous insight." John Dewey (1922, p. 30) similarly remarked that the "formation of ideas as well as their execution depends upon habit." In the pragmatist view, habit supports rather than obstructs rational deliberation. Without habit, reason is disempowered (Kilpinen 1999, 2000).

Veblen adopted a pragmatist theory of action in which activity and habit precede rational deliberation. By contrast, much social science takes it for granted, or by definition, that "action" is motivated exclusively by reasons based on beliefs. This proposition is undermined by modern psychology as well as the evolutionary outlook offered by Darwinism. Experiments show that conscious sensations are reported about half a second after neural events, and unconscious brain processes are discernable before any conscious decision to act (Libet 1985, 2004, Libet *et al.* 1983, Wegner 2002, 2003, Wegner and Wheatley 1999, Haynes and Rees 2005a, 2005b, Haynes *et al.* 2007). This evidence suggests that our dispositions are triggered before our actions are rationalized: we contrive reasons for actions already under way.

Contrary to much of twentieth century social science, the uniqueness of humanity does not lie in any relegation of instinct or habit, but in the critical supplementary deployment of conscious rational deliberation when a striking problem or novel situation demands it. Reasons and intentions emerge in continuous process of interaction with the world, while we are always driven by habits and other dispositions. As Veblen (1908d, p. 482 [in this volume]) wrote: "habits of thought are an outcome of habits of life." Veblen (1919c, p. 15) later explained:

> History teaches that men, taken collectively, learn by habituation rather than precept and reflection; particularly as touches those underlying principles of truth and validity on which the effectual scheme of law and custom finally rests.

30 This contrasts with neoclassical analyses, where habit is seen as based upon, and derivable from, preferences and rational behavior (Lluch 1974, Philips and Spinnewyn 1984, Becker and Murphy 1988). These accounts lack adequate explanations of the preference functions that are assumed to be foundational. Note also that Becker's (1992) definition of habit as serially correlated behavior is very different from that of a programmed disposition or propensity.

Reason is intimately connected with doing, because activity is the stimulus for habits of thought, and because reason and intelligence are deployed to guide action through problems and difficulties. Intelligence is "the selective effect of inhibitive complication" (Veblen 1906a, p. 358 [in this volume]). Deliberation and reason are deployed to make a choice when habits conflict or are insufficient to deal with the complex situation. In turn, these particular patterns of reason and deliberation themselves begin to become habituated, so that when we face a similar situation again, we may have learned to deal with it more effectively. Veblen (1906a, p. 357 [in this volume]) wrote that "knowledge is inchoate action inchoately directed to an end." For him all knowledge is "functional ... that it is of the nature of use." Hence knowledge is an adaptation to a problem situation; it stems from and assists activity. This "instrumental" or "adaptive" view of knowledge is characteristic of both Dewey (1922) and modern writers such as Plotkin (1994).

In sum, instinct is prior to habit, habit is prior to belief, and belief is prior to reason. That is the order in which they have evolved in our human ancestry over millions of years. That too is the order in which they appear in the ontogenetic development of each human individual. Lower elements in the hierarchy do not entirely determine the higher functions, but they impel them into their being, where they are formed in their respective natural and social context. The lower elements are necessary but not sufficient for the higher (Margolis 1987, 1994, Murphy 1994).

Veblen followed Darwin and James in regarding habit and instinct as the basis of motivation; they impel and dominate any rational calculation of individual interests or objectives. This was a key element in Veblen's critiques of both Marxism and neoclassical economics.

Veblen's criticisms of Marxism

Veblen was deeply interested in Marxism and socialism. He noted that Max Lorenz (1896, p. 50) had found a serious defect in the Marxian "materialist conception of history." In his own words, Veblen (1897b, p. 116 [in this volume]) wrote that in this Marxian conception of history

> it is nowhere pointed out what is the operative force at work in the process. ... The materialistic theory conceives of man as exclusively a social being, who counts in the process solely as a medium for the transmission and expression of social laws and changes; whereas he is, in fact, also an individual, acting out his own life as such.

Following Lorenz, Veblen indicated that Marxism lacked an adequate theory of human agency. It lacked an explanation of how social forces impel individual actors to think and act. Veblen addressed this hiatus in his subsequent work.

Paraphrasing and seemingly endorsing Lorenz, Veblen (1897b, p. 116 [in this volume]) rejected the proposition that the individual is "*exclusively* a social being, who counts in the process *solely* as a medium for the transmission and expression of social laws and changes" (emphasis added). Veblen did not believe that the individual's actions are formed entirely by his or her socio-economic circumstances.

But Veblen (1897b, p. 116 [in this volume]) did not deny that a human is "a social being" or "a medium for the transmission of social laws and changes." He simply rejected an exclusive stress on social determination and asserted that the human agent is "*also* an individual, acting out his own life as such" (emphasis added). This suggests that humans mould their circumstances just as they are molded by them.

As Veblen made clear in his later writings, explanations of socio-economic evolution must involve individual agents as well as institutions and structures. But the evolution of individuality must itself be explained. This need for an explanation of origin led Veblen to conceive the individual in both biological and socio-economic terms. But he also emphasized that socio-economic outcomes are irreducible to a biotic substratum.

Veblen developed his criticisms of Marxism, while retaining a strong Marxian influence in his thought. Veblen (1901a, p. 300 [in this volume]) observed that the theory of human motivation in Marxism is largely one of rational appraisal of class interest, without any explanation of how the criteria and procedures of rationality themselves evolve. Veblen (1906b, pp. 377–78 [in this volume]) also emphasized that any rational appraisal of interests does not itself explain how people acquire their beliefs and seek particular objectives. Veblen (1907, p. 392 [in this volume]) also brought Darwinism into his critique:

> Under the Darwinian norm it must be held that men's reasoning is largely controlled by other than logical, intellectual forces; that the conclusion reached by public or class opinion is as much, or more, a matter of sentiment than of logical inference; and that the sentiment which animates men, singly or collectively, is as much, or more, an outcome of habit and native propensity as of calculated material interest.

This crucial emphasis on habit as a key mechanism by which social conditions affect individual preferences and beliefs distinguished Veblen from Marx.[31] Veblen argued that the mere class position of an individual as a wage laborer or a capitalist tells us very little about the specific conceptions or habits of thought, and thereby the likely actions, of the individuals involved. Individual interests do not necessarily lead to accordant individual actions. As Veblen (1907, p. 392 [in this volume]) pointed out, and as sophisticated Marxists such as Antonio

---

31 In an attempt to synthesize Veblen and Marx, O'Hara (2000, p. 49) missed the point that Veblen found lacking in Marxism any explanation of the causal mechanisms by which social structures may affect human attitudes or behavior. It is true that both Veblen and Marx identified "structural conditions which fundamentally condition human behavior in groups." But the question is *how* social structures affect preferences or behavior. Veblen found this mechanism in his theory of habit. Marx proposed no equivalent mechanism.

Gramsci (1971, pp. 163–65) later emphasized, the members of the working class could perceive their own salvation just as much in terms of patriotism or nationalism as in socialist revolution. The class position of an agent – exploiter or exploited – does not itself lead to any particular view of reality or pattern of action. Marxism lacked an explanation of how structures or institutions affected individual purposes or inclinations. Abram Harris (1932, p. 743) later suggested that for Marx this was "the weakest link in his chain of reasoning."

From Veblen's evolutionary and Darwinian perspective, individual and social structure were in a process of coevolution, rather than one being the determinant of the other. Veblen's insistence on the evolution of individuality also led to critiques of some of the central propositions of orthodox economics, as noted below.

While Veblen shared many of Marx's perspectives, including the idea that individuals were molded by their social circumstances, he departed from Marx on key points. In particular, for Veblen, the fact that social institutions could profoundly affect individuals did not mean that individuals were infinitely impressionable. Much more than Marx, Veblen pointed to the biological, structural, and historical limits to human malleability. His discourse on human nature was not reduced to an account of social structure. He thus acknowledged variations between individuals, even in a single culture.

Veblen on methodological individualism and holism

By both supporters and critics, Veblen is sometimes described as a methodological collectivist or holist (Dugger and Sherman 1994, p. 107). Some cite passages such as the following, where Veblen (1909c, p. 519 [in this volume]) wrote:

> Not only is the individual's conduct hedged about and directed by his habitual relations to his fellows in the group, but these relations, being of an institutional character, vary as the institutional scheme varies. The wants and desires, the end and aim, the ways and means, the amplitude and drift of the individual's conduct are functions of an institutional variable that is of a highly complex and wholly unstable character.

Hence some commentators, whether approvingly or critically, describe Veblen as a "methodological collectivist" or "holist," who emphasized the determination of individuals by structures, institutions, or culture.[32] But Veblen did

---

32 For example, Broda (1998, p. 222) argues that for Veblen, "individual intentions are reduced to their institutional conditioning" leading to a "neutralization of the individual." This view is unsupported by any quotation from Veblen, and it is denied by Veblen's words quoted here. Khalil (1995, pp. 555–56) wrote: "Inspired by Veblen's legacy, old institutional economists generally tend to view the preferences of agents as, in the final analysis, determined by cultural norms." To be sure, some original institutionalists, particularly Ayres (1918, p. 57; 1936, p. 235; 1952, p. 41; 1961, p. 175), underestimated the role of the individual (Hodgson 2004). But this was not true of Veblen, who insisted that social science must "formulate its theoretical results in terms of individual conduct" (1909c, p. 519 [in this volume]).

not believe that social wholes entirely determine the individual parts. On the following page (p. 52 [in this volume]) he immediately goes on to emphasize that institutions are a product of individuals in a group, and institutions cannot exist without individuals:

> The growth and mutations of the institutional fabric are an outcome of the conduct of the individual members of the group, since it is out of the experience of the individuals, through the habituation of individuals, that institutions arise; and it is in this same experience that these institutions act to direct and define the aims and end of conduct. It is, of course, on individuals that the system of institutions imposes those conventional standards, ideals and canons of conduct that make up the community's scheme of life. Scientific inquiry in this field, therefore, must deal with individual conduct and must formulate its theoretical results in terms of individual conduct.

It cannot be more clear that while Veblen believed that institutions affect individual "wants and desires," he also insisted that social processes operate through individuals, that institutions "are an outcome of the conduct of the individual members of the group," and that it is "out of the experience of the individuals ... that institutions arise."

While Veblen took a balanced position, Malcolm Rutherford (1984, p. 345) quotes two of the former three sentences in isolation and concludes that Veblen was a methodological individualist. But Rutherford does not make it sufficiently clear what he means by this ambiguous term (Hodgson 2007). Clearly, Veblen does not state that explanations must *exclusively* be in terms of individuals, even if individuals are essential to the explanation. An appreciation of Veblen's broader methodological position is gained by placing the above statement in the context of the passages that precede, succeed, and qualify it.

Terms such as "methodological collectivism" and "methodological individualism" are used in a variety of different ways. Clearly, if "methodological collectivism" means that explanations of social phenomena must be entirely in terms of structures, institutions, or culture (and not individuals), then Veblen was not a methodological collectivist.

Similarly, despite its widespread usage, there is no consensus on a clear meaning of methodological individualism (Udéhn 2001, Hodgson 2007). If it means explanations in terms of individuals alone, then it is not implemented in practice (Arrow 1994). If it means explanations in terms of individuals *plus* relations between individuals, then it is difficult to find exceptions to this practice in modern social science. And if both individuals and their structural relations are important, then the one-sided emphasis on individuals in the term "methodological individualism" is misleading. Similar problems apply to methodological collectivism. If individuals are also included here in the *explanantia,* then the meanings of methodological collectivism and individualism converge!

At least if these terms retain strict and distinguishable meanings, Veblen was neither a methodological collectivist nor a methodological individualist (Hodgson 2004, 2007). For him, explanations of social phenomena could be reduced entirely to neither institutions, structures, culture, nor individuals. He saw both social institutions and individual agency as mutually constitutive. Both individuals and institutions were required in all explanations of social phenomena; it was possible to dispense with neither of these explanatory terms.

Veblen's critiques of neoclassical and Austrian economics

Veblen (1900a, p. 239 [in this volume]) coined the term "neo-classical" to refer to equilibrium-oriented economics in the genre of William Jevons, Alfred Marshall, John Bates Clark, and others.[33] Because of their assumptions of self-interest and utility maximization, he describes their economics as "hedonistic." This word was also applied to the Austrian school economics of Carl Menger and others.

Although some modern writers have modified neoclassical utility functions to include motivations beyond mere pleasure, and even forms of altruism (Collard 1978), these approaches are still "self-regarding" (Bowles 2004) and involve utility maximization. Accordingly, with a caveat, the core of Veblen's critique remains relevant.

Veblen also tended to lump together neoclassical and Austrian writers. Although Veblen overlooks the much more dynamic conception of the agent in the Austrian school, the charge that the Austrians take individual psychology, preferences, and purposes as given remains relevant (e.g. Hayek 1948, p. 67).

In one passage on the "hedonistic calculus," whereby "human conduct is conceived of and interpreted as a rational response to the exigencies of the situation in which mankind is placed," Veblen (1909c, p. 515 [in this volume]) identifies a deliberative version of utilitarianism. Understandably, he does not foresee the "as if" methodology of Milton Friedman (1953) and others, where attention is directed at behavior rather than the reasoning that leads to it. Nevertheless, his critique retains considerable force.

Veblen (1898b, p. 153 [in this volume]) argues that neoclassical and Austrian economists adopt "a passive and substantially inert and immutably given human nature." Then followed Veblen's famous critical lines:

> The hedonistic conception of man is that of a lightning calculator of pleasures and pains, who oscillates like a homogeneous globule of desire of happiness under the impulse of stimuli that shift him about the area, but leave him intact. He has neither antecedent nor consequent. He is an

---

33 See also Aspromourgos (1986) and Fayazmanesh (1998).

isolated, definitive human datum, in stable equilibrium except for the buffets of the impinging forces that displace him in one direction or another.

The ironic phrase "lightning calculator" points to the unwarranted assumption that agents have rapid and unlimited computational abilities. Veblen thus foreshadows Herbert Simon's (1957) notion of "bounded rationality." The point that "economic man" has "neither antecedent nor consequent" should also not pass unnoticed. It connects directly with Veblen's (1898b, p. 153 [in this volume]) argument that the requirement of a full evolutionary explanation of origin obliges us to abandon the assumption of the given individual:

> The economic life history of the individual is a cumulative process of adaptation of means to ends that cumulatively change as the process goes on, both the agent and his environment being at any point the outcome of the last process.

In place of "a passive and substantially inert and immutably given human nature," Veblen saw instincts and habits as the dynamic bases of intention and action. Veblen (1898b, p. 155 [in this volume]) then laid down his core methodological principle: "an evolutionary economics must be a theory of a process of cultural growth as determined by the economic interest, a theory of a cumulative sequence of economic institutions stated in terms of the process itself."

Veblen (1909c, p. 513 [in this volume]) observed that neoclassical economics is concerned with the distribution or allocation of goods, but neglects their production or consumption. Neoclassical analysis is static rather than dynamic because "as to the causes of change or the unfolding sequence of the phenomena of economic life they have had nothing to say hitherto." Veblen, by contrast, emphasized "the phenomena of growth and change" and took neither individuals, institutions, or technology as given.

Veblen also addressed capital theory. In about 1970, during the Cambridge capital theory debates (Harcourt 1972), Joan Robinson (1979, p. 95) came across Veblen's (1908a) critique of neoclassical capital theory and concluded that Veblen was "the most original economist born and bred in the USA." Veblen had come to the attention of Cambridge economists partly because he criticized orthodox theorists for confusing capital as material goods and capital as pecuniary or financial assets (Veblen 1908a, pp. 443–44 [in this volume], 1908e, pp. 467–68 [in this volume]). But Veblen goes further than this, anticipating many of the points made by the later critics of orthodoxy. For instance, he was one of the first to point out the concept of the "amount of capital" can only be derived through a process of valuation: "The value involved is, like all value, a matter of imputation" (Veblen 1908e, p. 468 [in this volume]). He thus hints at the problem of circular argumentation later identified by Joan Robinson (1953) and Piero Sraffa (1960).

Veblen's work differs from both Marxian theory, in which labor is the prime mover in production and the source of all "value," and from neoclassical theory, where output is related to a combination of two or more "factors."

For Veblen (1908a, pp. 413–14 [in this volume]) production is a matter of both tangible and intangible assets. Intangible assets involve "the accumulated, habitual knowledge of the ways and means involved ... the outcome of long experience and experimentation."

Furthermore, the "great body of commonplace knowledge made use of in an industry is the product and heritage of the group" (Veblen 1908a, p. 414 [in this volume]). "These immaterial industrial expedients are necessarily a product of the community, the immaterial residue of the community's experience, past and present; which has no existence apart from the community's life, and can be transmitted only in the keeping of the community at large" (Veblen 1908c, p. 455 [in this volume]). The group-based nature of the immaterial assets of production ill-fits the labor contract between employer and individual employee; such immaterial assets reside in the interstices of the social organization of the firm and its associated community. The importance of tacit, group-based knowledge in the firm is now recognized by leading evolutionary economists and theorists of technological change (Nelson and Winter 1982, Dosi 1988).

Veblen argues that orthodox capital theory overestimates the tangible assets to the detriment of the intangible, and individualizes an essentially social phenomenon. He abandons the capital–labor, "factors of production" approach, to propose a conception of production based on the structured interactions of groups of individuals and capital goods. Widespread recognition of this would mean that the orthodox theory of the "natural" distribution of incomes between labor and capital would "go up in the air" (Veblen 1908a, p. 422 [in this volume]). These points have enhanced relevance where intangible assets – especially knowledge – play an even greater role in the economy.

But while Veblen's critique of neoclassical theory has enduringly relevant features, such as his insights on the nature of knowledge and his critique of rationality, in other respects it is more limited. Veblen's critique of neoclassical economics explores neither the general ethical limitations of its utilitarianism nor the particular role of sentiments of morality and duty in sustaining real-world institutions. Veblen subsumes such deontic factors under habits of thought, and otherwise downplays the moral dimension of human interaction. In this respect his critique of neoclassical utilitarianism contrasts not only with modern thinkers who criticize the ethically flat individual in utilitarianism (Sen 1987, Etzioni 1988, Searle 1995), but also with some of Veblen's contemporaries who discussed moral issues in more depth, notably John Hobson (1902, 1914, 1929). Despite the emphasis on ideology by some of his interpreters, Veblen's frequent attempts to avoid normative judgments went too far by neglecting the objective study of the function of ethical norms.

The Veblenian dichotomy?

Veblen is widely associated with the idea that institutions come into conflict with technological development. According to Ayres (1973, p. v) he "made the dichotomy of technology and ceremonialism his master principle." Ayres

(1961, p. 30) also saw institutions as essentially ceremonial, and hence the "Veblenian dichotomy" between institutions and technology entered the literature (Waller 1982, 1994).

Veblen's writings tell a different and more nuanced story. The true dichotomy in his work is between "industrial" and "pecuniary" activities, or between "industry" and "business." Yet this dichotomy has its problems, and these will be discussed first. As shown below, there is much less evidence in his writings of a general dichotomy between institutions and technology.

Veblen (1899f, p. 277 [in this volume]) explains that this distinction between "pecuniary" and "industrial" employments "marks the difference between workmanship and bargaining," or production and distribution. For Veblen, industrial employment includes labor and management leading to production. Pecuniary employment relates to the valuation, marketing, and distribution of that which is produced.

The aim of the distinction is "to indicate the different economic value of the aptitudes and habits of thought fostered by the one and the other class of employments" (Veblen 1899f, p. 276 [in this volume]). As Veblen suggests, this dichotomy has its precursors in the classical distinction between productive and unproductive labor. Veblen (1899f, p. 278 [in this volume]) also refers approvingly to John Stuart Mill's claim that production – by contrast to distribution – is essentially a matter of the laws of nature.[34]

According to Veblen (1899f, p. 277 [in this volume]), pecuniary employments "rest on the institution of private property" while industrial employments "rest chiefly on the physical conditions of human life." Similarly, Veblen (1901a, p. 289 [in this volume]) suggests that while business centers on the "higgling of the market," industrial employments are aimed at "the shaping and guiding of material things and processes." Such industry is "primarily occupied with ... material serviceability rather than ... exchange value" and is to be understood in terms of "Physics and the other material sciences."

A problem here is that industrial output depends upon and is affected by the organization of the firm. Even if we avoid some of the extremes of modern social constructivism, there is a large literature testifying to the interaction and inseparability of social technology and organization.[35] From this viewpoint,

---

34 Mill (1871, Bk. 2, Ch. 1) wrote: "The laws and conditions of the production of wealth, partake of the character of physical truths. There is nothing optional, or arbitrary in them." Despite his earlier endorsement of Mill, in later writings there are signs that Veblen moved closer to a view that technology is socially conditioned and inextricably entwined with social relations. Veblen (1923, p. 280) wrote:

> The technological system is an organisation of intelligence, a structure of intangibles and imponderables, in the nature of habits of thought. It resides in the habits of thoughts of the community and comes to a head in the habits of thought of the technicians.

35 See for example Suchman (1987), Button (1993), Star (1995), Collins and Kusch (1998).

production is necessarily institutional and cannot be grounded on physical conditions without the inclusion of organizational and motivational matters as well.

Veblen (1901a, p. 289 [in this volume]) admits that pecuniary and industrial activities interact and "business activity may ... effect an enhancement of the aggregate material wealth of the community, or the aggregate serviceability of the means at hand." He acknowledges that particular business arrangements often lead to greater industrial output. Veblen (1901a, pp. 291–92 [in this volume]) goes as far as to admit that

> shrewd business management is a requisite to success in any industry that is carried on within the scope of the market. Pecuniary failure carries with it industrial failure ... In this way industrial results are closely dependent upon the presence of business ability.

But this admission has two defects. First, despite his institutionalism, he accounts for differences in output that are due to different business arrangements on output in terms of the "business ability" of individuals and omits the nature or structure of institutions.

Second, while assuming that it is possible, Veblen avoids the question of how industry could be organized outside "the scope of the market" and whether a greater or lesser industrial output would result. While he is normatively disposed toward nonmarket solutions, he does not explain in detail what they are or how they would work. He simply suggests that without a market system most "business" activities will be dispensable. Veblen (1914, p. 550 n. 10) also wrote that the "all-pervading modern institution of private property appears to have ... grown out of the self-regarding bias of men in their oversight of the community's material interests." This suggests that "the community's material interests" are not served by private property. But Veblen failed to give an account of how an alternative society could be organized without private property or markets – how knowledge would be tapped and used, how decisions would be delegated and made, how people would be incentivized to work effectively, and how the rewards of production would be distributed. Hence the institutionalist John Maurice Clark (1925, p. 57) objected:

> As for the technical processes, neither Veblen nor anyone else has ever shown how social efficiency can be organized on a technical basis alone. ... Veblen's antithesis [between business and industry], valuable as it is as a challenge to orthodoxy, cannot serve the purposes of a constructive search for the line of progress. This calls for an evolution of our scheme of values, not for a "technocracy" which ignores value.

Veblen (1921a, p. 100) declared: "Twentieth-century technology has outgrown the eighteenth-century system of vested rights." But he did not describe the system of economic organization and coordination that was appropriate for twentieth-century technology. He never gave a detailed picture of an alternative mode of organization of modern industrial society, other than his vague references to a "Soviet of engineers" or an "industrial directorate" of experts (Veblen 1921a, p. 144). With his insufficiently grounded presumption that private property and markets are entirely dispensable, Veblen converges with Marxism, despite his other analytical differences with that doctrine.

If production is inseparable from organization and motivation, then we have to face the question of organizational and other incentives. Are private property and markets essential spurs to innovation, entrepreneurship, and economic growth? No one has yet provided an adequately detailed and viable account of how a modern economy can be organized without some private property and some markets. Arguably, incentives could be maintained in a mixed economy where the state also plays a major role, as found in many modern economies. These questions are different and controversial. Sadly on such matters, Veblen is of little help.

We now return to the alleged dichotomy between technology, on the one hand, and institutions or ceremony, on the other. Ayres (1944, p. 99) proposed that Veblen was the first "to make this analytical distinction between technology and ceremony the point of departure of all further economic analysis." On the contrary, there is no evidence that Veblen used a "distinction between technology and ceremony" as an analytical "point of departure" of any kind. Veblen did not regard institutions as wholly noninstrumental, and he did not define them essentially in terms of ceremony. Furthermore, he saw strong institutional elements within technology itself. No writer has identified a passage in Veblen's writings that clearly indicates a belief in a general dichotomy between institutions and technology, rather than particular instances of such a clash (Hodgson 2004).

In *The Leisure Class*, Veblen (1899c, p. 253 [in this volume]) depicted institutions as "a conservative factor" involving "social inertia, psychological inertia, conservatism." But this passage does not mention technology. It is about a mismatch between the inherited "institutions of to-day" and the general "situation of to-day."

In the *The Theory of Business Enterprise*, Veblen (1904b, p. 303) remarked: "The factor in the modern situation that is alien to the ancient régime is the machine technology, with its many and wide ramifications." But this is not evidence of a general dichotomy between institutions and technology; it is between a specific (machine) technology and specific institutions.

A passage in *The Instinct of Workmanship* refers to the possibility that instincts such as "the parental bent or the sense of workmanship" may overturn "institutional elements at variance with the continued life-interests of the community" and "the bonds of custom, prescription, principles, precedent" may be broken. "But history records more spectacular instances of the triumph of imbecile institutions over life and culture" (Veblen 1914, p. 550

[in this volume]). Here he asserted that workmanship and other instincts *could* come into conflict with some institutions, and with different possible outcomes. Some "imbecile" institutions block these instinctive drives, but others prove more accommodating. He did *not* suggest that *all* institutions are "imbecile." Hence this passage does not give us the "Veblenian" dichotomy.

Not only is a general "Veblenian dichotomy" absent from Veblen's writings, but also some passages are inconsistent with the idea. For example, in *The Leisure Class*, Veblen (1899c, p. 363) wrote that "habits of thought which are so formed under the guidance of teachers and scholastic traditions have an economic value." Bearing in mind Veblen's own description of an institution as shared habits, this passage suggests that institutions can have a positive role. These extracts undermine the "Veblenian" dichotomy, by recognizing that some institutions can enhance the life process or serve acceptable economic interests. One of the clearest and most dramatic examples is in an amazingly prescient analysis of the Japanese socio-economic system. Veblen (1915b, p. 26) remarked:

> It is in this unique combination of a high-wrought spirit of feudalistic fealty and chivalric honor with the material efficiency given by the modern technology that the strength of the Japanese nation lies.

Such an observation is commonplace in the recent literature on the 1945–90 Japanese economic miracle. But Veblen made it well before the rise of modern Japan, and nevertheless saw the root of Japan's future strength. This strength does not lie in technology alone but in its *combination* with conservative and ceremonial institutions "of feudalistic fealty and chivalric honor." In sum, the notion of a conflict between institutions and technology is not only absent in Veblen's writings but it is contradicted by his own words and conceptions.

Veblen on the evolution of science and the machine process

One of Veblen's prominent concerns was to attempt to explain the origins of modern science and its institutions. Veblen (1908d, p. 478 [in this volume]) acknowledges the self-referential problem that any attempt at explaining the "scientific point of view which avowedly proceeds from this point of view itself has necessarily the appearance of an argument in a circle." His solution is to recruit Darwinism to help explain the evolution of science. Veblen is here a forerunner of more recent evolutionary analyses of science, such as those of David Hull (1988) and Philip Kitcher (1993). Veblen also emphasizes that science is governed by habits of thought, which themselves evolve. Here too he connects with contemporary views (Margolis 1994).

For Veblen (1908d, pp. 478–80 [in this volume]) the core of "modern science" is its attempt to explain "consecutive change" in terms of causal sequence or "the relation of cause and effect." For Veblen (1908d, p. 481 [in this volume]), "post-Darwinian science" involves "a new distribution of emphasis, whereby the process of causation, the interval of instability and transition between initial cause and definitive effect, has come to take the first place in the inquiry."

Veblen (1908d, pp. 484–86 [in this volume]) describes novelties in the development of scientific thought as "mutations." When scientific enquiry was the province of the aristocracy, science was detached from the immediate and "matter-of-fact" requirements of survival. Hence "mutations" were unchecked by experimental verification and divorced from "matter-of-fact" experience. By contrast, when the "institutional fabric … changes in such a manner as to throw the work-day experience into the foreground of attention … then the interval between the speculative realm of knowledge … and the work-day generalizations of fact … is likely to lessen, and the two ranges of knowledge are likely to converge more or less effectually upon a common ground." In these circumstances "something in the way of science has at least a chance to arise." Mutations remain essential for change, but their frequency and scope are usefully tested and constrained by experiment and experience (Kitcher 1993).

The Industrial Revolution and the "technological ascendancy of the machine-process, brought a new and characteristic discipline into the cultural situation." It took some time for this to take effect, but it led to the "habit of thinking in terms of process rather than in terms of the workmanlike efficiency of a given cause working to a given effect." But these new habits of thought had a lesser effect in "the sciences which lie farther afield from the technological domain," including ethics, political theory, and "even economics" (Veblen 1908d, pp. 490–91 [in this volume]).

Veblen considers what engine might drive the process and lead to scientific and technological advance. According to Veblen (1904b, pp. 66–67) the "machine process" inculcates and enforces a number of "habits of thought," involving "matter-of-fact" knowledge and "a standardization of conduct and of knowledge in terms of quantitative precision." For Veblen (1904b, p. 67), the machine process "inculcates a habit of apprehending and explaining facts in terms of material cause and effect."

Veblen (1904b, 1906a, 1914) repeated these arguments in several places but never provided an adequate explanation of how the machine process assisted the growth of these particular preconceptions or habits of thought. For Veblen (1906a, pp. 355, 364 [in this volume]), "matter-of-fact" meant "impersonal, dispassionate insight into the material facts with which mankind has to deal" and he wrote of "that matter-of-fact inquiry that constitutes scientific research." Veblen (1906a, p. 355 [in this volume]) proposed an evolutionary theory by which "matter-of-fact" habits of thought are selected in a "struggle for existence" against those habits of lesser efficacy or fitness:

> A civilization which is dominated by this matter-of-fact insight must prevail against any cultural scheme that lacks this element. This characteristic of western civilization comes to a head in modern science, and

finds its highest material expression in the technology of the machine industry.

For Veblen (1904b, p. 67) such habits of thought were "both a cause and an effect of the machine process." Habits of thought affected technology just as technology affected habits (Rutherford, 1984).

In a characteristic speculation, Veblen (1904b, p. 311) believed that "machine technology" could help to undermine "conventionally established rules of precedence," such as the rights of property. He upheld that the people most likely to be affected in this way were not necessarily the machine operatives, but skilled mechanics, supervisors and engineers (Layton 1962, Rutherford 1992, Knoedler and Mayhew 1999, Edgell 2001). He thus regarded the engineers as a force for radical change.

But Veblen's optimism that technological and "matter-of-fact" habits of thought can undermine outdated convention and prejudice is challenged by experience in the United States, the leading industrial nation throughout the twentieth century. Despite its technological lead, religion and creationism remain entrenched, even among scientists and engineers.

We do not learn causality directly from technological experience. Practical involvement, even with machines, does not itself make the philosophically complex and physically mysterious nature of causality clear. Humans are perfectly capable of erecting barriers within the mind, where scientific or technological knowledge of causal relations is compartmentalized from spiritual or religious beliefs.

Not only was Veblen overly optimistic about the power of technology to undermine obsolescent conventions, but also he hinted that industry could function without any established traditions at all. On the contrary, technology itself depends on the accumulated tradition of experiment and trial, with complex arrangements that cannot be causally dissected or optimized in every detail. Modern studies have shown that engineering is a partially conservative as well as an innovative evolutionary process: it progresses through evolutionary selection upon established usages and conventions (Rosenberg and Vincenti 1985, Vincenti 1990). New "mutations" have first to be developed, trialed, and reviewed within a scientific or technological community in order to become sufficiently effective and marketable.

Veblen's inspirational prescience

A major tragedy of Veblen's legacy is that while he develops the philosophical, psychological, and evolutionary foundations of a highly sophisticated approach, which has retained its power and relevance for over a century, neither he nor his followers ever developed a systematic theoretical superstructure to rest on these robust foundations. That task is still on our agenda today.

It is furthermore a diversion to look to Veblen for ideas on how a modern complex economy can be better organized. His criticisms of neoclassical apologetics and his satires on the status quo are all well and good, but he was insufficiently engaged with the analysis of practical alternatives to leave us with much of value in this area. He was a dissenting rather than a practical radical.

Nevertheless, Veblen's work remained inspirational for generations, even for those economists more concerned with theoretical or practical matters and less engaged with philosophical or psychological fundamentals. His combination of playful and forensic phraseology makes an enduring mark on the reader. He coined a number of witty and powerful phrases, such as "conspicuous consumption" (Veblen 1899c, ch. 4) and "invention is the mother of necessity" (Veblen 1914, p. 314).

Some of Veblen's analytical insights have an amazing prescience. As noted above, he not only identified sources of Japanese later economic dynamism (Veblen 1915b) but understood the root of Britain's relative decline in its ossified institutions and outdated technologies, thus foreshadowing later commentators (Elbaum and Lazonic 1986). Veblen (1915a, p. 132) wrote that Britain is "paying the penalty for having been thrown into the lead and so having shown the way." He also prefigured later institutional economists such as Mancur Olson (1982), who identified processes of institutional sclerosis or ossification.

Veblen (1904b, p. 48) also hinted at the concept of transaction costs by noting that "business consolidation" eliminates "the pecuniary element from the interstices of the system ... with the result that there is a saving of work and an avoidance of that systematic mutual hindrance that characterizes the competitive management of industry." He suggested that business integration can reduce costs relative to a disaggregated and market-driven mode of governance, prefiguring the work of Ronald Coase (1937) and Oliver Williamson (1975).

In an analysis of business fluctuations that retains immense relevance today, Veblen (1904b, pp. 185–267 and [in this volume] pp. 343–44) saw industrial cycles and depressions as rooted in the credit mechanism and in business psychology. This analysis had institutionalized business speculations and expectations at the center. Against the prevailing view that industrial recessions in market economies would automatically bring about the mechanisms of recovery, Veblen stressed that business depressions would feed cumulatively on their own results. Markets are not self-righting institutions.

Veblen (1904b, p. 185) also criticized Karl Marx (1894, ch. 15) and Mikhail Tugan-Baranovsky (1901) for approaching the analysis of business cycles from "the mechanical facts of production and consumption; rather than, from the side of business enterprise – the phenomena of price, earnings, and capitalization." Veblen saw the source of capitalist crises in financial institutions that promoted the excessive and irrational exuberance of the speculators. He focused on the institutional basis of earnings and capitalist expectations, rather than "mechanical facts of production and consumption" such as Marx's (1894) rising "organic composition of capital." Consequently, it has been rightly argued by some commentators (Vining 1939, Raines and Leathers 1996) that Veblen brilliantly foreshadowed the theory of business fluctuations and employment in the later work of John Maynard Keynes (1936).[36]

Despite his limitations, and because of the enduring relevance of his work, Veblen was one of the greatest economists of his time. Notwithstanding his omissions, he left us with an evolutionary research program and a philosophical outlook that retains its power and promise in the twenty-first century. The challenge today is not only to understand Veblen's legacy but to use it as a quarry of ideas for the further development of an incisive and relevant approach to institutional economics, evolutionary economics, business studies, and social theory.

The scope and nature of this volume

This volume differs from previous collections of Veblen's writings and is designed to provide twenty-first century scholars and students with an accessible, compact, and authoritative edition of the foundational works in Veblen's oeuvre. For this reason, the volume focuses on the years in Veblen's career from 1881 to 1914. The 38 selections include full texts of Veblen's most important essays and book reviews from this period as well as excerpts from the three books that he published during these years, *The Theory of the Leisure Class, The Theory of Business Enterprise*, and *The Instinct of Workmanship*.

As suggested above, our rationale for focusing on Veblen's work from these years is our belief that his most fundamental and important contributions to economics and to social theory date from this period, which begins when he is a young graduate student and concludes when he is a distinguished scholar in late middle age. This is not to deny that there is much of originality and value in the books and essays that Veblen produced in the final fifteen years of his life. Even so, Veblen's tendency in his later writings is to repeat earlier insights and to devote relatively less attention to philosophical, psychological, and theoretical fundamentals.

Aside from this temporal focus, this volume contrasts with the three major existing collections of Veblen's writings (Veblen 1919j, 1934b, 1973) in two significant ways. First, the following selections are presented (with a few very minor exceptions) in the chronological sequence in which Veblen published them during his lifetime.[37] No other collection of Veblen's writings adopts this

---

36 Veblen's theory of business cycles was partly inspired by others, particularly Hobson (1896), who was cited by Veblen (1904b) in several places. Keynes (1936) also acknowledged the seminal importance of Hobson's work in this area.

37 The few slight exceptions are due to the fact that, as we mention below, the volume combines the separate parts of articles that were published in multiple installments over the course of several months. We insert these multipart articles in our chronological arrangement of selections according to the publication date of the first installment of each, although in some cases the publication of a later installment of the same article occurred a few months *after* the selection that follows it in the volume.

chronological organization, which we believe is vital for understanding the evolution of Veblen's thought. Second, in the Introductions to Parts I–IV, we provide item-by-item commentaries that aim to clarify the central argument of each of the selections either by situating the selection in the intellectual-historical context in which Veblen originally wrote it or by locating the selection in relation to subsequent developments in social and economic thought. There has been no previous work that examines the unfolding of Veblen's ideas in this manner.

Of the 36 articles and notes that Veblen published between 1882 and 1914, this collection includes 27 items. In four cases (Selections 19, 31, 33, and 35), we have combined into one continuous selection the separate parts of articles that were originally published in installments. Viewed from the baseline of the "Complete List of Thorstein Veblen's Published Writings," which we include as the first of the three bibliographies at the end of this volume, our collection omits "The Overproduction Fallacy" (1892b), "The Price of Wheat since 1867" (1892c), "The Use of Loan Credit in Modern Business" (1903a), "Credit and Prices" (1905b), "Christian Morals and the Competitive System" (1910), and "The Blond Race and the Aryan Culture" (1913b) because the aspects of Veblen's thought shown in these articles are well represented, in our view, in other selections herein.[38] We have also omitted "The Army of the Commonweal" (1894c) and "Arts and Crafts" (1902a) because of their more restricted topical focus, and "An Early Experiment in Trusts" (1904a), where Veblen speculates on Viking collective organization.

With the exception of two of the just-mentioned items (1904a, 1913b), this volume includes all of the essays collected in *The Place of Science in Modern Civilisation* (Veblen 1919j), and it supercedes that anthology by correcting several dating and printing errors and omissions. The present volume also reproduces nine articles that were included in a later anthology, *Essays on Our Changing Order* (Veblen 1934b), and thirteen book reviews found in *Essays, Reviews and Reports* (Veblen 1973).

In all selections, we preserve the spelling used in Veblen's original publications, which is mostly American but sometimes British English. Throughout, we also correct obvious minor typographical errors, standardize punctuation, and replace footnotes originally indicated by character-symbols with numbered footnotes. We also remove signature lines and institutional affiliations as these were originally given at either the beginning or end of Veblen's articles and book reviews. In instances where Veblen quotes from foreign-language sources, we include translations of these passages in editorial footnotes.

---

38 Regarding our omission of "The Blond Race and the Aryan Culture" (Veblen 1913b), we also note that the account that Veblen here endorses of racial types and their European movements has been superseded by modern genetic and archaeological research (Cavalli-Sforza 2000, Wells 2002, Dunbar 2004, Oppenheimer 2004, Klein 2009).

With regard to the references that Veblen cites in these selections, we have adopted a middle course between reproducing his references in the manner in which he originally provided them and reformatting those references to conform with twenty-first century academic citation practices. After careful consideration, we decided that simply reproducing Veblen's sources in the somewhat casual fashion in which he referred to them would leave many of his citations sufficiently obscure that modern readers might have trouble identifying them. We felt at the same time, however, that recasting his citations according to present-day conventions would remove from the selections some of their distinctive historical characteristics. Our compromise has been to retain the original form of Veblen's references essentially intact throughout, but to insert slightly fuller author and title information where we thought readers might find this beneficial. Except in instances where these modifications involve only a few characters or a slight adjustment for consistency, we indicate them in square brackets. Insofar as we have detected minor dating or spelling errors in Veblen's references, we silently correct these mistakes.

For the benefit of students and scholars who seek to use this volume as a research tool, the selections include original page numbers within square brackets. We have inserted these bracketed numbers to mark the beginning of each new page in the source in which the reprinted selection was first published. *Throughout the volume, the bracketed number corresponds to the page in the original published source.*[39]

We also include three bibliographies: a complete bibliography of Veblen's published writings; a bibliography of all sources to which Veblen himself refers in the selections in the volume; and a bibliography of the sources that we cite in our introductory essays. This last bibliography is selective; although we make numerous references to the secondary literature on Veblen, this is so vast that we cannot claim that these listed citations are comprehensive. The challenge of understanding, critically appraising, and properly appropriating Veblen's ideas is ongoing, and the materials in this volume are presented to facilitate continuing inquiry into his work.

Acknowledgments

We gratefully acknowledge the encouragement of colleagues. We are also thankful for the generous help that we received from Elisabeth Anderson, Gregoire Mallard, and Carey Seal in translating the German, French, and Latin passages contained in these selections. Joshua Kaiser and Lila Strommer provided valuable technical assistance, for which we are also grateful.

---

39 In cases where the start of a new page occurs in the middle of a word, we indicate the new page number at the *end* of the word in question.

Introduction to Part I

1882–1898: early works

The 14 selections in Part I follow Thorstein Veblen's publications from age 24 to age 40. At the outset of this formative period, Veblen was a graduate student still in search of his intellectual coordinates; at the end of the period, he stood ready to publish the writings that laid the foundation of his seminal contributions to modern social and economic thought. Examining these works in the order in which they originally appeared, during the closing decades of the nineteenth century, offers a portal into the making of a major American thinker.

From first to last, these selections show a thinker of high ambition, who charged boldly into the vexed debates of his day and did not hesitate to engage the ideas of towering figures in the Western intellectual canon. Perhaps more surprisingly, the selections also document how firmly Veblen kept his ear to the ground and attended to the intellectual discourses that immediately surrounded him – moving from one large debate to another and confronting the ideas of different canonical figures, as his own intellectual location changed.

Selection 1 is a fragment of a paper that has not otherwise survived. Veblen wrote it in the fall of 1881 during the semester that he spent as a graduate student at Johns Hopkins. As part of his curriculum, Veblen took Richard T. Ely's[1] lecture course on the "History of Political Economy" and, in conjunction with this course, prepared a paper that spoke to a topic of interest to Ely and that addressed the writings of some of the economists with whom Ely's lectures dealt. After Ely approved the paper, Veblen presented it orally before a local meeting of the Historical and Political Science Association – the lofty title of a multidisciplinary graduate seminar that Hopkins historian Herbert B. Adams held on a monthly basis. Veblen's paper was one of several read on the evening of December 21, 1881, and the next issue of the *Johns Hopkins University Circular* carried the brief abstract that is Selection 1.

---

1 Ely had studied in Germany with members of the German historical school and was one of the founders of the American Economic Association (AEA). He was AEA secretary from 1885 to 1892 and its president from 1900 to 1901 (Hodgson 2001).

Entitled "Mill's Theory of the Taxation of Land," the paper may initially appear to be an early hint of the heterodox economist that Veblen later became. Denouncing the "unearned increment" that accrues to landowners (as against "all classes of the community") from rising ground rents, the paper explicitly champions the "nationalization of land" and the "redistribution of wealth." At the time, however, such ideas were far more commonplace than they are in our own day. By the early 1880s, they were stock phrases in academic and popular discourse in America and England alike, themes so familiar that fellow attendees at the seminar where Veblen gave his paper found the occasion "dull" rather than anything out of the ordinary.[2]

The notion that the "progress of society" confers on landowners an "unearned increment" in rent that the state should tax is an argument that Veblen draws directly from a widely discussed section of John Stuart Mill's *Principles of Political Economy* (1848, Bk. 5, Ch. 2, Sec. 5) and which, in part, had been broached as well by others in the tradition of classical economics, including David Ricardo and Herbert Spencer. In *Social Statics*, Spencer, staunch anti-socialist though he was, had gone so far as to advocate land nationalization as a means of righting the historical "robbery" of land from the "mass of mankind" and to propose "compensation to existing proprietors" for the necessary redistribution (1851, pp. 123–25). However, shortly before Veblen presented his paper, Spencer's compensation scheme had been prominently assaulted by the popular American writer Henry George, whose bestselling economic tract *Progress and Poverty* (1879) reignited concerns about the unearned increment of ground rents, while simultaneously criticizing proposals that would compensate landowners rather than subject them to heavy taxation.[3] In Selection 1, Veblen inserts himself into this debate among some of the contemporary luminaries of political economy, agreeing that the unearned increment was a consequential problem that taxation should address, but suggesting that state land purchases were an alternative means to compensate landlords who were opposed to paying rent taxes. As he formulates these points, Veblen also appeals to ideas, which George's book developed in detail, about population density and labor-saving improvements.

Selection 2, "Kant's Critique of Judgment," Veblen's first full-length article, appeared in July 1884 in the *Journal of Speculative Philosophy*, which was then America's premier philosophy journal. Earlier the same year, Veblen, who by this point had transferred from Hopkins to Yale, completed his doctorate in philosophy, with a dissertation that (apparently) compared the

---

2 The description is that of Veblen's classmate, future historian J. Franklin Jameson (J. Franklin Jameson Papers; Library of Congress, Container 2, Diary for 1881–82, entry for December 21). Statements in the text about Veblen's course of study at Johns Hopkins are based on Jameson's diaries and 1881–82 issues of the *Johns Hopkins University Circular.*

3 The entries on "Increment, The Unearned" and "Land, Nationalisation of" in Palgrave's *Dictionary of Political Economy* (1894–99) offer a useful introduction to this debate from the point of view of contemporaries.

teachings of Immanuel Kant and Herbert Spencer with regard to the ethics of retribution. How closely Veblen's article duplicated the Kant portion of his dissertation is unknown, as copies of the dissertation have never come to light. At the least, both the dissertation and the article attest to Veblen's deep engagement during these years with the work of Kant, which was then under extensive discussion as part of the "return to Kant" movement in European and American philosophy and the international centennial of Kant's *Critique of Pure Reason* (1781), in which several of Veblen's professors were involved.[4]

Indeed, at Hopkins, Veblen studied Kant's writings with philosopher George S. Morris, who was then composing what would become one of the two principal American treatises on Kant from this era, whereas, at Yale, Veblen's mentor and dissertation supervisor was philosopher Noah Porter, who was then completing the other major contemporary treatise on Kant.[5] The fact that Morris's book (1882) analyzed Kant's *Critique of Pure Reason*, while Porter's book (1886) dealt with Kant's *Critique of Practical Reason* (1788), perhaps drew Veblen – who, at the time, aspired to a faculty position in a department of philosophy – to undertake an article on Kant's lesser-known third critique, the as-yet-untranslated *Critique of Judgment* (1790). Be this as it may, like Porter, Veblen adopts in his article an approach to Kant's text that is mainly exegetical; and like Porter, who hailed Kant as a "sage [of] intellectual and moral greatness" (1882, p. 450), Veblen seeks to defend Kant against sundry critics. Although Veblen does not identify these critics by name, Morris himself, who rejected Porter's laudatory assessment and continually trumpeted Hegel over Kant, is among the plausible candidates, as is Morris's student, the young John Dewey, whose attack on Kant's "philosophic method" (Dewey 1884) had just appeared in the previous issue of the *Journal of Speculative Philosophy*.

Of the different possible interpretations of Kant's *Critique of Judgment*, Veblen's article presents the *Critique* as a work concerned primarily with the logic of inductive reasoning and with what induction can and cannot achieve. In viewing Kant's *Critique* from this specific angle, Veblen tacitly builds on the model of another of his teachers, philosopher C. S. Peirce; at Hopkins, Veblen had taken Peirce's course on "General Logic," which dealt extensively with induction, a topic on which Peirce's own ideas at the time were heavily beholden to Kant, whom Peirce regarded as "the greatest philosopher of modern times."[6] In Selection 2, Veblen lauds Kant for recognizing "the

---

4 Adamson (1882), Anon. (1881), Caird (1880), and Porter (1882) provide valuable contemporary accounts of the Kant revival and centennial. On Kant's place in late nineteenth-century American academic philosophy more generally, see Kuklick (2001).

5 While at Yale, Veblen also studied with yet another Kant specialist, philosopher and psychologist, George T. Ladd.

6 The words are Peirce's, as quoted by Forster (1997, p. 46) in a thorough analysis of the indebtedness of Peirce's early theory of logic – and his views of induction in particular – to Kant's work (see also Burks 1996).

indispensableness of th[e] power of inductive reasoning," meaning by "induction" the capacity of the knowledge-seeker "to find unity in [the] multiplicity" of particulars, as these are given through human experience, by ordering particulars into "a system under more general laws," which can then speak to the question that presses on the knowledge-seeker: "What is the cause of a given effect, and, still more, what *will be* the effect of a given cause" (pp. 55, 56, 57, 61). On Veblen's reading of Kant, this ordering capacity presumes, however, "a guiding principle beyond anything that experience gives"; and this is the "principle of adaptation," which impels the knowledge-seeker to conceive of "particular things ... as adapted to one another so as to form a systematic totality" and then "sets the mind hunting to find out how" (p. 61). In this sense, "inductive reasoning ... proceeds on subjective ground entirely," yielding "results [that are] only more or less probable" (p. 63). This limitation notwithstanding, Veblen – speaking for Kant and for himself – concludes that "hardly any part of our knowledge except that got by induction is of ... use for practical purposes," including the purposes of morality and science (pp. 63, 54).

Selection 3, "Some Neglected Points in the Theory of Socialism," Veblen's next publication, appeared seven years after his article on Kant and shows him returning to large economic issues that were at the center of extensive academic and popular discussion during this period. The piece ran in late 1891 in a recently founded journal for policy debate, *Annals of the American Academy of Political and Social Science*, and Veblen wrote it early in his tenure as a graduate student at Cornell. The article captures Veblen as he first puts before the public his emerging ideas about the evolution of economic and social institutions, wasteful expenditures for the purpose of social display, the role of emulation and envy in motivating such expenditures, and the prospects for more satisfactory social arrangements in the future. These were subjects that had occupied the attentions of some of Veblen's previous teachers – Ely at Hopkins, Sumner at Yale, and Clark at Carleton – and now the work of his new Cornell mentors – Laughlin, Tuttle, and Tyler – gave them renewed prominence.[7] In the selection, Veblen seeks to make use what he has learned up to this point.

Veblen takes as his occasion the publication of an essay by Herbert Spencer, which appeared in British author (and wine merchant) Thomas Mackay's volume *A Plea for Liberty: An Argument against Socialism and Socialistic Legislation* (1891). Although the essay and the volume were both generally regarded as containing little that Spencer and his followers had not said elsewhere (Dunning 1891), the great American "vogue of Spencer" was still well underway (Hofstadter 1944), thus making Spencer a highly visible adversary for Veblen to confront.

7 For an analysis of the work of all of these figures in relation to Veblen ideas, see Camic (2011). On Veblen's Cornell teachers, see also Viano (2009).

This Veblen does by raising two principal objections to the case that Spencer mounts against socialism. First, Veblen charges that Spencer misunderstands the source of the "widely prevalent discontent" that fuels "popular demands" for socialism (p. 65). Veblen traces this source to the fact that, as it has evolved, "the modern industrial system is based on the institution of private property under free competition" and, in consequence, engenders a "struggle to keep up appearances by otherwise unnecessary expenditure" on tokens of "economic success," including "articles of apparel" and "show[s] of luxury" – a struggle that breeds, among those who are "relatively poorer," "emulation and ... jealousy [of those who are in] possession and enjoyment of material goods" (pp. 66, 71, 68, 66, 69, 70). However, "with the abolition of private property," socialism will end this whole "wasteful" process, "very considerably lessen[ing] the aggregate amount of labor required for the support of the community" (pp. 65, 71). Second, Veblen deems as fallacious Spencer's assertion that, were socialism substituted for the existing "system of free competition," then "voluntary cooperation," based on contract, would necessarily give way to a ruthless bureaucratic regime governing by "compulsion" (p. 72). According to Veblen, Spencer's two alternatives are "not logically exhaustive"; they neglect the desirable form that socialism would likely assume if conjoined with "modern constitutional government – the system of modern free institutions. ... of the English-speaking people" (pp. 73, 75).

Selection 4, "Böhm-Bawerk's Definition of Capital, and the Source of Wages," is one of two publications from the first half of the following year (1892), which veer in a different direction to reveal a side of Veblen that is almost completely unknown: his (partial and perhaps temporary[8]) embrace of the intellectual tools of late ninetenth-century "mainstream" economics and his ability to work with those tools. Written while he was studying classical economics under Laughlin and in a decade when American economics was experiencing the infiltration of various streams of marginal utility theory, the article appeared as a short note in what was then America's leading journal in the field, the *Quarterly Journal of Economics*.

Veblen offers the article, eight paragraphs in all, as an intervention into one of the most heated debates in economics at this time: the wages-fund controversy. The controversy centered on a notion that dated to the start of the classical tradition and was reiterated in many sources, including Mill's *Principles of Economics*: the assumption that employers pay the wages of workers out of capital, understood as a fix fund that is the result of production carried out at a previous time. By the late nineteenth century, this

---

8 In lectures delivered in 1926–27, Veblen's former student Wesley Mitchell (1969, vol. 2, pp. 685–86) pointed out that "Veblen himself at times makes casual, implicit use of orthodox economic theory." Mitchell justified this by citing part of Veblen's *Theory of Business Enterprise* (1904).

doctrine was mired in dispute, as economists in Europe and the United States refuted it, defended it, and reformulated it on various grounds.[9]

In his note, Veblen audaciously claims that he has identified a conceptual move that enables him to resolve the conflict insofar as it relates to the "source of wages" (p. 77). He presents this move as analogous to one made in Eugen von Böhm-Bawerk's just-translated Austrian-marginalist treatise, *The Positive Theory of Capital* (1891), which American economists were widely praising. Commending Böhm-Bawerk for differentiating "private capital" from "social capital," but then slightly amending Böhm-Bawerk's own definition of social capital,[10] Veblen urges a parallel distinction between "wages" and "earnings," observing that "wages is a category having a different significance for economic theory from that of earnings or of goods consumed" (p. 79). Although admitting that this argument might seem a mere "point of classification" inside a "web of excessively fine-spun technicalities," Veblen nonetheless asserts that it reconciles the wages-fund doctrine in "its essential tenets" with the valid objections of its critics, thus bringing the controversy finally to an end (p. 79).

Veblen characterizes this article as a contribution to "pure theory" (p. 79), and during this period he published one more article (Veblen 1892b) in this same genre, before shifting his focus to a more empirical – though no less mainstream – topic in economics. This topic was the price of wheat, the subject of Veblen's next two publications, one of which is Selection 5, "The Food Supply and the Price of Wheat." Veblen took up this subject shortly after his departure with Laughlin from Cornell in mid-1892 for a fellowship at the University of Chicago. As part of his move to the University of Chicago, Laughlin agreed to found a new journal of economics, the *Journal of Political Economy*, in order to address the "practical problems of economics," such as "transportation, agriculture, socialism, taxation," and "the modern growth of large production" (1892, pp. 14–19). Veblen's two articles on wheat prices responded to this agenda and were both published in the *Journal's* first volume.

Selection 5, the second of the two articles, appeared in June 1893, in the context of a prolonged period of economic hardship in American agriculture,

---

9 Writing of the wages-fund doctrine, Frank Taussig (1896, p. 282) commented: "The varieties of opinion are endless; on no topic in the range of economic theory would it be so difficult to extract any consensus of opinion." Taussig's volume remains an excellent history of the controversy. See also Breit (1967).

10 In a later literature prompted by Coleman (1988) and Putnam (1995, 2000), "social capital" acquired a very different set of meanings, to refer (rather vaguely and without a consensus on its definition) to the social relations, networks, and institutions that sustain a modern complex society and economy. What is often overlooked is that "social capital" was widely used in the late nineteenth century, and influentially by Marshall (1890) among others, to refer (with lesser but still positive imprecision) to the collection of *tangible* capital goods held publicly or privately within the society at large. On the problems of broadening the definition of capital, see Fetter (1930) as well as others (Hodgson 2008). Veblen (1908b, p. 115) held that the term "capital" should not apply to persons.

which was then being exacerbated by the deepening national depression. In the selection, Veblen brandishes the teachings and the terminology of neo-classical economics, describing the decline in agricultural prices as "an object lesson to enforce the truth that there is a close dependence of price on supply" (p. 80), and invoking one of Mill's and Laughlin's favorite principles, "the law of diminishing returns" (p. 81). Chiefly, though, the article seeks, by means of a comparison of wheat prices and average acreage yields in Britain and America, to "forecast" US wheat production a decade into the future by elaborating several "premises [about] the normal increase in the demand for bread" and from these premises "deduc[ing the] possible advance in price" of wheat (pp. 82, 89, 84). For the time being, Veblen reflects critically on none of the concepts that he makes use of in his analysis.

The interest in the "practical problems of economics" that Laughlin imparted to the early volumes of the *Journal of Political Economy* affected as well the curriculum that he instituted for Chicago's Political Economy Department, which from the outset offered (*inter alia*) courses on American agriculture and on socialism. Beginning with Veblen's first year at Chicago, responsibility for courses on these topics fell naturally to him, as the department member who had recently written on both subjects. Likewise, as the primary teacher of courses on these subjects, Veblen quickly assumed the role of the *Journal of Political Economy*'s in-house reviewer of new books on socialism, agriculture, and related topics (e.g. Marxism, land ownership), publishing in the journal, in the years between 1893 and 1898, reviews of 20 titles in English, French, and German.[11] These book reviews document Veblen's close and critical engagement with the literature of the social sciences during the final decade of the nineteenth century, and nine of them appear as selections here in Part I.

Selection 6 is Veblen's 1893 review of British colonial administrator Henry Baden-Powell's massive three-volume treatise, *The Land-Systems of British India* (1892). A work of erudition that scholars admire even at the present time, Veblen lauds the book for recognizing the variety of land-tenure arrangements in India and for examining their diverse courses of historical development. In particular, Veblen approvingly spotlights the portion of the treatise where Baden-Powell discusses the "stages of property" and disputes the notion of a universal primitive stage during which "the whole tribe or clan regarded the land as really 'common' in a communistic or socialist sense" (1892, vol. 1, pp. 110–11). Even so, Veblen insists, with

---

11 With the fourth volume of the *Journal of Political Economy* in 1895, Veblen was also listed as the journal's managing editor, a task that perhaps involved him in locating reviewers for books that the journal received and, by extension, in taking on some of the reviews himself. Dorfman (1934, p. 95) is of the impression that Veblen's role at the journal began earlier and that "most of the burden of editing [it] fell upon Veblen's shoulders" during most of his time at Chicago (1934, p. 95). Also on Veblen's shoulders, at the instigation of his departmental colleagues, was the 800-page translation of German economist Gustav Cohn's *System der Finanzwissenschaft* (1889), which Veblen brought out in English in 1895 as *The Science of Finance*.

Baden-Powell, that "certain broad generalizations may be made, and may be made good use of" (p. 93). As he formulates these points, Veblen locates Baden-Powell's central achievement in what his research offers to "the student of economic institutions" regarding the "origins" of those institutions (pp. 93, 92).

Selection 7 is Veblen's review in early 1894 of *Der Parlamentarismus* (1893), a minor work by the prominent European Marxist theorist, politician, and journalist Karl Kautsky, whose prolific writings had at the time established him, after Friedrich Engels, as "the chief exponent of the naturalistic, evolutionist, determinist, Darwinist version of Marxism."[12] Like many others within the "Social Democratic"[13] wing of late nineteenth-century continental Marxism, Kautsky advocated a political middle course – favorable to a "parliamentary legislative body and the parliamentary method" (p. 94) – which contrasted with anarchists and syndicalists who wished the proletariat to avoid political and parliamentary issues *and* with revolutionary socialists who wanted workers to seize political power by force. Veblen's review strongly recommends Kautsky's alternative as set forth in his most recent book. Moreover, Veblen uses Kautsky's tract to support the view that he himself had urged two years before in his critique of Spencer: viz., that socialism can be rendered compatible with the "modern political institutions [of the] English-speaking people" (p. 95). Regarding this claim, Veblen now remarks further that socialism "will be reached *if at all* by an evolution from existing forms of social organization" and "will do its work [by perfecting] the means employed by the political republic" (p. 95, emphasis added). Veblen's position thus contrasted with that of Lenin, Trotsky, and the Bolsheviks, who a few years later proposed the global overthrow of all state institutions, including parliamentary democracies, and their replacement by workers' soviets.

Although Veblen wrote additional book reviews during this stage of his career, the next item, Selection 8, would be his last article for a period of nearly four years,[14] as he composed the body of work that makes up Part II. Published in late 1894, just before this period began, this substantial article is entitled "The Economic Theory of Woman's Dress," and it witnesses Veblen harking back to other themes found in his critique of Spencer. As he does so

---

12 The quotation here is from Kolakowski (1978, p. 51), whose volume provides a valuable discussion of the socialist factions described in the following sentence.

13 Note that left parties in several countries then described themselves as "Social Democratic" and welcomed Marxists into their ranks. It is only after the Second World War that "Social Democracy" became associated with more moderate positions, including advocates of a reformed capitalism.

14 Several months earlier, in the June 1894 issue of the *Journal of Political Economy*, Veblen also published a brief "note" on "the Army of the Commonweal" (Veblen 1894c), a band of unemployed men, formed in the depths of the nation's continuing depression, that had recently marched on Washington, DC, to demand (unsuccessfully) that the federal government release funds to pay the unemployed to build roads.

here, however, he elaborates his ideas – about wasteful consumption and the modern-day concern with maintaining appearances of economic success – in conjunction with another contemporary discussion that was unfolding around him.

At the center of this particular discussion was Frederick Starr, Veblen's colleague in the university's Department of Sociology and Anthropology, who in 1891 had delivered a set of public lectures on "Dress and Adornment," which he subsequently published as a series of articles in *Popular Science Monthly*, a widely read periodical designed to disseminate academic scholarship to the educated American public (see Starr 1891a, 1891b, 1891c, 1891d). Starr's series focused on bodily adornments among primitive peoples, which he characterized as "emblems of rank or power," "mark[s] of social inequality" that display "class distinctions" (1891c, p. 56). Two years later, *Popular Science Monthly* ran a companion article in which economist J. W. Black reiterated Starr's analysis but raised questions as to "how dress has developed [into] its present form among civilized peoples" and how women came to surpass men as the objects of conspicuous decoration (1893, pp. 395, 397).

Appearing in *Popular Science Monthly* the following year, Veblen's article on woman's dress took up these questions, while also responding to Laughlin's recent call to study "the economic effects of changes of fashion" within the "modern industrial system" (1894, p. 9). In the article, Veblen argues that woman's "'dress,' ... from the economic point of view, [constitutes a] 'display of wasteful expenditure'" on the part of the wearer (p. 98). In this way, dress provides an "index of the wealth of the economic unit which the wearer represents," thus furnishing a visible marker of the economic "success," or "pecuniary strength," of households in "the most advanced modern communities," which have as their norm the "conspicuously unproductive consumption of valuable goods" (pp. 97–100). It is in accord with this principle, according to Veblen, that such communities prize women's apparel to the extent that it is expensive, continually replaced, and sufficiently "cumbrous" to require "habitual idleness," a condition that compels from onlookers "observation of the fact that the wearer is manifestly incapable of doing anything that is of any use" (p. 100).

Selection 9 is Veblen's lengthy 1896 joint review of a recent reissue of Karl Marx's *Misère de la Philosophie* (1847) and of *Socialisme et Science Positive* (1896), the French edition of a major essay by Italian criminologist and socialist politician Enrico Ferri. Veblen's comment on Marx's volume is cursory, briefly acknowledging "the unabated authority with which the writings of the master still appeal to thoughtful and studious adherents of the school" (p. 104). In contrast, Veblen takes pains with his presentation of Ferri's text, albeit without disclosing much of his reaction to Ferri's elaborate effort to reconcile socialism with Darwinism. Veblen does, however, underscore in the essay two themes that signal issues that were moving to the forefront of his own attentions in these years. The first of these themes is Ferri's opposition to "injecting ... teleological meaning into the term 'fittest' as used by Darwin"

(p. 106). Ferri's book repudiated writers who equated "fittest" with "best adapted" because such an equation wrongly assumed "a teleology which saw in nature and history a finality to be attained by means of a continuous amelioration" (1896/1909, p. 38); and not only does Veblen emphasize this point, but he observes that it finds support in the research of respected European anthropologists such as Lapouge and Ammon. Second, Veblen flags Ferri's argument that, "while the profound revolution in science wrought by Darwinism and the Spencerian evolutionism has rehabilitated every department of physical, biological, and even the psychological sciences, [it has] barely rippled the surface of the still waters of that pool of orthodoxy in social science, Political Economy" (p. 108). Veblen voices no opinion as to Ferri's assertion that "the Marxian Materialistic Theory of History" offers the genuinely Darwinian way forward, though one may doubt that Ferri's was the only option that Veblen saw before him at this time.

That he was already thinking along different lines appears in Selection 10, Veblen's more admiring early 1897 review of the young German Marxist writer Richard Calwer's little-known *Einführung in der Socialismus* (1896). Here Veblen applauds Calwer for formulating a "greatly modernized" Marxism whose account of "social evolution" goes beyond the tenets of historical materialism to recognize that "the institutions of the community, whether socialistic or otherwise, rest on psychological ground" (pp. 110–11). In Veblen's view, Calwer rightly grasped that the "material circumstances of environment, and of industrial organization and methods, control the growth of institutions and social structure only as they affect the individual's habitual view of things" (p. 111). What is more, according to Veblen, Calwer claimed that the "motive force" that fuels "the discontent of the modern laborer ... is simply sentiment and is closely akin to envy, its basis being chiefly an invidious comparison of the laborer's lot with that of the propertied classes" (p. 111) – a claim akin to Veblen's own argument back in his critique of Spencer.

Of a piece with this review of Calwer is Selection 11, Veblen's review, a few months later, of *Essais sur la conception materialiste de l'histoire* (1897), the French translation of University of Rome philosophy professor Antonio Labriola's principal treatise. Little noticed at the time, Labriola's *Essais* would subsequently emerge as one of the classics of European Marxism, a nondogmatic alternative to the writings of Marx, Engels, and Kautsky;[15] and Veblen's ambivalent review seems to have been the first notice the book received in English. Veblen was perhaps drawn to the book by Georges Sorel's "Preface," which promised to Labriola's readers "substantial and valuable suggestion for the study of the origin and transformation of institutions" (quoted by Kerr 1904, p. 4), although on this score Veblen may well have come away disappointed. In any event, he characterizes Labriola's book – inasmuch as it goes beyond a "tedious" summary of the historical materialism

---

15 On Labriola, see Kolakowski (1978).

of the past – as typifying a welcome new trend among European socialists to cast aside the labor-theory of value and the theory of class struggle and, instead, to uphold "a conception of the evolution of social structure according to which economic activities, and the habits bred by them, determine the activities and habitual view of things in other directions than the economic" (pp. 113–14). "In this development," remarks Veblen, "socialists are drawing close to the position of a large and increasing class of economists who are accepting the materialist conception, or so much of it as [can] be affiliated with Darwinism" (p. 114) – a clear allusion to his own stance at this time.

Selection 12, from late 1897, is Veblen's review of still another *fin de siècle* reformulation of historical materialism, Max Lorenz's *Die Marxistische Socialdemokratie* (1896). Like Calver, Lorenz was an aspiring young German Marxist rethinking the ideas of Marx and Engels in ways that appealed to Veblen, though in this case the prose of his brief review is less evaluative. Even so, the few pages that Veblen singles out from Lorenz's book are telling, particularly on the assumption that (as in his reviews of Calver and Labriola) Veblen is using the author as a spokesperson for his own views. For, what Veblen emphasizes is Lorenz's effort to replace Marxism's understanding of man "solely as a medium for the transmission and expression of social laws and changes" with a conception of human nature that also recognizes the "individual [as] acting out his own life as such" (p. 116). "With the amendment so indicated," observes Veblen with apparent approval, historical materialism "becomes not only a theory of the method of social and economic changes, but a theory of social process considered as a substantial unfolding of life as well" (p. 116).[16]

In Selection 13, Veblen turns to a distinguished author familiar to all economists of the period, Gustav Schmoller, one of Germany's so-called "socialists of the chair," who was then the acknowledged head of the much-discussed historical school of economics, as well as rector of the University of Berlin.[17] The occasion for this mid-1898 review was the publication of one of Schmoller's lesser works, *Über einige Grundfragen der Socialpolitik und der Volkswirtschaftslehre* (1898), a short collection of essays from different

---

16 For a fuller discussion of this review, as well as those of Ferri and Labriola, see Hodgson (2004).

17 The term "socialists of the chair" – *Kathedersozialisten* – was an expression that contemporaries associated with the second ("younger") generation of nineteenth-century German historical economists, especially those who, along with Schmoller, participated in the 1872 congress that gave rise to the *Verein für Sozialpolitik* and generally supported, from their university "chairs," various reform measures of a "state socialist" nature. (See the entries on "Socialism, State" and "Socialists, of the Chair" in Palgrave's *Dictionary of Political Economy* (1894–99).) Gustav Cohn, the translation of whose treatise on finance Veblen published in 1895 (see n. 11 above), was a member of this group. Some historians have argued about the precision and utility of the expression, as well as the related notion of a "German Historical School" (see Grimmer-Solem 2003; Rodgers 1998), though such terms were in wide circulation in Veblen's time, especially as applied to Schmoller.

stages in his career. In the review, Veblen agrees with the central criticism that classical and marginalist economists had brought forth in response to Schmoller's attack on their use of deductive methods: namely, that, as evidenced by his early work, Schmoller's inductive method is antiscientific, producing nothing beyond "compilation and description" (p. 118). Against the critics, however, Veblen defends Schmoller's later work as a "prospectus for theoretical science" (p. 118). In support of this interpretation, his review translates long passages from Schmoller's later essays, choosing those passages that anticipate arguments that Veblen was then preparing to develop elsewhere (see Part II). Accordingly, he quotes Schmoller saying: that the "ideal of all knowledge [is] the explanation of all facts in terms of causation" (p. 119); that, although classification is essential to scientific thought, "normalization and taxonomic schedules are not science in the modern acceptance of the word" (p. 120); and that it is "incumbent on a practical science, such as economics, to carry its inquiry ... into the details of psychological processes" (pp. 119–20).

Selection 14 is Veblen's review, also from 1898, of a book of very different kind. Its author, W. H. Mallock, was a highly productive British man-of-letters, who had attained prominence in the 1880s and 1890s for relentless anti-socialist writings seeking to refute the notion that workers have a right to the product of their labor with the counter-argument that economic advance depends on the productive ability of capitalists. Popular among the British upper classes, Mallock's work had come under heavy criticism from economists such as J. A. Hobson as well as from socialist George Bernard Shaw;[18] and Veblen's long review of Mallock's latest book, *Aristocracy and Evolution* (1898), sides with the critics. Dismissing Mallock's "grotesquely devious ways of [formulating his] economic argument," Veblen devotes particular attention to dismantling the logic by which Mallock attributes productive ability chiefly to businessmen – whose relation to production is "always remote" – rather than to the inventors, engineers, and production supervisors who also figure in his account (pp. 125, 124). Searching for a feature of the book to compliment, Veblen commends Mallock for observing "the importance of a gifted minority as an element in the process of institutional growth," though without properly recognizing that this effect occurs mainly in "other fields than the economic" (p. 125). As regards Mallock's extended treatment of the topic of social evolution (1898, pp. 89–107), Veblen interestingly remains silent, just as his own views on the topic were about to issue forth.

---

18 On Mallock's career and ideas, as well as the response of his critics, see Mason (1980).

Selection 1

Mill's theory of the taxation of land

Source: *Johns Hopkins University Circulars*, February 1882 (vol. 13, p. 176).

Veblen (1882)

With the advance of society the rent of land increases. This increase is independent of any effort on the part of the landlord, being the product of the activity of the community. The State should, therefore, by a peculiar tax, appropriate this "unearned increment" and not permit it to go to the owner of the land. To obviate all injustice to owners who have bought land with the expectation of being permitted to enjoy the future increase of its rent, the State is to offer to buy the land of the owners at its market price as an alternative to their keeping it and paying to the State the increase in rent. As a consequence of such an alternative, land having a speculative value would be sold to the State in order to avoid loss to the owners. The measure would act as a fine on the holding of land, to the amount of the speculative value, and lead to an almost universal nationalization of land; differing, however, from generally entertained schemes for the State's getting possession of land, in that the expense of the change would be more equitably distributed on all classes of the community. No immediate redistribution of wealth would take place, but, neglecting all probable undesirable secondary effects of the change on the people, an advantage would accrue from an increased compactness of population, making possible a saving of labor.

Selection 2

Kant's *Critique of Judgment*

Source: *Journal of Speculative Philosophy*, July 1884
(vol. 43, pp. 260–74).

Veblen (1884)

The place of the *Critique of Judgment* in Kant's system of Philosophy is that
of a mean between the two *Critiques* of the Pure and of the Practical Reason.
A feeling of the lack of coherence between the other two critiques prompted
him to the elaboration of this one, and the Doctrine of Method at the close of
the [261] work is mainly a sketch of the way in which he conceived that the
results of this *Critique* were to be made useful in the system of Philosophy to
which he regarded all his critical work as preliminary. The outcome of *Critique of the Practical Reason* is the notion of freedom in the person; the outcome of the *Critique of Pure Reason* is the notion of strict determinism,
according to natural law, in the world. It will hardly do to say that the two
are contradictory, for they are so thoroughly disparate that, taken by themselves only and placed in juxtaposition, they do not even contradict each
other. It is well known that it was on account of this disparity of the two
notions that Kant was able to hold to the reality of personal freedom at the
same time that he held to the doctrine of unavoidable determination according to natural law. But while he found the disparity of the two indispensable
in order to the reality of freedom, he also found that, in order to free activity,
a mediation between the two was likewise indispensable.

The idea of freedom of moral action contains the requirement that the
concepts of morality are to be actualized in the sphere of natural law. Without the possibility of realizing the concepts of morality in the realm of
nature – without ability to affect events in the course of nature – morality
would be only a fiction, The free person must be only an absurdity; but, even
if it be granted that the person can and does come into the course of events as
an efficient cause, that is not enough. Thus far the conclusions of the *Critique
of Practical* reach, but Kant was not satisfied with that. The action of the
person must be capable of falling in with the activity of the causes among
which it comes; otherwise it will act blindly to no purpose. The agent must
know what will be the effect of this or that action, if his activity is not to be
nugatory, or worse than nugatory. And, in order to such a knowledge of the
results of a contemplated action, the knowledge furnished by simple experience is not sufficient. Simple experience, whether we accept Kant's doctrine
concerning the knowledge given by experience, as he has developed it in the

Critique of Pure Reason, or not, cannot forecast the future. Experience can, at the best, give what is or what has been, but cannot say what is to be. It gives data only, and data never go into the [262] future unaided and of their own accord. Data do not tell what the effect of action will be, except as we are able to judge the future by the help of the data given. Judgment must come in, if experience is to be any use, and morality anything more than a dream. The power of judgment, or of reasoning, must mediate between theoretical knowledge and moral action; and the kind of judgment that is required is inductive reasoning. All this is simple enough. It is so simple and is so obvious that it is difficult to see it until it has been pointed out, and after it has been pointed out it seems to have been unnecessary to speak of it. Though Kant, in giving his reasons for undertaking the *Critique of Judgment*, speaks mainly of the indispensableness of this power of inductive reasoning for the purposes of morality, it is evident that it is no less indispensable in every other part of practical life. To-day any attempt, in any science, which does not furnish us an induction, is counted good for nothing, and it is with this power of inductive reasoning that the most important part of the *Critique of Judgment* has to do.

In Kant's trichotomous scheme of the faculties and capacities of the intellect, the Power of Judgment lies in the middle, between the Understanding and the Reason, just as the faculty of pleasure and pain lies between the faculties of cognition and of desire, and affords a connection and mediation between the two. The Understanding has to do with cognition, and is *a priori* legislative for empirical knowledge; the pure Reason has to do with desire, and is *a priori* legislative for action; by analogy we should be able to say, at least provisionally, that the Power of Judgment has to do with the capacity of pleasure and pain, and legislates *a priori* concerning the adequate or subservient, the commensurate, appropriate, or adapted (*das Zweckmässige*).

The Power of Judgment is, in general, the power of thinking the particular under the universal. "If the universal (the rule, the principle, the law) is given, then the judgment which subsumes the particular under it is *determinative* [deductive reasoning]. But if only the particular is given, for which the judgment is to find a universal, then the judgment is only *reflective*" [inductive reasoning]. (*Kritik der Urtheilskraft*, ed. K. Kehrbach, 1878; *Einl.*, IV.) Inasmuch as this *Critique* is a critique of the *pure* Power of Judgment only – *i.e.*, of the Power of Judgment in so [263] far as none of the principles of its action are borrowed from elsewhere – it has to do only with the reflective judgment; for, in order that the judgment be determinative, the universal which is to serve it as a rule in the work of subsumption must be *given*, and so must be present as a premise, and will condition the action of the judgment working under it. The determinative judgment is simply the activity of the intellect in general in applying the laws given by Understanding and Reason, and, as such, its action has been analyzed in the two critiques which treat of those faculties. The determinative judgment, subsuming particular data under general laws which are also data, is nothing but the activity of the Understanding in combining simple experience into a synthetic whole, under those laws of the understanding which are a necessary condition of experience. Therefore the discussion of the determinative judgment belongs in the critique of the theoretical Reason. The reflective judgment passes beyond the simple data of experience and seeks a universal which is not given in empirical cognition; therefore it must proceed according to a principle not given to it from without. It has a power of self-direction, and therefore calls for a critique of its own.

This is the starting-point of the *Critique of Judgment*, and, if this had been borne in mind, it might have saved many of Kant's critics a good deal of mistaken criticism. As a rule, the criticisms offered on his doctrine of Teleology have gone to work as though his starting-point had been from the developed principle of Final Cause, and as though he had proceeded from that principle to the notions of adaptation, and thence to that of æsthetic appropriateness, which is precisely reversing the truth. They have taken up the *Critique* wrong end foremost, and it is no wonder that they have found fault with it. Kant's doctrine of Final Cause is arrived at from a consideration of the ways in which the reflective judgment works; the nature of the reflective judgment is not deduced from a preconceived notion about finality.

The office of the reflective judgment is to find unity in multiplicity, or to give unity to multiplicity. Its action is not only synthetic, but it is to make a synthesis which shall reach beyond, and include more than what is given in simple experience. The problem of this *Critique*, as of the other two, is: How are synthetic judgments *a priori* possible? but, while the faculties under consideration [264] in the other two *Critiques* have to do with laws unavoidably given and unavoidably applied to given data, the reflective judgment is the faculty of search. It is the faculty of adding to our knowledge something which is not and cannot be given in experience. It is to reduce the manifold of nature, the various concepts we have of the things in the world, to a synthetic totality. It has to bring the facts given in experience under laws and principles, and to bring empirical concepts under higher concepts. Whatever is ascertained, and so becomes an item of knowledge, becomes therewith a point of departure for the reflective judgment. The reflective judgment is continually reaching over beyond the known, and grasping at that which cannot come within experience. Its object is a synthesis, a systematization of whatever is known; and, in order to the attainment of a system, its procedure must be governed by some principle. As the result aimed at lies beyond experience, the principle according to which it is to proceed cannot be given by experience. The principle is not taken from outside the power of judgment, for, if such were the case, the judgment working under that principle would be determinative and not reflective; therefore the principle according to which the reflective judgment proceeds must originate with the reflective judgment itself; or, in other words, it must be an *a priori* principle of the intellect, and must hold its place as a principle only in relation to the reflective judgment. It cannot be the same principle, in the same form, as any of the principles governing the other faculties.

The nature of this principle is to be found from a consideration of the work it is to do. The reflective judgment is to generalize, to reduce our knowledge to a system under more general laws than any given by experience. Its office is to systematize, and to systematize is but another expression for reducing things to intelligent order; that is, to think things as though they had been made according to the laws of an understanding, to think them as though made by an intelligent cause. But to think things in a system *as though* they were made by an intelligent cause is not the same as to think that they are made by such a cause. So much is not required by the principle. All that is required is that the things be thought as falling under a system of law according [265] to which they adapt themselves to the laws of our understanding – that they are such in the manner of their being as they would be if they were made with a view to the exigencies of our capacity of knowing. The principle of the reflective judgment is, therefore, primarily the requirement of adaptation on the part of the object to the laws of the activity of our faculties of knowledge, or, briefly, adaptation to our faculties.

Now, whenever the intellect finds the objects of its knowledge to be such as to admit of the unhampered activity of the faculties employed about them, there results a gratification such as always felt on the attainment of an end striven for. The more nearly the concept of the object known approaches to what such a concept might have been if it had been constructed simply under the guidance of the laws of the mind's own activity and without being in any way hindered or modified by external reality – that is, the more nearly the activity of the mind in thinking a given thought coincides with what would be the mind's activity if that activity were guided by its own intrinsic laws alone and were not influenced or hampered by the environment – the more fully will the requirements of the mind's activity be realized and the more intense will be the gratification felt in contemplating the object of thought which so employs the mind. A feeling of gratification, or the contrary, accordingly, goes along with the activity of the reflective judgment as a sanction and a test of its normality.

What this feeling of gratification testifies to is, that the play of the faculties of the intellect is free, or but little hampered by the empirical element in its knowledge. It therefore indicates that the objects contemplated are, in the form in which they are present in thought, adapted to the faculties. This adaptation of knowledge to our faculties may take place in two different ways, or rather it may take place at two different stages in the elaboration of the material gained by the experience. A simple datum may be given to the apprehension such as to conform to the normal action of our faculty of knowledge, and, by its so conforming, it shows adaptation to the faculties that are employed about it. In such a case, the concept which is contemplated and found adapted is not thereby an item of knowledge which goes to make up our conception of world-system, or to make a part of any systematic or organized whole. As a datum of the apprehension, it is considered [266] singly by itself only in relation to the apprehending subject, no thought being given to its making or not making an integral part of our knowledge of reality. In so far as concerns the adaptation conceived to belong to the concept, it is no matter whether any external reality corresponds to the concept or not; and, therefore, it makes no difference, as to the adaptation, whether the concept is derived from experience or is a pure figment. The adaptation belonging to such a concept, which is only a datum of the apprehension, is, therefore, subjective only. It is only a question of the conformation or nonconformation of a simple concept (*Vorstellung*) to the norms of the apprehension. The question is, how far the concept given is suited to the normal activity of the faculty of cognition; whatever may be the objective validity of the concept, that does not enter into consideration at all. This being the case, the only way to judge of the adaptation of such a concept is to take cognizance of the way in which the faculties act on occasion of it, and the test can only be whether the faculties act unhampered and satisfactorily; and the only indication of the normal activity of the faculties, again, is the resulting feeling of gratification or dissatisfaction. If the concept, simply as such, pleases, it is normal or adapted; if it displeases, it is not. The object corresponding to such a concept, which pleases in its simple apprehension, is said to be beautiful, and the reflective judgment, in so far as it proceeds on the simple adaptation of the data of apprehension to the faculties of cognition, is æsthetic judgment. It is of a purely subjective character, and its action is not based on logical, but wholly on pathological grounds. The decision of the æsthetic judgment is made on the ground of the feeling called forth by the apprehension of the concept, and the feeling is, therefore, in this case, the only authority that has a voice in the matter.

From these considerations it follows that there can be no objective principle of æsthetic judgment. The principle which governs taste must accordingly exert its authority, not through the means of logical argument and proof, but by an appeal to the nature of men in respect to reflective judgment in general. "The principal of taste is the subjective principle of the judgment in general" (*Kritik der Urtheilskraft*, p. 148). The universal validity which a judgment in a matter of taste bespeaks can, therefore, rest only [267] on the assumption of an essential similarity of all men in respect to the feeling involved in such a judgment.

On the other hand, the data of cognition may also be contemplated, with reference to their adaptation, at the stage at which they are no longer simple data apprehension, but constitute a part of our knowledge of reality. That is, they (the concepts) may be considered as making a part of our knowledge of nature, and, consequently, as entering into a system in which they must stand in relation to other data. Their adaptation will consequently here be found, if at all, in the logical relations of concepts – items of empirical knowledge or laws of nature – to one another, and the conformity of these relations to the normal activity of the faculties; not in the immediate adaptation of particular items or data of experience to be taken up by the faculties, as was the case in the æsthetic judgment. And since the faculties, dealing with the relations of concepts as making up our knowledge of reality, have to do with the relations of real objects as known to us, the relations of the concepts, in which the adaptation is supposed to lie, are here conceived to be real relations of objects; the adaptation of these concepts, as standing in logical relations to one another, to the normal activity of the mind, therefore comes to be looked on as a quality of the objects contemplated. The objects are conceived to stand in such relations of dependence and interaction as correspond to the logical relations of the concepts we have of them. Now, as a matter of fact, the connection or relation of our concepts which will be found adapted to our faculties, and which answers the requirements of their normal action, is one according to which they make a systematic, connected whole. The relations of objects which shall correspond in the world of reality to this logical relation of our concepts are such relations of interaction and interdependence as will bind the particular things in the world of reality together into a whole, in which the existence of one thing is dependent on that of another, and in which no one thing can exist without mutually conditioning and being conditioned by every other. That is, the adaptation found, or sought to be found, in concepts when contemplated in their logical aspect, is conceived to be an adaptation of things to one another in such a way that each is at the same time the means and the end of the existence of every other. [268]

Such a conception of the world of reality, in which things are united into an organized whole, can proceed only on the assumption that the particular things which go to make up the organic whole are subject to laws of a character similar to that of the logical laws according to which our mind subsumes the particular under the general, and holds together all the material gained by our cognition in a systematic totality of knowledge; which is the same as saying that in such a conception is contained the idea that the world is made according to laws similar to the laws of understanding, and therefore that it is made by an intelligent cause, and made with intention and purpose. To put the same thing in another way: To conceive the world in the way required by the reflective judgment is to conceive it as being made so as to harmonize with the laws of our understanding; that is, in being made, it is adapted to our faculties, and therefore made by a cause of working according to laws like those of our understanding, and with a view to the exigencies of our understanding in comprehending the world. The cause producing the world must therefore be conceived to have worked it out according to a preconceived notion of what it was to be, and the realization of the form in which the world so created actually exists, accordingly, has its ground in an idea conceived by the cause which created it. The idea of what the world was to be precedes and conditions the world as it actually comes into existence – which is precisely what we mean when we say that the world was created by final cause.

All this argument for a final cause in the world rests on the action of the reflective judgment and its validity therefore extends only so far as the principle of the reflective judgment reaches. That principle is the requirement of adaptation, on the part of our knowledge, to the normal action of our faculties of knowing; it is therefore of subjective validity only, and can say nothing as to the nature of external reality. The finality which is attributed to external reality, on the ground of the adaptation found by the reflective judgment, is simply and only an imputed finality, and the imputation of it to reality is based on the same ground of feeling as every other act of the reflective judgment. Our imputation of finality to the things of the world, and our teleological arguments for an intelligent cause of the world, proceed on subjective grounds entirely, and give no knowledge of objective fact, and furnish no [269] proof that is available for establishing even a probability in favor of what is claimed.

What is proved by the tenacity with which we cling to our teleological conception of the world is, that the constitution of our intellect demands this conception – that our faculties, in their normal action, must arrive at this before they can find any halting-place. The mind is not satisfied with its knowledge of a thing, or of any event or fact, until it is able to say, not only how the thing or event has a purpose; the proposition may be put into this general form, and we may be obliged, oftentimes, to leave the matter in this state of generality; but we cannot believe, concerning anything, that there is not reason why it is, or why it is as it is. It is, of course, possible to give our attention to any item of knowledge – to employ ourselves about any object or any process or law in nature – without bringing in the notion of purpose; but our knowledge of it cannot be regarded as complete until we have asked the question why it is.

But though this question of teleology is of extreme importance, yet a knowledge of the teleological end of a given thing, or the purpose of an action or event as considered from the standpoint of the economy of the universe, is not absolutely necessary in order to human life, not even in order to a high degree of development in moral life. In truth, a knowledge of ultimate particular ends and purposes is of no use whatever in the affairs of everyday life; and, therefore, the principle of teleology, as being the principle of conscious purpose in the world, is not indispensable in order to such knowledge of things as is required by the exigencies of life. The knowledge we need and use can be got, and got in sufficient completeness for all purposes of utility, without any appeal to, or any aid from, the developed principle of finality; and, if the exercise of the reflective judgment, in its logical application, consisted in the decision of teleological questions alone, its value would be small enough. Such, however, is not the case.

The principle of the logical use of the reflective judgment was found to be the general principle of adaptation; and since, in its logical use, the judgment has to do with reality the principle [270] which shall govern the reflective judgment here will be that of objective adaptation; that is, adaptation which is *conceived* to belong to things objectively. The motive which leads to the application of this principle to our knowledge of things was found to be a feeling of dissatisfaction with our knowledge so long as it consists only in a chaotic manifold of concepts. We are dissatisfied with a conception of reality which makes it only a congeries of things, without connection, system, or order, beyond juxtaposition in space and succession and duration in time. Yet such a congeries is all that unaided experience can give; and the determinative (deductive) judgment can do little to bring further order into this chaos. It is true, we have the general law of cause and effect given, and it looks as though we ought to be able to establish some system by the aid of it, when the experience gives us the data to which the law applies; but further thought will show that we should be as helpless with that law as without it if no further principle came in to guide us in the application of it. We should have the law which says: "Every change has a cause and an effect": and all that the data of experience would enable us to say further would be, that this law in general applies to these data. The abstract law and the data, simply under the action of the determinative judgment, could never get so far as to afford us ground for asserting that a given effect has a given cause; still less, that a given cause will produce a given effect. The truth of this is shown by the nature of our knowledge of particular causes. We can never designate, with that certainty which belongs to every deliverance of the deductive judgment, what is the cause of any given effect. We may have no doubt as to what is the cause of a given effect; but still, if it should turn out that the effect under consideration has some other cause than the one we counted on, we should not, therefore, conclude than the world is out of joint. It is possible that we may be mistaken in our opinion as to particular cases of cause and effect – even the most certain of them – which would not be the case if we arrived at our knowledge of them by simple deductive reasoning from data of experience and an *a priori* law. There is always an element of probability, however slight, in our knowledge of particular causes; but simple experience – cognition – never has anything to say about probability; it only says what *is*, and leaves no room for doubt or probability. [271]

In order to find what is the cause of a given effect, and, still more, what *will be* the effect of a given cause, we need a guiding principle beyond anything that experience gives. We have to go beyond what is given us, and so we need a principle of search. That is what is afforded by this principle of adaptation. The mind is unsatisfied with things until it can see how they belong together. The principle of adaptation says that the particular things do belong together, and sets the mind hunting to find out how. The principle of adaptation says that, in order to the normal action of the faculties, things must be conceived as adapted to one another so as to form a systematic totality – that things must be conceived to be so co-ordinated in their action as to make up an organized whole – and the mind goes to work to make its knowledge of reality conform to its own normal activity; or, in other words, to find what particular case of interaction under the law of cause and effect will stand the test of the principle of adaptation. What the principle of adaptation does for us is, therefore, in the first place, that it makes us guess, and that it guides our guessing. If it were not that we are dissatisfied with our knowledge so long as it remains in the shape of a mere manifold, we should never seek to get beyond a congeries of things in time and space; and, if it were not that the principle of adaptation shows us what we are to seek further, we should never find anything further in our knowledge.

But the principle of adaptation cannot give us any new data, nor can it tell us anything new about the data we have. All it can do is to guide us in guessing about the given data, and then leave it to experience to credit or discredit our guesses. That is, it is a regulative, not a constitutive principle of knowledge, according to the distinction which Kant makes in his classification of *a priori* principles of the mind. Now, as has already been pointed out, the direction in which this principle will lead us is that of generalization, since no such principle is needed in order to deductive reasoning. In order to analyze the content of our empirical knowledge, there is no guessing necessary; all that is then required is that we take a more complete inventory of what we already know. The guessing, under the principle of adaptation, is in the direction of a higher systematization of what we know. The principle suggests that, in order to conform to the norms of [272] our faculties, things should fall into a system under laws of such or such a character; that they should stand in such or such relations of interaction and co-ordination; and that the laws which are given *a priori* as applying to things should apply to them in such or such a way; and so it leads to an hypothesis as to the nature of particular things and the laws of their connection. The principle guides us to an hypothesis in the world of reality. It proceeds on the basis of a feeling, and so it can decide whether the hypothesis suits the minds, but not at all whether it applies to reality. Experience alone can say whether the hypothesis fits the thing it is intended for; or, rather, it can say whether it appears to fit them, since, inasmuch as an hypothesis never can become an object of experience in the sense as things are objects of experience, it can also not have the empirical certainty which belongs to our knowledge of individual things. The testimony of experience as to the validity of the hypothesis can only be of a cumulative character, and all it can do is to give it a greater or less degree of probability. It is of the nature of circumstantial evidence.

The principle of adaptation, in its logical use, is accordingly the principle of inductive reasoning. The need felt by the mind of bringing order and systematic coherence into the knowledge it acquires, and therefore of conceiving the things about which it is engaged as adapted to one another, affords, at the same time, the motive and the guiding principle for induction. The unrest felt on account of the inharmonious and forced activity of the faculties, when engaged about a mere manifold or a discordant miscellany, drives the mind to seek a concord for its own activities, and, consequently, a reconciliation of the conflicting elements of its knowledge. The reason for the unrest felt in contemplating external things simply as individual and unconnected things lies in the fact that the mind is adapted to conceive the subject-matter of its knowledge in the form of a connected whole. If the mind had not an inherent capacity for thinking things as connected into a totality, or at least as being connected in a systematic way and under definite laws, it could not feel the lack of totality in contemplating things under the mere form of juxtaposition in time and space. It would not be dissatisfied with things as mere data if it knew of nothing better; and it would not seek anything [273] different if the conception of things, as a mere congeries, satisfied the requirements of its normal activity. But, the requirement of totality, of adaptation of part to part, being present, the mind has no alternative but to reflect and reflect on the material given it, and make the most it can out of it in the way of a systematic whole; and the requirement of adaptation points out the direction which its search must take. One consequence of this is that the search is never ended, as, from the nature of the case, the requirement can never be fulfilled. As soon as a result is obtained by the process of induction, that result becomes, for the purposes of the question in hand, a fact of empirical knowledge, and therefore acquires the character, not of a completed whole, but of an isolated and disconnected datum. As fast as one step of induction is completed it becomes a means to another step, which must inevitably follow it.

According to what has just been said, the motive and guiding principle of inductive reasoning, and, with it, of the teleological judgment, is the requirement of adaptation or totality in our knowledge. When we find this requirement answered, in greater or less degree, the consequence is more or less of a feeling of gratification, just as there is always a feeling of gratification on the successful completion of an undertaking, or the attainment of a desired end. This feeling of gratification may therefore be regarded as a sanction to the principles of the reflective judgment, and, in the last resort, it is this feeling of gratification alone which can decide whether the principle has been applied successfully in any given case.

Therefore, so far as concerns the distinctive characteristics of the reflective judgment – and, therefore, of inductive reasoning – it proceeds on subjective ground entirely. Its motive is subjective, and, though the evidence by which it seeks to establish the results aimed at is of empirical origin, yet the criterion, to which the result must conform in order to answer the purposes for which it is sought to be established, is subjective. The consequence of this subjectivity of the principle of induction is that the results it arrives at are only more or less probable. Yet, singular as it might seem, hardly any part of our knowledge except that got by induction is of any immediate use for practical purposes. For by induction alone can we reduce things to system and connection, [274] and so bring particular things and events under definite laws of interaction; therefore by induction alone can we get such knowledge as will enable us to forecast the future; and knowledge which shall help us to forecast the future – to tell what will take place under given circumstances and as the result of given actions – is the only knowledge which can serve as a guide in practical life, whether moral or otherwise.

Selection 3

Some neglected points in the theory of socialism

Source: *Annals of the American Academy of Political and Social Science*, November 1891 (vol. 2, pp. 345–62).

Veblen (1891)

The immediate occasion for the writing of this paper was given by the publication of Mr. Spencer's essay, "From Freedom to Bondage";[1] although it is not altogether a criticism of that essay. It is not my purpose to controvert the position taken by Mr. Spencer as regards the present feasibility of any socialist scheme. The paper is mainly a suggestion, offered in the spirit of the disciple, with respect to a point not adequately covered by Mr. Spencer's discussion, and which has received but very scanty attention at the hands of any other writer on either side of the socialist controversy. This main point is as to an economic ground, as a matter of fact, for the existing unrest that finds expression in the demands of socialist agitators.

I quote from Mr. Spencer's essay a sentence which does fair justice, so far as it goes, to the position taken by agitators: "In presence of obvious improvements, joined with that increase of longevity, which even alone yields conclusive proof of general amelioration, it is proclaimed, with increasing vehemence, that things are so bad that society must be pulled to pieces and reorganized on another plan." The most obtrusive feature of the change demanded by the advocates of socialism is governmental control of the industrial activities of society – the nationalization of industry. There is also, just at present, a distinct movement in practice, towards a more extended control of industry by the government, as Mr. Spencer has pointed out. This movement strengthens the position of the advocates of a complete nationalization of industry, by making it appear that the logic of events is on their side.

In America at least, this movement in the direction of a broader assertion of the paramount claims of the community, [346] and an extension of corporate action on part of the community in industrial matters, has not generally been connected with or based on an adherence to socialistic dogmas. This is perhaps truer of the recent past than of the immediate present. The motive of the movement has been, in large part, the expediency of each particular step taken. Municipal supervision, and, possibly, complete municipal control, has come to be a necessity in the case of such industries – mostly of recent

---

1 Introductory paper of *A Plea for Liberty*, edited by Thomas Mackay.

growth – as elementary education, street-lighting, water-supply, etc. Opinions differ widely as to how far the community should take into its own hands such industries as concern the common welfare, but the growth of sentiment may fairly be said to favor a wider scope of governmental control.

But the necessity of some supervision in the interest of the public extends to industries which are not simply of municipal importance. The modern development of industry and of the industrial organization of society makes it increasingly necessary that certain industries – often spoken of as "natural monopolies" – should be treated as being of a semi-public character. And through the action of the same forces a constantly increasing number of occupations are developing into the form of "natural monopolies."

The motive of the movement towards corporate action on the part of the community – State control of industry – has been largely that of industrial expediency. But another motive has gone with this one, and has grown more prominent as the popular demands in this direction have gathered wider support and taken more definite form. The injustice, the inequality, of the existing system, so far as concerns these natural monopolies especially, are made much of. There is a distinct unrest abroad, a discontent with things as they are, and the cry of injustice is the expression of this more or less widely prevalent discontent. This discontent is the truly socialistic element in the situation.

It is easy to make too much of this popular unrest. The clamor of the agitators might be taken to indicate a wider prevalence and a greater acuteness of popular discontent than actually exists; but after all due allowance is made for exaggeration [347] on the part of those interested in the agitation, there can still be no doubt of the presence of a chronic feeling of dissatisfaction with the working of the existing industrial system, and a growth of popular sentiment in favor of a leveling policy. The economic ground of this popular feeling must be found, if we wish to understand the significance, for our industrial system, of the movement to which it supplies the motive. If its causes shall appear to be of a transient character, there is little reason to apprehend a permanent or radical change of our industrial system as the outcome of the agitation; while if this popular sentiment is found to be the outgrowth of any of the essential features of the existing social system, the chances of its ultimately working a radical change in the system will be much greater.

The explanation offered by Mr. Spencer, that the popular unrest is due essentially to a feeling of *ennui* – to a desire for a change of posture on part of the social body, is assuredly not to be summarily rejected; but the analogy will hardly serve to explain the sentiment away. This may be a cause, but it can hardly be accepted as a sufficient cause.

Socialist agitators urge that the existing system is necessarily wasteful and industrially inefficient. That may be granted, but it does not serve to explain the popular discontent, because the popular opinion, in which the discontent resides, does notoriously not favor that view. They further urge that the existing system is unjust, in that it gives an advantage to one man over another. That contention may also be true, but it is in itself no explanation, for it is true only if it be granted that the institutions which make this advantage of one man over another possible are unjust, and that is begging the question. This last contention is, however, not so far out of line with popular sentiment. The advantage complained of lies, under modern conditions, in the possession of property, and there is a feeling abroad that the existing order of things affords an undue advantage to property, especially to owners of property whose possessions rise much above a certain rather indefinite average. This feeling of injured justice is not always [348] distinguishable from envy; but it is, at any rate, a factor that works towards a leveling policy. With it goes a feeling of slighted manhood, which works in the same direction. Both these elements are to a great extent of a subjective origin. They express themselves in the general, objective form, but it is safe to say that on the average they spring from a consciousness of disadvantage and slight suffered by the person expressing them, and by persons whom he classes with himself. No flippancy is intended in saying that the rich are not so generally alive to the necessity of any leveling policy as are people of slender means. Any question as to the legitimacy of the dissatisfaction, on moral grounds, or even on grounds of expediency, is not very much to the point; the question is as to its scope and its chances of persistence.

The modern industrial system is based on the institution of private property under free competition, and it cannot be claimed that these institutions have heretofore worked to the detriment of the material interests of the average member of society. The ground of discontent cannot lie in a disadvantageous comparison of the present with the past, so far as material interests are concerned. It is notorious, and, practically, none of the agitators deny, that the system of industrial competition, based on private property, has brought about, or has at least co-existed with, the most rapid advance in average wealth and industrial efficiency that the world has seen. Especially can it fairly be claimed that the result of the last few decades of our industrial development has been to increase greatly the creature comforts within the reach of the average human being. And, decidedly, the result has been an amelioration of the lot of the less favored in a relatively greater degree than that of those economically more fortunate. The claim that the system of competition has proved itself an engine for making the rich richer and the poor poorer has the fascination of epigram; but if its meaning is that the lot of the average, of the masses of humanity in civilized life, is worse to-day, as measured in the means of livelihood, than it was twenty, or fifty, or a hundred years [349] ago, then it is farcical. The cause of discontent must be sought elsewhere than in any increased difficulty in obtaining the means of subsistence or of comfort. But there is a sense in which the aphorism is true, and in it lies at least a partial explanation of the unrest which our conservative people so greatly deprecate. The existing system has not made, and does not tend to make, the industrious poor poorer as measured absolutely in means of livelihood; but it does tend to make them relatively poorer, in their own eyes, as measured in terms of comparative economic importance, and, curious as it may seem at first sight, that is what seems to count. It is not the abjectly poor that are oftenest heard protesting; and when a protest is heard in their behalf it is through spokesmen who are from outside their own class, and who are not delegated to speak for them. They are not a negligible element in the situation, but the unrest which is ground for solicitude does not owe its importance to them. The protest comes from those who do not habitually, or of necessity, suffer physical privation. The qualification "of necessity," is to be noticed. There is a not inconsiderable amount of physical privation suffered by many people in this country, which is not physically necessary. The cause is very often that what might be the means of comfort is diverted to the purpose of maintaining a decent appearance, or even a show of luxury.

Man as we find him to-day has much regard to his good fame – to his standing in the esteem of his fellow-men. This characteristic he always has had, and no doubt always will have. This regard for reputation may take the noble form of a striving after a good name; but the existing organization of society does not in any way pre-eminently foster that line of development. Regard for one's reputation means, in the average of cases, emulation. It is a striving to be, and more immediately to be thought to be, better than one's neighbor. Now, modern society, the society in which competition without prescription is predominant, is pre-eminently an industrial, economic society, and it is industrial – economic – excellence that most readily attracts the approving regard of that society. [350] Integrity and personal worth will, of course, count for something, now as always; but in the case of a person of moderate pretentions and opportunities, such as the average of us are, one's reputation for excellence in this direction does not penetrate far enough into the very wide environment to which a person is exposed in modern society to satisfy even a very modest craving for respectability. To sustain one's dignity – and to sustain one's self-respect – under the eyes of people who are not socially one's immediate neighbors, it is necessary to display the token of economic worth, which practically coincides pretty closely with economic success. A person may be well-born and virtuous, but those attributes will not bring respect to the bearer from people who are not aware of his possessing them, and these are ninety-nine out of every one hundred that one meets. Conversely, by the way, knavery and vulgarity in any person are not repro-bated by people who know nothing of the person's shortcomings in those respects.

In our fundamentally industrial society a person should be economically successful, if he would enjoy the esteem of his fellowmen. When we say that a man is "worth" so many dollars, the expression does not convey the idea that moral or other personal excellence is to be measured in terms of money, but it does very distinctly convey the idea that the fact of his possessing many dol-lars is very much to his credit. And, except in cases of extraordinary excel-lence, efficiency in any direction which is not immediately of industrial importance, and does not redound to a person's economic benefit, is not of great value as a means of respectability. Economic success is in our day the most widely accepted as well as the most readily ascertainable measure of esteem. All this will hold with still greater force of a generation which is born into a world already encrusted with this habit of a mind.

But there is a further, secondary stage in the development of this economic emulation. It is not enough to possess the talisman of industrial success. In order that it may mend one's good fame efficiently, it is necessary to display it. One does not "make much of a showing" in the eyes of the large [351] majority of the people whom one meets with, except by unremitting demonstration of ability to pay. That is practically the only means which the average of us have of impressing our respectability on the many to whom we are personally unknown, but whose transient good opinion we would so gladly enjoy. So it comes about that the appearance of success is very much to be desired, and is even in many cases preferred to the substance. We all know how nearly indispensable it is to afford whatever expenditure other people with whom we class ourselves can afford, and also that it is desirable to afford a little something more than others.

This element of human nature has much to do with the "standard of living." And it is of a very elastic nature, capable of an indefinite extension. After making proper allowance for individual exceptions and for the action of prudential restraints, it may be said, in a general way, that this emulation in expenditure stands ever ready to absorb any margin of income that remains after ordinary physical wants and comforts have been provided for, and, further, that it presently becomes as hard to give up that part of one's habitual "standard of living" which is due to the struggle for respectability, as it is to give up many physical comforts. In a general way, the need of expenditure in this direction grows as fast as the means of satisfying it, and, in the long run, a large expenditure comes no nearer satisfying the desire than a smaller one.

It comes about through the working of this principle that even the creature comforts, which are in themselves desirable, and, it may even be, requisite to a life on a passably satisfactory plane, acquire a value as a means of respectability quite independent of, and out of proportion to, their simple utility as a means of livelihood. As we are all aware, the chief element of value in many articles of apparel is not their efficiency for protecting the body, but for protecting the wearer's respectability; and that not only in the eyes of one's neighbors but even in one's own eyes. Indeed, it happens not very rarely that a person chooses to go ill-clad in order to be well dressed. [352] Much more than half the value of what is worn by the American people may confidently be put down to the element of "dress," rather than to that of "clothing." And the chief motive of dress is emulation – what I have ventured to designate as "economic emulation." The like is true, though perhaps in a less degree, of what goes to food and shelter.

This misdirection of effort through the cravings of human vanity is of course not anything new, nor is "economic emulation" a modern fact. The modern system of industry has not invented emulation, nor has even this particular form of emulation originated under that system. But the system of free competition has accentuated this form of emulation, both by exalting the industrial activity of man above the rank which it held under more primitive forms of social organization, and by in great measure cutting off other forms of emulation from the chance of efficiently ministering to the craving for a good fame. Speaking generally and from the standpoint of the average man, the modern industrial organization of society has practically narrowed the scope of emulation to this one line; and at the same time it has made the means of sustenance and comfort so much easier to obtain as very materially to widen the margin of human exertion that can be devoted to purposes of emulation. Further, by increasing the freedom of movement of the individual and widening the environment to which the individual is exposed – increasing the number of persons before whose eyes each one carries on his life, and, *pari passu*, decreasing the chances which such persons have of awarding their esteem on any other basis than that of immediate appearances, it has increased the relative efficiency of the economic means of winning respect through a show of expenditure for personal comforts.

It is not probable that further advance in the same direction will lead to a different result in the immediate future; and it is the *immediate* future we have to deal with. A further advance in the efficiency of our industry, and a further widening of the human environment to which the individual is exposed, should logically render emulation in this direction more intense. There [353] are, indeed, certain considerations to be set off against this tendency, but they are mostly factors of slow action, and are hardly of sufficient consequence to reverse the general rule. On the whole, other things remaining the same, it must be admitted that, within wide limits, the easier the conditions of physical life for modern civilized man become, and the wider the horizon of each and the extent of the personal contact of each with his fellowmen, and the greater the opportunity of each to compare notes with his fellows, the greater will be the preponderance of economic success as a means of emulation, and the greater the straining after economic respectability. Inasmuch as the aim of emulation is not any absolute degree of comfort or of excellence, no advance in the average well-being of the community can end the struggle or lessen the strain. A general amelioration cannot quiet the unrest whose source is the craving of everybody to compare favorably with his neighbor.

Human nature being what it is, the struggle of each to possess more than his neighbor is inseparable from the institution of private property. And also, human nature being what it is, one who possesses less will, on the average, be jealous of the one who possesses more; and "more" means not more than the average share, but more than the share of the person who makes the comparison. The criterion of complacency is, largely, the *de facto* possession or enjoyment; and the present growth of sentiment among the body of the people – who possess less – favors, in a vague way, a readjustment adverse to the interests of those who possess more, and adverse to the possibility of legitimately possessing or enjoying "more;" that is to say, the growth of sentiment favors a socialistic movement. The outcome of modern industrial development has been, so far as concerns the present purpose, to intensify emulation and the jealousy that goes with emulation, and to focus the emulation and the jealousy on the possession and enjoyment of material goods. The ground of the unrest with which we are concerned is, very largely, jealousy, – envy, if you choose; and the ground of this particular form of jealousy, that makes for [354] socialism, is to be found in the institution of private property. With private property, under modern conditions, this jealousy and unrest are unavoidable.

The corner-stone of the modern industrial system is the institution of private property. That institution is also the objective point of all attacks upon the existing system of competitive industry, whether open or covert, whether directed against the system as a whole or against any special feature of it. It is, moreover, the ultimate ground – and, under modern conditions, necessarily so – of the unrest and discontent whose proximate cause is the struggle for economic respectability. The inference seems to be that, human nature being what it is, there can be no peace from this – it must be admitted – ignoble form of emulation, or from the discontent that goes with it, this side of the abolition of private property. Whether a larger measure of peace is in store for us after that event shall have come to pass, is of course not a matter to be counted on, nor is the question immediately to the point.

This economic emulation is of course not the sole motive, nor the most important feature, of modern industrial life; although it is in the foreground, and it pervades the structure of modern society more thoroughly perhaps than any other equally powerful moral factor. It would be rash to predict that socialism will be the inevitable outcome of a continued development of this emulation and the discontent which it fosters, and it is by no means the purpose of this paper to insist on such an inference. The most that can be claimed is that this emulation is one of the causes, if not the chief cause, of the existing unrest and dissatisfaction with things as they are; that this unrest is inseparable from the existing system of industrial organization; and that the growth of popular sentiment under the influence of these conditions is necessarily adverse to the institution of private property, and therefore adverse to the existing industrial system of free competition.

The emulation to which attention has been called in the preceding section of this paper is not only a fact of importance to an understanding of the unrest that is urging us towards an [355] untried path in social development, but it has also a bearing on the question of the practicability of any scheme for the complete nationalization of industry. Modern industry has developed to such a degree of efficiency as to make the struggle for subsistence alone, under average conditions, relatively easy, as compared with the state of the case a few generations ago. As I have labored to show, the modern competitive system has at the same time given the spirit of emulation such a direction that the attainment of subsistence and comfort no longer fixes, even approximately, the limit of the required aggregate labor on the part of the community. Under modern conditions the struggle for existence has, in a very appreciable degree, been transformed into a struggle to keep up appearances. The ultimate ground of this struggle to keep up appearances by otherwise unnecessary expenditure, is the institution of private property. Under a régime which should allow no inequality of acquisition or of income, this form of emulation, which is due to the possibility of such inequality, would also tend to become obsolete. With the abolition of private property, the characteristic of human nature which now finds its exercise in this form of emulation, should logically find exercise in other, perhaps nobler and socially more serviceable, activities; it is at any rate not easy to imagine it running into any line of action more futile or less worthy of human effort.

Supposing the standard of comfort of the community to remain approximately at its present average, the abolition of the struggle to keep up economic appearances would very considerably lessen the aggregate amount of labor required for the support of the community. How great a saving of labor might be effected is not easy to say. I believe it is within the mark to suppose that the struggle to keep up appearances is chargeable, directly and indirectly, with one-half the aggregate labor, and abstinence from labor – for the standard of respectability requires us to shun labor as well as to enjoy the fruits of it – on part of the American people. This does not mean that the same community, under a system not allowing private property, could make its way with half the labor [356] we now put forth; but it means something more or less nearly approaching that. Anyone who has not seen our modern social life from this point of view will find the claim absurdly extravagant, but the startling character of the proposition will wear off with longer and closer attention to this aspect of the facts of everyday life. But the question of the exact amount of waste due to this factor is immaterial. It will not be denied that it is a fact of considerable magnitude, and that is all that the argument requires.

It is accordingly competent for the advocates of the nationalization of industry and property to claim that even if their scheme of organization should prove less effective for production of goods than the present, as measured absolutely in terms of the aggregate output of our industry, yet the community might readily be maintained at the present average standard of comfort. The required aggregate output of the nation's industry would be considerably less than at present, and there would therefore be less necessity for that close and strenuous industrial organization and discipline of the members of society under the new régime, whose evils unfriendly critics are apt to magnify. The chances of practicability for the scheme should logically be considerably increased by this lessening of the necessity for severe application. The less irksome and exacting the new régime, the less chance of a reversion to the earlier system.

Under such a social order, where common labor would no longer be a mark of peculiar economic necessity and consequent low economic rank on part of the laborer, it is even conceivable that labor might practically come to assume that character of nobility in the eyes of society at large, which it now sometimes assumes in the speculations of the well-to-do, in their complacent moods. Much has sometimes been made of this possibility by socialist speculators, but the inference has something of a utopian look, and no one, certainly, is entitled to build institutions for the coming social order on this dubious ground.

What there seems to be ground for claiming is that a society [357] which has reached our present degree of industrial efficiency would not go into the Socialist or Nationalist state with as many chances of failure as a community whose industrial development is still at the stage at which strenuous labor on the part of nearly all members is barely sufficient to make both ends meet.

In Mr. Spencer's essay, in conformity with the line of argument of his "Principles of Sociology," it is pointed out that, as the result of constantly operative social forces, all social systems, as regards the form of organization, fall into the one or the other of Sir Henry Maine's two classes – the system of status or the system of contract. In accordance with this generalization it is concluded that whenever the modern system of contract or free competition shall be displaced, it will necessarily be replaced by the only other known system – that of status; the type of which is the military organization, or, also, a hierarchy, or a bureaucracy. It is something after the fashion of the industrial organization of ancient Peru that Mr. Spencer pictures as the inevitable sequel of the demise of the existing competitive system. Voluntary coöperation can be replaced only by compulsory coöperation, which is identified with the system of status and defined as the subjection of man to his fellow-man.

Now, at least as a matter of speculation, this is not the only alternative. These two systems, of status, or prescription, and of contract, or competition, have divided the field of social organization between them in some proportion or other in the past. Mr. Spencer has shown that, very generally, where human progress in its advanced stages has worked towards the amelioration of the lot of the average member of society, the movement has been away from the system of status and towards the system of contract. But there is at least one, if not more than one exception to the rule, as concerns the recent past. The latest development of the industrial organization among civilized nations – perhaps in an especial degree in the case of the American people – has not been entirely a continuation of the approach to a régime of free contract. It is also, [358] to say the least, very doubtful if the movement has been towards a régime of status, in the sense in which Sir Henry Maine uses the term. This is especially evident in the case of the great industries which we call "natural monopolies;" and it is to be added that the present tendency is for a continually increasing proportion of the industrial activities of the community to fall into the category of "natural monopolies." No revolution has been achieved; the system of competition has not been discarded, but the course of industrial development is not in the direction of an extension of that system at all points; nor does the principle of status always replace that of competition wherever the latter fails.

The classification of methods of social organization under the two heads of status or of contract, is not logically exhaustive. There is nothing in the meaning of the terms employed which will compel us to say that whenever man escapes from the control of his fellow man, under a system of status, he thereby falls into a system of free contract. There is a conceivable escape from the dilemma, and it is this conceivable, though perhaps impracticable, escape from both these systems that the socialist agitator wishes to effect. An acquaintance with the aims and position of the more advanced and consistent advocates of a new departure leaves no doubt but that the principles of contract and of status, both, are in substance familiar to their thoughts – though often in a vague and inadequate form – and that they distinctly repudiate both. This is perhaps less true of those who take the socialist position mainly on ethical grounds.

As bearing on this point it may be remarked that while the industrial system, in the case of all communities with whose history we are acquainted, has always in the past been organized according to a scheme of status or of contract, or of the two combined in some proportion, yet the social organization has not in all cases developed along the same lines, so far as concerns such social functions as are not primarily industrial. Especially is this true of the later stages in the development of those communities whose institutions we are [359] accustomed to contemplate with the most complacency, *e.g.*, the case of the English-speaking peoples. The whole system of modern constitutional government in its latest developed forms, in theory at least, and, in a measure, in practice, does not fall under the head of either contract or status. It is the analogy of modern constitutional government through an impersonal law and impersonal institutions, that comes nearest doing justice to the vague notions of our socialist propagandists. It is true, some of the most noted among them are fond of the analogy of the military organization, as a striking illustration of one feature of the system they advocate, but that must after all be taken as an *obiter dictum*.

Further, as to the manner of the evolution of existing institutions and their relation to the two systems spoken of. So far as concerns the communities which have figured largely in the civilized world, the political organization has had its origin in a military system of government. So, also, has the industrial organization. But while the development of industry, during its gradual escape from the military system of status, has been, at least until lately, in the direction of a system of free contract, the development of the political organization, so far as it has escaped from the régime of status, has not been in that direction. The system of status is a system of subjection to personal authority, – of prescription and class distinctions, and privileges and immunities; the system of constitutional government, especially as seen at its best among a people of democratic traditions and habits of mind, is a system of subjection to the will of the social organism, as expressed in an impersonal law. This difference between the system of status and the "constitutional system" expresses a large part of the meaning of the boasted free institutions of the English-speaking people. Here, subjection is not to the person of the public functionary, but to the powers vested in him. This has, of course, something of the ring of latter-day popular rhetoric, but it is after all felt to be true, not only speculatively, but in some measure also in practice. [360]

The right of eminent domain and the power to tax, as interpreted under modern constitutional forms, indicate something of the direction of development of the political functions of society at a point where they touch the province of the industrial system. It is along the line indicated by these and kindred facts that the socialists are advancing; and it is along this line that the later developments made necessary by the exigencies of industry under modern conditions are also moving. The aim of the propagandists is to sink the industrial community in the political community; or perhaps better, to identify the two organizations; but always with insistence on the necessity of making the political organization, in some further developed form, the ruling and only one in the outcome. Distinctly, the system of contract is to be done away with; and equally distinctly, no system of status is to take its place.

All this is pretty vague, and of a negative character, but it would quickly pass the limits of legitimate inference from the accepted doctrines of the socialists if it should attempt to be anything more. It does not have much to say as to the practicability of any socialist scheme. As a matter of speculation, there seems to be an escape from the dilemma insisted on by Mr. Spencer. We may conceivably have nationalism without status and without contract. In theory, both principles are entirely obnoxious to that system. The practical question, as to whether modern society affords the materials out of which an industrial structure can be erected on a system different from either of these, is a problem of constructive social engineering which calls for a consideration of details far too comprehensive to be entered on here. Still, in view of the past course of development of character and institutions on the part of the people to which we belong, it is perhaps not extravagant to claim that no form of organization which should necessarily eventuate in a thorough-going system of status could endure among us. The inference from this proposition may be, either that a near approach to nationalization of industry would involve a régime of status, a bureaucracy, which would be unendurable, and which would therefore [361] drive us back to the present system before it had been entirely abandoned; or that the nationalization would be achieved with such a measure of success, in conformity with the requirements of our type of character, as would make it preferable to what we had left behind. In either case the ground for alarm does not seem so serious as is sometimes imagined.

A reversion to the system of free competition, after it had been in large part discarded, would no doubt be a matter of great practical difficulty, and the experiment which should demonstrate the necessity of such a step might involve great waste and suffering, and might seriously retard the advance of the race toward something better than our present condition; but neither a permanent deterioration of human society, nor a huge catastrophe, is to be confidently counted on as the outcome of the movement toward nationalization, even if it should prove necessary for society to retrace its steps.

It is conceivable that the application of what may be called the "constitutional method" to the organization of industry – for that is essentially what the advocates of Nationalization demand – would result in a course of development analogous to what has taken place in the case of the political organization under modern constitutional forms. Modern constitutional government – the system of modern free institutions – is by no means an unqualified success, in the sense of securing to each the rights and immunities which in theory are guaranteed to him.

Our modern republics have hardly given us a foretaste of that political millennium whereof they proclaim the fruition. The average human nature is as yet by no means entirely fit for self-government according to the "constitutional method." Shortcomings are visible at every turn. These shortcomings are grave enough to furnish serious arguments against the practicability of our free institutions. On the continent of Europe the belief seems to be at present in the ascendant that man must yet, for a long time, remain under the tutelage of absolutism before he shall be fit to organize himself into an [362] autonomous political body. The belief is not altogether irrational. Just how great must be the advance of society and just what must be the character of the advance, preliminary to its advantageously assuming the autonomous – republican – form of political organization, must be admitted to be an open question. Whether we, or any people, have yet reached the required stage of the advance is also questioned by many. But the partial success which has attended the movement in this direction, among the English-speaking people for example, goes very far towards proving that the point in the development of human character at which the constitutional method may be advantageously adopted in the political field, lies from this side at which human nature shall have become completely adapted for that method. That is to say, it does not seem necessary, as regards the functions of society which we are accustomed to call political, to be entirely ready for nationalization before entering upon it. How far the analogy of this will hold when applied to the industrial organization of society is difficult to say, but some significance the analogy must be admitted to possess.

Certainly, the fact that constitutional government – the nationalization of political functions – seems to have been a move in the right direction is not to be taken as proof of the advisability of forthwith nationalizing the industrial functions. At the same time this fact does afford ground for the claim that a movement in this direction may prove itself in some degree advantageous, even if it takes place at a stage in the development of human nature at which mankind is still far from being entirely fit for the duties which the new system shall impose. The question, therefore, is not whether we have reached the perfection of character which would be necessary in order to a perfect working of the scheme of nationalization of industry, but whether we have reached such a degree of development as would make an imperfect working of the scheme possible.

Selection 4

Böhm-Bawerk's definition of capital and the source of wages

Source: *Quarterly Journal of Economics*, January 1892 (vol. 6, 247–50).

Veblen (1892a)

In his exposition of the term "capital," Professor Böhm-Bawerk briefly touches on the wages-fund doctrine, so far as to reject summarily the proposition that the means of subsistence of productive laborers is drawn from the capital of the community, although, from the point of view of the employer, these "real wages" are to he regarded as drawn from his private capital. With the distinction which the discussion establishes between social capital and private capital, this position is, of course, in itself perfectly consistent. The position is, indeed, contained in the definition of capital previously arrived at (pp. 42, 43, and 21). The ground of the position taken is the unquestioned or, at all events, unquestionable truth that the laborer is a member of society, and his consumption of products is, in a broad view, a fact of the same kind, and of like theoretical significance with consumption on the part of any other member of society. The satisfaction of wants, whether it be the wants of the laborer or of any other, is the end, not the means, of productive activity.

While the exposition at this point undeniably sheds a strong light on the question, it can hardly be said to have finally disposed of all ground for difference of opinion, still less to have explained away the wages-fund controversy, or that point of the controversy which concerns the question of the source of wages. And that controversy has been of such extent and earnestness as to raise the presumption that something is to be said for both sides of the dispute, and to leave little hope of its being finally put at rest by any other method than that of explaining away the ground of difference. For reaching this end, I believe Professor Böhm-Bawerk's exposition of capital has given us the means. [248]

It is to be remarked, by the way, however, that there is a lacuna in the exposition at this point, which seems, at least, not of first-rate theoretical consequence, and is, perhaps, the result of oversight of a not very important point, but which might afford a foothold for carping criticism. It will be best to speak of it at the outset, and put it out of the way before going on. This difficulty arises from the inclusion, as a subhead under Social Capital, of "stocks of goods for consumption which are still in the hands of producers or dealers" (p. 70); that is to say, goods which have not yet passed that final stage of preparation for consumption which consists in their transfer, through the mechanism of exchange, into the ownership of the ultimate consumer.

Now, this classification may afford ground for persons unduly given to nice distinctions to take the exception to Professor Böhm-Bawerk's position on the question of the source of wages that, (1) inasmuch as the payment of wages, actually for the most part, and in theory normally, is a transfer to the laborer not of the particular goods he wants, but of an item of value by means of which he may obtain the particular goods through this final productive step of exchange, therefore the payment of wages simply gives the recipient a claim on goods which have not yet passed the final stage of production, and so are as yet a part of the general capital by the terms of the definition, and which will pass that stage only in consequence of this claim; (2) that, without regard to the mechanism by which the transaction is carried out, the claim on the goods, which accrues to the laborer in the payment of wages, constitutes a drain on the stocks in the hands of producers or merchants, and tends to diminish such stocks, and this without regard to the point of time of the payment, relative to the production of the goods, which ultimately go to satisfy the laborer's wants. The payment of the wages, as a matter to be considered in a theory of the methods of production, precedes the consumption, or the ownership on the part of the recipient, of the goods which the claim so transferred to him ultimately puts into his hands for consumption, and so is a claim that can be satisfied only by drawing on a class of goods included under the head of social capital. This criticism, it will be [249] seen, touches a point of classification, and may perhaps be avoided without deranging the main structure of the theory.

Now, as to the theory of the source of wages, in the light of Professor Böhm-Bawerk's definition of capital. It is not too much to say that the controversy has owed much of its bitterness and sterility to inadequate definition of the terms employed, especially to a lack of accuracy in the concept of capital. The *Positive Theorie des Kapitales* has given to the concept of capital, and of its relation to other elements of economic theory, a conciseness and adequacy of which earlier speculators were sorely in need. If the distinction which this discussion formulates between social and private capital had been apprehended earlier, with the same full and clear consciousness, the means would have been at hand by which the wages-fund controversy might have been put at rest. But the completed definition of capital does not of itself dispose of the question. A further analysis in the same direction is necessary. It seems to me that economic theory is at this point in the presence of a distinction necessary to be made between "the laborer's share of consumable goods," or "earnings," on the one hand, and "wages," on the other, analogous to the distinction taken by Wagner – and perfected by Professor Böhm-Bawerk – between capital as "a purely economic category" and capital "in a juridico-historical sense." Wages, in this stricter definition, and private capital both are facts of usage, while the laborer's income, or earnings, and social capital both are facts intrinsic and fundamental to any theory of industrial society.

Wages is a fact incident to the relation of employer and employed. It is, in the sense fixed by colloquial use, an economic category whose scope is entirely within the theory of production as carried on by the method based on that relation; and the term is not used in precisely the same sense when the discussion shifts to the standpoint of production simply as such, still less when the point of view is that of distribution or consumption. It is by an unconscious equivocation, in shifting the point of view, that wages is identified with earnings and spoken of as an element in the theory of distribution or consumption. The laborer, from the point of [250] view of consumption of products, is no longer "laborer": he is a member of society simply, and his share of the product of industry is the share of an individual member of society. As consumer, he is not "laborer," and his share of consumable goods is not "wages," in the strict technical sense of the term. Wages may coincide in range of comprehension with the laborer's share of product, – with earnings, – and may likewise coincide with the aggregate of his consumption; but wages is a category having a different significance for economic theory from that of earnings or of goods consumed. The item of value, which from the point of view of production as carried on by the method of private capital is wages, is, from the point of view of the laborer, as being productively employed in his own interest, earnings. From the point of view of consumption of goods produced, neither of these terms can be employed with entirely the same meaning as they have in the use just specified.

If this distinction be allowed as theoretically legitimate, it appears that Professor Böhm-Bawerk's discussion does not upset the wages-fund doctrine in any of its essential tenets. The one proposition, that the sustenance of men while productively employed is drawn from the product of past industry, is of course not impugned: the other, that wages are paid out of capital, is conceded in conceding that it will hold true when capital is understood to mean private capital; for it is only then that the term "wages," in the strict technical sense, can properly be employed. At the same time this discrimination of terms leaves the position of the opponents of the wages-fund doctrine, as to this particular point, perfectly tenable; for whenever "wages" is used in the sense of "earnings," as, I believe, is invariably the case in the usage of these writers, they are undoubtedly drawn from the product of industry, inasmuch as earnings are the product, to the laborer, of his labor.

All this may seem to be a web of excessively fine-spun technicalities, but in apology it is to be said that it is also directed exclusively to a point of pure theory. And the whole controversy about the source of wages has also been in the region of pure theory, having never directly involved questions of physical fact or of expediency.

Selection 5

The food supply and the price of wheat

Source: *Journal of Political Economy*, June 1893
(vol. 1, pp. 365–79).

Veblen (1893c)

In 1879, in an address before the London Statistical Society, Mr. G. Shaw-Lefevre, said: "If I were to venture a prediction on so difficult and obscure a question, I would incline to the opinion that wheat has during the past year reached its lowest point."

This forecast was made a couple of years before the beginning of the great protracted decline in the prices of all agricultural produce that set in in the early years of the eighties. The forces which brought on the decline were already at work, and had been at work for some years before Mr. Shaw-Lefevre made his prediction; but the causes which seem very obvious after the fact may be quite obscure before it, and the causes that make for a permanent decline in agricultural produce are commonly more uncertain of prevision than those that make for a permanent rise. The former are apt to be of the nature of innovations, whose scope and efficacy can not well be foretold, while the latter are as apt to be simply the cumulative action of factors with whose scope and method we are already familiar.

Recognising, then, the chance of an unforeseen decline, and recognising, also, that there is more than one known factor already at work to bring about a decline in agricultural products in the near future, the purpose of this paper is to attempt an estimate of the possible maximum advance in the price of wheat (as a representative product of agriculture), supposing the factors that make for a decline to remain in abeyance for the next ten years.

The great permanent fall in prices that took place during the first half of the last decade has served as an object lesson to enforce the truth that there is a close dependence of price on supply. The fact of this dependence has been made much of both by those who hope for an advance in prices of farm produce, and by [366] those who deprecate the approach of a scarcity of bread. The assumption has been freely made that the date at which the land available for tillage shall have been definitively occupied is near at hand, and that when that day arrives a great and "sudden" advance in agricultural prices is to be looked for, with its consequences, of great gains for the farmer – for the American farmer perhaps, in an especial degree – and of distress for all peoples who get their supply of food largely from other countries. This sweeping generalisation merits some scrutiny.

It is unquestionably true that the price of wheat depends on the supply, but it is no less true that, other things being the same, the annual average supply of wheat depends, in the long run, on its price. The control exercised by the supply over the price is direct and transient. That exercised by the price over the annual average supply is of slower action, but it is also more permanent. We have therefore not said the last word in saying that when the demand shall have outgrown the present annual supply, the price of wheat will advance. The converse is also true; when the price of wheat begins to advance appreciably beyond what will barely remunerate the growers of wheat to-day, the supply will presently increase. The date of the definitive occupation of the tillable area yet available will no doubt mark an advance in the price of wheat, other things remaining unchanged; but the date of a definitive advance in price will no less surely mark an increase in the output from the acreage already under cultivation in the older wheat-growing sections. When this event comes to pass the farmers in the older sections will find it to their advantage to give their land such additional attention as will increase the yield per acre from the land already in cultivation, and so to some extent cover the shortage to which the rise in price is due and break the force of the advance. At the same time recourse will be had in an increasing degree to lands which are scarcely profitable for tillage at the prices which have been ruling for some years past.

The increased demand that is expected to advance the price of wheat will come as a result of an increase of the population [367] of bread-eating countries. An increased demand for wheat accordingly implies an increase of approximately the same proportions in the demand for other food products; therefore any considerable increase of the acreage sown to wheat will be practicable only as a feature in the general increase of the acreage of arable land. The increased supply of wheat, as of other food products, will therefore have to be obtained, in part, by an increased yield per acre from the acreage already in cultivation.

While we have by no means reached – or nearly reached – the limit of the possible extension of the wheat area in America, it is probably true that we are fast approaching the point beyond which there is no considerable additional amount of wheat lands equally fertile and otherwise equally available with the last ten or twenty million acres already brought under cultivation. It can hardly be said that the spread of cultivation in America during the past ten or twelve years has been to less fertile or less available lands; but for the next ten or twelve years, barring unforeseen developments, any considerable further spread of the area of cultivation can not take place without recourse to less available lands. The practical working of the law of diminishing returns will therefore assume an importance for our farming which it has not had for some time past. This practical working of the law will appear in the relation between the price and the yield per acre.

The yield per acre and the prices of farm produce vary considerably as between the different sections of the country, and, so far as concerns the older sections, they vary together, with some regularity; but the difference in prices between different localities is too slight, and the difference in other respects is too great to afford satisfactory figures from which to infer what is the effect, on the yield, of a given local advantage in price. The divergence in price is not pronounced nor easily ascertainable, as between states which are in other respects available for our comparison. Evidently no value can attach to a comparison of the newer, spring-wheat states with the older, winter-wheat states. But it may be remarked that Vermont, Massachusetts and Connecticut [368] show a higher yield than any of the Ohio Valley states.

It will be more to the purpose, because the divergence both in price and in yield is great enough to afford tangible evidence of the efficacy of the forces at work, to compare the price and yield per acre in Great Britain with the price in Chicago and the yield per acre in the winter-wheat states lying about Chicago. The yield per acre of wheat in Great Britain is very considerably greater than in the states about Chicago. The immediate cause of its being so is the higher price obtained for wheat, and for other farm produce, by the British farmers; and the degree of effectiveness of the inducement offered them in the way of higher prices ought to help us to forecast the probable efficacy of an appeal of the same kind to the industry of their American competitors.

The winter-wheat states centering about Chicago and the great lakes – Ohio, Indiana, Illinois, Wisconsin and Michigan – may, in some respects, not unfairly be compared with Great Britain. They are like that country in being a country of mixed farming, and, as regards wheat production, mainly a winter-wheat country. Their farm lands have also been under cultivation for such a length of time as in large measure to obviate the complications which the "virgin soil" would introduce into any comparison of the newer states of the west with the countries of Europe. In some respects these states do not afford a close parallel to the farming lands of Great Britain. The climate is not the same, and the faults of the climate are not of the same kind. In the states mentioned there is more danger from drought than from wet seasons; in the United Kingdom it is all the other way. A bad season in England is sure to be a year of deficient heat, or excessive moisture, or both. Further, the soil of these states does not closely resemble the British soil in point of adaptation to wheat culture. These states do, however, afford as nearly fair a comparison with British soil and climate as any part of America that is a sufficiently representative wheat-growing region, and at every point where the comparison seems to be vitiated by inherent [369] differences the difference is in favor of the states, as a superior country for wheat-growing and for mixed farming. The American soil is more fertile and more easily tilled; the climate of the states is better adapted for wheat-growing; the American farmers are probably not at all inferior to the British in intelligence or enterprise. So far as the inherent difference in natural advantages may lead us astray in drawing any inferences from a comparison of this group of states with Great Britain, the error would be in the direction of too low an estimate of the wheat-growing capacity of the states under the stimulus of a higher price. And as the object of the inquiry is to estimate the probable minimum effect on supply of a given permanent advance in price, rather than the maximum capacity of the states under such a stimulus, this is not a danger that need be specially guarded against.

An objection of greater weight may be found in the difference between British and American prices of staples, other than agricultural produce. The higher general level of prices of what the American farmer has to buy places him at a disadvantage, as compared with the British farmer, in precisely the same way as the lower price he gets for what he has to sell. The hindering effect of the higher price of staples must accordingly be allowed for in calculating the effect which a given rise in the price of farm products will have in the way of increasing the intensity of culture.

This higher range of prices does not comprise all articles of consumption used by the farmer. Lumber, and forest products generally, are lower here than in England. Farm implements of most kinds are rather cheaper; leather goods are scarcely higher; many of the staple food products are cheaper. But after all has been said, it is not to be questioned that the American farmer has to pay a somewhat higher average range of prices for what he buys (outside of agricultural products) than his British competitor. The American tariff, to the extent to which it is protective, increases the price of the articles on which it is laid, and among these articles are many important items of the farmer's necessary consumption. [370]

It is difficult to say, even approximately, how much of a handicap this added cost is to American farming. It assuredly does not amount to more than 20 percent of the value of our farm products at Chicago prices; probably the actual additional cost to the farmers is considerably less than 20 percent of the value of their products.

Against this higher cost of necessaries in America may be offset the lower margin of cultivation in Great Britain, – using the term in the sense of a resort to poorer soils. The natural fertility of the poorest soils in cultivation in Great Britain, in the system of mixed farming of which wheat culture is an integral part, is greatly lower than that of the poorest class of soils cultivated in the states named. This implies a correspondingly greater average cost of production of the products of British farming,[1] and it affects also the cost of many of the necessaries of life to the British farmer.

The advantage is as definitely on the side of the states with respect to the margin of cultivation, as it is on the side of Great Britain with respect to the range of general prices. Here, again, it is impossible to say how great the

---

1 This statement does not imply that rent is an element in the cost of production. What is claimed is that Great Britain, as a whole, because of its lower margin of cultivation, gets the products of its soil at a greater average expenditure than do the states, and that a given increment in the price will induce a less increment in yield at this lower margin than at the higher margin of cultivation existing in the states.

advantage of the one over the other may be, but it is not unlikely that the disadvantage of the British farmer in this respect may completely offset the disadvantage which the American farmer has in the matter of higher general prices.

It may be thought that the fact that the agricultural depression in Great Britain during the whole of the period chosen for comparison (1884–92) has been severer than in America, would vitiate any British data for comparison with our own in any case where the point at issue turns on the question of a remunerative price. This difficulty is not a very serious one in any case, and does not affect the question in hand at all. What is required for the validity of the argument is: (1) that the inducements to [371] wheat culture in Great Britain, relatively to other tillage, should not be greater than in the states; and (2) that the least fertile lands cultivated in the British system of farming should not be intrinsically superior to the lands similarly at the margin of cultivation in the states. It needs no argument to establish that both these conditions are fully met and will continue to hold for an indefinite time to come.[2]

If the considerations adduced are admitted to be valid, to the extent that wheat growing in a system of mixed farming in the states named lies under no other or greater disadvantage as compared with wheat growing in Great Britain than that indicated by the difference in the price of a given grade of wheat between Chicago and Liverpool, then we have the premises from which to deduce approximately what will be the maximum possible advance in price required to induce a given increase in the average yield per acre of wheat in the states. And this will afford some indication of what will be the maximum possible advance in price resulting from a given increase in the consumption of wheat.

The prices selected for comparison are average prices of American No. 2 Red Winter Wheat in Liverpool and in Chicago, since 1884.

While this grade of wheat is not grown in England, the quotations for this grade are quite as significant for wheat prices in England as any quotations obtainable. The Gazette averages, which are usually quoted, are for British wheat, without respect to quality; and the average quality of the grain from which the quotations are made up will accordingly vary from year to year, with the character of the harvest. Gazette averages are useless for any exact comparison. [372]

The reason for not making up the averages for a comparison of prices from a series of years reaching back of 1884 is obvious. Wheat culture had

2 The depression in British farming, so far as it is not due to bad harvests, is due to the decline in prices; and this decline has affected grain production rather more strongly than other tillage. Its most pronounced economic result has been a readjustment of rents on a lowered basis. Apart from adverse seasons, the British farmers' chief real grievance is too high rents. Prices have fallen some 30 percent or more; money rents, except in isolated cases, have not been lowered to correspond. In addition to this, the farmers have suffered from a depreciation of the capital they have had invested in farming; which is also a considerable item.

not, until that time, adjusted itself to the changed conditions of the market that supervened about 1880–82. The years immediately preceding 1884–85 were years of great changes in the price and acreage of wheat. By 1884 the decline was completed, and the price of wheat has moved on a lower level since that time than before. About the same time the decline in acreage in the states selected had also practically ceased;[3] though a slight tendency to a further narrowing of the acreage has been perceptible since that time, at least until 1890.

The average yield per acre of wheat for the eight years since 1885[4] in the states selected has been about 13¾ bushels.[5] This average includes the extra-ordinary harvest of 1891 (17½ bushels per acre). But even counting 1891, this average is probably slightly short of the normal average yield for these states, the seasons during the latter half of the eighties having been, on the [373] whole, rather unfavorable for winter wheat. The average yield of the same states for the years 1877–83, when the seasons were, on the whole, very favorable, was 14¾ bushels. The lower average yield during later years seems to be due, in a slight degree, to a partial displacement of wheat by other crops on some of the more fertile and better-tilled soils; or perhaps more exactly, to a relative neglect of wheat-growing by some of the more capable and better equipped farmers; but the great cause of this discrepancy lies, no doubt, in the

---

3 The extraordinary decline in wheat acreage in the Ohio valley group of states in 1885 was due quite as much to an unfavorable season as to a voluntary narrowing of the area. The acreage regained in 1886 more than half of what had been lost in 1885. The definitive effect on acreage of the decline in price that ended in 1884, was not had until the following year. In studying the movement of acreage under the influence of the new level of prices then established, the new period is to be considered as having begun with 1885.

4 The average yield for the years 1885–92 has been taken, as, for the present purpose, answering to the price during the years 1884–91. The yield for the year 1884 was the same as the average for 1885–92.

5 The average annual yield has been:

Year	In the States; bushels (Winchester)	In Great Britain; bushels (Imperial)
1885	11.19	31.31
1886	14.41	26.89
1887	13.38	32.07
1888	12.02	28.05
1889	14.91	29.89
1890	11.74	30.74
1891	17.49	31.26
1892	14.40	26.38
Average.	13.78	29.57

character of the seasons. When due weight is allowed to all these factors, we shall be very near the truth in assuming 14 bushels per acre to be the present normal average yield of wheat in these states.

For Great Britain the officially assumed normal average yield of wheat is 28.80 bushels per acre. The actual annual average for the eight years since 1885 is 29.57 bushels.[6] It is difficult to say whether the officially assumed normal average is nearer the true normal than the recorded actual average. The *London Economist*, as well as some other authorities, claims the true normal average to exceed 29 bushels. The seasons during the eighties have been, on the whole, rather more favorable for wheat than the average of a long series of years. If this were the sole modifying circumstance the official normal average would have to be accepted as very near the true normal. But this circumstance does not account for the whole of the discrepancy between the average yield of today and that of some years ago. It has been pointed out that the average has also probably been raised by the dropping of some of the inferior soils out of wheat cultivation. At the same time, improvements in agriculture seem also to have affected the average yield in the same direction. It will be safe to take 29 bushels per acre as the actual normal average yield of wheat in Great Britain.

The average yield in Great Britain exceeds the yield in the states by about 107 percent (15 bushels). The annual average price of American No. 2 Red Winter Wheat in Liverpool, for the years 1884–91, exceeds the average price of the same grade in [374] Chicago by a trifle over 20 percent (18.095 cents per Winchester bushel).[7] It ought to be a safe inference that a gradual advance in the price of wheat in the Chicago market to the present level of the price in Liverpool (accompanied, as in the normal course of things it would be, by a corresponding advance in the prices of other farm produce) would result in such an advance in the intensity of culture in the

6 See note 5, page 85.
7 Annual average price of No. 2 Red Winter Wheat, in cents per bushel:

Year	Chicago	Liverpool
1884	89.3	107.2
1885	88.3	103.1
1886	77.6	99.6
1887	77.2	98.7
1888	92.5	107.4
1889	85.2	102.8
1890	89.5	105.3
1891	97.3	117.7
Average.	87.13	105.225

states lying about Chicago as to increase the average yield of wheat, during the early stages of the advance, in the same proportion as the British yield is higher on account of the higher British price. That is to say, a sufficiently gradual and permanent moderate advance, of a given percent, in price, in the Chicago market, should result in an increase in the yield per acre of wheat in these states, of at least five times as many percent. Twenty percent (18 cents per bushel) advantage in price in Liverpool carries with it 107 percent (15 bushels) advantage in the yield per acre in Great Britain. A gradual advance of 5 percent (4.36 cents per bushel) in the annual average price in Chicago ought to bring an increase of more than 20 percent (2.8 bushels) in the yield per acre of wheat in the states lying about Chicago, supposing the conditions of production otherwise to remain unchanged.

The aggregate annual production of the five states named, for the eight years 1885–92, has averaged slightly over 140 million bushels. If the price of wheat in Chicago were to advance permanently to 95.84 cents per bushel (10 per cent) we should have to expect the total annual production of these states to rise to not much less than 210 million bushels (50 percent). [375] Assuming that the advance in price would have an equivalent effect on the output in the other wheat regions (and the chances would seem to be that the effect would be relatively at least as great in the remoter wheat fields, since the percent advance in price in the remoter local markets would be appreciably greater, and any inability to increase the yield on the newer wheat lands would be fully offset by an extension of the area), and considering also that such an advance in price would induce some increase in acreage in all the wheat producing country, an ordinary average price of 96 cents in the Chicago markets might be expected to bring out an aggregate annual product of not less than 800 million bushels.

Conversely, No. 2 Red Winter Wheat cannot advance permanently to 96 cents in Chicago until there is a customary demand for about 800 million bushels of American wheat at the increased price. A ten percent advance in price presumes something near a fifty percent increase in the demand.

The increase in the demand for wheat will coincide approximately with the increase of the bread-eating population. Judging of the future by the past, it will be a liberal estimate to say that the bread-eating population of the countries which draw on the supplies of the general market to which America contributes, may be expected to increase by ten percent in ten years. It has perhaps reached that rate of growth during the last decade, and it would be extravagant to expect that rate to be exceeded during the next decade.

The price which it would be necessary to offer for wheat in order to meet this increased demand by an increased production is more a matter of surmise than the probable rate of growth of population. If we could answer this question, we should know approximately what prices our farmers may look for in payment for their produce during the opening years of the twentieth century. There is reason to believe that, barring unforeseen innovations, at the point in the growth of the demand for food at which there will be an effective demand for one-and-one-half times as much American wheat as at present, the price will have to be [376] advanced by not more than nine cents above the present ordinary average price in Chicago. In the meantime, a less increase in the demand could be met at a less advance in price. An increase of ten percent (200,000,000 bushels) in the world's consumption of wheat would mean, if the demand were distributed as it is at present, an increase of about 50 million bushels in the portion ordinarily required of America. This additional demand could be met, without increase of acreage, by an addition of about 1¼ bushels to the present average yield per acre of wheat; and this additional 1¼ bushels would be forthcoming without its being necessary to advance the price in the local markets by as much as two cents per bushel above the average of the last eight or nine years.

But the additional demand will not fall *pro rata* on the countries which now supply the world with wheat; and the like is true to almost the same extent of the supply of other agricultural products. America now, of late years, supplies rather less than one-fourth of the total wheat product. She will certainly be called on to contribute more than one-fourth of the additional 200 bushels that will be required before the end of another ten years, unless some unforeseen contingency should come in to change the complexion of things.

An advance in price would have some effect on the intensity of culture in all agricultural countries, but the effect would probably be very slight in such regions as the wheat lands of Russia and India, especially the latter. In these countries, as well as in large portions of Western Europe, notably in France, agriculture is in the hands of a population that does not respond readily to promptings from without. Whatever addition may be made to the wheat supply furnished by those countries – apart from additions due to improved facilities for transportation – will be made slowly, and will at best be inconsiderable for some time to come. The new demand will fall first and most heavily on the American, Australian and South American wheat lands, and on such portions of Europe as Great Britain, Austria, parts of Germany, &c., together with some contributions due to an increase of acreage in Russia. [377]

This fact, that the intensity of culture of a considerable portion of the present wheat-producing area of the world will be but partially and feebly affected by a moderate advance in the price, will necessitate a higher production on the part of that portion which will more readily respond to the call. It results in a virtual narrowing of the area from which the additional supply can be obtained, so as to include little else than the newer wheat-growing countries, with portions of Western Europe. These regions will therefore be called on to furnish more than their *pro rata* contingent to the increase, and this greater rate of production in these countries will be obtained only at the cost of a greater advance in price.

Of these more manageable countries, not all would respond to the demand with equal alacrity. It is, for example, easier for America to add one-tenth to her average yield of 12¼ bushels than it is for England to add one-tenth to her yield of 29 bushels.[8]

This fact goes in the same direction and adds further to the necessity of a higher price in the American market than would have been required if America were called on to furnish her *pro rata* increase only.

America has of late contributed something less than one-quarter of the world's annual wheat supply. If the facts above recited are allowed the extreme weight implied in looking to this country for one-half instead of one-fourth of the additional 200 million bushels that will be required by the end of another ten years, then it will be necessary to increase the yield of wheat in America, not by one-tenth, as was assumed above, but by one-fifth; that is, from 12⅓ bushels to 14.8 bushels per acre for the whole country, or from 14 bushels to 16.8 bushels per acre for the five states named. To maintain such an increase in the American yield of wheat would require an advance [378] of less than 4½ percent (3.8 cents per bushel) in the price of wheat in Chicago.

But as some increase in acreage is sure to result from any advance in price, allowance must be made for the increased supply to be obtained by this means. How great the effect on the acreage will be, it is impossible to say. On the other hand, it is pretty certainly true that any advance in price will not have as great an effect in increasing the yield in the newer states, especially in the spring-wheat country, as in the group of states with which we set out. The chief increase in product in the newer states will, for some time to come, be got by increasing the acreage. It may be accepted without much risk that this increase in acreage will fully make up for the slighter increase in the yield per acre, so that the conclusion already arrived at need not be modified on that account.

If, therefore, these premises are accepted as sound and adequate, there is small chance that the normal increase in the demand for bread will permanently raise the average price of No. 2 wheat above 91 cents in the Chicago market within the next ten years.

This estimate proceeds on the supposition that no considerable advance is taking place or will take place the next few years in the methods of farming or in any of the industries that have to do directly or indirectly with the food supply. This of course is an extreme position. If, as is quite probable, improved industrial knowledge and processes should appreciably lessen the cost of production of grain in the newer wheat countries, this estimate would probably prove too high. And if, as is still more probable, the prices of staple articles of consumption in

---

8 It must not be supposed that England, or any part of Europe, is near the limit of productivity. The *London Economist* of September 13, 1890, says: "High authorities have estimated that we might double the produce of the soil in the United Kingdom even under our existing system of farming. As it is, there are farmers who grow nearly double the average of grain crops for the kingdom as a whole, and many who produce twice the average weight of roots and potatoes."

America should decline, relatively to those of farm produce, the chance of any advance in wheat or in farm products generally, would be still further narrowed. If, for example, American import duties on staples should be lowered within the next ten years sufficiently to diminish the cost of the farmer's necessary articles of consumption by 20 percent (and such a result is possible), the chance of any permanent advance in wheat for the present would disappear. [379]

Even apart from any lowering of the cost of articles of necessary consumption, it is fully within the possibilities of the situation that no permanent advance in farm products need take place at all for a generation or more. Better methods and a more intimate knowledge of the natural processes concerned in farming are probably capable, as competent authorities insist, of so adding to the efficiency of our farming as not to admit of prices going higher than they are.

Agriculture is fast assuming the character of an "industry," in the modern sense, and the development of the next few decades may not improbably show us, in farming as in other occupations, a continual improvement in methods and a steady decline in cost of production, even in the face of a considerably increased demand.

Selection 6

Review of *The Land-Systems of British India* by B. H. Baden-Powell

Source: *Journal of Political Economy*, December 1893 (vol. 2, pp. 112–15).

Veblen (1893d)

Mr. Baden-Powell's work is a manual of Indian land systems, for the use, primarily, of Indian revenue officers. But while admirably adapted, as near as may be judged at this distance, for this its immediate purpose, it also contains a great deal of material of first-rate importance to the student of tenures and other agrarian questions.

Something more than one-half (386 pages) of the first volume is occupied with a general discussion of Indian land tenures and revenue systems, by way of gaining a historical and theoretical standpoint for the detailed discussion of the particular systems in effect in the various provinces of the Indian Empire. This general portion (book i.) is followed in the same volume by book ii., dealing in detail with Bengal. Book iii., occupying the whole of the second volume, discusses the system of village settlements, in its many local varieties. Volume iii. (book iv.) treats of the Raiyatwári and allied systems.

The work is a monument to the intricacy and extent of the British-Indian land revenue system, as well as to the author's industry and erudition. One may open the book at almost any of its more than two thousand pages and find that the special subject dealt with at any given point has received scant treatment, rather than the contrary. At least it will seem so to anyone reading with a view to inform himself on the details relating to any question in which he may be specially interested. The space required for the treatment of the subject, and the multiplicity of definitions and distinctions, and varieties of detail, [113] serve to enforce the greatness and the wide range of British India, geographically, historically, culturally and ethnologically. Within almost any geographical sub-division treated of, we have to do with tenures ranging in complexity and degree of development from the simplest to the most elaborate and intricate known. Where successive waves of conquest have superposed one system of tenures upon another, leaving in most cases a residuum of customary rights to represent the displaced proprietary claims of the supplanted owner or occupier, and to be gradually modified and differentiated by the passage of time, the resulting structure is a sufficiently formidable one. Where, on the other hand, as in the case of the Tódas, in the Nílgiri District, conquest and invasion by alien peoples have not disturbed the ancient order, at least within historic times, the system, and the prevalent concepts with respect to land tenure, which the English found in vogue on acquiring the over-lordship of the country, were of such a simple and primitive character as to baffle the officials by affording no features comparable to the concepts familiar to European habits of thought. This latter proposition holds even now, after all that has been achieved by the researches of the past hundred years into land tenures and the development of the concept of property. Witness Mr. Baden-Powell's discussion of the "Supposed Rights of the Tódas" (vol. iii. pp. 187–88).

It is interesting to find a writer of such wide and intimate acquaintance with the subject from the practical side, holding a detailed, and, to a great extent, independent view of the origin (or origins) and life history of the Indian village, "under its varied conditions". He finds that "there can hardly be any doubt that the formation of village groups ... is not peculiar to Hindu races, either original or converted. It is found in India, among the great races which were certainly antecedent to the Hindus, and which still survive (with their institutions) in widely distant parts of the country. The village – apart from questions of particular forms – is not so much the result of any system as it is of a natural instinct. We find it everywhere, especially in the plain country, where circumstances invited it." (vol. i. p. 106.) "And then, there is not one type of village community, but two very distinct types, one of which, again, has marked and curious forms and varieties. And without anticipating details, which must come later, I may say at once that these two types are distinct in origin." (p. 106.) The group belonging to one of these two types [114] claim and acknowledge no joint ownership of the whole estate, or joint liability for burdens imposed by the state. "In the other type ... a strong joint-body ... has pretensions to be of higher caste or superior title to the 'tenants' who live on the estate. As a matter of fact, the first type of village is the one most closely connected with Hindu government and Hindu ideas." (p. 107.) Mr. Baden-Powell holds (p. 112) that "If we look to the earliest villages formed under the Aryans, or before that, we have no evidence (other than that of the [periodical] re-distribution, which I do not regard as conclusive) of a tribal stage; and even among the later Panjáb tribes, where tribal occupation and allotment are clearly discernible, any previous stage of the *joint* holding by the tribe collectively, hardly seems deducible from the known facts." "Family" property, however, he finds to prevail as regards most villages.

"We must conclude that the first (and, as far as we know, the oldest) form of village is where the cultivators – practically owners of their several family holdings – live under a common headman, with certain common officers and artisans who serve them ... ; and there is no landlord (class or individual) over the whole." (p. 129.) This is the "Raiyatwári" or "Non-landlord Village," and this type, the author inclines to think, is of Dravidian rather than Aryan origin. The second type of village is held to have arisen (*a*) out of this first type, by superposition of a landlord in one of several different ways enumerated, or (*b*) "from the original conquest and occupation of land – as far as we know – previously occupied." Under (*a*), the active factor in producing a joint ownership, vested in a class "of higher caste and superior title," has been the institution of family property and family inheritance. "When the original acquirer of such (landlord) rights dies, and a body of joint heirs succeeds, *we soon find a number of co-sharers*, all equally entitled, claiming the whole estate, and (whether remaining joint or partitioning the fields) forming what is called a 'joint village community'."

The author leaves but scant and dubious room for the "primitive Aryan village community", in the sense of a patriarchal-communistic tribal group.

A large portion, perhaps the greater portion of the part given up to the general discussion, deals with the history and description of legislation and administrative practice. The later portions are perhaps even to a greater extent occupied with matters of this somewhat [115] technical nature. While serving their immediate purpose of usefulness to the revenue official, they serve a no less useful purpose for the student of economic institutions (the author is as much a student as an official). It comes out clearly in the course of the narrative and exposition of what has been done and aimed at, that the officials who have had to do with the vast complex of the land system, have had repeatedly to learn from their own failures, and from the failure in one place of methods that had approved themselves by experience in another, how concrete and individual the situation in each particular locality is. Each little district, one might almost say each village, is in some sense a case by itself, with what might be called personal idiosyncracies of its own. And still, it appears at the same time that certain broad generalizations may be made, and may be made good use of. It is also evident that, while the officials, especially since the evil effect of the Cornwallis settlement became manifest, have striven to understand and to adapt themselves to the circumstances as they have found them, their own European habits of mind have to a large extent decided the point of view from which they have studied the situation. And this fact, that the administrative, as well as the legislative functionaries of the British–Indian system, have been men inheriting a common tradition and a common point of view, has left its visible effects in the trend toward unity and homogeneity in the development of the system. While Mr. Baden-Powell's exposition brings out in strong colors the variety and contrast of local systems and usages, it also brings out the fact (slight though the actual achievements in that direction may be) that the British occupation and administration of India is at work to make "India" something more than "a geographical expression," in spite of Mr. Baden-Powell's declaration (vol. i. p. 5), that the term is at present nothing more. His own book – the possibility of such a work of generalization and orderly statement – is testimony to the fact that "India" is a term connoting more of homogeneity and solidarity to-day than the same "geographical expression" would have covered in the days when scores of petty sovereign governments were each pulling its own way, and each developing particolored systems of its own.

The three volumes are a credit to the printer as well as to the author, and are copiously supplied with excellent maps and contain two good indexes.

Selection 7

Review of *Der Parlamentarismus, die Volksgesetzgebung und die Socialdemokratie* by Karl Kautsky

Source: *Journal of Political Economy*, March 1894 (vol. 2, pp. 312–14).

Veblen (1894a)

The traditional attitude of socialists, both in Germany and elsewhere, has generally been hostile to "parliamentarism." The name of the "Social-Democrats" of Germany is significant of their leaning toward the primitive democratic organization of society, which has no use for a parliament. Socialists have made much of the direct participation of the people in legislation, almost universally to the extent of urging the Referendum, Initiative, and Imperative Mandate, and very generally advocating a close circumscription of the powers of the representative body. At the same time they have held in theory that the members should be delegates only, and not representatives in the full sense. Extremists have held that representative legislatures have no place in the republic of the future, and have even discountenanced participation in elections of members of parliamentary bodies.

Mr. Kautsky takes exception to this view. He expresses the view of what is probably a strong section and apparently a growing section of European socialism, that a parliamentary legislative body, and the parliamentary method, is not simply a necessary evil under existing circumstances, but is the best means known for embodying the popular will in law and enforcing the execution of the law. It is urged that direct legislation by the people belongs to the same primitive stage of culture with direct administration of justice by the people, and that both of these become impossible as the community increases in numbers and complexity. In a large and highly developed republic it would take all the time of all the citizens to enact the necessary laws and watch over their execution. The most that can be left to direct popular action is what is comprised in the Referendum and the Initiative, and the purpose of these two institutions is not to abolish the parliamentary body, but only to render it more immediately dependent on popular influence and control. [313]

It is pointed out that not only is the trend of development toward the employment of parliamentary methods in all civil bodies, but even in voluntary organizations of all kinds and for all purposes the same method necessarily prevails. And by no class is the parliamentary idea carried out more rigorously than by the laboring population, from whose members the socialist organizations are made up. They, the substance and exponent of the coming socialist State, delegate powers to their representatives, when occasion demands, with more freedom, and submit to their decision with less reserve, than any other class. No class or party has the same sense of party discipline and solidarity.

The author points out that direct legislation by the people, together with its complement, direct administration of justice, logically belong in the anarchist scheme. It is, in fact, the characteristic feature that distinguishes anarchism from socialism.

While its purpose is the refutation of what the author considers an unsocialistic position – the position that the powers of parliamentary (representative) bodies should be closely limited and legislation by the body of the people insisted on at all points, the argument serves a purpose more interesting to students of the socialist movement. It indicates that the attitude of socialism, in the persons of the leaders of the movement, is with an increasing degree of consciousness coming to be that of an aspiration towards the republic, in the same sense which that term conveys to English-speaking people. Parliamentarism is the form and method whereby socialism is to work out the salvation of mankind. Patriarchal absolutism has virtually ceased some time past to occupy the socialist's thoughts, and the idea of government by a committee of delegates is likewise becoming discredited. The modern socialistic movement has outlived the bitter antagonism to all things belonging to the existing social order, which characterized its early utterances at the middle of the century, and is casting about to find and make use of whatever is good and serviceable for the cause in modern political institutions. A livelier appreciation of the meaning of the dogma that socialism is the "next stage in social evolution," that it will be reached if at all by an evolution from existing forms of social organization, is bringing into fuller consciousness the implication that socialism is the industrial republic, not industrial democracy, and that the means by which it will do its work must be, if anything, a further development and a perfected form of the means employed by the political republic in its sphere. [314]

Perhaps the first reflection which this change, or growth, will suggest to conservative members of society, is that it renders socialism all the more effective an engine for mischief, the more reasonable it becomes on all other heads than its chief characteristic of antagonism to the institution of private ownership.

Selection 8

The economic theory of woman's dress

Source: *Popular Science Monthly*, December 1894
(vol. 2, pp. 198–205).

Veblen (1894g)

In human apparel the element of dress is readily distinguishable from that of clothing. The two functions – of dress and of clothing the person – are to a great extent subserved by the same material goods, although the extent to which the same material serves both purposes will appear very much slighter on second thought than it does at first glance. A differentiation of materials has long been going on, by virtue of which many things that are worn for the one purpose no longer serve, and are no longer expected to serve, the other. The differentiation is by no means complete. Much of human apparel is worn both for physical comfort and for dress; still more of it is worn ostensibly for both purposes. But the differentiation is already very considerable and is visibly progressing.

But, however united in the same object, however the two purposes may be served by the same material goods, the purpose of physical comfort and that of a reputable appearance are not to be confounded by the meanest understanding. The elements of clothing and of dress are distinct; not only that, but they even verge on incompatibility; the purpose of either is frequently best subserved by special means which are adapted to perform only a single line of duty. It is often true, here as elsewhere, that the most efficient tool is the most highly specialized tool.

Of these two elements of apparel dress came first in order of development, and it continues to hold the primacy to this day. The element of clothing, the quality of affording comfort, was from the beginning, and to a great extent it continues to be, in some sort an afterthought.

The origin of dress is sought in the principle of adornment. This is a well-accepted fact of social evolution. But that principle furnished the point of departure for the evolution of dress rather than the norm of its development. It is true of dress, as of so much else of the apparatus of life, that its initial purpose has not remained its sole or dominant purpose throughout the course of its later growth. It may be stated broadly that adornment, in the naïve æsthetic sense, is a factor of relatively slight importance in modern dress.

The line of progress during the initial stage of the evolution of apparel was from the simple concept of adornment of the person by supplementary accessions from without, to the complex concept of an adornment that should render the person pleasing, or of an enviable presence, and at the same time serve to indicate the possession [199] of other virtues than that of a well-favored person only. In this latter direction lies what was to evolve into dress. By the time dress emerged from the primitive efforts of the savage to beautify himself with gaudy additions to his person, it was already an economic factor of some importance. The change from a purely æsthetic character (ornament) to a mixture of the æsthetic and economic took place before the progress had been achieved from pigments and trinkets to what is commonly understood by apparel. Ornament is not properly an economic category, although the trinkets which serve the purpose of ornament may also do duty as an economic factor, and in so far be assimilated to dress. What constitutes dress an economic fact, properly falling within the scope of economic theory, is its function as an index of the wealth of its wearer – or, to be more precise, of its owner, for the wearer and owner are not necessarily the same person. It will hold with respect to more than one half the values currently recognized as "dress," especially that portion with which this paper is immediately concerned – woman's dress – that the wearer and the owner are different persons. But while they need not be united in the same person, they must be organic members of the same economic unit; and the dress is the index of the wealth of the economic unit which the wearer represents. Under the patriarchal organization of society, where the social unit was the man (with his dependents), the dress of the women was an exponent of the wealth of the man whose chattels they were. In modern society, where the unit is the household, the woman's dress sets forth the wealth of the household to which she belongs. Still, even to-day, in spite of the nominal and somewhat celebrated demise of the patriarchal idea, there is that about the dress of women which suggests that the wearer is something in the nature of a chattel; indeed, the theory of woman's dress quite plainly involves the implication that the woman is a chattel.

In this respect the dress of women differs from that of men. With this exception, which is not of first-rate importance, the essential principles of woman's dress are not different from those which govern the dress of men; but even apart from this added characteristic the element of dress is to be seen in a more unhampered development in the apparel of women. A discussion of the theory of dress in general will gain in brevity and conciseness by keeping in view the concrete facts of the highest manifestation of the principles with which it has to deal, and this highest manifestation of dress is unquestionably seen in the apparel of the women of the most advanced modern communities.

The basis of the award of social rank and popular respect is the success, or more precisely the efficiency, of the social unit, as evidenced by its visible success. When efficiency eventuates in [200] possessions, in pecuniary strength, as it eminently does in the social system of our time, the basis of the award of social consideration becomes the visible pecuniary strength of the social unit. The immediate and obvious index of pecuniary strength is the visible ability to spend, to consume unproductively; and men early learned to put in evidence their ability to spend by displaying costly goods that afford no return to their owner, either in comfort or in gain. Almost as early did a differentiation set in, whereby it became the function of woman, in a peculiar degree, to exhibit the pecuniary strength of her social unit by means of a conspicuously unproductive consumption of valuable goods.

Reputability is in the last analysis, and especially in the long run, pretty fairly coincident with the pecuniary strength of the social unit in question. Woman, primarily, originally because she was herself a pecuniary possession, has become in a peculiar way the exponent of the pecuniary strength of her social group; and with the progress of specialization of functions in the social organism this duty tends to devolve more and more entirely upon the woman. The best, most advanced, most highly developed societies of our time have reached the point in their evolution where it has (ideally) become the great, peculiar, and almost the sole function of woman in the social system to put in evidence her economic unit's ability to pay. That is to say, woman's place (according to the ideal scheme of our social system) has come to be that of a means of conspicuously unproductive expenditure.

The admissible evidence of the woman's expensiveness has considerable range in respect of form and method, but in substance it is always the same. It may take the form of manners, breeding, and accomplishments that are, *prima facie*, impossible to acquire or maintain without such leisure as bespeaks a considerable and relatively long-continued possession of wealth. It may also express itself in a peculiar manner of life, on the same grounds and with much the same purpose. But the method in vogue always and everywhere, alone or in conjunction with other methods, is that of dress. "Dress," therefore, from the economic point of view, comes pretty near being synonymous with "display of wasteful expenditure."

The extra portion of butter, or other unguent, with which the wives of the magnates of the African interior anoint their persons, beyond what comfort requires, is a form of this kind of expenditure lying on the border between primitive personal embellishment and incipient dress. So also the brass-wire bracelets, anklets, etc., at times aggregating some thirty pounds in weight, worn by the same class of persons, as well as, to a less extent, by the male population of the same countries. So also the pelt of the arctic fur seal, which the women of civilized countries prefer to [201] fabrics that are preferable to it in all respects but that of expense. So also the ostrich plumes and the many curious effigies of plants and animals that are dealt in by the milliners. The list is inexhaustible, for there is scarcely an article of apparel of male or female, civilized or uncivilized, that does not partake largely of this element, and very many may be said, in point of economic principle, to consist of virtually nothing else.

It is not that the wearers or the buyers of these wasteful goods desire the waste. They desire to make manifest their ability to pay. What is sought is not the *de facto* waste, but the appearance of waste. Hence there is a constant effort on the part of the consumers of these goods to obtain them at as good a bargain as may be; and hence also a constant effort on the part of the producers of these goods to lower the cost of their production, and consequently to lower the price. But as fast as the price of the goods declines to such a figure that their consumption is no longer *prima facie* evidence of a considerable ability to pay, the particular goods in question fall out of favor, and consumption is diverted to something which more adequately manifests the wearer's ability to afford wasteful consumption.

This fact, that the object sought is not the waste but the display of waste, develops into a principle of pseudo-economy in the use of material; so that it has come to be recognized as a canon of good form that apparel should not show lavish expenditure simply. The material used must be chosen so as to give evidence of the wearer's (owner's) capacity for making it go as far in the way of display as may be; otherwise it would suggest incapacity on the part of the owner, and so partially defeat the main purpose of the display. But what is more to the point is that such a mere display of crude waste would also suggest that the means of display had been acquired so recently as not to have permitted that long-continued waste of time and effort required for mastering the most effective methods of display. It would argue recent acquisition of means; and we are still near enough to the tradition of pedigree and aristocracy of birth to make long-continued possession of means second in point of desirability only to the possession of large means. The greatness of the means possessed is manifested by the volume of display; the length of possession is, in some degree, evidenced by the manifestation of a thorough habituation to the methods of display. Evidence of a knowledge and habit of good form in dress (as in manners) is chiefly to be valued because it argues that much time has been spent in the acquisition of this accomplishment; and as the accomplishment is in no wise of direct economic value, it argues pecuniary ability to waste time and labor. Such accomplishment, therefore, when possessed in a high degree, is evidence of a life (or of more than [202] one life) spent to no useful purpose; which, for purposes of respectability, goes as far as a very considerable unproductive consumption of goods. The offensiveness of crude taste and vulgar display in matters of dress is, in the last analysis, due to the fact that they argue the absence of ability to afford a reputable amount of waste of time and effort.

Effective use of the means at hand may, further, be taken to argue efficiency in the person making the display; and the display of efficiency, so long as it does not manifestly result in pecuniary gain or increased personal comfort, is a great social desideratum. Hence it happens that, surprising as it may seem at first glance, a principle of pseudo-economy in the use of materials has come to hold a well-secured though pretty narrowly circumscribed place in the theory of dress, as that theory expresses itself in the facts of life. This principle, acting in concert with certain other requirements of dress, produces some curious and otherwise inexplicable results, which will be spoken of in their place.

The first principle of dress, therefore, is conspicuous expensiveness. As a corollary under this principle, but of such magnificent scope and consequence as to claim rank as a second fundamental principle, there is the evidence of expenditure afforded by a constant supersession of one wasteful garment or trinket by a new one. This principle inculcates the desirability, amounting to a necessity wherever circumstances allow, of wearing nothing that is out of date. In the most advanced communities of our time, and so far as concerns the highest manifestations of dress – e.g., in ball dress and the apparel worn on similar ceremonial occasions, when the canons of dress rule unhampered by extraneous considerations – this principle expresses itself in the maxim that no outer garment may be worn more than once.

This requirement of novelty is the underlying principle of the whole of the difficult and interesting domain of fashion. Fashion does not demand continual flux and change simply because that way of doing is foolish; flux and change and novelty are demanded by the central principle of all dress – conspicuous waste.

This principle of novelty, acting in concert with the motive of pseudo-economy already spoken of, is answerable for that system of shams that figures so largely, openly and aboveboard, in the accepted code of dress. The motive of economy, or effective use of material, furnishes the point of departure, and this being given, the requirement of novelty acts to develop a complex and extensive system of pretenses, ever varying and transient in point of detail, but each imperative during its allotted time – facings, edgings, and the many (pseudo) deceptive contrivances that will occur to any one that is at all familiar with the technique of dress. This pretense of deception is often developed into a pathetic, child-like [203] make-believe. The realities which it simulates, or rather symbolizes, could not be tolerated. They would be in some cases too crudely expensive, in others inexpensive and more nearly adapted to minister to personal comfort than to visible expense; and either alternative is obnoxious to the canons of good form.

But apart from the exhibition of pecuniary strength afforded by an aggressive wasteful expenditure, the same purpose may also be served by conspicuous abstention from useful effort. The woman is, by virtue of the specialization of social functions, the exponent of the economic unit's pecuniary strength, and it consequently also devolves on her to exhibit the unit's capacity to endure this passive form of pecuniary damage. She can do this by putting in evidence the fact (often a fiction) that she leads a useless life. Dress is her chief means of doing so. The ideal of dress, on this head, is to demonstrate to all observers, and to compel observation of the fact, that the wearer is manifestly incapable of doing anything that is of any use. The modern civilized woman's dress attempts this demonstration of habitual idleness, and succeeds measurably.

Herein lies the secret of the persistence, in modern dress, of the skirt and of all the cumbrous and otherwise meaningless drapery which the skirt typifies. The skirt persists because it is cumbrous. It hampers the movements of the wearer and disables her, in great measure, for any useful occupation. So it serves as an advertisement (often disingenuous) that the wearer is backed by sufficient means to be able to afford the idleness, or impaired efficiency, which the skirt implies. The like is true of the high heel, and in less degree of several other features of modern dress. Herein is also to be sought the ground of the persistence (probably not the origin) of the one great mutilation practiced by civilized Occidental womankind – the constricted waist, as well as of the analogous practice of the abortive foot among their Chinese sisters. This modern mutilation of woman is perhaps not to be classed strictly under the category of dress; but it is scarcely possible to draw the line so as to exclude it from the theory, and it is so closely coincident with that category in point of principle that an outline of the theory would be incomplete without reference to it.

A corollary of some significance follows from this general principle. The fact that voluntarily accepted physical incapacity argues the possession of wealth practically establishes the futility of any attempted reform of woman's dress in the direction of convenience, comfort, or health. It is of the essence of dress that it should (appear to) hamper, incommode, and injure the wearer, for in so doing it proclaims the wearer's pecuniary ability to endure idleness and physical incapacity. [204]

It may be noted, by the way, that this requirement, that women must appear to be idle in order to be respectable, is an unfortunate circumstance for women who are compelled to provide their own livelihood. They have to supply not only the means of living, but also the means of advertising the fiction that they live without any gainful occupation; and they have to do all this while encumbered with garments specially designed to hamper their movements and decrease their industrial efficiency.

The cardinal principles of the theory of woman's dress, then, are these three:

1 Expensiveness: Considered with respect to its effectiveness as clothing, apparel must be uneconomical. It must afford evidence of the ability of the wearer's economic group to pay for things that are in themselves of no use to any one concerned – to pay without getting an equivalent in comfort or in gain. From this principle there is no exception.
2 Novelty: Woman's apparel must afford *prima facie* evidence of having been worn but for a relatively short time, as well as, with respect to many articles, evidence of inability to withstand any appreciable amount of wear. Exceptions from this rule are such things as are of sufficient permanence to become heirlooms, and of such surpassing expensiveness as normally to be possessed only by persons of superior (pecuniary) rank. The possession of an heirloom is to be commended because it argues the practice of waste through more than one generation.
3 Ineptitude: It must afford *prima facie* evidence of incapacitating the wearer for any gainful occupation; and it should also make it apparent that she is

permanently unfit for any useful effort, even after the restraint of the apparel is removed. From this rule there is no exception.

Besides these three, the principle of adornment, in the æsthetic sense, plays some part in dress. It has a certain degree of economic importance, and applies with a good deal of generality; but it is by no means imperatively present, and when it is present its application is closely circumscribed by the three principles already laid down. Indeed, the office of the principle of adornment in dress is that of handmaid to the principle of novelty, rather than that of an independent or co-ordinate factor. There are, further, minor principles that may or may not be present, some of which are derivatives of the great central requisite of conspicuous waste; others are of alien origin, but all are none the less subject to the controlling presence of the three cardinal principles enumerated above. These three are essential and constitute the substantial norm of woman's dress, and no exigency can permanently set them aside so long as the chance of rivalry between [205] persons in respect of wealth remains. Given the possibility of a difference in wealth, and the sway of this norm of dress is inevitable. Some spasm of sense, or sentiment, or what not, may from time to time create a temporary and local diversion in woman's apparel; but the great norm of "conspicuous waste" can not be set aside or appreciably qualified so long as this its economic ground remains.

To single out an example of the temporary effect of a given drift of sentiment, there has, within the past few years, come, and very nearly gone, a recrudescence of the element of physical comfort of the wearer, as one of the usual requirements of good form in dress. The meaning of this proposition, of course, is not what appears on its face; that seldom happens in matters of dress. It was the show of personal comfort that was lately imperative, and the show was often attained only at the sacrifice of the substance. This development, by the way, seems to have been due to a ramification of the sentimental athleticism (flesh-worship) that has been dominant of late; and now that the crest of this wave of sentiment has passed, this alien motive in dress is also receding.

The theory of which an outline has now been given is claimed to apply in full force only to modern woman's dress. It is obvious that if the principles arrived at are to be applied as all-deciding criteria, "woman's dress" will include the apparel of a large class of persons who, in the crude biological sense, are men. This feature does not act to invalidate the theory. A classification for the purpose of economic theory must be made on economic grounds alone, and can not permit considerations whose validity does not extend beyond the narrower domain of the natural sciences to mar its symmetry so far as to exclude this genial volunteer contingent from the ranks of womankind.

There is also a second, very analogous class of persons, whose apparel likewise, though to a less degree, conforms to the canons of woman's dress.

This class is made up of the children of civilized society. The children, with some slight reservation of course, are, for the purpose of the theory, to be regarded as ancillary material serving to round out the great function of civilized womankind as the conspicuous consumers of goods. The child in the hands of civilized woman is an accessory organ of conspicuous consumption, much as any tool in the hands of a laborer is an accessory organ of productive efficiency.

Selection 9

Review of *Misère de la philosophie* by Karl Marx, and of *Socialisme et science positive* by Enrico Ferri

Source: *Journal of Political Economy*, December 1896 (vol. 5, pp. 97–103).

Veblen (1896)

This reprint of Marx's earliest exposition of his peculiar economic views is notable, not in point of novelty, nor because it adds to what is already currently known by students of Marx with regard to his early position, but because it is evidence of the unabated authority with which the writings of the master still appeal to the thoughtful and studious adherents of the school. It may be noted in this connection that a German translation of the book (by men as eminent in the socialist world as Bernstein and Kautsky) has also recently (1892) appeared. The present reprint is an unaltered reproduction of the book as it originally appeared in 1847, in Marx's polemical onslaught on Proudhon, except for the incorporation of certain minor corrections made by the author in the margins of his private copy of the volume. There are also added, by way of appendices, three briefer papers by Marx, – a condemnatory letter on Proudhon, reprinted from the *Socialdemokrat* (Berlin) of 1865; an extract from *Zur Kritik der politischen Oekonomie*, going to disprove Proudhon's claim to originality in his proposed *banque du peuple*; and the address on free trade before the Democratic Association of Brussels. These supplementary documents go to enforce the impression made by Engels's preface, that the purpose of the reprint is in some measure a polemical one. The preface is directed to the disproof of any possible indebtedness of Marx to Rodbertus, as well as to the definitive confutation of all who may claim any originality or other merit for Rodbertus, whether as against Marx or otherwise in connection with economic discussion. Although Engels's preface dates from 1884, it may not be out of place to repeat, for the good of Rodbertus's admirers and champions at this day, certain characteristic claims and assertions here made by Marx's lifelong intimate friend, "the most [98] truthful of the socialists." After referring for details to his prospective discussion of the relation between Marx and Rodbertus in the subsequently published preface to the fourth edition of Marx's *Kapital*, he goes on to say:

> It will be sufficient here to say that when Rodbertus accuses Marx of having "despoiled" him and "of having in his *Kapital* drawn extensively on,

but without citing," his work, *Zur Erkenntniss*, etc., he has allowed himself to be led into a calumny which can be explained only through the ill humor naturally to be expected of an unappreciated genius, and through his remarkable ignorance of things which took place outside of Prussia, and more especially his ignorance of economic and socialistic literature. Neither these complaints nor Rodbertus's work above cited had ever come under Marx's eyes; he had no acquaintance with Rodbertus beyond the three *Sozialen Briefe*, and even these assuredly not prior to 1858 or 1859.

Professor Ferri's work, which has now come to hand in a French edition, is no less laudatory of Marx. The juxtaposition of names in the sententious subtitle ("Darwin, Spencer, Marx") is of itself a sufficient promise of an appreciatory discussion of Marx's writings and of his place in the science. The eminent Italian criminologist gives in his adhesion to the tenets of scientific socialism without equivocation, and sets out with a promise to justify the claims of that dogma to be the complement, on the side of the social sciences, of that theory of development for which, in its general features, Darwin's name serves as catchword in the biological sciences.

Part I (pp. 13–85) of the volume is in great measure taken up with a refutation of what Professor Ferri regards as the three fundamental objections that have been made against socialism on grounds of evolutionary theory. These three points of alleged contradiction between Darwinism and socialism are: (*a*) Socialism demands equality of individuals, while the evolutionary process constantly accentuates that inequality between individuals which alone affords play for the selective adaptation of the species or the type; (*b*) socialism demands the survival, in comfort and fullness of life, of all individuals, whereas Darwinism (taking the term here, as elsewhere in the book, in the broad sense in which it is popularly used) requires the destruction, through the struggle for existence, of the great majority of individuals; (*c*) the struggle for existence secures a progressive elimination of the unfit and a survival of the superior individuals, resulting in a progressive amelioration of the selected minority of individuals that are [99] in this way delegated to carry on the development of the species or of the type, whereas socialism, by giving all an even chance of life, reduces the aggregate of individuals to a dead level of democratic uniformity, in which the superior merits of the "fit" count for nothing.

Of these objections to socialism Haeckel is regarded as the best and most effective spokesman that has yet appeared; other and later restatements, of which the number is by no means small, being taken only as feebler variants of the apology for natural selection made by the great German apostle of Darwinism. The alleged contradictions are reviewed somewhat in detail, and the socialist position which claims a full accord between the teachings of evolutionary science and the prospectus of revolutionary evolution offered by spokesmen of Marxism are summarized and restated in a telling manner, though with somewhat more of a declamatory turn than would be required for the purpose of an enumeration of the data bearing on the question of human evolution and a formulation of the inferences to be drawn from these data. The three contradictions which are passed under review are disposed of by showing, in rather more convincing form than is usual with the scientific apologists of socialism, (*a*) that the equality of individuals demanded by the socialist scheme is an equality of opportunities rather than an identity of function or of the details of life; (*b*) that the struggle for existence, as applied within the field of social evolution, is a struggle between groups and institutions rather than a competition *à outrance* between the individuals of the group, and that this struggle can lead to socially desirable results only as it is carried on on the basis of a large measure of group solidarity and co-operation between the individuals of the group; that the "normal" *milieu* for the competitive development of individuals in society in the direction of availability for the social purpose and a fuller and more truly human life is afforded only by an environment which secures the members of the community a competent and equitable – if not equal – immunity from the sordid cares of a life of pecuniary competition. Only under such an environment can we look for the development and fixation of a type of man which shall best meet the requirements of associated human life. That is to say, the closer an approach is made to a condition of pecuniary equality and solidarity the better are the chances of a survival of the "fittest," in the sense of the most efficient for the purposes of the collective life. And this brings us to the consideration [100] of the third alleged contradiction between the socialist scheme and Darwinism – that an abolition of the pecuniary struggle would abolish the evolutionary factor of a selective survival of the fittest individuals. It is (*c*) only by injecting a wholly illegitimate teleological meaning into the term "fittest," as used by Darwin and the Darwinists that the expression "survival of the fittest" is made to mean a survival of the socially desirable individuals. This whole objection, therefore, is a sophism which proceeds on a teleological pre-conception – a survival in modern discussion of a concept which belongs among the mental furniture of the metaphysical speculations of the pre-Darwinian times. A sober review of well-known facts, we are told, shows that the present competitive system does not by any means uniformly result in a working out of favorable results by a process of natural selection. "It is well known that in the modern civilized world the action of natural selection is vitiated by the presence of a military selection, by matrimonial selection, and especially by economic selection" (p. 49). Professor Ferri here develops very briefly, and turns to socialist account, the theory of "social selection" of types originated by Broca, and more recently developed with greater fullness and effect by Lapouge, Ammon, and Loria. It is only in the "*milieu normal*" afforded by such an equality of pecuniary competence as the socialist scheme contemplates that the factor of "choice" has a chance to act and to award the victory to "the most normal individuals" and types.

The struggle for existence, and therefore the fact of a selective adaptation, is a fact inseparable from the life process, and therefore inseparable from the life of mankind; but while its scope remains unaltered, the forms under which it expresses itself in the life of society change as the development of collective life proceeds. The most striking general modification which the struggle has suffered in the past growth of society, and the feature which most immediately concerns the present discussions, is seen in the transformation of this struggle for existence in the communities of the occidental culture into a struggle for equality.

> During the historical period of development, Græco-Latin society in the first place carried on a struggle for *civil* equality (abolition of slavery); this struggle was triumphant, but it did not stop there, for life and struggle are the same facts stated in different words; society during the Middle Ages carried on its struggle for *religious* equality, achieved it, but did not stop there; and at the close of the last century the struggle was for *political* equality. Is [101] society now to come to a standstill and to stagnate in its present phase? Today the struggle of society is for *economic* equality; not for an absolute pecuniary equality, but for an equality of that more consequential kind of which I have spoken above. And everything goes to impress upon us with mathematical certainty that when this victory is achieved it must in turn give place to further struggles and new ideals among the generations that are to succeed us (pp. 37–38).

This struggle for equality, as is to some extent true of any other expression of the struggle within a given society, takes the form of a struggle between classes, and necessarily so. It is therefore a struggle for existence on the basis of solidarity and co-operation. The discovery of this law of cultural evolution, "of this grand conception," "is the imperishable glory of Marx, which secures him a place in sociology such as that occupied by Darwin in biology, and by Spencer in natural philosophy" (p. 71).

According to Professor Ferri socialism is atheistic, as a matter of course; but he regards the antagonism of the religious organizations, as well as the quasi-socialistic endeavors of the Roman Catholic church, with the utmost complacency; being fully persuaded that in this matter of irreligiousness as a requisite of socialistic reform the course of events will effectually take care of itself. No thought need be taken for the education of humanity away from the theistic cults, since the cults, with their entire theistic content, will disappear from man's habits of thought as fast as the chief positions of evolutionary science are accepted. This is the meaning to be attached to the declaration of the Erfurt programme that religion is a private affair with which the socialist propaganda will not concern itself. Education – a familiarity with the views and the point of view of modern science – will obliterate the faiths; therefore the socialist propaganda need take no thought for erasing them (pp. 56–63).

Similarly, although the scheme of socialism is, fundamentally and of necessity, republican – being but a reorganization of the industrial community on republican lines – the office of republicanizing society, as a step pre-paratory to its socialization, may without misgiving be left to bourgeois lib-eralism, which must necessarily work out such a result as its logical outcome.

Incidentally, in so far as it is not altogether relevant to the main point of the book, but somewhat at large, in so much as the discussion runs through some twenty-five pages, the great Italian criminologist [102] has a word of kindly admonition to say to the students of Sociology and Political Economy. This discussion (Part III of the volume) is headed: "Sociology and Socialism," and the two chapters of which it is made up bear the captions: The Sterility of Sociology, and Marx the Complement of Darwin and Spencer.

> One of the most curious facts in the history of scientific thought during the nineteenth century is this, that while the profound revolution in sci-ence wrought by Darwinism and the Spencerian evolutionism has reha-bilitated every department of physical, biological, and even the psychological sciences, and endowed them with a new youth, this same scientific revolution has, upon reaching the domain of the social sciences, barely rippled the surface of the still waters of that pool of orthodoxy in social science, Political Economy.
>
> It is true, there was a move made by Auguste Comte … toward the creation of a new science, Sociology, which was intended, in conjunction with the natural history of human society, to form the glorious consummation of a new edifice of science erected by the empirical method (p. 145).

It is admitted that some substantial work has been done in the descriptive or "anatomical" branches of the science that deals with the social organism, but after all has been said it is to be admitted that in all this, with the exception of the author's own special department of Criminal Sociology, the results hitherto achieved have been meager in the extreme.

> So soon as the discussion comes in contact with the live political and social questions, the new science of Sociology is overtaken by some sort of hypnotic slumber, and remains in a state of indecision in the limbo of sterile and colorless generalities, such as will permit the sociologues to continue, in questions of the public economy as well as in politics, as conservatives or as radicals just as their caprice or inclination may dictate (p. 146).
>
> The secret of this curious phenomenon lies not alone in the fact poin-ted out by Malagodi that the science is still in the period of scientific analysis and has not yet reached the period of synthesis, but more espe-cially in this, that the logical consequences of Darwinism and of scientific evolutionism, when applied to the study of human society, lead inexorably to socialism (p. 147).

As a remedy for this desperate state of the science, Professor Ferri recommends sociological and economic students to seek somewhere the courage necessary to accept the logical consequences of their own argument. And for scientific method they are frankly commended to [103] turn to Karl Marx as the only competent guide. The Marxian Materialistic Theory of History, and the Theory of Class Struggle, together with the Theory of Surplus Labor, point the way which Sociology and Political Economy must follow if they are to take a place as modern sciences of the post-Darwinian epoch.

Selection 10

Review of *Einführung in den Socialismus* by Richard Calwer

Source: *Journal of Political Economy*, March 1897
(vol. 5, pp. 270–72).

Veblen (1897a)

An elementary text-book in socialism written by a socialist and primarily for the instruction of adherents of the socialist creed is not altogether a new departure in literature, but there are few efforts of the kind which are on the whole as acceptable and effective a presentation of their subject as this. The immediate aim of the book is to combat the spirit of petty personal and local interest which is becoming a hindrance to effective co-operation for the larger and remoter ends of the socialist movement in Germany. At the same time it is not a controversial work. Its purpose is sought to be accomplished by so explaining the meaning and trend of the socialist movement as to leave no legitimate ground for the tendency which it deprecates.

That the author is a Marxian goes almost without saying; but his Marxism is of a greatly modernized, softened, conciliatory kind. It is a doctrine of economic evolution, or perhaps better of social evolution primarily on an economic basis, but a doctrine in which the "materialistic theory of history" is no longer obtrusively present in the crude form at every step, although it still remains the fundamental premise. There is no hint of the catastrophic method of reform, nor is there any urging of revolutionary measures. The industrial evolution, we are told, is visibly furthering the socialization of industry day by day. And this not only at certain points, – in certain salient features to which socialistic writers have been in the habit of pointing as evidence of the approach to socialism, – but in all branches of industry, including agriculture, which most socialist teachers have hitherto been content to pass over as a "backward" industry somewhat doubtfully to be included in the scheme for immediate socialization. A characteristic instance of Mr. Calwer's ingenious use of everyday facts in support of this thesis is his pointing out (p. 71) that all statistical determination of industrial methods and of the extent and range of the production and consumption of industrial products contributes to make an eventual collective control of these branches of industry easier. Not only the collective organization of industry under the direction of trusts and syndicates, therefore, but all canvassing of the markets and the industrial situation, by trade journals as well as by students of practical economics, is labor in the service of the socialist movement.

But while the evolution of industry, it is claimed, assures the rapid [271] and inevitable socialization of industry, these mechanical facts and technological events do not immediately or of themselves afford the basis for that growth of institutions which the socialist republic involves. The institutions of the community, whether socialistic or otherwise, rest on psychological ground. The material situation, the state of industry and the arts, may condition the growth of institutions in accordance with the materialistic theory of history, but these material circumstances of environment and of industrial organization and methods control the growth of institutions and social structure only as they affect the individual's habitual view of things. This psychological factor which is to afford the motive to socialistic reconstruction is conceived in quite modern terms. The discontent of the modern laborer, which is to work out the revolution, is no longer conceived to be of the nature of a calm resolution, the outcome of dispassionate ratiocination. It is bluntly recognized (pp. 138–42, 159, 163) that this motive force is simply sentiment and is closely akin to envy, its basis being chiefly an invidious comparison of the laborer's lot with that of the propertied classes. The decisive fact is the distastefulness of the laborer's social position as compared with his employer. Improvement in material comfort measured in absolute terms counts for very little. "You may feed the laborer well, you may clothe him decently, you may provide him with a modest dwelling, in short, you may keep him as a well-to-do man keeps his domestic animals – still the laborer will not be beguiled into overlooking the fact that his place in life is determined by accidents and circumstances which do not permit him to lead the life of a man" (p. 139).

The exposition (Part III) of the aim and methods of the socialistic movement is also temperate and conciliatory in tone, though it leaves no doubt as to its radical character in substance. It deprecates all violence, and even enters a caution against the free use of what a socialist would consider peaceable and legitimate measures, such as strikes and boycotts. "Socialism is essentially a peaceable development of a struggle between different interests … and so long as the socialists are a minority and the industrial situation is not yet ripe for the socialistic régime, so long the socialists must yield, willing or unwilling, to the majority – to those that hold the power. But the time is coming when the majority of the people will be on the socialist side, and then it will depend on the ruling class, which will then have fallen into the position of a minority, whether they are wise enough and shrewd enough [272] to let the further development of the nation's life go on undisturbed or not" (pp. 218, 219). The militarism of European countries is decried as inconsistent with the socialistic evolution, not because war as such is to be deplored, but because war and armaments weaken a nation industrially, and hinder the process of industrial evolution. While no speculation as to the "future state" is indulged in, some reference is made to the probable future of certain institutions and to the attitude of the socialist toward these institutions. So, for instance, (pp. 203–4) socialism is said to hold an entirely neutral position with regard to religion, but this is uttered with an evident conviction that the church and the creeds are alien to socialism and irreconcilable with it in detail. Similarly, socialism is not unpatriotic, although it is international, but the patriotism of the German socialist is in abeyance through the government's fault rather than his own. Little is said about the family, but it is plainly implied that the traditional form of the family is in an advanced stage of obsolescence so far as regards the working classes. It is conceded that the marriage relation at present sanctioned by the law may for the present and for an indefinite time to come be the form best suited for the well-to-do classes.

Selection 11

Review of *Essais sur la conception matérialiste de l'histoire* by Antonio Labriola

Source: *Journal of Political Economy*, June 1897
(vol. 5, pp. 390–91).

Veblen (1897c)

Of these two essays the first (*En memoire du Manifeste du parti communiste*) recalls the attention to what was the meaning, in its author's mind, of the phrase which affords the title of this book. This central Marxian position says that the exigencies of the industrial process determine the features of the society's life process in all its other aspects – social, political, and intellectual. The rest of what the famous *Manifesto* has to say is to be read in the light of this principle which gives the socialist point of view. All the rest, even the doctrine of the class struggle and the Marxian theory of surplus-value, is by comparison provisional and tentative, although in point of fact, it is held, the whole of this further development of the theory is substantially correct. The office of this "materialistic conception" is that of a guiding principle (*Leitfaden*) in the study of social life and of social structure. These economic exigencies afford the definitive test of fitness in the adaptation of all human institutions by a process of selective elimination of the economically unfit. They also, through the industrial process through which they work their effect, determine the development of thought and science; the materialistic conception is itself, at the second remove, a product of the industrial process.

The second essay (*Le materialisme historique*) expands and expounds this position further; and it reiterates, with an insistence that sometimes grows tedious, that, "given the conditions of the development of industry and its appliances, the economic structure of society will determine ... primarily and directly all the rest of the practical activity of the members, as well as the variations of this activity, which are met within the process that we call history – that is to say, the formation, dissensions, conflicts, and erosion of classes. ... And it determines, secondarily, also the tendency, and in an indirect way, in great part, the objects which shall occupy thought and fancy, in art, religion, and science" (p. 239).

The book is notable not as a unique presentation of its thesis nor as a new departure in economic speculation, but as being, on the contrary, a typical example of the theoretical position at present occupied by socialist writers. For the theoretical writers among the socialists, and for the popular discussion in a less pronounced degree, socialist economics no longer revolves about the labor-value dogma that did [391] such ubiquitous service for the propaganda in its day. Nor is the class-struggle dogma any longer so unfaltering a recourse as it once was, even among the Marxists of the stricter observance. These doctrines and their various ramifications are to an extent giving way before an interpretation of the materialistic conception which does not, in its fundamental position, go much beyond a conception of the evolution of social structure according to which the economic activities, and the habits bred by them, determine the activities and the habitual view of things in other directions than the economic one. And in this development the socialists are drawing close to the position of a large and increasing class of economists who are accepting the materialistic conception, or so much of it as is conveniently to be affiliated with Darwinism, whether they accept it under the style and title approved by their socialist mentors or under designations chosen by themselves. These economists of the new evolutionist or socialist departure are nowhere more numerous or more favorably received than among Professor Labriola's countrymen.

Selection 12

Review of *Die Marxistische Socialdemokratie* by Max Lorenz

Source: *Journal of Political Economy*, December 1897 (vol. 6, pp. 136–137).

Veblen (1897f)

There are two features of the Marxian teaching that seem to me to be of definitive significance for today and for the future: the stress laid on the concept of society, with no complacent parade of philanthropy expressing itself in soup-kitchens and alms, but asserting itself as a dominant principle which in strain and struggle resistlessly pervades the entire cultural development, – this is the first; the second is Marx's insistence on the connection between the so-called material or economic movement and the so-called spiritual movement in the evolution of society. ... It is true, Marx has exaggerated the bearing and importance of both these points, because his work, like that of any other man, was conditioned by the circumstances of his time. But on both heads Marx has also shed such light as no one before him, nor in his time, nor – at least until the present – since his time; and that comes of the pre-eminent greatness of the man (pp. viii–ix.).

There is yet a further remark to be made: It is frequently assumed that the substantial core of the Marxian doctrine is the theory of labor-value and surplus-value, and that Marx arrives at his communistic demands directly from his surplus-value theory, on the basis of some assumed principle of justice or morality which requires communism as its fulfillment. ... But Engels disclaims, for Marx and for himself, any such ... "application of Morals to Economics." ... What comes about comes, according to Marx, not for equity's or morality's sake, but it comes as a causally, historically necessary phase of social evolution. The question is then as to the character of this causal, historical necessity in Marx's apprehension. Hence, our first effort must be directed to a presentation of the so-called "Materialistic Conception of History" (pp. xi–xii).

With a reverent hand, the author then enters on a discussion of this materialistic conception, which occupies the first of the four chapters (73 pages) of the volume. He insists on the antithesis between this and the individualistic conception – the conception which has dominated all the writings of the professed historians. After [137] some exposition, and some criticism of its philosophical short-comings, he reaches (p. 50) the consideration of a serious if not irremediable defect in the Marxian theory. While the materialistic interpretation of history points out how social development goes on – by a class struggle that proceeds from maladjustment between economic structure and economic function – it is nowhere pointed out what is the operative force at work in the process. It denies that human discretion and effort seeking a better adjustment can furnish such a force, since it makes man the creature of circumstances. This defect reduces itself under the author's hand to a misconception of human nature and of man's place in the social development. The materialistic theory conceives of man as exclusively a social being, who counts in the process solely as a medium for the transmission and expression of social laws and changes; whereas he is, in fact, also an individual, acting out his own life as such. Hereby is indicated not only the weakness of the materialistic theory, but also the means of remedying the defect pointed out. With the amendment so indicated, it becomes not only a theory of the method of social and economic change, but a theory of social process considered as a substantial unfolding of life as well.

It is as an expression of this materialistic theory of Marx and Engels that the Marxian Socialism is taken up in chapter II and examined point by point. The third chapter is a criticism of the aims and views of socialists as regards the outcome of the development. The author finds the extreme conclusions reached by the socialists – the dissolution of the state and the family, the disappearance of religion, etc. – are reached by a one-sided and arbitrarily limited application of their own principles. The author takes up the materialistic argument and carries it out to its logical consequences, with the result of reducing the socialistic millennium to absurdity, at least to his own satisfaction. In the hands of the social democracy, the teachings of Marx have hardened into a system and a creed, incapable of growth and incapable of meeting the practical exigencies of an unfolding political and social life. While the work of Marx was great and fruitful, "Marxism is but an episode."

Selection 13

Review of *Über einige Grundfragen der Socialpolitik und der Volkswirtschaftslehre* by Gustav Schmoller

Source: *Journal of Political Economy*, June 1898 (vol. 6, pp. 416–19).

Veblen (1898a)

The volume reproduces in collected form three well-known essays of various dates: (1) the polemical chapters of Professor Schmoller's controversy with Treitschke (*Über einige Grundfragen des Rechts und der Volkswirtschaft* – 1874–75); (2) the essay on the Scope and Method of Economic Science (*Die Volkswirtschaft, die Volkswirtschaftslehre und ihre Methode* – 1895), originally written for Conrad's *Handwörterbuch*; and (3) the Inaugural Address of October last, delivered on the occasion of Professor Schmoller's induction into the rectorship at the University of Berlin (*Wechselnde Theorien und feststehende Wahrheiten im Gebiete der Staats – und Socialwissenschaften und die heutige deutsche Volkswirtschaftslehre* – 1897). It is notable as indicating the extent and the character of the changes that have passed over the "historical method" during the past twenty-five years. The earlier of the essays gives Professor Schmoller's position at the time when he first came prominently forward as the champion of that method, and its defender against those who spoke for a return to a rehabilitated classicism. It marks the supersession of Roscher's "historico-physiological" by the "historical" method, through discontinuing, or at least discountenancing, the use of the physiological analogy in economic theory. On the basis of this early controversy with Treitschke, Professor Schmoller got the reputation, not altogether gratuitous, at the hands of his critics, of being spokesman for the view that economic science is, and of right ought to be, without form and void. But if this construction of his views was not altogether gratuitous, still less was it altogether well grounded. The elements of his later methodological work are visible in this early essay, but they are most readily visible and most significant when seen in the light of his later utterances on the same head. Without the consistency and application given to these elements in his later work, it is doubtful if there would have been occasion seriously to qualify the disparaging opinion [417] passed upon his efforts by his Austrian critics. What gives added color to the contentions of those who carp at the historical method, as shown in Schmoller's exposition, is the fact that very much of his constructive work has been of a character to bear out the criticisms leveled at him on methodological grounds.

Much of his own work, as well as the greater part of the voluminous work carried on under his hands by his many disciples, has been of the nature of compilation and description – narrative, often discursive and fragmentary. But as to this prevalent character of his published work, it is to be said that he has, professedly, been occupied with the foundations of a prospective theoretical science of economics. And this prospective science "is, as regards its foundation, descriptive" (p. 226). The second of the essays contained in the volume leaves no ground for the objection that Professor Schmoller makes the science an undisciplined congeries of data. He gives, in concise and telling form, a prospectus for a theoretical science, such that, whatever strictures may be offered by his critics, it can assuredly not be characterized as being without form and void.

> The method of any given science is determined (1) by the general standpoint which human knowledge, taken as a whole, has reached at the time; that is to say, by the generic features of the ideals and methods of knowledge which are in vogue at the time, and which are fundamentally of the same character for all directions of human thinking and knowledge. ... (2) Scientific method depends on the nature of the subject-matter under inquiry. So mathematics follows a different method of procedure from physics, and the latter a different one from physiology, etc. ... (3) The method employed in any given science at any given point of time depends on the degree of development which the science has reached at the time. In its crude beginnings knowledge always proceeds by half truths and sweeping generalizations; only little by little is the method of procedure improved and subtilized; emphasis falls now on observation and description, now on classification, and again, attention may be centered upon the causal explanation of phenomena (pp. 228–30).

It is this third count that seems to have been most insistently present in Professor Schmoller's mind in shaping his work in the past, especially his published writings. Economics has hitherto, in Professor Schmoller's apprehension, been in the inchoate stage only, and the method proper to the science, has, therefore, been conceived to be description and collation. In his lectures, and in the guidance [418] given his students, especially during later years, the same scrupulous regard for the requirements of economics as an inchoate science simply has not been so decisive, at least not to the full extent. It is evident both from the character which his work is now assuming and from the tone of this essay that the science is now felt to be rapidly passing this inchoate stage, and that the economists may now legitimately turn to constructive theoretical work.

Several chapters (iv–x. pp. 231–76) are given to a discussion of the methods and aims of economic science in the past; to an exposition, in outline, of the part which observation and description must play as preliminary to constructive work; to the use of statistical inquiry; to a characterization of the true historical method, and the relation of historical inquiry to economics; and last, but not least, to the important place of a taxonomic discipline – definitions, concepts and classification – in the science. In this latter discussion, it may not be out of place to point out, Professor Schmoller gives but scant acknowledgment to the really large and substantial deserts of the classical writers under this head. The most substantial and characteristic move in advance made by Professor Schmoller in the methodological discussion then follows under xi (*Die Urschen*).

> Observation and description, definition and classification are preparatory work only. What we seek by these means is an apprehension of economic phenomena as a connected whole. ... Our insight in this respect can never be complete or fully adequate. ... But, in any case, the more we confine ourselves to seeking an explanation of the facts at hand on the basis of what has immediately gone before, the more nearly will we succeed in this undertaking. And, in any event, there must remain before our eyes, as the ideal of all knowledge, the explanation of all facts in terms of causation. The natural sciences have accustomed us to apprehend every event as conditioned by causes, which we conceive of as forces (p. 277).
>
> As causes at work in the sequence of economic phenomena we have mechanical and organic forces on the one side, and psychical forces on the other, which meet as two independent groups of causes contributing to the results to be studied. Whatever opinions we may hold as to the relation between physical and psychical life; however much we may be inclined to emphasize the fact that our spiritual life is conditioned by the facts of our nervous system; although we may, with full justification, hold that all our sensations and feelings are inseparable from certain physiological processes; this much remains beyond question, that the coexistence and sequence of spiritual phenomena are not to be explained through nerve changes simply, and that [419] for the present, and apparently for all time to come, the ultimate ascertainable facts of material existence and the most rudimentary adjustments of the spiritual life are ranged over against one another as independent and self explaining groups of phenomena. Hence all efforts to explain the actions of men through direct recourse to merely physical or biological factors must be declared mistaken or inadequate (p. 278).

Hence the causes in terms of which economic theory must in the last resort formulate its results are psychical facts – facts of human motives and propensities.

> There is no science possible outside the range of the universal law of causation – not even in the domain of the spiritual life. But the causes at work in the psychical sequence are essentially different from the mechanical ones. And hence it becomes incumbent on a practical science,

such as economics, to carry its inquiry, as far as may be needed, into the details of psychological processes (pp. 286–87).

The aim of economics, as of any science, adopting any method, must be the determination of uniformities and laws (pp. 298–307). But the descriptive, empirical generalization of uniformities, simply, must not be accepted as a determination of the laws of the phenomena under inquiry. Normalization and taxonomic schedules are not science in the modern acceptance of the word.

> We are no longer content to call empirically ascertained uniformities laws, but only those uniformities the causes of which we have been able to seize and fix (p. 302). Economics is now in a fair way to become such a science. History and philosophy have brought it back to a realizing sense of the phenomena of collective life; statistics and industrial history have shown the way to a methodologically adequate empiricism; and psychology holds up before the science as its only competent purpose the quest for the substantially decisive causes of all human affairs (p. 309).

Selection 14

Review of *Aristocracy and Evolution: A Study of the Rights, the Origins and the Social Functions of the Wealthier Classes* by William H. Mallock

Source: *Journal of Political Economy*, June 1898 (vol. 6, pp. 430–35).

Veblen (1898b)

On a cursory acquaintance with this volume one is tempted to dismiss it with the comment that Mr. Mallock has written another of his foolish books. The objective point of the new book is still the enforcement of the author's pet fallacy, which he has expounded so felicitously on many a former occasion. It is restated here with somewhat greater circumstance than before, and is backed by much telling illustration and some substantial information that might well have served a more useful purpose. A fuller acquaintance with its contents, however, will convince the reader that the book has substantial merits, although these merits do not belong with the economic side of the argument.

While the present volume covers a wider range of phenomena and traces the working of the great man's dominating efficiency through a greater variety of human relations than Mr. Mallock's earlier books have done, the chief point of the argument is still the productive efficiency of the great man in industry and the bearing of this productive efficiency upon the equitable claim of the wealthy classes to a superior share of the product. What is to be proven is the equity and the expediency of a system of distribution in which a relatively large share of the product of industry goes to the owners of capital and the directors of business. For this purpose "the great man" in industry is tacitly identified with the captain of industry or the owner of capital. It is right that the great man, so understood, should receive a large share, because he produces a large proportion of the product of industry (book iii; pp. 197–267). And it is expedient that exceptional gains should come to this exceptional wealth-producer, because on no other terms can he be induced to take care of the economic welfare of the community – and, in the nature of things, [431] the welfare of the community, of the many, lies unreservedly in the hands of the minority of great men (book iv; pp. 271–380).

The few are the chief producers.

> All the democratic formulas which for the past hundred years have represented the employed as the producers of wealth, and the capitalistic employers as the appropriators of it, are, instead of being, as they claim

to be, the expressions of a profound truth, related to truth only as being direct inversions of it. Whatever appearances may seem to show to the contrary, it is the few and not the many who, in the domain of economic production, are essentially and permanently the chief repositories of power (pp. 174–75).

The case of labour directed by different great men is the same as the case of labour applied to different qualities of land. The great men produce the increment. Labour, however, must be held to produce that minimum necessary to the support of the labourers, both in agriculture and in all kinds of production. The great man produces the increment that would not be produced by labour if his influence ceased. Labour, it is true, is essential to the production of the increment, also; but we cannot draw any conclusions from the hypothesis of labour ceasing; for the labourers would have to labor whether the great men were there or no (pp. 202–6, margin). The efficiency of labour itself is practically constant; and for the student of wealth-production the principal force to be studied is the ability of the few, by which the labour of the many is multiplied, and which only exerts itself under special social circumstances (p. 209, note).

We are thus enabled to discriminate arithmetically between the share of the product due to the great men and that due to the many.

Let us take the case of the United Kingdom, and consider the amount per head that was annually produced by the population a hundred years ago. This amount was about £14. At the present time it is something like £35. ... Now, if we attribute the entire production of this country, at the close of the last century, to common or average labour (which is plainly an absurd concession), we shall gain some idea of what the utmost limits of the independent productivity of the ordinary man are; for the ordinary man's talents as a producer, when directed by nobody but himself, have, as has been said already, not appreciably increased in the course of two thousand years, and have certainly not increased within the past three generations. The only thing that has increased has been the concentration on the ordinary man's productive talents of the productive talents of the exceptional man. The talents of the exceptional man, in fact, have been the only variant in the problem; and, accordingly, the minimum which these talents produce is the total difference between £14 and £35. [432]

This argument may be restated in a more concise arithmetical form after adding a further premise, which is implied, though not fully taken account of, in Mr. Mallock's exposition. The talents of the ordinary man have not changed within the past three generations, or if they have changed it is but by a variation so small that it can only be indicated, not quantitatively registered; the like is true of the talents of the exceptional man. This latter feature of the premises has not been brought out by Mr. Mallock, although his claim that human talents have remained constant plainly involves it. The traits of human nature have not appreciably changed within the period in question. The race of British subjects is much the same as it has been. But in order to allow for a possible, though inappreciable change, in the talents of the two classes, the conceivable infinitesimal change may be indicated by the use of accents. The arithmetical problem in hand will then present the following result:

(1) o (ordinary) × g (great man) = 14.

(2) $o' \times g' = 35$.

But since 35 may be broken up and written 14 + 21, it follows that, in the second equation, 21 of the entire product (35) is the product of g' alone. *Q. E. D.*

This traverses the ancient traditions of arithmetic, but it is to be said in legitimation of this procedure that it would be extremely difficult to get the same result by a different method. Any man encumbered with a hide-bound arithmetic would find himself constrained to look for some other variable in the problem than a special segment of that human nature which is by sup-position declared invariable; nor would such a one have the courage to por-tion out the *meum* and *tuum* as between two factors of a joint product. But Mr. Mallock is without fear.

Some account, though scant, is taken by Mr. Mallock of the phenomena of transmitted knowledge, usages, and methods of work; but these facts are not allowed to count as against the primacy of the great man. And as regards this great man, where he is first characterized and expounded, in the chapter especially devoted to him ("Great Men, as the True Cause of Progress," pp. 55–88), the chief variants of him that concern economic theory are the inventor, the overseer of industrial processes, and the business man. The impression is conveyed in this early chapter that for the industrial pur-pose the greatest of these is the inventor, and next him ranks the director of [433] mechanical processes, while the business man comes into view as a wealth-producer chiefly in an indirect way by influencing the motions of the two former, and, through them, the motions of "ordinary men" engaged in manual labor. At a later point, when the question comes to concern the appraisement of productivity and the equitable apportionment of the product, the inventor, the engineer and the foreman disappear behind the business man's ledger, as the peppercorn disappears behind the nutshell, and "the great man" becomes synonymous with "the captain of industry." By a curious inversion of his own main position, Mr. Mallock reaches the broad verdict that consumable goods are mainly produced by the captain of industry. His main position, so far as regards industrial efficiency, is that the greatness and efficiency of the great man lie in his superior knowledge, which he is able to impose upon others and so direct their efforts to the result aimed at. "The master of knowledge, as applied to production, is the inventor" (p. 138). "The inventor ... is an agent of 'social progression' only because the particularized knowledge of which his invention consists is embodied either in models, or drawings, or written or spoken orders, and thus affects the technical action of whole classes of other men" (p. 139). Under the capitalistic wage system "productive power has increased because capital ... has enabled a few men to apply, with the most constant and intense effort, their intellectual faculties to industry in its minutest details" (p. 161). Productive efficiency, therefore, is a matter of detailed knowledge of the technical processes of industry, and the application of this knowledge through directing the technical movements of others. Yet the type of productive efficiency in the advanced portion of Mr. Mallock's argument is taken to be the counting-house activity of the business man, who frequently does not, and pretty uniformly need not, have any technical knowledge of the industry that goes on under his hand. His relation to the mechanical processes is always remote, and usually of a permissive kind only. This is especially true of the director of a large business, who is by that fact, if he is successful, a highly efficient great man. He delegates certain men, perhaps at the second or third remove, to assume discretion and set certain workmen and machines in motion under the guidance of technical knowledge possessed by them, not by him. The captain's efficiency is not to be called in question, but it is bold irony to call it productive efficiency under the definition of productivity set up by Mr. Mallock. [434]

Most modern men would have been content to justify the business man's claim to a share in the product on the ground of his serviceability to the community, without specifically imputing to him the major part in the production of goods; but Mr. Mallock's abounding faith in the canons of natural rights compels him naïvely to account for the business man's income in terms of productive efficiency simply. The argument of the book as is evident especially in the concluding portion (book iv; pp. 271–380), is chiefly directed to the confutation of the socialists. And in this confutation it is the ancient, now for the most part abandoned, socialist position that is made the point of attack. This early socialist position was summed up in the claim that to the laborer should belong the entire product of his labor. The claim is a crude application of a natural-rights dogma, and for the living generation of socialists it may fairly be said to be a discarded standpoint. It is this dead dog that Mr. Mallock chiefly belabors. Together with this, the similarly obsolete natural-rights formula that all men are born free and equal comes in for a portion of his polemical attention. In all this, the polemic proceeds on the lost ground of natural rights. Objection is taken not to the obvious groundlessness of the whole natural-rights structure, but to the scope of the application given the dogmas and to the excessive narrowness of the definitions employed.

Through it all, however, Mr. Mallock very effectively presents the current arguments going to show that the pecuniary incentive is indispensable to modern industry, and he shows, with great detail and with good effect, the weakness of the socialist contentions on this head. He goes with the socialists to the length of showing that the pecuniary incentive – the desire of wealth – is in large part a desire for distinction only, not in the last analysis a desire for the material, consumable goods. But he denies flatly – what they affirm – that an emulative incentive of another kind might serve the turn if the pecuniary incentive were to fall away. No other method of gauging success and distinction will take the place of this one as an incentive to wealth-production, whatever seems to be true as regard other directions of effort (book iv. chap. ii; pp. 284–323). It is to be regretted that nothing beyond asseveration is put forward in support of this denial, which is the central feature of the refutation of socialism. No decisive argument for the denial is adduced, but through the assertion made there runs an implication that, in order to serve their purpose at all effectively, the inducements offered the wealth-producer [435] must mechanically resemble the results to be worked out. As on the homeopathic principle like is to be cured by like, so in industry the repugnance to effort spent on material goods must be overcome by a remedial application of material goods. While it seems to be present in the reasoning, it is by no means clear, it should be remarked, that this axiom of similarity has been present in the reasoner's mind.

Mr. Mallock is a master of pleasing diction, and his arguments are presented in a lucid and forcible way that makes the book very attractive reading. And the grotesquely devious ways of its economic argument do not prevent it from being a suggestive contribution to the discussion of cultural development. At many points it brings out in a strong light the importance of a gifted minority as an element in the process of institutional growth, although even here it is curious, and in a sense instructive, to note that as representative spokesmen of the modern social sciences, Mr. Mallock has been constrained to cite George, Laveleye, and Mr. Kidd. The discussion of the great man's place in the cultural process is at its best where it deals with other fields than the economic. Unfortunately, it is the economic bearing of the argument alone that can be taken up here.

The volume suffers from a meretricious increase of bulk, due to an excessive use of large type, wide margins and heavy paper. It should be added that the printer's work is altogether above reproach.

Introduction to Part II

1898–99: intellectual efflorescence

The seven selections in this section cover a short but decisive interval in Veblen's intellectual career, the momentous twenty-month period, from July 1898 to February 1900,[1] during which he published an interconnected set of writings that laid the foundations for institutional economics and would subsequently become classics of modern social theory.

In contrast to Veblen's previous articles and reviews, which witness him ranging from subject to subject in response to changing intellectual stimuli in the academic settings surrounding him, Veblen's writings during this second phrase of his career all trace their root to a larger intellectual program that he set forth for himself during the mid-1890s, shortly after his move to the University of Chicago. Encapsulating the breadth of his intellectual experiences up to that point, Veblen boldly outlined this program to his former student Sarah Hardy[2] as follows in a letter of January 23, 1896:

> I have a theory which I wish to propound. ... My theory touches the immediate future development of economic science. ... It is ... that the work of the [coming] generation of economists ... is to consist substantially in a rehabilitation of the science on modern lines. Economics is to be brought into line with modern evolutionary science, which it has not been hitherto. The point of departure for this rehabilitation, or rather the basis of it, will be the modern anthropological and psychological sciences. ... Starting from [the] study of usages, aptitudes, propensities and habits of thought, ... the science, taken generally, is to shape itself into the science of the evolution of economic institutions. (cited in Jorgensen and Jorgensen 1999, 194)

---

1 This period was even more intensive than this twenty-month figure suggests. With the exception of the last part of Selection 19, all the other items in this section appeared in the thirteen-month period from July 1898 to July 1899.

2 Hardy was more than a student; at this time, Veblen was in love with her (see the General Introduction to this volume).

Veblen penned these words as a 38-year-old faculty associate in a Department of Political Economy at an historical moment when the entire field of economics stood, in the eyes of contemporary political economists and outside observers alike, in a state of intense ferment on both sides of the Atlantic (Hutchison 1953, Hodgson 2001, Samuels *et al.* 2003). To some contemporaries, this situation meant a stultifying theoretical and methodological impasse, and the resulting sense of crisis was the source of much soul-searching in the *fin de siècle* literature of economics. For his part, however, Veblen does not shrink from the occasion, but rather believes that he himself has identified a way to "rehabilitate" economics and to set the direction for its "future development."[3]

While Veblen's book reviews from 1894 to June 1898 contain scattered hints regarding the nature of this plan as he worked it out during these years (see Part I), articles where he articulates his new agenda for economics began to appear in print only in the second half of 1898. By this point, Veblen evidently made the decision to present his emerging ideas in two different ways. In the articles included here as Selection 15 and the three parts of Selection 19, he adopts a predominately critical posture, minutely analyzing the misconceptions that had prevented earlier economists from erecting economics "on modern lines," but himself stopping short of elaborating his own alternative approach. In contrast, in Selections 16, 17, 18, and 21, Veblen offers several positive examples of his program for economics, albeit without the same detailed engagement with the economic theories that he is criticizing and attempting to transcend. This bifurcation in his writings between critical attacks on the work of other economists, on the one hand, and piecemeal positive illustrations of his proposed alternative, on the other hand, impaired comprehension of Veblen's program in his own time and has continued to have this effect down to the present.

Unlike present-day readers, however, Veblen's original turn-of-the-century audience was at least positioned to understand certain references in his vocabulary, which were then standard fixtures in everyday academic discourse but which would subsequently disappear from regular usage or take on different associations. In regard to the selections in Part II, three of these references bear special notice.

The first of these is the tripartite classification of writings in the field of political economy and also of periods in the history of economic thought. The economic literature of the late nineteenth century routinely spoke of three broad "schools" of political economy: the Classical School, the Historical School, and the Austrian School. Then as now, "classical" typically referenced the genre associated with the names of Adam Smith, David Ricardo, John Stuart Mill, and (by some accounts) Karl Marx, and with issues connected with the so-called cost-of-production theory of value. As well, "classical"

---

3 Veblen was not alone. As Pearson (2000, p. 938) has observed, the turn-of-the-century era brought forth "interventions [aimed at the] rectification of economy theory" not only from economists but also from "ethnologists, geographers, anthropologists, sociologists, and historians."

applied to other writers from 1870s onward who tied political economy more explicitly to utilitarianism and presented their analysis in the form of deductive theories based on allegedly universal axioms about the hedonistic behavior of "economic man." Veblen (1900a, p. 239 [in this volume]) coined the term "neo-classical" to describe this post-1870 group. The "Historical School" denominated a heterogeneous group of mid-nineteenth to early-twentieth century authors, located principally in Germany but represented elsewhere in Europe as well, who criticized the abstractions of classical economics and championed inductive research into the historical development of economic conditions, practices, and organizations (Hodgson 2001). The "Austrian School" designated economists who, following the lead of Carl Menger (1871), appealed to universal and ahistorical principles concerning human nature to propound a "subjective" or "psychological" version of the "marginal utility" theory of value.

In his early writings (see Part I) Veblen engaged ideas from all three schools briefly, and in the selections in this section he offers a more comprehensive analysis as part of his effort to open an intellectual space for his own very different approach. In so doing, he follows his contemporaries in including among the classical political economists not only Adam Smith and some of Smith's fore-runners (the French Physiocrats, David Hume), but a then-familiar litany of subsequent figures: David Ricardo, Robert Torrens, Nassau Senior, and John Stuart Mill. Veblen devotes particular attention to the since-forgotten writings of J. E. Cairnes, one of the leading academic economists in the British Isles in the late nineteenth century (see Koot 1987). In addition, he cites several contemporary "neoclassical" economists, William Stanley Jevons, Alfred Marshall, Edwin Cannan, and John Neville Keynes in England, along with Arthur Hadley and John Bates Clark (Veblen's own former teacher) in the United States. By contrast, while his knowledge of the Historical School was broad, in the selections Veblen tends to speak of the School *en masse*, though he points to it more specifically when he mentions Germans Wilhelm Roscher (one of the School's founders) and Gustav Schmoller, Wilhelm Hasbach, and Karl Bücher (members of the School's younger generation), as well as British authors William Cunningham and W. J. Ashley. When Veblen writes of the "Austrian School" he refers principally to Carl Menger and Eugen Böhm-Bawerk. Significantly, Veblen does not dwell on the differences between the Austrian School and neoclassical writers, which later scholars have tended to widen (Streissler 1972, Jaffé 1976). Hence Veblen sometimes lumps together the Austrians and neoclassicals, along with other sundry kindred figures, such as William Smart, James Bonar, Nicholas Pierson and Achille Loria.[4]

4 For a sense of how these schools appeared to contemporaries, see the entries on "Classical Economists," "Historical School of Economists," and "Austrian School of Economists" in Palgrave's *Dictionary of Political Economy* (1896). See also Ingram (1888). In recent decades, some scholars have stressed similarities between the theory of the Austrian School and that of institutionalists such as Veblen (Boettke 1989, Samuels 1989, Wynarczyk 1992).

Veblen's writings in the 1898–1900 period also draw upon a second common-place set of terms – albeit a set of terms that is likely to seem far more jarring from the perspective of the twenty-first century. Already prevalent in various elite discourses during the eighteenth century, this terminology gained wide currency in Western Europe and the United States from the 1860s onward as the field of anthropology emerged and took shape in conjunction with an explosion of scholarly and popular interest in "ethnology" – i.e. the study the physical, linguistic, and socio-cultural characteristics of non-European peoples. Serving as a metric to calibrate these characteristics in relation to features of American and European societies, these terms were "savage," "barbarian," and "civilized" – or (in alternative noun form) "savagery," "barbarism," and "civilization."[5]

By the time Veblen was writing in the closing years of the nineteenth century, the elements in this triplet had undergone considerable internal subdivision (lower, middle, and upper savagery; lower, middle, and upper barbarism), and they had been incorporated into a diverse range of social theories, including those that regarded savage and barbarian groups as fundamentally different from civilized Western societies *and* those that saw these same groups as representing evolutionary stages through which Western societies had previously progressed. Despite these complications, however, the trio of terms had nonetheless acquired generally accepted connotations, with "savagery" describing peaceful seminomadic bands engaged in gathering, fishing, and the hunting of small prey; "barbarism" referring to tribes, increasingly settled in villages, involved in big game hunting, agriculture, the domestication of animals, and the use of iron tools and simple machines, in tandem with widespread inter-tribal warfare; and "civilization" signaling (*inter alia*) the arrival of the phonetic alphabet, the emergence of cities (and eventual transformation of warring city-states into warring nations), and the growth of manufacturing technologies, industry, and science. Such, for example, was the position of leading American ethnologists Lewis Henry Morgan (1877) and John Wesley Powell (1888), and Veblen's anthropological colleagues at the University of Chicago, Starr (1893) and Thomas (1896, 1897, 1898) echoed this same usage. In the selections below, the same holds for Veblen himself when he speaks of "savage" and "barbarian" cultures, though he follows the literature of economic history in substituting two successive historical epochs for the ethnologists' "civilization," the era of handicraft production and the era of modern industrial production.[6]

5 For a valuable discussion of this set of concepts in relation to the history of anthropology, see Stocking (1968, 1987), on whose analysis we draw heavily in this paragraph and the one that follows.
6 In addition to drawing the distinction between savagery and barbarism from ethnology, Veblen (in Selection 21) makes use of a related strand in contemporary anthropology, the differentiation of the so-called "races" of Europe into "dolichocephalic" (long-faced, tall, blond) and "brachycephalic" (round-faced, short, brunette). Veblen's colleague in the Political Economy Department at the University of Chicago, Carlos C. Closson, was among the leading American exponents of this kind of work, which took its lead from the European anthropologists Otto Ammon and Georges Lapouge, to whose writings Veblen refers.

The third late-century referent that Veblen implicitly appeals to in these selections derives from the field of psychology. The final decades of the nineteenth century were, as Veblen's contemporaries were well aware, a turbulent time in psychology, a period during which psychological authors were actively at work formulating a variety of new theories highly critical not only of the viewpoints that had traditionally dominated the European and American literature on psychological topics, but also of the psychological postulates found in many other social-scientific literatures, including the writings of ethnologists and of economists of the Classical, Historical, and Austrian Schools (e.g. Sklansky 2002). In Veblen's judgment, as he indicates in his 1896 letter to Sarah Hardy, some of these new lines of psychological thinking had clear implications for his own program for economics, and his knowledge of these developments was extensive. This was especially so with regard to the developments occurring immediately around him at the University of Chicago, where John Dewey and his collaborators were gaining prominence for their efforts to advance the "pragmatist" perspective in psychology, which Veblen had previously encountered in nascent form at Johns Hopkins as a student of C. S. Peirce (as well as in the writings of William James).

Of the several aspects of this emerging pragmatist psychology, most relevant to Veblen in the following selections is the pragmatists' contention that human beings are agents active in relation to conditions around them, rather than passive units responding to stimuli – especially to sensations and feelings of pleasure or pain – which impinge upon them from without, as had been assumed by many older psychologies, including the British associationist approach on which the Classical economists had built. Dewey asserted this newer view vigorously in the course of the mid-1890s, urging "a psychology which states the mental life in active terms" – i.e. in terms of the focal individual's developing impulses, instincts, goals, and habits – "instead of in passive terms, mere feelings of pleasure and pain" (1894, p. 405). Attacking the very notion of a stimulus separable from and antecedent to the individual's own particular orbit of activity, Dewey (1896, pp. 361, 365) famously illustrated the point with regard to the mundane occurrence of "a loud, unexpected sound":

> If one is reading a book, if one is hunting, if one is watching in a dark place on a lonely night, if one is performing a chemical experiment, in each case, the noise has a very different psychical value; it is a different experience. …
> The fact is that the stimulus and response are not distinctions of existence, but teleological distinctions, that is, distinctions of function, or part played, with reference to reaching or maintaining an end [for the given individual].

In the selections in Part II, Veblen has no need to elaborate arguments of this kind as he indicates his own psychological position, for the pragmatist conception of action was, by the late 1890s, almost as familiar to those in his audience as were the divisions of savage, barbarian, and civilized peoples and of Classical, Historical, and Austrian economists.

In borrowing these common terminological tools, however, Veblen immediately turns them to the larger programmatic purpose foreshadowed in his letter to Hardy, as he looks to set economics on a "modern" path of development. His opening salvo toward this end comes in Selection 15. Appearing as the lead article in the July 1898 issue of the prestigious Harvard-based *Quarterly Journal of Economics*, the selection addresses the query in its title: "Why Is Economics Not an Evolutionary Science?" Grappling with this "why" question, rather than establishing the fact that economics is not yet an evolutionary field, is uppermost for Veblen because the fact itself was not by this date in serious dispute. Evolutionary thinking, in diverse forms, was ubiquitous in the local, national, and international intellectual contexts where Veblen was situated; and "turn-of-the-century social scientists were evolutionists almost to a man" (Stocking 1968, p. 112), at least outside the domain of political economy. Not surprisingly, therefore, as Veblen mentions at the outset of the article, critiques of economics for being "helplessly behind the times and unable to handle its subject-matter in a way to entitle it to standing as a modern science" (p. 143) were commonplace, even among economists.

Contemporary observers of economics were less agreed, however, as to the specific way in which the field lagged behind the evolutionary sciences, and this is the issue that Veblen's own analysis seeks to address. For Veblen, economics remained "pre-evolutionary" as a result of the outmoded attitude – the "archaic point of view" (p. 147) – from which economists conduct their work.[7] In contrast to modern evolutionary scientists, whose concern is with "an unfolding sequence" of cause and effect (p. 144) and with formulating a theory that renders this process as a "colorless impersonal sequence" of "cumulative causation" (p. 146), economists, in Veblen's view, occupy themselves building and elaborating "a system of economic taxonomy" (p. 149).

By describing much of the work of the discipline as "taxonomy," Veblen is intentionally associating economics with what his contemporaries would have recognized as the losing side in a battle that had recently occurred in the field of botany between the taxonomic rearguard, dedicated to the traditional "systematic botany" of plant classification (which critics ridiculed as "pigeon-holing" and "juggling with nomenclature"), and the evolutionary vanguard, committed to a "genetic" approach which sought to "recognize ... every plant [as] a living thing with a history" (quoting Coulter 1891, pp. 244–46; see also Bessey 1893). Veblen's frequent use of

---

7 In an allusion to the work of anthropologist E. B. Tylor (1871), Veblen describes this attitude as "primitive animism" (379), a point he elaborates in Selection 19.

botanical terms throughout the article aims to reinforce this negative association.[8] Evidence to justify this comparison with taxonomists abounds, according to Veblen's account, in economists' efforts at differentiating definitional categories, such as "value," "wages," "rents," and "profits," and at then distinguishing further categories – deriving from the metaphysical notion that economic processes obey beneficent "natural laws" – such as "normal value," "normal wages," "normal rent," and "normal profits," in relation to conditions of "normal equilibrium,"[9] a conceptual procedure that relegates all else to the pigeonhole of "abnormal cases" (p. 149). Granting that these classifying tendencies are less pronounced in the work of the Historical and Austrian Schools than among late Classical School writers such as Cairnes, Veblen nonetheless holds that "Economics … still shows too many reminiscences of the 'natural' and the 'normal' … to be classed as an evolutionary science" (p. 148).

Having diagnosed the problem of economics in this manner, Veblen's article proceeds to trace the source of the problem to economists' defective "psychological and anthropological preconceptions" (p. 153) – preconceptions that he hopes to replace with a more pragmatist viewpoint on human conduct, as he explains:

> the human material with which [economics has dealt has been] conceived in hedonistic terms; that is to say, in terms of a passive and substantially inert and immutably given human nature. … The later psychology … gives a different conception of human nature. According to this conception, it is the characteristic of man to do something, not simply to suffer pleasures and pains. … [This conception views human nature as] a coherent structure of propensities and habits which seeks realization and expression in an unfolding activity. (pp. 152–53)

Applying this newer conception to the economic realm, Veblen urges attention to the unfolding of "economic action," which he describes as the "teleological" use of historically available "material objects and circumstances" to accomplish the present "economic interest" of communities of individuals via "a change in habits of thought," or in "habitual methods of procedure"

---

8 The highpoint of this use of botanical terminology comes in Veblen's droll comment about "the taxonomy of a monocotyledonous wage doctrine and a cryptogamic theory of interest, with involute, loculicidal, tomentous, and moniliform variants" (p. 151). Veblen's fluency in this language was due in part to his wife, who had recently been a graduate student in botany.

9 With the examples here, we go slightly beyond the text of Veblen's article to supply illustrations that Veblen's contemporaries would have found superfluous. We draw these illustrations from a prominent source to which Veblen refers, Marshall (1890).

(pp. 154, 151). Veblen spells out the implications of this perspective in the following manner:

> The economic life history of any community is its life history in so far as it is shaped by men's interest in the material means of life. This economic interest has counted for much in shaping the cultural growth of all communities. Primarily, ... it has guided the formation, the cumulative growth, of that range of conventionalities and methods of life that are currently recognized as economic institutions; but the same interest has also pervaded the community's life and its cultural growth at points [that] are not chiefly and most immediately of an economic bearing. ... This is necessarily the case since the base of action – the point of departure – at any step in the process is the entire organic complex of habits of thought that have been shaped by the past process. (pp. 154–55)

Lacking this understanding of ongoing economic action, the Classical, the Austrian, and even the Historical Schools inevitably fell short, in Veblen's view, of "evolutionary economics" – an expression that he first introduces in this article (p. 144).[10] Forecasting what a genuine economics of this modern type would offer, Veblen concludes the selection by envisioning a "theory of a process of cultural growth as determined by the economic interest, a theory of cumulative sequence of economic institutions stated in terms of the process itself" – where "economic institutions," although never a "neatly isolatable range of cultural phenomena," consist chiefly of "those institutions ... which most immediately and with least limitation are of an economic bearing" (p. 155).

In Selections 16, 17, and 18, Veblen offers his earliest empirical illustrations of this kind of economics. Originating in papers that he presented in the late spring of 1898 to the Graduate Club at the University of Chicago,[11] these short companion articles appeared between September 1898 and January 1899 in consecutive issues of the *American Journal of Sociology* (*AJS*), a new

---

10 We have found no earlier use of "evolutionary economics," and the available evidence seems to suggest that the expression originates with Veblen, despite its frequent subsequent association with the work of Joseph Schumpeter – an association seen, for example, in Nelson and Winter (1982), among others. Eaton (1984) astutely notes that Nelson and Winter's own work shows a greater – if unacknowledged – affinity to Veblen than to Schumpeter.

11 The Graduate Club was an association of graduate students from different departments at University of Chicago. According to its description, the club held monthly meetings "at which short addresses are made, on topics of general interest, usually by persons not connected with the University." That Veblen, as member of the Chicago faculty, addressed the group on topics of somewhat more specialized interest may reflect the circumstance that his student, the future institutional economist Wesley Mitchell, was the club's vice president at this time (*University of Chicago Annual Register* 1899, p. 155).

academic journal edited by Veblen's colleagues in the university's Department of Sociology and Anthropology.[12] In each of the three pieces, Veblen considers an economic phenomenon that Classical and Austrian economists generally regarded as "normal" or "natural" and reexamines it as a matter of the evolution of economic institutions.

Veblen embarks on this agenda in Selection 16 by taking up what economists called "the natural aversion to labor." Remarking that "one of the commonplaces of the received economic theory [has been] that work" – "useful labor" – "is irksome" to humans and something they desire to avoid (p. 158), Veblen finds little evidence for this resistant attitude toward work among the "small, rude peaceable group[s] of savages" that existed during "early social evolution" (p. 166). Rather, "throughout the history of human culture, the great body of the people have almost everywhere, in their everyday life, been at work to turn things to human use" in accord with humankind's "proclivity for purposeful action," or what Veblen's calls the "instinct for workmanship" (pp. 161, 163).[13] In his view, this proclivity is a potent force. It confers to humans a "great advantage over other species in the struggle for survival" (p. 159); "by long and consistent habituation," combined with the tendency of members of social groups to seek mutual approval and to give such approval to useful activities that exhibit "industrial efficiency," workmanship acquires the status of an esteemed virtue and becomes a dominant "canon of conduct" (pp. 162–64); and it results in "a selective elimination of those individuals and lines of descent that do not conform to the required canon of knowledge and conduct" (pp. 163–64) – as Veblen discusses in the Darwinian language that he begins to use more liberally from this point onward in his career.[14]

However, according to Veblen, actual habits of work change significantly as the savage "group passes, by force of circumstances, from the archaic condition of poverty-stricken peace to a stage of predatory life" – i.e. to the "barbarian" stage – using improved tools and weapons in "pursuit of large game and ... of conflict between groups" (p. 166). Veblen describes the long-term result of this evolutionary transformation as follows (making allusion to corroborating ethnological evidence, but not naming the authorities that he is drawing upon):

12 In this period, *AJS* published a number of other articles drawing broadly, as Veblen does, on the ethnological literature of the time, and his friend Thomas (1896, 1897, 1898, 1899a, 1899b, 1899c, 1901) authored several of these. Indeed, on some disputed ethnological points, it seems that Veblen and Thomas were engaged in a polite argument with each other and they went back-and-forth across successive issues of *AJS*.

13 Veblen may have taken the expression "instinct of workmanship" from Sarah Hardy (Bartley and Bartley 1997). In Selection 16, Veblen does not as of yet define "instinct," though he does so in his later work (see the General Introduction and the Introduction to Part IV in this volume).

14 On the circumstances that may have spurred Veblen in this direction, see Hodgson (2004, pp. 134–42).

As the predatory culture reaches a fuller development, there comes a distinction between employments. The tradition of prowess, as the virtue *par excellence*, gains in scope and consistency until prowess comes near being recognized as the sole virtue. Those employments alone are then worthy and reputable which involve the exercise of this virtue. Other employments, in which men are occupied with tamely shaping inert material to human use, become unworthy and end with becoming debasing. ... [Henceforth,] labor carries a taint, and all contamination from vulgar employments must be shunned by self-respecting men. (pp. 166–67)

Seen in this light, the "aversion to labor" becomes for Veblen not the "natural" condition that it was for economists but rather a "conventional" or "cultural fact," its continuing and widespread presence in modern society the "heritage" of an "ancient tradition that has come down from early barbarism" (p. 167).[15]

In Selection 17, "The Beginnings of Ownership," Veblen makes a parallel argument with respect to the so-called "natural rights of property" and individual property ownership. Claims regarding such rights were part of the intellectual stock-in-trade of political economy, deriving as corollaries from the economists' postulate of isolated individual producers and the related assumption "that, in the normal case, wealth is distributed in proportion to – and ... because of – the recipient's contribution to the product" (p. 169).

Again, though, Veblen sees nothing "natural" about such phenomena. Looking back to early savage cultures, Veblen finds neither isolated producers nor any notion of ownership (whether individual or collective). Instead, he maintains that "the earliest occurrence of ownership seems to fall in the early stage of barbarism," since "with the advent of predatory life comes the practice of plundering," i.e. of seizing from the enemy both goods and persons, women in particular (pp. 175–76). Because the sorts of goods that exist at this stage are "habitually consumed in common by the group," however, they are too ephemeral to constitute objects of individual ownership. In this way, goods differ significantly from captive women, who "serve the purpose of trophies very effectually," thereby making it "worth while for their captor to trace and keep in evidence his relation to them as their captor" (pp. 176–77) – a situation that eventually gives rise to the "great institutions" of marriage-by-capture and the patriarchal household, both of which originate in tandem with the beginning of individual property ownership (p. 177). For this reason, individual property ownership, too, stands as "a conventional fact, ... a cultural fact which has grown into an institution in the past through a long course of habituation, and which is transmitted from generation to generation as all cultural facts are" (p. 174).

---

15 As Veblen's readers would have recognized, he is here applying anthropologist E. B. Tylor's (1871) concept of a "survival." In the present selection, Veblen does not actually include Tylor's term, though he does so subsequently, as our discussion of Selection 21 will note.

Selection 18, "The Barbarian Status of Women," resumes this line of analysis about marriage-by-capture and patriarchy – favorite topics of inquiry
among Victorian anthropologists (see Stocking 1987) and subjects of likely
personal interest to Veblen himself.[16] The shortest and seemingly slightest of
three *AJS* articles, the selection not only considers these institutions in
themselves, but briefly uses them as well as a window onto an even larger
issue, namely, the intertwined origins of the division of labor and of social
class distinctions (subjects that Veblen mentions in passing in his two previous
articles). Written again against the backdrop of a large literature in economics
that had naturalized such arrangements – in an often quoted passage Adam
Smith (1776) spoke of the "natural division and distribution of labour"[17] –
Veblen appeals again to the ethnological record to observe that, in early
savage cultures, "there was but the very slightest beginning of a system of
status, with little of invidious distinction between classes and little of the
corresponding division of employments" (p. 179).

In regard to all of these developments, the evolutionary turning point lies
once more with the transition to barbarian culture, as Veblen explains:

> The work of the predatory barbarian group is gradually specialized and
> differentiated under the dominance of [the] ideal of prowess, so as to
> give rise to a system of status in which the non-fighters fall into a position
> of subservience to the fighters. … The group divides itself conventionally
> into a fighting and a peace-keeping class, with a corresponding division
> of labor. Fighting, together with other work that involves a serious element
> of exploit, becomes the employment of able-bodied men; the uneventful
> everyday work of the group falls to the women and the infirm.
> (pp. 181, 180)

In this circumstance, women come to constitute "a subservient and low
class," at the same time as "women's employments" undergo widespread
denigration (pp. 180, 182). Deepening this original class division are situations in which the woman is acquired as "a trophy of the raid" and forced, as
an enemy captive, into a "coercive ownership-marriage" (p. 182). Still further,
marriage according to this model soon gains "acceptance as the only beautiful
and virtuous form" of marriage and calls forth, when the supply of "wives by
capture" dwindles, the ceremonial "practice of mock-seizure or mock-capture,
and hence the formal profession of fealty and submission on the part of the
woman in the marriage rites of peoples among whom the household with a
male head prevails" (pp. 182–84). In marriage of this particular kind,
according to Veblen, there accordingly occurs – alongside "individual

16 Toward the end of the selection, Veblen pointedly contrasts coercive capture-type marriages
   with unions that are "terminable at will by either party" (p. 514) – the latter an arrangement
   that perhaps appealed to him in the face of his own marital problems at this time.
17 In Selection 19 (p. 208), Veblen explicitly draws attention to this aspect of Smith's work.

ownership, the system of status, and the paternal household" – another "predatory institution" of far-reaching economic consequences that "has been handed down from the barbarian past of the peoples of the western culture" (pp. 186, 184). In this instance, however, Veblen hints at a more recent "change of circumstances" due to which "this type of the marriage relation ... is at present visibly breaking down in modern civilized communities" (p. 187).

Selection 19 combines into one piece the three parts of "The Preconceptions of Economic Science," which appeared in installments in the *Quarterly Journal of Economics* (QJE), beginning (as the lead article) in January 1899 and concluding in February 1900. In it, Veblen leaves the ethnological terrain of his three *AJS* articles to expand upon the argument of "Why Is Economics Not an Evolutionary Science?" – now buttressing his critique of economics by means of a more thorough examination of the history of economic thought. His purpose in doing this, as he indicates, is to repudiate the claims of contemporary economists who held that their field was in the process of transforming itself into an evolutionary science. Conceding that *fin de siècle* economics had recently donned a few of the outward trappings of evolutionism, Veblen seeks to channel attention away from the externals of economic analysis to its underlying metaphysical principles – its taken-for-granted "preconceptions" – as he advances the argument that "the living generation [of economists] has not seen [the] disappearance of the metaphysics that fixed the point of view of the early classical political economy" (pp. 226–27).

In support of this thesis, Veblen methodically retraces the history of the Classical School, considering the work of the Physiocrats, Smith, the utilitarians, J. S. Mill, Cairnes, J. N. Keynes, Marshall, and others in the familiar line of descent. As he does so, he appropriates the central theme of Irish Historical-School-style economist J. K. Ingram's best-selling *History of Political Economy* (1888), which had presented economic doctrines in relation to the historical period and circumstances in which those doctrines were formulated (Koot 1987, Hodgson 2001). Like Ingram, Veblen maintains that "the point of view ... of a given generation of economists is [an] outgrowth of the ideals and preconceptions current in the world about them" (p. 190). Veblen qualifies this proposition, however, by remarking on economists' tendency to remain insulated from the immediate effect of the surrounding world due to their privileged class location. This situation enables them to cling to "ancient" ways of thinking, as contrasted with the "matter-of-fact habit[s] of mind," which the "exigencies of life in a modern industrial community breed in men exposed to their unmitigated impact" and which find intellectual expression in the modern evolutionary sciences when they examine "cumulative causal sequence[s]" (pp. 189, 242).

To describe the economists' pre-modern approach, Veblen's article makes heavy use of the belittling term "animism," which anthropologist E. B. Tylor had famously applied to characterize "the general belief in spiritual beings" that predominates in savage and barbarian cultures but finds certain survivals as well in "the midst of high modern culture" (1871, p. 426).[18] Veblen sees animism – which he equates with the mental habit of anthropomorphizing natural phenomena (p. 199) – as lying at the root of economists' belief that there is in economic life a "benign order" that operates by "immutable natural laws" that guide economic events in accord with an implicit "teleology" or "meliorative developmental trend" (pp. 229, 192, 236, 227). Denouncing this insidious form of teleological thinking,[19] Veblen attributes to it all the cardinal defects of the Classical School (as well as its Austrian progeny): its profusion of "normalizing" concepts and categories (p. 215); its reliance on taxonomy; its wrongheaded hedonistic assumptions about economic man; its vacuous theory of value (and resulting neglect of actual consumption); and its failure to examine "the developmental variation of economic institutions" (p. 242). In his view, these defects were neither separable problems nor problems that economists would overcome by occasional nods towards "processes" and "causes" or further piecemeal adjustments to their theories, but only by extirpating all vestiges of their inherited animistic preconceptions and extending "evolutionist methods [to] the facts with which their own science" needed to deal: viz., "the cumulative modification and diversification of human activities through the economic interest" (p. 242).

Selection 20 contains Veblen's long review, in the *Annals of the American Academy of Political and Social Science*, of *The Development of English Thought* by Simon Patten, a prominent American economist, loosely allied with the Historical School, who was then on the faculty of the Wharton School of Finance at the University of Pennsylvania. It is the only book review that Veblen published in 1899 amid all his other work that year, and he presumably agreed to the assignment because of the ostensible correspondence between his own interests at the time and the topics addressed in Patten's book, as Patten too was concerned with the historical development of the Classical School (among other ideas) and sought to connect changes in patterns of thought to larger economic changes.

Like other contemporary reviewers, however, Veblen's reaction to the book is strongly negative. Viewing the study from the theoretical side, Veblen sees many of the flaws that his writings had identified in the work of other economists also exhibited in Patten's book, including a hedonistic psychology, the

---

18 For a valuable discussion of Veblen in relation to Tylor, see Dawson (1993), who speculates that Frederick Starr introduced Veblen to Tylor's work. In this period, W. I. Thomas also taught a course at the University of Chicago entitled "Animism."

19 In here attacking economists for ascribing teleological trends to economic events, Veblen simultaneously reaffirms his Deweyian conviction that human beings themselves act "teleologically" in pursuit of their economic ends – a point that he once again faults economists for neglecting as a consequence of their hedonistic assumptions. In Veblen's view, these two teleological issues were directly related and admitted of a single solution: "when less of a teleological continuity [is] imputed to the course of events, more [is] thereby imputed to man's life process" (p. 231) – and properly so in Veblen's opinion.

postulate of a "meliorative trend" in economic events, and a "resort to normality" (p. 244). As well, Veblen objects that Patten's analysis of historical development treats each historical era as "entirely new" and overlooks the role of legacies from the past, "the continuity of tradition and usages" (p. 247). But Veblen appears less interested in elaborating these theoretical points than in criticizing the book on factual grounds. In his view, Patten seriously neglects "the evidence from ethnology" as found in "the published accounts of existing primitive communities" (pp. 246, 247), such as – to use Veblen's words – "the Australians, Bushmen, or Eskimo," the Fuegians, the Ainu, the Haida, the Mexicans and Pueblos, and so on. Drawing confidently on these studies to refute particular economic arguments in Patten's book, Veblen here shows a depth and breadth of ethnological knowledge that his work nowhere else displays in such concrete detail.[20]

Selection 21 concludes Part II with a chapter from Veblen's celebrated first book, *The Theory of the Leisure Class*. Published in March 1899, the book was a project on which Veblen had been actively at work since 1895, composing it at the same time he was writing Selections 9–19 in this volume,[21] though the text is continuous as well with his 1891 article on "Socialism" (Selection 3) and his 1894 article on "Woman's Dress" (Selection 8). The announcement for the book, which Veblen presumably authorized (if he did not in fact author) read: *The Theory of the Leisure Class* "deals with the leisure class as an institution, its history and its place as a factor in culture today" – an apt one-sentence summary of the book's subject matter.

In content, *The Theory of the Leisure Class* more closely resembles Veblen's three prior *AJS* articles (Selections 17–19) than it does his critiques of economics in the *QJE* articles (Selections 15 and 19), although the book's original subtitle – *An Economic Study of the Evolution of Institutions* – leaves little doubt that Veblen saw the book as a step toward making economics the evolutionary science that he had criticized the field for not having yet become. When discussing the beginnings of several other predatory institutions in the *AJS* articles, Veblen mentions in passing the absence of a "leisure class" in "primitive savage hordes" (p. 175) and the dramatic change that occurs in barbarian cultures "when some wealth has been accumulated and the members of the community fall into a servile class, on the one hand, and a leisure class, on the other" (p. 167). Taking up from this point in *The Theory of the Leisure Class*, Veblen – now using Darwinian concepts extensively and in detail, along with ideas drawn from psychology and

---

20 Although Veblen does not give the titles and the authors of the accounts to which he refers, this information would have been familiar to most of his readers.

21 The last two parts of Selection 19 as well as Selection 20 appeared in print shortly *after* the publication of *The Theory of the Leisure Class*. We place our excerpt from the book as the final item in Part II, however, because the book is the capstone of all of Veblen's writings during this period of his career.

anthropology – greatly elaborates this institutional origin story and carries the evolutionary account forward in time to his own era, examining the practices of "conspicuous consumption" and "conspicuous leisure" on the part of those in the leisure class and how "emulation" of such practices by members of less privileged groups engenders far-reaching economic and cultural effects.

While no single excerpt from this book can substitute for the text in its entirety, Selection 21 presents Chapter 8, "Industrial Exemption and Conservatism," where Veblen furnishes one of his most general accounts of the evolution of economic institutions. Conceiving of institutions as "habitual method[s] of responding to the stimuli which ... circumstances afford," Veblen here describes "a process of natural selection of institutions," i.e. "the selection of [their] favourable variations," in relation to "the changing environment" (pp. 251–52) – the last term his shorthand for "advance[s] in technical methods, in population, or in industrial organisation" (p. 254). In the chapter, the aspect of this process that Veblen particularly emphasizes is "that the institutions of to-day ... do not entirely fit of the situation of today," because present-day institutions have been "received from an earlier time, ... are the products of the past process, are adapted to past circumstances, and are therefore never in full accord with the requirements of the present" (pp. 261, 252) – a passage that closely mirrors E. B. Tylor's famous definition of "survivals in culture" (1871, p. 71).

To Veblen, the modern leisure class – the "propertied non-industrial class" (p. 261) – constitutes a prime example of such a survival.[22] In his view, adjustment to environmental changes "depends in great measure on ... the degree of exposure of the individual members [of a community] to the constraining forces of the environment" (p. 253). However, when a social class "is sheltered from the action of the environment in any essential respect," that class will "retard the process of social transformation" – and "[t]he wealthy leisure class is in such a sheltered position with respect to the economic forces that make for change and readjustment" (p. 253). As such, it is "a parasitic character" in the social body, a force of economic, political, and cultural conservatism and inertia not only within itself, but also due to the "prescriptive example of conspicuous waste" that the leisure class sets for other classes, at the same time as it "withdraw[s] from them as much as it may of the means of sustenance" (pp. 261, 259). On these grounds, Veblen, in implied ridicule of the "meliorative developmental trend" that Classical School

---

22 Because of Veblen's penchant for varying his word choices, the term "survival" in its Tylorian sense does not itself appear in the present selection. Given how often Veblen uses Tylor's concept explicitly elsewhere in *The Theory of the Leisure Class*, however, his readers would have taken the concept for granted in the excerpted chapter. Later in the book, when referring back to the argument of the chapter, Veblen speaks directly of "the survival of the leisure class" (1899c, p. 337).

economists had ascribed to economic affairs, offers the general principle that, with respect to economic institutions, "Whatever is, is wrong" – that is to say, maladjusted "to some extent" to the ever-changing societal environment in which such institutions exist (p. 260). In this axiom lies, for Veblen, one of the first great lessons of institutional economics as he brings it to life in *The Theory of the Leisure Class.*

Selection 15

Why is economics not an evolutionary science?

Source: *Quarterly Journal of Economics*, July 1898
(vol. 12, pp. 373–97).

Veblen (1898c)

M. G. de Lapouge recently said, "Anthropology is destined to revolutionize the political and the social sciences as radically as bacteriology has revolutionized the science of medicine."[1] In so far as he speaks of economics, the eminent anthropologist is not alone in his conviction that the science stands in need of rehabilitation. His words convey a rebuke and an admonition, and in both respects he speaks the sense of many scientists in his own and related lines of inquiry. It may be taken as the consensus of those men who are doing the serious work of modern anthropology, ethnology, and psychology, as well as of those in the biological sciences proper, that economics is helplessly behind the times, and unable to handle its subject-matter in a way to entitle it to standing as a modern science. The other political and social sciences [374] come in for their share of this obloquy, and perhaps on equally cogent grounds. Nor are the economists themselves buoyantly indifferent to the rebuke. Probably no economist to-day has either the hardihood or the inclination to say that the science has now reached a definitive formulation, either in the detail of results or as regards the fundamental features of theory. The nearest recent approach to such a position on the part of an economist of accredited standing is perhaps to be found in Professor Marshall's Cambridge address of a year and a half ago.[2] But these utterances are so far from the jaunty confidence shown by the classical economists of half a century ago that what most forcibly strikes the reader of Professor Marshall's address is the exceeding modesty and the uncalled-for humility of the spokesman for the "old generation." With the economists who are most attentively looked to for guidance, uncertainty as to the definitive value of what has been and is being done, and as to what we may, with effect, take to next, is so common as to

---

1 "The Fundamental Laws of Anthropo-sociology," *Journal of Political Economy*, December, 1897, p. 54. The same paper, in substance, appears in the *Rivista Italiana di Sociologia* for November, 1897.
2 "The Old Generation of Economists and the New," in this journal [*Quarterly Journal of Economics*] for January, 1897, p. 133.

suggest that indecision is a meritorious work. Even the Historical School, who made their innovation with so much home-grown applause some time back, have been unable to settle down contentedly to the pace which they set themselves.

The men of the sciences that are proud to own themselves "modern" find fault with the economists for being still content to occupy themselves with repairing a structure and doctrines and maxims resting on natural rights, utilitarianism, and administrative expediency. This aspersion is not altogether merited, but is near enough to the mark to carry a sting. These modern sciences are evolutionary sciences, and their adepts contemplate that characteristic of their work with some complacency. Economics is not an evolutionary science – by the confession of its [375] spokesmen; and the economists turn their eyes with something of envy and some sense of baffled emulation to these rivals that make broad their phylacteries with the legend, "Up to date."

Precisely wherein the social and political sciences, including economics, fall short of being evolutionary sciences, is not so plain. At least, it has not been satisfactorily pointed out by their critics. Their successful rivals in this matter – the sciences that deal with human nature among the rest – claim as their substantial distinction that they are realistic: they deal with facts. But economics, too, is realistic in this sense: it deals with facts, often in the most painstaking way, and latterly with an increasingly strenuous insistence on the sole efficacy of data. But this "realism" does not make economics an evolutionary science. The insistence on data could scarcely be carried to a higher pitch than it was carried by the first generation of the Historical School; and yet no economics is farther from being an evolutionary science than the received economics of the Historical School. The whole broad range of erudition and research that engaged the energies of that school commonly falls short of being science, in that, when consistent, they have contented themselves with an enumeration of data and a narrative account of industrial development, and have not presumed to offer a theory of anything or to elaborate their results into a consistent body of knowledge.

Any evolutionary science, on the other hand, is a close-knit body of theory. It is a theory of a process, of an unfolding sequence. But here, again, economics seems to meet the test in a fair measure, without satisfying its critics that its credentials are good. It must be admitted, *e.g.*, that J. S. Mill's doctrines of production, distribution, and exchange, are a theory of certain economic processes, and that he deals in a consistent and effective fashion with the sequences of fact that make up his subject-matter. So, [376] also, Cairnes's discussion of normal value, of the rate of wages, and of international trade, are excellent instances of a theoretical handling of economic processes of sequence and the orderly unfolding development of fact. But an attempt to cite Mill and Cairnes as exponents of an evolutionary economics will produce no better effect than perplexity, and not a great deal of that. Very much of monetary theory might be cited to the same purpose and with the like effect. Something similar is true even of late writers who have avowed some penchant for the evolutionary point of view; as, *e.g.*, Professor Hadley, – to cite a work of unquestioned merit and unusual reach. Measurably, he keeps the word of promise to the ear; but any one who may cite his *Economics* as having brought political economy into line as an evolutionary science will convince neither himself nor his interlocutor. Something to the like effect may fairly be said of the published work of that later English strain of economists represented by Professors Cunningham and Ashley, and Mr. Cannan, to name but a few of the more eminent figures in the group.

Of the achievements of the classical economists, recent and living, the science may justly be proud; but they fall short of the evolutionist's standard of adequacy, not in failing to offer a theory of a process or of a developmental relation, but through conceiving their theory in terms alien to the evolutionist's habits of thought. The difference between the evolutionary and the pre-evolutionary sciences lies not in the insistence on facts. There was a great and fruitful activity in the natural sciences in collecting and collating facts before these sciences took on the character which marks them as evolutionary. Nor does the difference lie in the absence of efforts to formulate and explain schemes of process, sequence, growth, and development in the pre-evolutionary days. Efforts of this kind abounded, in number and diversity; and many schemes of development of great subtlety and beauty, [377] gained a vogue both as theories of organic and inorganic development and as schemes of the life history of nations and societies. It will not even hold true that our elders overlooked the presence of cause and effect in formulating their theories and reducing their data to a body of knowledge. But the terms which were accepted as the definitive terms of knowledge were in some degree different in the early days from what they are now. The terms of thought in which the investigators of some two or three generations back definitively formulated their knowledge of facts, in their last analyses, were different in kind from the terms in which the modern evolutionist is content to formulate his results. The analysis does not run back to the same ground, or appeal to the same standard of finality or adequacy, in the one case as in the other.

The difference is a difference of spiritual attitude or point of view in the two contrasted generations of scientists. To put the matter in other words, it is a difference in the basis of valuation of the facts for the scientific purpose, or in the interest from which the facts are appreciated. With the earlier as with the later generation the basis of valuation of the facts handled is, in matters of detail, the causal relation which is apprehended to subsist between them. This is true to the greatest extent for the natural sciences. But in their handling of the more comprehensive schemes of sequence and relation – in their definitive formulation of the results – the two generations differ. The modern scientist is unwilling to depart from the test of causal relation or quantitative sequence. When he asks the question, Why? he insists on an answer in terms of cause and effect. He wants to reduce his solution of all problems to terms of the conservation of energy or the persistence of quantity. This is his last recourse.

And this last recourse has in our time been made available for the handling of schemes of development and theories of a comprehensive process by the [378] notion of a cumulative causation. The great deserts of the evolutionist leaders – if they have great deserts as leaders – lie, on the one hand, in their refusal to go back of the colorless sequence of phenomena and seek higher ground for their ultimate syntheses, and, on the other hand, in their having shown how this colorless impersonal sequence of cause and effect can be made use of for theory proper, by virtue of its cumulative character.

For the earlier natural scientists, as for the classical economists, this ground of cause and effect is not definitive. Their sense of truth and substantiality is not satisfied with a formulation of mechanical sequence. The ultimate term in their systematization of knowledge is a "natural law." This natural law is felt to exercise some sort of a coercive surveillance over the sequence of events, and to give a spiritual stability and consistence to the causal relation at any given juncture. To meet the high classical requirement, a sequence – and a developmental process especially – must be apprehended in terms of a con-sistent propensity tending to some spiritually legitimate end. When facts and events have been reduced to these terms of fundamental truth and have been made to square with the requirements of definitive normality, the investigator rests content. Any causal sequence which is apprehended to traverse the imputed propensity in events is a "disturbing factor." Logical congruity with the apprehended propensity is, in this view, adequate ground of procedure in building up a scheme of knowledge or of development. The objective point of the efforts of the scientists working under the guidance of this classical tradition, is to formulate knowledge in terms of absolute truth; and this absolute truth is a spiritual fact. It means a coincidence of facts with the deliverances of an enlightened and deliberate common sense.

The development and the attenuation of this preconception of normality or of a propensity in events might be [379] traced in detail from primitive ani-mism down through the elaborate discipline of faith and metaphysics, over-ruling Providence, order of nature, natural rights, natural law, underlying principles. But all that may be necessary here is to point out that, by descent and by psychological content, this constraining normality is of a spiritual kind. It is for the scientific purpose an imputation of spiritual coherence to the facts dealt with. The question of interest is how this preconception of normality has fared at the hands of modern science, and how it has come to be super-seded in the intellectual primacy by the latter-day preconception of a non-spiritual sequence. This question is of interest because its answer may throw light on the question as to what chance there is for the indefinite persistence of this archaic habit of thought in the methods of economic science.

Under primitive conditions, men stand in immediate personal contact with the material facts of the environment; and the force and discretion of the individual in shaping the facts of the environment count obviously, and to all appearance solely, in working out the conditions of life. There is little of impersonal or mechanical sequence visible to primitive men in their every-day life; and what there is of this kind in the processes of brute nature about them is in large part inexplicable and passes for inscrutable. It is accepted as malignant or beneficent, and is construed in the terms of personality that are familiar to all men at first hand, – the terms known to all men by first-hand knowledge of their own acts. The inscrutable movements of the seasons and of the natural forces are apprehended as actions guided by discretion, will power, or propensity looking to an end, much as human actions are. The processes of inanimate nature are agencies whose habits of life are to be learned, and who are to be coerced, outwitted, circumvented, and turned to account, [380] much as the beasts are. At the same time the community is small, and the human contact of the individual is not wide. Neither the industrial life nor the non-industrial social life forces upon men's attention the ruthless impersonal sweep of events that no man can withstand or deflect, such as becomes visible in the more complex and comprehensive life process of the larger community of the later day. There is nothing decisive to hinder men's knowledge of facts and events being formulated in terms of personality – in terms of habit and propensity and will power.

As time goes on and as the situation departs from this archaic character, – where it does depart from it, – the circumstances which condition men's systematization of facts change in such a way as to throw the impersonal character of the sequence of events more and more into the foreground. The penalties for failure to apprehend facts in dispassionate terms fall surer and swifter. The sweep of events is forced home more consistently on men's minds. The guiding hand of a spiritual agency or a propensity in events becomes less readily traceable as men's knowledge of things grows ampler and more searching. In modern times, and particularly in the industrial countries, this coercive guidance of men's habits of thought in the realistic direction has been especially pronounced; and the effect shows itself in a somewhat reluctant but cumulative departure from the archaic point of view. The departure is most visible and has gone farthest in those homely branches of knowledge that have to do immediately with modern mechanical processes, such as engineering designs and technological contrivances generally. Of the sciences, those have wandered farthest on this way (of integration or disintegration, according as one may choose to view it) that have to do with mechanical sequence and process; and those have best and longest retained the archaic point of view intact which – like the [381] moral, social, or spiritual sciences – have to do with process and sequence that is less tangible, less traceable by the use of the senses, and that therefore less immediately forces upon the attention the phenomenon of sequence as contrasted with that of propensity.

There is no abrupt transition from the pre-evolutionary to the post-evolutionary standpoint. Even in those natural sciences which deal with the processes of life and the evolutionary sequence of events the concept of dispassionate cumulative causation has often and effectively been helped out by the notion that there is in all this some sort of a meliorative trend that exercises a constraining guidance over the course of causes and effects. The faith in this meliorative trend as a concept useful to the science has gradually weakened, and it has repeatedly been disavowed; but it can scarcely be said to have yet disappeared from the field.

The process of change in the point of view, or in the terms of definitive formulation of knowledge, is a gradual one; and all the sciences have shared, though in an unequal degree, in the change that is going forward. Economics is not an exception to the rule, but it still shows too many reminiscences of the "natural" and the "normal," of "verities" and "tendencies," of "controlling principles" and "disturbing causes," to be classed as an evolutionary science. The history of the science shows a long and devious course of disintegrating animism, – from the days of the scholastic writers, who discussed usury from the point of view of its relation to the divine suzerainty, to the Physiocrats, who rested their case on an "*ordre naturel*" and a "*loi naturelle*" that decides what is substantially true and, in a general way, guides the course of events by the constraint of logical congruence. There has been something of a change from Adam Smith, whose recourse in perplexity was to the guidance of "an unseen hand," to Mill and Cairnes, who formulated the [382] laws of "natural" wages and "normal" value, and the former of whom was so well content with his work as to say, "Happily, there is nothing in the laws of Value which remains for the present or any future writer to clear up: the theory of the subject is complete."[3] But the difference between the earlier and the later point of view is a difference of degree rather than of kind.

The standpoint of the classical economists, in their higher or definitive syntheses and generalizations, may not inaptly be called the standpoint of ceremonial adequacy. The ultimate laws and principles which they formulated were laws of the normal or the natural, according to a preconception regarding the ends to which, in the nature of things, all things tend. In effect, this preconception imputes to things a tendency to work out what the instructed common sense of the time accepts as the adequate or worthy end of human effort. It is a projection of the accepted ideal of conduct. This ideal of conduct is made to serve as a canon of truth, to the extent that the investigator contents himself with an appeal to its legitimation for premises that run back of the facts with which he is immediately dealing, for the "controlling principles" that are conceived intangibly to underlie the process discussed, and for the "tendencies" that run beyond the situation as it lies before him. As instances of the use of this ceremonial canon of knowledge may be cited the "conjectural history" that plays so large a part in the classical treatment of economic institutions, such as the normalized accounts of the beginnings of barter in the transactions of the putative hunter, fisherman, and boat-builder, or the man with the plane and the two planks, or the two men with the basket of apples and the basket of nuts.[4] Of a similar import is the

---

3 *Political Economy*, Book III. chap. i.
4 Marshall, *Principles of Economics* (2d ed.), Book V. chap. ii. p. 395, note.

characterization of money as "the great wheel of circulation"[5] or as "the medium of exchange." [383] Money is here discussed in terms of the end which, "in the normal case," it should work out according to the given writer's ideal of economic life, rather than in terms of causal relation.

With later writers especially, this terminology is no doubt to be commonly taken as a convenient use of metaphor, in which the concept of normality and propensity to an end has reached an extreme attenuation. But it is precisely in this use of figurative terms for the formulation of theory that the classical normality still lives in its attenuated life in modern economics; and it is this facile recourse to inscrutable figures of speech as the ultimate terms of theory that has saved the economists from being dragooned into the ranks of modern science. The metaphors are effective, both in their homiletical use and as a labor-saving device, – more effective than their user designs them to be. By their use the theorist is enabled serenely to enjoin himself from following out an elusive train of causal sequence. He is also enabled, without misgivings, to construct a theory of such an institution as money or wages or land-owner-ship without descending to a consideration of the living items concerned, except for convenient corroboration of his normalized scheme of symptoms. By this method the theory of an institution or a phase of life may be stated in conventionalized terms of the apparatus whereby life is carried on, the apparatus being invested with a tendency to an equilibrium at the normal, and the theory being a formulation of the conditions under which this putative equilibrium supervenes. In this way we have come into the usufruct of a cost-of-production theory of value which is pungently reminiscent of the time when Nature abhorred a vacuum. The ways and means and the mechanical structure of industry are formulated in a conventionalized nomenclature, and the observed motions of this mechanical apparatus are then reduced to a normalized scheme of relations. The scheme so arrived at is spiritually [384] binding on the behavior of the phenomena contemplated. With this normalized scheme as a guide, the permutations of a given segment of the apparatus are worked out according to the values assigned the several items and features comprised in the calculation; and a ceremonially consistent formula is constructed to cover that much of the industrial field. This is the deductive method. The formula is then tested by comparison with observed permutations, by the polariscopic use of the "normal case"; and the results arrived at are thus authenticated by induction. Features of the process that do not lend themselves to interpretation in the terms of the formula are abnormal cases and are due to disturbing causes. In all this the agencies or forces causally at work in the economic life process are neatly avoided. The outcome of the method, at its best, is a body of logically consistent propositions concerning the normal relations of things – a system of economic taxonomy. At its worst, it is a body of maxims for the conduct of business and a polemical discussion of disputed points of policy.

---

5 Adam Smith, *Wealth of Nations* (Bohn ed.), Book II. chap. ii. p. 289.

In all this, economic science is living over again in its turn the experiences which the natural sciences passed through some time back. In the natural sciences the work of the taxonomist was and continues to be of great value, but the scientists grew restless under the régime of symmetry and system-making. They took to asking why, and so shifted their inquiries from the structure of the coral reefs to the structure and habits of life of the polyp that lives in and by them. In the science of plants, systematic botany has not ceased to be of service; but the stress of investigation and discussion among the botanists to-day falls on the biological value of any given feature of structure, function, or tissue rather than on its taxonomic bearing. All the talk about cytoplasm, centrosomes, and karyokinetic process, means that the inquiry now looks consistently to the life process, and aims to explain it in terms of cumulative causation. [385]

What may be done in economic science of the taxonomic kind is shown at its best in Cairnes's work, where the method is well conceived and the results effectively formulated and applied. Cairnes handles the theory of the normal case in economic life with a master hand. In his discussion the metaphysics of propensity and tendencies no longer avowedly rules the formulation of theory, nor is the inscrutable meliorative trend of a harmony of interests confidently appealed to as an engine of definitive use in giving legitimacy to the economic situation at the given time. There is less of an exercise of faith in Cairnes's economic discussions than in those of the writers that went before him. The definitive terms of the formulation are still the terms of normality and natural law, but the metaphysics underlying this appeal to normality is so far removed from the ancient ground of the beneficent "order of nature" as to have become at least nominally impersonal and to proceed without a constant regard to the humanitarian bearing of the "tendencies" which it formulates. The metaphysics has been attenuated to something approaching in colorlessness the naturalist's conception of natural law. It is a natural law which, in the guise of "controlling principles," exercises a constraining surveillance over the trend of things; but it is no longer conceived to exercise its constraint in the interest of certain ulterior human purposes. The element of beneficence has been well-nigh eliminated, and the system is formulated in terms of the system itself. Economics as it left Cairnes's hand, so far as this theoretical work is concerned, comes near being taxonomy for taxonomy's sake.

No equally capable writer has come as near making economics the ideal "dismal" science as Cairnes in his discussion of pure theory. In the days of the early classical writers economics had a vital interest for the laymen of the time, because it formulated the common sense metaphysics of the time in its application to a department [386] of human life. But in the hands of the later classical writers the science lost much of its charm in this regard. It was no longer a definition and authentication of the deliverances of current common sense as to what ought to come to pass; and it, therefore, in large measure lost the support of the people out of doors, who were unable to take an interest in what did not concern them; and it was also out of touch with that realistic or evolutionary habit of mind which got under way about the middle of the century in the natural sciences. It was neither vitally metaphysical nor matter-of-fact, and it found comfort with very few outside of its own ranks. Only for those who by the fortunate accident of birth or education have been able to conserve the taxonomic animus has the science during the last third of a century continued to be of absorbing interest. The result has been that from the time when the taxonomic structure stood forth as a completed whole in its symmetry and stability the economists themselves, beginning with Cairnes, have been growing restive under its discipline of stability, and have made many efforts, more or less sustained, to galvanize it into movement. At the hands of the writers of the classical line these excursions have chiefly aimed at a more complete and comprehensive taxonomic scheme of permutations; while the historical departure threw away the taxonomic ideal without getting rid of the preconceptions on which it is based; and the later Austrian group struck out on a theory of process, but presently came to a full stop because the process about which they busied themselves was not, in their apprehension of it, a cumulative or unfolding sequence.

But what does all this signify? If we are getting restless under the taxonomy of a monocotyledonous wage doctrine and a cryptogamic theory of interest, with involute, loculicidal, tomentous and moniliform variants, [387] what is the cytoplasm, centrosome, or karyokinetic process to which we may turn, and in which we may find surcease from the metaphysics of normality and controlling principles? What are we going to do about it? The question is rather, What are we doing about it? There is the economic life process still in great measure awaiting theoretical formulation. The active material in which the economic process goes on is the human material of the industrial community. For the purpose of economic science the process of cumulative change that is to be accounted for is the sequence of change in the methods of doing things, – the methods of dealing with the material means of life.

What has been done in the way of inquiry into this economic life process? The ways and means of turning material objects and circumstances to account lie before the investigator at any given point of time in the form of mechanical contrivances and arrangements for compassing certain mechanical ends. It has therefore been easy to accept these ways and means as items of inert matter having a given mechanical structure and thereby serving the material ends of man. As such, they have been scheduled and graded by the economists under the head of capital, this capital being conceived as a mass of material objects serviceable for human use. This is well enough for the purposes of taxonomy; but it is not an effective method of conceiving the matter for the purpose of a theory of the developmental process. For the latter purpose, when taken as items in a process of cumulative change or as items in the scheme of life, these productive goods are facts of human knowledge, skill, and predilection; that is to say, they are, substantially, prevalent habits of thought, and it is as such that they enter into the process of industrial development. The physical properties of the materials accessible to man are constants: it is the human agent that changes, – his insight [388] and his appreciation of what these things can be used for is what develops. The accumulation of goods already on hand conditions his handling and utilization of the materials offered, but even on this side – the "limitation of industry by capital" – the limitation imposed is on what men can do and on the methods of doing it. The changes that take place in the mechanical contrivances are an expression of changes in the human factor. Changes in the material facts breed further change only through the human factor. It is in the human material that the continuity of development is to be looked for; and it is here, therefore, that the motor forces of the process of economic development must be studied if they are to be studied in action at all. Economic action must be the subject-matter of the science if the science is to fall into line as an evolutionary science.

Nothing new has been said in all this. But the fact is all the more significant for being a familiar fact. It is a fact recognized by common consent throughout much of the later economic discussion, and this current recognition of the fact is a long step towards centering discussion and inquiry upon it. If economics is to follow the lead or the analogy of the other sciences that have to do with a life process, the way is plain so far as regards the general direction in which the move will be made.

The economists of the classical trend have made no serious attempt to depart from the standpoint of taxonomy and make their science a genetic account of the economic life process. As has just been said, much the same is true for the Historical School. The latter have attempted an account of developmental sequence, but they have followed the lines of pre-Darwinian speculations on development rather than lines which modern science would recognize as evolutionary. They have given a narrative survey of phenomena, not a genetic account of an unfolding process. In this work they have, no doubt, achieved [389] results of permanent value; but the results achieved are scarcely to be classed as economic theory. On the other hand, the Austrians and their precursors and their coadjutors in the value discussion have taken up a detached portion of economic theory, and have inquired with great nicety into the process by which the phenomena within their limited field are worked out. The entire discussion of marginal utility and subjective value as the outcome of a valuation process must be taken as a genetic study of this range of facts. But here, again, nothing further has come of the inquiry, so far as regards a rehabilitation of economic theory as a whole. Accepting Menger as their spokesman on this head, it must be said that the Austrians have on the whole showed themselves unable to break with the classical tradition that economics is a taxonomic science.

The reason for the Austrian failure seems to lie in a faulty conception of human nature, – faulty for the present purpose, however adequate it may be for any other. In all the received formulations of economic theory, whether at the hands of English economists or those of the Continent, the human material with which the inquiry is concerned is conceived in hedonistic terms; that is to say, in terms of a passive and substantially inert and immutably given human nature. The psychological and anthropological preconceptions of the economists have been those which were accepted by the psychological and social sciences some generations ago. The hedonistic conception of man is that of a lightning calculator of pleasures and pains, who oscillates like a homogeneous globule of desire of happiness under the impulse of stimuli that shift him about the area, but leave him intact. He has neither antecedent nor consequent. He is an isolated, definitive human datum, in stable equilibrium except for the buffets of the impinging forces that displace him in one direction or another. Self-poised in elemental space, [390] he spins symmetrically about his own spiritual axis until the parallelogram of forces bears down upon him, whereupon he follows the line of the resultant. When the force of the impact is spent, he comes to rest, a self-contained globule of desire as before. Spiritually, the hedonistic man is not a prime mover. He is not the seat of a process of living, except in the sense that he is subject to a series of permutations enforced upon him by circumstances external and alien to him.

The later psychology, re-enforced by modern anthropological research, gives a different conception of human nature. According to this conception, it is the characteristic of man to do something, not simply to suffer pleasures and pains through the impact of suitable forces. He is not simply a bundle of desires that are to be saturated by being placed in the path of the forces of the environment, but rather a coherent structure of propensities and habits which seeks realization and expression in an unfolding activity. According to this view, human activity, and economic activity among the rest, is not apprehended as something incidental to the process of saturating given desires. The activity is itself the substantial fact of the process, and the desires under whose guidance the action takes place are circumstances of temperament which determine the specific direction in which the activity will unfold itself in the given case. These circumstances of temperament are ultimate and definitive for the individual who acts under them, so far as regards his attitude as agent in the particular action in which he is engaged. But, in the view of the science, they are elements of the existing frame of mind of the agent, and are the outcome of his antecedents and his life up to the point at which he stands. They are the products of his hereditary traits and his past experience, cumulatively wrought out under a given body of traditions, conventionalities, and material circumstances; and they afford the point of departure for [391] the next step in the process. The economic life history of the individual is a cumulative process of adaptation of means to ends that cumulatively change as the process goes on, both the agent and his environment being at any point the outcome of the past process. His methods of life to-day are enforced upon him by his habits of life carried over from yesterday and by the circumstances left as the mechanical residue of the life of yesterday.

What is true of the individual in this respect is true of the group in which he lives. All economic change is a change in the economic community, – a change in the community's methods of turning material things to account. The change is always in the last resort a change in habits of thought. This is true even of changes in the mechanical processes of industry. A given contrivance for effecting certain material ends becomes a circumstance which affects the further growth of habits of thought – habitual methods of procedure – and so becomes a point of departure for further development of the methods of compassing the ends sought and for the further variation of ends that are sought to be compassed. In all this flux there is no definitively adequate method of life and no definitive or absolutely worthy end of action, so far as concerns the science which sets out to formulate a theory of the process of economic life. What remains as a hard and fast residue is the fact of activity directed to an objective end. Economic action is teleological, in the sense that men always and everywhere seek to do something. What, in specific detail, they seek, is not to be answered except by a scrutiny of the details of their activity; but, so long as we have to do with their life as members of the economic community, there remains the generic fact that their life is an unfolding activity of a teleological kind.

It may or may not be a teleological process in the sense that it tends or should tend to any end that is conceived to be worthy or adequate by the inquirer or by the consensus [392] of inquirers. Whether it is or is not is a question with which the present inquiry is not concerned; and it is also a question of which an evolutionary economics need take no account. The question of a tendency in events can evidently not come up except on the ground of some preconception or prepossession on the part of the person looking for the tendency. In order to search for a tendency, we must be possessed of some notion of a definitive end to be sought, or some notion as to what is the legitimate trend of events. The notion of a legitimate trend in a course of events is an extra-evolutionary preconception, and lies outside the scope of an inquiry into the causal sequence in any process. The evolutionary point of view, therefore, leaves no place for a formulation of natural laws in terms of definitive normality, whether in economics or in any other branch of inquiry. Neither does it leave room for that other question of normality, What should be the end of the developmental process under discussion?

The economic life history of any community is its life history in so far as it is shaped by men's interest in the material means of life. This economic interest has counted for much in shaping the cultural growth of all communities. Primarily and most obviously, it has guided the formation, the cumulative growth, of that range of conventionalities and methods of life that are currently recognized as economic institutions; but the same interest has also pervaded the community's life and its cultural growth at points where the resulting structural features are not chiefly and most immediately of an economic bearing. The economic interest goes with men through life, and it goes with the race throughout its process of cultural development. It affects the cultural structure at all points, so that all institutions may be said to be in some measure economic institutions. This is necessarily the case, since the base of action – the point of departure – at any step [393] in the process is the entire organic complex of habits of thought that have been shaped by the past process. The economic interest does not act in isolation, for it is but one of several vaguely isolable interests on which the complex of teleological activity carried out by the individual proceeds. The individual is but a single agent in each case; and he enters into each successive action as a whole, although the specific end sought in a given action may be sought avowedly on the basis of a particular interest; as *e.g.*, the economic, æsthetic, sexual, humanitarian, devotional interests. Since each of these passably isolable interests is a propensity of the organic agent man, with his complex of habits of thought, the expression of each is affected by habits of life formed under the guidance of all the rest. There is, therefore, no neatly isolable range of cultural phenomena that can be rigorously set apart under the head of economic institutions, although a category of "economic institutions" may be of service as a convenient caption, comprising those institutions in which the economic interest most immediately and consistently finds expression, and which most immediately and with the least limitation are of an economic bearing.

From what has been said it appears that an evolutionary economics must be the theory of a process of cultural growth as determined by the economic interest, a theory of a cumulative sequence of economic institutions stated in terms of the process itself. Except for the want of space to do here what should be done in some detail if it is done at all, many efforts by the later economists in this direction might be cited to show the trend of economic discussion in this direction. There is not a little evidence to this effect, and much of the work done must be rated as effective work for this purpose. Much of the work of the Historical School, for instance, and that of its later exponents especially, is too noteworthy to be passed over in silence, even with all due regard to the limitations space. [394]

We are now ready to return to the question why economics is not an evolutionary science. It is necessarily the aim of such an economics to trace the cumulative working out of the economic interest in the cultural sequence. It must be a theory of the economic life process of the race or the community. The economists have accepted the hedonistic preconceptions concerning human nature and human action, and the conception of the economic interest which a hedonistic psychology gives does not afford material for a theory of the development of human nature. Under hedonism the economic interest is not conceived in terms of action. It is therefore not readily apprehended or appreciated in terms of a cumulative growth of habits of thought, and does not provoke, even if it did lend itself to, treatment by the evolutionary method. At the same time the anthropological preconceptions current in that common-sense apprehension of human nature to which economists have habitually turned has not enforced the formulation of human nature in terms of a cumulative growth of habits of life. These received anthropological preconceptions are such as have made possible the normalized conjectural accounts of primitive barter with which all economic readers are familiar, and the no less normalized conventional derivation of landed property and its rent, or the sociologico-philosophical discussion of the "function" of this or that class in the life of society or of the nation.

The premises and the point of view required for an evolutionary economics have been wanting. The economists have not had the materials for such a science ready to their hand, and the provocation to strike out in such a direction has been absent. Even if it has been possible at any time to turn to the evolutionary line of speculation in economics, the possibility of a departure is not enough to bring it about. So long as the habitual view taken of a given range of facts is of the taxonomic kind and the [395] material lends itself to treatment by that method, the taxonomic method is the easiest, gives the most gratifying immediate results, and best fits into the accepted body of knowledge of the range of facts in question. This has been the situation in economics. The other sciences of its group have likewise been a body of taxonomic discipline, and departures from the accredited method have lain under the odium of being meretricious innovations. The well-worn paths are easy to follow and lead into good company. Advance along them visibly furthers the accredited work which the science has in hand. Divergence from the paths means tentative work, which is necessarily slow and fragmentary and of uncertain value.

It is only when the methods of the science and the syntheses resulting from their use come to be out of line with habits of thought that prevail in other matters that the scientist grows restive under the guidance of the received methods and standpoints, and seeks a way out. Like other men, the economist is an individual with but one intelligence. He is a creature of habits and propensities given through the antecedents, hereditary and cultural, of which he is an outcome; and the habits of thought formed in any one line of experience affect his thinking in any other. Methods of observation and of handling facts that are familiar through habitual use in the general range of knowledge, gradually assert themselves in any given special range of knowledge. They may be accepted slowly and with reluctance where their acceptance involves innovation; but, if they have the continued backing of the general body of experience, it is only a question of time when they shall come into dominance in the special field. The intellectual attitude and the method of correlation enforced upon us in the apprehension and assimilation of facts in the more elementary ranges of knowledge that have to do with brute facts assert themselves also when the attention is directed to those phenomena of the life [396] process with which economics has to do; and the range of facts which are habitually handled by other methods than that in traditional vogue in economics has now become so large and so insistently present at every turn that we are left restless, if the new body of facts cannot be handled according to the method of mental procedure which is in this way becoming habitual.

In the general body of knowledge in modern times the facts are apprehended in terms of causal sequence. This is especially true of that knowledge of brute facts which is shaped by the exigencies of the modern mechanical industry. To men thoroughly imbued with this matter-of-fact habit of mind the laws and theorems of economics, and of the other sciences that treat of the normal course of things, have a character of "unreality" and futility that bars out any serious interest in their discussion. The laws and theorems are "unreal" to them because they are not to be apprehended in the terms which these men make use of in handling the facts with which they are perforce habitually occupied. The same matter-of-fact spiritual attitude and mode of procedure have now made their way well up into the higher levels of scientific knowledge, even in the sciences which deal in a more elementary way with the same human material that makes the subject-matter of economics, and the economists themselves are beginning to feel the unreality of their theorems about "normal" cases. Provided the practical exigencies of modern industrial life continue of the same character as they now are, and so continue to enforce the impersonal method of knowledge, it is only a question of time when that (substantially animistic) habit of mind which proceeds on the notion of a definitive normality shall be displaced in the field of economic inquiry by that (substantially materialistic) habit of mind which seeks a comprehension of facts in terms of a cumulative sequence.

The later method of apprehending and assimilating [397] facts and handling them for the purposes of knowledge may be better or worse, more or less worthy or adequate, than the earlier; it may be of greater or less ceremonial or æsthetic effect; we may be move to regret the incursion of underbred habits of thought into the scholar's domain. But all that is beside the present point. Under the stress of modern technological exigencies, men's every-day habits of thought are falling into the lines that in the sciences constitute the evolutionary method; and knowledge which proceeds on a higher, more archaic plain is becoming alien and meaningless to them. The social and political sciences must follow the drift, for they are already caught in it.

Selection 16

The instinct of workmanship and the irksomeness of labor

Source: *American Journal of Sociology*, September 1898 (vol. 4, pp. 187–201).

Veblen (1898d)

It is one of the commonplaces of the received economic theory that work is irksome. Many a discussion proceeds on this axiom that, so far as regards economic matters, men desire above all things to get the goods produced by labor and to avoid the labor by which the goods are produced. In a general way the common-sense opinion is well in accord with current theory on this head. According to the common-sense ideal, the economic beatitude lies in an unrestrained consumption of goods, without work; whereas the perfect economic affliction is unremunerated labor. Man instinctively revolts at effort that goes to supply the means of life.

No one will accept the proposition when stated in this bald fashion, but even as it stands it is scarcely an overstatement of what is implied in the writings of eminent economists. If such an aversion to useful effort is an integral part of human nature, then the trail of the Edenic serpent should be plain to all men, for this is a unique distinction of the human species. A consistent aversion to whatever activity goes to maintain the life of the species is assuredly found in no other species of animal. Under the selective process through which species are held to have emerged and gained their stability there is no chance for the survival of a species gifted with such an aversion to the furtherance of its own life process. If man alone is an exception from the selective norm, then the alien propensity in question must have been intruded into his make-up by some malevolent *deus ex machina*.

Yet, for all the apparent absurdity of the thing, there is the fact. With more or less sincerity, people currently avow an aversion to useful effort. The avowal does not cover all effort, but only such as is of some use; it is, more particularly, such effort as is vulgarly recognized to be useful labor. Less [188] repugnance is expressed as regards effort which brings gain without giving a product that is of human use, as, for example, the effort that goes into war, politics, or other employments of a similar nature. And there is commonly no avowed aversion to sports or other similar employments that yield neither a pecuniary gain nor a useful product. Still, the fact that a given line of effort is useless does not of itself save it from being odious, as is shown by the case of menial service; much of this work serves no useful end, but it is none the less repugnant to all people of sensibility.

"The economic man," whose lineaments were traced in outline by the classical economists and filled in by their caricaturists, is an anomaly in the animal word; and yet, to judge by everyday popular expressions of inclination, the portrait is not seriously overdrawn. But if this economic man is to serve as a lay figure upon which to fit the garment of economic doctrines, it is incumbent upon the science to explain what are his limitations and how he has achieved his emancipation from the law of natural selection. His emancipation from the law is, indeed, more apparent than substantial. The difference in this respect between man and his sometime competitors in the struggle for survival lies not in a slighter but in a fuller adjustment of his propensities to the purposes of the life of the species. He distanced them all in this respect long ago, and by so wide an interval that he is now able, without jeopardy to the life of the species, to play fast and loose with the spiritual basis of its survival.

Like other animals, man is an agent that acts in response to stimuli afforded by the environment in which he lives. Like other species, he is a creature of habit and propensity. But in a higher degree than other species, man mentally digests the content of the habits under whose guidance he acts, and appreciates the trend of these habits and propensities. He is in an eminent sense an intelligent agent. By selective necessity he is endowed with a proclivity for purposeful action. He is possessed of a discriminating sense of purpose, by force of which [189] all futility of life or of action is distasteful to him. There may be a wide divergence between individuals as regards the form and the direction in which this impulse expresses itself, but the impulse itself is not a matter of idiosyncrasy, it is a generic feature of human nature. It is not a trait that occurs sporadically in a few individuals. Cases occur in which this proclivity for purposeful action is wanting or is present in obviously scant measure, but persons endowed in this stepmotherly fashion are classed as "defective subjects." Lines of descent which carry this defective human nature dwindle and decay even under the propitious circumstances of modern life. The history of hereditarily dependent or defective families is evidence to this effect.

Man's great advantage over other species in the struggle for survival has been his superior facility in turning the forces of the environment to account. It is to his proclivity for turning the material means of life to account that he owes his position as lord of creation. It is not a proclivity to effort, but to achievement – to the compassing of an end. His primacy is in the last resort an industrial or economic primacy. In his economic life man is an agent, not an absorbent; he is an agent seeking in every act the accomplishment of some concrete, objective, impersonal end. As this pervading norm of action guides the life of men in all the use they make of material things, so it must also serve as the point of departure and afford the guiding principle for any science that aims to be a theory of the economic life process. Within the purview of economic theory, the last analysis of any given phenomenon must run back to this ubiquitous human impulse to do the next thing.

All this seems to contradict what has just been said of the conventional aversion to labor. But the contradiction is not so sheer in fact as it appears to be at first sight. Its solution lies in the fact that the aversion to labor is in great part a conventional aversion only. In the intervals of sober reflection, when not harassed with the strain of overwork, men's common sense speaks unequivocally under the guidance of the instinct of workmanship. They like to see others spend their life to some purpose, and they like to reflect that their own life is of some use. All men [190] have this quasi-æsthetic sense of economic or industrial merit, and to this sense of economic merit futility and inefficiency are distasteful. In its positive expression it is an impulse or instinct of workmanship; negatively it expresses itself in a deprecation of waste. This sense of merit and demerit with respect to the material furtherance or hindrance of life approves the economically effective act and deprecates economic futility. It is needless to point out in detail the close relation between this norm of economic merit and the ethical norm of conduct, on the one hand, and the æsthetic norm of taste, on the other. It is very closely related to both of these, both as regards its biological ground and as regards the scope and method of its award.

This instinct of workmanship apparently stands in sheer conflict with the conventional antipathy to useful effort. The two are found together in full discord in the common run of men; but whenever a deliberate judgment is passed on conduct or on events, the former asserts its primacy in a pervasive way which suggests that it is altogether the more generic, more abiding trait of human nature. There can scarcely be a serious question of precedence between the two. The former is a human trait necessary to the survival of the species; the latter is a habit of thought possible only in a species which has distanced all competitors, and then it prevails only by sufferance and within limits set by the former. The question between them is, Is the aversion to labor a derivative of the instinct of workmanship? and, How has it arisen and gained consistency in spite of its being at variance with that instinct?

Until recently there has been something of a consensus among those who have written on early culture, to the effect that man, as he first emerged upon the properly human plane, was of a contentious disposition, inclined to isolate his own interest and purposes from those of his fellows, and with a penchant for feuds and brawls. Accordingly, even where the view is met with that men are by native proclivity inclined to action, there is still evident a presumption that this native proclivity to action is a proclivity to action of a destructive kind. It is held that men are inclined to fight, not to work – that the end of [191] action in the normal case is damage rather than repair. This view would make the proclivity to purposeful action an impulse to sportsmanship rather than to workmanship. In any attempt to fit this view into an evolutionary scheme of culture it would carry the implication that in the prehuman or proto-anthropoid phase of its life the race was a predaceous species, and that the initial phase of human culture, as well as the later cultural development, has been substantially of a predatory kind.

There is much to be said for this view. If mankind is by derivation a race not of workmen but of sportsmen, then there is no need of explaining the conventional aversion to work. Work is unsportsmanlike and therefore distasteful, and perplexity then arises in explaining how men have in any degree become reconciled to any but a predaceous life. Apart from the immediate convenience of this view, it is also enforced by much evidence. Most peoples at a lower stage of culture than our own are of a more predatory habit than our people. The history of mankind, as conventionally written, has been a narrative of predatory exploits, and this history is not commonly felt to be one-sided or misinformed. And a sportsmanlike inclination to warfare is also to be found in nearly all modern communities. Similarly, the sense of honor, so-called, whether it is individual or national honor, is also an expression of sportsmanship. The prevalence of notions of honor may, therefore, be taken as evidence going in the same direction. And as if to further fortify the claim of sportsmanship to antiquity and prescriptive standing, the sense of honor is also noticeably more vivid in communities of a somewhat more archaic culture than our own.

Yet there is a considerable body of evidence, both from cultural history and from the present-day phenomena of human life, which traverses this conventionally accepted view that makes man generically a sportsman. Obscurely but persistently, throughout the history of human culture, the great body of the people have almost everywhere, in their everyday life, been at work to turn things to human use. The proximate aim of all industrial improvement has been the better performance of some workmanlike task. Necessarily this work has, on the one hand, [192] proceeded on the basis of an appreciative interest in the work to be done; for there is no other ground on which to obtain anything better than the aimless performance of a task. And necessarily also, on the other hand, the discipline of work has acted to develop a workmanlike attitude. It will not do to say that the work accomplished is entirely due to compulsion under a predatory régime, for the most striking advances in this respect have been wrought where the coercive force of a sportsmanlike exploitation has been least.

The same view is borne out by the expressions of common sense. As has already been remarked, whenever they dispassionately take thought and pass a judgment on the value of human conduct, the common run of mature men approve workmanship rather than sportsmanship. At the best, they take an apologetic attitude toward the latter. This is well seen in the present (May, 1898) disturbance of the popular temper. While it may well be granted that the warlike raid upon which this community is entering is substantially an access of sportsmanlike exaltation, it is to be noticed that nearly all those who speak for war are at pains to find some colorable motive of another kind. Predatory exploit, simply as such, is not felt to carry its own legitimation, as it should in the apprehension of any species that is primarily of a predaceous character. What meets unreserved approval is such conduct as furthers human life on the whole, rather than such as furthers the invidious or predatory interest of one as against another.

The most ancient and most consistent habits of the race will best assert themselves when men are not speaking under the stress of instant irritation. Under such circumstances the ancient bent may even bear down the immediate conventional canons of conduct. The archaic turn of mind that inclines men to commend workmanlike serviceability is the outcome of long and consistent habituation to a course of life of such a character as is reflected by this inclination.

Man's life is activity; and as he acts, so he thinks and feels. This is necessarily so, since it is the agent man that does the [193] thinking and feeling. Like other species, man is a creature of habits and propensities. He acts under the guidance of propensities which have been imposed upon him by the process of selection to which he owes his differentiation from other species. He is a social animal; and the selective process whereby he has acquired the spiritual make-up of a social animal has at the same time made him substantially a peaceful animal. The race may have wandered far from the ancient position of peacefulness, but even now the traces of a peaceful trend in men's everyday habits of thought and feeling are plain enough. The sight of blood and the presence of death, even of the blood or death of the lower animals, commonly strike inexperienced persons with a sickening revulsion. In the common run of cases, the habit of complacency with slaughter comes only as the result of discipline. In this respect man differs from the beasts of prey. He differs, of course, most widely in this respect from the solitary beasts, but even among the gregarious animals his nearest spiritual relatives are not found among the carnivora. In his unarmed frame and in the slight degree to which his muscular force is specialized for fighting, as well as in his instinctive aversion to hostile contact with the ferocious beasts, man is to be classed with those animals that owe their survival to an aptitude for avoiding direct conflict with their competitors, rather than with those which survive by virtue of overcoming and eating their rivals.

"Man is the weakest and most defenseless of all living things," and, according to the Law of the Jungle, it is his part to take advice and contrive and turn divers things to account in ways that are incomprehensible to the rest. Without tools he is not a dangerous animal, as animals go. And he did not become a formidable animal until he had made some considerable advance in the contrivance of implements for combat. In the days before tools had been brought into effective use – that is to say, during by far the greater part of the period of human evolution – man could not be primarily an agent of destruction or a disturber of the peace. He was of a peaceable and retiring disposition by force of circumstances. With the use of tools the possibility of [194] his acquiring a different disposition gradually began, but even then the circumstances favoring the growth of a contentious disposition supervened only gradually and partially. The habits of life of the race were still perforce of a peaceful and industrial character, rather than contentious and destructive.

Tools and implements, in the early days, must have served chiefly to shape facts and objects for human use, rather than for inflicting damage and discomfort. Industry would have to develop far before it became possible for one group of men to live at the cost of another; and during the protracted evolution of industry before this point had been reached the discipline of associated life still consistently ran in the direction of industrial efficiency, both as regards men's physical and mental traits and as regards their spiritual attitude.

By selection and by training, the life of man, before a predaceous life became possible, would act to develop and to conserve in him instinct for workmanship. The adaptation to the environment which the situation enforced was of an industrial kind; it required men to acquire facility in shaping things and situations for human use. This does not mean the shaping of things by the individual to his own individual use simply; for archaic man was necessarily a member of a group, and during this early stage, when industrial efficiency was still inconsiderable, no group could have survived except on the basis of a sense of solidarity strong enough to throw self-interest into the background. Self-interest, as an accepted guide of action, is possible only as the concomitant of a predatory life, and a predatory life is possible only after the use of tools has developed so far as to leave a large surplus of product over what is required for the sustenance of the producers. Subsistence by predation implies something substantial to prey upon.

Early man was a member of a group which depended for its survival on the industrial efficiency of its members and on their singleness of purpose in making use of the material means at hand. Some competition between groups for the possession of the fruits of the earth and for advantageous locations there would be even at a relatively early stage, but much hostile contact [195] between groups there could not be; not enough to shape the dominant habits of thought.

What men can do easily is what they do habitually, and this decides what they can think and know easily. They feel at home in the range of ideas which is familiar through their everyday line of action. A habitual line of action constitutes a habitual line of thought, and gives the point of view from which facts and events are apprehended and reduced to a body of knowledge. What is consistent with the habitual course of action is consistent with the habitual line of thought, and gives the definitive ground of knowledge as well as the conventional standard of complacency or approval in any community. Conversely, a process or method of life, once understood, assimilated in thought works into the scheme of life and becomes a norm of conduct, simply because the thinking, knowing agent is also the acting agent. What is apprehended with facility and is consistent with the process of life and knowledge is thereby apprehended as right and good. All this applies with added force where the habituation is not simply individual and sporadic, but is enforced upon the group or the race by a selective elimination of those individuals and lines of descent that do not conform to the required canon of knowledge and conduct. Where this takes place, the acquired proclivity passes from the status of habit to that of aptitude or propensity. It becomes a transmissible trait, and action under its guidance becomes right and good, and the longer and more consistent the selective adaptation through which the aptitude arises, the more firmly is the resulting aptitude settled upon the race, and the more unquestioned becomes the sanction of the resulting canon of conduct.

So far as regards his relation to the material means of life, the canon of thought and of conduct which was in this way enforced upon early man was what is here called the instinct of workmanship. The interest which men took in economic facts on the basis of this propensity, in the days before spoliation came into vogue, was not primarily of a self-regarding character. The necessary dominance of a sense of group solidarity would [196] preclude that. The selective process must eliminate lines of descent unduly gifted with a self-regarding bias. Still, there was some emulation between individuals, even in the most indigent and most peaceable groups. From the readiness with which a scheme of emulation is entered upon where late circumstances favor its development, it seems probable that the proclivity to emulation must have been present also in the earlier days in sufficient force to assert itself to the extent to which the exigencies of the earlier life of the group would permit. But this emulation could not run in the direction of an individual acquisition or accumulation of goods, or of a life consistently given to raids and tumults. It would be emulation such as is found among the peaceable gregarious animals generally; that is to say, it was primarily and chiefly sexual emulation, recurring with more or less regularity. Beyond this there must also have been some wrangling in the distribution of goods on hand, but neither this nor the rivalry for subsistence could have been the dominant note of life.

Under the canon of conduct imposed by the instinct of workmanship, efficiency, serviceability, commends itself, and inefficiency or futility is odious. Man contemplates his own conduct and that of his neighbors, and passes a judgment of complacency or of dispraise. The degree of effectiveness with which he lives up to the accepted standard of efficiency in great measure determines his contentment with himself and his situation. A wide or persistent discrepancy in this respect is a source of abounding spiritual discomfort.

Judgment may in this way be passed on the intention of the agent or on the serviceability of the act. In the former case the award of merit or demerit is to be classed as moral; and with award of merit of this kind this paper is not concerned. As regards serviceability or efficiency, men do not only take thought at first hand of the facts of their own conduct; they are also sensitive to rebuke or approval from others. Not only is the immediate consciousness of the achievement of a purpose gratifying and stimulating, but the imputation of [197] efficiency by one's fellows is perhaps no less gratifying or stimulating.

Sensitiveness to rebuke or approval is a matter of selective necessity under the circumstances of associated life. Without it no group of men could carry on a collective life in a material environment that requires shaping to the ends of man. In this respect, again, man shows a spiritual relationship with the gregarious animals rather than with the solitary beasts of prey.

Under the guidance of this taste for good work, men are compared with one another and with the accepted ideals of efficiency, and are rated and graded by the common sense of their fellows according to a conventional scheme of merit and demerit. The imputation of efficiency necessarily proceeds on evidence of efficiency. The visible achievement of one man is, therefore, compared with that of another, and the award of esteem comes habitually to rest on an invidious comparison of persons instead of on the immediate bearing of the given line of conduct upon the approved end of action. The ground of esteem in this way shifts from a direct appreciation of the expediency of conduct to a comparison of the abilities of different agents. Instead of a valuation of serviceability, there is a gauging of capability on the ground of visible success. And what comes to be compared in an invidious comparison of this kind between agents is the force which the agent is able to put forth, rather than the serviceability of the agent's conduct. So soon, therefore, and in so far, as the esteem awarded to serviceability passes into an invidious esteem of one agent as compared with another, the end sought in action will tend to change from naïve expediency to the manifestation of capacity or force. It becomes the proximate end of effort to put forth evidence of power, rather than to achieve an impersonal end for its own sake, simply as an item of human use. So that, while in its more immediate expression the norm of economic taste stands out as an impulse to workmanship or a taste for serviceability and a distaste for futility, under given circumstances of associated life it comes in some degree to take on the character of an emulative demonstration of force. [198]

Since the imputation of efficiency and of invidious merit goes on the evidence afforded by visible success, the appearance of evil must be avoided in order to escape dispraise. In the early savage culture, while the group is small and while the conditions favorable to a predatory life are still wanting, the resulting emulation between the members of the group runs chiefly to industrial efficiency. It comes to be the appearance of industrial incapacity that is to be avoided. It is in this direction that force or capacity can be put in evidence most consistently and with the best effect for the good name of the individual. It is, therefore, in this direction that a standard of merit and a canon of meritorious conduct will develop. But even for a growth of emulation in the productive use of brain and muscle, the small, rude, peaceable group of savages is not fertile ground. The situation does not favor a vigorous emulative spirit. The conditions favorable to the growth of a habit of emulative demonstration of force are (1) the frequent recurrence of conjunctures that call for a great and sudden strain, and (2) exposure of the individual to a large, and especially to a shifting, human environment whose approval is sought. These conditions are not effectually met on the lower levels of savagery, such as human culture must have been during the early days of the use of tools. Accordingly, relatively little of the emulative spirit is seen in communities that have retained the archaic, peaceable constitution, or that have reverted to it from a higher culture. In such communities a low standard of culture and comfort goes along with an absence of strenuous application to the work in hand, as well as a relative absence of jealousy and gradations of rank. Notions of economic rank and discrimination between persons, whether in point of possessions or in point of comfort, are almost, if not altogether, in abeyance.

With a further development of the use of tools and of human command over the forces of the environment, the habits of life of the savage group change. There is likely to be more of aggression, both in the way of a pursuit of large game and in the way of conflict between groups. As the industrial efficiency of the group increases, and as weapons are brought to greater perfection, [199] the incentives to aggression and the opportunities for achievement along this line increase. The conditions favorable to emulation are more fully met. With the increasing density of population that follows from a heightened industrial efficiency, the group passes, by force of circumstances, from the archaic condition of poverty-stricken peace to a stage of predatory life. This fighting stage – the beginning of barbarism – may involve aggressive predation, or the group may simply be placed on the defensive. One or the other, or both the lines of activity – and commonly both, no doubt – will be forced upon the group, on pain of extermination. This has apparently been the usual course of early social evolution.

When a group emerges into this predatory phase of its development, the employments which most occupy men's attention are employments that involve exploit. The most serious concern of the group, and at the same time the direction in which the most spectacular effect may be achieved by the individual, is conflict with men and beasts. It becomes easy to make a telling comparison between men when their work is a series of exploits carried out against these difficult adversaries or against the formidable movements of the elements. The assertion of the strong hand, successful aggression, usually of a destructive character, becomes the accepted basis of repute. The dominant life interest of the group throws its strong light upon this creditable employment of force and sagacity, and the other, obscurer ways of serving the group's life fall into the background. The guiding animus of the group becomes a militant one, and men's actions are judged from the standpoint of the fighting man. What is recognized, without reflection and without misgiving, as serviceable and effective in such a group is fighting capacity. Exploit becomes the conventional ground of invidious comparison between individuals, and repute comes to rest on prowess.

As the predatory culture reaches a fuller development, there comes a distinction between employments. The tradition of prowess, as the virtue *par excellence*, gains in scope and consistency until prowess comes near being recognized as the sole virtue. Those employments alone are then worthy and reputable [200] which involve the exercise of this virtue. Other employments, in which men are occupied with tamely shaping inert materials to human use, become unworthy and end with becoming debasing. The honorable man must not only show capacity for predatory exploit, but he must also avoid entanglement with the occupations that do not involve exploit. The tame employments, those that involve no obvious destruction of life and no spectacular coercion of refractory antagonists, fall into disrepute and are relegated to those members of the community who are defective in predatory capacity; that is to say, those who are lacking in massiveness, agility, or ferocity. Occupation in these employments argues that the person so occupied falls short of that decent modicum of prowess which would entitle him to be graded as a man in good standing. In order to an unsullied reputation, the appearance of evil must be avoided. Therefore the able-bodied barbarian of the predatory culture, who is at all mindful of his good name, severely leaves all uneventful drudgery to the women and minors of the group. He puts in his time in the manly arts of war and devotes his talents to devising ways and means of disturbing the peace. That way lies honor.

In the barbarian scheme of life the peaceable, industrial employments are women's work. They imply defective force, incapacity for aggression or devastation, and are therefore not of good report. But whatever is accepted as a conventional mark of a shortcoming or a vice comes presently to be accounted intrinsically base. In this way industrial occupations fall under a polite odium and are apprehended to be substantially ignoble. They are unsportsmanlike. Labor carries a taint, and all contamination from vulgar employments must be shunned by self-respecting men.

Where the predatory culture has developed in full consistency, the common-sense apprehension that labor is ignoble has developed into the further refinement that labor is wrong – for those who are not already beneath reproach. Hence certain well-known features of caste and tabu. In the further cultural development, when some wealth has been accumulated and the members of the community fall into a servile class on the one hand [201] and a leisure class on the other, the tradition that labor is ignoble gains an added significance. It is not only a mark of inferior force, but it is also a perquisite of the poor. This is the situation today. Labor is morally impossible by force of the ancient tradition that has come down from early barbarism, and it is shameful by force of its evil association with poverty. It is indecorous.

The irksomeness of labor is a spiritual fact; it lies in the indignity of the thing. The fact of its irksomeness is, of course, none the less real and cogent for its being of a spiritual kind. Indeed, it is all the more substantial and irremediable on that account. Physical irksomeness and distastefulness can be borne, if only the spiritual incentive is present. Witness the attractiveness of warfare, both to the barbarian and to the civilized youth. The most commonplace recital of a campaigner's experience carries a sweeping suggestion of privation, exposure, fatigue, vermin, squalor, sickness, and loathsome death; the incidents and accessories of war are said to be unsavory, unsightly, unwholesome beyond the power of words; yet warfare is an attractive employment if one only is gifted with a suitable habit of mind. Most sports, and many other polite employments that are distressing but creditable, are evidence to the same effect.

Physical irksomeness is an incommodity which men habitually make light of if it is not reinforced by the sanction of decorum; but it is otherwise with the spiritual irksomeness of such labor as is condemned by polite usage. That is a cultural fact. There is no remedy for this kind of irksomeness, short of a subversion of that cultural structure on which our canons of decency rest. Appeal may of course be made to taste and conscience to set aside the conventional aversion to labor; such an appeal is made from time to time by well-meaning and sanguine persons, and some fitful results have been achieved in that way. But the commonplace, common-sense man is bound by the deliverances of common-sense decorum on this head – the heritage of an unbroken cultural line of descent that runs back to the beginning.

Selection 17

The beginnings of ownership

Source: *American Journal of Sociology*, November 1898
(vol. 4, pp. 352–65).

Veblen (1898f)

In the accepted economic theories the ground of ownership is commonly conceived to be the productive labor of the owner. This is taken, without reflection or question, to be the legitimate basis of property; he who has produced a useful thing should possess and enjoy it. On this head the socialists and the economists of the classical line – the two extremes of economic speculation – are substantially at one. The point is not in controversy, or at least it has not been until recently; it has been accepted as an axiomatic premise. With the socialists it has served as the ground of their demand that the laborer should receive the full product of his labor. To classical economists the axiom has, perhaps, been as much trouble as it has been worth. It has given them no end of bother to explain how the capitalist is the "producer" of the goods that pass into his possession, and how it is true that the laborer gets what he produces. Sporadic instances of ownership quite dissociated from creative industry are recognized and taken account of as departures from the normal; they are due to disturbing causes. The main position is scarcely questioned, that in the normal case wealth is distributed in proportion to – and in some cogent sense because of – the recipient's contribution to the product.

Not only is the productive labor of the owner the definitive ground of his ownership today, but the derivation of the institution of property is similarly traced to the productive labor of that putative savage hunter who produced two deer or one beaver or twelve fish. The conjectural history of the origin of property, so far as it has been written by the economists, has been constructed out of conjecture proceeding on the preconceptions of Natural Rights and a coercive Order of Nature. To anyone who approaches the question of ownership with only an incidental interest in its solution (as is true of the classical, pre-evolutionary economists), and fortified with the preconceptions [353] of natural rights, all this seems plain. It sufficiently accounts for the institution, both in point of logical derivation and in point of historical development. The "natural" owner is the person who has "produced" an article, or who, by a constructively equivalent expenditure of productive force, has found and appropriated an object. It is conceived that such a person becomes the owner of the article by virtue of the immediate logical inclusion of the idea of ownership under the idea of creative industry.

This natural-rights theory of property makes the creative effort of an isolated, self-sufficing individual the basis of the ownership vested in him. In so
doing it overlooks the fact that there is no isolated, self-sufficing individual.
All production is, in fact, a production in and by the help of the community,
and all wealth is such only in society. Within the human period of the race
development, it is safe to say, no individual has fallen into industrial isolation,
so as to produce any one useful article by his own independent effort alone.
Even where there is no mechanical coöperation, men are always guided by
the experience of others. The only possible exceptions to this rule are those
instances of lost or cast-off children nourished by wild beasts, of which half-
authenticated accounts have gained currency from time to time. But the
anomalous, half-hypothetical life of these waifs can scarcely have affected
social development to the extent of originating the institution of ownership.

Production takes place only in society – only through the coöperation of an
industrial community. This industrial community may be large or small; its
limits are commonly somewhat vaguely defined; but it always comprises a
group large enough to contain and transmit the traditions, tools, technical
knowledge, and usages without which there can be no industrial organization
and no economic relation of individuals to one another or to their environment. The isolated individual is not a productive agent. What he can do at
best is to live from season to season, as the non-gregarious animals do. There
can be no production without technical knowledge; hence no accumulation
and no wealth to be owned, in severalty or otherwise. [354] And there is no
technical knowledge apart from an industrial community. Since there is no
individual production and no individual productivity, the natural-rights preconception that ownership rests on the individually productive labor of the
owner reduces itself to absurdity, even under the logic of its own assumptions.

Some writers who have taken up the question from the ethnological side
hold that the institution is to be traced to the customary use of weapons and
ornaments by individuals. Others have found its origin in the social group's
occupation of a given piece of land, which it held forcibly against intruders,
and which it came in this way to "own." The latter hypothesis bases the collective ownership of land on a collective act of seizure, or tenure by prowess,
so that it differs fundamentally from the view which bases ownership on
productive labor.

The view that ownership is an outgrowth of the customary consumption of
such things as weapons and ornaments by individuals is well supported by
appearances and has also the qualified sanction of the natural-rights preconception. The usages of all known primitive tribes seem at first sight
to bear out this view. In all communities the individual members exercise a
more or less unrestrained right of use and abuse over their weapons, if they
have any, as well as over many articles of ornament, clothing, and the toilet.
In the eyes of the modern economist this usage would count as ownership. So
that, if the question is construed to be simply a question of material fact, as
to the earliest emergence of usages which would in the latter-day classification

be brought under the head of ownership, then it would have to be said that ownership must have begun with the conversion of these articles to individual use. But the question will have to be answered in the contrary sense if we shift our ground to the point of view of the primitive men whose institutions are under review. The point in question is the origin of the institution of ownership, as it first takes shape in the habits of thought of the early barbarian. The question concerns the derivation of the idea of ownership or property. What is of interest for the present purpose is not whether we, [355] with our preconceptions, would look upon the relation of the primitive savage or barbarian to his slight personal effects as a relation of ownership, but whether that is his own apprehension of the matter. It is a question as to the light in which the savage himself habitually views these objects that pertain immediately to his person and are set apart for his habitual use. Like all questions of the derivation of institutions, it is essentially a question of folk-psychology, not of mechanical fact; and, when so conceived, it must be answered in the negative.

The unsophisticated man, whether savage or civilized, is prone to conceive phenomena in terms of personality; these being terms with which he has a first-hand acquaintance. This habit is more unbroken in the savage than in civilized men. All obvious manifestations of force are apprehended as expressions of conation – effort put forth for a purpose by some agency similar to the human will. The point of view of the archaic culture is that of forceful, pervading personality, whose unfolding life is the substantial fact held in view in every relation into which men or things enter. This point of view in large measure shapes and colors all the institutions of the early culture – and in a less degree the later phases of culture. Under the guidance of this habit of thought, the relation of any individual to his personal effects is conceived to be of a more intimate kind than that of ownership simply. Ownership is too external and colorless a term to describe the fact.

In the apprehension of the savage and the barbarian the limits of his person do not coincide with the limits which modern biological science would recognize. His individuality is conceived to cover, somewhat vaguely and uncertainly, a pretty wide fringe of facts and objects that pertain to him more or less immediately. To our sense of the matter these items lie outside the limits of his person, and to many of them we would conceive him to stand in an economic rather than in an organic relation. This quasi-personal fringe of facts and objects commonly comprises the man's shadow; the reflection of his image in water or any similar surface; his name; his peculiar tattoo [356] marks; his totem, if he has one; his glance; his breath, especially when it is visible; the print of his hand and foot; the sound of his voice; any image or representation of his person; any excretions or exhalations from his person; parings of his nails; cuttings of his hair; his ornaments and amulets; clothing that is in daily use, especially what has been shaped to his person, and more particularly if there is wrought into it any totemic or other design peculiar to him; his weapons, especially his favorite weapons and those which he habitually carries. Beyond these there is a great number of other, remoter things which may or may not be included in the quasi-personal fringe.

As regards this entire range of facts and objects, it is to be said that the "zone of influence" of the individual's personality is not conceived to cover them all with the same degree of potency; his individuality shades off by insensible, penumbral gradations into the external world. The objects and facts that fall within the quasi-personal fringe figure in the habits of thought of the savage as personal to him in a vital sense. They are not a congeries of things to which he stands in an economic relation and to which he has an equitable, legal claim. These articles are conceived to be his in much the same sense as his hands and feet are his, or his pulse-beat, or his digestion, or the heat of his body, or the motions of his limbs or brain.

For the satisfaction of any who may be inclined to question this view, appeal may be taken to the usages of almost any people. Some such notion of a pervasive personality, or a penumbra of personality, is implied, for instance, in the giving and keeping of presents and mementos. It is more indubitably present in the working of charms; in all sorcery; in the sacraments and similar devout observances; in such practices as the Tibetan prayer-wheel; in the adoration of relics, images, and symbols; in the almost universal veneration of consecrated places and structures; in astrology; in divination by means of hair-cuttings, nail-parings, photographs, etc. Perhaps the least debatable evidence of belief in such a quasi-personal fringe is afforded by the practices of sympathetic magic; and the practices are strikingly similar in substance the world over – from [357] the love-charm to the sacrament. Their substantial ground is the belief that a desired effect can be wrought upon a given person through the means of some object lying within his quasi-personal fringe. The person who is approached in this way may be a fellow-mortal, or it may be some potent spiritual agent whose intercession is sought for good or ill. If the sorcerer or anyone who works a charm can in any way get at the "penumbra" of a person's individuality, as embodied in his fringe of quasi-personal facts, he will be able to work good or ill to the person to whom the fact or object pertains; and the magic rites performed to this end will work their effect with greater force and precision in proportion as the object which affords the point of attack is more intimately related to the person upon whom the effect is to be wrought. An economic relation, simply, does not afford a handle for sorcery. It may be set down that whenever the relation of a person to a given object is made use of for the purposes of sympathetic magic, the relation is conceived to be something more vital than simple legal ownership.

Such meager belongings of the primitive savage as would under the nomenclature of a later day be classed as personal property are not thought of by him as his property at all; they pertain organically to his person. Of the things comprised in his quasi-personal fringe all do not pertain to him with the same degree of intimacy or persistency; but those articles which are more remotely or more doubtfully included under his individuality are not therefore conceived to be partly organic to him and partly his property simply. The alternative does not lie between this organic relation and ownership. It may easily happen that a given article lying along the margin of the quasi-personal fringe is eliminated from it and is alienated, either by default through lapse of time or by voluntary severance of the relation. But when this happens the article is not conceived to escape from the organic relation into a remoter category of things that are owned by and external to the person in question. If an object escapes in this way from the organic sphere of one person, it may pass into the sphere of another; or, if it is an [358] article that lends itself to common use, it may pass into the common stock of the community.

As regards this common stock, no concept of ownership, either communal or individual, applies in the primitive community. The idea of a communal ownership is of relatively late growth, and must by psychological necessity have been preceded by the idea of individual ownership. Ownership is an accredited discretionary power over an object on the ground of a conventional claim; it implies that the owner is a personal agent who takes thought for the disposal of the object owned. A personal agent is an individual, and it is only by an eventual refinement – of the nature of a legal fiction – that any group of men is conceived to exercise a corporate discretion over objects. Ownership implies an individual owner. It is only by reflection, and by extending the scope of a concept which is already familiar, that a quasi-personal corporate discretion and control of this kind comes to be imputed to a group of persons. Corporate ownership is quasi-ownership only; it is therefore necessarily a derivative concept, and cannot have preceded the concept of individual ownership of which it is a counterfeit.

After the idea of ownership has been elaborated and has gained some consistency, it is not unusual to find the notion of pervasion by the user's personality applied to articles owned by him. At the same time a given article may also be recognized as lying within the quasi-personal fringe of one person while it is owned by another – as, for instance, ornaments and other articles of daily use which in a personal sense belong to a slave or to an inferior member of a patriarchal household, but which as property belong to the master or head of the household. The two categories, (*a*) things to which one's personality extends by way of pervasion and (*b*) things owned, by no means coincide; nor does the one supplant the other. The two ideas are so far from identical that the same object may belong to one person under the one concept and to another person under the other; and, on the other hand, the same person may stand in both relations to a given object without the one concept being lost in the other. A given article may change owners without passing out of the [359] quasi-personal fringe of the person under whose "self" it has belonged, as, for instance, a photograph or any other memento. A familiar instance is the mundane ownership of any consecrated place or structure which in the personal sense belongs to the saint or deity to whom it is sacred.

The two concepts are so far distinct, or even disparate, as to make it extremely improbable that the one has been developed out of the other by a process of growth. A transition involving such a substitution of ideas could scarcely take place except on some notable impulse from without. Such a step would amount to the construction of a new category and a reclassification of certain selected facts under the new head. The impulse to reclassify the facts and things that are comprised in the quasi-personal fringe, so as to place some of them, together with certain other things, under the new category of ownership, must come from some constraining exigency of later growth than the concept whose province it invades. The new category is not simply an amplified form of the old. Not every item that was originally conceived to belong to an individual by way of pervasion comes to be counted as an item of his wealth after the idea of wealth has come into vogue. Such items, for instance, as a person's footprint, or his image or effigy, or his name, are very tardily included under the head of articles owned by him, if they are eventually included at all. It is a fortuitous circumstance if they come to be owned by him, but they long continue to hold their place in his quasi-personal fringe. The disparity of the two concepts is well brought out by the case of the domestic animals. These non-human individuals are incapable of ownership, but there is imputed to them the attribute of a pervasive individuality, which extends to such items as their footprints, their stalls, clippings of hair, and the like. These items are made use of for the purposes of sympathetic magic even in modern civilized communities. An illustration that may show this disparity between ownership and pervasion in a still stronger light is afforded by the vulgar belief that the moon's phases may have a propitious or sinister effect on human affairs. The inconstant moon is conceived to work good or ill through a [360] sympathetic influence or spiritual infection which suggests a quasi-personal fringe, but which assuredly does not imply ownership on her part.

Ownership is not a simple and instinctive notion that is naïvely included under the notion of productive effort on the one hand, nor under that of habitual use on the other. It is not something given to begin with, as an item of the isolated individual's mental furniture; something which has to be unlearned in part when men come to coöperate in production and make working arrangements and mutual renunciations under the stress of associated life – after the manner imputed by the social-contract theory. It is a conventional fact and has to be learned; it is a cultural fact which has grown into an institution in the past through a long course of habituation, and which is transmitted from generation to generation as all cultural facts are.

On going back a little way into the cultural history of our own past, we come upon a situation which says that the fact of a person's being engaged in industry was *prima facie* evidence that he could own nothing. Under serfdom and slavery those who work cannot own, and those who own cannot work. Even very recently – culturally speaking – there was no suspicion that a woman's work, in the patriarchal household, should entitle her to own the products of her work. Farther back in the barbarian culture, while the patriarchal household was in better preservation than it is now, this position was accepted with more unquestioning faith. The head of the household alone could hold property; and even the scope of his ownership was greatly qualified if he had a feudal superior. The tenure of property is a tenure by prowess, on the one hand, and a tenure by sufferance at the hands of a superior, on the other hand. The recourse to prowess as the definitive basis of tenure becomes more immediate and more habitual the farther the development is traced back into the early barbarian culture; until, on the lower levels of barbarism or the upper levels of savagery, "the good old plan" prevails with but little mitigation. There are always certain conventions, a certain understanding as to what are the [361] legitimate conditions and circumstances that surround ownership and its transmission, chief among which is the fact of habitual acceptance. What has been currently accepted as the *status quo* – vested interest – is right and good so long as it does not meet a challenge backed by irresistible force. Property rights sanctioned by immemorial usage are inviolable, as all immemorial usage is, except in the face of forcible dispossession. But seizure and forcible retention very shortly gain the legitimation of usage, and the resulting tenure becomes inviolable through habituation. *Beati possidentes.*

Throughout the barbarian culture, where this tenure by prowess prevails, the population falls into two economic classes: those engaged in industrial employments, and those engaged in such non-industrial pursuits as war, government, sports, and religious observances. In the earlier and more naïve stages of barbarism the former, in the normal case, own nothing; the latter own such property as they have seized, or such as has, under the sanction of usage, descended upon them from their forebears who seized and held it. At a still lower level of culture, in the primitive savage horde, the population is not similarly divided into economic classes. There is no leisure class resting its prerogative on coercion, prowess, and immemorial status; and there is also no ownership.

It will hold as a rough generalization that in communities where there is no invidious distinction between employments, as exploit, on the one hand, and drudgery, on the other, there is also no tenure of property. In the cultural sequence, ownership does not begin before the rise of a canon of exploit; but it is to be added that it also does not seem to begin with the first beginning of exploit as a manly occupation. In these very rude early communities, especially in the unpropertied hordes of peaceable savages, the rule is that the product of any member's effort is consumed by the group to which he belongs; and it is consumed collectively or indiscriminately, without question of individual right or ownership. The question of ownership is not brought up by the fact that an article has been produced or is at hand in finished form for consumption. [362]

The earliest occurrence of ownership seems to fall in the early stages of barbarism, and the emergence of the institution of ownership is apparently a concomitant of the transition from a peaceable to a predatory habit of life. It is a prerogative of that class in the barbarian culture which leads a life of exploit rather than of industry. The pervading characteristic of the barbarian culture, as distinguished from the peaceable phase of life that precedes it, is the element of exploit, coercion, and seizure. In its earlier phases ownership is this habit of coercion and seizure reduced to system and consistency under the surveillance of usage.

The practice of seizing and accumulating goods on individual account could not have come into vogue to the extent of founding a new institution under the peaceable communistic régime of primitive savagery; for the dissensions arising from any such resort to mutual force and fraud among its members would have been fatal to the group. For a similar reason individual ownership of consumable goods could not come in with the first beginnings of predatory life; for the primitive fighting horde still needs to consume its scanty means of subsistence in common, in order to give the collective horde its full fighting efficiency. Otherwise it would succumb before any rival horde that had not yet given up collective consumption.

With the advent of predatory life comes the practice of plundering – of seizing goods from the enemy. But in order that the plundering habit should give rise to individual ownership of the things seized, these things must be goods of a somewhat lasting kind, and not immediately consumable means of subsistence. Under the primitive culture the means of subsistence are habitually consumed in common by the group, and the manner in which such goods are consumed is fixed according to an elaborate system of usage. This usage is not readily broken over, for it is a substantial part of the habits of life of every individual member. The practice of collective consumption is at the same time necessary to the survival of the group, and this necessity is present in men's minds and exercises a surveillance over the formation of habits of thought as to what is right [363] and seemly. Any propensity to aggression at this early stage will, therefore, not assert itself in the seizure and retention of consumable goods; nor does the temptation to do so readily present itself, since the idea of individual appropriation of a store of goods is alien to the archaic man's general habits of thought.

The idea of property is not readily attached to anything but tangible and lasting articles. It is only where commercial development is well advanced – where bargain and sale is a large feature in the community's life – that the more perishable articles of consumption are thought of as items of wealth at all. The still more evanescent results of personal service are still more difficult to bring in under the idea of wealth. So much so that the attempt to classify services as wealth is meaningless to laymen, and even the adept economists hold a divided opinion as to the intelligibility of such a classification. In the commonsense apprehension the idea of property is not currently attached to any but tangible, vendible goods of some durability. This is true even in modern civilized communities, where pecuniary ideas and the pecuniary point of view prevail. In a like manner and for a like reason, in an earlier, non-commercial phase of culture there is less occasion for and greater difficulty in applying the concept of ownership to anything but obviously durable articles.

But durable articles of use and consumption which are seized in the raids of a predatory horde are either articles of general use or they are articles of immediate and continued personal use to the person who has seized them. In the former case the goods are consumed in common by the group, without giving rise to a notion of ownership; in the latter case they fall into the class of things that pertain organically to the person of their user, and they would, therefore, not figure as items of property or make up a store of wealth.

It is difficult to see how an institution of ownership could have arisen in the early days of predatory life through the seizure of goods, but the case is different with the seizure of persons. Captives are items that do not fit into the scheme of communal [364] consumption, and their appropriation by their individual captor works no manifest detriment to the group. At the same time these captives continue to be obviously distinct from their captor in point of individuality, and so are not readily brought in under the quasi-personal fringe. The captives taken under rude conditions are chiefly women. There are good reasons for this. Except where there is a slave class of men, the women are more useful, as well as more easily controlled, in the primitive group. Their labor is worth more to the group than their maintenance, and as they do not carry weapons, they are less formidable than men captives would be. They serve the purpose of trophies very effectually, and it is therefore worth while for their captor to trace and keep in evidence his relation to them as their captor. To this end he maintains an attitude of dominance and coercion toward women captured by him; and, as being the insignia of his prowess, he does not suffer them to stand at the beck and call of rival warriors. They are fit subjects for command and constraint; it ministers to both his honor and his vanity to domineer over them, and their utility in this respect is very great. But his domineering over them is the evidence of his prowess, and it is incompatible with their utility as trophies that other men should take the liberties with his women which serve as evidence of the coercive relation of captor.

When the practice hardens into custom, the captor comes to exercise a customary right to exclusive use and abuse over the women he has seized; and this customary right of use and abuse over an object which is obviously not an organic part of his person constitutes the relation of ownership, as naïvely apprehended. After this usage of capture has found its way into the habits of the community, the women so held in constraint and in evidence will commonly fall into a conventionally recognized marriage relation with their captor. The result is a new form of marriage, in which the man is master. This ownership-marriage seems to be the original both of private property and of the patriarchal household. Both of these great institutions are, accordingly, of an emulative origin.

The varying details of the development whereby ownership [365] extends to other persons than captured women cannot be taken up here; neither can the further growth of the marriage institution that came into vogue at the same time with ownership. Probably at a point in the economic evolution not far subsequent to the definitive installation of the institution of ownership-marriage comes, as its consequence, the ownership of consumable goods. The women held in servile marriage not only render personal service to their master, but they are also employed in the production of articles of use. All the non-combatant or ignoble members of the community are habitually so employed. And when the habit of looking upon and claiming the persons identified with my invidious interest, or subservient to me, as "mine" has become an accepted and integral part of men's habits of thought, it becomes a relatively easy matter to extend this newly achieved concept of ownership to the products of the labor performed by the persons so held in ownership. And the same propensity for emulation which bears so great a part in shaping the original institution of ownership extends its action to the new category of things owned. Not only are the products of the women's labor claimed and valued for their serviceability in furthering the comfort and fullness of life of the master, but they are valuable also as a conspicuous evidence of his possessing many and efficient servants, and they are therefore useful as an evidence of his superior force. The appropriation and accumulation of consumable goods could scarcely have come into vogue as a direct outgrowth of the primitive horde-communism, but it comes in as an easy and unobtrusive consequence of the ownership of persons.

Selection 18

The barbarian status of women

Source: *American Journal of Sociology*, January 1899
(vol. 4, pp. 503–14).

Veblen (1899a)

It seems altogether probable that in the primitive groups of mankind, when
the race first took to a systematic use of tools and so emerged upon the
properly human plane of life, there was but the very slightest beginning
of a system of status, with little of invidious distinction between classes
and little of a corresponding division of employments. In an earlier paper,
published in this journal,[1] it has been argued that the early division of labor
between classes comes in as the result of an increasing efficiency of labor,
due to a growing effectiveness in the use of tools. When, in the early cultural
development, the use of tools and the technical command of material
forces had reached a certain degree of effectiveness, the employments
which occupy the primitive community would fall into two distinct groups –
(*a*) the honorific employments, which involve a large element of prowess, and
(*b*) the humiliating employments, which call for diligence and into which the
sturdier virtues do not enter. An appreciable advance in the use of tools must
precede this differentiation of employments, because (1) without effective
tools (including weapons) men are not sufficiently formidable in conflict with
the ferocious beasts to devote themselves so exclusively to the hunting
of large game as to develop that occupation into a conventional mode of
life reserved for a distinct class; (2) without tools of some efficiency, industry
is not productive enough to support a dense population, and therefore
the groups into which the population gathers will not come into such a
habitual hostile contact with one another as would give rise to a life of
warlike prowess; (3) until industrial methods and knowledge have made
some advance, the work of getting a livelihood is too exacting to admit
of the consistent exemption of any portion of the community from
vulgar labor; [504] (4) the inefficient primitive industry yields no such disposable surplus of accumulated goods as would be worth fighting for, or
would tempt an intruder, and therefore there is little provocation to warlike
prowess.

1 "The Instinct of Workmanship and the Irksomeness of Labor," [*American Journal of Sociology*],
September, 1898. [Selection 16 in this volume.]

With the growth of industry comes the possibility of a predatory life; and if the groups of savages crowd one another in the struggle for subsistence, there is a provocation to hostilities, and a predatory habit of life ensues. There is a consequent growth of a predatory culture, which may for the present purpose be treated as the beginning of the barbarian culture. This predatory culture shows itself in a growth of suitable institutions. The group divides itself conventionally into a fighting and a peace-keeping class, with a corresponding division of labor. Fighting, together with other work that involves a serious element of exploit, becomes the employment of the able-bodied men; the uneventful everyday work of the group falls to the women and the infirm.

In such a community the standards of merit and propriety rest on an invidious distinction between those who are capable fighters and those who are not. Infirmity, that is to say incapacity for exploit, is looked down upon. One of the early consequences of this deprecation of infirmity is a tabu on women and on women's employments. In the apprehension of the archaic, animistic barbarian, infirmity is infectious. The infection may work its mischievous effect both by sympathetic influence and by transfusion. Therefore it is well for the able-bodied man who is mindful of his virility to shun all undue contact and conversation with the weaker sex and to avoid all contamination with the employments that are characteristic of the sex. Even the habitual food of women should not be eaten by men, lest their force be thereby impaired. The injunction against womanly employments and foods and against intercourse with women applies with especial rigor during the season of preparation for any work of manly exploit, such as a great hunt or a warlike raid, or induction into some manly dignity or society or mystery. Illustrations of this seasonal tabu abound in the early history of all peoples that have had a warlike or barbarian past. [505] The women, their occupations, their food and clothing, their habitual place in the house or village, and in extreme cases even their speech, become ceremonially unclean to the men. This imputation of ceremonial uncleanness on the ground of their infirmity has lasted on in the later culture as a sense of the unworthiness or Levitical inadequacy of women; so that even now we feel the impropriety of women taking rank with men, or representing the community in any relation that calls for dignity and ritual competency; as for instance, in priestly or diplomatic offices, or even in representative civil offices, and likewise, and for a like reason, in such offices of domestic and body servants as are of a seriously ceremonial character – footmen, butlers, etc.

The changes that take place in the everyday experiences of a group or horde when it passes from a peaceable to a predatory habit of life have their effect on the habits of thought prevalent in the group. As the hostile contact of one group with another becomes closer and more habitual, the predatory activity and the bellicose animus become more habitual to the members of the group. Fighting comes more and more to occupy men's everyday thoughts, and the other activities of the group fall into the background and become subsidiary to the fighting activity. In the popular apprehension the substantial core of such a group – that on which men's thoughts run when the community and the community's life is thought of – is the body of fighting men. The collective fighting capacity becomes the most serious question that occupies men's minds, and gives the point of view from which persons and conduct are rated. The scheme of life of such a group is substantially a scheme of exploit. There is much of this point of view to be found even in the common-sense views held by modern populations. The inclination to identify the community with its fighting men comes into evidence today whenever warlike interests occupy the popular attention in an appreciable degree.

The work of the predatory barbarian group is gradually specialized and differentiated under the dominance of this ideal of prowess, so as to give rise to a system of status in which the non-fighters [506] fall into a position of subservience to the fighters. The accepted scheme of life or consensus of opinions which guides the conduct of men in such a predatory group and decides what may properly be done, of course comprises a great variety of details; but it is, after all, a single scheme – a more or less organic whole – so that the life carried on under its guidance in any case makes up a somewhat consistent and characteristic body of culture. This is necessarily the case, because of the simple fact that the individuals between whom the consensus holds are individuals. The thinking of each one is the thinking of the same individual, on whatever head and in whatever direction his thinking may run. Whatever may be the immediate point or object of his thinking, the frame of mind which governs his aim and manner of reasoning in passing on any given point of conduct is, on the whole, the habitual frame of mind which experience and tradition have enforced upon him. Individuals whose sense of what is right and good departs widely from the accepted views suffer some repression, and in case of an extreme divergence they are eliminated from the effective life of the group through ostracism. Where the fighting class is in the position of dominance and prescriptive legitimacy, the canons of conduct are shaped chiefly by the common sense of the body of fighting men. Whatever conduct and whatever code of proprieties has the authentication of this common sense is definitively right and good, for the time being, and the deliverances of this common sense are, in their turn, shaped by the habits of life of the able-bodied men. Habitual conflict acts, by selection and by habituation, to make these male members tolerant of any infliction of damage and suffering. Habituation to the sight and infliction of suffering, and to the emotions that go with fights and brawls, may even end in making the spectacle of misery a pleasing diversion to them. The result is in any case a more or less consistent attitude of plundering and coercion on the part of the fighting body, and this animus is incorporated into the scheme of life of the community. The discipline of predatory life makes for an attitude of mastery on the part of the able-bodied men in all their relations with the weaker members of the group, and especially in their [507] relations with the women. Men who are trained in predatory ways of life and modes of thinking come by habituation to apprehend this form of the relation between the sexes as good and beautiful.

All the women in the group will share in the class repression and depreciation that belongs to them as women, but the status of women taken from hostile groups has an additional feature. Such a woman not only belongs to a subservient and low class, but she also stands in a special relation to her captor. She is a trophy of the raid, and therefore an evidence of exploit, and on this ground it is to her captor's interest to maintain a peculiarly obvious relation of mastery toward her. And since, in the early culture, it does not detract from her subservience to the life of the group, this peculiar relation of the captive to her captor will meet but slight, if any, objection from the other members of the group. At the same time, since his peculiar coercive relation to the woman serves to mark her as a trophy of his exploit, he will somewhat jealously resent any similar freedom taken by other men, or any attempt on their part to parade a similar coercive authority over her, and so usurp the laurels of his prowess, very much as a warrior would under like circumstances resent a usurpation or an abuse of the scalps or skulls which he had taken from the enemy.

After the habit of appropriating captured women has hardened into custom, and so given rise on the one hand to a form of marriage resting on coercion, and on the other hand to a concept of ownership,[2] a development of certain secondary features of the institution so inaugurated is to be looked for. In time this coercive ownership-marriage receives the sanction of the popular taste and morality. It comes to rest in men's habits of thought as the right form of marriage relation, and it comes at the same time to be gratifying to men's sense of beauty and of honor. The growing predilection for mastery and coercion, as a manly trait, together with the growing moral and æsthetic approbation of marriage on a basis of coercion and ownership, [508] will affect the tastes of the men most immediately and most strongly; but since the men are the superior class, whose views determine the current views of the community, their common sense in the matter will shape the current canons of taste in its own image. The tastes of the women also, in point of morality and of propriety alike, will presently be affected in the same way. Through the precept and example of those who make the vogue, and through selective repression of those who are unable to accept it, the institution of ownership-marriage makes its way into definitive acceptance as the only beautiful and virtuous form of the relation. As the conviction of its legitimacy grows stronger in each succeeding generation, it comes to be appreciated unreflectingly as a deliverance of common sense and enlightened reason that the good and beautiful attitude of the man toward the woman is an attitude of coercion. "None but the brave deserve the fair."

---

2 For a more detailed discussion on this point see a paper on "The Beginnings of Ownership" in this journal [*American Journal of Sociology*], November, 1898. [Selection 17 in this volume.]

As the predatory habit of life gains a more unquestioned and undivided sway, other forms of the marriage relation fall under a polite odium. The masterless, unattached woman consequently loses caste. It becomes imperative for all men who would stand well in the eyes of their fellows to attach some woman or women to themselves by the honorable bonds of seizure. In order to a decent standing in the community a man is required to enter into this virtuous and honorific relation of ownership-marriage, and a publicly acknowledged marriage relation which has not the sanction of capture becomes unworthy of able-bodied men. But as the group increases in size, the difficulty of providing wives by capture becomes very great, and it becomes necessary to find a remedy that shall save the requirements of decency and at the same time permit the marriage of women from within the group. To this end the status of women married from within the group is sought to be mended by a mimic or ceremonial capture. The ceremonial capture effects an assimilation of the free woman into the more acceptable class of women who are attached by bonds of coercion to some master, and so gives a ceremonial legitimacy and decency to the resulting marriage relation. The probable motive for adopting the free women into the honorable [509] class of bond women in this way is not primarily a wish to improve their standing or their lot, but rather a wish to keep those good men in countenance who, for dearth of captives, are constrained to seek a substitute from among the home-bred women of the group. The inclinations of men in high standing who are possessed of marriageable daughters would run in the same direction. It would not seem right that a woman of high birth should irretrievably be outclassed by any chance-comer from outside.

According to this view, marriage by feigned capture within the tribe is a case of mimicry – "protective mimicry," to borrow a phrase from the naturalists. It is substantially a case of adoption. As is the case in all human relations where adoption is practiced, this adoption of the free women into the class of the unfree proceeds by as close an imitation as may be of the original fact for which it is a substitute. And as in other cases of adoption, the ceremonial performance is by no means looked upon as a fatuous make-believe. The barbarian has implicit faith in the efficiency of imitation and ceremonial execution as a means of compassing a desired end. The entire range of magic and religious rites is testimony to that effect. He looks upon external objects and sequences naïvely, as organic and individual things, and as expressions of a propensity working toward an end. The unsophisticated common sense of the primitive barbarian apprehends sequences and events in terms of will-power or inclination. As seen in the light of this animistic preconception, any process is substantially teleological, and the propensity imputed to it will not be thwarted of its legitimate end after the course of events in which it expresses itself has once fallen into shape or got under way. It follows logically, as a matter of course, that if once the motions leading to a desired consummation have been rehearsed in the accredited form and sequence, the same substantial result will be attained as that produced by the process imitated. This is the ground of whatever efficiency is imputed to ceremonial observances on all planes of culture, and it is especially the chief element in formal adoption and initiation. Hence, probably, the practice of mock-seizure or [510] mock-capture, and hence the formal profession of fealty and submission on the part of the woman in the marriage rites of peoples among whom the household with a male head prevails. This form of the household is almost always associated with some survival or reminiscence of wife-capture. In all such cases, marriage is, by derivation, a ritual of initiation into servitude. In the words of the formula, even after it has been appreciably softened under the latter-day decay of the sense of status, it is the woman's place to love, honor, and obey.

According to this view, the patriarchal household, or, in other words, the household with a male head, is an outgrowth of emulation between the members of a warlike community. It is, therefore, in point of derivation, a predatory institution. The ownership and control of women is a gratifying evidence of prowess and high standing. In logical consistency, therefore, the greater the number of women so held, the greater the distinction which their possession confers upon their master. Hence the prevalence of polygamy, which occurs almost universally at one stage of culture among peoples which have the male household. There may, of course, be other reasons for polygamy, but the ideal development of polygamy which is met with in the harems of very powerful patriarchal despots and chieftains can scarcely be explained on other grounds. But whether it works out in a system of polygamy or not, the male household is in any case a detail of a system of status under which the women are included in the class of unfree subjects. The dominant feature in the institutional structure of these communities is that of status, and the groundwork of their economic life is a rigorous system of ownership.

The institution is found at its best, or in its most effectual development, in the communities in which status and ownership prevail with the least mitigation; and with the decline of the sense of status and of the extreme pretensions of ownership, such as has been going on for some time past in the communities of the western culture, the institution of the patriarchal household has also suffered something of a disintegration. There has been some weakening and slackening of the bonds, and this [511] deterioration is most visible in the communities which have departed farthest from the ancient system of status, and have gone farthest in reorganizing their economic life on the lines of industrial freedom. And the deference for an indissoluble tie of ownership-marriage, as well as the sense of its definitive virtuousness, has suffered the greatest decline among the classes immediately engaged in the modern industries. So that there seems to be fair ground for saying that the habits of thought fostered by modern industrial life are, on the whole, not favorable to the maintenance of this institution or to that status of women which the institution in its best development implies. The days of its best development are in the past, and the discipline of modern life – if not supplemented by a prudent inculcation of conservative ideals – will scarcely afford the psychological basis for its rehabilitation.

This form of marriage, or of ownership, by which the man becomes the head of the household, the owner of the woman, and the owner and discretionary consumer of the household's output of consumable goods, does not of necessity imply a patriarchal system of consanguinity. The presence or absence of maternal relationship should, therefore, not be given definite weight in this connection. The male household, in some degree of elaboration, may well coexist with a counting of relationship in the female line, as, for instance, among many North American tribes. But where this is the case it seems probable that the ownership of women, together with the invidious distinctions of status from which the practice of such an ownership springs, has come into vogue at so late a stage of the cultural development that the maternal system of relationship had already been thoroughly incorporated into the tribe's scheme of life. The male household in such cases is ordinarily not developed in good form or entirely free from traces of a maternal household. The traces of a maternal household which are found in these cases commonly point to a form of marriage which disregards the man rather than places him under the surveillance of the woman. It may well be named the household of the unattached woman. This condition of things argues that the tribe or race in question [512] has entered upon a predatory life only after a considerable period of peaceable industrial life, and after having achieved a considerable development of social structure under the régime of peace and industry, whereas the unqualified prevalence of the patriarchate, together with the male household, may be taken to indicate that the predatory phase was entered early, culturally speaking.

Where the patriarchal system is in force in fully developed form, including the paternal household, and hampered with no indubitable survivals of a maternal household or a maternal system of relationship, the presumption would be that the people in question has entered upon the predatory culture early, and has adopted the institutions of private property and class prerogative at an early stage of its economic development. On the other hand, where there are well-preserved traces of a maternal household, the presumption is that the predatory phase has been entered by the community in question at a relatively late point in its life history, even if the patriarchal system is, and long has been, the prevalent system of relationship. In the latter case the community, or the group of tribes, may, perhaps for geographical reasons, not have independently attained the predatory culture in accentuated form, but may at a relatively late date have contracted the agnatic system and the paternal household through contact with another, higher, or characteristically different, culture, which has included these institutions among its cultural furniture. The required contact would take place most effectually by way of invasion and conquest by an alien race occupying the higher plane or divergent line of culture. Something of this kind is the probable explanation, for instance, of the equivocal character of the household and relationship system in the early Germanic culture, especially as it is seen in such outlying regions as Scandinavia. The evidence, in this latter case, as in some other communities lying farther south, is somewhat obscure, but it points to a long-continued coexistence of the two forms of the household; of which the maternal seems to have held its place most tenaciously among the subject or lower classes of the population, while the [513] paternal was the honorable form of marriage in vogue among the superior class. In the earliest traceable situation of these tribes there appears to have been a relatively feeble, but growing, preponderance of the male household throughout the community. This mixture of marriage institutions, as well as the correlative mixture or ambiguity of property institutions associated with it in the Germanic culture, seems most easily explicable as being due to the mingling of two distinct racial stocks, whose institutions differed in these respects. The race or tribe which had the maternal household and common property would probably have been the more numerous and the more peaceable at the time the mixing process began, and would fall into some degree of subjection to its more warlike consort race.

No attempt is hereby made to account for the various forms of human marriage, or to show how the institution varies in detail from place to place and from time to time, but only to indicate what seems to have been the range of motives and of exigencies that have given rise to the paternal household, as it has been handed down from the barbarian past of the peoples of the western culture. To this end, nothing but the most general features of the life history of the institution have been touched upon, and even the evidence on which this much of generalization is based is, per force, omitted. The purpose of the argument is to point out that there is a close connection, particularly in point of psychological derivation, between individual ownership, the system of status, and the paternal household, as they appear in this culture.

This view of the derivation of private property and of the male household, as already suggested, does not imply the prior existence of a maternal household of the kind in which the woman is the head and master of a household group and exercises a discretionary control over her husband or husbands and over the household effects. Still less does it imply a prior state of promiscuity. What is implied by the hypothesis and by the scant evidence at hand is rather the form of the marriage relation above characterized as the household of the unattached woman. The characteristic feature of this marriage seems to [514] have been an absence of coercion or control in the relation between the sexes. The union (probably monogamic and more or less enduring) seems to have been terminable at will by either party, under the constraint of some slight conventional limitations. The substantial difference introduced into the marriage relation on the adoption of ownership-marriage is the exercise of coercion by the man and the loss on the part of the woman of the power to terminate the relation at will. Evidence running in this direction, and in part hitherto unpublished, is to be found both in the modern and in the earlier culture of Germanic communities.

It is only in cases where circumstances have, in an exceptional degree, favored the development of ownership-marriage that we should expect to find the institution worked out to its logical consequences. Wherever the predatory phase of social life has not come in early and has not prevailed in unqualified form for a long time, or wherever a social group or race with this form of the household has received a strong admixture of another race not possessed of the institution, there the prevalent form of marriage should show something of a departure from this paternal type. And even where neither of these two conditions is present, this type of the marriage relation might be expected in the course of time to break down with the change of circumstances, since it is an institution that has grown up as a detail of a system of status, and, there-fore, presumably fits into such a social system, but does not fit into a system of a different kind. It is at present visibly breaking down in modern civilized communities, apparently because it is at variance with the most ancient habits of thought of the race, as well as with the exigencies of a peaceful, industrial mode of life. There may seem some ground for holding that the same reas-sertion of ancient habits of thought which is now apparently at work to dis-integrate the institution of ownership-marriage may be expected also to work a disintegration of the correlative institution of private property; but that is perhaps a question of speculative curiosity rather than of urgent theoretical interest.

Selection 19

The preconceptions of economic science

Source: *Quarterly Journal of Economics*, January 1899 (vol. 13, pp. 121–50), July 1899 (vol. 13, pp. 396–426), February 1900 (vol. 14, pp. 240–69).

Veblen (1899b, 1899d, 1900a)

Part I

In an earlier paper[1] the view has been expressed that the economics handed down by the great writers of a past generation is substantially a taxonomic science. A view of much the same purport, so far as concerns the point here immediately in question, is presented in an admirably lucid and cogent way by Professor Clark in a recent number of this journal.[2] There is no wish hereby to burden Professor Clark with a putative sponsorship of any ungraceful or questionable generalizations reached in working outward from this main position, but expression may not be denied the comfort which his unintended authentication of the main position affords. It is true, Professor Clark does not speak of taxonomy, but employs the term [122] "statics," which is perhaps better suited to his immediate purpose. Nevertheless, in spite of the high authority given the term "statics," in this connection, through its use by Professor Clark and by other writers eminent in the science, it is fairly to be questioned whether the term can legitimately be used to characterize the received economic theories. The word is borrowed from the jargon of physics, where it is used to designate the theory of bodies at rest or of forces in equilibrium. But there is much in the received economic theories to which the analogy of bodies at rest or of forces in equilibrium will not apply. It is perhaps not too much to say that those articles of economic theory that do not lend themselves to this analogy make up the major portion of the received doctrines. So, for instance, it seems scarcely to the point to speak of the statics of production, exchange, consumption, circulation. There are, no doubt, appreciable elements in the theory of these several processes that may fairly be characterized as statical features of the theory; but the doctrines handed down are after all, in the main,

---

1 [Veblen,] "Why is Economics not an Evolutionary Science?" *Quarterly Journal of Economics*, July, 1898. [Selection 15 in this volume.].

2 [John Bates Clark,] "The Future of Economic Theory," *Quarterly Journal of Economics*, October, 1898.

theories of the process discussed under each head, and the theory of a process does not belong in statics. The epithet "statical" would, for instance, have to be wrenched somewhat ungently to make it apply to Quesnay's classic *Tableau Économique* or to the great body of Physiocratic speculations that take their rise from it. The like is true for Books II. and III. of Adam Smith's *Wealth of Nations*, as also for considerable portions of Ricardo's work, or, to come down to the present generation, for much of Marshall's *Principles*, and for such a modern discussion as Smart's *Studies in Economics*, as well as for the fruitful activity of the Austrians and of the later representatives of the Historical School.

But to return from this terminological digression. While economic science in the remoter past of its history has been mainly of a taxonomic character, later [123] writers of all schools show something of a divergence from the taxonomic line and an inclination to make the science a genetic account of the economic life process, sometimes even without an ulterior view to the taxonomic value of the results obtained. This divergence from the ancient canons of theoretical formulation is to be taken as an episode of the movement that is going forward in latter-day science generally; and the progressive change which thus affects the ideals and the objective point of the modern sciences seems in its turn to be an expression of that matter-of-fact habit of mind which the prosy but exacting exigencies of life in a modern industrial community breed in men exposed to their unmitigated impact.

In speaking of this matter-of-fact character of the modern sciences it has been broadly characterized as "evolutionary"; and the evolutionary method and the evolutionary ideals have been placed in antithesis to the taxonomic methods and ideals of pre-evolutionary days. But the characteristic attitude, aims, and ideals which are so designated here are by no means peculiar to the group of sciences that are professedly occupied with a process of development, taking that term in its most widely accepted meaning. The latter-day inorganic sciences are in this respect like the organic. They occupy themselves with "dynamic" relations and sequences. The question which they ask is always, What takes place next, and why? Given a situation wrought out by the forces under inquiry, what follows as the consequence of the situation so wrought out? or what follows upon the accession of a further element of force? Even in so non-evolutionary a science as inorganic chemistry the inquiry consistently runs on a process, an active sequence, and the value of the resulting situation as a point of departure for the next step in an interminable cumulative sequence. The last step in the chemist's experimental inquiry into any substance is, What comes of the substance determined? What will it [124] do? What will it lead to, when it is made the point of departure in further chemical action? There is no ultimate term, and no definite solution except in terms of further action. The theory worked out is always a theory of a genetic succession of phenomena, and the relations determined and elaborated into a body of doctrine are always genetic relations. In modern chemistry no cognizance is taken of the honorific bearing of reactions or molecular formulæ. The modern chemist, as contrasted with this ancient congener, knows nothing of the worth, elegance, or cogency of the relations that may subsist between the particles of matter with which he busies himself, for any other than the genetic purpose. The spiritual element and the elements of worth and propensity no longer count. Alchemic symbolism and the hierarchical glamour and virtue that once hedged about the nobler and more potent elements and reagents are almost altogether a departed glory of the science. Even the modest imputation of propensity involved in the construction of a scheme of coercive normality, for the putative guidance of reactions, finds little countenance with the later adepts of chemical science. The science has outlived that phase of its development at which the taxonomic feature was the dominant one.

In the modern sciences, of which chemistry is one, there has been a gradual shifting of the point of view from which the phenomena that the science treats of are apprehended and passed upon; and to the historian of chemical science this shifting of the point of view must be a factor of great weight in the development of chemical knowledge. Something of a like nature is true for economic science; and it is the aim here to present, in outline, some of the successive phases that have passed over the spiritual attitude of the adepts of the science, and to point out the manner in which the transition from one point of view to the next has been made. [125]

As has been suggested in the paper already referred to, the characteristic spiritual attitude or point of view of a given generation or group of economists is shown not so much in their detail work as in their higher syntheses – the terms of their definitive formulations – the grounds of their final valuation of the facts handled for the purpose of theory. This line of recondite inquiry into the spiritual past and antecedents of the science has not often been pursued seriously or with singleness of purpose, perhaps because it is, after all, of but slight consequence to the practical efficiency of the present-day science. Still, not a little substantial work has been done towards this end by such writers as Hasbach, Oncken, Bonar, Cannan, and Marshall. And much that is to the purpose is also due to writers outside of economics, for the aims of economic speculation have never been insulated from the work going forward in other lines of inquiry. As would necessarily be the case, the point of view of economists has always been in large part the point of view of the enlightened common sense of their time. The spiritual attitude of a given generation of economists is therefore in good part a special outgrowth of the ideals and preconceptions current in the world about them.

So, for instance, it is quite the conventional thing to say that the speculations of the Physiocrats were dominated and shaped by the preconception of Natural Rights. Account has been taken of the effect of natural-rights preconceptions upon the Physiocratic schemes of policy and economic reform, as well as upon the details of their doctrines.[3] But little has been said

---

3 See, for instance, Hasbach, *Allgemeine philosophische Grundlagen der von François Quesnay und Adam Smith begründeten politischen Oekonomie.*

of the significance of these preconceptions for the lower courses of the Physiocrats' theoretical structure. And yet that habit of mind to which the natural-rights view is wholesome and adequate is answerable both for the point of departure and [126] for the objective point of the Physiocratic theories, both for the range of facts to which they turned and for the terms in which they were content to formulate their knowledge of the facts which they handled. The failure of their critics to place themselves at the Physiocratic point of view has led to much destructive criticism of their work; whereas, when seen through Physiocratic eyes, such doctrines as those of the net product and of the barrenness of the artisan class appear to be substantially true.

The speculations of the Physiocrats are commonly accounted the first articulate and comprehensive presentation of economic theory that is in line with later theoretical work. The Physiocratic point of view may, therefore, well be taken as the point of departure in an attempt to trace that shifting of aims and norms of procedure that comes into view in the work of later economists when compared with earlier writers.

Physiocratic economics is a theory of the working-out of the Law of Nature (*loi naturelle*) in its economic bearing, and this Law of Nature is a very simple matter.

> Les lois naturelles sont ou physiques ou morales.
>
> On entend ici, par loi physique, *le cours réglé de tout événement physique de l'ordre naturel, évidemment le plus avantageux au genre humain.*
>
> On entend ici, par loi morale, *la règle de toute action humaine de l'ordre morale, conforme à l'ordre physique évidemment le plus advantageux au genre humain.*
>
> Ces lois forment ensemble ce qu'on appelle la *loi naturelle*. Tous les hommes et toutes les puissances humaines doivent être soumis à ces lois souveraines, instituées par l'Être-Suprême: elles sont immuables et irréfragables, et les meilleures lois possible.[4]

The settled course of material facts tending beneficently to the highest welfare of the human race, – this is the final term in the Physiocratic speculations. This is the touch-stone of substantiality. Conformity to these "immutable [127] and unerring" laws of nature is the test of economic truth. The laws are

---

4 [Natural laws are either physical or moral. The term "physical law" refers to the ordered pattern of physical events in the natural realm – it encompasses those events most beneficial to the human species, of course. The term "moral law" refers to the rule guiding any human conduct of a moral character to the extent that it, of course, conforms with the most beneficial physical order of the human species. These laws form what we call "natural law". All men and all human powers must submit to these sovereign laws, instituted by the Supreme Being: they are permanent and irrefragable laws, and the best possible ones. – Eds.] Quesnay, *Le Droit Naturel*, ch. v. (ed. Daire, *Les Physiocrates*, pp. 52–53).

immutable and unerring, but that does not mean that they rule the course of events with a blind fatality that admits of no exception and no divergence from the direct line. Human nature may, through infirmity or perversity, willfully break over the beneficent trend of the laws of nature; but to the Physiocrat's sense of the matter the laws are none the less immutable and irrefragable on that account. They are not empirical generalizations on the course of phenomena, like the law of falling bodies or of the angle of reflection; although many of the details of their action are to be determined only by observation and experience, helped out, of course, by interpretation of the facts of observation under the light of reason. So, for instance, Turgot, in his *Réflections*, empirically works out a doctrine of the reasonable course of development through which wealth is accumulated and reaches the existing state of unequal distribution; so also his doctrines of interest and of money. The immutable natural laws are rather of the nature of canons of conduct governing nature than generalizations of mechanical sequence, although in a general way the phenomena of mechanical sequence are details of the conduct of nature working according to these canons of conduct. The great law of the order of nature is of the character of a propensity working to an end, to the accomplishment of a purpose. The processes of nature working under the quasi-spiritual stress of this immanent propensity may be characterized as nature's habits of life. Not that nature is conscious of its travail, and knows and desires the worthy end of its endeavors; but for all that there is a quasi-spiritual nexus between antecedent and consequent in the scheme of operation in which nature is engaged. Nature is not uneasy about interruptions of its course or occasional deflections from the direct line through an untoward conjunction of mechanical causes, nor does the validity of [128] the great overruling law suffer through such an episode. The introduction of a mere mechanically effective causal factor cannot thwart the course of nature from reaching the goal to which she animistically tends. Nothing can thwart this teleological propensity of nature except counter-activity or divergent activity of a similarly teleological kind. Men can break over the law, and have short-sightedly and willfully done so; for men are also agents who guide their actions by an end to be achieved. Human conduct is activity of the same kind – on the same plane of spiritual reality or competency – as the course of nature, and it may therefore traverse the latter. The remedy for this short-sighted traffic of misguided human nature is enlightenment, – "instruction publique et privée des lois de l'ordre naturel."[5]

The nature in terms of which all knowledge of phenomena – for the present purpose economic phenomena – is to be finally synthesized is, therefore, substantially of a quasi-spiritual or animistic character. The laws of nature are in the last resort teleological: they are of the nature of a propensity. The

---

5 [Public and private instruction regarding the laws of the natural order. – Eds.] Quesnay, *Le Droit Naturel*, ch. v. (ed. Daire, *Les Physiocrates*, p. 53).

substantial fact in all the sequences of nature is the end to which the sequence naturally tends, not the brute fact of mechanical compulsion or causally effective force. Economic theory is accordingly the theory (1) of how the efficient causes of the *ordre naturel* work in an orderly unfolding sequence, guided by the underlying natural laws – the propensity immanent in nature to establish the highest well-being of mankind, and (2) of the conditions imposed upon human conduct by these natural laws in order to reach the ordained goal of supreme human welfare. The conditions so imposed on human conduct are as definitive as the laws and the order by force of which they are imposed; and the theoretical conclusions reached, when these laws and this order are known, are therefore expressions [129] of absolute economic truth. Such conclusions are an expression of reality, but not necessarily of fact.

Now, the objective end of this propensity that determines the course of nature is human well-being. But economic speculation has to do with the workings of nature only so far as regards the *ordre physique*. And the laws of nature in the *ordre physique*, working through mechanical sequence, can only work out the physical well-being of man, not necessarily the spiritual. This propensity to the physical well-being of man is therefore the law of nature to which economic science must bring its generalizations, and this law of physical beneficence is the substantial ground of economic truth. Wanting this, all our speculations are vain; but having its authentication they are definitive. The great, typical function, to which all the other functioning of nature is incidental if not subsidiary, is accordingly that of the alimentation, nutrition of mankind. In so far, and only in so far as the physical processes contribute to human sustenance and fulness of life, can they, therefore, further the great work of nature. Whatever processes contribute to human sustenance by adding to the material available for human assimilation and nutrition, by increasing the substance disposable for human comfort, therefore count towards the substantial end. All other processes, however serviceable in other than this physiological respect, lack the substance of economic reality. Accordingly, human industry is productive, economically speaking, if it heightens the effectiveness of the natural processes out of which the material of human sustenance emerges; otherwise not. The test of productivity, or economic reality in material facts, is the increase of nutritive material. Whatever employment of time or effort does not afford an increase of such material is unproductive, however profitable it may be to the person employed, and however useful or indispensable it may be to the community. [130] The type of such productive industry is the husbandman's employment, which yields a substantial (nutritive) gain. The artisan's work may be useful to the community and profitable to himself, but its economic effect does not extend beyond an alteration of the form in which the material afforded by nature already lies at hand. It is formally productive only, not really productive. It bears no part in the creative or generative work of nature; and therefore it lacks the character of economic substantiality. It does not enhance nature's output of vital force. The artisan's labors, therefore, yield no net product, whereas the husbandman's labors do.

Whatever constitutes a material increment of this output of vital force is wealth, and nothing else is. The theory of value contained in this position has not to do with value according to men's appraisement of the valuable article. Given items of wealth may have assigned to them certain relative values at which they exchange, and these conventional values may differ more or less widely from the natural or intrinsic value of the goods in question; but all that is beside the substantial point. The point in question is not the degree of predilection shown by certain individuals or bodies of men for certain goods. That is a matter of caprice and convention, and it does not directly touch the substantial ground of the economic life. The question of value is a question of the extent to which the given item of wealth forwards the end of nature's unfolding process. It is valuable, intrinsically and really, in so far as it avails the great work which nature has in hand.

Nature, then, is the final term in the Physiocratic speculations. Nature works by impulse and in an unfolding process, under the stress of a propensity to the accomplishment of a given end. This propensity, taken as the final cause that is operative in any situation, furnishes the basis on which to co-ordinate all our knowledge of those [131] efficient causes through which Nature works to her ends. For the purpose of economic theory proper, this is the ultimate ground of reality to which our quest of economic truth must penetrate. But back of Nature and her works there is, in the Physiocratic scheme of the universe, the Creator, by whose all-wise and benevolent power the order of nature has been established in all the strength and beauty of its inviolate and immutable perfection. But the Physiocratic conception of the Creator is essentially a deistic one: he stands apart from the course of nature which he has established, and keeps his hands off. In the last resort, of course, "Dieu seul est producteur. Les hommes travaillent, receuillent, économisent, conservent; mais *économiser* n'est par *produire*."[6] But this last resort does not bring the Creator into economic theory as a fact to be counted with in formulating economic laws. He serves a homiletical purpose in the Physiocratic specula- tions rather than fills an office essential to the theory. He comes within the purview of the theory by way of authentication rather than as a subject of inquiry or a term in the formulation of economic knowledge. The Physiocratic God can scarcely be said to be an economic fact, but it is otherwise with that nature whose ways and means constitute the subject-matter of the Physiocratic inquiry.

When this natural system of the Physiocratic speculations is looked at from the side of the psychology of the investigators, or from that of the logical premises employed, it is immediately recognized as essentially animistic. It runs consistently on animistic ground; but it is animism of a high grade, – highly integrated and enlightened, but, after all, retaining very much of that

---

6 [Only God can produce things. Men work, they collect things, they save them, they keep them; but saving is not the same as producing. – Eds.] Dupont de Nemours, Correspondence avec J.-B. Say (ed. Daire, *Les Physiocrates*, p. 399).

primitive force and naïveté which characterize the animistic explanations of phenomena in vogue among the untroubled barbarians [132]. It is not the disjected animism of the vulgar, who see a willful propensity – often a willful perversity – in given objects or situations to work towards a given outcome, good or bad. It is not the gambler's haphazard sense of fortuitous necessity or the housewife's belief in lucky days, numbers or phases of the moon. The Physiocrat's animism rests on a broader outlook, and does not proceed by such an immediately impulsive imputation of propensity. The teleological element – the element of propensity – is conceived in a large way, unified and harmonized, as a comprehensive order of nature as a whole. But it vindicates its standing as a true animism by never becoming fatalistic and never being confused or confounded with the sequence of cause and effect. It has reached the last stage of integration and definition, beyond which the way lies downward from the high, quasi-spiritual ground of animism to the tamer levels of normality and causal uniformities.

There is already discernible a tone of dispassionate and colorless "tendency" about the Physiocratic animism, such as to suggest a wavering towards the side of normality. This is especially visible in such writers as the half-protestant Turgot. In his discussion of the development of farming, for instance, Turgot speaks almost entirely of human motives and the material conditions under which the growth takes place. There is little metaphysics in it, and that little does not express the law of nature in an adequate form. But, after all has been said, it remains true that the Physiocrat's sense of substantiality is not satisfied until he reaches the animistic ground; and it remains true also that the arguments of their opponents made little impression on the Physiocrats so long as they were directed to other than this animistic ground of their doctrine. This is true in great measure even of Turgot, as witness his controversy with Hume. Whatever criticism is directed against them on other grounds is met [133] with impatience, as being inconsequential, if not disingenuous.[7]

To an historian of economic theory the source and the line of derivation whereby this precise form of the order-of-nature preconception reached the Physiocrats are of first-rate importance; but it is scarcely a question to be taken up here, – in part because it is too large a question to be handled here, in part because it has met with adequate treatment at more competent hands,[8] and in part because it is somewhat beside the immediate point under discussion. This point is the logical, or perhaps better the psychological, value of the Physiocrats' preconception, as a factor in shaping their point of view and the terms of their definitive formulation of economic knowledge.

---

7 So, for instance, the concluding chapters of La Rivière's *L'Ordre naturel et essential des sociétiés politiques*.
8 E.g., Hasbach, loc. cit.; Bonar, *Philosophy and Political Economy*, Book II.; Ritchie, *Natural Rights*.

For this purpose it may be sufficient to point out that the preconception in question belongs to the generation in which the Physiocrats lived, and that it is the guiding norm of all serious thought that found ready assimilation into the common-sense views of that time. It is the characteristic and controlling feature of what may be called the common-sense metaphysics of the eighteenth century, especially so far as concerns the enlightened French community.

It is to be noted as a point bearing more immediately on the question in hand that this imputation of final causes to the course of phenomena expresses a spiritual attitude which has prevailed, one might almost say, always and everywhere, but which reached its finest, most effective development, and found its most finished expression, in the eighteenth-century metaphysics. It is nothing recondite; for it meets us at every turn, as a matter of course, in the vulgar thinking of to-day, – in the pulpit and in the market place, – although it is not so ingenuous, [134] nor does it so unquestionedly hold the primacy in the thinking of any class to-day as it once did. It meets us likewise, with but little change of features, at all past stages of culture, late or early. Indeed, it is the most generic feature of human thinking, so far as regards a theoretical or speculative formulation of knowledge. Accordingly, it seems scarcely necessary to trace the lineage of this characteristic preconception of the era of enlightenment, through specific channels, back to the ancient philosophers or the jurists of the empire. Some of the specific forms of its expression – as, for instance, the doctrine of Natural Rights – are no doubt traceable through mediæval channels to the teachings of the ancients; but there is no need of going over the brook for water, and tracing back to specific teachings the main features of that habit of mind or spiritual attitude of which the doctrines of Natural Rights and the Order of Nature are specific elaborations only. This dominant habit of mind came to the generation of the Physiocrats on the broad ground of group inheritance, not by lineal devolution from any one of the great thinkers of past ages who had thrown its deliverances into a similarly competent form for the use of his own generation.

In leaving the Physiocratic discipline and the immediate sphere of Physiocratic influence for British ground, we are met by the figure of Hume. Here, also, it will be impracticable to go into details as to the remoter line of derivation of the specific point of view that we come upon on making the transition, for reasons similar to those already given as excuse for passing over the similar question with regard to the Physiocratic point of view. Hume is, of course, not primarily an economist; but that placid unbeliever is none the less a large item in any inventory of eighteenth-century economic thought. Hume was not gifted with a facile acceptance of the group inheritance [135] that made the habit of mind of his generation. Indeed, he was gifted with an alert, though somewhat histrionic, skepticism touching everything that was well received. It is his office to prove all things, though not necessarily to hold fast that which is good.

Aside from the strain of affectation discernible in Hume's skepticism, he may be taken as an accentuated expression of that characteristic bent which distinguishes British thinking in his time from the thinking of the Continent, and more particularly of the French. There is in Hume, and in the British community, an insistence on the prosy, not to say the seamy, side of human affairs. He is not content with formulating his knowledge of things in terms of what ought to be or in terms of the objective point of the course of things. He is not even content with adding to the teleological account of phenomena a chain of empirical, narrative generalizations as to the usual course of things. He insists, in season and out of season, on an exhibition of the efficient causes engaged in any sequence of phenomena; and he is skeptical – irreverently skeptical – as to the need or the use of any formulation of knowledge that outruns the reach of his own matter-of-fact, step-by-step argument from cause to effect.

In short, he is too modern to be wholly intelligible to those of his con-temporaries who are most neatly abreast of their time. He out-Britishes the British; and, in his foot-sore quest for a perfectly tame explanation of things, he finds little comfort, and indeed scant courtesy, at the hands of his own generation. He is not in sufficiently naïve accord with the range of preconceptions then in vogue.

But, while Hume may be an accentuated expression of a national char-acteristic, he is not therefore an untrue expression of this phase of British eighteenth-century thinking. The peculiarity of point of view and of method for which he stands has sometimes been called the critical [136] attitude, sometimes the inductive method, sometimes the materialistic or mechanical, and again, though less aptly, the historical method. Its characteristic is an insistence on matter of fact.

This matter-of-fact animus that meets any historian of economic doctrine on his introduction to British economics is a large, but not the largest, feature of the British scheme of early economic thought. It strikes the attention because it stands in contrast with the relative absence of this feature in the contemporary speculations of the Continent. The most potent, most for-mative habit of thought concerned in the early development of economic teaching on British ground is best seen in the broader generalizations of Adam Smith, and this more potent factor in Smith is a bent that is sub-stantially identical with that which gives consistency to the speculations of the Physiocrats. In Adam Smith the two are happily combined, not to say blended; but the animistic habit still holds the primacy, with the matter-of-fact as a subsidiary though powerful factor. He is said to have combined deduction with induction. The relatively great prominence given the latter marks the line of divergence of British from French economics, not the line of coincidence; and on this account it may not be out of place to look more narrowly into the circumstances to which the emergence of this relatively greater penchant for a matter-of-fact explanation of things in the British community is due.

To explain the characteristic animus for which Hume stands on grounds that might appeal to Hume, we should have to inquire into the peculiar cir-cumstances – ultimately material circumstances – that have gone to shape the habitual view of things within the British community, and that so have acted to differentiate the British preconceptions from the French, or from the general range of preconceptions prevalent on the Continent. These peculiar [137] formative circumstances are no doubt to some extent racial peculiarities; but the racial complexion of the British community is not widely different from the French, and especially not widely different from certain other Continental communities which are for the present purpose roughly classed with the French. Race difference can therefore not wholly, nor indeed for the greater part, account for the cultural difference of which this difference in preconceptions is an outcome. Through its cumulative effect on institutions the race difference must be held to have had a considerable effect on the habit of mind of the community; but, if the race difference is in this way taken as the remoter ground of an institutional peculiarity, which in its turn has shaped prevalent habits of thought, then the attention may be directed to the proximate causes, the concrete circumstances, through which this race difference has acted, in conjunction with other ulterior circumstances, to work out the psychological phenomena observed. Race differences, it may be remarked, do not so nearly coincide with national lines of demarcation as differences in the point of view from which things are habitually apprehended or differences in the standards according to which facts are rated.

If the element of race difference be not allowed definitive weight in discussing national peculiarities that underlie the deliverances of common sense, neither can these national peculiarities be confidently traced to a national difference in the transmitted learning that enters into the common-sense view of things. So far as concerns the concrete facts embodied in the learning of the various nations within the European culture, these nations make up but a single community. What divergence is visible does not touch the character of the positive information with which the learning of the various nations is occupied. Divergence is visible in the higher syntheses, the methods of handling the material of knowledge, the basis of valuation [138] of the facts taken up, rather than in the material of knowledge. But this divergence must be set down to a cultural difference, a difference of point of view, not to a difference in inherited information. When a given body of information passes the national frontiers it acquires a new complexion, a new national, cultural physiognomy. It is this cultural physiognomy of learning that is here under inquiry, and a comparison of early French economics (the Physiocrats) with early British economics (Adam Smith) is here entered upon merely with a view to making out what significance this cultural physiognomy of the science has for the past progress of economic speculation.

The broad features of economic speculation, as it stood at the period under consideration, may be briefly summed up, disregarding the element of policy, or expediency, which is common to both groups of economists, and attending to their theoretical work alone. With the Physiocrats, as with Adam Smith, there are two main points of view from which economic phenomena are treated: (*a*) the matter-of-fact point of view or preconception, which yields a discussion of causal sequences and correlations; and (*b*) what, for want of a more expressive word, is here called the animistic point of view or preconception, which yields a discussion of teleological sequences and correlations, – a discussion of the function of this and that "organ," of the legitimacy of this or the other range of facts. The former preconception is allowed a larger scope in the British than in the French economics: there is more of "induction" in the British. The latter preconception is present in both, and is the definitive element in both: but the animistic element is more colorless in the British, it is less constantly in evidence, and less able to stand alone without the support of arguments from cause to effect. Still, the animistic element is the controlling factor in the higher syntheses of both; and for both alike it affords the definitive [139] ground on which the argument finally comes to rest. In neither group of thinkers is the sense of substantiality appeased until this quasi-spiritual ground, given by the natural propensity of the course of events, is reached. But the propensity in events, the natural or normal course of things, as appealed to by the British speculators, suggests less of an imputation of will-power, or personal force, to the propensity in question. It may be added, as has already been said in another place, that the tacit imputation of will-power or spiritual consistency to the natural or normal course of events has progressively weakened in the later course of economic speculation, so that in this respect, the British economists of the eighteenth century may be said to represent a later phase of economic inquiry than the Physiocrats.

Unfortunately, but unavoidably, if this question as to the cultural shifting of the point of view in economic science is taken up from the side of the causes to which the shifting is traceable, it will take the discussion back to ground on which an economist must at best feel himself to be but a raw layman, with all a layman's limitations and ineptitude, and with the certainty of doing badly what might be done well by more competent hands. But, with a reliance on charity where charity is most needed, it is necessary to recite summarily what seems to be the psychological bearing of certain cultural facts.

A cursory acquaintance with any of the more archaic phases of human culture enforces the recognition of this fact, – that the habit of construing the phenomena of the inanimate world in animistic terms prevails pretty much universally on these lower levels. Inanimate phenomena are apprehended to work out a propensity to an end; the movements of the elements are construed in terms of quasi-personal force. So much is well authenticated by the observations on which anthropologists and ethnologists draw [140] for their materials. This animistic habit, it may be said, seems to be more effectual and far-reaching among those primitive communities that lead a predatory life.

But along with this feature of archaic methods of thought or of knowledge, the picturesqueness of which has drawn the attention of all observers, there goes a second feature, no less important for the purpose in hand, though less obtrusive. The latter is of less interest to the men who have to do with the theory of cultural development, because it is a matter of course. This second feature of archaic thought is the habit of also apprehending facts in non-animistic, or impersonal, terms. The imputation of propensity in no case extends to all the mechanical facts in the case. There is always a substratum of matter of fact, which is the outcome of an habitual imputation of causal sequence, or, perhaps better, an imputation of mechanical continuity, if a new term be permitted. The agent, thing, fact, event, or phenomenon, to which propensity, will-power, or purpose, is imputed, is always apprehended to act in an environment which is accepted as spiritually inert. There are always opaque facts as well as self-directing agents. Any agent acts through means which lend themselves to his use on other grounds than that of spiritual compulsion, although spiritual compulsion may be a large feature in any given case.

The same features of human thinking, the same two complementary methods of correlating facts and handling them for the purposes of knowledge, are similarly in constant evidence in the daily life of men in our own community. The question is, in great part, which of the two bears the greater part in shaping human knowledge at any given time and within any given range of knowledge or of facts.

Other features of the growth of knowledge, which are remoter from the point under inquiry, may be of no less [141] consequence to a comprehensive theory of the development of culture and of thought; but it is of course out of the question here to go farther afield. The present inquiry will have enough to do with these two. No other features are correlative with these, and these merit discussion on account of their intimate bearing on the point of view of economics. The point of interest with respect to these two correlative and complementary habits of thought is the question of how they have fared under the changing exigencies of human culture; in what manner they come, under given cultural circumstances, to share the field of knowledge between them; what is the relative part of each in the composite point of view in which the two habits of thought express themselves at any given cultural stage.

The animistic preconception enforces the apprehension of phenomena in terms generically identical with the terms of personality or individuality. As a certain modern group of psychologists would say, it imputes to objects and sequences an element of habit and attention similar in kind, though not necessarily in degree, to the like spiritual attitude present in the activities of a personal agent. The matter-of-fact preconception, on the other hand, enforces a handling of facts without imputation of personal force or attention, but with an imputation of mechanical continuity, substantially the preconception which has reached a formulation at the hands of scientists under the name of conservation of energy or persistence of quantity. Some appreciable resort to the latter method of knowledge is unavoidable at any cultural stage, for it is indispensable to all industrial efficiency. All technological processes and all mechanical contrivances rest, psychologically speaking, on this ground. This habit of thought is a selectively necessary consequence of industrial life, and, indeed, of all human experience in making use of the material means of life.

It should therefore follow that, in [142] a general way, the higher the culture, the greater the share of the mechanical preconception in shaping human thought and knowledge, since, in a general way, the stage of culture attained depends on the efficiency of industry. The rule, while it does not hold with anything like extreme generality, must be admitted to hold to a good extent; and to that extent it should hold also that, by a selective adaptation of men's habits of thought to the exigencies of those cultural phases that have actually supervened, the mechanical method of knowledge should have gained in scope and range. Something of the sort is borne out by observation.

A further consideration enforces the like view. As the community increases in size, the range of observation of the individuals in the community also increases; and continually wider and more far-reaching sequences of a mechanical kind have to be taken account of. Men have to adapt their own motives to industrial processes that are not safely to be construed in terms of propensity, predilection, or passion. Life in an advanced industrial community does not tolerate a neglect of mechanical fact; for the mechanical sequences through which men, at an appreciable degree of culture, work out their livelihood, are no respecters of persons or of will-power. Still, on all but the higher industrial stages, the coercive discipline of industrial life, and of the scheme of life that inculcates regard for the mechanical facts of industry, is greatly mitigated by the largely haphazard character of industry, and by the great extent to which man continues to be the prime mover in industry. So long as industrial efficiency is chiefly a matter of the handicraftsman's skill, dexterity, and diligence, the attention of men in looking to the industrial process is met by the figure of the workman, as the chief and characteristic factor; and thereby it comes to run on the personal element in industry.

But, with or without mitigation, the scheme of life [143] which men perforce adopt under exigencies of an advanced industrial situation shapes their habits of thought on the side of their behavior, and thereby shapes their habits of thought to some extent for all purposes. Each individual is but a single complex of habits of thought, and the same psychical mechanism that expresses itself in one direction as conduct expresses itself in another direction as knowledge. The habits of thought formed in the one connection, in response to stimuli that call for a response in terms of conduct, must, therefore, have their effect when the same individual comes to respond to stimuli that call for a response in terms of knowledge. The scheme of thought or of knowledge is in good part a reverberation of the scheme of life. So that, after all has been said, it remains true that with the growth of industrial organization and efficiency there must, by selection and by adaptation, supervene a greater resort to the mechanical or dispassionate method of apprehending facts.

But the industrial side of life is not the whole of it, nor does the scheme of life in vogue in any community or at any cultural stage comprise industrial conduct alone. The social, civic, military, and religious interests come in for their share of attention, and between them they commonly take up by far the larger share of it. Especially is this true so far as concerns those classes among whom we commonly look for a cultivation of knowledge for knowledge's sake. The discipline which these several interests exert does not commonly coincide with the training given by industry. So the religious interest, with its canons of truth and of right living, runs exclusively on personal relations and the adaptation of conduct to the predilections of a superior personal agent. The weight of its discipline, therefore, falls wholly on the animistic side. It acts to heighten our appreciation of the spiritual bearing of phenomena and to discountenance a matter-of-fact [144] apprehension of things. The skeptic of the type of Hume has never been in good repute with those who stand closest to the accepted religious truths. The bearing of this side of our culture upon the development of economics is shown by what the mediæval scholars had to say on economic topics.

The disciplinary effects of other phases of life, outside of the industrial and the religious, is not so simple a matter; but the discussion here approaches nearer to the point of immediate inquiry, – namely, the cultural situation in the eighteenth century, and its relation to economic speculation, – and this ground of interest in the question may help to relieve the topic of the tedium that of right belongs to it.

In the remoter past of which we have records, and even in the more recent past, Occidental man, as well as man elsewhere, has eminently been a respecter of persons. Wherever the warlike activity has been a large feature of the community's life, much of human conduct in society has proceeded on a regard for personal force. The scheme of life has been a scheme of personal aggression and subservience, partly in the naïve form, partly conventionalized in a system of status. The discipline of social life for the present purpose, in so far as its canons of conduct rest on this element of personal force in the unconventionalized form, plainly tends to the formation of a habit of apprehending and co-ordinating facts from the animistic point of view. So far as we have to do with life under a system of status, the like remains true, but with a difference. The régime of status inculcates an unremitting and very nice discrimination and observance of distinctions of personal superiority and inferiority. To the criterion of personal force, or will-power, taken in its immediate bearing on conduct, is added the criterion of personal excellence-in-general, regardless of the first-hand potency of the given person as an agent. This criterion of conduct requires [145] a constant and painstaking imputation of personal value, regardless of fact. The discrimination enjoined by the canons of status proceeds on an invidious comparison of persons in respect of worth, value, potency, virtue, which must, for the present purpose, be taken as putative. The greater or less personal value assigned a given individual or a given class under the canons of status is not assigned on the ground of visible efficiency, but on the ground of a dogmatic allegation accepted on the strength of an uncontradicted categorical affirmation simply. The canons of status hold their ground by force of pre-emption. Where distinctions of status are based on a putative worth transmitted by descent from honorable antecedents, the sequence of transmission to which appeal is taken as the arbiter of honor is of a putative and animistic character rather than a visible mechanical continuity. The habit of accepting as final what is prescriptively right in the affairs of life has as its reflex in the affairs of knowledge the formula, *Quid ab omnibus, quid ubique creditur credendum est.*[9]

Even this meagre account of the scheme of life that characterizes a régime of status should serve to indicate what is its disciplinary effect in shaping habits of thought, and therefore in shaping the habitual criteria of knowledge and of reality. A culture whose institutions are a framework of invidious comparisons implies, or rather involves and comprises, a scheme of knowledge whose definitive standards of truth and substantiality are of an animistic character; and, the more undividedly the canons of status and ceremonial honor govern the conduct of the community, the greater the facility with which the sequence of cause and effect is made to yield before the higher claims of a spiritual sequence or guidance in the course of events. Men consistently trained to an unremitting discrimination of honor, worth, and personal force in their daily conduct, and to whom these criteria [146] afford the definitive ground of sufficiency in co-ordinating facts for the purposes of life, will not be satisfied to fall short of the like definitive ground of sufficiency when they come to co-ordinate facts for the purposes of knowledge simply. The habits formed in unfolding his activity in one direction, under the impulse of a given interest, assert themselves when the individual comes to unfold his activity in any other direction, under the impulse of any other interest. If his last resort and highest criterion of truth in conduct is afforded by the element of personal force and invidious comparison, his sense of substantiality or truth in the quest of knowledge will be satisfied only when a like definitive ground of animistic force and invidious comparison is reached. But when such ground is reached he rests content and pushes the inquiry no farther. In his practical life he has acquired the habit of resting his case on an authentic deliverance as to what is absolutely right. This absolutely right and good final term in conduct has the character of finality only when conduct is construed in a ceremonial sense; that is to say, only when life is conceived as a scheme of conformity to a purpose outside and beyond the process of living. Under the régime of status this ceremonial finality is found in the concept of worth or honor. In the religious domain it is the concept of virtue, sanctity, or tabu. Merit lies in what one is, not in what one does. The habit of appeal to ceremonial finality, formed in the school of status, goes with the individual in his quest of knowledge, as a dependence upon a similarly authentic norm of absolute truth, – a similar seeking of a final term outside and beyond the range of knowledge.

The discipline of social and civic life under a régime of status, then, re-inforces the discipline of the religious life; and the outcome of the resulting habituation is that the canons of knowledge are cast in the animistic mould and converge to a ground of absolute truth, and this absolute [147]

---

9 [What is believed by everyone, everywhere, should be believed. – Eds.]

truth is of a ceremonial nature. Its subject-matter is a reality regardless of fact. The outcome, for science, of the religious and social life of the civilization of status, in Occidental culture, was a structure of quasi-spiritual appreciations and explanations, of which astrology, alchemy, and mediæval theology and metaphysics are competent, though somewhat one-sided, exponents. Throughout the range of this early learning the ground of correlation of phenomena is in part the supposed relative potency of the facts correlated; but it is also in part a scheme of status, in which facts are scheduled according to a hierarchical gradation of worth or merit, having only a ceremonial relation to the observed phenomena. Some elements (some metals, for instance) are noble, others base; some planets, on grounds of ceremonial efficacy, have a sinister influence, others a beneficent one; and it is a matter of serious consequence whether they are in the ascendant, and so on.

The body of learning through which the discipline of animism and invidious comparison transmitted its effects to the science of economics was what is known as natural theology, natural rights, moral philosophy, and natural law. These several disciplines or bodies of knowledge had wandered far from the naïve animistic standpoint at the time when economic science emerged, and much the same is true as regards the time of the emergence of other modern sciences. But the discipline which makes for an animistic formulation of knowledge continued to hold the primacy in modern culture, although its dominion was never altogether undivided or unmitigated. Occidental culture has long been largely an industrial culture; and, as already pointed out, the discipline of industry, and of life in an industrial community, does not favor the animistic preconception. This is especially true as regards industry which makes large use of mechanical contrivances. The difference in these respects between Occidental industry and [148] science, on the one hand, and the industry and science of other cultural regions, on the other hand, is worth noting in this connection. The result has been that the sciences, as that word is understood in later usage, have come forward gradually, and in a certain rough parallelism with the development of industrial processes and industrial organization. It is possible to hold that both modern industry (of the mechanical sort) and modern science centre about the region of the North Sea. It is still more palpably true that within this general area the sciences, in the recent past, show a family likeness to the civil and social institutions of the communities in which they have been cultivated, this being true to the greatest extent of the higher or speculative sciences; that is, in that range of knowledge in which the animistic preconception can chiefly and most effectively find application. There is, for instance, in the eighteenth century a perceptible parallelism between the divergent character of British and Continental culture and institutions, on the one hand, and the dissimilar aims of British and Continental speculation, on the other hand.

Something has already been said of the difference in preconceptions between the French and the British economists of the eighteenth century. It remains to point out the correlative cultural difference between the two communities, to which it is conceived that the difference in scientific animus is in great measure due. It is, of course, only the general features, the general attitude of the speculators, that can be credited to the difference in culture. Differences of detail in the specific doctrines held could be explained only on a much more detailed analysis than can be entered on here, and after taking account of facts which cannot here be even allowed for in detail.

Aside from the greater resort to mechanical contrivances and the larger scale of organization in British industry, the further cultural peculiarities of the British community [149] run in the same general direction. British religious life and beliefs had less of the element of fealty – personal or discretionary mastery and subservience – and more of a tone of fatalism. The civil institutions of the British had not the same rich personal content as those of the French. The British subject owned allegiance to an impersonal law rather than to the person of a superior. Relatively, it may be said that the sense of status, as a coercive factor, was in abeyance in the British community. Even in the warlike enterprise of the British community a similar characteristic is traceable. Warfare is, of course, a matter of personal assertion. Warlike communities and classes are necessarily given to construing facts in terms of personal force and personal ends. They are always superstitious. They are great sticklers for rank and precedent, and zealously cultivate those distinctions and ceremonial observances in which a system of status expresses itself. But, while warlike enterprise has by no means been absent from the British scheme of life, the geographical and strategic isolation of the British community has given a characteristic turn to their military relations. In recent times British warlike operations have been conducted abroad. The military class has consequently in great measure been segregated out from the body of the community, and the ideals and prejudices of the class have not been transfused through the general body with the same facility and effect that they might otherwise have had. The British community at home has seen the campaign in great part from the standpoint of the "sinews of war."

The outcome of all these national peculiarities of circumstance and culture has been that a different scheme of life has been current in the British community from what has prevailed on the Continent. There has resulted the formation of a different body of habits of thought and a different animus in their handling of facts. The preconception of causal sequence has been allowed larger scope [150] in the correlation of facts for purposes of knowledge; and, where the animistic preconception has been resorted to, as it always has in the profounder reaches of learning, it has commonly been an animism of a tamer kind.

Taking Adam Smith as an exponent of this British attitude in theoretical knowledge, it is to be noted that, while he formulates his knowledge in terms of a propensity (natural laws) working teleologically to an end, the end or objective point which controls the formulation has not the same rich content of vital human interest or advantage as is met with in the Physiocratic speculations. There is perceptibly less of an imperious tone in Adam Smith's natural laws than in those of the contemporary French economists. It is true, he sums up the institutions with which he deals in terms of the ends which they should subserve, rather than in terms of the exigencies and habits of life out of which they have arisen; but he does not with the same tone of finality appeal to the end subserved as a final cause through whose coercive guidance the complex of phenomena is kept to its appointed task. Under his hands the restraining, compelling agency retires farther into the background, and appeal is taken to it neither so directly nor on so slight provocation.

But Adam Smith is too large a figure to be disposed of in a couple of concluding paragraphs. At the same time his work and the bent which he gave to economic speculation are so intimately bound up with the aims and bias that characterize economics in its next stage of development that he is best dealt with as the point of departure for the Classical School rather than merely as a British counterpart of Physiocracy. Adam Smith will accordingly be considered in immediate connection with the bias of the classical school and the incursion of utilitarianism into economics.

Part II

Adam Smith's animistic bent asserts itself more plainly and more effectually in the general trend and aim of his discussion than in the details of theory. "Adam Smith's *Wealth of Nations* is, in fact, so far as it has one single purpose, a vindication of the unconscious law present in the separate actions of men when these actions are directed by a certain strong personal motive."[10] Both in the *Theory of the Moral Sentiments* and in the *Wealth of Nations* there are many passages that testify to his abiding conviction that there is a wholesome trend in the natural course of things, and the characteristically optimistic tone in which he speaks for natural liberty is but an expression of this conviction. An extreme resort to this animistic ground occurs in his plea for freedom of investment.[11]

In the proposition that men are "led by an invisible hand," Smith does not fall back on a meddling Providence who is to set human affairs straight when they are in danger of going askew. He conceives the Creator to be very continent in the matter of interference with the natural course of things. The

---

10 Bonar, *Philosophy and Political Economy*, pp. 177, 178.
11 "Every individual is continually exerting himself to find out the most advantageous employment for whatever capital he can command. It is his own advantage, and not that of the society, which he has in view. But the study of his own advantage naturally, or rather necessarily, leads him to prefer that employment which is most advantageous to the society. ... By directing that industry in such a manner as its produce may be of the greatest value, he intends only his own gain; and he is in this, as in many other cases, led by an invisible hand to promote an end which was no part of his intention. Nor is it always the worse for society that it was no part of it. By pursuing his own interest he frequently promotes that of the society more effectually than when he really intends to promote it." *Wealth of Nations*, Book IV. chap. ii.

Creator has established [397] the natural order to serve the ends of human welfare; and he has very nicely adjusted the efficient causes comprised in the natural order, including human aims and motives, to this work that they are to accomplish. The guidance of the invisible hand takes place not by way of interposition, but through a comprehensive scheme of contrivances established from the beginning. For the purpose of economic theory, man is conceived to be consistently self-seeking; but this economic man is a part of the mechanism of nature, and his self-seeking traffic is but a means whereby, in the natural course of things, the general welfare is worked out. The scheme as a whole is guided by the end to be reached, but the sequence of events through which the end is reached is a causal sequence which is not broken into episodically. The benevolent work of guidance was performed in first establishing an ingenious mechanism of forces and motives capable of accomplishing an ordained result, and nothing beyond the enduring constraint of an established trend remains to enforce the divine purpose in the resulting natural course of things.

The sequence of events, including human motives and human conduct, is a causal sequence; but it is also something more, or, rather, there is also another element of continuity besides that of brute cause and effect, present even in the step-by-step process whereby the natural course of things reaches its final term. The presence of such a quasi-spiritual or non-causal element is evident from two (alleged) facts. (1) The course of things may be deflected from the direct line of approach to that consummate human welfare which is its legitimate end. The natural trend of things may be overborne by an untoward conjuncture of causes. There is a distinction, often distressingly actual and persistent, between the legitimate and the observed course of things. If "natural," in Adam Smith's use, meant necessary, in the sense [398] of causally determined, no divergence of events from the natural or legitimate course of things would be possible. If the mechanism of nature, including man, were a mechanically competent contrivance for achieving the great artificer's design, there could be no such episodes of blundering and perverse departure from the direct path as Adam Smith finds in nearly all existing arrangements. Institutional facts would then be "natural."[12] (2) When things have gone wrong, they will right themselves if interference with the natural course ceases; whereas, in the case of a causal sequence simply, the mere cessation of interference will not leave the outcome the same as if no interference had taken place. This recuperative power of nature is of an extra-mechanical character. The continuity of sequence by force of which the natural course of things prevails is, therefore, not of the nature of cause and effect, since it

---

12 The discrepancy between the actual, causally determined situation and the divinely intended consummation is the metaphysical ground of all that inculcation of morality and enlightened policy that makes up so large a part of Adam Smith's work. The like, of course, holds true for all moralists and reformers who proceed on the assumption of a providential order.

bridges intervals and interruptions in the causal sequence.[13] Adam Smith's use of the term "real" in statements of theory – as, for example, "real value," "real price"[14] – is evidence to this effect. "Natural" commonly has the same meaning as "real" in this connection.[15] Both "natural" and "real" are placed in contrast with the actual; and, in Adam Smith's apprehension, both have a substantiality [399] different from and superior to facts. The view involves a distinction between reality and fact, which survives in a weakened form in the theories of "normal" prices, wages, profits, costs, in Adam Smith's successors.

This animistic prepossession seems to pervade the earlier of his two monumental works in a greater degree than the latter. In the *Moral Sentiments* recourse is had to the teleological ground of the natural order more freely and with perceptibly greater insistence. There seems to be reason for holding that the animistic preconception weakened or, at any rate, fell more into the background as his later work of speculation and investigation proceeded. The change shows itself also in some details of his economic theory, as first set forth in the *Lectures*, and afterwards more fully developed in the *Wealth of Nations*. So, for instance, in the earlier presentation of the matter, "the division of labor is the immediate cause of opulence"; and this division of labor, which is the chief condition of economic well-being, "flows from a direct propensity in human nature for one man to barter with another."[16] The "propensity" in question is here appealed to as a natural endowment immediately given to man with a view to the welfare of human society, and without any attempt at further explanation of how man has come by it. No causal explanation of its presence or character is offered. But the corresponding passage of the *Wealth of Nations* handles the question more cautiously.[17] Other parallel passages

---

13 "In the political body, however, the wisdom of nature has fortunately made ample provision for remedying many of the bad effects of the folly and injustice of man; in the same manner as it has done in the natural body, for remedying those of his sloth and intemperance." *Wealth of Nations*, Book IV. chap. ix.

14 *E.g.*, "the real measure of the exchangeable value of all commodities." *Wealth of Nations*, Book I. chap. v., and repeatedly in the like connection.

15 *E.g.*, Book I. chap. vii.: "When the price of any commodity is neither more nor less than what is sufficient to pay the rent of the land, the wages of the labor, and the profits of the stock employed in raising, preparing, and bringing it to market, according to their *natural* rates, the commodity is then sold for what may be called its *natural* price." "The actual price at which any commodity is commonly sold is called its market price. It may be either above or below or exactly the same with its natural price."

16 [Smith], *Lectures [on Justice, Police, Revenue and Arms]* (ed. Cannan, 1896), p. 169.

17 "This division of labor, from which so many advantages are derived, is not originally the effect of any human wisdom, which foresees and intends that general opulence to which it gives occasion. It is the necessary though very slow and gradual consequence of a certain propensity in human nature which has in view no such extensive utility, – the propensity to truck, barter, and exchange one thing for another. Whether this propensity be one of those original principles in human nature of which no further account can be given, or whether, as seems more probable, it be the necessary consequence of the faculties of reason and speech, it belongs not to our present subject to inquire." *Wealth of Nations*, Book I. chap. ii.

might be compared with much the same effect. The [400] guiding hand has withdrawn farther from the range of human vision.

However, these and other like filial expressions of a devout optimism need, perhaps, not be taken as integral features of Adam Smith's economic theory, or as seriously affecting the character of his work as an economist. They are the expression of his general philosophical and theological views, and are significant for the present purpose chiefly as evidences of an animistic and optimistic bent. They go to show what is Adam Smith's accepted ground of finality, – the ground to which all his speculations on human affairs converge; but they do not in any great degree show the teleological bias guiding the formulation of economic theory in detail.

The effective working of the teleological bias is best seen in Smith's more detailed handling of economic phenomena – in his discussion of what may loosely be called economic institutions – and in the criteria and principles of procedure by which he is guided in incorporating these features of economic life into the general structure of his theory. A fair instance, though perhaps not the most telling one, is the discussion of the "real and nominal price," and of the "natural and market price" of commodities, already referred to above.[18] The "real" price of commodities is their value in terms of human life. At this point Smith differs from the Physiocrats, with whom the ultimate terms of value are afforded by human sustenance taken as a product of the functioning of brute nature; the cause of the difference being that the Physiocrats conceived the natural order which works towards [401] the material well-being of man to comprise the non-human environment only, whereas Adam Smith includes man in this concept of the natural order, and, indeed, makes him the central figure in the process of production. With the Physiocrats, production is the work of nature: with Adam Smith, it is the work of man and nature, with man in the foreground. In Adam Smith, therefore, labor is the final term in valuation. This "real" value of commodities is the value imputed to them by the economist under the stress of his teleological preconception. It has little, if any, place in the course of economic events, and no bearing on human affairs, apart from the sentimental influence which such a preconception in favor of a "real value" in things may exert upon men's notions of what is the good and equitable course to pursue in their transactions. It is impossible to gauge this real value of goods; it cannot be measured or expressed in concrete terms. Still, if labor exchanges for a varying quantity of goods, "it is their value which varies, not that of the labor which purchases them."[19] The values which practically attach to goods in men's handling of them are conceived to be determined without regard to the real value which Adam Smith imputes to the goods; but, for all that, the substantial fact with respect to these market values is their presumed approximation to the real

18 *Wealth of Nations*, Book I. chaps. v.–vii.
19 *Wealth of Nations*, Book I. chap. v.

values teleologically imputed to the goods under the guidance of inviolate natural laws. The real, or natural, value of articles has no causal relation to the value at which they exchange. The discussion of how values are determined in practice runs on the motives of the buyers and sellers, and the relative advantage enjoyed by the parties to the transaction.[20] It is a discussion of a process of valuation, quite unrelated to the "real," or "natural," price of things, and [402] quite unrelated to the grounds on which things are held to come by their real, or natural, price; and yet, when the complex process of valuation has been traced out in terms of human motives and the exigencies of the market, Adam Smith feels that he has only cleared the ground. He then turns to the serious business of accounting for value and price theoretically, and making the ascertained facts articulate with his teleological theory of economic life.[21]

The occurrence of the words "ordinary" and "average" in this connection need not be taken too seriously. The context makes it plain that the equality which commonly subsists between the ordinary or average rates, and the natural rates, is a matter of coincidence, not of identity. Not only are there temporary deviations, but there may be a permanent divergence between the ordinary and the natural price of a commodity; as in case of a monopoly or of produce grown under peculiar circumstances of soil or climate.[22]

The natural price coincides with the price fixed by competition, because competition means the unimpeded play of those efficient forces through which the nicely adjusted mechanism of nature works out the design to accomplish which it was contrived. The natural price is reached through the free interplay of the factors of [403] production, and it is itself an outcome of production. Nature, including the human factor, works to turn out the goods; and the natural value of the goods is their appraisement from the standpoint of this productive process of nature. Natural value is a category of production: whereas, notoriously, exchange value or market price is a

---

20 As, *e.g.*, the entire discussion of the determination of Wages, Profits, and Rent, in Book I. chaps. viii.–xi.

21 "There is in every society or neighborhood an ordinary or average rate both of wages and profit in every different employment of labor and stock. This rate is naturally regulated, ... partly by the general circumstances of the society. ... There is, likewise, in every society or neighborhood an ordinary or average rate of rent, which is regulated, too. ... These ordinary or average rates may be called the natural rates of wages, profit, and rent, at the time and place in which they commonly prevail. When the price of any commodity is neither more nor less than what is sufficient to pay the rent of the land, the wages of the labor, and the profits of the stock employed in raising, preparing, and bringing it to market, according to their natural rates, the commodity is then sold for what may be called its natural price." *Wealth of Nations*, Book I. chap. vii.

22 "Such commodities may continue for whole centuries together to be sold at this high price; and that part of it which resolves itself into the rent of land is, in this case, the part which is generally paid above its natural rate." Book I. chap. vii.

category of distribution. And Adam Smith's theoretical handling of market price aims to show how the factors of human predilection and human wants at work in the higgling of the market bring about a result in passable consonance with the natural laws that are conceived to govern production.

The natural price is a composite result of the blending of the three "component parts of the price of commodities," – the natural wages of laborer, the natural profits of stock, and the natural rent of land; and each of these three components is in its turn the measure of the productive effect of the factor to which it pertains. The further discussion of these shares in distribution aims to account for the facts of distribution on the ground of the productivity of the factors which are held to share the product between them. That is to say, Adam Smith's preconception of a productive natural process as the basis of his economic theory dominates his aims and procedure, when he comes to deal with phenomena that cannot be stated in terms of production. The causal sequence in the process of distribution is, by Adam Smith's own showing, unrelated to the causal sequence in the process of production; but, since the latter is the substantial fact, as viewed from the standpoint of a teleological natural order, the former must be stated in terms of the latter before Adam Smith's sense of substantiality, or "reality," is satisfied. Something of the same kind is, of course, visible in the Physiocrats and in Cantillon. It amounts to an extension of the natural-rights preconception to economic theory. Adam Smith's discussion of distribution as a function of productivity might be traced in [404] detail through his handling of Wages, Profits, and Rent; but, since the aim here is a brief characterization only, and not an exposition, no farther pursuit of this point seems feasible.

It may, however, be worth while to point out another line of influence along which the dominance of the teleological preconception shows itself in Adam Smith. This is the normalization of data, in order to bring them into consonance with an orderly course of approach to the putative natural end of economic life and development. The result of this normalization of data is, on the one hand, the use of what James Steuart calls "conjectural history" in dealing with past phases of economic life, and, on the other hand, a statement of present-day phenomena in terms of what legitimately ought to be according to the God-given end of life rather than in terms of unconstrued observation. Account is taken of the facts (supposed or observed) ostensibly in terms of causal sequence, but the imputed causal sequence is construed to run on lines of teleological legitimacy.

A familiar instance of this "conjectural history," in a highly and effectively normalized form, is the account of "that early and rude state of society which precedes both the accumulation of stock and the appropriation of land."[23] It is needless at this day to point out that this "early and rude state," in which

---

23 *Wealth of Nations*, Book I. chap. vi.; also chap. viii.

"the whole produce of labor belongs to the laborer," is altogether a figment. The whole narrative, from the putative origin down, is not only suppositious, but it is merely a schematic presentation of what should have been the course of past development, in order to lead up to that ideal economic situation which would satisfy Adam Smith's preconception.[24] As the narrative comes nearer the region of [405] known latter-day facts, the normalization of the data becomes more difficult and receives more detailed attention; but the change in method is a change of degree rather than of kind. In the "early and rude state" the coincidence of the "natural" and the actual course of events is immediate and undisturbed, there being no refractory data at hand; but in the later stages and in the present situation, where refractory facts abound, the co-ordination is difficult, and the coincidence can be shown only by a free abstraction from phenomena that are irrelevant to the teleological trend and by a laborious interpretation of the rest. The facts of modern life are intricate, and lend themselves to statement in the terms of the theory only after they have been subjected to a "higher criticism."

The chapter "Of the Origin and Use of Money"[25] is an elegantly normalized account of the origin and nature of an economic institution, and Adam Smith's further discussion of money runs on the same lines. The origin of money is stated in terms of the purpose which money should legitimately serve in such a community as Adam Smith considered right and good, not in terms of the motives and exigencies which have resulted in the use of money and in the gradual rise of the existing method of payment and accounts. Money is "the great wheel of circulation," which effects the transfer of goods in process of production and the distribution of the finished goods to the consumers. It is an organ of the economic commonwealth rather than an expedient of accounting and a conventional repository of wealth.

It is perhaps superfluous to remark that to the "plain man," who is not concerned with the "natural course of things" in a consummate *Geldwirtschaft*,[26] the money that passes his hand is not a "great wheel of circulation." To the Samoyed, for instance, the reindeer which serves him [406] as unit of value is wealth in the most concrete and tangible form. Much the same is true of coin, or even of bank-notes, in the apprehension of unsophisticated people among ourselves to-day. And yet it is in terms of the habits and conditions of life of these "plain people" that the development of money will have to be accounted for if it is to be stated in terms of cause and effect.

The few scattered passages already cited may serve to illustrate how Adam Smith's animistic or teleological bent shapes the general structure of his

24 For an instance of how these early phases of industrial development appear, when not seen in the light of Adam Smith's preconception, see, among others, Bücher, *Entstehung der Volkswirtschaft*.
25 Book I. chap. iv.
26 [Money economy. – Eds.]

theory and gives it consistency. The principle of definitive formulation in Adam Smith's economic knowledge is afforded by a putative purpose that does not at any point enter causally into the economic life process which he seeks to know. This formative or normative purpose or end is not freely conceived to enter as an efficient agent in the events discussed, or to be in any way consciously present in the process. It can scarcely be taken as an animistic agency engaged in the process. It sanctions the course of things, and gives legitimacy and substance to the sequence of events, so far as this sequence may be made to square with the requirements of the imputed end. It has therefore a ceremonial or symbolical force only, and lends the discussion a ceremonial competency; although with economists who have been in passable agreement with Adam Smith as regards the legitimate end of economic life this ceremonial consistency, or consistency *de jure*, has for many purposes been accepted as the formulation of a causal continuity in the phenomena that have been interpreted in its terms. Elucidations of what normally ought to happen, as a matter of ceremonial necessity, have in this way come to pass for an account of matters of fact.

But, as has already been pointed out, there is much more to Adam Smith's exposition of theory than a formulation of what ought to be. Much of the advance he [407] achieved over his predecessors consists in a larger and more painstaking scrutiny of facts, and a more consistent tracing out of causal continuity in the facts handled. No doubt, his superiority over the Physiocrats, that characteristic of his work by virtue of which it superseded theirs in the farther growth of economic science, lies to some extent in his recourse to a different, more modern ground of normality, – a ground more in consonance with the body of preconceptions that have had the vogue in later generations. It is a shifting of the point of view from which the facts are handled; but it comes in great part to a substitution of a new body of preconceptions for the old, or a new adaptation of the old ground of finality, rather than an elimination of all metaphysical or animistic norms of valuation. With Adam Smith, as with the Physiocrats, the fundamental question, the answer to which affords the point of departure and the norm of procedure, is a question of substantiality or economic "reality." With both, the answer to this question is given naïvely, as a deliverance of common sense. Neither is disturbed by doubts as to this deliverance of common sense or by any need of scrutinizing it. To the Physiocrats this substantial ground of economic reality is the nutritive process of Nature. To Adam Smith it is Labor. His reality has the advantage of being the deliverance of the common sense of a more modern community, and one that has maintained itself in force more widely and in better consonance with the facts of latter-day industry. The Physiocrats owe their preconception of the productiveness of nature to the habits of thought of a community in whose economic life the dominant phenomenon was the owner of agricultural land. Adam Smith owes his preconception in favor of labor to a community in which the obtrusive economic feature of the immediate past was handicraft and agriculture, with commerce as a scarcely secondary phenomenon. [408]

So far as Adam Smith's economic theories are a tracing out of the causal sequence in economic phenomena, they are worked out in terms given by these two main directions of activity, – human effort directed to the shaping of the material means of life, and human effort and discretion directed to a pecuniary gain. The former is the great, substantial productive force: the latter is not immediately, or proximately, productive.[27] Adam Smith still has too lively a sense of the nutritive purpose of the order of nature freely to extend the concept of productiveness to any activity that does not yield a material increase of the creature comforts. His instinctive appreciation of the substantial virtue of whatever effectually furthers nutrition, even leads him into the concession that "in agriculture nature labors along with man," although the general tenor of his argument is that the productive force with which the economist always has to count is human labor. This recognized substantiality of labor as productive is, as has already been remarked, accountable for his effort to reduce to terms of productive labor such a category of distribution as exchange value.

With but slight qualification, it will hold that, in the causal sequence which Adam Smith traces out in his economic theories proper (contained in the first three books of the *Wealth of Nations*), the causally efficient factor is conceived to be human nature in these two relations, – of productive efficiency and pecuniary gain through exchange. Pecuniary gain – gain in the material means of life through barter – furnishes the motive force to the economic activity of the individual; although productive efficiency is the legitimate, normal end of the community's economic life. To such an extent does this concept of man's seeking his ends through "truck, barter, and exchange" pervade Adam Smith's treatment of economic [409] processes that he even states production in its terms, and says that "labor was the first price, the original purchase-money, that was paid for all things."[28] The human nature engaged in this pecuniary traffic is conceived in somewhat hedonistic terms, and the motives and movements of men are normalized to fit the requirements of a hedonistically conceived order of nature. Men are very much alike in their native aptitudes and propensities;[29] and, so far as economic theory need take account of these aptitudes and propensities, they are aptitudes for the production of the "necessaries and conveniences of life," and propensities to secure as great a share of these creature comforts as may be.

Adam Smith's conception of normal human nature – that is to say, the human factor which enters causally in the process which economic theory

---

27 See *Wealth of Nations*, Book II. chap. v., "Of the Different Employment of Capitals."

28 *Wealth of Nations*, Book I. chap. v. See also the plea for free trade, Book IV. chap. ii.: "But the annual revenue of every society is always precisely equal to the exchangeable value of the whole annual produce of its industry, or, rather, is precisely the same thing with that exchangeable value."

29 "The difference of natural talents in different men is in reality much les than we are aware of." *Wealth of Nations*, Book I. chap. ii.

discusses – comes, on the whole, to this: Men exert their force and skill in a mechanical process of production, and their pecuniary sagacity in a competitive process of distribution, with a view to individual gain in the material means of life. These material means are sought in order to the satisfaction of men's natural wants through their consumption. It is true, much else enters into men's endeavors in the struggle for wealth, as Adam Smith points out; but this consumption comprises the legitimate range of incentives, and a theory which concerns itself with the natural course of things need take but incidental account of what does not come legitimately in the natural course. In point of fact, there are appreciable "actual," though scarcely "real," departures from this rule. They are spurious and insubstantial departures, and do not properly come [410] within the purview of the stricter theory. And, since human nature is strikingly uniform, in Adam Smith's apprehension, both the efforts put forth and the consumptive effect accomplished may be put in quantitative terms and treated algebraically, with the result that the entire range of phenomena comprised under the head of consumption need be but incidentally considered; and the theory of production and distribution is complete when the goods or the values have been traced to their disappearance in the hands of their ultimate owners. The reflex effect of consumption upon production and distribution is, on the whole, quantitative only.

Adam Smith's preconception of a normal teleological order of procedure in the natural course, therefore, affects not only those features of theory where he is avowedly concerned with building up a normal scheme of the economic process. Through his normalizing the chief causal factor engaged in the process, it affects also his arguments from cause to effect.[30] What makes this latter feature worth particular attention is the fact that his successors carried this normalization farther, and employed it with less frequent reference to the mitigating exceptions which Adam Smith notices by the way.

The reason for that farther and more consistent normalization of human nature which gives us the "economic man" at the hands of Adam Smith's successors lies, in great part, in the utilitarian philosophy that entered in force

---

30 "Mit diesen philosophischen Ueberzengungen tritt nun Adam Smith an die Welt der Enfahrung heran, und es ergiebt sich ihm die Richtigkeit der Principien. Der Reiz der Smith'schen Schriften beruht zum grossen Teile darauf, dass Smith die Principien in so innige Verbindung mit dem Thatsächlichen gebracht. Hie und da werden dann auch die Principien, was durch diese Verbindung veranlasst wird, an ihren Spitzen etwas abgeschliffen, ihre allzuscharfe Ausprägung dadurch vermieden. Nichtsdestoweniger aber bleiben sie stets die leitenden Grundgedanken." (With these philosophical hypotheses, then, Adam Smith tackles the empirical world, and it confirms the correctness of his principles. The attraction of the Smithian writings is grounded primarily in [the fact that] Smith so closely connects principles with reality. Due to the requirements of this connection, the sharpness of the principles is here and there somewhat dulled, thereby avoiding an overly narrow precision. The principles nevertheless always remain guiding fundamental ideas [of Smith's work]. – Eds.) Richard Zeyss, *Adam Smith und der Eigennutz* (Tübingen. 1889), p. 110.

and in consummate form at about the turning of the century. Some credit in the work of normalization is due [411] also to the farther supersession of handicraft by the "capitalistic" industry that came in at the same time and in pretty close relation with the utilitarian views.

After Adam Smith's day, economics fell into profane hands. Apart from Malthus, who, of all the greater economists, stands nearest to Adam Smith on such metaphysical heads as have an immediate bearing upon the premises of economic science, the next generation do not approach their subject from the point of view of a divinely instituted order; nor do they discuss human interests with that gently optimistic spirit of submission that belongs to the economist who goes to his work with the fear of God before his eyes. Even with Malthus the recourse to the divinely sanctioned order of nature is somewhat sparing and temperate. But it is significant for the later course of economic theory that, while Malthus may well be accounted the truest continuer of Adam Smith, it was the undevout utilitarians that became the spokesmen of the science after Adam Smith's time.

There is no wide breach between Adam Smith and the utilitarians, either in details of doctrine or in the concrete conclusions arrived at as regards questions of policy. On these heads Adam Smith might well be classed as a moderate utilitarian, particularly so far as regards his economic work. Malthus has still more of a utilitarian air, – so much so, indeed, that he is not infrequently spoken of as a utilitarian. This view, convincingly set forth by Mr. Bonar,[31] is no doubt well borne out by a detailed scrutiny of Malthus's economic doctrines. His humanitarian bias is evident throughout, and his weakness for considerations of expediency is the great blemish of his scientific work. But, for all that, in order to an appreciation of the change that came over classical economics with the [412] rise of Benthamism, it is necessary to note that the agreement in this matter between Adam Smith and the disciples of Bentham, and less decidedly that between Malthus and the latter, is a coincidence of conclusions rather than an identity of preconceptions.[32]

With Adam Smith the ultimate ground of economic reality is the design of God, the teleological order; and his utilitarian generalizations, as well as the hedonistic character of his economic man, are but methods of the working out of this natural order, not the substantial and self-legitimating ground. Shifty as Malthus's metaphysics are, much the same is to be said for him.[33] Of the utilitarians proper the converse is true, although here, again, there is by no

---

31 See, *e.g.*, *Malthus and his Work*, especially Book III., as also the chapter on Malthus in *Philosophy and Political Economy*, Book III., Modern Philosophy: Utilitarian Economics, chap. i., "Malthus."

32 Ricardo is here taken as a utilitarian of the Benthamite color, although he cannot be classed as a disciple of Bentham. His hedonism is but the uncritically accepted metaphysics comprised in the common sense of his time, and his substantial coincidence with Bentham goes to show how well diffused the hedonist preconception was at the time.

33 *Cf.* Bonar, *Malthus and his Work*, pp. 323–36.

means utter consistency. The substantial economic ground is pleasure and pain: the teleological order (even the design of God, where that is admitted) is the method of its working out. It may be unnecessary here to go into the farther implications, psychological and ethical, which this preconception of the utilitarians involves. And even this much may seem a taking of excessive pains with a distinction that marks no tangible difference. But a reading of the classical doctrines, with something of this metaphysics of political economy in mind, will show how, and in great part why, the later economists of the classical line diverged from Adam Smith's tenets in the early years of the century, until it has been necessary to interpret Adam Smith somewhat shrewdly in order to save him from heresy.

The post-Bentham economics is substantially a theory of value. This is altogether the dominant feature of the [413] body of doctrines; the rest follows from, or is adapted to, this central discipline. The doctrine of value is of very great importance also in Adam Smith; but Adam Smith's economics is a theory of the production and apportionment of the material means of life.[34] With Adam Smith, value is discussed from the point of view of production. With the utilitarians, production is discussed from the point of view of value. The former makes value an outcome of the process of production: the latter makes production the outcome of a valuation process.

The point of departure with Adam Smith is the "productive power of labor."[35] With Ricardo it is a pecuniary problem concerned in the distribution of ownership;[36] but the classical writers are followers of Adam Smith, and improve upon and correct the results arrived at by him, and the difference of point of view, therefore, becomes evident in their divergence from him, and the different distribution of emphasis, rather than in a new and antagonistic departure.

The reason for this shifting of the centre of gravity from production to valuation lies, proximately, in Bentham's revision of the "principles" of morals. Bentham's philosophical position is, of course, not a self-explanatory phenomenon, nor does the effect of Benthamism extend only to those who are avowed followers of Bentham; for Bentham is the exponent of a cultural change that affects the habits of thought of the entire community. [414] The immediate point of Bentham's work, as affecting the habits of thought of the educated community, is the substitution of hedonism (utility) in place of achievement of

34 His work is an inquiry into "the Nature and Causes of the Wealth of Nations."
35 "The annual labor of every nation is the fund which originally supplies it with all the necessaries and conveniences of life which it annually consumes, and which consist always either in the immediate produce of that labor or in what is purchased with that produce from other nations." *Wealth of Nations*, "Introduction and Plan," opening paragraph.
36 "The produce of the earth – all that is derived from its surface by the united application of labor, machinery, and capital – is divided among three classes of the community. ... To determine the laws which regulate this distribution is the principal problem of political economy." *Political Economy*, Preface.

purpose, as a ground of legitimacy and a guide in the normalization of knowledge. Its effect is most patent in speculations on morals, where it inculcates determinism. Its close connection with determinism in ethics points the way to what may be expected of its working in economics. In both cases the result is that human action is construed in terms of the causal forces of the environment, the human agent being, at the best, taken as a mechanism of commutation, through the workings of which the sensuous effects wrought by the impinging forces of the environment are, by an enforced process of valuation, transmuted without quantitative discrepancy into moral or economic conduct, as the case may be. In ethics and economics alike the subject-matter of the theory is this valuation process that expresses itself in conduct, resulting, in the case of economic conduct, in the pursuit of the greatest gain or least sacrifice.

Metaphysically or cosmologically considered, the human nature into the motions of which hedonistic ethics and economics inquire is an intermediate term in a causal sequence, of which the initial and the terminal members are sensuous impressions and the details of conduct. This intermediate term conveys the sensuous impulse without loss of force to its eventuation in conduct. For the purpose of the valuation process through which the impulse is so conveyed, human nature may, therefore, be accepted as uniform; and the theory of the valuation process may be formulated quantitatively, in terms of the material forces affecting the human sensory and of their equivalents in the resulting activity. In the language of economics, the theory of value may be stated in terms of the consumable goods that afford the incentive to effort and the expenditure undergone in order to procure them. [415] Between these two there subsists a necessary equality; but the magnitudes between which the equality subsists are hedonistic magnitudes, not magnitudes of kinetic energy nor of vital force, for the terms handled are sensuous terms. It is true, since human nature is substantially uniform, passive, and unalterable in respect of men's capacity for sensuous affection, there may also be presumed to subsist a substantial equality between the psychological effect to be wrought by the consumption of goods, on the one side, and the resulting expenditure of kinetic or vital force, on the other side; but such an equality is, after all, of the nature of a coincidence, although there should be a strong presumption in favor of its prevailing on an average and in the common run of cases. Hedonism, however, does not postulate uniformity between men except in the respect of sensuous cause and effect.

The theory of value which hedonism gives is, therefore, a theory of cost in terms of discomfort. By virtue of the hedonistic equilibrium reached through the valuation process, the sacrifice or expenditure of sensuous reality involved in acquisition is the equivalent of the sensuous gain secured. An alternative statement might perhaps be made, to the effect that the measure of the value of goods is not the sacrifice or discomfort undergone, but the sensuous gain that accrues from the acquisition of the goods; but this is plainly only an alternative statement, and there are special reasons in the economic life of the time why the statement in terms of cost, rather than in terms of "utility," should commend itself to the earlier classical economists.

On comparing the utilitarian doctrine of value with earlier theories, then, the case stands somewhat as follows. The Physiocrats and Adam Smith contemplate value as a measure of the productive force that realizes itself in the valuable article. With the Physiocrats this productive force is the "anabolism" of Nature (to resort to [416] a physiological term): with Adam Smith it is chiefly human labor directed to heightening the serviceability of the materials with which it is occupied. Production causes value in either case. The post-Bentham economics contemplates value as a measure of, or as measured by, the irksomeness of the effort involved in procuring the valuable goods. As Mr. E. C. K. Gonner has admirably pointed out,[37] Ricardo – and the like holds true of classical economics generally – makes cost the foundation of value, not its cause. This resting of value on cost takes place through a valuation. Any one who will read Adam Smith's theoretical exposition to as good purpose as Mr. Gonner has read Ricardo will scarcely fail to find that the converse is true in Adam Smith's case. But the causal relation of cost to value holds only as regards "natural" or "real" value in Adam Smith's doctrine. As regards market price, Adam Smith's theory does not differ greatly from that of Ricardo on this head. He does not overlook the valuation process by which market price is adjusted and the course of investment is guided, and his discussion of this process runs in terms that should be acceptable to any hedonist.

The shifting of the point of view that comes into economics with the acceptance of utilitarian ethics and its correlate, the associationist psychology, is in great part a shifting to the ground of causal sequence as contrasted with that of serviceability to a preconceived end. This is indicated even by the main fact already cited, – that the utilitarian economists make exchange value the central feature of their theories, rather than the conduciveness of industry to the community's material welfare. Hedonistic exchange value is the outcome of a valuation process enforced by the apprehended pleasure-giving capacities of the items valued. And in the utilitarian [417] theories of production, arrived at from the standpoint so given by exchange value, the conduciveness to welfare is not the objective point of the argument. This objective point is rather the bearing of productive enterprise upon the individual fortunes of the agents engaged, or upon the fortunes of the several distinguishable classes of beneficiaries comprised in the industrial community; for the great immediate bearing of exchange values upon the life of the collectivity is their bearing upon the distribution of wealth. Value is a category of distribution. The result is that, as is well shown by Mr. Cannan's discussion,[38] the theories of production offered by the classical economists have been sensibly scant, and have

---

37 In the introductory essay to his edition of Ricardo's *Political Economy.* See, e.g., paragraphs 9 and 24.

38 *Theories of Production and Distribution,* 1776–1848.

been carried out with a constant view to the doctrines on distribution. An incidental but telling demonstration of the same facts is given by Professor Bücher;[39] and in illustration may be cited Torrens's *Essay on the Production of Wealth*, which is to a good extent occupied with discussions of value and distribution. The classical theories of production have been theories of the production of "wealth"; and "wealth," in classical usage, consists of material things having exchange value. During the vogue of the classical economics the accepted characteristic by which "wealth" has been defined has been its amenability to ownership. Neither in Adam Smith nor in the Physiocrats is this amenability to ownership made so much of, nor is it in a similar degree accepted as a definite mark of the subject-matter of the science.

As their hedonistic preconception would require, then, it is to the pecuniary side of life that the classical economists give their most serious attention, and it is the pecuniary bearing of any given phenomenon or of any institution that commonly shapes the issue of the argument [418]. The causal sequence about which the discussion centres is a process of pecuniary valuation. It runs on distribution, ownership, acquisition, gain, investment, exchange.[40] In this way the doctrines on production come to take a pecuniary coloring; as is seen in a less degree also in Adam Smith, and even in the Physiocrats, although these earlier economists very rarely, if ever, lose touch with the concept of generic serviceability as the characteristic feature of production. The tradition derived from Adam Smith, which made productivity and serviceability the substantial features of economic life, was not abruptly put aside by his successors, though the emphasis was differently distributed by them in following out the line of investigation to which the tradition pointed the way. In the classical economics the ideas of production and of acquisition are not commonly held apart, and very much of what passes for a theory of production is occupied with phenomena of investment and acquisition. Torrens's *Essay* is a case in point, though by no means an extreme case.

This is as it should be; for to the consistent hedonist the sole motive force concerned in the industrial process is the self-regarding motive of pecuniary gain, and industrial activity is but an intermediate term between the expenditure or discomfort undergone and the pecuniary gain sought. Whether the end and outcome is an invidious gain for the individual (in contrast with or at the cost of his neighbors), or an enhancement of the facility of human life on the whole, is altogether a by-question in any discussion of the range of incentives by which men are prompted to their work or the direction which their efforts

---

39 *Entstehung der Volkswirtschaft* (second edition). *Cf.* especially chaps. ii., iii., vi., and vii.

40 "Even if we put aside all questions which involve a consideration of the effects of industrial institutions in modifying the habits and character of the classes of the community, ... that enough still remains to constitute a separate science, the mere enumeration of the chief terms of economies – wealth, value, exchange, credit money, capital, and commodity – will suffice to show." Shirres, *Analysis of the Ideas of Economics* (London, 1893), pp. 8 and 9.

take. The serviceability of the given line of activity [419], for the life purposes of the community or for one's neighbors, "is not of the essence of this contract." These features of serviceability come into the account chiefly as affecting the vendibility of what the given individual has to offer in seeking gain through a bargain.[41]

In hedonistic theory the substantial end of economic life is individual gain; and for this purpose production and acquisition may be taken as fairly coincident, if not identical. Moreover, society, in the utilitarian philosophy, is the algebraic sum of the individuals; and the interest of the society is the sum of the interests of the individuals. It follows by easy consequence, whether strictly true or not, that the sum of individual gains is the gain of the society, and that, in serving his own interest in the way of acquisition, the individual serves the collective interest of the community. Productivity or serviceability is, therefore, to be presumed of any occupation or enterprise that looks to a pecuniary gain; and so, by a roundabout path, we get back to the ancient conclusion of Adam Smith, that the remuneration of classes or persons engaged in industry coincides with their productive contribution to the output of services and consumable goods.

A felicitous illustration of the working of this hedonistic norm in classical economic doctrine is afforded by the theory of the wages of superintendence, – an element in distribution which is not much more than suggested in Adam Smith, but which receives ampler and more painstaking attention as the classical body of doctrines reaches a fuller development. The "wages of superintendence" are the gains due to pecuniary management. They are the gains that come to the director of the "business," – not those that go to the director of the mechanical process [420] or to the foreman of the shop. The latter are wages simply. This distinction is not altogether clear in the earlier writers, but it is clearly enough contained in the fuller development of the theory.

The undertaker's work is the management of investment. It is altogether of a pecuniary character, and its proximate aim is "the main chance." If it leads, indirectly, to an enhancement of serviceability or a heightened aggregate output of consumable goods, that is a fortuitous circumstance incident to that heightened vendibility on which the investor's gain depends. Yet the classical doctrine says frankly that the wages of superintendence are the remuneration of superior productivity,[42] and the classical theory of production is in good

---

41 "If a commodity were in no way useful, ... it would be destitute of exchangeable value; ... (but), possessing utility, commodities derive their exchangeable value from two sources," etc. Ricardo, *Political Economy*, chap. i. sect. 1.

42 *Cf.*, for instance, Senior, *Political Economy* (London, 1872), particularly pp. 88, 89, and 130–35, where the wages of superintendence are, somewhat reluctantly, classed under profits; and the work of superintendence is thereupon conceived as being, immediately or remotely, an exercise of "abstinence" and a productive work. The illustration of the bill-broker is particularly apt. The like view of the wages of superintendence is an article of theory with more than one of the later descendents of the classical line.

part a doctrine of investment in which the identity of production and pecuniary gain is taken for granted.

The substitution of investment in the place of industry as the central and substantial fact in the process of production is due not to the acceptance of hedonism simply, but rather to the conjunction of hedonism with an economic situation of which the investment of capital and its in management for gain was the most obvious feature. The situation which shaped the common-sense apprehension of economic facts at the time was what has since been called a capitalistic system, in which pecuniary enterprise and the phenomena of the market were the dominant and tone-giving facts. But this economic situation was also the chief ground for the vogue of hedonism in economics; so that hedonistic economics may be taken as an interpretation of human nature in terms of the market-place. The market and the "business world," to which the business [421] man in his pursuit of gain was required to adapt his motives, had by this time grown so large that the course of business events was beyond the control of any one person; and at the same time those far-reaching organizations of invested wealth which have latterly come to prevail and to coerce the market were not then in the foreground. The course of market events took its passionless way without traceable relation or deference to any man's convenience and without traceable guidance towards an ulterior end. Man's part in this pecuniary world was to respond with alacrity to the situation, and so adapt his vendible effects to the shifting demand as to realize something in the outcome. What he gained in his traffic was gained without loss to those with whom he dealt, for they paid no more than the goods were worth to them. One man's gain need not be another's loss; and, if it is not, then it is net gain to the community.

Among the striking remoter effects of the hedonistic preconception, and its working out in terms of pecuniary gain, is the classical failure to discriminate between capital as investment and capital as industrial appliances. This is, of course, closely related to the point already spoken of. The appliances of industry further the production of goods, therefore capital (invested wealth) is productive; and the rate of its average remuneration marks the degree of its productiveness.[43] The most obvious fact limiting the pecuniary gain secured by means of invested wealth is the sum invested. Therefore, capital limits the productiveness of industry; and the chief and indispensable condition to an advance in material well-being is the accumulation of invested wealth. In discussing the conditions of industrial improvement, it is usual to assume that "the state of the arts remains unchanged," which is, [422] for all purposes but that of a doctrine of profits percent, an exclusion of the main fact. Investments may, further, be transferred from one

---

43 *Cf.* Böhm-Bawerk, *Capital and Interest*, Books II. and IV., as well as the Introduction and chaps. iv. and v. of Book I. Böhm-Bawerk's discussion bears less immediately on the present point than the similarity of the terms employed would suggest.

enterprise to another. Therefore, and in that degree, the means of production are "mobile."

Under the hands of the great utilitarian writers, therefore, political economy is developed into a science of wealth, taking that term in the pecuniary sense, as things amenable to ownership. The course of things in economic life is treated as a sequence of pecuniary events, and economic theory becomes a theory of what should happen in that consummate situation where the permutation of pecuniary magnitudes takes place without disturbance and without retardation. In this consummate situation the pecuniary motive has its perfect work, and guides all the acts of economic man in a guileless, colorless unswerving quest of the greatest gain at the least sacrifice. Of course, this perfect competitive system, with its untainted "economic man," is a feat of the scientific imagination, and is not intended as a competent expression of fact. It is an expedient of abstract reasoning; and its avowed competency extends only to the abstract principles, the fundamental laws of the science, which hold only so far as the abstraction holds. But, as happens in such cases, having once been accepted and assimilated as real, though perhaps not as actual, it becomes an effective constituent in the inquirer's habits of thought, and goes to shape his knowledge of facts. It comes to serve as a norm of substantiality or legitimacy; and facts in some degree fall under its constraint, as is exemplified by many allegations regarding the "tendency" of things.

To this consummation, which Senior speaks of as "the natural state of man,"[44] human development tends by force of the hedonistic character of human nature; and in terms of its approximation to this natural state, therefore, the immature actual situation had best be stated. The [423] pure theory, the "hypothetical science" of Cairnes, "traces the phenomena of the production and distribution of wealth up to their causes, in the principles of human nature and the laws and events – physical, political, and social – of the external world."[45] But since the principles of human nature that give the outcome in men's economic conduct, so far as it touches the production and distribution of wealth, are but the simple and constant sequence of hedonistic cause and effect, the element of human nature may fairly be eliminated from the problem, with great gain in simplicity and expedition. Human nature being eliminated, as being a constant intermediate term, and all institutional features of the situation being also eliminated (as being similar constants under that natural or consummate pecuniary *régime* with which the pure theory is concerned), the laws of the phenomena of wealth may be formulated in terms of the remaining factors. These factors are the vendible items that men handle in these processes of production and distribution; and economic laws come, therefore, to be

---

44 *Political Economy*, p. 87.
45 *Character and Logical Method of Political Economy* (New York, 1875), p. 71. Cairnes may not be altogether representative of the high tide of classicism, but his characterization of the science is none the less to the point.

expressions of the algebraic relations subsisting between the various elements of wealth and investment, – capital, labor, land, supply and demand of one and the other, profits, interest, wages. Even such items as credit and population become dissociated from the personal factor, and figure in the computation as elemental factors acting and reacting through a permutation of values over the heads of the good people whose welfare they are working out.

To sum up: the classical economics, having primarily to do with the pecuniary side of life, is a theory of a process of valuation. But since the human nature at whose hands and for whose behoof the valuation takes place is simple and constant in its reaction to pecuniary stimulus, [424] and since no other feature of human nature is legitimately present in economic phenomena than this reaction to pecuniary stimulus, the valuer concerned in the matter is to be overlooked or eliminated; and the theory of the valuation process then becomes a theory of the pecuniary interaction of the facts valued. It is a theory of valuation with the element of valuation left out, – a theory of life stated in terms of the normal paraphernalia of life.

In the preconceptions with which classical economics set out were comprised the remnants of natural rights and of the order of nature, infused with that peculiarly mechanical natural theology that made its way into popular vogue on British ground during the eighteenth century and was reduced to a neutral tone by the British penchant for the commonplace – stronger at this time than at any earlier period. The reason for this growing penchant for the commonplace, for the explanation of things in causal terms, lies partly in the growing resort to mechanical processes and mechanical prime movers in industry, partly in the (consequent) continued decline of the aristocracy and the priesthood, and partly in the growing density of population and the consequent greater specialization and wider organization of trade and business. The spread of the discipline of the natural sciences, largely incident to the mechanical industry, counts in the same direction; and obscurer factors in modern culture may have had their share.

The animistic preconception was not lost, but it lost tone; and it partly fell into abeyance, particularly so far as regards its avowal. It is visible chiefly in the unavowed readiness of the classical writers to accept as imminent and definitive any possible outcome which the writer's habit or temperament inclined him to accept as right and good. Hence the visible inclination of classical economists to a doctrine of the harmony of interests, and their somewhat uncircumspect readiness to state their [425] generalizations in terms of what ought to happen according to the ideal requirements of that consummate *Geldwirtschaft*[46] to which men "are impelled by the provisions of nature."[47] By virtue of their hedonistic preconceptions, their habituation to

46 [Money economy. – Eds.].
47 Senior, *Political Economy*, p. 87.

the ways of a pecuniary culture, and their unavowed animistic faith that nature is in the right, the classical economists knew that the consummation to which, in the nature of things, all things tend, is the frictionless and beneficent competitive system. This competitive ideal, therefore, affords the normal, and conformity to its requirements affords the test of absolute economic truth. The standpoint so gained selectively guides the attention of the classical writers in their observation and apprehension of facts, and they come to see evidence of conformity or approach to the normal in the most unlikely places. Their observation is, in great part, interpretative, as observation commonly is. What is peculiar to the classical economists in this respect is their particular norm of procedure in the work of interpretation. And, by virtue of having achieved a standpoint of absolute economic normality, they became a "deductive" school, so called, in spite of the patent fact that they were pretty consistently employed with an inquiry into the causal sequence of economic phenomena.

The generalization of observed facts becomes a normalization of them, a statement of the phenomena in terms of their coincidence with, or divergence from, that normal tendency that makes for the actualization of the absolute economic reality. This absolute or definitive ground of economic legitimacy lies beyond the causal sequence in which the observed phenomena are conceived to be interlinked. It is related to the concrete facts neither as cause nor as effect in any such way that the causal relation may be traced in a concrete instance. It has little causally to do either with the "mental" or with the "physical" [426] data with which the classical economist is avowedly employed. Its relation to the process under discussion is that of an extraneous – that is to say, a ceremonial – legitimation. The body of knowledge gained by its help and under its guidance is, therefore, a taxonomic science.

So, by way of a concluding illustration, it may be pointed out that money, for instance, is normalized in terms of the legitimate economic tendency. It becomes a measure of value and a medium of exchange. It has become primarily an instrument of pecuniary commutation, instead of being, as under the earlier normalization of Adam Smith, primarily a great wheel of circulation for the diffusion of consumable goods. The terms in which the laws of money, as of the other phenomena of pecuniary life, are formulated, are terms which connote its normal function in the life history of objective values as they live and move and have their being in the consummate pecuniary situation of the "natural" state. To a similar work of normalization we owe those creatures of the myth-maker, the quantity theory and the wages-fund.

Part III

In what has already been said, it has appeared that the changes which have supervened in the preconceptions of the earlier economists constitute a somewhat orderly succession. The feature of chief interest in this development has been a gradual change in the received grounds of finality to which the successive generations of economists have brought their theoretical output, on which they have been content to rest their conclusions, and beyond which they have not been moved to push their analysis of events or their scrutiny of phenomena. There has been a fairly unbroken sequence of development in what may be called the canons of economic reality, or, to put it in other words, there has been a precession of the point of view from which facts have been handled and valued for the purpose of economic science.

The notion which has in its time prevailed so widely, that there is in the sequence of events a consistent trend which it is the office of the science to ascertain and turn to account, – this notion may be well founded or not. But that there is something of such a consistent trend in the sequence of the canons of knowledge under whose guidance the scientist works is not only a generalization from the past course of things, but lies in the nature of the case; for the canons of knowledge are of the nature of habits of thought, and habit does not break with the past, nor do the hereditary aptitudes that find expression in habit vary gratuitously with the mere lapse of time. What is true in this respect, for instance, in the domain of law and institutions is true, likewise, in the domain of [241] science. What men have learned to accept as good and definitive for the guidance of conduct and of human relations remains true and definitive and unimpeachable until the exigencies of a later, altered situation enforce a variation from the norms and canons of the past, and so give rise to a modification of the habits of thought that decide what is, for the time, right in human conduct. So in science the ancient ground of finality remains a good and valid test of scientific truth until the altered exigencies of later life enforce habits of thought that are not wholly in consonance with the received notions as to what constitutes the ultimate, self-legitimating term – the substantial reality – to which knowledge in any given case must penetrate.

This ultimate term or ground of knowledge is always of a metaphysical character. It is something in the way of a preconception, accepted uncritically, but applied in criticism and demonstration of all else with which the science is concerned. So soon as it comes to be criticised, it is in a way to be superseded by a new, more or less altered formulation; for criticism of it means that it is no longer fit to survive unaltered in the altered complex of habits of thought to which it is called upon to serve as fundamental principle. It is subject to natural selection and selective adaptation, as are other conventions. The underlying metaphysics of scientific research and purpose, therefore, changes gradually and, of course, incompletely, much as is the case with the metaphysics underlying the common law and the schedule of civil rights. As in the legal framework the now avowedly useless and meaningless preconceptions of status and caste and precedent are even yet at the most metamorphosed and obsolescent rather than overpassed, – witness the facts of inheritance, vested interests, the outlawry of debts through lapse of time, the competence of the State to coerce individuals into support of a given policy, – so in the science the living [242] generation has not seen an abrupt and traceless disappearance of the metaphysics that fixed the point of view of the early classical political economy. This is true even for those groups of economists who have most incontinently protested against the absurdity of the classical doctrines and methods. In Professor Marshall's words, "There has been no real breach of continuity in the development of the science."

But, while there has been no breach, there has none the less been change, – more far-reaching change than some of us are glad to recognize; for who would not be glad to read his own modern views into the convincing words of the great masters?

Seen through modern eyes and without effort to turn past gains to modern account, the metaphysical or preconceptional furniture of political economy as it stood about the middle of this century may come to look quite curious. The two main canons of truth on which the science proceeded, and with which the inquiry is here concerned, were: (*a*) a hedonistic-associational psychology, and (*b*) an uncritical conviction that there is a meliorative trend in the course of events, apart from the conscious ends of the individual members of the community. This axiom of a meliorative developmental trend fell into shape as a belief in an organic or quasi-organic (physiological)[48] life process on the part of the economic community or of the nation; and this belief carried with it something of a constraining sense of self-realizing cycles of growth, maturity and decay in the life history of nations or communities.

Neglecting what may for the immediate purpose be negligible in this outline of fundamental tenets, it will bear the following construction. (*a*) On the ground of the hedonistic or associational psychology, all spiritual continuity and any consequent teleological trend is tacitly denied so far as regards individual conduct, where the [243] later psychology, and the sciences which build on this later psychology, insist upon and find such a teleological trend at every turn. (*b*) Such a spiritual or quasi-spiritual continuity and teleological trend is uncritically affirmed as regards the non-human sequence or the sequence of events in the affairs of collective life, where the modern sciences diligently assert that nothing of the kind is discernible, or that, if it is discernible, its recognition is beside the point, so far as concerns the purposes of the science.

This position, here outlined with as little qualification as may be admissible, embodies the general metaphysical ground of that classical political economy that affords the point of departure for Mill and Cairnes, and also for Jevons. And what is to be said of Mill and Cairnes in this connection will apply to the later course of the science, though with a gradually lessening force.

By the middle of the century the psychological premises of the science are no longer so neat and succinct as they were in the days of Bentham and James Mill. At J. S. Mill's hands, for instance, the naïvely quantitative hedonism of Bentham is being supplanted by a sophisticated hedonism, which makes much of an assumed qualitative divergence between the different

---

48 So, *e.g.*, Roscher, Comte, the early socialists, J. S. Mill, and later Spencer, Schaeffle, Wagner.

kinds of pleasures that afford the motives of conduct. This revision of hedonistic dogma, of course, means a departure from the strict hedonistic ground.
Correlated with this advance more closely in the substance of the change than
in the assignable dates, is a concomitant improvement – at least, set forth as
an improvement – upon the received associational psychology, whereby
"similarity" is brought in to supplement "contiguity" as a ground of connection between ideas. This change is well shown in the work of J. S. Mill and
Bain. In spite of all the ingenuity spent in maintaining the associational
legitimacy of this new article of theory, it remains a patent innovation and a
departure from the [244] ancient standpoint. As is true of the improved
hedonism, so it is true of the new theory of association that it is no longer
able to construe the process which it discusses as a purely mechanical process,
a concatenation of items simply. Similarity of impressions implies a comparison of impressions by the mind in which the association takes place, and
thereby it implies some degree of constructive work on the part of the perceiving subject. The perceiver is thereby construed to be an agent engaged in
the work of perception; therefore, he must be possessed of a point of view and
an end dominating the perceptive process. To perceive the similarity, he must
be guided by an interest in the outcome, and must "attend." The like applies
to the introduction of qualitative distinctions into the hedonistic theory of
conduct. Apperception in the one case and discretion in the other cease to be
the mere registration of a simple and personally uncolored sequence of permutations enforced by the factors of the external world. There is implied a
spiritual – that is to say, active – "teleological" continuity of process on the
part of the perceiving or of the discretionary agent, as the case may be.

It is on the ground of their departure from the stricter hedonistic promises
that Mill and, after him, Cairnes are able, for instance, to offer their
improvement upon the earlier doctrine of cost of production as determining
value. Since it is conceived that the motives which guide men in their choice
of employments and of domicile differ from man to man and from class to
class, not only in degree, but in kind, and since varying antecedents, of heredity and of habit, variously influence men in their choice of a manner of life,
therefore the mere quantitative pecuniary stimulus cannot be depended on to
decide the outcome without recourse. There are determinable variations in the
alacrity with which different classes or communities respond to the pecuniary
stimulus; and in so far as this condition prevails, the classes or communities in
[245] question are non-competing. Between such non-competing groups the
norm that determines values is not the unmitigated norm of cost of production taken absolutely, but only taken relatively. The formula of cost of production is therefore modified into a formula of reciprocal demand. This
revision of the cost-of-production doctrine is extended only sparingly, and the
emphasis is thrown on the pecuniary circumstances on which depend
the formation and maintenance of non-competing groups. Consistency with
the earlier teaching is carefully maintained, so far as may be; but extra-
pecuniary factors are, after all, even if reluctantly, admitted into the body of

the theory. So also, since there are higher and lower motives, higher and lower pleasures, – as well as motives differing in degree, – it follows that an unguided response even to the mere quantitative pecuniary stimuli may take different directions, and so may result in activities of widely differing outcome. Since activities set up in this way through appeal to higher and lower motives are no longer conceived to represent simply a mechanically adequate effect of the stimuli, working under the control of natural laws that tend to one beneficent consummation, therefore the outcome of activity set up even by the normal pecuniary stimuli may take a form that may or may not be serviceable to the community. Hence *laissez-faire* ceases to be a sure remedy for the ills of society. Human interests are still conceived normally to be at one; but the detail of individual conduct need not, therefore, necessarily serve these generic human interests.[49] Therefore, other inducements than the unmitigated impact of pecuniary [246] exigencies may be necessary to bring about a coincidence of class or individual endeavor with the interests of the community. It becomes incumbent on the advocate of *laissez-faire* to "prove his minor premise." It is no longer self-evident that: "Interests left to themselves tend to harmonious combinations, and to the progressive preponderance of the general good."[50]

The natural-rights preconception begins to fall away as soon as the hedonistic mechanics have been seriously tampered with. Fact and right cease to coincide, because the individual in whom the rights are conceived to inhere has come to be something more than the field of intersection of natural forces that work out in human conduct. The mechanics of natural liberty – that assumed constitution of things by force of which the free hedonistic play of the laws of nature across the open field of individual choice is sure to reach the right outcome – is the hedonistic psychology; and the passing of the doctrine of natural rights and natural liberty, whether as a premise or as a dogma, therefore coincides with the passing of that mechanics of conduct on the validity of which the theoretical acceptance of the dogma depends. It is, therefore, something more than a coincidence that the half-century which has seen the disintegration of the hedonistic faith and of the associational psychology has also seen the dissipation, in scientific speculations, of the concomitant faith in natural rights and in that benign order of nature of which the natural-rights dogma is a corollary.

It is, of course, not hereby intended to say that the later psychological views and premises imply a less close dependence of conduct on environment than

49 "Let us not confound the statement that *human* interests are at one with the statement that *class* interests are at one. The latter I believe to be as false as the former is true. ... But accepting the major premises of the syllogism, that the interests of human beings are fundamentally the same, how as to the minor? – how as to the assumption that people know their interests in the sense in which they are identical with the interests of others, and that they spontaneously follow them *in this sense?*" Cairnes, *Essays in Political Economy* (London, 1873), p. 245. This question cannot consistently be asked by an adherent of the stricter hedonism.
50 Bastiat, quoted by Cairnes, *Essays*, p. 319.

do the earlier ones. Indeed, the reverse may well be held to be true. The pervading characteristic of later thinking is the constant recourse to a detailed analysis of phenomena in causal terms. The modern catchword, in the present connection. [247] is "response to stimulus"; but the manner in which this response is conceived has changed. The fact, and ultimately the amplitude, at least in great part, of the reaction to stimulus, is conditioned by the forces in impact; but the constitution of the organism, as well as its attitude at the moment of impact, in great part decides what will serve as a stimulus, as well as what the manner and direction of the response will be.

The later psychology is biological, as contrasted with the metaphysical psychology of hedonism. It does not conceive the organism as a causal hiatus. The causal sequence in the "reflex arc" is, no doubt, continuous; but the continuity is not, as formerly, conceived in terms of spiritual substance transmitting a shock: it is conceived in terms of the life activity of the organism. Human conduct, taken as the reaction of such an organism under stimulus, may be stated in terms of tropism, involving, of course, a very close-knit causal sequence between the impact and the response, but at the same time imputing to the organism a habit of life and a self-directing and selective attention in meeting the complex of forces that make up its environment. The selective play of this tropismatic complex that constitutes the organism's habit of life under the impact of the forces of the environment counts as discretion.

So far, therefore, as it is to be placed in contrast with the hedonistic phase of the older psychological doctrines, the characteristic feature of the newer conception is the recognition of a selectively self-directing life process in the agent. While hedonism seeks the causal determinant of conduct in the (probable) outcome of action, the later conception seeks this determinant in the complex of propensities that constitutes man a functioning agent, that is to say, a personality. Instead of pleasure ultimately determining what human conduct shall be, the tropismatic propensities that eventuate in conduct ultimately determine [248] what shall be pleasurable. For the purpose in hand, the consequence of the transition to the altered conception of human nature and its relation to the environment is that the newer view formulates conduct in terms of personality, whereas the earlier view was content to formulate it in terms of its provocation and its by-product. Therefore, for the sake of brevity, the older preconceptions of the science are here spoken of as construing human nature in inert terms, as contrasted with the newer, which construes it in terms of functioning.

It has already appeared above that the second great article of the metaphysics of classical political economy – the belief in a meliorative trend or a benign order of nature – is closely connected with the hedonistic conception of human nature; but this connection is more intimate and organic than appears from what has been said above. The two are so related as to stand or fall together, for the latter is but the obverse of the former. The doctrine of a trend in events imputes purpose to the sequence of events; that is, it invests this sequence with a discretionary, teleological character, which asserts itself in a constraint over all the steps in the sequence by which the supposed objective point is reached. But discretion touching a given end must be single, and must alone cover all the acts by which the end is to be reached. Therefore, no discretion resides in the intermediate terms through which the end is worked out. Therefore, man being such an intermediate term, discretion cannot be imputed to him without violating the supposition. Therefore, given an indefeasible meliorative trend in events, man is but a mechanical intermediary in the sequence. It is as such a mechanical intermediate term that the stricter hedonism construes human nature.[51] Accordingly, when more of [249] teleological activity came to be imputed to man, less was thereby allowed to the complex of events. Or it may be put in the converse form: when less of a teleological continuity came to be imputed to the course of events, more was thereby imputed to man's life process. The latter form of statement probably suggests the direction in which the causal relation runs, more nearly than the former. The change whereby the two metaphysical premises in question have lost their earlier force and symmetry, therefore, amounts to a (partial) shifting of the seat of putative personality from inanimate phenomena to man.

It may be mentioned in passing, as a detail lying perhaps afield, yet not devoid of significance for latter-day economic speculation, that this elimination of personality, and so of teleological content, from the sequence of events, and its increasing imputation to the conduct of the human agent, is incident to a growing resort to an apprehension of phenomena in terms of process rather than in terms of outcome, as was the habit in earlier schemes of knowledge. On this account the categories employed are, in a gradually increasing degree, categories of process, – "dynamic" categories. But categories of process applied to conduct, to discretionary action, are teleological categories: whereas categories of process applied in the case of a sequence where the members of the sequence are not conceived to be charged with discretion, are, by the force of this conception itself, non-teleological, quantitative categories. The continuity comprised in the concept of process as applied to conduct is consequently a spiritual, teleological continuity: whereas the concept of process under the second head, the non-teleological sequence, comprises a continuity of a quantitative, causal kind, substantially the conservation of energy. In its turn the growing resort to categories of process in the formulation of knowledge is probably due to the epistemological discipline of modern mechanical industry, the technological exigencies of which [250] enforce a constant recourse to the apprehension of phenomena in terms of process, differing therein from the earlier forms of industry, which neither

---

51 It may be remarked, by the way, that the use of the differential calculus and similar mathematical expedients in the discussion of marginal utility and the like, proceeds on this psychological ground, and that the theoretical results so arrived at are valid to the full extent only if this hedonistic psychology is accepted.

obtruded visible mechanical process so constantly upon the apprehension nor so imperatively demanded an articulate recognition of continuity in the processes actually involved. The contrast in this respect is still more pronounced between the discipline of modern life in an industrial community and the discipline of life under the conventions of status and exploit that formerly prevailed.

To return to the benign order of nature, or the meliorative trend, – its passing, as an article of economic faith, was not due to criticism levelled against it by the later classical economists on grounds of its epistemological incongruity. It was tried on its merits, as an alleged account of facts; and the weight of evidence went against it. The belief in a self-realizing trend had no sooner reached a competent and exhaustive statement – *e.g.*, at Bastiat's hands, as a dogma of the harmony of interests specifically applicable to the details of economic life – than it began to lose ground. With his usual concision and incisiveness, Cairnes completed the destruction of Bastiat's special dogma, and put it forever beyond a rehearing. But Cairnes is not a destructive critic of the classical political economy, at least not in intention: he is an interpreter and continuer – perhaps altogether the clearest and truest continuer – of the classical teaching. While he confuted Bastiat and discredited Bastiat's peculiar dogma, he did not thereby put the order of nature bodily out of the science. He qualified and improved it, very much as Mill qualified and improved the tenets of the hedonistic psychology. As Mill and the ethical speculation of his generation threw more of personality into the hedonistic psychology, so Cairnes and the speculators on scientific method (such as Mill and Jevons) attenuated the imputation of personality or teleological content to the process [251] of material cause and effect. The work is of course, by no means, an achievement of Cairnes alone; but he is, perhaps, the best exponent of this advance in economic theory. In Cairnes's redaction this foundation of the science became the concept of a colorless normality.

It was in Cairnes's time the fashion for speculators in other fields than the physical sciences to look to those sciences for guidance in method and for legitimation of the ideals of scientific theory which they were at work to realize. More than that, the large and fruitful achievements of the physical sciences had so far taken men's attention captive as to give an almost instinctive predilection for the methods that had approved themselves in that field. The ways of thinking which had on this ground become familiar to all scholars occupied with any scientific inquiry, had permeated their thinking on any subject whatever. This is eminently true of British thinking.

It had come to be a commonplace of the physical sciences that "natural laws" are of the nature of empirical generalizations simply, or even of the nature of arithmetical averages. Even the underlying preconception of the modern physical sciences – the law of the conservation of energy, or persistence of quantity – was claimed to be an empirical generalization, arrived at inductively and verified by experiment. It is true the alleged proof of the law took the whole conclusion for granted at the start, and used it constantly as a tacit axiom at every step in the argument which was to establish its truth; but that fact serves rather to emphasize than to call in question the abiding faith which these empiricists had in the sole efficacy of empirical generalization. Had they been able overtly to admit any other than an associational origin of knowledge, they would have seen the impossibility of accounting on the mechanical grounds of association for the premise on which [252] all experience of mechanical fact rests. That any other than a mechanical origin should be assigned to experience, or that any other than a so-conceived empirical ground was to be admitted for any general principle, was incompatible with the prejudices of men trained in the school of the associational psychology, however widely they perforce departed from this ideal in practice. Nothing of the nature of a personal element was to be admitted into these fundamental empirical generalizations; and nothing, therefore, of the nature of a discretionary or teleological movement was to be comprised in the generalizations to be accepted as "natural laws." Natural laws must in no degree be imbued with personality, must say nothing of an ulterior end; but for all that they remained "laws" of the sequences subsumed under them. So far is the reduction to colorless terms carried by Mill, for instance, that he formulates the natural laws as empirically ascertained sequences simply, even excluding or avoiding all imputation of causal continuity, as that term is commonly understood by the unsophisticated. In Mill's ideal no more of organic connection or continuity between the members of a sequence is implied in subsuming them under a law of causal relationship than is given by the ampersand. He is busied with dynamic sequences, but he persistently confines himself to static terms.

Under the guidance of the associational psychology, therefore, the extreme of discontinuity in the deliverances of inductive research is aimed at by those economists – Mill and Cairnes being taken as typical – whose names have been associated with deductive methods in modern science. With a fine sense of truth they saw that the notion of causal continuity, as a premise of scientific generalization, is an essentially metaphysical postulate; and they avoided its treacherous ground by denying it, and construing causal sequence to mean a uniformity of coexistences and successions simply. But, since a strict [253] uniformity is nowhere to be observed at first hand in the phenomena with which the investigator is occupied, it has to be found by a laborious interpretation of the phenomena and a diligent abstraction and allowance for disturbing circumstances, whatever may be the meaning of a disturbing circumstance where causal continuity is denied. In this work of interpretation and expurgation the investigator proceeds on a conviction of the orderliness of the natural sequence. *Natura non facit saltum*:[52] a maxim which has no meaning within the stricter limits of the associational theory of knowledge.

Before anything can be said as to the orderliness of the sequence, a point of view must be chosen by the speculator, with respect to which the sequence in

---

52 [Nature makes no leap. – Eds.]

question does or does not fulfil this condition of orderliness; that is to say, with respect to which it is a sequence. The endeavor to avoid all metaphysical premises fails here as everywhere. The associationists, to whom economics owes its transition from the older classical phase to the modern or quasi-classical, chose as their guiding point of view the metaphysical postulate of congruity, – in substance, the "similarity" of the associationist theory of knowledge. This must be called their *proton pseudos*, if associationism pure and simple is to be accepted. The notion of congruity works out in laws of resemblance and equivalence, in both of which it is plain to the modern psychologist that a metaphysical ground of truth, antecedent to and controlling empirical data, is assumed. But the use of the postulate of congruence as a test of scientific truth has the merit of avoiding all open dealing with an imputed substantiality of the data handled, such as would be involved in the overt use of the concept of causation. The data are congruous among themselves, as items of knowledge; and they may therefore be handled in a logical synthesis and concatenation on the basis of this congruence alone, without committing the scientist to an [254] imputation of a kinetic or motor relation between them. The metaphysics of process is thereby avoided, in appearance. The sequences are uniform or consistent with one another, taken as articles of theoretical synthesis simply; and so they become elements of a system or discipline of knowledge in which the test of theoretical truth is the congruence of the system with its premises.

In all this there is a high-wrought appearance of matter-of-fact, and all metaphysical subreption of a non-empirical or non-mechanical standard of reality or substantiality is avoided in appearance. The generalizations which make up such a system of knowledge are, in this way, stated in terms of the system itself; and when a competent formulation of the alleged uniformities has been so made in terms of their congruity or equivalence with the prime postulates of the system, the work of theoretical inquiry is done.

The concrete premises from which proceeds the systematic knowledge of this generation of economists are certain very concise assumptions concerning human nature, and certain slightly less concise generalizations of physical fact,[53] presumed to be mechanically empirical generalizations. These postulates afford the standard of normality. Whatever situation or course of events can be shown to express these postulates without mitigation is normal; and wherever a departure from this normal course of things occurs, it is due to disturbing causes, – that is to say, to causes not comprised in the main premises of the science, – and such departures are to be taken account of by way of qualification. Such departures and such qualification are constantly present in the facts to be handled by the science; but, being not congruous with the underlying postulates, they have no place in the body of the science. The laws of the science, that which makes up the economist's theoretical knowledge,

---

53 See, *e.g.*, Cairnes, *Character and Logical Method* (New York), p. 71.

are laws of the normal case. [255] The normal case does not occur in concrete fact. These laws are, therefore, in Cairnes's terminology, "hypothetical" truths; and the science is a "hypothetical" science. They apply to concrete facts only as the facts are interpreted and abstracted from, in the light of the underlying postulates. The science is, therefore, a theory of the normal case, a discussion of the concrete facts of life in respect of their degree of approximation to the normal case. That is to say, it is a taxonomic science.

Of course, in the work actually done by these economists this standpoint of rigorous normality is not consistently maintained; nor is the unsophisticated imputation of causality to the facts under discussion consistently avoided. The associationist postulate, that causal sequence means empirical uniformity simply, is in great measure forgotten when the subject-matter of the science is handled in detail. Especially is it true that in Mill the dry light of normality is greatly relieved by a strong common sense. But the great truths or laws of the science remain hypothetical laws; and the test of scientific reality is congruence with the hypothetical laws, not coincidence with matter-of-fact events.

The earlier, more archaic metaphysics of the science, which saw in the orderly correlation and sequence of events a constraining guidance of an extra-causal, teleological kind, in this way becomes a metaphysics of normality which asserts no extra-causal constraint over events, but contents itself with establishing correlations, equivalencies, homologies, and theories concerning the conditions of an economic equilibrium. The movement, the process of economic life, is not overlooked, and it may even be said that it is not neglected; but the pure theory, in its final deliverances, deals not with the dynamics, but with the statics of the case. The concrete subject-matter of the science is, of course, the process of economic life, – that is unavoidably the case, – and in so far the discussion [256] must be accepted as work bearing on the dynamics of the phenomena discussed; but even then it remains true that the aim of this work in dynamics is a determination and taxis of the outcome of the process under discussion rather than a theory of the process as such. The process is rated in terms of the equilibrium to which it tends or should tend, not conversely. The outcome of the process, taken in its relation of equivalence within the system, is the point at which the inquiry comes to rest. It is not primarily the point of departure for an inquiry into what may follow. The science treats of a balanced system rather than of a proliferation. In this lies its characteristic difference from the later evolutionary sciences. It is this characteristic bent of the science that leads its spokesman, Cairnes, to turn so kindly to chemistry rather than to the organic sciences, when he seeks an analogy to economics among the physical sciences.[54] What Cairnes has in mind in his appeal to chemistry is, of course, the received, extremely taxonomic (systematic) chemistry of his own time, not the tentatively genetic theories of a slightly later day.

---

54 *Character and Logical Method*, p. 62.

It may seem that in the characterization just offered of the standpoint of normality in economics there is too strong an implication of colorlessness and impartiality. The objection holds as regards much of the work of the modern economists of the classical line. It will hold true even as to much of Cairnes's work; but it cannot be admitted as regards Cairnes's ideal of scientific aim and methods. The economists whose theories Cairnes received and developed, assuredly did not pursue the discussion of the normal case with an utterly dispassionate animus. They had still enough of the older teleological metaphysics left to give color to the accusation brought against them that they were advocates of *laissez-faire*. The preconception of the utilitarians, – in substance the natural-rights preconception. [257] – that unrestrained human conduct will result in the greatest human happiness, retains so much of its force in Cairnes's time as is implied in the then current assumption that what is normal is also right. The economists, and Cairnes among them, not only are concerned to find out what is normal and to determine what consummation answers to the normal, but they also are at pains to approve that consummation. It is this somewhat uncritical and often unavowed identification of the normal with the right that gives colorable ground for the widespread vulgar prejudice, to which Cairnes draws attention,[55] that political economy "sanctions" one social arrangement and "condemns" another. And it is against this uncritical identification of two essentially unrelated principles or categories that Cairnes's essay on "Political Economy and Laissez-faire," and in good part also that on Bastiat, are directed. But, while this is one of the many points at which Cairnes has substantially advanced the ideals of the science, his own concluding argument shows him to have been but half-way emancipated from the prejudice, even while most effectively combating it.[56] It is needless to point out that the like prejudice is still present in good vigor in many later economists who have had the full benefit of Cairnes's teachings on this head.[57] Considerable as Cairnes's achievement in this matter undoubtedly was, it effected a mitigation rather than an elimination of the untenable metaphysics against which he contended.

The advance in the general point of view from animistic teleology to taxonomy is shown in a curiously succinct manner in a parenthetical clause of Cairnes's in the chapter [258] on Normal Value.[58] With his acceptance of the later point of view involved in the use of the new term, Cairnes becomes the interpreter of the received theoretical results. The received positions are not

---

55 *Essays in Political Economy*, pp. 260–64.

56 See especially *Essays*, pp. 263, 264.

57 It may be interesting to point out that the like identification of the categories of normality and right gives the dominant note of Mr. Spencer's ethical and social philosophy, and that later economists of the classical line are prone to be Spencerians.

58 "Normal value (called by Adam Smith and Ricardo 'natural value,' and by Mill 'necessary value,' but best expressed, it seems to me, by the term which I have used)." *Leading Principles* (New York), p. 45.

subjected to a destructive criticism. The aim is to complete them where they fall short and to cut off what may be needless or what may run beyond the safe ground of scientific generalization. In his work of redaction, Cairnes does not avow – probably he is not sensible of – any substantial shifting of the point of view or any change in the accepted ground of theoretic reality. But his advance to an unteleological taxonomy none the less changes the scope and aim of his theoretical discussion. The discussion of Normal Value may be taken in illustration.

Cairnes is not content to find (with Adam Smith) that value will "naturally" coincide with or be measured by cost of production, or even (with Mill) that cost of production must, in the long run, "necessarily" determine value. "This ... is to take a much too limited view of the range of this phenomenon."[59] He is concerned to determine not only this general tendency of values to a normal, but all those characteristic circumstances as well which condition this tendency and which determine the normal to which values tend. His inquiry pursues the phenomena of value in a normal economic system rather than the manner and rate of approach of value relations to a teleologically or hedonistically defensible consummation. It therefore becomes an exhaustive but very discriminating analysis of the circumstances that bear upon market values, with a view to determine what circumstances are normally present; that is to say, what circumstances conditioning value are commonly effective and at the same time in consonance with the premises of economic [259] theory. These effective conditions, in so far as they are not accounted anomalous and, therefore, to be set aside in the theoretical discussion, are the circumstances under which a hedonistic valuation process in any modern industrial community is held perforce to take place, – the circumstances which are held to enforce a recognition and rating of the pleasure-bearing capacity of facts. They are not, as under the earlier cost-of-production doctrines, the circumstances which determine the magnitude of the forces spent in the production of the valuable article. Therefore, the normal (natural) value is no longer (as with Adam Smith, and even to some extent with his classical successors) the primary or initial fact in value theory, the substantial fact of which the market value is an approximate expression and by which the latter is controlled. The argument does not, as formerly, set out from that expenditure of personal force which was once conceived to constitute the substantial value of goods, and then construe market value to be an approximate and uncertain expression of this substantial fact. The direction in which the argument runs is rather the reverse of this. The point of departure is taken from the range of market values and the process of bargaining by which these values are determined. This latter is taken to be a process of discrimination between various kinds and degrees of discomfort, and the average or consistent outcome of such a process of bargaining constitutes normal value. It is

59 *Leading Principles*, p. 45.

only by virtue of a presumed equivalence between the discomfort undergone and the concomitant expenditure, whether of labor or of wealth, that the normal value so determined is conceived to be an expression of the productive force that goes into the creation of the valuable goods. Cost being only in uncertain equivalence with sacrifice or discomfort, as between different persons, the factor of cost falls into the background; and the process of bargaining, which is in the foreground, being a process [260] of valuation, a balancing of individual demand and supply, it follows that a law of reciprocal demand comes in to supplant the law of cost. In all this the proximate causes at work in the determination of values are plainly taken account of more adequately than in earlier cost-of-production doctrines; but they are taken account of with a view to explaining the mutual adjustment and interrelation of elements in a system rather than to explain either a developmental sequence or the working out of a foreordained end.

This revision of the cost-of-production doctrine whereby it takes the form of a law of reciprocal demand is in good part effected by its consistent reduction of cost to terms of sacrifice, – a reduction more consistently carried through by Cairnes than it had been by earlier hedonists, and extended by Cairnes's successors with even more far-reaching results. By this step the doctrine of cost is not only brought into closer accord with the neo-hedonistic premises, in that it in a greater degree throws the stress upon the factor of personal discrimination, but it also gives the doctrine a more general bearing upon economic conduct and increases its serviceability as a comprehensive principle for the classification of economic phenomena. In the further elaboration of the hedonistic theory of value at the hands of Jevons and the Austrians the same principle of sacrifice comes to serve as the chief ground of procedure.

Of the foundations of later theory, in so far as the postulates of later economists differ characteristically from those of Mill and Cairnes, little can be said in this place. Nothing but the very general features of the later development can be taken up; and even these general features of the existing theoretic situation can not be handled with the same confidence as the corresponding features of a past phase of speculation. With respect to writers of [261] the present or the more recent past the work of natural selection, as between variants of scientific aim and animus and between more or less divergent points of view, has not yet taken place; and it would be over-hazardous to attempt an anticipation of the results of the selection that lies in great part yet in the future. As regards the directions of theoretical work suggested by the names of Professor Marshall, Mr. Cannan, Professor Clark, Mr. Pierson, Professor Loria, Professor Schmoller, the Austrian group, – no off-hand decision is admissible as between these candidates for the honor, or, better, for the work, of continuing the main current of economic speculation and inquiry. No attempt will here be made even to pass a verdict on the relative claims of the recognized two or three main "schools" of theory, beyond the somewhat obvious finding that, for the purpose in hand, the so-called Austrian school is scarcely distinguishable from the neo-classical, unless it be in the different distribution of emphasis. The divergence between the modernized classical views, on the one hand, and the historical and Marxist schools, on the other hand, is wider, – so much so, indeed, as to bar out a consideration of the postulates of the latter under the same head of inquiry with the former. The inquiry, therefore, confines itself to the one line standing most obviously in unbroken continuity with that body of classical economics whose life history has been traced in outline above. And, even for this phase of modernized classical economics, it seems necessary to limit discussion, for the present, to a single strain, selected as standing peculiarly close to the classical source, at the same time that it shows unmistakable adaptation to the later habits of thought and methods of knowledge.

For this later development in the classical line of political economy, Mr. Keynes's book may fairly be taken as the maturest exposition of the aims and ideals of the science; [262] while Professor Marshall excellently exemplifies the best work that is being done under the guidance of the classical antecedents. As, after a lapse of a dozen or fifteen years from Cairnes's days of full conviction, Mr. Keynes interprets the aims of modern economic science, it has less of the "hypothetical" character assigned it by Cairnes; that is to say, it confines its inquiry less closely to the ascertainment of the normal case and the interpretative subsumption of facts under the normal. It takes fuller account of the genesis and developmental continuity of all features of modern economic life, gives more and closer attention to institutions and their history. This is, no doubt, due, in part at least, to impulse received from German economists; and in so far it also reflects the peculiarly vague and bewildered attitude of protest that characterizes the earlier expositions of the historical school. To the same essentially extraneous source is traceable the theoretic blur embodied in Mr. Keynes's attitude of tolerance towards the conception of economics as a "normative" science having to do with "economic ideals," or an "applied economics" having to do with "economic precepts."[60] An inchoate departure from the consistent taxonomic ideal shows itself in the tentative resort to historical and genetic formulations, as well as in Mr. Keynes's pervading inclination to define the scope of the science, not by exclusion of what are conceived to be non-economic phenomena, but by disclosing a point of view from which all phenomena are seen to be economic facts. The science comes to be characterized not by the delimitation of a range of facts, as in Cairnes,[61] but as an inquiry into the bearing which all facts have upon men's economic activity. It is no longer that certain phenomena belong within the science, but rather that the science is concerned with any and all phenomena as seen from the point of [263] view of the economic interest. Mr. Keynes does not go fully to the length which this last proposition

60 *Scope and Method of Political Economy* (London, 1891), chaps. i. and ii.
61 *Character and Logical Method*; *e.g.*, Lecture II., especially pp. 53, 54, and 71.

indicates. He finds[62] that political economy "treats of the phenomena arising out of the economic activities of mankind in society": but, while the discussion by which he leads up to this definition might be construed to say that all the activities of mankind in society have an economic bearing, and should therefore come within the view of the science, Mr. Keynes does not carry out his elucidation of the matter to that broad conclusion. Neither can it be said that modern political economy has, in practice, taken on the scope and character which this extreme position would assign it.

The passage from which the above citation is taken is highly significant also in another and related bearing, and it is at the same time highly characteristic of the most effective modernized classical economics. The subject-matter of the science has come to be the "economic activities" of mankind, and the phenomena in which these activities manifest themselves. So Professor Marshall's work, for instance, is, in aim, even if not always in achievement, a theoretical handling of human activity in its economic bearing, – an inquiry into the multiform phases and ramifications of that process of valuation of the material means of life by virtue of which man is an economic agent. And still it remains an inquiry directed to the determination of the conditions of an equilibrium of activities and a quiescent normal situation. It is not in any eminent degree an inquiry into cultural or institutional development as affected by economic exigencies or by the economic interest of the men whose activities are analyzed and portrayed. Any sympathetic reader of Professor Marshall's great work – and that must mean every reader – comes away with a sense of swift and smooth movement and interaction of parts; but it is the movement of a [264] consummately conceived and self-balanced mechanism, not that of a cumulatively unfolding process or an institutional adaptation to cumulatively unfolding exigencies. The taxonomic bearing is, after all, the dominant feature. It is significant of the same point that even in his discussion of such vitally dynamic features of the economic process as the differential effectiveness of different laborers or of different industrial plants, as well as of the differential advantages of consumers, Professor Marshall resorts to an adaptation of so essentially taxonomic a category as the received concept of rent. Rent is a pecuniary category, a category of income, which is essentially a final term, not a category of the motor term work or interest.[63] It is not a factor or a feature of the process of industrial life, but a phenomenon of the pecuniary situation which emerges from this process under given conventional circumstances. However far-reaching and various the employment of the rent concept in economic theory has been, it has through all permutations remained, what it was to begin with, a rubric in the classification of incomes. It is a pecuniary, not an industrial category. In so far as resort is had to the rent concept in the formulation of a theory of the

---

62 *Scope and Method of Political Economy*, chap. iii., particularly p. 97.
63 "Interest" is, of course, here used in the sense which it has in modern psychological discussion.

industrial process, – as in Professor Marshall's work, – it comes to a statement of the process in terms of its residue. Let it not seem presumptuous to say that, great and permanent as is the value of Professor Marshall's exposition of quasi-rents and the like, the endeavor which it involves to present in terms of a concluded system what is of the nature of a fluent process has made the exposition unduly bulky, unwieldy, and inconsequent.

There is a curious reminiscence of the perfect taxonomic day in Mr. Keynes's characterization of political economy as a "positive science," "the sole province of which is to establish economic uniformities";[64] and, in this resort to [265] the associationist expedient of defining a natural law as a "uniformity," Mr. Keynes is also borne out by Professor Marshall.[65] But this and other survivals of the taxonomic terminology, or even of the taxonomic canons of procedure, do not hinder the economists of the modern school from doing effective work of a character that must be rated as genetic rather than taxonomic. Professor Marshall's work in economics is not unlike that of Asa Gray in botany, who, while working in great part within the lines of "systematic botany" and adhering to its terminology, and on the whole also to its point of view, very materially furthered the advance of the science outside the scope of taxonomy.

Professor Marshall shows an aspiration to treat economic life as a development; and, at least superficially, much of his work bears the appearance of being a discussion of this kind. In this endeavor his work is typical of what is aimed at by many of the later economists. The aim shows itself with a persistent recurrence in his *Principles*. His chosen maxim is, *Natura non facit saltum*,[66] – a maxim that might well serve to designate the prevailing attitude of modern economists towards questions of economic development as well as towards questions of classification or of economic policy. His insistence on the continuity of development and of the economic structure of communities is a characteristic of the best work along the later line of classical political economy. All this gives an air of evolutionism to the work. Indeed, the work of the neo-classical economics might be compared, probably without offending any of its adepts, with that of the early generation of Darwinians, though such a comparison might somewhat shrewdly have to avoid any but superficial features. Economists of the present day are commonly evolutionists, in a general way. They commonly [266] accept, as other men do, the general results of the evolutionary speculation in those directions in which the evolutionary method has made its way. But the habit of handling by evolutionist methods the facts with which their own science is concerned has made its way among the economists to but a very uncertain degree.

---

64 *Scope and Method of Political Economy*, p. 46.
65 *Principles of Economics*, vol. i., Book I., chap. vi., sect. 6, especially p. 105 (3d edition).
66 [Nature makes no leap. – Eds.]

The prime postulate of evolutionary science, the preconception constantly underlying the inquiry, is the notion of a cumulative causal sequence; and writers on economics are in the habit of recognizing that the phenomena with which they are occupied are subject to such a law of development. Expressions of assent to this proposition abound. But the economists have not worked out or hit upon a method by which the inquiry in economics may consistently be conducted under the guidance of this postulate. Taking Professor Marshall as exponent, it appears that, while the formulations of economic theory are not conceived to be arrived at by way of an inquiry into the developmental variation of economic institutions and the like, the theorems arrived at are held, and no doubt legitimately, to apply to the past,[67] and with due reserve also to the future, phases of the development. But these theorems apply to the various phases of the development not as accounting for the developmental sequence, but as limiting the range of variation. They say little, if anything, as to the order of succession, as to the derivation and the outcome of any given phase, or as to the causal relation of one phase of any given economic convention or scheme of relations to any other. They indicate the conditions of survival to which any innovation is subject, supposing the innovation to have taken place, not the conditions of variational growth. The economic laws, the "statements of uniformity," are therefore, when construed in an evolutionary bearing, theorems [267] concerning the superior or the inferior limit of persistent innovations, as the case may be.[68] It is only in this negative, selective bearing that the current economic laws are held to be laws of developmental continuity; and it should be added that they have hitherto found but relatively scant application at the hands of the economists, even for this purpose.

Again, as applied to economic activities under a given situation, as laws governing activities in equilibrium, the economic laws are, in the main, laws of the limits within which economic action of a given purpose runs. They are theorems as to the limits which the economic (commonly the pecuniary) interest imposes upon the range of activities to which the other life interests of men incite, rather than theorems as to the manner and degree in which the economic interest creatively shapes the general scheme of life. In great part they formulate the normal inhibitory effect of economic exigencies rather than the cumulative modification and diversification of human activities through the economic interest, by initiating and guiding habits of life and of thought. This, of course, does not go to say that economists are at all slow to credit the economic exigencies with a large share in the growth of culture; but, while claims of this kind are large and recurrent, it remains true that

---

67 See, *e.g.*, Professor Marshall's "Reply" to Professor Cunningham in the *Economic Journal* for 1892, pp. 507–519.

68 This is well illustrated by what Professor Marshall says of the Ricardian law of rent in his "Reply," cited above [in note 67 in this Selection].

the laws which make up the framework of economic doctrine are, when construed as generalizations of causal relation, laws of conservation and selection, not of genesis and proliferation. The truth of this, which is but a commonplace generalization, might be shown in detail with respect to such fundamental theorems as the laws of rent, of profits, of wages, of the increasing or diminishing returns of industry, of population, of competitive prices, of cost of production.

In consonance with this quasi-evolutionary tone of the [268] neo-classical political economy, or as an expression of it, comes the further clarified sense that nowadays attaches to the terms "normal" and economic "laws." The laws have gained in colorlessness, until it can no longer be said that the concept of normality implies approval of the phenomena to which it is applied.[69] They are in an increasing degree laws of conduct, though they still continue to formulate conduct in hedonistic terms; that is to say, conduct is construed in terms of its sensuous effect, not in terms of its teleological content. The light of the science is a drier light than it was, but it continues to be shed upon the accessories of human action rather than upon the process itself. The categories employed for the purpose of knowing this economic conduct with which the scientists occupy themselves are not the categories under which the men at whose hands the action takes place themselves apprehend their own action at the instant of acting. Therefore, economic conduct still continues to be somewhat mysterious to the economists; and they are forced to content themselves with adumbrations whenever the discussion touches this central, substantial fact.

All this, of course, is intended to convey no dispraise of the work done, nor in any way to disparage the theories which the passing generation of economists have elaborated or the really great and admirable body of knowledge which they have brought under the hand of the science; but only to indicate the direction in which the inquiry in its later phases – not always with full consciousness – is shifting as regards its categories and its point of view. The discipline of life in a modern community, particularly the industrial life, strongly re-enforced by the modern sciences, has divested our knowledge of non-human phenomena of that fulness of self-directing life that was once imputed to them, and has reduced this knowledge to terms [269] of opaque causal sequence. It has thereby narrowed the range of discretionary, teleological action to the human agent alone; and so it is compelling our knowledge of human conduct, in so far as it is distinguished from the non-human, to fall into teleological terms. Foot-pounds, calories, geometrically progressive procreation, and doses of capital have not been supplanted by the equally uncouth denominations of habits, propensities, aptitudes, and conventions, nor does there seem to be any probability that they will be; but the discussion which continues to run in terms of the former class of concepts is in an increasing degree seeking support in concepts of the latter class.

---

69 See, *e.g.*, Marshall, *Principles*, Book I., chap. vi., sect. 6, pp. 105–8. The like dispassionateness is visible in most other modern writers on theory; as, *e.g.*, Clark, Cannan, and the Austrians.

Selection 20

Review of *The Development of English Thought: A Study in the Economic Interpretation of History* by Simon N. Patten

Source: *Annals of the American Academy of Political and Social Science*, July 1899 (vol. 14, pp. 125–31).

Veblen (1899e)

If the term be taken in a general sense, Mr. Patten's "Development of English Thought" is a working out of a materialistic conception of history, although his "materialistic conception" is not nearly the same as that to which Marx and Engels gave a vogue in socialistic circles. It is needless to say that it is a marked advance over the somewhat crude form in which the great socialists left their fundamental concept. While they were content with an appeal to class interest and antagonism as a sufficient explanation of the control of cultural development through the economic situation, Mr. Patten's modern scientific animus leads him to look more closely into the causal relation between the economic situation and the resulting culture. The resulting theory is not a doctrine of a class struggle. In Mr. Patten's view the economic situation shapes culture by shaping human character and habits of thought. It does this somewhat directly, through a process of habituation as well as through a concomitant process of selection between habits and between different styles of temperament. The causal relation between the situation ("environment") and the cultural outcome, therefore, lies through the psychological development of the individuals who are exposed to this environment.

Some part of the theoretical ground on which this materialistic doctrine proceeds has already been set forth, in greater detail, in an earlier monograph on "The Theory of Social Forces." The elements of that theory are (1) a frankly and uncritically accepted, though modified, associational psychology, such as had general vogue until a generation ago, with its accompanying hedonism, and (2) a rationalistic doctrine of evolution, stated in terms of the consummation to which the development should tend in order to meet the author's ideal. It is part of the tacit premises of this doctrine that evolution means improvement, amelioration, progress; hence there is occasional reference to the "normal line" of development, and some phases of the development are spoken of as departures and detours from the normal. This resort to normality and a more or less constraining meliorative trend is scarcely a modern feature.

The normal line of development is conceived to run from an earlier "pain economy" to a subsequent "pleasure economy." This distinction, it may be remarked, seems to have no ground in fact and to serve no useful purpose. Under the regime of the archaic "pain economy," [126]

> "fear and the avoidance of pain are the prominent motives for action. The sensory ideas are so grouped that they give early intimation of the presence of every possible foe or evil. ... Man must have an instinctive fear of evil. The sensory and motor powers must unite in emphasizing any quality or person that may be the forerunner of suffering, or the means of avoiding it. Such activities and such a type of mind appear in primitive men, and wherever they are dominant a pain economy results" (p. 8).

Even a hasty and fragmentary comparison of this theory of primitive habits of life and thought with what is known of existing primitive communities will show its irrelevancy. It appears, for instance, that in such communities as those of the Australians, Bushmen or Eskimo, where life is precarious and the environment local, all this does not seem to hold. "Motor ideas" (to accept, without criticising, Mr. Patten's terminology) do not here crowd out "sensory ideas" to the extent which the theory would seem to demand; nor do these bearers of the lower culture bend their thoughts with utter consistency to the avoidance of pain. To some extent – in the case of many Australian tribes to a very great extent—they seem to court pain. Of these latter it is quite safe to say that there is more blood shed by them peacefully and deliberately, in self-torture and ceremonial scarification, than all that is lost in hostile encounter with men and beasts. Their times of peace are times of blood and wounds. Illustrations to the same effect abound in the accounts of other peoples at or near the same cultural level. And far from the "motor ideas" shutting out all other thought processes than a strenuous application to the struggle against a refractory environment, there is on this cultural level a very large and free development of legends and ceremonial myths that have no obvious relation to "fear and the avoidance of pain." And the body of what passes for knowledge among these people is comprehensive and intricate, and shows no peculiarly close correlation with an effective avoidance of evils. "The sensory ideas are" not in any especial degree "so grouped that they give early intimation of the presence of every foe or evil." On the contrary, they are in great part so grouped as to be ineffective for that purpose. In point of fact, most of the known primitive communities are saddled with a stupendous fabric of magical conceits and ceremonials that frequently hinder their avoidance of patent evils. They are also, if the consensus of observers is to be accepted, notably indolent, light-hearted and careless of any evil that is not already upon them. *Dolce far niente*[1] and merry-making, often hideously exuberant,

1 [Sweet doing nothing, or pleasant idleness. – Eds.]

claim a very large portion of their time and attention. It is behind the man on horseback that black care sits; the savage of the earlier, more unmitigated "pain economy" knows little of worry. And the evils which he seriously [127] seeks to avoid are for the most part figments – high-wrought complications of "sensory ideas" that are not controlled by relevant "motor ideas." The evidence from ethnology seems to say that care and deliberation for the avoidance of evils find no place in the early culture until the necessity of taking thought is forced home upon the luckless by a successful incursion from without; and such an incursion commonly comes from men who seek an increase of pleasures through booty, – the "sensualists" of Mr. Patten's nomenclature, that are bred in a "pleasure economy."

The predilection for sharp antitheses and striking transitions that shows itself in the overdrawn contrast between a "pain economy" and a "pleasure economy" appears again in the repeated insistence on the epochal character of historical development. Mr. Patten finds that history proceeds by epochs, each of which begins with a transition to a new and novel environment and affords an entirely new and unprejudiced point of departure. The impression conveyed is that of an extreme segmentation of the sequence.

> "Each succeeding environment will … create a new series of economic, æsthetic, moral, and religious ideas which will have their basis in the economic conditions of the epoch. The history of each epoch is thus practically independent, starting from its own conditions and developing in its own way. In studying an epoch, the economic conditions must be studied first, then the economic doctrines that flow from them, and last the æsthetic, moral, and religious ideas which the epoch produces."
>
> "The different groups of ideas cannot be traced independently, because the ideas of each epoch do not grow out of the similar ideas of the preceding epoch, but are formed anew from the new conditions" (p. 44).
>
> "History, to be valuable, must be studied in epochs, and each group of ideas [economic, æsthetic, moral, religious] be connected with its roots in the underlying conditions, and not with its antecedents in the same group. The blending of the old and the new groups of ideas happens after the new conditions have exerted their force, or at least have brought out what is most peculiar to them" (p. 45).

The notion of a sheer transition and a fresh start is mitigated rather than superseded by the subsequent statement that each succeeding temporary environment

> "has given to the race certain characteristics that become a part of the national character. And thus character is the one enduring growing element in a civilization; all else when compared with it is temporary and fleeting"

for it remains true that

"in each new environment a new nation grows up almost as distinct from its predecessors as were the new nations of ancient times from the nations that preceded them" (p. 46–47).

That continuity of traditions and usages that has so impressed students of institutions and folklore, as well as that persistence of [128] physical type and temperamental bent that makes the burden of the teachings of the modern anthropologists, seem to have passed harmless over Mr. Patten.

The antecedents of English thought (ch. ii) are proximately racial, more remotely climatic; but the analysis is pushed back of the racial to the climatic with a freedom which indicates that in Mr. Patten's view the sequence covered by these terms is by no means a long one. The character of the race is created by an economic (climatic) situation which imposes certain traits upon men. These traits may be imposed by a relatively brief discipline, but after they have once been imposed they persist with an extreme tenacity. Further changes in the "character" of the race take place by the imposition of added traits, rather than by an organic change or selective variation of hereditary temperament or by an alteration in the individual's habits of thought. One gets the impression that traits are conceived to make up a mechanical aggregate, which is the race character, and to which new items may be added without essentially disturbing the previously existing aggregation (see pp. 4–21, 50–52, 57–66).

Mr. Patten's theoretical handling of the antecedents of English thought will be found at many points to traverse received notions of the primitive growth of culture, and his statements of fact in this connection also do not easily fit into the framework of the published accounts of existing primitive communities. Under the former head there is a characteristically bold departure from current notions as to the origin, nature, and functional relations of the clan (p. 109). Again, Mr. Patten says that "the northern man conquers nature, while the southern man yields to it" (pp. 5–8). An American reader will instinctively call to mind the Aleutian and Alaskan tribes on the one hand, and the Yucatanese and Mexican civilizations on the other, and the juxtaposition of the author's generalization with the specific facts leaves the effect of a drawn game.

> "In wet, cold countries, natural forces act regularly, and the social surplus is small. Here men unite into strongly knit social groups, with a well-developed feeling of the solidarity of responsibility. Vigorous and aggressive, they react promptly against sources of pain" (p. 64).

This again calls up the Eskimo, the Fuegians, the Ainu, whose social groups are not seriously to be weighed in the balance of solidarity. And to make the bewilderment complete one might add the Haida, except for the fact that with them the food supply ("social surplus") was not scant, while their social groups were "strongly knit."

So again, in contrast, [129]

> "These concepts of peace and obedience do not come naturally to people living in hot, dry countries, where nature is arbitrary. ... As their privations seem to be due to their own shortcomings, they develop readily the concept of sin and of a fallen nature. But peace they do not look for, and obedience they do not yield. On the contrary, they have inclinations toward a life of asceticism and individual freedom. Among these people there is no powerful priesthood and no concept of God except as a being to fear and avoid" (p. 63).

The Mexicans and Pueblos should afford illustration of this text, but credible accounts say that they do not altogether. The Pueblos, for instance, probably as clear a case as may be found, are currently held by students of their culture to be peaceable, obedient to their chosen authorities, not noticeably conscious of their own shortcoming, not perceptibly inclined to asceticism, with a priesthood constituting the strongest power among them, with an extensive and well-grown mythology and an intricate and elaborate cult, constantly resorting for comfort to their divinities, of whom they have but little fear.

This anthropological-economic verification of Mr. Patten's underlying principles of interpretation might be continued at considerable length without coming closer to a conviction of their adequacy. But all this touches only the preliminaries and premises of the discussion, not the main work of interpretation itself. It may seem gratuitous and ungraceful to apply these preliminary generalizations to the case of peoples that lie outside of that European culture with which alone his argument is occupied; but if the generalizations are to apply with such force as to afford a point of departure within the European culture they should be of such a consistency as to avoid the appearance of having been constructed *ad hoc*.

It is to be regretted that, even at points that are not peculiarly recondite or difficult, in the handling of the main question, faults of the same kind occur again. So, in the distinction made between his three typical civilizations, German, Semitic and Roman, Mr. Patten overlooks that difference of racial stocks that anthropologists make much of, and resorts instead to an unnecessarily bald appeal to the economic situation (p. 64). Similarly, the like persistent racial difference traceable between Catholics and Protestants, and in a less degree between Calvinists and Lutherans, is neglected at a later point (ch. ii, also pp. 110–42).

> "The character of the early German was due mainly to the damp, cold climate in which he lived, and to the meagre food products upon which he subsisted" (p. 65).

The evidence of the German's food products being meagre is not easy to find; where evidence of the early dietary is most available, as, for instance, in the case of the older Scandinavian communities, [130] it goes the other way. Nor does the statement (p. 66) that in Germany the equilibrium of population was maintained by pressing against nature for the means of subsistence comport with the other statement, on the same page, that "their migrations seem to have been actuated, not by starvation, but by greed." So also it seems paradoxical to say that the character of that Germanic stock that won its way by the sword "has few of the traits which war creates."

But paradox and the inversion of received views are not among the things which this book avoids. Wide divergence from the common-place interpretations meets the reader at almost all points of first-rate consequence. At first one is struck with the novelty and force of the new formulations, and one has a feeling that Mr. Patten must have discovered and will unfold a wealth of evidence that shall substantiate the new positions taken. But with further progress this feeling (perhaps unwarrantably) wears off, as the proliferation of novel ideas and the paucity of documentation goes on. The matter-of-fact material handled in the body of the volume raises fewer questions of authenticity than the striking statements made in the hundred-odd pages of theoretical groundwork, but there are few portions of the book in the reading of which one quite escapes the apprehension that the facts cited are speaking under constraint. And Mr. Patten's handling of the theme is so flexuous and multiform, and to one not in entire sympathy with his premises and his point of view it seems at times so whimsical and inconsequent, that a detailed scrutiny of the argument would be a large and by no means attractive employment and could scarcely avoid the appearance of captiousness.

It is a book of which it is not easy to say much in the way of commendation that shall be specific enough to bear itemized statement. But none the less it will afford valuable suggestion and incentive, and, indeed, guidance, to the economic study of many features of European culture. It abounds in irrelevant generalizations, but there is also much of shrewd observation, with many new and cogent characterizations of the writers and tenets with which the book deals. We may not be able to accept Mr. Patten's position that antagonism to Puritan enthusiasm was the deciding motive and guide in Locke's work; nor may many students find conviction in the characterization of Darwin as a "philosopher on the downward curve," or of Hume as an economist changed into a philosopher. But the pointed contrast of Mr. Patten's views on these heads as against what has passed current will at least have a salutary effect in directing the attention of students to features in the development of thought which have commonly been passed over too lightly. The account given of the development of the English "home" and of the cultural causes and effects of the English [131] status of women does not seem conclusive, in view of the fact that a passably equivalent economic situation in other communities, where race, religion, or social traditions have been different, has not worked out like results. But here again the discussion throws an effective light upon the questions in hand, though it is perhaps to be rated as a side light. One is somewhat at a loss to account for the very high degree of efficacy imputed to the Christian religion – an intrusive cult – in Germanic and English culture, in a discussion whose first, if not sole, postulate is that the economic situation shapes the cultural sequence without help or hindrance from any outside spiritual force or from any antecedent tradition or tenet. And still, inconsistent as it may be, his handling of this intrusive cult as a formative element in English spiritual life is by no means the least effective of Mr. Patten's work.

On one point at least, of general bearing, Mr. Patten's conclusion seems blind to those who do not see all these matters through his eyes. In chapter iii (p. 188–89) and again in his concluding remarks (p. 378) it is broadly stated that the English have shown a conspicuous incapacity for the development of political institutions. This raises a question as to what may be meant by a capacity for political life – in that economic relation with which Mr. Patten is avowedly occupied – beyond such an adequate adjustment to their economic situation as Mr. Patten shows the English to be eminently possessed of.

Selection 21

The Theory of the Leisure Class: An Economic Study in the Evolution of Institutions

Source: Chapter VIII, pp. 188–211. New York: Macmillan, 1899.

Veblen (1899c)

Industrial exemption and conservatism

The life of man in society, just like the life of other species, is a struggle for existence, and therefore it is a process of selective adaptation. The evolution of social structure has been a process of natural selection of institutions. The progress which has been and is being made in human institutions and in human character may be set down, broadly, to a natural selection of the fittest habits of thought and to a process of enforced adaptation of individuals to an environment which has progressively changed with the growth of the community and with the changing institutions under which men have lived. Institutions are not only themselves the result of a selective and adaptive process which shapes the prevailing or dominant types of spiritual attitude and aptitudes; they are at the same time special methods of life and of human relations, and are therefore in their turn efficient factors of selection. So that the changing institutions in their turn make for a further selection of individuals endowed with the fittest temperament, and a further adaptation of individual temperament and habits to the changing environment through the formation of new institutions. [189]

The forces which have shaped the development of human life and of social structure are no doubt ultimately reducible to terms of living tissue and material environment; but proximately, for the purpose in hand, these forces may best be stated in terms of an environment, partly human, partly non-human, and a human subject with a more or less definite physical and intellectual constitution. Taken in the aggregate or average, this human subject is more or less variable; chiefly, no doubt, under a rule of selective conservation of favourable variations. The selection of favourable variations is perhaps in great measure a selective conservation of ethnic types. In the life history of any community whose population is made up of a mixture of divers ethnic elements, one or another of several persistent and relatively stable types of body and of temperament rises into dominance at any given point. The situation, including the institutions in force at any given time, will favour the survival and dominance of one type of character in preference to another; and the type of man so selected to continue and to further elaborate the institutions handed down from the past will in some considerable measure shape these institutions in his own likeness. But apart from selection as between relatively stable types of character and habits of mind, there is no doubt simultaneously going on a process of selective adaptation of habits of thought within the general range of aptitudes which is characteristic of the dominant ethnic type or types. There may be a variation in the fundamental character of any population by selection between relatively stable types; but there is [190] also a variation due to adaptation in detail within the range of the type, and to selection between specific habitual views regarding any given social relation or group of relations.

For the present purpose, however, the question as to the nature of the adaptive process – whether it is chiefly a selection between stable types of temperament and character, or chiefly an adaptation of men's habits of thought to changing circumstances – is of less importance than the fact that, by one method or another, institutions change and develop. Institutions must change with changing circumstances, since they are of the nature of an habitual method of responding to the stimuli which these changing circumstances afford. The development of these institutions is the development of society. The institutions are, in substance, prevalent habits of thought with respect to particular relations and particular functions of the individual and of the community; and the scheme of life, which is made up of the aggregate of institutions in force at a given time or at a given point in the development of any society, may, on the psychological side, be broadly characterised as a prevalent spiritual attitude or a prevalent theory of life. As regards its generic features, this spiritual attitude or theory of life is in the last analysis reducible to terms of a prevalent type of character.

The situation of to-day shapes the institutions of tomorrow through a selective, coercive process, by acting upon men's habitual view of things, and so altering or fortifying a point of view or a mental attitude handed [191] down from the past. The institutions – that is to say the habits of thought – under the guidance of which men live are in this way received from an earlier time; more or less remotely earlier, but in any event they have been elaborated in and received from the past. Institutions are products of the past process, are adapted to past circumstances, and are therefore never in full accord with the requirements of the present. In the nature of the case, this process of selective adaptation can never catch up with the progressively changing situation in which the community finds itself at any given time; for the environment, the situation, the exigencies of life which enforce the adaptation and exercise the selection, change from day to day; and each successive situation of the community in its turn tends to obsolescence as soon as it has been established. When a step in the development has been taken, this step itself constitutes a change of situation which requires a new adaptation; it becomes the point of departure for a new step in the adjustment, and so on interminably.

It is to be noted then, although it may be a tedious truism, that the institutions of to-day – the present accepted scheme of life – do not entirely fit the situation of to-day. At the same time, men's present habits of thought tend to persist indefinitely, except as circumstances enforce a change. These institutions which have so been handed down, these habits of thought, points of view, mental attitudes and aptitudes, or what not, are therefore themselves a conservative factor. This is the factor of social inertia, psychological inertia, conservatism. [192]

Social structure changes, develops, adapts itself to an altered situation, only through a change in the habits of thought of the several classes of the community; or in the last analysis, through a change in the habits of thought of the individuals which make up the community. The evolution of society is substantially a process of mental adaptation on the part of individuals under the stress of circumstances which will no longer tolerate habits of thought formed under and conforming to a different set of circumstances in the past. For the immediate purpose it need not be a question of serious importance whether this adaptive process is a process of selection and survival of persistent ethnic types or a process of individual adaptation and an inheritance of acquired traits.

Social advance, especially as seen from the point of view of economic theory, consists in a continued progressive approach to an approximately exact "adjustment of inner relations to outer relations"; but this adjustment is never definitively established, since the "outer relations" are subject to constant change as a consequence of the progressive change going on in the "inner relations." But the degree of approximation may be greater or less, depending on the facility with which an adjustment is made. A readjustment of men's habits of thought to conform with the exigencies of an altered situation is in any case made only tardily and reluctantly, and only under the coercion exercised by a stipulation which has made the accredited views untenable. The readjustment of institutions and habitual views to an altered environment is made in response to [193] pressure from without; it is of the nature of a response to stimulus. Freedom and facility of readjustment, that is to say capacity for growth in social structure, therefore depends in great measure on the degree of freedom with which the situation at any given time acts on the individual members of the community – the degree of exposure of the individual members to the constraining forces of the environment. If any portion or class of society is sheltered from the action of the environment in any essential respect, that portion of the community, or that class, will adapt its views and its scheme of life more tardily to the altered general situation; it will in so far tend to retard the process of social transformation. The wealthy leisure class is in such a sheltered position with respect to the economic forces that make for change and readjustment. And it may be said that the forces which make for a readjustment of institutions, especially in the case of a modern industrial community, are, in the last analysis, almost entirely of an economic nature.

Any community may be viewed as an industrial or economic mechanism, the structure of which is made up of what is called its economic institutions. These institutions are habitual methods of carrying on the life process of the community in contact with the material environment in which it lives. When given methods of unfolding human activity in this given environment have been elaborated in this way, the life of the community will express itself with some facility in these habitual directions. The community will make use of the forces of the environment for the purposes of its [194] life according to methods learned in the past and embodied in these institutions. But as population increases, and as men's knowledge and skill in directing the forces of nature widen, the habitual methods of relation between the members of the group, and the habitual method of carrying on the life process of the group as a whole, no longer give the same result as before; nor are the resulting conditions of life distributed and apportioned in the same manner or with the same effect among the various members as before. If the scheme according to which the life process of the group was carried on under the earlier conditions gave approximately the highest attainable result – under the circumstances – in the way of efficiency or facility of the life process of the group, then the same scheme of life unaltered will not yield the highest result attainable in this respect under the altered conditions. Under the altered conditions of population, skill, and knowledge, the facility of life as carried on according to the traditional scheme may not be lower than under the earlier conditions; but the chances are always that it is less than might be if the scheme were altered to suit the altered conditions.

The group is made up of individuals, and the group's life is the life of individuals carried on in at least ostensible severalty. The group's accepted scheme of life is the consensus of views held by the body of these individuals as to what is right, good, expedient, and beautiful in the way of human life. In the redistribution of the conditions of life that comes of the altered method of dealing with the environment, the outcome [195] is not an equable change in the facility of life throughout the group. The altered conditions may increase the facility of life for the group as a whole, but the redistribution will usually result in a decrease of facility or fulness of life for some members of the group. An advance in technical methods, in population, or in industrial organisation will require at least some of the members of the community to change their habits of life, if they are to enter with facility and effect into the altered industrial methods; and in doing so they will be unable to live up to the received notions as to what are the right and beautiful habits of life.

Any one who is required to change his habits of life and his habitual relations to his fellow-men will feel the discrepancy between the method of life required of him by the newly arisen exigencies, and the traditional scheme of life to which he is accustomed. It is the individuals placed in this position who have the liveliest incentive to reconstruct the received scheme of life and are most readily persuaded to accept new standards; and it is through the need of the means of livelihood that men are placed in such a position. The pressure exerted by the environment upon the group, and making for a read-justment of the group's scheme of life, impinges upon the members of the group in the form of pecuniary exigencies; and it is owing to this fact – that external forces are in great part translated into the form of pecuniary or eco-nomic exigencies – that we can say that the forces which count toward a readjustment of institutions in any modern industrial community are chiefly economic forces; or [196] more specifically, these forces take the form of pecuniary pressure. Such a readjustment as is here contemplated is sub-stantially a change in men's views as to what is good and right, and the means through which a change is wrought in men's apprehension of what is good and right is in large part the pressure of pecuniary exigencies.

Any change in men's views as to what is good and right in human life make its way but tardily at the best. Especially is this true of any change in the direction of what is called progress; that is to say, in the direction of diver-gence from the archaic position – from the position which may be accounted the point of departure at any step in the social evolution of the community. Retrogression, reapproach to a standpoint to which the race has been long habituated in the past, is easier. This is especially true in case the development away from this past standpoint has not been due chiefly to a substitution of an ethnic type whose temperament is alien to the earlier standpoint.

The cultural stage which lies immediately back of the present in the life his-tory of Western civilisation is what has here been called the quasi-peaceable stage. At this quasi-peaceable stage the law of status is the dominant feature in the scheme of life. There is no need of pointing out how prone the men of to-day are to revert to the spiritual attitude of mastery and of personal sub-servience which characterises that stage. It may rather be said to be held in an uncertain abeyance by the economic exigencies of to-day, than to have been definitely supplanted by a habit of mind that is [197] in full accord with these later-developed exigencies. The predatory and quasi-peaceable stages of eco-nomic evolution seem to have been of long duration in the life history of all the chief ethnic elements which go to make up the populations of the Western culture. The temperament and the propensities proper to those cultural stages have, therefore, attained such a persistence as to make a speedy reversion to the broad features of the corresponding psychological constitution inevitable in the case of any class or community which is removed from the action of those forces that make for a maintenance of the later-developed habits of thought.

It is a matter of common notoriety that when individuals, or even con-siderable groups of men, are segregated from a higher industrial culture and exposed to a lower cultural environment, or to an economic situation of a more primitive character, they quickly show evidence of reversion toward the spiritual features which characterise the predatory type; and it seems probable that the dolicho-blond type of European man is possessed of a greater facility for such reversion to barbarism than the other ethnic elements with which that type is associated in the Western culture. Examples of such a reversion on a small scale abound in the later history of migration and colonisation. Except for the fear of offending that chauvinistic patriotism which is so characteristic a feature of the predatory culture, and the presence of which is frequently the most striking mark of reversion in modern communities, the case of the American colonies might be cited as an example of [198] such a reversion on an unusually large scale, though it was not a reversion of very large scope.

The leisure class is in great measure sheltered from the stress of those economic exigencies which prevail in any modern, highly organised industrial community. The exigencies of the struggle for the means of life are less exacting for this class than for any other; and as a consequence of this privileged position we should expect to find it one of the least responsive of the classes of society to the demands which the situation makes for a further growth of institutions and a readjustment to an altered industrial situation. The leisure class is the conservative class. The exigencies of the general economic situation of the community do not freely or directly impinge upon the members of this class. They are not required under penalty of forfeiture to change their habits of life and their theoretical views of the external world to suit the demands of an altered industrial technique, since they are not in the full sense an organic part of the industrial community. Therefore these exigencies do not readily produce, in the members of this class, that degree of uneasiness with the existing order which alone can lead any body of men to give up views and methods of life that have become habitual to them. The office of the leisure class in social evolution is to retard the movement and to conserve what is obsolescent. This proposition is by no means novel; it has long been one of the commonplaces of popular opinion.

The prevalent conviction that the wealthy class is by [199] nature conservative has been popularly accepted without much aid from any theoretical view as to the place and relation of that class in the cultural development. When an explanation of this class conservatism is offered, it is commonly the invidious one that the wealthy class opposes innovation because it has a vested interest, of an unworthy sort, in maintaining the present conditions. The explanation here put forward imputes no unworthy motive. The opposition of the class to changes in the cultural scheme is instinctive, and does not rest primarily on an interested calculation of material advantages; it is an instinctive revulsion at any departure from the accepted way of doing and of looking at things – a revulsion common to all men and only to be overcome by stress of circumstances. All change in habits of life and of thought is irksome. The difference in this respect between the wealthy and the common run of mankind lies not so much in the motive which prompts to conservatism as in the degree of exposure to the economic forces that urge a change. The members of the wealthy class do not yield to the demand for innovation as readily as other men because they are not constrained to do so.

This conservatism of the wealthy class is so obvious a feature that it has even come to be recognised as a mark of respectability. Since conservatism is a characteristic of the wealthier and therefore more reputable portion of the community, it has acquired a certain honorific or decorative value. It has become prescriptive to such an extent that an adherence to conservative views is comprised as a matter of course in our notions [200] of respectability; and it is imperatively incumbent on all who would lead a blameless life in point of social repute. Conservatism, being an upper-class characteristic, is decorous; and conversely, innovation, being a lower-class phenomenon, is vulgar. The first and most unreflected element in that instinctive revulsion and reprobation with which we turn from all social innovators is this sense of the essential vulgarity of the thing. So that even in cases where one recognises the substantial merits of the case for which the innovator is spokesman – as may easily happen if the evils which he seeks to remedy are sufficiently remote in point of time or space or personal contact – still one cannot but be sensible of the fact that the innovator is a person with whom it is at least distasteful to be associated, and from whose social contact one must shrink. Innovation is bad form.

The fact that the usages, actions, and views of the well-to-do leisure class acquire the character of a prescriptive canon of conduct for the rest of society, gives added weight and reach to the conservative influence of that class. It makes it incumbent upon all reputable people to follow their lead. So that, by virtue of its high position as the avatar of good form, the wealthier class comes to exert a retarding influence upon social development far in excess of that which the simple numerical strength of the class would assign it. Its prescriptive example acts to greatly stiffen the resistance of all other classes against any innovation, and to fix men's affections upon the good institutions handed down from an earlier generation. [201]

There is a second way in which the influence of the leisure class acts in the same direction, so far as concerns hindrance to the adoption of a conventional scheme of life more in accord with the exigencies of the time. This second method of upper-class guidance is not in strict consistency to be brought under the same category as the instinctive conservatism and aversion to new modes of thought just spoken of; but it may as well be dealt with here, since it has at least this much in common with the conservative habit of mind that it acts to retard innovation and the growth of social structure. The code of proprieties, conventionalities, and usages in vogue at any given time and among any given people has more or less of the character of an organic whole; so that any appreciable change in one point of the scheme involves something of a change or readjustment at other points also, if not a reorganisation all along the line. When a change is made which immediately touches only a minor point in the scheme, the consequent derangement of the structure of conventionalities may be inconspicuous; but even in such a case it is safe to say that some derangement of the general scheme, more or less far-reaching, will follow. On the other hand, when an attempted reform involves the suppression or thorough-going remodelling of an institution of first-rate importance in the conventional scheme, it is immediately felt that a serious derangement of the entire scheme would result; it is felt that a readjustment of the structure to the new form taken on by one of its chief elements would be a painful and tedious, if not a doubtful process. [202]

In order to realise the difficulty which such a radical change in any one feature of the conventional scheme of life would involve, it is only necessary to suggest the suppression of the monogamic family, or of the agnatic system of consanguinity, or of private property, or of the theistic faith, in any country of the Western civilisation; or suppose the suppression of ancestor worship in China, or of the caste system in India, or of slavery in Africa, or the establishment of equality of the sexes in Mohammedan countries. It needs no argument to show that the derangement of the general structure of conventionalities in any of these cases would be very considerable. In order to effect such an innovation a very far-reaching alteration of men's habits of thought would be involved also at other points of the scheme than the one immediately in question. The aversion to any such innovation amounts to a shrinking from an essentially alien scheme of life.

The revulsion felt by good people at any proposed departure from the accepted methods of life is a familiar fact of everyday experience. It is not unusual to hear those persons who dispense salutary advice and admonition to the community express themselves forcibly upon the far-reaching pernicious effects which the community would suffer from such relatively slight changes as the disestablishment of the Anglican Church, an increased facility of divorce, adoption of female suffrage, prohibition of the manufacture and sale of intoxicating beverages, abolition or restriction of inheritances, etc. Any one of these innovations would, we are told, "shake the social structure to its base," "reduce society to chaos," [203] "subvert the foundations of morality," "make life intolerable," "confound the order of nature," etc. These various locutions are, no doubt, of the nature of hyperbole; but, at the same time, like all overstatement, they are evidence of a lively sense of the gravity of the consequences which they are intended to describe. The effect of these and like innovations in deranging the accepted scheme of life is felt to be of much graver consequence than the simple alteration of an isolated item in a series of contrivances for the convenience of men in society. What is true in so obvious a degree of innovations of first-rate importance is true in a less degree of changes of a smaller immediate importance. The aversion to change is in large part an aversion to the bother of making the readjustment which any given change will necessitate; and this solidarity of the system of institutions of any given culture or of any given people strengthens the instinctive resistance offered to any change in men's habits of thought, even in matters which, taken by themselves, are of minor importance.

A consequence of this increased reluctance, due to the solidarity of human institutions, is that any innovation calls for a greater expenditure of nervous energy in making the necessary readjustment than would otherwise be the case. It is not only that a change in established habits of thought is distasteful.

The process of readjustment of the accepted theory of life involves a degree of mental effort – a more or less protracted and laborious effort to find and to keep one's bearings under the altered circumstances. This process requires a certain expenditure of energy, and so presumes, for its successful [204] accomplishment, some surplus of energy beyond that absorbed in the daily struggle for subsistence. Consequently it follows that progress is hindered by underfeeding and excessive physical hardship, no less effectually than by such a luxurious life as will shut out discontent by cutting off the occasion for it. The abjectly poor, and all those persons whose energies are entirely absorbed by the struggle for daily sustenance, are conservative because they cannot afford the effort of taking thought for the day after to-morrow; just as the highly prosperous are conservative because they have small occasion to be discontented with the situation as it stands to-day.

From this proposition it follows that the institution of a leisure class acts to make the lower classes conservative by withdrawing from them as much as it may of the means of sustenance, and so reducing their consumption, and consequently their available energy, to such a point as to make them incapable of the effort required for the learning and adoption of new habits of thought. The accumulation of wealth at the upper end of the pecuniary scale implies privation at the lower end of the scale. It is a commonplace that, wherever it occurs, a considerable degree of privation among the body of the people is a serious obstacle to any innovation.

This direct inhibitory effect of the unequal distribution of wealth is seconded by an indirect effect tending to the same result. As has already been seen, the imperative example set by the upper class in fixing the canons of reputability fosters the practice of conspicuous consumption. The prevalence of conspicuous [205] consumption as one of the main elements in the standard of decency among all classes is of course not traceable wholly to the example of the wealthy leisure class, but the practice and the insistence on it are no doubt strengthened by the example of the leisure class. The requirements of decency in this matter are very considerable and very imperative; so that even among classes whose pecuniary position is sufficiently strong to admit a consumption of goods considerably in excess of the subsistence minimum, the disposable surplus left over after the more imperative physical needs are satisfied is not infrequently diverted to the purpose of a conspicuous decency, rather than to added physical comfort and fulness of life. Moreover, such surplus energy as is available is also likely to be expended in the acquisition of goods for conspicuous consumption or conspicuous hoarding. The result is that the requirements of pecuniary reputability tend (1) to leave but a scanty subsistence minimum available for other than conspicuous consumption, and (2) to absorb any surplus energy which may be available after the bare physical necessities of life have been provided for. The outcome of the whole is a strengthening of the general conservative attitude of the community. The institution of a leisure class hinders cultural development immediately (1) by the inertia proper to the class itself, and (2) through its prescriptive example of conspicuous waste and of conservatism, and (3) indirectly through that system of unequal distribution of wealth and sustenance on which the institution itself rests.

To this is to be added that the leisure class has also [206] a material interest in leaving things as they are. Under the circumstances prevailing at any given time this class is in a privileged position, and any departure from the existing order may be expected to work to the detriment of the class rather than the reverse. The attitude of the class, simply as influenced by its class interest, should therefore be to let well-enough alone. This interested motive comes in to supplement the strong instinctive bias of the class, and so to render it even more consistently conservative than it otherwise would be.

All this, of course, has nothing to say in the way of eulogy or deprecation of the office of the leisure class as an exponent and vehicle of conservatism or reversion in social structure. The inhibition which it exercises may be salutary or the reverse. Whether it is the one or the other in any given case is a question of casuistry rather than of general theory. There may be truth in the view (as a question of policy) so often expressed by the spokesmen of the conservative element, that without some such substantial and consistent resistance to innovation as is offered by the conservative well-to-do classes, social innovation and experiment would hurry the community into untenable and intolerable situations; the only possible result of which would be discontent and disastrous reaction. All this, however, is beside the present argument.

But apart from all deprecation, and aside from all question as to the indispensability of some such check on headlong innovation, the leisure class, in the nature of things, consistently acts to retard that adjustment to [207] the environment which is called social advance or development. The characteristic attitude of the class may be summed up in the maxim: "Whatever is, is right"; whereas the law of natural selection, as applied to human institutions, gives the axiom: "Whatever is, is wrong." Not that the institutions of to-day are wholly wrong for the purposes of the life of to-day, but they are, always and in the nature of things, wrong to some extent. They are the result of a more or less inadequate adjustment of the methods of living to a situation which prevailed at some point in the past development; and they are therefore wrong by something more than the interval which separates the present situation from that of the past. "Right" and "wrong" are of course here used without conveying any reflection as to what ought or ought not to be. They are applied simply from the (morally colourless) evolutionary standpoint, and are intended to designate compatibility or incompatibility with the effective evolutionary process. The institution of a leisure class, by force of class interest and instinct, and by precept and prescriptive example, makes for the perpetuation of the existing maladjustment of institutions, and even favours a reversion to a somewhat more archaic scheme of life; a scheme which would be still farther out of adjustment with the exigencies of life under the existing situation even than the accredited, obsolescent scheme that has come down from the immediate past.

But after all has been said on the head of conservation of the good old ways, it remains true that institutions [208] change and develop. There is a cumulative growth of customs and habits of thought; a selective adaptation of conventions and methods of life. Something is to be said of the office of the leisure class in guiding this growth as well as in retarding it; but little can be said here of its relation to institutional growth except as it touches the institutions that are primarily and immediately of an economic character. These institutions – the economic structure – may be roughly distinguished into two classes or categories, according as they serve one or the other of two divergent purposes of economic life.

To adapt the classical terminology, they are institutions of acquisition or of production; or to revert to terms already employed in a different connection in earlier chapters, they are pecuniary or industrial institutions; or in still other terms, they are institutions serving either the invidious or the non-invidious economic interest. The former category have to do with "business," the latter with industry, taking the latter word in the mechanical sense. The latter class are not often recognised as institutions, in great part because they do not immediately concern the ruling class, and are, therefore, seldom the subject of legislation or of deliberate convention. When they do receive attention they are commonly approached from the pecuniary or business side; that being the side or phase of economic life that chiefly occupies men's deliberations in our time, especially the deliberations of the upper classes. These classes have little else than a business interest in things economic, and on them at the same time it is [209] chiefly incumbent to deliberate upon the community's affairs.

The relation of the leisure (that is, propertied non-industrial) class to the economic process is a pecuniary relation – a relation of acquisition, not of production; of exploitation, not of serviceability. Indirectly their economic office may, of course, be of the utmost importance to the economic life process; and it is by no means here intended to depreciate the economic function of the propertied class or of the captains of industry. The purpose is simply to point out what is the nature of the relation of these classes to the industrial process and to economic institutions. Their office is of a parasitic character, and their interest is to divert what substance they may to their own use, and to retain whatever is under their hand. The conventions of the business world have grown up under the selective surveillance of this principle of predation or parasitism. They are conventions of ownership; derivatives, more or less remote, of the ancient predatory culture. But these pecuniary institutions do not entirely fit the situation of to-day, for they have grown up under a past situation differing somewhat from the present. Even for effectiveness in the pecuniary way, therefore, they are not as apt as might be. The changed industrial life requires changed methods of acquisition; and the pecuniary classes have some interest in so adapting the pecuniary institutions as to give them the best effect for acquisition of private gain that is compatible with the continuance of the industrial process out of which this gain arises. Hence there is a more or less consistent trend [210] in the leisure-class guidance of institutional growth, answering to the pecuniary ends which shape leisure-class economic life.

The effect of the pecuniary interest and the pecuniary habit of mind upon the growth of institutions is seen in those enactments and conventions that make for security of property, enforcement of contracts, facility of pecuniary transactions, vested interests. Of such bearing are changes affecting bankruptcy and receiverships, limited liability, banking and currency, coalitions of labourers or employers, trusts and pools. The community's institutional furniture of this kind is of immediate consequence only to the propertied classes, and in proportion as they are propertied; that is to say, in proportion as they are to be ranked with the leisure class. But indirectly these conventions of business life are of the gravest consequence for the industrial process and for the life of the community. And in guiding the institutional growth in this respect, the pecuniary classes, therefore, serve a purpose of the most serious importance to the community, not only in the conservation of the accepted social scheme, but also in shaping the industrial process proper.

The immediate end of this pecuniary institutional structure and of its amelioration is the greater facility of peaceable and orderly exploitation; but its remoter effects far outrun this immediate object. Not only does the more facile conduct of business permit industry and extra-industrial life to go on with less perturbation; but the resulting elimination of disturbances and complications calling for an exercise of astute discrimination in [211] everyday affairs acts to make the pecuniary class itself superfluous. As fast as pecuniary transactions are reduced to routine, the captain of industry can be dispensed with. This consummation, it is needless to say, lies yet in the indefinite future. The ameliorations wrought in favour of the pecuniary interest in modern institutions tend, in another field, to substitute the "soulless" joint-stock corporation for the captain, and so they make also for the dispensability of the great leisure-class function of ownership. Indirectly, therefore, the bent given to the growth of economic institutions by the leisure-class influence is of very considerable industrial consequence.

Introduction to Part III

1899–1906: critiques and further developments

The writings collected together in this part cover the period from after the publication of Veblen's *Theory of the Leisure Class* in 1899, which brought him to the attention of a wider public, to his departure from the University of Chicago in 1906. This interval includes *The Theory of Business Enterprise* (1904b), which was his second book.

Selection 22 is Veblen's response to a long, critical review by John Cummings (1899) in the *Journal of Political Economy* of Veblen's *Theory of the Leisure Class*. Cummings was then at Harvard University but later became a colleague in Chicago. In 1906 Cummings took over the editorship of the *Journal of Political Economy* from Veblen. From his limited publications he appears as an empirically oriented and middle-of-the-road Marshallian.

In his review Cummings (1899, p. 425) accused Veblen of "an incomplete survey of the facts" and being "influenced by personal animus." Cummings argued that the "economist accepts individual wants uncritically" (p. 429) and regards waste as that which does not meet those given wants. At stake here was whether it was possible to elaborate standards or want or waste that applied to society as a whole. By contrast, Cummings regarded the preferences of each individual as the ultimate arbiter in such matters. Cummings also accused Veblen of using judgmental terms such as "invidious," "predatory," and "archaic" that were unworthy of a scientific treatise devoted to explanation rather than moral deprecation.

Veblen's response clarifies his position on a number of issues. He rejects the view that evaluations of want or waste are devolved entirely to individuals. He explains that within given cultures there is some degree of consensus on their meanings. Indeed, because of such shared evaluations, social order is possible. Veblen thus implies that his deprecations of waste are based on current and commonly held evaluations.

Against Cummings, Veblen also defends his distinction between "industrial" and "pecuniary" employments. Cummings was not its only critic. As noted in the General Introduction to this collection, Veblen expanded on this characteristic theme elsewhere.

Another interesting feature of Veblen's response is the way that he deals with Cummings's accusations of impartiality and inadequate scientific objectivity. Veblen succeeds in showing that Cummings himself is guilty of normative bias. But it does not end there. Contrary to some writers today, Veblen did not claim that judgments of value and judgments of fact *are the same thing*. Hence the final passages of Veblen's reply must be taken seriously. There Veblen calls for a "dispassionate" approach to enquiry in economics that focuses on matters of cause and effect (p. 279). Veblen takes a similar stance in his 1901 critique of Gustav Schmoller (Selection 25).

Many years later, Cummings signed the 1925 petition nominating Veblen for President of the American Economic Association (Veblen 1973, p. 668). After Veblen's death Cummings acknowledged that he had overlooked the importance and value of *The Leisure Class*:

> I did not at the time fairly appreciate the contribution Veblen was making to our economic and social philosophy. I have often wondered how I could have been so blind. ... In the years since we have all seen the accumulating evidence of the widespread influence of Veblen's analysis of social and economic behavior, as set forth in his *Theory of the Leisure Class*. ... I know that I would write a very different review ... today. (Dorfman 1934, p. 508)

Veblen's brief review of Gabriel Tarde's *Social Laws: An Outline of Sociology* (Selection 23) exposes the distance between Veblen and the then fashionable French sociologist, and gives hints concerning Veblen's own methodological approach. Tarde has since been largely forgotten, but significantly a century later he has been described as a "forefather of memetics" (Marsden, 2000) – an approach to the theory of social and cultural evolution that (after Dawkins 1976) treats the vaguely defined "meme" as its basic unit.

Tarde and Veblen might on the surface appear similar, as they both favored evolutionary and Darwinian approaches to social science. Veblen seems to have seized such opportunities to clarify his own views by engaging critically with others, and publicly proclaiming such differences in the form of a book review. In part, his propensity to review such items in these years is likely to be an elaborate exercise to triangulate his own position.[1]

Tarde (1890, 1899, 1903) searched for some kind of uniformity that was distinctly social, and could not be reduced to biological or physical terms. This he found in the "laws of imitation." He saw imitation as a mechanism of "social memory" and noted its similarities with biological inheritance. But Tarde did not see this memory as involving social structures or institutions. Neither did he provide an adequate social equivalent to natural selection.

---

1 Without observing any difference, the influential American sociologist Edward Alsworth Ross (1903, p. 444) lumped Veblen and Tarde together as joint discoverers of "the laws that govern the expansion of human wants."

Veblen was dismissive of Tarde's work, which had been widely praised by his contemporaries. Veblen criticized Tarde's "elastic," "ambiguous," and superficial formulations, noting that "the volume may contribute materially to curtail the vogue of M. Tarde's sociological doctrines" (p. 280). In a later review (Selection 26), Veblen extends his critique of Tarde's theoretical system.

In this earlier review Veblen shows that he is suspicious of approaches based on "bold and dexterous use of metaphor and analogy" (p. 280). This suggests that Veblen's own attempts to apply Darwinian principles to social evolution are not primarily matters of analogy or metaphor. While Veblen himself employs general concepts, he is opposed to generalization that is bereft of substance. Generalization must always be supported by a detailed examination of particular causes and effects. Relatedly, Veblen is also suspicious of ungrounded conceptions of evolution involving "spiritually guided progress" (p. 280). Instead of elusive teleological causes, Veblen always insists on psychological or material causal details.

The long essay on "industrial and pecuniary employments" (Selection 24) covers a number of classical Veblenian themes. Veblen starts with his claim that the three-fold delineation of factors of production as land, labor, and capital has its roots in conceptions of a natural or normal order where the output or product is regarded as in some sense "the equivalent of the expenditure of forces, or of the effort, or what not, that has gone into the process out of which the product emerges" (p. 282). Upon this implicit "law of the conservation of economic energy" (p. 282), economists have erected a theory of rights by which owners of an input make claim to a corresponding portion of the product.

Veblen notes that economists have had some difficulty with the three-fold division of factors, particularly when they have pondered the contribution of the undertaker or entrepreneur. Veblen argues that it is possible to distinguish the undertaker from workers "mechanically engaged in the production of goods" (p. 288). On this basis he draws a line between "business and industry." As Veblen suggests, this has its precursors in the classical distinction between productive and unproductive labor. For classical economists such as Smith and Ricardo, productive labor increased value via saleable commodities, as against allegedly unproductive laborers such as servants. Veblen's own distinction is discussed in more detail in the General Introduction to this volume.

In another passage of this essay, Veblen (p. 296) further pursues the application of the Darwinian principle of "natural selection" to human institutions that he developed in *The Theory of the Leisure Class*. But as in that volume, he makes it clear that such evolution in human society does not necessarily lead to the most efficient outcomes.

Concerning the nature of capital, Veblen (p. 297) urges "that care be taken to distinguish between capital as a pecuniary category, and capital as an industrial category." For this reason Veblen was cited by Joan Robinson (1975, p. vii; 1979, pp. 37–40, 94–95, 116) and others in the Cambridge capital debates of the 1960s and 1970s (Harcourt 1972).

Veblen's review essay on Gustav Schmoller's *Grundriss* (Selection 25) is significant for a number of reasons. It tells us much about Veblen's opinion of the German historical school. It also gives insights on Veblen's views on several other matters of enduring importance.

Wilhelm Roscher is said to have founded this school with the publication of his *Grundriss* in 1843. As a representative of a later generation, Schmoller was responsible for major developments in this school, particularly after the famous *Methodenstreit* (clash of methods) with Carl Menger in the 1880s. Despite Menger's (1883) criticisms of the historical school, Schmoller remained enormously influential, and remained highly rated by Alfred Marshall among others (Hodgson 2001, 2005).

Veblen credits Schmoller with moving away from the kind unexplained description that had prevailed in earlier works in the school, and moving towards scientific explanations of the causes of the phenomena at hand. For Veblen, science uncovers connections of cause and effect and dispenses with explanations in terms of final goals or ideals. He regarded the Hegelian view of society as unfolding "by inner necessity" as inadequate in this respect, because the inner driving force is unexplained. In its rejection of Divine creation, Veblen saw Darwinism as the apogee of modern science. Veblen (p. 314) thus credits Schmoller as surpassing earlier historical school writers by aiming at a "Darwinistic account of the origin, growth, persistence, and variation of institutions."

But for Veblen, Schmoller's scientific efforts are diluted when he periodically abandons a "dispassionate analysis and exposition of the causal complex at work" and preoccupies himself with "the question of what ought to be and what modern society must do to be saved" (p. 317). This essay gives us clear and extensive evidence that Veblen saw scientific explanation as the priority over normative proclamations.

In Selection 26 a volume by Tarde is criticized on a number of counts. It mistakenly addresses the process of production in terms of its material outputs, "instead of dealing with the producers and their relations to one another in the productive process" (p. 323). Veblen conceded that Tarde's book shows that "social and economic institutional structure is always and everywhere an outcome of the play of psychological forces" (p. 325). This also is one of the key strengths of Veblen's work. But Veblen regarded Tarde's efforts as overly and unconvincingly schematic. He described its theoretical foundations as "behind the times." Like other writings by Tarde, its "penchant for system making and symmetry gives it an air of completeness and definitiveness which is not borne out by substantial results" (p. 324).

Selection 27 gives more insight on Veblen's views of the German historical school, in this case in a review of a major work by Werner Sombart. Although Veblen was not attracted by Sombart's style, he found that the German author had adopted a distinction between business and industry similar to his own. In his review, Veblen largely devotes himself to sketching the outlines of this two-volume work to an English-speaking audience.

Selection 28 is significant because it is a review of a major (and since scandalously neglected) work by the brilliant American sociologist Lester Frank Ward. In 1906 Ward was elected as the first president of the newly founded American Sociological Association. Like Veblen (1899c), Ward (1883, 1893, 1903) argued at length that the outcome of evolution, whether in nature or society, was rarely, if ever optimal. Hence the use of evolutionary theory in the social sciences could not be used to justify an economic policy of *laissez-faire*. Enlightened government intervention was required to guide the more spontaneous processes of social evolution on a relatively beneficial course. In *Pure Sociology* Ward developed a hierarchical ontology in which the social levels depended upon the psychological and biological levels below, but could not be analytically reduced to them. Ward (1906) also attacked eugenics and argued that social environment and conditioning were most important in human development.

Ward (1900) had written a very favorable review of *The Theory of the Leisure Class* and had described the book "as one of the most brilliant productions of the country." Ward also nominated Veblen to the prestigious *Institut International de Sociologie*, which was limited to 100 members, including at that time Alfred Marshall, Carl Menger, Eugen von Böhm-Bawerk, Adolph Wagner, Alchille Loria, and Gustav Schmoller (Dorfman 1934, pp. 254–57, Jorgensen and Jorgensen 1999, pp. 78–84).

Selection 29 is one chapter of Veblen's important work *The Theory of Business Enterprise*. The work as a whole combined two key research programs, the first on the role of expectations and financial speculation in business cycles, the second on the alleged influence of the machine process on habits of thought. The first theme proved influential. It inspired Veblen's student Wesley Mitchell on an entire career of research. Later Veblen was credited with foreshadowing some of the key ideas on business fluctuations in the economics of John Maynard Keynes (Vining 1939, Raines and Leathers 1996).

The second theme must be understood in terms of Veblen's Kantian leanings and his enthusiasm for Darwinism. It was an attempt to understand the material basis of the modern scientific point of view. Some doubts about this argument are raised elsewhere (Hodgson 2004). Nevertheless, *The Theory of Business Enterprise* remains as one of Veblen's most important and inspiring works.

The particular chapter reprinted here contains a number of interesting features. Veblen notes that the capital value of an enterprise is based not only on its material assets but also its earning capacity and goodwill. Veblen develops his persistent and characteristic argument "that there unavoidably results a discrepancy, not uncommonly a divergence, between the industrial needs of the community and the business needs of the corporations" (p. 346). Veblen also observes that the "ready vendibility of corporate capital has in great measure dissociated the business interest of the directorate from that of the corporation whose affairs they direct and whose business policy they dictate" (p. 346), and "the management is separated from the ownership of the property, more and more widely as the scope of corporation finance widens" (p. 354). This has since been described in terms of the separation of ownership and control (Means 1931). In line with this later literature, Veblen observes that in a modern capitalist economy trade in corporate financial assets tends to drive economic development, rather than the direct needs of industry itself or the demands of its managers.

It is notable that, unlike much of the so-called "theory of the firm" during the twentieth century, Veblen pays particular attention to legal forms. He underlines the emergence of the corporate form and the device of limited liability. He argues that "with the assumption of the corporate form is associated a more modern method of capitalization and a freer use of credit" (p. 338). Here Veblen very briefly foreshadows a modern argument that the legal structure of the corporation is relevant to understand its nature and dynamism, whereby the corporation has the capacity to attract and "lock-in" capital, and to shield it from the personal creditors of its owners (Blair 1999, 2003, Hansmann *et al.* 2006, Gindis 2007, 2009). Like these modern theorists, Veblen indicated that the legal corporate structure of the firm has important economic consequences, and goes a long way to explain the accelerated growth of capitalism in the nineteenth century.

In Selection 30 Veblen took up an issue that he had considered in his *Theory of Business Enterprise,* namely the problem of explaining the origins of modern scientific culture. He argued, in brief, that the growth of modern science was itself stimulated by the rational "habits of thought" that were said to be associated with the spread of machines. This machine-powered explanation of "The Place of Science in Modern Civilization" was the title of this essay published in 1906, which incidentally Veblen himself considered to be his best (Dorfman, 1934 p. 260). This same essay gave its title to Veblen's (1919j) most important collection of essays, and was misleadingly and anachronistically placed at the head of the collection.

We do not regard this as Veblen's best essay, but it is certainly one of the most interesting and important. It contains a number of important philosophical insights and gives us a view into the core presuppositions of Veblen's thought. Veblen proposed a Darwinian evolutionary theory by which "matter-of-fact" habits of thought are selected in a "struggle for existence" against those habits of lesser efficacy or fitness.

As well as outlining Veblen's theory of the origins of science, the essay makes several other interesting – and arguably more durable – points. For example, against the positivist trend of thinking that prevailed in many quarters until the last quarter of the twentieth century, Veblen made it clear that facts alone cannot produce theories and "metaphysical imputation" is unavoidable in science, particularly in the case of the assumption of cause and effect (see above, p. 13). Veblen points out, as has been securely established in philosophy since David Hume, that this assumption cannot itself be verified empirically.

There are also insights on Veblen's view of the role of human agency. Veblen wrote: "While knowledge is construed in teleological terms, in terms of personal interest and attention, this teleological aptitude is itself reducible to a product of unteleological natural selection" (pp. 357–58). In other words, human intentionality is itself an outcome of a Darwinian evolutionary process. Veblen's view of knowledge as "functional" chimes in perfectly with both his contemporary and the modern pragmatist view of knowledge as an evolutionary adaptation (James 1890, Dewey 1910, 1922, Joas 1993, 1996, Plotkin 1994, Kilpinen 1998).

Selection 31 was published in two parts in the *Quarterly Journal of Economics,* and is based on a series of four lectures on Marxism that Veblen delivered at Harvard University in April 1906. At that time Veblen was still at the University of Chicago, but the second part was published after his transfer to Stanford in August 1906 and the original text of this part bears this institutional affiliation at its end.

Veblen's critique of Marxism ranks as one of the most powerful and well-informed of all time. Its strength derives not only from Veblen's scholarly familiarity with the English and German texts, but also the manner in which he uses Darwinian theory to wedge open the cracks in the Marxian system. Veblen sees the materialistic conception of history at the core of Marxism as essentially Hegelian in derivation. Veblen finds in Marxism the same Hegelian notion of history having an immanent tendency to gravitate towards ends – "self-conditioned and self-acting ... unfolding by inner necessity" (p. 376). This is transformed by Marxism into the impetus toward communism. But it is profoundly in contrast to the "unteleological" Darwinian notion of evolution (p. 377), which depends critically on the selective pressure of the environment and knows neither inevitable progress, nor definitive equilibrium, nor final ends.

The second forceful part of Veblen's critique derives from a focus on the necessary motivational forces that must lie behind the class struggle, which is seen by Marxists as the main driver of historical change. According to Marxism, social classes come into conflict because of their incompatible interests in obtaining the material means of life. But Veblen points out that the impetus to struggle must also be based on "human desire and passion" and a particular "human consciousness," which in turn must be explained. It is not essentially a class of "brute material forces" (p. 377). Impoverishment does not automatically lead to rebellion. Human behavior depends on perceptions and reflections upon circumstances. Veblen regards the inadequate theory of human motivation in Marxism as having something in common with utilitarianism and "quite out of harmony with the later results of psychological inquiry" (p. 378).

Veblen is highly skeptical of the labor theory of value, which he regards as assumed rather than proved. Veblen mocks Marx's attempts to substantiate the theory as involving "a self-satisfied superior's playful mystification of those readers (critics) whose limited powers do not enable them to see that his proposition is self-evident" (p. 379). For Veblen, the labor theory of value is neither the keystone nor pinnacle of Marx's achievement.

In the second part Veblen turns to the doctrines of later Marxists. He notes the views of "revisionists" such as Eduard Bernstein. But in a manner that betrays some lack of systemic structure in his writing, he repeats and expands upon his former point concerning the contrast between the teleological notion of history in Marxism and the Darwinian "scheme of blindly cumulative causation, in which there is no trend, no final term, no consummation" (p. 389). Veblen also expands on the contrasting treatments of human motivation, where Darwinism sees "the sentiment which animates men" as much, or more, "an outcome of habit and native propensity as of calculated material interest" (p. 392). Consequently, there is no ground to regard the socialist revolution as inevitable, because adverse material circumstances can lead to patriotic as much as socialistic sentiments. These shining nuggets overcome their poorly ordered position in the overall structure of the two-part work.

Veblen observes a significant shift of opinion in the later Marxism. Despite earlier promulgations of international peace, an "infection of jingoism" – particularly in Germany – led some by 1906 to "stand for national aggrandizement first and for international comity second" (p. 399). Veblen thus acutely noted the erosion of antiwar ideals within the political movement inspired by Marxism, which was to be dramatically exhibited eight years later, when many leftists endorsed the involvement of their national governments in the First World War.

Selection 22

Mr. Cummings's strictures on *The Theory of the Leisure Class*

Source: *Journal of Political Economy*, December 1899
(vol. 8, pp. 106–17).

Veblen (1899f)

In the last issue of this journal is a paper of some length by Mr. John Cummings,[1] criticising a book lately published for me under the title, *The Theory of the Leisure Class*. The paper is notable for its earnestness no less than for its graceful and cogent discussion. It is needless for me here to express my high appreciation of the attention which the volume has received at Mr. Cummings's hands. But circumstances have made it necessary for me to take this means of calling attention to certain passages in Mr. Cummings's discussion, where the criticism is directed rather against the apparent than against the intended drift of the argument set forth in the volume.

As editor of the *Journal* it should have been my place, and my privilege, to forestall what I might conceive to be misdirected criticism by making the necessary suggestions to Mr. Cummings before his paper appeared in print; and, but for the untoward chance that the issue in which the paper appears was printed during my absence, this [107] would have been done. As it is, I am constrained to offer my explanations in the ungracious form of a reply to his criticism. There is the more excuse for so doing, since what has proved to be obscure to so acute a critic as Mr. Cummings may be expected to offer at least as great difficulties to others who may have the patience to read the book. Had I had the good fortune to say what I intended, and no more, my critic would, I believe, have been saved a good share of the corrections which he is good enough to offer, as well as much of the annoyance which he is at pains to conceal. Indeed, to such an extent does this appear to be true that the greater portion and the weightier of Mr. Cummings's criticisms appears to proceed on misapprehension that might have been obviated by a more facile use of language.

But to speak first of a point on which the difference between the book and its critic is apparently not of this verbal complexion. Mr. Cummings (p. 426) gravely distrusts any "attempt to read modern psychology into primitive conditions," together with attempts at "a psychological reconstruction of

---

1 ["The Theory of the Leisure Class"], *Journal of Political Economy*, September 1899.

primitive society." To the first count I plead guilty, only if "modern" psychology is taken to mean the latest views of psychological science known to me, as contrasted with older theories. Whether this constitutes an offense is, of course, not within my competency to inquire. As to the second count, I plead that any theory of culture, late or early, must have recourse to a psychological analysis, since all culture is substantially a psychological phenomenon. In any modern discussion of culture, and of cultural development, where this recourse is not had openly it is had covertly.

Mr. Cummings's criticism is directed to three main heads: (1) The theory of waste (pp. 427–34); (2) the relation of the leisure class to cultural change (pp. 436–39); (3) the justification of leisure-class incomes (pp. 439–53). On the first of these heads the difference between the book and its critic seems to be apparent only, due to a misconception caused by want of explicitness in the argument. As to the second, the difference between Mr. Cummings's views and mine is, I believe, less by half than appears from Mr. Cummings's strictures. Under the third head, running through some fourteen pages, Mr. Cummings develops a point of doctrine with which the book does not concern itself.

Exception is taken (p. 427) to my attempted definition of waste. It should be said that the definition in question aims to promulgate no [108] novel doctrine; the aim being to state discursively what is the content of a judgment concerning waste or futility. The definition may be unfortunate, but its ineptitude does not eliminate the concept of waste from men's habits of thought, nor does it eliminate the word from everyday speech. Men do currently pass opinions on this and that as being wasteful or not wasteful, and there is much evidence that they have long been in the habit of doing so. Sumptuary legislation and the much preaching of the moralists of all ages against lavish habits of life is evidence to this effect. There is also a good deal of a consensus as to what manner of things are wasteful. The brute fact that the word is current shows that. Without something of a passable consensus on that head the word would not be intelligible; that is to say, we should have no such word. As Mr. Cummings earnestly contends (p. 428), it is always the individual that passes an opinion of this kind – as must manifestly be conceded with respect to all opinions. But the consensus that prevails shows that the opinions of individuals on matters touching "the generically human" passably coincide – which, I gather, Mr. Cummings is (p. 428) unwilling to admit. If it were in place to offer instruction here, I should suggest some reason for this coincidence of views is to be found in a community of descent, traditions, and circumstances, past and present, among men living in any given community, and in a less degree among men in all communities. It is because men's notions of the generically human, of what is the legitimate end of life, does not differ incalculably from man to man that men are able to live in communities and to hold common interests.

It is the use of the word "impersonal," in the sense of non-invidious or non-emulative, that seems particularly to have proved misleading. And this, probably, has provoked Mr. Cummings (p. 429) unguardedly to deny the practical possibility of waste. This result of my escapade, I need not say, I deeply regret. The like is true for the word "invidious," though on this term the critic's quarrel is with the current use of the word, not with any misuse of it at my hands. My critic's discussion at this point also carries the implication that any item of consumption which is in any degree useful, as, e.g., "costly church edifices," cannot at the same time be in any degree wasteful. This seems an unwarranted application of the logical expedient of "exclusion." As bearing on this passage (p. 429), it may be added that even if "the labor expended on the church edifice ... be considered in [109] any sense wasteful," that need not imply that the edifice or its consumption according to the accepted method is disallowed by economic theory. It is, for all I can see, competent for an economist to inquire how far such an edifice and the employment of time and effort involved in its use may be industrially unproductive, or even industrially disserviceable, if such should be the outcome of the inquiry. Such an endeavor, I believe, need bring no obloquy upon the economist, nor need he thereby invade the moralist's peculiar domain, nor need it flutter the keepers of the idols of the tribe. The economic bearing of any institution is not its only bearing, nor its weightiest. The ends of human culture are manifold and multiform and it is but the meaner of them, if any, that are fairly comprised in that petty side of life into which it is the economist's lot to inquire. An electrician might, without blame, speak of the waste of energy that is inseparable from the use of storage batteries. Indeed, if he is discussing the efficiency of this means of utilising a source of power, he could not avoid a detailed inquiry into this feature of their use. But his endeavor to determine the magnitude of the unavoidable or of the ordinary waste involved would not commit him to a condemnation of the batteries, nor would it make him an object of suspicion in the eyes of his fellow-electricians.

The like critical use of exclusion, applied to alternatives which it had not occurred to me to conceive of as exclusive alternatives, recurs in Mr. Cummings's observations on the conservatism of the leisure class (e.g., pp. 437–38), and on the differentiation of employments between the pecuniary and the industrial occupations (pp. 443–53). It is on the strength of such a needless application of exclusion that Mr. Cummings is able to say (p. 432): "In Dr. Veblen's philosophy, all our judgments are based on invidiousness." This should be so amended as to read: "*Some of* our judgments are *in part* based on invidiousness." It will be seen that such an amendment would materially affect Mr. Cummings's further development of the theme, particularly as regards his strictures on the views advanced in the book. Similarly the *reductio ad absurdum* on page 434, where the view that elegance of diction and orthography serve an invidious purpose is taken logically to contain the further position that speech can serve no purpose but an invidious one, and that the origin and sole use of language lies in the invidious distinction which it lends the user. This resort to excluded middle is in touch with the rhyme of a modern poet, who sings: [110]

I'd rather have fingers than toes;
I'd rather have ears than a nose;
etc.,[2]

overlooking the possibility of combining these several features in a single organism.

These pages (428–35) are a source of comfort and of despair to me. Of comfort in that I find in them a cogent exposition of views which I had attempted to set forth; of despair in showing how my attempted exposition has proved unintelligible even to a reader who had already beforehand reached an articulate recognition of very much of what I attempted to say. For, if I am not mistaken, Mr. Cummings's views on the subject of waste, as set forth fragmentarily in these pages, passably coincide with those intended to be expressed in the volume which he criticises.

Much the same is true for what Mr. Cummings has to say (pp. 436–39) on the conservative effect of the institution of a leisure class. The point at which his development of theory on this head chiefly differs from that of the book – as I had conceived it – is his insistence that this conservative effect is, always and in the nature of things, of a salutary kind. On this I had, perhaps weakly, reserved decision, as I am still compelled to do. Similarly as regards Mr. Cummings's conviction (p. 437) that "Theoretically there is but one right course of social evolution, while the number of wrong courses is infinite." For my part, I have not had the fortune to reach a conclusion, or to attempt one, on this point. I am at a loss to understand what such a thesis may mean to an evolutionist, and I believe it would get the assent of fewer men today than at any previous time. But the main drift of Mr. Cummings's development I gladly assent to. In particular, I am at one with him in his view (p. 437) – which reads like a summary restatement of the argument of the book – that "whatever is, is clearly, at one and the same time, both right and wrong." This proposition Mr. Cummings has, by an unfortunate oversight, placed in contrast with a partial statement of the same view as expressed in the book.

Attention may be called to a further point of detail in this connection. Mr. Cummings (p. 442) takes exception to the view that man's environment changes with the growth of culture. He finds that the environment is "relatively fixed"; that "climate and soil make up pretty much all there is at the basis of that environment, and these [111] change but little." All this is no doubt true if environment be taken to mean climate and topography; but for the purpose of my inquiry – an inquiry as to why and how the habits of life and of thought of the individual come to be modified – for this purpose customs, conventions, and methods of industry are no less effective elements in the environment than climate and topography, and these vary incontinently.

2 Gelett Burgess, *The Purple Cow*, San Francisco, 1898.

Mr. Cummings also (pp. 440–44, 449–52) offers a theory as to the equity of the existing distribution of property and of the incomes that accrue to the various classes in the community. This discussion is directed to a point not touched upon in my inquiry. But since my critic has been led to read into my argument certain implications on this head which he finds it necessary to refute, it is not improbable that others may read the argument in the same sense and feel the same need of refutation. It may therefore be in place to point out why I have not entered upon a discussion of this topic. The reason is that the whole question of such a justification is beside the point. The argument of the book deals with the causal, not with the moral competence of the phenomena which it takes up. The former is a question for the economist, the latter for the moralist. The manner in which Mr. Cummings has misread the argument – as I conceive it – may be illustrated by citing several specific propositions which are mistakenly conceived to bear upon the argument. He says (p. 440): "The accumulation at one end is conceived to be at the expense of the other end in the sense that the other end would have more if it had *its just deserts.*" This should read: "is *not* conceived to be at the expense of the other end in the sense," etc. In particular, there is in the volume no reference, express or by implication, to "just deserts." Similarly, unless I am mistaken, it contains no suggestion that a "confiscation" (p. 449) of the products of the "productive laborers" takes place. It does not raise the question as to whether the captain of industry on the one hand or the laborer on the other hand "earn" (pp. 440, 441) their respective incomes. Mr. Cummings (pp. 440–52) assumes the validity of the natural-rights dogma that property rests on production. This relation between production and property rights is a moral, not a causal relation, if it is assumed to subsist at all. As regards Mr. Cummings's advocacy of the claims of the captain of industry to his income, on this ground, it proceeds on the bold though ancient metaphor by force of which bargaining is conceived to produce goods. And as regards the claims of the laborer to a property right [112] in his product, an exhaustive analysis would probably show that they rest on similarly inconclusive grounds. I am therefore unable, in view of well-known facts, to go with Mr. Cummings in his view (p. 453) that a person who does not produce wealth cannot acquire it except by a miracle. One might cite the trite case of the man with the nutshells and the peppercorn, when the miraculous element is, at the best, held to be apparent only.

In a similar connection (p. 448) Mr. Cummings, in a restatement of my argument, says: "it is a game of chance, not of skill, this game of ownership, and the risks assumed are devoid of economic significance." This should read: "*in some part* of chance, *though chiefly of skill,*" and "the risks assumed are *of the gravest economic significance.*" Also (p. 448): "since individual members of the wealthy leisure class resort to chicanery and fraud, therefore nobody else does." This is an instance of Mr. Cummings's use of exclusion. It should read: "individual members of the wealthy leisure class resort to chicanery and fraud, *as do also many other persons.*" Again (p. 449): "The unscrupulous man is not, by virtue of his unscrupulousness, a member of any class." To this I beg to give a cordial assent; as also to the proposition (p. 451) that "labor alone [unaided by intelligence] does not produce." So, again, I accept, with a covetous acknowledgment of its aptness, Mr. Cummings's proposition (p. 447) that, instead of its being the sole player in the game, the leisure class "is peculiar in that in playing this game of ownership in which all engage, *its members have succeeded conspicuously.*" This statement contains the central position of the argument against which it is directed. The chief difference between the leisure and the industrial classes is conceived to be a larger endowment on the part of the former in respect of those aptitudes and propensities which make for pecuniary success.

In the pages which Mr. Cummings devotes to a defense of the captain of industry and his income the point of serious difference between his exposition and the argument of the book is his rejection of the distinction between "pecuniary" and "industrial" employments. He insists that there is no tenable distinction between the employment of the financier and that of the day laborer, both alike being "productive" and both alike owing their productivity and their income yielding character to the intelligence exercised. This does not run altogether on the same ground as the argument in the volume, and it seems a less conclusive objection to me than it appears to have [113] been to Mr. Cummings. It seems necessary to explain that the intended point of the argument concerning "pecuniary" and "industrial" employments was to indicate the different economic value of the aptitudes and habits of thought fostered by the one and the other class of employments. The question turns on a difference of kind, not on a difference of degree, in the intelligence and spiritual attitude called for by the different employments, in such a way that the one line of employment calls for more of one range of aptitudes while the other line of employments calls for more of the other. It is the ethological bearing of employments that is chiefly in question, my endeavor being to point out how employments differ, for the purpose in hand, in respect of the training and the selective stress to which the character of these employments subjects the persons employed. "The distinction here made between classes of employments is by no means a hard and fast distinction between classes of persons." Few persons escape having some experience of both lines of employment, but the one or the other line of employment commonly is accountable for the greater portion of the serious occupation of any given person. So that while the disciplinary effect of either is seldom unmitigated in any concrete case, still the existing differentiation of occupations commonly confines the attention of any given person chiefly to the one or the other line of employment, and gives his training a bent in the one or the other direction. In the earlier phases of modern industry, where the owner was at the same time the foreman of the shop and the manager of the "business," as well as in those modern industries in which the division of labor is relatively slight, the distinction does not obtrude itself on the attention because the separation of employments is not marked. Probably on this account the distinction is, at least commonly, not made in the received discussions of economic theory, which have for the most part taken their shape under the traditions of a less highly developed differentiation of employments than the existing one. Still, even then the different, or divergent, disciplinary trend of the pecuniary and the industrial activities of any given individual must be held to have had its force, although the unblended effect of the one or the other may not be shown in any concrete case. It is to be added that in the somewhat numerous marginal cases, where these lines of employment cross and blend, as, e.g., in retail shopkeeping, in newspaper work, in popular art, in preaching, in sleight-of-hand, etc., it is perhaps impossible for the nicest discrimination to draw a neat distinction between them. [114]

Since the distinction in question is not an accepted article of economic theory, it need occasion no surprise that my critic should fail to apprehend it or to admit it; but his failure to apprehend the distinction does not affect its reality. As I conceive it, the distinction at its clearest marks the difference between workmanship and bargaining. Both equally are economic activities, but both are not in the same sense industrial. The "industrial" activities, whose characteristic is workmanship, of course include the work of directing the processes of industry as well as of contriving the aims and ideals of industry – such work as that of the artist, the inventor, the designer, the engineer, and the foreman. This range of employments has to do with adapting the material means of life, and the processes of valuation constantly involved in the work run on the availability of goods and on the material serviceability of the contrivances, materials, persons, or mechanical expedients employed. They have to do with relations of physical cause and effect. In the received scheme of economic theory these employments fall under the head of "Production." The "pecuniary" employments, on the other hand, should, in the received scheme, fall under the head of "Distribution." They have to do with the distribution of wealth – not necessarily with the distribution of goods to consumers. The processes of valuation involved in this work run on the exchange values of goods and on the vendibility of the items with which they are concerned, and on the necessities, solvency, cupidity, or gullibility of the persons whose actions may affect the transaction contemplated. These valuations look to the pecuniary serviceability of the persons and expedients employed. The objective point of the former range of valuations is material use, of the latter pecuniary gain. Indirectly this latter class of employments may have a very considerable effect in shaping industrial life, as witness, e.g., the industrial changes incident to the formation of trusts; and it is this indirect effect that has commonly received the attention of the economists. Similarly, of course, the "industrial" employments rarely if ever are without a pecuniary bearing.

It may be said by way of further characterisation that the pecuniary employments, and the pecuniary institutions to which they give rise, rest on the institution of private property and affect the industrial process by grace of that institution; while the industrial employments, and the industrial differentiation to which they give rise, rest chiefly on the physical conditions of human life; but they have their pecuniary [115] bearing by virtue of the institution of ownership, since all pecuniary phenomena lie within the range of that institution. As J. S. Mill might be conceived to say – as, indeed, he has virtually said – the pecuniary employments are conditioned by human convention, the industrial by the unalterable laws of nature.

Either line of employment may be said to require and to foster a certain intelligence or sagacity in the persons so employed, but the intelligence so fostered is not the same in both cases. The sagacity characteristic of the pecuniary employments is a sagacity in judging what persons will do in the face of given pecuniary circumstances; the sagacity required by the industrial employments is chiefly a sagacity in judging what inanimate things will do under given mechanical conditions. When well developed, sagacity of the former complexion may be expected to make a shrewd salesman, investor, or promoter; intelligence of the latter kind, a competent engineer or mechanician. With the former goes an interest in gain and in contests of shrewdness and personal advantage; with the latter goes an interest in workmanlike efficiency and in the play of inanimate forces. It is needless to add that men whose occupations are made up of the latter class of employments also commonly have something of the pecuniary aptitudes and find more or less frequent exercise for them; but it is also bootless to contend that there is no difference between the "pecuniary" and the "industrial" employments in respect of their disciplinary and selective effect upon the character of the persons employed. Neither should it be necessary to point out that the pecuniary employments, with the aptitudes and inclinations that give success in them, are, in their immediate bearing, in no degree serviceable to the community, since their aim is a competitive one. Whereas the latter commonly are serviceable in their immediate effects, except in so far as they are, commonly under the guidance of the pecuniary interest, led into work that is wasteful or disserviceable to the community.

I have permitted myself to speak at length and in this expository way on this point because Mr. Cummings's criticism has shown that the earlier discussion on this topic must have been lacking in clearness, while it has also raised the apprehension in my mind that the distinction between "pecuniary" and "industrial" aptitudes and employments may be more novel and more recondite than I had appreciated.

In conclusion Mr. Cummings speaks in terms of high appreciation of the "clever" use of terminological expedients which he finds in the [116] volume. There is, however, a suggestion that, with all its cleverness, this consummate diction is charged with some malign potency, somewhat after the manner of the evil eye. Sincere, and withal kindly, as may be the intention of these comments on the "consummate cleverness" shown in the choice of terms, I cannot but mistrust that they express the impulses of my critic's heart rather than the deliverances of a serene intelligence. I apprehend they will not commend themselves to thoughtful readers of the volume. For instance, so serious a person as Mr. D. Collin Wells would be able at the most to give but a very materially qualified assent to Mr. Cummings's eulogy. Mr. Wells[3] expresses disappointment on precisely the point that stirs Mr. Cummings's admiration. Indeed, I catch, in Mr. Wells's observations on this matter, something of an inflection of sadness, such as argues a profound solicitude together with a baffled endeavor to find that the diction employed expresses any meaning whatever. In this bewilderment Mr. Wells, I regret to say, is not alone. The difficulty has been noted also by others, and to meet it is a good part of the purpose of what has been said above.

But, while he finds the terminology clever, Mr. Cummings deprecates the resort to terms which, in their current use, convey an attitude of approval or disapproval on the part of those who use them. This, of course, comes to a deprecation of the use of everyday words in their everyday meaning. In their discourse and in their thinking, men constantly and necessarily take an attitude of approval or disapproval toward the institutional facts of which they speak, for it is through such everyday approval or disapproval that any feature of the institutional structure is upheld or altered. It is only to be regretted that a trained scientist should be unable to view these categories of popular thought in a dispassionate light, for these categories, with all the moral force with which they are charged, designate the motive force of cultural development, and to forgo their use in a genetic handling of this development means avoidance of the substantial facts with which the discussion is concerned. A scientist inquiring into cultural growth, and an evolutionist particularly, must take account of this dynamic content of the categories of popular thought as the most important material with which he has to work. Many persons may find it difficult to divest themselves of the point of view of morality or policy, from which these categories are habitually employed, and to [117] take them up from the point of view of the scientific interest simply. But this difficulty does not set the scientific necessity aside. His inability to keep the cultural value and the moral content of these categories apart may reflect credit upon the state of such a person's sentiments, but it detracts from his scientific competence.

If the free use of unsophisticated vulgar concepts, with whatever content of prejudice and sentiment they may carry, is proscribed, the alternative is a resort to analogies and other figures of speech, such as have long afflicted economics and have given that science its reputed character of sterility. In extenuation of my fault, therefore, if such it must be, it should be said that, if one would avoid paralogistic figures of speech in the analysis of institutions, one must resort to words and concepts that express the thoughts of the men whose habits of thought constitute the institutions in question.

3 [David Collin Wells, review of Thorstein Veblen, *The Theory of the Leisure Class*], *Yale Review*, August 1899, p. 218.

Selection 23

Review of *Social Laws: An Outline of Sociology* by Gabriel Tarde

Source: *Journal of Political Economy*, September 1900 (vol. 8, pp. 562–63).

Veblen (1900e)

As the editor of the volume remarks, M. Tarde has here summarized his theoretical work and shown it to constitute a system. In this reduction of the system to its outlines its great ingenuity is [563] impressed upon the reader much more forcibly than by the detailed presentation contained in M. Tarde's larger works. At the same time the essential artificiality of the doctrines likewise comes out in plainer relief, proceeding as they do, for the most part, and particularly as regards their general features, on a bold and dexterous use of metaphor and analogy. It seems not improbable that, as a result of the conciseness, not to say boldness, with which the ingenious artifices of the theory are here brought out, the volume may contribute materially to curtail the vogue of M. Tarde's sociological doctrines.

The essential superficiality of the formulations offered is shown, e.g., in such generalizations as this: "Habit is merely a sort of internal heredity, just as heredity is only externalized habit. Heredity, then, is the form of repetition appropriate to life, just as undulation, or periodic movement, is its physical, and imitation its social form" (p. 22). Again: "Every real opposition implies a relation between two forces, tendencies, or directions" (p. 88). Under this elastic, not to say ambiguous term, "opposition," are comprised such diverse phenomena as mechanical action and reaction, arithmetical positive and negative, variations of degree, war, industrial competition, discussion, hesitation. It is plainly by a felicitous use of analogy alone that the comprehensive term "opposition" can be made to serve in the discussion of matters so disparate as these. All this is of a character to suggest the moralizing speculations of the eighteenth century and prepares one to meet the metaphysical conception of a spiritually guided progress, expressed in the conclusion that, "It would appear ... that the strife of opposition fulfills the role of a middle term in the social as it does in the organic and inorganic worlds" (p. 133).

Selection 24

Industrial and pecuniary employments

Source: *Publications of the American Economic Association*, Series 3, February 1901 (vol. 2, pp. 190–235).

Veblen (1901a)

For purposes of economic theory, the various activities of men and things about which economists busy themselves were classified by the early writers according to a scheme which has remained substantially unchanged, if not unquestioned, since their time. This scheme is the classical three-fold division of the factors of production under Land, Labor, and Capital. The theoretical aim of the economists in discussing these factors and the activities for which they stand has not remained the same throughout the course of economic discussion, and the three-fold division has not always lent itself with facility to new points of view and new purposes of theory, but the writers who have shaped later theory have, on the whole, not laid violent hands on the sacred formula. These facts must inspire the utmost reserve and circumspection in anyone who is moved to propose even a subsidiary distinction of another kind between economic activities or agents. The terminology and the conceptual furniture of economics are complex and parti-colored enough without gratuitous innovation.

It is accordingly not the aim of this paper to set aside the time-honored classification of factors, or even to formulate an iconoclastic amendment, but rather to indicate how and why this classification has proved inadequate for certain purposes of theory which were not contemplated by the men who elaborated it. To this end a bit of preface may be in place as regards the aims which led to its formulation and the uses which the three-fold classification originally served. [191]

The economists of the late eighteenth and early nineteenth centuries were believers in a Providential order, or an order of Nature. How they came by this belief need not occupy us here; neither need we raise a question as to whether their conviction of its truth was well or ill grounded. The Providential order or order of Nature is conceived to work in an effective and just way toward the end to which it tends; and in the economic field this objective end is the material welfare of mankind. The science of that time set itself the task of interpreting the facts with which it dealt, in terms of this natural order. The material circumstances which condition men's life fall within the scope of this natural order of the universe, and as members of the universal scheme of things men fall under the constraining guidance of the laws of Nature, who does all things well. As regards their purely theoretical work, the early economists are occupied with bringing the facts of economic life under natural laws conceived somewhat after the manner indicated; and when the facts handled have been fully interpreted in the light of this fundamental postulate the theoretical work of the scientist is felt to have been successfully done.

The economic laws aimed at and formulated under the guidance of this preconception are laws of what takes place "naturally" or "normally," and it is of the essence of things so conceived that in the natural or normal course there is no wasted or misdirected effort. The standpoint is given by the material interest of mankind, or, more concretely, of the community or "society" in which the economist is placed; the resulting economic theory is formulated as an analysis of the "natural" course of the life of the community, the ultimate theoretical [192] postulate of which might, not unfairly, be stated as in some sort a law of the conservation of economic energy. When the course of things runs off naturally or normally, in accord with the exigencies of human welfare and the constraining laws of nature, economic income and outgo balance one another. The natural forces at play in the economic field may increase indefinitely through accretions brought in under man's dominion and through the natural increase of mankind, and, indeed, it is of the nature of things that an orderly progress of this kind should take place; but within the economic organism, as within the larger organism of the universe, there prevails an equivalence of expenditure and returns, an equilibrium of flux and reflux, which is not broken over in the normal course of things. So it is, by implication, assumed that the product which results from any given industrial process or operation is, in some sense or in some unspecified respect, the equivalent of the expenditure of forces, or of the effort, or what not, that has gone into the process out of which the product emerges.

This theorem of equivalence is the postulate which lies at the root of the classical theory of distribution, but it manifestly does not admit of proof – or of disproof either, for that matter; since neither the economic forces which go into the process nor the product which emerges are, in the economic respect, of such a tangible character as to admit of quantitative determination. They are in fact incommensurable magnitudes. To this last remark the answer may conceivably present itself that the equivalence in question is an equivalence in utility or in exchange value, and that the quantitative determination of the various items in terms of exchange value or of utility is, theoretically, not impossible; but when it is called [193] to mind that the forces or factors which go to the production of a given product take their utility or exchange value from that of the product, it will easily be seen that the expedient will not serve. The equivalence between the aggregate factors of production in any given case and their product remains a dogmatic postulate whose validity cannot be demonstrated in any terms that will not reduce the whole proposition to an aimless fatuity, or to metaphysical grounds which have now been given up.

The point of view from which the early, and even the later classical, economists discussed economic life was that of "the society" taken as a collective whole and conceived as an organic unit. Economic theory sought out and formulated the laws of the normal life of the social organism, as it is conceived to work out in that natural course whereby the material welfare of society is attained. The details of economic life are construed, for purposes of general theory, in terms of their subservience to the aims imputed to the collective life process. Those features of detail which will bear construction as links in the process whereby the collective welfare is furthered, are magnified and brought into the foreground, while such features as will not bear this construction are treated as minor disturbances. Such a procedure is manifestly legitimate and expedient in a theoretical inquiry whose aim is to determine the laws of health of the social organism and the normal functions of this organism in a state of health. The social organism is, in this theory, handled as an individual endowed with a consistent life purpose and something of an intelligent apprehension of what means will serve the ends which it seeks. With these collective ends the interests of the individual members are conceived [194] to be fundamentally at one; and, while men may not see that their own individual interests coincide with those of the social organism, yet, since men are members of the comprehensive organism of nature and consequently subject to beneficent natural law, the ulterior trend of unrestrained individual action is, on the whole, in the right direction.

The details of individual economic conduct and its consequences are of interest to such a general theory chiefly as they further or disturb the beneficent "natural" course. But if the aims and methods of individual conduct were of minor importance in such an economic theory, that is not the case as regards individual rights. The early political economy was not simply a formulation of the natural course of economic phenomena, but it embodied an insistence on what is called "natural liberty." Whether this insistence on natural liberty is to be traced to utilitarianism or to a less specific faith in natural rights, the outcome for the purpose in hand is substantially the same. To avoid going too far afield, it may serve the turn to say that the law of economic equivalence, or conservation of economic energy, was, to early economics, backed by this second corollary of the order of nature, the closely related postulate of natural rights. The classical doctrine of distribution rests on both of these, and it is consequently not only a doctrine of what must normally take place as regards the course of life of society at large, but it also formulates what ought of right to take place as regards the remuneration for work and the distribution of wealth among men.

Under the resulting natural-economic law of equivalence and equity, it is held that the several participants or factors in the economic process severally get the [195] equivalent of the productive force which they expend. They severally get as much as they produce; and conversely, in the normal case they severally produce as much as they get. In the earlier formulations, as, for example, in the authoritative formulation of Adam Smith, there is no clear or consistent pronouncement as regards the terms in which this equivalence between production and remuneration runs. With the later, classical economists, who had the benefit of a developed utilitarian philosophy, it seems to be somewhat consistently conceived in terms of an ill-defined serviceability.

With some later writers it is an equivalence of exchange values; but as this latter reduces itself to tautology, it need scarcely be taken seriously. When we are told in the later political economy that the several agents or factors in production normally earn what they get, it is perhaps fairly to be construed as a claim that the economic service rendered the community by any one of the agents in production equals the service received by the agent in return. In terms of serviceability, then, if not in terms of productive force,[1] the individual agent, or at least the class or group of agents to which the individual belongs, normally gets as much as he contributes and contributes as much as he gets. This applies to all those employments or occupations which are ordinarily carried on in any community, throughout the aggregate of men's dealings with the material means of life. All activity which touches industry comes in under this law of equivalence and equity.

Now, to a theorist whose aim is to find the laws governing [196] the economic life of a social organism, and who for this purpose conceives the economic community as a unit, the features of economic life which are of particular consequence are those which show the correlation of efforts and the solidarity of interests. For this purpose, such activities and such interests as do not fit into the scheme of solidarity contemplated are of minor importance, and are rather to be explained away or construed into subservience to the scheme of solidarity than to be incorporated at their face value into the theoretical structure. Of this nature are what are here to be spoken of under the term "pecuniary employments," and the fortune which these pecuniary employments have met at the hands of classical economic theory is such as is outlined in the last sentence.

In a theory proceeding on the premise of economic solidarity, the important bearing of any activity that is taken up and accounted for, is its bearing upon the furtherance of the collective life process. Viewed from the standpoint of the collective interest, the economic process is rated primarily as a process for the provision of the aggregate material means of life. As a late representative of the classical school expresses it: "Production, in fact, embraces every economic operation except consumption."[2] It is this aggregate productivity, and the bearing of all details upon the aggregate productivity, that constantly occupies the attention of the classical economists. What partially diverts their attention from this central and ubiquitous interest, is their persistent lapse into natural-rights morality.

The result is that acquisition is treated as a sub-head under production, and effort directed to acquisition is [197] construed in terms of production, The pecuniary activities of men, efforts directed to acquisition and operations

---

1 Some late writers, as, e.g., J. B. Clark, apparently must be held to conceive the equivalence in terms of productive force rather than of serviceability; or, perhaps, in terms of serviceability on one side of the equation and productive force on the other.

2 J. B. Clark, *The Distribution of Wealth*, p. 20.

incident to the acquisition or tenure of wealth, are treated as incidental to the distribution to each of his particular proportion in the production of goods. Pecuniary activities, in short, are handled as incidental features of the process of social production and consumption, as details incident to the method whereby the social interests are served, instead of being dealt with as the controlling factor about which the modern economic process turns.

Apart from the metaphysical tenets indicated above as influencing them, there are, of course, reasons of economic history for the procedure of the early economists in so relegating the pecuniary activities to the background of economic theory. In the days of Adam Smith, for instance, economic life still bore much of the character of what Professor Schmoller calls *Stadtwirtschaft*.[3] This was the case to some extent in practice, but still more decidedly in tradition. To a greater extent than has since been the case, households produced goods for their own consumption, without the intervention of sale; and handicraftsmen still produced for consumption by their customers, without the intervention of a market. In a considerable measure, the conditions which the Austrian marginal-utility theory supposes, of a producing seller and a consuming buyer, actually prevailed. It may not be true that in Adam Smith's time the business operations, the bargain and sale of goods, were, in general, obviously subservient to their production and consumption, but it comes nearer being true at that time than at any time since then. And the tradition having once been put into form and authenticated by Adam Smith, that such was the place of pecuniary [198] transactions in economic theory, this tradition has lasted on in the face of later and further changes. Under the shadow of this tradition the pecuniary employments are still dealt with as auxiliary to the process of production, and the gains from such employments are still explained as being due to a productive effect imputed to them.

According to ancient prescription, then, all normal, legitimate economic activities carried on in a well regulated community serve a materially useful end, and so far as they are lucrative they are so by virtue of and in proportion to a productive effect imputed to them. But in the situation as it exists at any time there are activities and classes of persons which are indispensable to the community, or which are at least unavoidably present in modern economic life, and which draw some income from the aggregate product, at the same time that these activities are not patently productive of goods and can not well be classed as industrial, in any but a highly sophisticated sense. Some of these activities, which are concerned with economic matters but are not patently of an industrial character, are integral features of modern economic life, and must therefore be classed as normal; for the existing situation, apart from a few minor discrepancies, is particularly normal in the apprehension of present-day economists. Now, the law of economic equivalence and equity says that those who normally receive an income must perforce serve some productive end; and, since the existing organization of society is conceived to be eminently normal, it becomes

---

3 [The urban economy. – Eds.]

imperative to find some ground on which to impute industrial productivity to those classes and employments which do not at the first view appear to be industrial at all. [199] Hence there is commonly visible in the classical political economy, ancient and modern, a strong inclination to make the schedule of industrially productive employments very comprehensive; so that a good deal of ingenuity has been spent in economically justifying their presence by specifying the productive effect of such non-industrial factors as the courts, the army, the police, the clergy, the schoolmaster, the physician, the opera singer.

But these non-economic employments are not so much to the point in the present inquiry; the point being employments which are unmistakably economic, but not industrial in the naïve sense of the word industry, and which yield an income.

Adam Smith analyzed the process of industry in which he found the community of his time engaged, and found the three classes of agents or factors: Land, Labor, and Capital (stock). The productive factors engaged being thus determined, the norm of natural-economic equivalence and equity already referred to above, indicated what would be the natural sharers in the product. Later economists have shown great reserve about departing from this three-fold division of factors, with its correlated three-fold division of sharers of remuneration; apparently because they have retained an instinctive, indefeasible trust in the law of economic equivalence which underlies it. But circumstances have compelled the tentative intrusion of a fourth class of agent and income. The undertaker and his income presently came to be so large and ubiquitous figures in economic life that their presence could not be overlooked by the most normalizing economist. The undertaker's activity has been interpolated in the scheme of productive factors, as [200] a peculiar and fundamentally distinctive kind of labor, with the function of coördinating industrial processes. Similarly, his income has been interpolated in the scheme of distribution, as a peculiar kind of wages, proportioned to the heightened productivity given the industrial process by his work.[4] His work is discussed in expositions of the theory of production. In discussions of his functions and his income the point of the argument is, how and in what degree does his activity increase the output of goods, or how and in what degree does it save wealth to the community. Beyond his effect in enhancing the effective volume of the aggregate wealth the undertaker receives but scant attention, apparently for the reason that so soon as that point has been disposed of the presence of the undertaker and his income has been reconciled with the tacitly accepted natural law of equivalence between productive service and remuneration. The normal balance has been established, and the undertaker's function has been justified and subsumed under the ancient law that Nature does all things well and equitably.

---

4 The undertaker gets an income; therefore he must produce goods. But human activity directed to the production of goods is labor; therefore the undertaker is a particular kind of laborer. There is, of course, some dissent from this position.

This holds true of the political economy of our grandfathers. But this aim and method of handling the phenomenon of life for theoretical ends, of course, did not go out of vogue abruptly in the days of our grandfathers.[5] There is a large sufficiency of the like aim and animus [201] in the theoretical discussions of a later time; but specifically to cite and analyse the evidence of its presence would be laborious, nor would it conduce to the general peace of mind.

Some motion towards a further revision of the scheme is to be seen in the attention which has latterly been given to the function and the profits of that peculiar class of undertakers whom we call speculators. But even on this head the argument is apt to turn on the question of how the services which the speculator is conceived to render the community are to be construed into an equivalent of his gains.[6] The difficulty of interpretation encountered at this point is considerable, partly because it is not quite plain whether the speculators as a class come out of their transactions with a net gain or with a net loss. A systematic net loss, or a no-profits balance, would, on the theory of equivalence, mean that the class which gets this loss or doubtful gain is of no service to the community; yet we are, out of the past, committed to the view that the speculator is useful – indeed economically indispensable – and shall therefore have his reward. In the discussions given to the speculator and his function some thought is commonly given to the question of the "legitimacy" of the speculator's traffic. The legitimate speculator is held to earn his gain by services of an economic kind rendered to the community. The recourse to this epithet, "legitimate," is chiefly of interest as showing that the tacit postulate of a natural order is still in force. Legitimate are such speculative dealings as are, by the theorist, [202] conceived to serve the ends of the community, while illegitimate speculation is that which is conceived to be disserviceable to the community.

The theoretical difficulty about the speculator and his gains (or losses) is that the speculator *ex professo* is quite without interest in or connection with any given industrial enterprise or any industrial plant. He is, industrially speaking, without visible means of support. He may stake his risks on the gain or on the loss of the community with equal chances of success, and he may shift from one side to the other without winking.

The speculator may be treated as an extreme case of undertaker, who deals exclusively with the business side of economic life rather than with the industrial side. But he differs in this respect from the common run of business men in degree rather than in kind. His traffic is a pecuniary traffic, and it touches industry only remotely and uncertainly; while the business man as commonly

---

5 The change which has supervened as regards the habitual resort to a natural law of equivalence is in large part a change with respect to the degree of immediacy and "reality" imputed to this law, and to a still greater extent a change in the degree of overtness with which it is avowed.

6 See, e.g., a paper by H. C. Emery, in Proceedings of the Twelfth Annual Meeting of the American Economic Association, on "The Place of the Speculator in the Theory of Distribution," and more particularly the discussion following the paper.

conceived is more or less immediately interested in the successful operation of some concrete industrial plant. But since the undertaker first broke into economic theory, some change has also taken place as regards the immediacy of the relations of the common run of undertakers to the mechanical facts of the industries in which they are interested. Half a century ago it was still possible to construe the average business manager in industry, as an agent occupied with the superintendence of the mechanical processes involved in the production of goods or services. But in the later development the connection between the business manager and the mechanical processes has, on an average, grown more remote; so much so, that his superintendence of the plant or of the processes is frequently visible only to the scientific imagination. That activity by [203] virtue of which the undertaker is classed as such makes him a business man, not a mechanic or foreman of the shop. His superintendence is a superintendence of the pecuniary affairs of the concern, rather than of the industrial plant; especially is this true in the higher development of the modern captain of industry. As regards the nature of the employment which characterizes the undertaker, it is possible to distinguish him from the men who are mechanically engaged in the production of goods, and to say that his employment is of a business or pecuniary kind, while theirs is of an industrial or mechanical kind. It is not possible to draw a similar distinction between the undertaker who is in charge of a given industrial concern, and the business man who is in business but is not interested in the production of goods or services. As regards the character of employment, then, the line falls not between legitimate and illegitimate pecuniary transactions, but between business and industry.

The distinction between business and industry has, of course, been possible from the beginning of economic theory, and, indeed, the distinction has from time to time temporarily been made in the contrast frequently pointed out between the proximate interest of the business man and the ulterior interest of society at large. What appears to have hindered the reception of the distinction into economic doctrine, is the constraining presence of a belief in an order of Nature and the habit or conceiving the economic community as an organism. The point of view given by these postulates has made such a distinction between employments not only useless, but even disserviceable for the ends to which theory has been directed. But the fact has come to be gradually more and more patent that there are constantly, [204] normally present in modern economic life an important range of activities and classes of persons who work for an income but of whom it cannot be said that they, either proximately or remotely, apply themselves to the production of goods. Their services, proximate or remote, to society are often of quite a problematical character. They are ubiquitous, and it will scarcely do to say that they are anomalous, for they are of ancient prescription, they are within the law and within the pale of popular morals.

Of these strictly economic activities that are lucrative without necessarily being serviceable to the community, the greater part are to be classed as "business." Perhaps the largest and most obvious illustration of these legitimate business employments is afforded by the speculators in securities. By way of further illustration may be mentioned the extensive and varied business of real-estate men (land-agents) engaged in the purchase and sale of property for speculative gain or for a commission; so, also, the closely related business of promoters and boomers of other than real-estate ventures; as also attorneys, brokers, bankers, and the like, although the work performed by these latter will more obviously bear interpretation in terms of social serviceability. The traffic of these business men shades off insensibly from that of the *bona fide* speculator who has no ulterior end of industrial efficiency to serve, to that of the captain of industry or entrepreneur as conventionally set forth in the economic manuals.

The characteristic in which these business employments resemble one another, and in which they differ from the mechanical occupations as well as from other non-economic employments, is that they are concerned primarily with the phenomena of value – with exchange [205] or market values and with purchase and sale – and only indirectly and secondarily, if at all, with mechanical processes. What holds the interest and guides and shifts the attention of men within these employments is the main chance. These activities begin and end within what may broadly be called "the higgling of the market." Of the industrial employments, in the stricter sense, it may be said, on the other hand, that they begin and end outside the higgling of the market. Their proximate aim and effect is the shaping and guiding of material things and processes. Broadly, they may be said to be primarily occupied with the phenomena of material serviceability, rather than with those of exchange value. They are taken up with phenomena which make the subject matter of Physics and the other material sciences.

The business man enters the economic life process from the pecuniary side, and so far as he works an effect in industry he works it through the pecuniary dispositions which he makes. He takes thought most immediately of men's convictions regarding market values; and his efforts as a business man are directed to the apprehension, and commonly also to the influencing of men's beliefs regarding market values. The objective point or business is the diversion of purchase and sale into some particular channel, commonly involving a diversion from other channels. The laborer and the man engaged in directing industrial processes, on the other hand, enter the economic process from the material side; in their characteristic work they take thought most immediately of mechanical effects, and their attention is directed to turning men and things to account for the compassing of some material end. The ulterior aim, and the ulterior effect, of these industrial [206] employments may be some pecuniary result; work of this class commonly results in an enhancement, or at least an alteration, of market values. Conversely, business activity may, and in a majority of cases it perhaps does, effect an enhancement of the aggregate material wealth of the community, or the aggregate serviceability of the means at hand; but such an industrial outcome is by no means bound to follow from the nature of the business man's work.

From what has just been said it appears that, if we retain the classical division of economic theory into Production, Distribution, and Consumption, the pecuniary employments do not properly fall under the first of these divisions, Production, if that term is to retain the meaning commonly assigned to it. In an earlier and less specialized organization of economic life, particularly, the undertaker frequently performs the work of a foreman or a technological expert, as well as the work or business management. Hence in most discussions of his work and his theoretical relations his occupation is treated as a composite one. The technological side of his composite occupation has even given a name to his gains (wages of superintendence), as if the undertaker were primarily a master-workman. The distinction at this point has been drawn between classes of persons instead of between classes of employments; with the result that the evident necessity of discussing his technological employment under production has given countenance to the endeavor to dispose of the undertaker's business activity under the same head. This endeavor has, of course, not wholly succeeded.

In the later development, the specialization of work in the economic field has at this point progressed so far, and the undertaker now in many cases comes so near [207] being occupied with business affairs alone, to the exclusion of technological direction and supervision, that, with this object lesson before us, we no longer have the same difficulty in drawing a distinction between business and industrial employments. And even in the earlier days of the doctrines, when the aim was to dispose of the undertaker's work under the theoretical head of Production, the business side of his work persistently obtruded itself for discussion in the books and chapters given to Distribution and Exchange. The course taken by the later theoretical discussion of the entrepreneur, leaves no question but that the characteristic fact about his work is that he is a business man, occupied with pecuniary affairs.

Such pecuniary employments, of which the purely fiscal or financiering forms of business are typical, are nearly all and nearly throughout, conditioned by the institution of property or ownership – an institution which, as John Stuart Mill remarks, belongs entirely within the theoretical realm of Distribution. Ownership, no doubt, has its effect upon productive industry, and, indeed, its effect upon industry is very large, both in scope and range, even if we should not be prepared to go the length of saying that it fundamentally conditions all industry; but ownership is not itself primarily or immediately a contrivance for production. Ownership directly touches the results of industry, and only indirectly the methods and processes of industry. If the institution of property be compared with such another feature of our culture, for instance, as the domestication of plants or the smelting of iron, the meaning of what has just been said may seem clearer.

So much then of the business man's activity as is conditioned by the institution of property, is not to be [208] classed, in economic theory, as productive or industrial activity at all. Its objective point is an alteration of the distribution of wealth. His business is, essentially, to sell and buy – sell in order to buy cheaper, buy in order to sell dearer.[7] It may or may not, indirectly, and in a sense incidentally, result in enhanced production. The business man may be

---

7 Cf., e.g., Marx's *Das Kapital* especially bk. I, ch. IV.

equally successful in his enterprise, and he may be equally well remunerated, whether his activity does or does not enrich the community. Immediately and directly, so long as it is confined to the pecuniary or business sphere, his activity is incapable of enriching or impoverishing the community as a whole except, after the fashion conceived by the mercantilists, through his dealings with men of other communities. The circulation and distribution of goods incidental to the business man's traffic is commonly, though not always or in the nature of the case, serviceable to the community; but the distribution of goods is a mechanical, not a pecuniary transaction, and it is not the objective point of business nor its invariable outcome. From the point of view of business, the distribution or circulation of goods is a means of gain, not an end sought.

It is true, industry is closely conditioned by business. In a modern community, the business man finally decides what may be done in industry, or at least in the greater number and the more conspicuous branches of industry. This is particularly true of those branches that are currently thought of as peculiarly modern. Under existing circumstances of ownership, the discretion in economic matters, industrial or otherwise, ultimately rests in the hands of the business men. It is their business to have to do with property, and property means [209] the discretionary control of wealth. In point of character, scope and growth, industrial processes and plants adapt themselves to the exigencies of the market, wherever there is a developed market, and the exigencies of the market are pecuniary exigencies. The business man, through his pecuniary dispositions, enforces his choice of what industrial processes shall be in use. He can, of course, not create or initiate methods or aims for industry; if he does so he steps out of the business sphere into the material domain of industry. But he can decide whether and which of the known processes and industrial arts shall be practised, and to what extent. Industry must be conducted to suit the business man in his quest for gain; which is not the same as saying that it must be conducted to suit the needs or the convenience of the community at large. Ever since the institution of property was definitely installed, and in proportion as purchase and sale has been practiced, some approach has been made to a comprehensive system of control of industry by pecuniary trans-actions and for pecuniary ends, and the industrial organization is nearer such a consummation now than it ever has been. For the great body of modern industry the final term of the sequence is not the production of the goods but their sale; the endeavor is not so much to fit the goods for use as for sale. It is well known that there are many lines of industry in which the cost of marketing the goods equals the cost of making and transporting them.

Any industrial venture which falls short in meeting the pecuniary exigencies of the market declines and yields ground to others that meet them with better effect. Hence shrewd business management is a requisite to success in any industry that is carried on within the scope of the market. Pecuniary failure carries with [210] it industrial failure, whatever may be the cause to which the pecuniary failure is due – whether it be inferiority of the goods produced, lack of salesmanlike tact, popular prejudice, scanty or ill-devised advertising, excessive truthfulness, or what not. In this way industrial results are closely dependent upon the presence of business ability; but the cause of this dependence of industry upon business in a given case is to be sought in the fact that other rival ventures have the backing of shrewd business management, rather than in any help which business management in the aggregate affords to the aggregate industry of the community. Shrewd and farsighted business management is a requisite of survival in the competitive pecuniary struggle in which the several industrial concerns are engaged, because shrewd and farsighted business management abounds and is employed by all the competitors. The ground of survival in the selective process is fitness for pecuniary gain, not fitness for serviceability at large. Pecuniary management is of an emulative character and gives, primarily, relative success only. If the change were equitably distributed, an increase or decrease of the aggregate or average business ability in the community need not immediately affect the industrial efficiency or the material welfare of the community. The like can not be said with respect to the aggregate or average industrial capacity of the men at work. The latter are, on the whole, occupied with production of goods; the business men, on the other hand, are occupied with the acquisition of them.

Theoreticians who are given to looking beneath the facts and to contemplating the profounder philosophical meaning of life speak of the function of the undertaker [211] as being the guidance and coördination of industrial processes with a view to economies of production. No doubt, the remoter effect of business transactions often is such coördination and economy, and, no doubt also, the undertaker has such economy in view and is stimulated to his manoeuvers of combination by the knowledge that certain economies of this kind are feasible and will inure to his gain if the proper business arrangements can be effected. But it is practicable to class even this indirect furthering of industry by the undertaker as a permissive guidance only. The men in industry must first create the mechanical possibility of such new and more economical methods and arrangements, before the undertaker sees the chance, makes the necessary business arrangements, and gives directions that the more effective working arrangements be adopted.

It is notorious, and it is a matter upon which men dilate, that the wide and comprehensive consolidations and coördinations of industry, which often add so greatly to its effectiveness, take place at the initiative of the business men who are in control. It should be added that the fact of their being in control precludes such coördination from being effected except by their advice and consent. And it should also be added, in order to a passably complete account of the undertaker's function, that he not only can and does effect economizing coördinations of a large scope, but he also can and does at times inhibit the process of consolidation and coördination. It happens so frequently that it might fairly be said to be the common run that business interests and undertaker's maneuvers delay consolidation, combination, coördination, for some appreciable time after they have become patently advisable on industrial grounds. The industrial advisability or practicability is not the decisive [212] point. Industrial advisability must wait on the eventual convergence of jarring pecuniary interests and on the strategical moves of business men playing for position.

Which of these two offices of the business man in modern industry, the furthering or the inhibitory, has the more serious or more far-reaching consequences is, on the whole, somewhat problematical. The furtherance of coördination by the modern captain of industry bulks large in our vision, in great part because the process of widening coördination is of a cumulative character. After a given step in coördination and combination has been taken, the next step takes place on the basis of the resulting situation. Industry, that is to say the working force engaged in industry, has a chance to develop new and larger possibilities to be taken further advantage of. In this way each successive move in the enhancement of the efficiency of industrial processes, or in the widening of coördination in industrial processes, pushes the captain of industry to a further concession, making possible a still farther industrial growth. But as regards the undertaker's inhibitory dealings with industrial coördination the visible outcome is not so striking. The visible outcome is simply that nothing of the kind then takes place in the premises. The potential cumulative sequence is cut off at the start, and so it does not figure in our appraisement of the disadvantage incurred. The loss does not commonly take the more obtrusive form of an absolute retreat, but only that of a failure to advance where the industrial situation admits of an advance.

It is, of course, impracticable to foot up and compare gain and loss in such a case, where the losses, being of the nature of inhibited growth, cannot be ascertained. [213] But since the industrial serviceability of the captain of industry is, on the whole, of a problematical complexion, it should be advisable for a cautious economic theory not to rest its discussion of him on his serviceability.[8] [214]

---

8 It is not intended to depreciate the services rendered the community by the captain of industry in his management of business. Such services are no doubt rendered and are also no doubt of substantial value. Still less is it the intention to decry the pecuniary incentive as a motive to thrift and diligence. It may well be that the pecuniary traffic which we call business is the most effective method of conducting the industrial policy of the community; not only the most effective that has been contrived, but perhaps the best that can be contrived. But that is a matter of surmise and opinion. In a matter of opinion on a point that can not be verified, a reasonable course is to say that the majority are presumably in the right. But all that is beside the point. However probable or reasonable such a view may be, it can find no lodgment in modern scientific theory, except as a corollary of secondary importance. Nor can scientific theory build upon the ground it may be conceived to afford. Policy may so build, but science can not. Scientific theory is a formulation of the laws of phenomena in terms of the efficient forces at work in the sequence of phenomena. So long as (under the old dispensation of the order of nature) the animistically conceived natural laws, with their God-given objective end, were considered to exercise a constraining guidance over the course of events whereof they were claimed to be laws, so long it was legitimate scientific procedure for economists to formulate their theory in terms of these laws of the natural course; because so long they were speaking in terms of what was, to them, the efficient forces at work. But so soon as these natural laws were reduced to the plane of colorless empirical generalization as to what commonly happens, while the efficient forces at work are

It appears, then, as all economists are no doubt aware, that there is in modern society a considerable range of activities, which are not only normally present, but which constitute the vital core of our economic system; which are not directly concerned with production, but which are nevertheless lucrative. Indeed, the group comprises most of the highly remunerative employments in modern economic life. The gains from these employments must plainly be accounted for on other grounds than their productivity, since they need have no productivity.

But it is not only as regards the pecuniary employments that productivity and remuneration are constitutionally out of touch. It seems plain, from what has already been said, that the like is true for the remuneration gained in the industrial employments. Most wages, particularly those paid in the industrial employments proper, as contrasted with those paid for domestic or personal service, are paid on account of pecuniary serviceability to the employer, not on grounds of material [215] serviceability to mankind at large. The product is valued, sought and paid for on account of and in some proportion to its vendibility, not for more recondite reasons of ulterior human welfare at large. It results that there is no warrant, in general theory, for claiming that the work of highly paid persons (more particularly that of highly paid business men) is of greater substantial use to the community than that of the less highly paid. At the same time, the reverse could, of course, also not be claimed. Wages, resting on a pecuniary basis, afford no consistent indication of the relative productivity of the recipients, except in comparisons between persons or classes whose products are identical except in amount, – that is to

---

conceived to be of quite another cast, so soon must theory abandon the ground of the natural course, sterile for modern scientific purposes, and shift to the ground of the causal sequence, where alone it will have to do with the forces at work as they are conceived in our time. The generalizations regarding the normal course, as "normal" has been defined in economics since J. S. Mill, are not of the nature of theory, but only rule-of-thumb. And the talk about the "function" of this and that factor of production, etc., in terms of the collective life purpose, goes to the same limbo; since the collective life purpose is no longer avowedly conceived to cut any figure in the every-day guidance of economic activities or the shaping of economic results.

The doctrine of the social-economic function of the undertaker may for the present purpose be illustrated by a suppositious parallel from [214] Physics. It is an easy generalization, which will scarcely be questioned, that, in practice, pendulums commonly vibrate in a plane approximately parallel with the nearest wall of the clock-case in which they are placed. The normality of this parallelism is fortified by the further observation that the vibrations are also commonly in a plane parallel with the nearest wall of the room; and when it is further called to mind that the balance which serves the purpose of a pendulum in watches similarly vibrates in a plane parallel with the walls of its case, the absolute normality of the whole arrangement is placed beyond question. It is true, the parallelism is not claimed to be related to the working of the pendulum, except as a matter of fortuitous convenience; but it should be manifest from the generality of the occurrence that in the normal case, in the absence of disturbing cases, and in the long run, all pendulums will "naturally" tend to swing in a plane faultlessly parallel with the nearest wall. The use which has been made of the "organic concept," in economics and in social science at large, is fairly comparable with this suppositious argument concerning the pendulum.

say, where a resort to wages as an index of productivity would be of no use anyway.[9]

A result of the acceptance of the theoretical distinction here attempted between industrial and pecuniary employments and an effective recognition of the pecuniary basis of the modern economic organization would be to dissociate the two ideas of productivity and remuneration. In mathematical language, remuneration could no longer be conceived and handled as a "function" of productivity, – unless productivity be taken to mean pecuniary serviceability to the person who pays the remuneration. In modern life remuneration is, in the last analysis, uniformly obtained by virtue of an agreement between individuals who commonly proceed [216] on their own interest in point of pecuniary gain. The remuneration may, therefore, be said to be a "function" of the pecuniary service rendered the person who grants the remuneration; but what is pecuniarily serviceable to the individual who exercises the discretion in the matter need not be productive of material gain to the community as a whole. Nor does the algebraic sum of individual pecuniary gains measure the aggregate serviceability of the activities for which the gains are got.

In a community organized, as modern communities are, on a pecuniary basis, the discretion in economic matters rests with the individuals, in severalty; and the aggregate of discrete individual interests nowise expresses the collective interest. Expressions constantly recur in economic discussions which imply that the transactions discussed are carried out for the sake of the collective good or at the initiative of the social organism, or that "society" rewards so and so for their services. Such expressions are commonly of the nature of figures of speech and are serviceable for homiletical rather than for scientific use. They serve to express their user's faith in a beneficent order of nature, rather than to convey or to formulate information in regard to facts.

Of course, it is still possible consistently to hold that there is a natural equivalence between work and its reward, that remuneration is naturally, or normally, or in the long run, proportioned to the material service rendered the community by the recipient; but that proposition will hold true only if "natural" or "normal" be taken in such a sense as to admit of our saying that the natural does not coincide with the actual; and it must be recognized that such a doctrine of the "natural" apportionment of wealth or of income disregards the [217] efficient facts of the case. Apart from effects of this kind in the way of equitable arrangements traceable to grounds of sentiment, the only recourse which modern science would afford the champion of a doctrine of

---

9 Since the ground of payment of wages is the vendibility of the product, and since the ground of a difference in wages is the different vendibility of the product acquired through the purchase of the labor for which the wages are paid, it follows that wherever the difference in vendibility rests on a difference in the magnitude of the product alone, there wages should be somewhat in proportion to the magnitude of the product.

natural distribution, in the sense indicated, would be a doctrine of natural selection; according to which all disserviceable or unproductive, wasteful employments would, perforce, be weeded out as being incompatible with the continued life of any community that tolerated them. But such a selective elimination of unserviceable or wasteful employments would presume the following two conditions, neither of which need prevail: (1) It must be assumed that the disposable margin between the aggregate productivity of industry and the aggregate necessary consumption is so narrow as to admit of no appreciable waste of energy or of goods; (2) it must be assumed that no deterioration of the condition of society in the economic respect does or can "naturally" take place. As to the former of these two assumptions, it is to be said that in a very poor community, and under exceptionally hard economic circumstances, the margin of production may be as narrow as the theory would require. Something approaching this state of things may be found, for instance, among some Eskimo tribes. But in a modern industrial community – where the margin of admissible waste probably always exceeds fifty per cent of the output of goods – the facts make no approach to the hypothesis. The second assumed condition is, of course, the old-fashioned assumption of a beneficent, providential order or meliorative trend in human affairs. As such, it needs no argument at this day. Instances are not far to seek of communities in which economic deterioration has taken place while the system of distribution, both [218] of income and of accumulated wealth, has remained on a pecuniary basis.

I am sensible of having dwelt at an unseemly length on this question of an organic or natural equivalence between social service and remuneration, on the one hand, and on the bearing of the attempted distinction between industrial and pecuniary employments upon this theory of a natural equivalence, on the other hand. My excuse for so doing is that this doctrine of a natural equivalence has had a far-reaching and enduring effect upon the received theories of distribution and production, and that, with a change of phrase rather than of substance, it still continues to afford ground for further elaboration of like theories; while at the same time it seems plain that a scrutiny of the metaphysics of the doctrine of equivalence must immediately put it out of court as being groundless as well as useless for the purposes of modern science. I am also sensible of having said very little in the course of this long argument that is not already contained, explicitly or by broad implication, in the accepted body of doctrines. What has been attempted is to follow out the direction of latter-day economic discussion one step beyond the point at which those who have been making economic science have been content to rest their analysis of phenomena. This one step crosses the frontier between the normal and the actual, at a point where the line has not usually been crossed.

To return to the main drift of the argument. The pecuniary employments have to do with wealth in point of ownership, with market values, with transactions of exchange, purchase and sale, bargaining for the purpose of pecuniary gain. These employments make up the [219] characteristic occupations of business men, and the gains of business are derived from successful endeavors of the pecuniary kind. These business employments are the characteristic activity (constitute the "function") of what are in theory called undertakers. The dispositions which undertakers, qua business men, make are pecuniary dispositions – whatever industrial sequel they may or may not have – and are carried out with a view to pecuniary gain. The wealth of which they have the discretionary disposal may or may not be in the form of "production goods"; but in whatever form the wealth in question is conceived to exist, it is handled by the undertakers in terms of values and is disposed of by them in the pecuniary respect. When, as may happen, the undertaker steps down from the pecuniary plane and directs the mechanical handling and functioning of "production goods," he becomes for the time a foreman. The undertaker, if his business venture is of the industrial kind, of course takes cognizance of the aptness of a given industrial method or process for his purpose, and he has to choose between different industrial processes in which to invest his values; but his work as undertaker, simply, is the investment and shifting of the values under his hand from the less to the more gainful point of investment. When the investment takes the form of material means of industry, or industrial plant, the sequel of a given business transaction is commonly some particular use of such means; and when such industrial use follows, it commonly takes place at the hands of other men than the undertaker, although it takes place within limits imposed by the pecuniary exigencies of which the undertaker takes cognizance. Wealth turned to account in the way of investment or business management may or may not, in consequence, [220] be turned to account, materially, for industrial effect. Wealth, values, so employed for pecuniary ends is capital in the business sense of the word.[10] Wealth, material means of industry, physically employed for industrial ends is capital in the industrial sense. Theory, therefore, would require that care be taken to distinguish between capital as a pecuniary category, and capital as an industrial category, if the term capital is retained to cover the two concepts.[11] The distinction here made substantially coincides with a distinction which many late writers have arrived at from a different point of approach and have, with varying success, made use of under different terms.[12]

---

10 All wealth so used is capital, but it does not follow that all pecuniary capital is social wealth.
11 In current theory the term capital is used in these two senses; while in business usage it is employed pretty consistently in the former sense alone. The current ambiguity in the term capital has often been adverted to by economists, and there may be need of a revision of the terminology at this point; but this paper is not concerned with that question.
12 Professor Fetter, in a recent paper (*Quarterly Journal of Economics*, November, 1900) is, perhaps, the writer who has gone the farthest in this direction in the definition of the capital concept. Professor Fetter wishes to confine the term capital to pecuniary capital, or rather to such pecuniary capital as is based on the ownership of material goods. The wisdom of such a terminological expedient is, of course, not in question here.

A further corollary touching capital may be pointed out. The gains derived from the handling of capital in the pecuniary respect have no immediate relation, stand in no necessary relation of proportion, to the productive effect compassed by the industrial use of the material means over which the undertaker may dispose; although the gains have a relation of dependence to the effects achieved in point of vendibility. But vendibility need not, even approximately, coincide with serviceability, [221] except serviceability be construed in terms of marginal utility or some related conception, in which case the outcome is a tautology. Where, as in the case commonly assumed by economists as typical, the investing undertaker seeks his gain through the production and sale of some useful article, it is commonly also assumed that his effort is directed to the most economical production of as large and serviceable a product as may be, or at least it is assumed that such production is the outcome of his endeavors in the natural course of things. This account of the aim and outcome of business enterprise may be natural, but it does not describe the facts. The facts being, of course, that the undertaker in such a case seeks to produce economically as vendible a product as may be. In the common run vendibility depends in great part on the serviceability of the goods, but it depends also on several other circumstances; and to that highly variable, but nearly always considerable extent to which vendibility depends on other circumstances than the material serviceability of the goods, the pecuniary management of capital must be held not to serve the ends of production. Neither immediately, in his purely pecuniary traffic, nor indirectly, in the business guidance of industry through his pecuniary traffic, therefore, can the undertaker's dealings with his pecuniary capital be accounted a productive occupation, nor can the gains of capital be taken to mark or to measure the productivity due to the investment. The "cost of production" of goods in the case contemplated is to an appreciable, but indeterminable, extent a cost of production of vendibility – an outcome which is often of doubtful service to the body of consumers, and which often counts in the aggregate as waste. The material serviceability of the means employed [222] in industry, that is to say the functioning of industrial capital in the service of the community at large, stands in no necessary or consistent relation to the gainfulness of capital in the pecuniary respect. Productivity can accordingly not be predicated of pecuniary capital. It follows that productivity theories of interest should be as difficult to maintain as productivity theories of the gains of the pecuniary employments, the two resting on the same grounds.

It is, further, to be remarked that pecuniary capital and industrial capital do not coincide in respect of the concrete things comprised under each. From this and from the considerations already indicated above, it follows that the magnitude of pecuniary capital may vary independently of variations in the magnitude of industrial capital – not indefinitely, perhaps, but within a range which, in its nature, is indeterminate. Pecuniary capital is a matter of market values, while industrial capital is, in the last analysis, a matter of mechanical efficiency, or rather of mechanical effects not reducible to a common measure or a collective magnitude. So far as the latter may be spoken of as a homo-genous aggregate – itself a doubtful point at best – the two categories of capital are disparate magnitudes, which can be mediated only through a pro-cess of valuation conditioned by other circumstances besides the mechanical efficiency of the material means valued. Market values being a psychological outcome, it follows that pecuniary capital, an aggregate of market values, may vary in magnitude with a freedom which gives the whole an air of caprice, – such as psychological phenomena, particularly the psychological phenomena of crowds, frequently present, and such as becomes strikingly noticeable in times of panic or of [223] speculative inflation. On the other hand, industrial capital, being a matter of mechanical contrivances and adaptation, cannot similarly vary through a revision of valuations. If it is taken as an aggregate, it is a physical magnitude, and as such it does not alter its complexion or its mechanical efficiency in response to the greater or less degree of appreciation with which it is viewed. Capital pecuniarily considered rests on a basis of subjective value; capital industrially considered rests on material circumstances reducible to objective terms of mechanical, chemical and physiological effect.

The point has frequently been noted that it is impossible to get at the aggregate social (industrial) capital by adding up the several items of indivi-dual (pecuniary) capital. A reason for this, apart from variations in the market values of given material means of production, is that pecuniary capital comprises not only material things but also conventional facts, psychological phenomena not related in any rigid way to material means in production, – as e.g., good will, fashions, customs, prestige, effrontery, personal credit. What-ever ownership touches, and whatever affords ground for pecuniary discre-tion, may be turned to account for pecuniary gain and may therefore be comprised in the aggregate of pecuniary capital. Ownership, the basis of pecuniary capital, being itself a conventional fact, that is to say a matter of habits of thought, it is intelligible that phenomena of convention and opinion should figure in an inventory of pecuniary capital; whereas, industrial capital being of a mechanical character, conventional circumstances do not affect it – except as the future production of material means to replace the existing outfit may be guided by convention – and items having but a conventional existence are, therefore, not comprised in [224] its aggregate. The disparity between pecuniary and industrial capital, therefore, is something more than a matter of an arbitrarily chosen point of view, as some recent discussions of the capital concept would have us believe; just as the difference between the pecuniary and the industrial employments, which are occupied with the one or the other category of capital, means something more than the same thing under different aspects.

But the distinction here attempted has a farther bearing, beyond the possi-ble correction of a given point in the theory of distribution. Modern eco-nomic science is to an increasing extent concerning itself with the question of what men do and how and why they do it, as contrasted with the older question of how Nature, working through human nature, maintains a favorable balance in the output of goods. Neither the practical questions of our generation, nor the pressing theoretical questions of the science, run on the adequacy or equity of the share that goes to any class in the normal case. The questions are rather such realistic ones as these: Why do we, now and again, have hard times and unemployment in the midst of excellent resources, high efficiency and plenty of unmet wants? Why is one-half our consumable product contrived for consumption that yields no material benefit? Why are large coördinations of industry, which greatly reduce cost of production, a cause of perplexity and alarm? Why is the family disintegrating among the industrial classes, at the same time that the wherewithal to maintain it is easier to compass? Why are large and increasing portions of the community penniless in spite of a scale of remuneration which is very appreciably above the subsistence [225] minimum? Why is there a widespread disaffection among the intelligent workmen who ought to know better? These and the like questions, being questions of fact, are not to be answered on the grounds of normal equivalence. Perhaps it might better be said that they have so often been answered on those grounds, without any approach to disposing of them, that the outlook for help in that direction has ceased to have a serious meaning. These are, to borrow Professor Clark's phrase, questions to be answered on dynamic, not on static grounds. They are questions of conduct and sentiment, and so far as their solution is looked for at the hands of economists it must be looked for along the line of the bearing which economic life has upon the growth of sentiment and canons of conduct. That is to say, they are questions of the bearing of economic life upon the cultural changes that are going forward.

For the present it is the vogue to hold that economic life, broadly, conditions the rest of social organization or the constitution of society. This vogue of the proposition will serve an excuse from going into an examination of the grounds on which it may be justified, as it is scarcely necessary to persuade any economist that it has substantial merits even if he may not accept it in an unqualified form. What the Marxists have named the "Materialistic Conception of History" is assented to with less and less qualification by those who make the growth of culture their subject of inquiry. This materialistic conception says that institutions are shaped by economic conditions; but, as it left the hands of the Marxists, and as it still functions in the hands of many who knew not Marx, it has very little to say regarding the efficient force, the channels, or the [226] methods by which the economic situation is conceived to have its effect upon institutions. What answer the early Marxists gave to this question, of how the economic situation shapes institutions, was to the effect that the causal connection lies through a selfish, calculating class interest. But, while class interest may count for much in the outcome, this answer is plainly not a competent one, since, for one thing, institutions by no means change with the alacrity which the sole efficiency of a reasoned class interest would require.

Without discrediting the claim that class interest counts for something in the shaping of institutions, and to avoid getting entangled in preliminaries, it may be said that institutions are of the nature of prevalent habits of thought, and that therefore the force which shapes institutions is the force or forces which shape the habits of thought prevalent in the community. But habits of thought are the outcome of habits of life. Whether it is intentionally directed to the education of the individual or not, the discipline of daily life acts to alter or re-enforce the received habits of thought, and so acts to alter or fortify the received institutions under which men live. And the direction in which, on the whole, the alteration proceeds is conditioned by the trend of the discipline of daily life. The point here immediately at issue is the divergent trend of this discipline in those occupations which are prevailingly of an industrial character, as contrasted with those which are prevailingly of a pecuniary character. So far as regards the different cultural outcome to be looked for on the basis of the present economic situation as contrasted with the past, therefore, the question immediately in hand is as to the greater or less degree in which occupations are differentiated into [227] industrial and pecuniary in the present as compared with the past.

The characteristic feature which is currently held to differentiate the existing economic situation from that out of which the present has developed, or out of which it is emerging, is the prevalence of the machine industry with the consequent larger and more highly specialized organization of the market and of the industrial force and plant. As has been pointed out above, and as is well enough known from the current discussions of the economists, industrial life is organized on a pecuniary basis and managed from the pecuniary side. This, of course, is true in a degree both of the present and of the nearer past, back at least as far as the middle ages. But the larger scope of organizations in modern industry means that the pecuniary management has been gradually passing into the hands of a relatively decreasing class, whose contact with the industrial classes proper grows continually less immediate. The distinction between employments above spoken of is in an increasing degree coming to coincide with a differentiation of occupations and of economic classes. Some degree of such specialization and differentiation there has, of course, been, one might almost say, always. But in our time, in many branches of industry, the specialization has been carried so far that large bodies of the working population have but an incidental contact with the business side of the enterprise, while a minority have little if any other concern with the enterprise than its pecuniary management. This was not true, e.g., at the time when the undertaker was still salesman, purchasing agent, business manager, foreman of the shop, and master workman. Still less was it true in the days of the self-sufficing manor or household, or in the [228] days of the closed town industry. Neither is it true in our time of what we call the backward or old-fashioned industries. These latter have not been and are not organized on a large scale, with a consistent division of labor between the owners and business managers on the one side and the operative employees on the other. Our standing illustrations of this less highly organized class of industries are the surviving handicrafts and the common run of farming as carried on by relatively small proprietors. In that earlier phase of economic life, out of which the modern situation has gradually grown, all the men engaged had to be constantly on their guard, in a pecuniary sense, and were constantly disciplined in the husbanding of their means and in the driving of bargains, – as is still true, e.g., of the American farmer. The like was formerly true also of the consumer, in his purchases, to a greater extent than at present. A good share of the daily attention of those who were engaged in the handicrafts was still perforce given to the pecuniary or business/side of their trade. But for that great body of industry which is conventionally recognized as eminently modern, specialization of function has gone so far as, in great measure, to exempt the operative employees from taking thought of pecuniary matters.

Now, as to the bearing of all this upon cultural changes that are in progress or in the outlook. Leaving the "backward," relatively unspecialized, industries on one side, as being of an equivocal character for the point in hand and as not differing characteristically from the corresponding industries in the past so far as regards their disciplinary value; modern occupations may, for the sake of the argument, be broadly distinguished. as economic employments have been distinguished [229] above, into business and industrial. The modern industrial and the modern business occupations are fairly comparable as regards the degree of intelligence required in both, if it be borne in mind that the former occupations comprise the highly trained technological experts and engineers as well as the highly skilled mechanics. The two classes of occupations differ in that the men in the pecuniary occupations work within the lines and under the guidance of the great institution of ownership, with its ramifications of custom, prerogative, and legal right; whereas those in the industrial occupations are, in their work, relatively free from the constraint of this conventional norm of truth and validity. It is, of course, not true that the work of the latter class lies outside the reach of the institution of ownership; but it is true that, in the heat and strain of the work, when the agent's powers and attention are fully taken up with the work which he has in hand, that of which he has perforce to take cognizance is not conventional law, but the conditions impersonally imposed by the nature of material things. This is the meaning of the current commonplace that the required close and continuous application of the operative in mechanical industry bars him out of all chance for an all-around development of the cultural graces and amenities. It is the periods of close attention and hard work that seem to count for most in the formation of habits of thought.

An *a priori* argument as to what cultural effects should naturally follow from such a difference in discipline between the occupations, past and present, would probably not be convincing, as *a priori* arguments from half-authenticated premises commonly are not. And the experiments along this line which later economic [230] developments have so far exhibited have been neither neat enough, comprehensive enough, nor long continued enough to give definite results. Still, there is something to be said under this latter head, even if this something may turn out to be somewhat familiar.

It is, e.g., a commonplace of current vulgar discussions of existing economic questions, that the classes engaged in the modern mechanical or factory industries are improvident and apparently incompetent to take care of the pecuniary details of their own life. In this indictment may well be included not only factory hands, but the general class of highly skilled mechanics, inventors, technological experts. The rule does not hold in any hard and fast way, but there seems to be a substantial ground of truth in the indictment in this general form. This will be evident on comparison of the present factory population with the class of handicraftsmen of the older culture whom they have displaced, as also on comparison with the farming population of the present time, especially the small proprietors of this and other countries. The inferiority which is currently conceded to the modern industrial classes in this respect is not due to scantier opportunities for saving, whether they are compared with the earlier handicraftsmen or with the modern farmer or peasant. This phenomenon is commonly discussed in terms which impute to the improvident industrial classes something in the way of total depravity, and there is much preaching of thrift and steady habits. But the preaching of thrift and self-help, unremitting as it is, is not producing an appreciable effect. The trouble seems to run deeper than exhortation can reach. It seems to be of the nature of habit rather than of reasoned conviction. Other causes may be present and [231] may be competent partially to explain the improvidence of these classes; but the inquiry is at least a pertinent one; how far the absence of property and thrift among them may be traceable to the relative absence of pecuniary training in the discipline of their daily life. If, as the general lay of the subject would indicate, this peculiar pecuniary situation of the industrial classes is in any degree due to comprehensive disciplinary causes, there is material in it for an interesting economic inquiry.

The surmise that the trouble with the industrial class is something of this character is strengthened by another feature of modern vulgar life, to which attention is directed as a further, and, for the present, a concluding illustration of the character of the questions that are touched by the distinction here spoken for. The most insidious and most alarming malady, as well as the most perplexing and unprecedented, that threatens the modern social and political structure is what is vaguely called socialism. The point of danger to the social structure, and at the same time the substantial core of the socialistic disaffection, is a growing disloyalty to the institution of property, aided and abetted as it is by a similarly growing lack of deference and affection for other conventional features of social structure. The classes affected by socialistic vagaries are not consistently averse in a competent organization and control of society, particularly not in the economic respect, but they are averse to organization and control on conventional lines. The sense of solidarity does not seem to be either defective or in abeyance, but the ground of solidarity is new and unexpected. What their constructive ideals may be need not concern nor detain us; they are vague and inconsistent [232] and for the most part negative. Their disaffection has been set down to discontent with their lot by comparison with others, and to a mistaken view of their own interests; and much and futile effort has been spent in showing them the error of their ways of thinking. But what the experience of the past suggests that we should expect under the guidance of such motives and reasoning as these would be a demand for a redistribution of property, a reconstitution of the conventions of ownership on such new lines as the apprehended interests of these classes would seem to dictate. But such is not the trend of socialistic thinking, which contemplates rather the elimination of the institution of property. To the socialists property or ownership does not seem inevitable or inherent in the nature of things; to those who criticise and admonish them it commonly does.

Compare them in this respect with other classes who have been moved by hardship or discontent, whether well or ill advised, to put forth denunciations and demands for radical economic changes; as e.g., the American farmers in their several movements, of grangerism, populism, and the like. These have been loud enough in their denunciations and complaints, and they have been accused of being socialistic in their demand for a virtual redistribution of property. They have not felt the justice of the accusation, however, and it is to be noted that their demands have consistently run on a rehabilitation of property on some new basis of distribution, and have been uniformly put forth with the avowed purpose of bettering the claimants in point of owner-ship. Ownership, property "honestly" acquired, has been sacred to the rural malcontents, here and elsewhere; what they have aspired to do has been to remedy what [233] they have conceived to be certain abuses under the institution, without questioning the institution itself.

Not so with the socialists, either in this country or elsewhere. Now, the spread of socialistic sentiment shows a curious tendency to affect those classes particularly who are habitually employed in the specialized industrial occu-pations, and are thereby in great part exempt from the intellectual discipline of pecuniary management. Among these men, who by the circumstances of their daily life are brought to do their serious and habitual thinking in other than pecuniary terms, it looks as if the ownership preconception were becoming obsolescent through disuse. It is the industrial population, in the modern sense, and particularly the more intelligent and skilled men employed in the mechanical industries, that are most seriously and widely affected. With exceptions both ways, but with a generality that is not to be denied, the socialistic disaffection spreads through the industrial towns, chiefly and most potently among the better classes of operatives in the mechanical employ-ments; whereas the relatively indigent and unintelligent regions and classes, which the differentiation between pecuniary and industrial occupations has not reached, are relatively free from it. In like manner the upper and middle classes, whose employments are of a pecuniary character, if any, are also not seriously affected; and when avowed socialistic sentiment is met with among these upper and middle classes it commonly turns out to be merely a humanitarian aspiration for a more "equitable" redistribution of wealth – a readjustment of ownership under some new and improved method of control – not a contemplation of the traceless disappearance of ownership.

Socialism, in the sense in which the word connotes a [234] subversion of the economic foundations of modern culture, appears to be found only sporadically and uncertainly outside the limits, in time and space, of the discipline exercised by the modern mechanical, non-pecuniary occupations. This state of the case need of course not be due solely to the disciplinary effects of the industrial employments, nor even solely to effects traceable to those employments whether in the way of disciplinary results, selective development, or what not. Other factors, particularly factors of an ethnic character, seem to coöperate to the result indicated; but, so far as evidence bearing on the point is yet in hand and has been analyzed, it indicates that this differentiation of occupations is a necessary requisite to the growth of a consistent body of socialistic sentiment; and the indication is also that wherever this differentiation prevails in such a degree of accentuation and affects such considerable and compact bodies of people as to afford ground for a consistent growth of common sentiment, a result is some form of iconoclastic socialism. The differentiation may of course have a selective as well as a disciplinary effect upon the population affected, and an off-hand separation of these two modes of influence can of course not be made. In any case, the two modes of influence seem to converge to the outcome indicated; and, for the present purpose of illustration simply, the tracing out of the two strands of sequence in the case neither can nor need be undertaken. By force of this differentiation, in one way and another, the industrial classes are learning to think in terms of material cause and effect, to the neglect of prescription and conventional grounds of validity; just as, in a faintly incipient way, the economists are also learning to do in their discussion of the life of these classes. The resulting decay of the popular sense of conventional validity of [235] course extends to other matters than the pecuniary conventions alone, with the outcome that the socialistically affected industrial classes are pretty uniformly affected with an effortless iconoclasm in other directions as well. For the discipline to which their work and habits of life subject them gives not so much a training away from the pecuniary conventions, specifically, as a positive and somewhat unmitigated training in methods of observation and inference proceeding on grounds alien to all conventional validity. But the practical experiment going on in the specialization of discipline, in the respect contemplated, appears still to be near its beginning, and the growth of aberrant views and habits of thought due to the peculiar disciplinary trend of this late and unprecedented specialization of occupations has not yet had time to work itself clear.

The effects of the like one-sided discipline are similarly visible in the highly irregular, conventionally indefensible attitude of the industrial classes in the current labor and wage disputes, not of an avowedly socialistic aim. So also as regards the departure from the ancient norm in such non-economic, or secondarily economic matters as the family relation and responsibility, where the disintegration of conventionalities in the industrial towns is said to threaten the foundations of domestic life and morality; and again as regards the growing inability of men trained to materialistic, industrial habits of thought to appreciate, or even to apprehend, the meaning of religious appeals and consolations that proceed on the old fashioned conventional or metaphysical grounds of validity. But these and other like directions in which the cultural effects of the modern specialization of occupations, whether in industry or in business, may be traceable need not be followed up here.

Selection 25

Gustav Schmoller's economics

Source: *Quarterly Journal of Economics*, November 1901 (vol. 16, pp. 69–93).

Veblen (1901b)

Professor Schmoller's *Grundriss*[1] is an event of the first importance in economic literature. It appears from later advices that the second and concluding volume of the work is hardly to be looked for at as early a date as the author's expressions in his preface had led us to anticipate. What lies before Professor Schmoller's readers, therefore, in this first volume of *The Outlines* is but one-half of the compendious statement which he here purposes making of his theoretical position and of his views and exemplification of the scope and method of economic science. It may accordingly seem adventurous to attempt a characterization of his economic system on the basis of this avowedly incomplete statement. And yet such an endeavor is not altogether gratuitous, nor need it in any great measure proceed on hypothetical grounds. The introduction comprised in the present volume sketches the author's aim in an outline sufficiently full to afford a convincing view of the "system" of science for which he speaks; and the two books by which the introduction is followed show Professor Schmoller's method of inquiry consistently carried out, as well as the reach and nature of the theoretical conclusions which he considers to lie within the competency of economic science. And with regard to an economist who is so much of an innovator, – not to say so much of an iconoclast, – and whose work touches the foundations of the science so intimately and profoundly, the interest of his critics and associates must, at least for the present, center chiefly about these questions as to the scope and nature assigned to the theory by his discussion, as to the range and character of the material of which he makes use, and as to the methods of inquiry [70] which his sagacity and experience commend. So, therefore, while *The Outlines* is yet incomplete, considered as a compendium of details of doctrine, the work in its unfinished state need not thereby be an inadequate expression of Professor Schmoller's relation to economic science.

Herewith for the first time economic readers are put in possession of a fully advised deliverance on economic science at large as seen and cultivated by

---

1 *Grundriss der allgemeinen Volkswirtschaftslehre*, Erster Teil. Leipzig, 1900.

that modernized historical school of which Professor Schmoller is the authoritative exponent. Valuable and characteristic as his earlier discussions on the scope and method of the science are, they are but preliminary studies and tentative formulations as compared with this maturer work, which not only avows itself a definitive formulation, but has about it an air of finality perceptible at every turn. But this comes near saying that it embodies the sole comprehensive working-out of the scientific aims of the historical school. Discussions partially covering the field, monographs and sketches there are in great number, allowing the manner of economic theory that was to be looked for as an outcome of the "historical diversion." Some of these, especially some of the later ones, are extremely valuable in the results they offer, as well as significant of the trend which the science is taking under the hands of the German students.[2] But a comprehensive work, aiming to formulate a body of economic theory on the basis afforded by the "historical method," has not hitherto been seriously attempted.

To the broad statement just made exception might perhaps be taken in favor of Schaeffle's half-forgotten work of the seventies, together possibly with several other less notable and less consistent endeavors of a similar kind, dating back to the early decades of the school. Probably none of the younger generation of economists [71] would be tempted to cite Roscher's work as invalidating such a statement as the one made above. Although time has been allowed for the acceptance and authentication of these endeavors of the earlier historical economists in the direction of a system of economic theory, – that is to say, of an economic science, – they have failed of authentication at the hands of the students of the science; and there seems no reason to regard this failure as less than definitive.

During the last two decades the historical school has branched into two main directions of growth, somewhat divergent, so that broad general statements regarding the historical economists can be less confidently made to-day than perhaps at any earlier time. Now, as regards the more conservative branch, the historical economists of the stricter observance, – these modern continuers of what may be called the elder line of the historical school can scarcely be said to cultivate a science at all, their aim being not theoretical work. Assuredly, the work of the elder line, of which Professor Wagner is the unquestioned head, is by no means idle. It is work of a sufficiently important and valuable order, perhaps it is indispensable to the task which the science has in hand, but, broadly speaking, it need not be counted with in so far as it touches directly upon economic theory. This elder line of German economics, in its numerous modern representatives, shows both insight and impartiality; but as regards economic theory their work bears the character of eclecticism rather

---

2 E.g., K. Bücher's *Entstehung der Volkswirtschaft* and *Arbeit und Rhythmus*, R. Hildebrand's *Recht und Sitte*, Knapp's *Grundherrschaft und Rittergut*, Ehrenberg's *Zeitalter der Fugger*, R. Mucke's various works.

than that of a constructive advance. Frequent and peremptory as their utterances commonly are on points of doctrine, it is only very rarely that these utterances embody theoretical views arrived at or verified by the economists who make them or by such methods of inquiry as are characteristic of these economists. Where these expressions of doctrine are not of the nature of maxims of expediency, they are, as is well known, commonly [72] borrowed somewhat uncritically from classical sources. Of constructive scientific work – that is to say, of theory – this elder line of German economics is innocent; nor does there seem to be any prospect of an eventual output of theory on the part of that branch of the historical school, unless they should unexpectedly take advice, and make the scope, and therefore the method, of their inquiry something more than historical in the sense of which that term is currently accepted. The historical economics of the conservative kind seems to be a barren field in the theoretical respect.

So that whatever characteristic articles of general theory the historical school may enrich the science with are to he looked for at the hands of those men who, like Professor Schmoller, have departed from the strict observance of the historical method. A peculiar interest, therefore, attaches to his work as the best accepted and most authoritative spokesman of that branch of historical economics which professes to cultivate theoretical inquiry. It serves to show in what manner and degree this more scientific wing of the historical school have outgrown the original "historical" standpoint and range of conceptions, and how they have passed from a distrust of all economic theory to an eager quest of theoretical formulations that shall cover all phenomena of economic life to better purpose than the body of doctrine received from the classical writers and more in consonance with the canons of contemporary science at large. That this should have been the outcome of the half-century of development through which the school has now passed might well seem unexpected, if not incredible, to any who saw the beginning of that divergence within the school, a generation ago, out of which this modernized, theoretical historical economics has arisen.

Professor Schmoller entered the field early, in the sixties, as a protestant against the aims and ideals then [73] in vogue in economics. His protest ran not only against the methods and results of the classical writers, but also against the views professed by the leaders of the historical school, both as regards the scope of the science and as regards the character of the laws or generalizations sought by the science. His early work, in so far as he was at variance with his colleagues, was chiefly critical; and there is no good evidence that he then had a clear conception of the character of that constructive work to which it has been his persistent aim to turn the science. Hence he came to figure in common repute as an iconoclast and an extreme exponent of the historical school, in that he was held practically to deny the feasibility of a scientific treatment of economic matters and to aim at confining economics to narrative, statistics, and description. This iconoclastic or critical phase of his economic discussion is now past, and with it the uncertainty as to the trend and outcome of his scientific activity.

To understand the significance of the diversion created by Professor Schmoller as regards the scope and method of economics, it is necessary, very briefly, to indicate the position occupied by that early generation of historical economists from which his teaching diverged, and more particularly those points of the older canon at which he has come to differ characteristically from the views previously in vogue.

As regards the situation in which the historical school, as exemplified by its leaders, was then placed, it is, of course, something of a commonplace that by the end of its first twenty years of endeavor in the reform of economic science the school had, in point of systematic results, scarcely got beyond preliminaries. And even these preliminaries were not in all respects obviously to the purpose. A new and wider scope had been indicated [74] for economic inquiry, as well as a new aim and method for theoretical discussion. But the new ideals of theoretical advance, as well as the ways and means indicated for their attainment, still had mainly a speculative interest. Nothing substantial had been done towards the realization of the former or the *mise en œuvre* of the latter. The historical economists can scarcely be said at that time to have put their hand to the new engines which they professed to house in their workshop. Apart from polemics and speculation concerning ideals, the serious interest and endeavors of the school had up to that time been in the field of history rather than in that of economics, except so far as the adepts of the new school continued in a fragmentary way to inculcate and, in some slight and uncertain degree, to elaborate the dogmas of the classical writers whom they sought to discredit.

The character of historical economics at the time when Professor Schmoller entered on his work of criticism and revision is fairly shown by Roscher's writings. Whatever may be thought to-day of Roscher's rank as an economist, in contrast with Knies and Hildebrand, it will scarcely be questioned that at the close of the first quarter-century of the life history of the historical school it was Roscher's conception of the scope and method of economics that found the widest acceptance and that best expressed the animus of that body of students who professed to cultivate economics by the historical method. For the purpose in hand Roscher's views may, therefore, be taken as typical, all the more readily since for the very general purpose here intended there are no serious discrepancies between Roscher and his two illustrious contemporaries. The chief difference is that Roscher is more naïve and more specific. He has also left a more considerable volume of results achieved by the professed use of his method.

Roscher's professed method was what he calls the "historico-physiological" method. This he contrasts with the [75] "philosophical" or "idealistic" method. But his air of depreciation as regards "philosophical" methods in economics must not be taken to mean that Roscher's own economic speculations were devoid of all philosophical or metaphysical basis. It only means that his philosophical postulates were different from those of the economists whom he discredits, and that they were regarded by him as self-evident.

As must necessarily be the case with a writer who had neither a special aptitude for nor special training in philosophical inquiries, Roscher's metaphysical postulates are, of course, chiefly tacit. They are the common-sense, commonplace metaphysics afloat in educated German circles in the time of Roscher's youth, – during the period when his growth and education gave him his outlook on life and knowledge and laid the basis of his intellectual habits; which means that these postulates belong to what Höffding has called the "Romantic" school of thought, and are of a Hegelian complexion. Roscher being not a professed philosophical student, it is neither easy nor safe to particularize closely as regards his fundamental metaphysical tenets; but, as near as so specific an identification of his philosophical outlook is practicable, he must be classed with the Hegelian "Right." But since the Hegelian metaphysics had in Roscher's youth an unbroken vogue in reputable German circles, especially in those ultra-reputable circles within which lay the gentlemanly life and human contact of Roscher, the postulates afforded by the Hegelian metaphysics were accepted simply as a matter of course, and were not recognized as metaphysical at all. And in this his metaphysical affiliation Roscher is fairly typical of the early historical school of economics.

The Hegelian metaphysics, in so far as bears upon the matter in hand, is a metaphysics of a self-realizing life process. This life process, which is the central and substantial fact of the universe, is of a spiritual nature, – [76] "spiritual," of course, being here not contrasted with "material." The life process is essentially active, self-determining, and unfolds by inner necessity, – by necessity of its own substantially active nature. The course of culture, in this view, is an unfolding (exfoliation) of the human spirit; and the task which economic science has in hand is to determine the laws of this cultural exfoliation in its economic aspect. But the laws of the cultural development with which the social sciences, in the Hegelian view, have to do are at one with the laws of the process of the universe at large; and, more immediately, they are at one with the laws of the life process at large. For the universe at large is itself a self-unfolding life process, substantially of a spiritual character, of which the economic life process which occupies the interest of the economist is but a phase and an aspect. Now, the course of the processes of unfolding life in organic nature has been fairly well ascertained by the students of natural history and the like; and this, in the nature of the case, must afford a clew to the laws of cultural development, in its economic as well as in any other of its aspects or bearings, – the laws of life in the universe being all substantially spiritual and substantially at one. So we arrive at a physiological conception of culture after the analogy of the ascertained physiological processes seen in the biological domain. It is conceived to be physiological after the Hegelian manner of conceiving a physiological process, which is, however, not the same as the modern scientific conception of a physiological process.[3] [77]

Since this quasi-physiological process of cultural development is conceived to be an unfolding of the self-realizing human spirit, whose life history it is, it is of the nature of the case that the cultural process should run through a certain sequence of phases – a certain life history prescribed by the nature of the active, unfolding spiritual substance. The sequence is determined on the whole, as regards the general features of the development, by the nature of life on the human plane. The history of cultural growth and decline necessarily repeats itself, since it is substantially the same human spirit that seeks to realize itself in every comprehensive sequence of cultural development, and since this human spirit is the only factor in the case that has substantial force. In its generic features the history of past cultural cycles is, therefore, the history of the future. Hence the importance, not to say the sole efficacy for economic science, of an historical scrutiny of culture. A well-authenticated sequence of cultural phenomena in the history of the past is conceived to have much the same binding force for the sequence of cultural phenomena in the future as a "natural law," as the term has been understood in physics or physiology, is conceived to have as regards the course of phenomena in the life history of the human body; for the onward cultural course of the human spirit, actively unfolding by inner necessity, is an organic process, following logically from the nature of this self-realizing spirit. If the process is conceived to meet with obstacles or varying conditions, it adapts itself to the circumstances in any [78] given case, and it then goes on along the line of its own logical bent until it eventuates in the consummation given by its own nature. The environment, in this view, if it is not to be conceived simply as a function of the spiritual force at work, is, at the most, of subsidiary and transient consequence only. Environmental conditions can at best give rise to minor perturbations; they do not initiate a cumulative sequence which can profoundly affect the outcome or the ulterior course of the cultural

3 A physiological conception of society, or of the community, had been employed before – e.g., by the Physiocrats, – and such a concept was reached also by English speculators – e.g., Herbert Spencer – during Roscher's lifetime; but these physiological conceptions of society are reached by a different line of approach from that which led up to the late-Hegelian physiological or biological conception of human culture as a spiritual structure and process. The outcome is also a different one, both as regards the use made of the analogy and as regards the theoretical result reached by its aid.

It may be remarked, by the way, that neo-Hegelianism, of the "Left," [77] likewise gave rise to a theory of a self-determining cultural exfoliation; namely, the so-called "Materialistic Conception of History" of the Marxian socialists. This Marxian conception, too, had much of a physiological air; but Marx and his coadjutors had an advantage over Roscher and his following, in that they were to a greater extent schooled in the Hegelian philosophy, instead of being uncritical receptacles of the Romantic commonplaces left by Hegelianism as a residue in popular thought. They were therefore more fully conscious of the bearing of their postulates and less *naïve* in their assumptions of self-sufficiency.

process. Hence the sole, or almost sole, importance of historical inquiry in determining the laws of cultural development, economic or other.

The working conception which this romantic-historical school had of economic life, therefore, is, in its way, a conception of development, or evolution; but it is not to be confused with Darwinism or Spencerianism. Inquiry into the cultural development under the guidance of such preconceptions as these has led to generalizations, more or less arbitrary, regarding uniformities of sequence in phenomena, while the causes which determine the course of events, and which make the uniformity or variation of the sequence, have received but scant attention. The "natural laws" found by this means are necessarily of the nature of empiricism, colored by the bias or ideals of the investigator. The outcome is a body of aphoristic wisdom, perhaps beautiful and valuable after its kind, but quite fatuous when measured by the standards and aims of modern science. As is well known, no substantial theoretical gain was made along this romantic-historical line of inquiry and speculation, for the reason, apparently, that there are no cultural laws of the kind aimed at, beyond the unprecise generalities that are sufficiently familiar beforehand to all passably intelligent adults.

It has seemed necessary to offer this much in characterization of that "historical" aim and method which afforded [79] a point of departure for Professor Schmoller's work of revision. When he first raised his protest against the prevailing ideals and methods, as being ill-advised and not thorough-going, he does not seem himself to have been entirely free from this Romantic, or Hegelian, bias. There is evidence to the contrary in his early writings.[4] It cannot even be said that his later theoretical work does not show something of the same animus, as, e.g., when he assumes that there is an ameliorative trend in the course of cultural events.[5] What has differentiated his work from that of the group of writers which has above been called the elder line of historical economics is the weakness or relative absence of this bias in his theoretical work. Particularly, he has refused to bring his researches in the field of theory definitely to rest on ground given by the Hegelian, or Romantic, school of thought. He was from the first unwilling to accept classificatory statements of uniformity or of normality as an adequate answer to questions of scientific theory. He does not commonly deny the truth or the importance of the empirical generalizations aimed at by the early historical economists. Indeed, he makes much of them and has been notoriously urgent for a full survey of historical data and a painstaking digestion of materials with a view to a comprehensive work of empirical generalization. As is well known, in his earlier work of criticism and methodological controversy he was led to

---

4 *E.g.*, in his controversy with Treitschke. See *Grundfragen der Socialpolitik und der Volkswirtschaftslehre*, particularly pp. 24, 25.

5 *E.g.*, *Grundriss*, pp. 225, 409, 411.

contend that for at least one generation economists must be content to spend their energies on descriptive work of this kind; and he thereby earned the reputation of aiming to reduce economics to a descriptive knowledge of details and to confine its method to the Baconian ground of generalization by simple enumeration. But this exhaustive historical scrutiny and description of detail has always, in Professor Schmoller's [80] view, been preliminary to an eventual theory of economic life. The survey of details and the empirical generalizations reached by its help are useful for the scientific purpose only as they serve the end of an eventual formulation of the laws of causation that work out in the process of economic life. The ulterior question, to which all else is subsidiary, is a question of the causes at work rather than a question of the historical uniformities observable in the sequence of phenomena. The scrutiny of historical details serves this end by defining the scope and character of the several factors causally at work in the growth of culture, and, what is of more immediate consequence, as they are at work in the shaping of the economic activities and the economic aims of men engaged in this unfolding cultural process as it lies before the investigator in the existing situation.

In the preliminary work, then, of defining and characterizing the causes or factors of economic life, historical investigation plays a large, if not the largest, part; but it is by no means the sole line of inquiry to which recourse is had for this purpose. Nor, it may be added, is this the sole use of historical inquiry. To the like end a comparative study of the climatic, geographical, and geological features of the community's environment is drawn into the inquiry; and more particularly there is a careful study of ethnographic parallels and a scrutiny of the psychological foundations of culture and the psychological factors involved in cultural change.

Hence it appears that Professor Schmoller's work differs from that of the elder line of historical economics in respect of the scope and character of the preliminaries of economic theory no less than in the ulterior aim which he assigns the science. It is only by giving a very broad meaning to the term that this latest development of the science can be called an "historical" economics. It is Darwinian rather than Hegelian, although with the ear-marks [81] of Hegelian affiliation visible now and again; and it is "historical" only in a sense similar to that in which a Darwinian account of the evolution of economic institutions might be called historical. For the distinguishing characteristic of Professor Schmoller's work, that wherein it differs from the earlier work of the economists of his general class, is that it aims at a Darwinistic account of the origin, growth, persistence, and variation of institutions, in so far as these institutions have to do with the economic aspect of life either as cause or as effect. In much of what he has to say, he is at one with his contemporaries and predecessors within the historical school; and he shows at many points both the excellences and weaknesses due to his "historical" antecedents. But his striking and characteristic merits lie in the direction of a post-Darwinian, causal theory of the origin and growth of species in institutions. In this line of theoretical inquiry Professor Schmoller is not alone, nor does he, perhaps, go so far or with such singleness of purpose in this direction as some others do at given points; but the seniority belongs to him, and he is also in the lead as regards the comprehensiveness of his work.

But to return to the *Grundriss*, to which recourse must be had to substantiate the characterization here offered. The entire work as projected comprises an Introduction and four Books, of which the introduction and the first two books are contained in the volume already published. The two books yet to be published, in a second volume, promise to be of a length corresponding to the first two. The present volumes should accordingly contain approximately three-fifths of the whole, counted by bulk. The scheme of the work is as follows: An Introduction (pp. 1–124) treats of (1) the Concept of Economics, (2) the Psychical, Ethical (or Conventional, *sittliche*), and Legal Foundations of Economic Life and of Culture, and (3) the [82] Literature and Method of the Science. This is followed by Book I (pp. 125–228) on Land, Population, and the Industrial Arts, considered as collective phenomena and factors in economic life, and Book II (pp. 229–457), on the Constitution of Economic Society, its chief organs and the causal factors to which they are due. Books III and IV are to deal with the Circulation of Goods and the Distribution of Income, and to give a genetic account of the Development of Economic Society.

The course outlined differs noticeably from what has been customary in treatises on economics. The point of departure is a comprehensive general survey of the factors which enter into the growth of culture, with special reference to their economic bearing. This survey runs chiefly on psychological and ethnographic ground, historical inquiry in the stricter sense being relatively scant and obviously of secondary consequence. It is followed up with a more detailed and searching discussion of the factors engaged in the economic process in any given situation. The factors, or "collective phenomena," in question are not the time-honored Land, Labor, and Capital, but rather population, material environment, and technological conditions. Here, too, the discussion has to do with ethnographic rather than with properly historical material. The question of population concerns not the numerical force of laborers, but rather the diversity of race characteristics and the bearing of race endowment upon the growth of economic institutions. The discussion of the material environment, again, has relatively little to say of the fertility of the soil, and gives much attention to diversities of climate, geographical situation, and geological and biological conditions. And this first book closes with a survey of the growth of technological knowledge and the industrial arts.

In all this the significant innovation lies not so much in the character of the details. They are for the most [83] part commonplace enough as details of the sciences from which they are borrowed. They are shrewdly chosen and handled in such a way as to bring out their bearing upon the ulterior questions about which the economist's interest centers; but there is, as might be expected, little attempt to go back of the returns given by specialists in the several lines of research that are laid under contribution. But the significance of it all lies rather in the fact that material of this kind should have been drawn upon for a foundation for economic theory, and that it should have seemed necessary to Professor Schmoller to make this introductory survey so comprehensive and so painstaking as it is. Its meaning is that these features of human nature and these forces of nature and circumstances of environment are the agencies out of whose interaction the economic situation has arisen by a cumulative process of change, and that it is this cumulative process of development, and its complex and unstable outcome, that are to be the economist's subject-matter. The theoretical outcome for which such a foundation is prepared is necessarily of a genetic kind. It necessarily seeks to know and explain the structure and functions of economic society in terms of how and why they have come to be what they are, not, as so many economic writers have explained them, in terms of what they are good for and what they ought to be. It means, in other words, a deliberate attempt to substitute an inquiry into the efficient causes of economic life in the place of empirical generalizations, on the one hand, and speculations as to the eternal fitness of things, on the other hand.

It follows from the nature of the case that an economics of this genetic character, working on grounds of the kind indicated, comprises nothing in the way of advice or admonition, no maxims of expediency, and no economic, political, or cultural creed. How nearly Professor Schmoller conforms to this canon of continence is [84] another question. The above indicates the scope of such doctrines as are consistently derivable from the premises with which the work under review starts out, not the scope of its writer's speculations on economic matters.

The second book, by the help of prehistoric and ethnographic material as well as history, deals with the evolution of the methods of social organization, – the growth of institutions in so far as this growth shapes or is shaped by the exigencies of economic life. The "organs," or social-economic institutions, whose life history is passed in review are: the family; the methods of settlement and domicile, in town and country; the political units of control and administration; differentiation of functions between industrial and other classes and groups; ownership, its growth and distribution; social classes and associations; business enterprise, industrial organizations and corporations.

As regards the singleness of purpose with which Professor Schmoller has carried out the scheme of economic theory for which he has sketched the outlines and pointed the way, it is not possible to speak with the same confidence as of his preliminary work. It goes without saying that this further work of elaboration is excellent after its kind; and this excellence, which was to be looked for at Professor Schmoller's hands, may easily divert the reader's attention from the shortcomings of the work in respect of kind rather than of quality. Now, while a broad generalization on this head may be hazardous and is to be taken with a large margin, still, with due allowance, the following generalization will probably stand, so far as regards this first volume. So long as the author is occupied with the life history of institutions down to contemporary developments, so long his discussion proceeds by the dry light of the scientific interest, simply, as the term "scientific" is understood among the modern adepts of the natural sciences; but so soon as he comes to close quarters with [85] the situation of to-day, and reaches the point where a dispassionate analysis and exposition of the causal complex at work in contemporary institutional changes should begin, so soon the scientific light breaks up into all the colors of the rainbow, and the author becomes an eager and eloquent counselor, and argues the question of what ought to be and what modern society must do to be saved. The argument at this point loses the character of a genetic explanation of phenomena, and takes on the character of appeal and admonition, urged on grounds of expediency, of morality, of good taste, of hygiene of political ends, and even of religion. All this, of course, is what we are used to in the common run of writers of the historical school; but those students whose interest centers in the science rather than in the ways and means of maintaining the received cultural forms of German society have long fancied they had ground to hope for something more to the purpose when Professor Schmoller came to put forth his great systematic work. Brilliant and no doubt valuable in its way and for its end, this digression into homiletics and reformatory advice means that the argument is running into the sands just at the stage where the science can least afford it. It is precisely at this point, where men of less years and breadth and weight would find it difficult to hold tenaciously to the course of cause and effect through the maze of jarring interests and sentiments that make up the contemporary situation, – it is precisely at this point that a genetic theory of economic life most needs the guidance of the firm, trained, dispassionate hand of the master. And at this point his guidance all but fails us.

What has just been said applies generally to Professor Schmoller's treatment of contemporary economic development, and it should be added that it applies at nearly all points with more or less of qualification. But the qualifications required are not large enough to belie the general [86] characterization just offered. It would be asking too large an indulgence to follow the point up in this place through all the discussions of the volume that fairly come under this criticism. The most that may be done is to point for illustration to the handling which two or three of the social-economic "organs" receive. So, for instance, Book II opens with an account of the family and its place and function in the structure of economic society. The discussion proceeds along the beaten paths of ethnographic research, with repeated and well-directed recourse to the psychological knowledge that Professor Schmoller always has well in hand. Coming down into recent times, the discussion still proceeds to show how the large economic changes of late mediæval and early modern times acted to break down the patriarchal régime of the earlier culture; but at the same time there comes into sight (pp. 245–49) a bias in favor of the recent as against the earlier form of the household. The author is no longer content to show the exigencies which set the earlier patriarchal household aside in favor of the modified patriarchal household of more recent times. He also offers reasons why the later, modified form is intrinsically the more desirable; reasons, it should perhaps be said, which may be well taken, but which are beside the point so far as regards a scientific explanation of the changes under discussion.

The closing paragraphs of the section (91) dwell with a kindly insistence on the many elements of strength and beauty possessed by the form of household organization handed down from the past generation to the present. The facts herewith recited by the author are, no doubt, of weight, and must be duly taken account of by any economist who ventures on a genetic discussion of the present situation and the changing fortunes of the received household. But Professor Schmoller has failed even to point out in what manner these elements of [87] strength and beauty have in the recent past or may in the present and immediate future causally affect the fortunes of the institution. The failure to turn the material in question to scientific account becomes almost culpable in Professor Schmoller, since there are few, if any, who are in so favorable a position to outline the argument which a theoretical account of the situation at this point must take. Plainly, as shown by Professor Schmoller's argument, economic exigencies are working an incessant cumulative change in the form of organization of the modern household; but he has done little towards pointing out in what manner and with what effect these exigencies come into play. Neither has he gone at all into the converse question, equally grave as a question of economic theory, of how the persistence, even though qualified, of the patriarchal family has modified and is modifying economic structure and function at other points and qualifying or accentuating the very exigencies themselves to which the changes wrought in the institution are to be traced. Plainly, too, the strength and beauty of the traditionally received form of the household – that is to say, the habits of life and of complacency which are bound up with this household – are elements of importance in the modern situation as affects the degree of persistence and the direction of change which this institution shows under modern circumstances. They are psychological facts, facts of habit and propensity and spiritual fitness, the efficiency of which as live forces making for survival or variation is in this connection probably second to that of no other factors that could be named. We had, therefore, almost a right to expect that Professor Schmoller's profound and comprehensive erudition in the fields of psychology and cultural growth should turn these facts to better ends than a preachment concerning an intrinsically desirable consummation.

Regarding the present visible disintegration of the family, [88] and the closely related "woman question," Professor Schmoller's observations are of much the same texture. He notes the growing disinclination to the old-fashioned family life on the part of the working population, and shows that there are certain economic causes for this growth or deterioration of sentiment.

What he has to offer is made up of the commonplaces of latter-day social-economic discussion, and is charged with a strong undertone of deprecation. What the trend of the causes at work to alter or fortify this body of sentiment may be, counts for very little in what he says on the present movement or on the immediate future of the institution. The best he has to offer on the "woman question" is an off-hand reference of the ground of sentiment on which it rests to a recrudescence of the eighteenth century spirit of *égalité*. This notion of the equality of the sexes he refutes in graceful and affecting terms, and he pleads for the unbroken preservation of woman's sphere and man's primacy; as if the matter of superiority or inferiority between the sexes could conceivably be anything more than a conventional outcome of the habits of life imposed upon the community by the circumstances under which they live. How it has come to pass that under the economic exigencies of the past the physical and temperamental diversity between the sexes has been conventionally construed into a superiority of the man and an inferiority of the woman, – on this head he has no more to say or to suggest than on the correlate question of why this conventional interpretation of the facts has latterly not been holding its ancient ground. The discussion of the family and of the relation of the sexes, in modern culture, is marked throughout by unwillingness or inability to penetrate behind the barrier of conventional finality.

The discussion of the family just cited occupies the opening chapter of Book II. For a further instance of Professor Schmoller's handling of a modern economic [89] problem, reference may be had to the closing chapter of Book I, on the "Development of Technological Expedients and its Economic Significance," but more particularly the sections (84–86) on the modern machine industry (pp. 211–28). In this discussion, also, the point of interest is the attention given to the latter-day phenomena of machine industry, and the author's method and animus in dealing with them. There is (pp. 211–18) a condensed and competent presentation of the main characteristics of the modern "machine age," followed (pp. 218–28) by a critical discussion of its cultural value. The customary eulogy, but with more than the customary discrimination, is given to the advantages of the régime of the machine in point of economy, creature comforts, and intellectual sweep; and it is pointed out how the régime of the machine has brought about a redistribution of wealth and of population and a reorganization and redistribution of social and economic structures and functions. It is pointed out (p. 223) that the gravest social effect of the machine industry has been the creation of a large class of wage laborers. The material circumstances into which this class has been thrown, particularly in point of physical comfort, are dealt with in a sober and discriminating way; and it is shown (p. 224) that in the days of its fuller development the machine's régime has evolved a class of trained laborers who not only live in comfort, but are sound and strong in mind and body. But with the citation of these facts the pursuit of the chain of cause and effect in this modern machine situation comes to an end. The remainder of the space given to the subject is occupied with extremely sane and well-advised criticism, moral and æsthetic, and indications of what the proper ideals and ends of endeavor should be.

Professor Schmoller misses the opportunity he here has of dealing with this material in a scientific spirit and with some valuable results for economic theory. He could, it [90] is not too bold to assume, have sketched for us an effective method and line of research to be pursued, for instance, in following up the scientific question of what may be the cultural, spiritual effects of the machine's régime upon this large body of trained workmen, and what this body of trained workmen in its turn counts for as a factor in shaping the institutional growth of the present and the economic and cultural situation of to-morrow. Work of this kind, there is reason to believe, Professor Schmoller could have done with better effect than any of his colleagues in the science; for he is, as already noticed above, possessed of the necessary qualifications in the way of psychological training, broad knowledge of the play of cause and effect in cultural growth, and an ability to take a scientific point of view. Instead of this he harks back again to the dreary homiletical waste of the traditional *Historismus*. It seems as if a topic which he deals with as an objective matter so long as it lies outside the sphere of every-day humanitarian and social solicitude, becomes a matter to be passed upon by conventional standards of taste, dignity, morality, and the like, so soon as it comes within the sweep of latter-day German sentiment.

This habit of treating a given problem from these various and shifting points of view at times gives a kaleidoscopic effect that is not without interest. So in the matter of the technically trained working population in the machine industry, to which reference has already been made, something of an odd confusion appears when expressions taken from diverse phases of the discussion are brought side by side. He speaks of this class at one point (p. 224) as "sound, strong, spiritually and morally advancing," superior in all these virtues to the working classes of other times and places. At another point (pp. 250–53) he speaks of the same popular element, under the designation of "socialists," as perverse, degenerate, and reactionary. This latter characterization may [91] be substantially correct, but it proceeds on grounds of taste and predilection, not on grounds of scientifically determinate cause and effect. And the two characterizations apply to the same elements of population; for the substantial core and tone-giving factor of the radical socialistic element in the German community is, notoriously, just this technically trained population of the industrial towns where the discipline of the machine industry has been at work with least mitigation. The only other fairly isolable element of a radical socialistic complexion is found among the students of modern science. Now, further, in his speculations on the relation of technological knowledge to the advance of culture, Professor Schmoller points out (e.g. p. 226) that a high degree of culture connotes, on the whole, a high degree of technological efficiency, and conversely. In this connection he makes use of the terms

Halbkulturvölker and *Ganzkulturvölker*[6] to designate different degrees of cultural maturity. It is curious to reflect, in the light of what he has to say on these several heads, that if the socialistically affected, technically trained population of the industrial towns, together with the radical-socialistic men of science, were abstracted from the German population, leaving substantially the peasantry, the slums, and the aristocracy great and small, the resulting German community would unquestionably have to be classed as a *Halbkulturvölker* in Professor Schmoller's scheme. Whereas the elements abstracted, if taken by themselves, would as unquestionably be classed among the *Ganzkulturvölker*.

In conclusion, one may turn to the concluding chapter (Book II, Chapter vii.) of the present volume for a final illustration of Professor Schmoller's method and animus in handling a modern economic problem. All the more so as this chapter on business enterprise better sustains that scientific attitude which the introductory outline leads the reader to look for throughout. It shows how modern [92] business enterprise is in the main an outgrowth of commercial activity, as also that it has retained the commercial spirit down to the present. The motive force of business enterprise is the self-seeking quest of dividends; but Professor Schmoller shows, with more dispassionate insight than many economists, that this self-seeking motive is hemmed in and guided at all points in the course of its development by considerations and conventions that are not of a primarily self-seeking kind. He is not content to point to the beneficent working of a harmony of interests, but sketches the play of forces whereby a self-seeking business traffic has come to serve the interests of the community. Business enterprise has gradually emerged and come into its present central and dominant position in the community's industry as a concomitant of the growth of individual ownership and pecuniary discretion in modern life. It is therefore a phase of the modern cultural situation; and its survival and the direction of its further growth are therefore conditioned by the exigencies of the modern cultural situation. What this modern cultural situation is and what are the forces, essentially psychological, which shape the further growth of the situation, no one is better fitted to discuss than Professor Schmoller; and he has also given valuable indications (pp. 428–57) of what these factors are and how the inquiry into their working must be conducted. But even here, where a dispassionate tracing-out of the sequence of cause and effect should be easier to undertake, because less readily blurred with sentiment, than in the case, *e.g.*, of the family, the work of tracing the developmental sequence tapers off into advice and admonition proceeding on the assumption that the stage now reached is, or at least should be, final. The attention in the later pages diverges from the process of growth and its conditioning circumstances, to the desirability of maintaining the good results attained and to the ways and means of holding fast that which is good in the

6 [Half-cultured people; fully-cultured people. – Eds.]

[93] outcome already achieved. The question to which an answer is sought in discussing the present phase of the development is not a question as to what is taking place as respects the institution of business enterprise, but rather a question as to what form should be given to an optimistic policy of fostering business enterprise and turning it to account for the common good. At this point, as elsewhere, though perhaps in a less degree than elsewhere, the existing form of the institution is accepted as a finality. All this is disappointing in view of the fact that at no other point do modern economic institutions bear less of an air of finality than in the forms and conventions of business organizations and relations. As Professor Schmoller remarks (p. 455), the scope and character of business undertakings necessarily conform to the circumstances of the time, not to any logical scheme of development from small to great or from simple to complex. So also, one might be tempted to say, the expediency and the chance of ultimate survival of business enterprise is itself an open question, to be answered by a scrutiny of the forces that make for its survival or alteration, not by advice as to the best method of sustaining and controlling it.

What has here been said in criticism of Professor Schmoller's work, particularly as regards his departure from the path of scientific research in dealing with present-day phenomena, may, of course, have to be qualified, if not entirely set aside, when his work is completed with the promised genetic survey of modern institutions to be set forth in the concluding fourth book. Perhaps it may even be said that there is fair hope, on general grounds, of such a consummation; but the present volume does not afford ground for a confident expectation of this kind. It is perhaps needless, perhaps gratuitous, to add that the strictures offered indicate, after all, but relatively slight shortcomings in a work of the first magnitude.

Selection 26

Review of *Psychologie économique* by Gabriel Tarde

Source: *Journal of Political Economy*, December 1902 (vol. 11, pp. 146–48).

Veblen (1902c)

In its general plan M. Tarde's book is an application of his well-known "social laws" to economics, together with a recasting of the received scheme of economic theory to fit the scheme of his social laws. The economics to whose revision he addresses himself is a somewhat old-fashioned economics; approximately, one might say, some half-a-century old, more or less. Later discussion, with the exception of what M. Gide has contributed, has not in any appreciable degree affected M. Tarde's apprehension of what economics aims at as regards either its scope, its method, or the range of phenomena which engage its attention. He finds fault with the received scheme of Production, Circulation, Distribution, and Consumption (Book I, chap. iii), and rejects these several captions one by one as being in part artificial and incompetent subdivisions of the subject-matter, and in part as not belonging within the scope of the science. Circulation (following Gide) is but a corollary of the division of labor (p. 98), hence this drops out without further comment; consumption is either inseparable from production, or it is extra-economic, so that also drops out; by distribution M. Tarde appears to understand the "diffusion" of the products of industry, which, again, cannot be fairly considered a distinct head of theory, but falls under the same general head with production (*reproduction*). But the remaining head of Production fares no better. It is condemned because as it stands it has regard simply to objective entities, products, instead of dealing with the producers and their relations to one another in the productive process (pp. 99, 100).

Instead of the worn-out scheme of economics as it has hitherto stood, M. Tarde proposes to discuss economic conduct under his own scheme of social-psychological laws: Repetition, Opposition, and Adaptation. The scheme is the same as has been expounded on several earlier occasions by M. Tarde, most succinctly and comprehensively in his *Lois Sociales*. The discussion which economic phenomena get in the three books in which these several heads are taken up is, on the whole, more suggestive than convincing. In Book I, chapter ii, on the "Economic Function of Opinion" (*Croyance*), and vi, on "Money," may be singled out as of peculiar value. The former

aims to show how opinions, ideas regarding the desirability of certain products, for instance, grow up and spread through the body of consumers under
the guidance of advertising and the like; and how, on the other hand, the
opinions and predilections of consumers influence the conduct of [147] producers. Chapter vi offers an analysis of the psychological processes involved in
the establishment of a standard of value as well as in the use of money. Of
Book II, on "Economic Opposition," it is difficult to single out any particular
portion that is peculiarly worth while; it contains little else than well-worn
general reflections on prices, competition, crises, and the like, with some slight
illustrative material. Of Book III, on "Economic Adaptation," the valuable
portions are in the main comprised in chapter ii, on "The Economic Imagination," which offers some suggestive passages on the part played by imagination in invention, in the direction and organization of industry, and in
commercial enterprise.

On the whole, M. Tarde's book is not a work with which economic science
will have to count. The author's familiarity with economics is patently scanty,
and has a perfunctory air. The book has the faults that habitually attach to
M. Tarde's writings: it is unnecessarily bulky, diffuse, and discursive, at the
same time that the penchant for system making and symmetry gives it an air
of completeness and definitiveness which is not borne out by substantial
results. M. Tarde's psychology is in much the same case as his economics: it is
somewhat behind the times; its outlook over its field is narrow, and is subject
to essentially mechanical limitations; it deals in catchwords and mechanical
schematization of phenomena rather than with causal relations and the
springs of human conduct. This applies, of course, to M. Tarde's psychology
generally, as it is set forth in his earlier works, as well as in the present book.

After a busy life spent in this field, M. Tarde has come in sight of the central principle of modern psychology, which has been the common property of
American and English psychologists of the last generation, ever since Professor James broke away from the earlier empiricism: but it cannot be said
that he has assimilated this modern standpoint which he has approached, nor,
perhaps, that he sees the outcome of his own speculations in this respect.

As is well known, though perhaps not always known under this phrase, the
point of departure of modern psychological inquiry is the empirical generalization that The Idea is Essentially Active. By a painstaking, somewhat
mechanical process of generalization, illuminated with many happy turns of
expression, M. Tarde has worked out his "laws" of repetition, opposition, and
adaptation; the general upshot of which is nothing more than the concept
covered by this phrase. Had he been so fortunate as to make this well-assured
concept [148] his point of departure, his detailed theories of social forces
would unavoidably have fallen into the form of corollaries under this main
thesis. The resulting theories of social conduct would of course not have taken
the same form of expression, nor showed the same structural relations as the
present body of psychological doctrines offered by M. Tarde – the apparatus
by which he has made his approach to this point of departure.

But after all has been said, M. Tarde's work will always be of high value, both for economic and sociological students, in that it will greatly lighten the work of any fairly-equipped student who may take up the inquiry on the ground given by modern psychological science, and push it outward over the field which M. Tarde has traversed. It will also continue to be valuable on account of that easy and graceful presentation which has given his work its wide vogue, as well as on account of the cogent manner in which he argues for, and illustrates, the thesis that social and economic institutional structure is always and everywhere an outcome of the play of psychological forces.

Selection 27

Review of *Der moderne Kapitalismus* by Werner Sombart

Source: *Journal of Political Economy*, March 1903
(vol. 11, pp. 300–05).

Veblen (1903b)

Mr. Sombart's *Kapitalismus* is the most considerable essay in economic theory yet made on lines independent of the classical English political economy, by an economist affiliated to the historical school. As is well known, the adherents of the historical method have not until recently entered the theoretical field, except by way of adaptation or criticism of doctrines already in vogue; and where they have made the attempt it has commonly not had substantial results.

Mr. Sombart is not a *Historiker*, although his work shows the training of the "historical method." In standpoint and animus his work blends the historical outlook with Marxist materialism. But his Marxism is very appreciably modified by the spirit of modern, post-Darwinian scientific inquiry; so that the latter element may perhaps be said to predominate. At least no preconceptions of *Historismus* or *Materialismus* are allowed to divert the inquiry from scientific theory, as that phrase is understood in the latter-day work of the material sciences. More than once (as *e.g.*, Vol. I, p. xxxii) he cautions the reader that the inquiry which he has in hand aims at an explanation of the economic situation in causal terms; although the caution is scarcely necessary for any one who will follow the discussion attentively, which is no difficult or tedious task, since Mr. Sombart is a master of a lucid and cogent style.

The work is as ambitious as anyone could desire. Indeed, it has an air of conviction and self-sufficiency at times quite cavalier. It condemns the work of predecessors and contemporaries in such harsh and flippant terms as sometimes to remind one of Marx's vituperative outbreaks. But, again like Marx, a large and ready command of the materials and a tenacious grasp of the many converging lines of his argument save Mr. Sombart's work from the damage which it would otherwise suffer on account of his jaunty self-complacency and his discourteous treatment of those who have the fortune to differ with him. While the work is theoretical throughout, it brings in much of the [301] material used in a somewhat comprehensive manner. So much so, indeed, as to make these two volumes the most available general guide to the materials of the subject. At times the argument comes near losing itself in an excess of illustrative detail, such as had better been dealt with in monographic form apart from the theoretical development. A more serious weakness of the book is an excess of terminological innovation. There is throughout an uncontrolled penchant for discarding definitions and distinctions already familiar to economic students and substituting for them new terms and distinctions that are not always more serviceable than those which they displace. And new distinctions are also multiplied with unnecessary alacrity; so that the new categories are not always useful to Mr. Sombart, and it is very doubtful if many of them will be of service to anyone else. No doubt, some, perhaps most, of the new categories that are of a general character and a broad bearing are necessary to the argument and constitute a substantial theoretical advance; but, also no doubt, a great part of the fine-drawn distinctions elaborately worked out and designated without apparently serving any theoretical end might advantageously have been left out. It is within the mark to say that if excessive detail of classification and such materials as are of the nature of collateral only had been omitted, the substance of the two volumes might conveniently have been brought within the compass of one.

The two volumes already published are but the beginning of a comprehensive systematic work, eventually to be completed in some three or four additional volumes. So that any present appraisement of the work as a whole must be taken as provisional only, so far as regards its adequacy for the theoretical purpose at which it aims. But as regards its scope and character these two volumes afford a sufficiently unequivocal indication. It is a genetic account of modern capitalism; that is to say, of modern business enterprise, as an English writer might phrase it. Vol. I, on "The Genesis of Capitalism," traces the origin of modern business enterprise from the small beginnings of the Middle Ages, through the handicraft and petty trade of early modern times, down to the full-grown capitalistic enterprise as it came to prevail in industrial business in the course of the nineteenth century. Vol. II, on "The Theory of Capitalistic Development," is occupied with "The Modern Foundations of Business" (Book I), "The Reorganization of Business Traffic" (Book II), and "The Theory of Business Competition" (Book III). These three books of Vol. II deal with the present situation, that is to say, the [302] situation as it stands since capitalistic enterprise has come to dominate industrial business.

Characteristic of Mr. Sombart's point of view and significant of the aim of his inquiry is the careful distinction with which he sets out (chap. i), between business (*Wirtschaft*) and industry (*Betrieb*).

Betrieb ist Arbeitsgemeinschaft; Wirtschaft ist Verwertungsgemeinschaft. Es liegt mir viel daran, diese Unterscheidung zwischen Wirtschaft und Betrieb zu einem sicheren Besitzstande unserer Wissenschaft zu machen, da ich ihr, wie sich im folgenden zeigen wird, eine grosse Bedeutung für die richtige Beurteilung des Wirtschaftslebens beimesse.[1]

Accordingly, it is the genesis and the ramifications of that modern form of business enterprise called "capitalism" that the inquiry pursues; and it does not concern itself with diversities and changes of the mechanical methods of industry, except so far as they condition or are conditioned by the methods and aims of business. In tracing the genesis of capitalistic enterprise there are two main factors of the development to be accounted for: the accumulation of capitalizable funds (Book II, Part II), and the rise of the spirit of business enterprise (Book II, Part III). Capitalizable funds, Mr. Sombart finds, gradually accumulated toward the close of the Middle Ages in the hands of the landed gentry, particularly such of the nobility as held urban real property. To the growth of accumulations in the hands of the landless merchants of the towns he assigns an altogether secondary importance. A great, perhaps the decisive, auxiliary of this landed property was the influx of the precious metals. This new supply of money at the same time tempted to investment in adventures of the commercial kind by holding out large chances of gain, as it also familiarized men with the notion of trafficking for increase of wealth rather than (as had been the case) for the means of a decent livelihood.

The capitalistic spirit, the habit of mind involved in diligently seeking gain for gain's sake, was new when the modern era set in; and its gradual spread and ultimate dominance in the economic life of the western nations is a phenomenon which not only itself needs explanation, but which is conditioned by, and in turn conditions, the habits of life, the institutions, the industrial methods, and the methods of business traffic of these nations. Mr. Sombart's inquiries on these heads run chiefly on German ground. He looks to the early German situation primarily, and to the growth in those communities (particularly Italian) with which the early German business community stood in [303] close relations. And it is from the German situation outward that his investigations chiefly run in working out the course of business growth. In so looking to Germany (and Italy) as the quasi-independent "area of characterization" of modern business enterprise, it is scarcely to be doubted that Mr. Sombart is following a mistaken lead. It need not, certainly it cannot, be disputed that both in Germany and in Italy, on the transition from mediaeval to modern times, business enterprise flourished both in commerce, banking, and industry; that the transition was effectively made, from the mediaeval spirit of handicraft and petty trade carried on for a livelihood and governed by corporate regulations designed to safeguard a livelihood, to the modern

---

1 [Industry is an association of work; business is an association of exploitation. It is important to me firmly to establish the distinction between business and industry in our scientific discipline because, as I will demonstrate in what follows, I attach great significance to this distinction with respect to a correct evaluation of economic life. – Eds.]

spirit of capitalistic investment for a profit, governed by some measure of free contract and presuming freedom of competition. This early start on the continent might be taken to signify that modern business enterprise took its rise from these continental cultural areas, and that it embodies the spirit of their traditions, and rests on their institutional substructure. But to that view there are two counter considerations to be offered. As it is notorious, among students of these matters, that business enterprise arose and rapidly grew great within these continental communities, so it is also notorious that it presently decayed and all but disappeared from among those nations when the era of politics, wars, and church dissensions set in. Those communities carried over into the new era that dates from the late eighteenth century nothing in the way of a business spirit or business tradition that is at all comparable with what the English community then had to offer. The question of how much the English community may have borrowed from continental examples of business methods and the like, is not much to the point, since the conditions out of which modern business enterprise has arisen prevailed in such effective force in the English community that nothing more substantial than an acceleration of the growth could be ascribed to the continental influence. "Materialistic" as his bias is, Mr. Sombart is not inclined to rate an inquiry into chronological precedence high as compared with the economic causes at work, the conditioning circumstances out of which this modern institutional fact of business enterprise has arisen. And so far as regards these decisive circumstances, material and cultural, the English situation in that late modern time to which current business enterprise takes back was favorable to business, whereas the continental situation was then decisively unfavorable. The circumstances favorable to the growth of business principles had in very great [304] measure disappeared from the continental, particularly the German and Italian, situation, so that it was only during the course of the nineteenth century, and only under the tutelage of that modern spirit of business and mechanical technology that spread outward from the English-speaking community after the Napoleonic era, that these countries again fell into line and recovered the degree of development which they had lost a couple of centuries earlier.

These considerations go to say that the connection of the present situation with the past, in point of continuous growth, is to be sought within the English-speaking communities, and that any historical study of the antecedents and character of modern business enterprise had best be directed to the British development. These considerations are strongly backed by Mr. Sombart's own answer, in the second volume, to the question: "What were the forces which created modern business enterprise?" There is neither place nor occasion here to follow out in detail the solution of this question, for that would require a recital of the substance of the second volume, but it is worth while in this connection to point out what is said in Book I of this volume on the institutional and material foundations of modern business enterprise and to call to mind that these institutional and material conditions are of British derivation and are not found in their best development outside of the English-speaking communities. This Book I, on "Die Neubegründung des Wirtschaftslebens," comprises these chapters: "Das neue Recht," "Die neue Technik," and "Der neue Stil des Wirtschaftslebens." The substance of the chapter on "The New Legal Basis" may be summed up in a few words. It is the system of natural liberty; that is to say, in its economic bearing, inviolability and equality of property rights, freedom of contract, free competition. This institutional foundation of business enterprise is embodied in the English common law; it was worked out on British ground, gradually, from the time of the Tudors; it is to be found ingrained in the commonsense of all English-speaking peoples and prevails nowhere else in anything like the same degree of consistency and tenacity. Institutionally speaking, the British natural-rights development affords the only practicable foundations for a consummate business life, and the other peoples of western Europe are on this head borrowers and imitators of the British, driven in good part by the exigencies imposed by the British competition. In proportion as the institutional situation in any of these neighboring communities departs sensibly from the British natural-rights pattern, they are handicapped [305] for the business purpose. Those who (practically) come nearest the British pattern, as, *e.g.*, Germany, are most fortunately placed for purposes of business enterprise.

So also as to the material, the technological basis of business enterprise. The industrial revolution, which brought in the technology of the machine process and so laid the material foundations of modern business, is, of course, broadly an English fact – whatever fragmentary technological elements the English community may once have borrowed from southern Europe. And from the time when the modern machine industry got under way the lead in this matter has remained with the English-speaking peoples. It is only in the immediate present, and then doubtfully, that other than the English-speaking peoples have come into the first rank as creative factors in industrial technology. The aptitude, or the habit, of consecutive and aggressive thinking in terms of the machine process is by no means confined within the limits of English speech, but the boldest and widest prevalence of this habit of materialistic thought lies within those limits; and this habit of mind is the spiritual ground of the modern technology. That its prevalence, or its vogue, should roughly coincide with English speech and English institutions need not bring surprise, since an analysis of its character and derivation will show that it comes of the same range of cultural factors that have given rise to the characteristically English institutions.

It is on this institutional and technological ground that modern business traffic rests, and it is accordingly not a matter of surprise that business methods and business enterprise – *der neue Stil des Wirtschaftslebens*,[2] as Mr. Sombart calls it – have reached their freest swing and their maturest expression among the English-speaking peoples. And it is to be regretted that Mr. Sombart's masterly analysis of the growth and the current phenomena of

2 [The new manner of economic life. – Eds.]

business enterprise should not have taken the British and American situation as the typical, central body of the development, by comparison with which the ramifications of business enterprise through the rest of the industrial world are best to be appreciated. Instead of this he has chosen as his immediate subject of inquiry the, essentially outlying, business community of Germany, and has taken account of the main (English) line of growth only by way of qualification. The result is a slightly more roundabout discussion, a slightly less clear insight into the working of the mechanism, a slightly less true perspective in the presentation, than might have been had from a more fortunately chosen historical point of departure.

Selection 28

Review of *Pure Sociology: A Treatise Concerning the Origin and Spontaneous Development of Society* by Lester Ward

Source: *Journal of Political Economy*, September 1903
(vol. 11, pp. 655–56).

Veblen (1903h)

Of the value of this great treatise for the general science of sociology it is not the place of an economic journal to speak. Nor may one who is not himself a lifelong specialist in the science presume to pass an opinion of praise or dispraise on the culminating work of a man to whom the science owes so extraordinary a debt as to Dr. Ward. But even a lay reader may see and say this much, that *Pure Sociology* is a captivating volume by reason of lucid and forcible presentation as well as by its great range and command of information and its engaging style. It is a work of theory, presents a system wrought out symmetrically and in detail, with the maturity and poise of half-a-century's unremitting work and with the fire of unfailing youth.

Dr. Ward succeeds in what others have attempted. He has brought the aims and method of modern science effectively into sociological inquiry. This method is the genetic one, which deals with the forces and sequence of development and seeks to understand the outcome by finding out how and why it has come about. The aim is to organize social phenomena into a theoretical structure in causal terms. The resulting system is too comprehensive, with too many ramifications, to admit of anything like an abstract or a general survey being presented in a brief space.

What is of direct interest to economic students is found, chiefly, in chap. xiii, on "Autogenetic Forces," chaps. xvi and xvii, on "The Directive Agent" and "Biologic Origin of the Objective Faculties," and in chaps. xix, and xx, on "The Conquest of Nature" and "The Socialization of Achievement." It is only scattered sections and paragraphs of these chapters that are of direct interest to economic theory, the main line of the argument, of course, bearing throughout on general sociological theory of which Dr. Ward's economic views are only a ramification. The chapter on the autogenetic forces deals with the human agent in the process of production, and very suggestively discusses the place and method of intelligence in industry. Broad and general as this discussion is, it contrasts in an illuminating way with the itemized and mechanical schematism that commonly does duty as a psychology of industry in the received doctrines, or even in such a special treatise as Tarde's *Psychologie economique*. In chap. xvii, the sections on "Indirection" offer a bold analysis of the motives and methods of business traffic, of which the dominant note is given in the [656] proposition (p. 487) that "deception may almost be called the foundation of business." For economic purposes, Dr. Ward's views on the "Socialization of Achievement" (chap. xx) converge to the outcome that the trend of cultural growth sets indefeasibly toward collectivism, toward which he finds, on an analysis of the available data, that the most advanced of the industrial peoples have made the most substantial approaches.

Selection 29

The Theory of Business Enterprise

Source: Chapter VI, pp. 133–76. New York: Charles Scribners, 1904.

Veblen (1904b)

Modern business capital

What has been said on the use of loan credit has anticipated much of what is peculiar in modern business capital. Such is necessarily the case, since it is in the extensive use of credit that the later phases of the management of capital contrast most strikingly with the corresponding features of earlier business traffic. To follow the terminological precedents set by German writers, the late-modern scheme of economic life is a "credit economy," as contrasted with the "money economy" that characterizes early-modern times. The nature of business capital and its relations to the industrial process under the later, more fully developed, credit economy is in some degree different from what it was before the full and free use of credit came to occupy its present central position in business traffic; and more particularly is it at variance with the theoretical expositions of the economists of the past generation.

It has been the habit of economists and others to speak of "capital" as a stock of the material means by which industry is carried on, – industrial [134] equipment, raw materials, and means of subsistence. This view is carried over from the situation in which business and industry stood at the time of Adam Smith and of the generation before Adam Smith, from whose scheme of life and of thought he drew the commonplace materials and conceptions with which his speculations were occupied. It further carries over the point of view occupied by Adam Smith and the generation to whom he addressed his speculations. That is to say, the received theoretical formulations regarding business capital and its relations to industry proceed on the circumstances that prevailed in the days of the "money economy," before credit and the modern corporation methods became of first-class consequence in economic affairs. They canvass these matters from the point of view of the material welfare of the community at large, as seen from the standpoint of the utilitarian philosophy. In this system of social philosophy the welfare of the community at large is accepted as the central and tone-giving interest, about which a comprehensive, harmonious order of nature circles and gravitates. These early speculations on business traffic turn about the bearing of this traffic upon the wealth of nations, particularly as the wealth of nations would stand in a "natural" scheme of things, in which all things should work together for the welfare of mankind. [135]

The theory, or what there is in the way of a theory, of business capital in the received body of doctrines is worked out from the point of view and for the theoretical purposes of the eighteenth century scheme of natural liberty, natural rights, and natural law; and the received theorems concerning the part played by capital and by the capitalist are substantially of the character of laws of nature, as that term was understood during the period to which these theorems owe their genesis. What these received theorems declare concerning the nature and normal function of capital and of the capitalist need not be recited here; their content is familiar enough to all readers, lay and learned. Also the merits of such a point of view for purposes of economic theory, and the adequacy of the received concept of capital for the purposes to which it was originally applied, need not detain the inquiry. Modern business management does not take that point of view, nor does "capital" carry such a meaning to the modern business man; because the guiding circumstances under which modern business is carried on are not those supposed to be given by a beneficent order of nature, nor do the controlling purposes of business traffic include that general wellbeing which constituted the final term of Adam Smith's social philosophy.

As a business proposition, "capital" means a fund of money values; and since the credit economy [136] and corporation finance have come to be the ruling factors in industrial business, this fund of money values (taken as an aggregate) bears but a remote and fluctuating relation to the industrial equipment and the other items which may (perhaps properly) be included under the old-fashioned concept of industrial capital.[1]

Capital has been spoken of as the capitalized (aggregated) cost of industrial equipment, etc.,[2] – a view which had its significance for economic theory a hundred years ago; but since corporation finance has come to pervade the

1 The distinction between business capital and "industrial capital" or "capital goods" has been shown by Knies, *Geld und Credit*, vol. I. ch. II. pp. 40–60. Distinctions having a very similar effect in some bearings are to be found in Rodbertus ("private capital" and "national capital"), in Böhm-Bawerk ("acquisitive capital" and "productive capital," or "private capital" and "social capital"), in Clark ("capital" and "capital goods"). Similar distinctions are made by various writers to help out the incompetency of the received definition of the term. The merit of these distinctions does not concern the present inquiry, since they are made for other purposes than that here aimed at. The distinction made above is not an attempt to recast the terminology of economic theory, but is simply an expedient for present use. It amounts to an unqualified acceptance of the concept (more or less well defined) which business men habitually attach to the term "capital." Mr. F. A. Fetter has latterly spoken for the restriction of "capital," as a technical term, practically to what is here called "business capital." Mr. Fetter's "capital concept," however, should probably not be taken to cover intangible assets. The practical distinction is visible in the testimony of various witnesses before the [United States] Industrial Commission, as also in the special report on "Securities," *Report [of the Industrial Commission]*, vol. XIII.
2 Even so late and competent a student of corporate capital as J. von Körösi is bound by this antique preconception, and his work has suffered in consequence. See *Finanzielle Ergebnisse der Actiengesellschaften*, p. 3.

management of [137] business this view is no longer of particular use for a theoretical handling of the facts. To avoid the tedium of argument it may be conceded that under the old dispensation, of partnerships and individual management in business, the basis of capitalization was the cost of the material equipment owned by any given concern; and so far as the methods of partnership and private firms still prevails such may still be the current method of capitalization, especially *de jure*. But in so far as business procedure and business conceptions have been shaped in the image of the modern corporation (or limited liability company), the basis of capitalization has gradually shifted, until the basis is now no longer given by the cost of material equipment owned, but by the earning-capacity of the corporation as a going concern.[3]

A given corporation's capital is, of course, *de jure* a magnitude fixed in the past by an act of legislature chartering the company, or by an issuance of stock by the company under the terms of its charter or of the acts which enable it. But this *de jure* capitalization is nominal only, and there are few, if any, cases in which the effective capital of a company coincides with its *de jure* [138] capital. Such could be the case only so long as all the securities which go to make up the company's capital were quoted at par on the market. The effective capitalization of any modern company, that is to say, the capitalization which is effective for current business purposes as distinct from the formal requirements of the charter, is given by the quotations of the company's securities, or by some similar but less overt market valuation in case the company's capital is not quotable on the market. The effective (business) capitalization, as distinct from the *de jure* capitalization, is not fixed permanently and inflexibly by a past act of incorporation or stock issue. It is fixed for the time being only, by an ever recurring valuation of the company's properties, tangible and intangible, on the basis of their earning-capacity.[4]

In this capitalization of earning-capacity the nucleus of the capitalization is not the cost of the plant, but the concern's good-will, so called, as has appeared in the last preceding chapter.[5] [139] "Good-will" is a somewhat

---

3 This state of the case is brought out, in a veiled manner, by the well-known proposition, expounded in varying form by various writers, that the cost of equipment on which capitalization must, in theory, take place is the cost of reproduction of all valuable items included, tangible and intangible.

4 "Nothing is more illusive and delusive than the idea that if a corporation's stock be only paid in money at the outset it is therefore better off than one that has issued its stock for property that could not be converted for one cent on the dollar. The question is what assets the corporation has got at the time of the particular transaction, and that can be ascertained only by present inquiry." – Testimony of F. L. Stetson, [United States Industrial Commission,] *Report of the Industrial Commission*, vol. I. p. 976. Cf. Meade, *Trust Finance*, ch. XVI. and XVIII.

5 Earning-capacity is practically accepted as the effective basis of capitalization for corporate business concerns, particularly for those [139] whose securities are quoted on the market. It is in the stock market that this effective capitalization takes place. But the law does not recognize such a basis of capitalization; nor are business men generally ready to adopt it in set form, although they constantly have recourse to it, in effect, in operations of investment and of credit extension.

extensible term, and latterly it has a more comprehensive meaning than it once had. Its meaning has, in fact, been gradually extended to meet the requirements of modern business methods. Various items, of very diverse character, are to be included under the head of "good-will"; but the items included have this much in common that they are "immaterial wealth," "intangible assets"; which, it may parenthetically be remarked, signifies among other things that these assets are not serviceable to the community, but only to their owners. Good-will taken in its wider meaning comprises such things as established customary business relations, reputation for upright dealing, franchises and privileges, trademarks, brands, patent rights, copy-rights, exclusive use of special processes guarded by law or by secrecy, exclusive control of particular sources of materials. All these items give a differential advantage to their owners, but they [140] are of no aggregate advantage to the community.[6] They are wealth to the individuals concerned – differential wealth; but they make no part of the wealth of nations.[7]

It is in the industrial corporations that this capitalization of good-will is seen to the best advantage – including, under the term "industrial corporations," railway companies, iron and steel concerns, mines, etc., as well as what are known in the stock market specifically as "industrials." The corporation is, of course, not the only form of business concern in the industrial field, but it is the typical, characteristic form of business organization for the management of industry in modern times, and the peculiarities of modern capital are therefore best seen in these modern corporations. Many of these corporations have grown out of partnerships and firms previously existing, and such is still the genesis of many of the corporations that come forward from time to time. In such a case of conversion from partnership or firm to corporation the rule is that the new corporation [141] takes over a body of good-will, under one form and name or another, previously pertaining to the partnership which it displaces. Conversely, when a flourishing partnership or similar private firm has gained an assured footing of good-will, in the way of any or all of the items enumerated under that term above, its lot, as prescribed by modern business exigencies, is to go up into a corporation, either by simple conversion

---

Cf. [United States Industrial Commission,] *Report of the Industrial Commission*, vol. I. pp. 6, 17, 21 (Test. F. B. Thurber); p. 967 (Test. F. L. Stetson); pp. 585–587 (Test. H. H. Rogers); pp. 110–111, 124 (Test. H. O. Havemeyer); pp. 1021, 1032 (Test. J. W. Gates); pp. 1054–1055 (Test S. Dodd); vol. XIII. pp. 287–288 (Test. H. Burn); p. 388 (Test. J. Morris); pp. 107–108 (Test. E. R. Chapman). See [Chester W. Wright,] *Quarterly Journal of Economics*, February 1903, pp. 344–345, "The Holyoke Water Case," for an illustrative decision.

6 The advantages afforded their owners by these intangible assets have latterly been discussed by economists under such headings as "Rent" or "Quasi-Rent." These discussions, it is believed, are of great theoretical weight. In business practice, however, the items in question are treated as capital, which must avail as an excuse for including them here in business capital.

7 Compare Böhm-Bawerk's and Clark's distinctions between "private" and "social" capital, and between "capital" and "capital goods."

into the corporate form or through coalition with other firms into a larger corporate whole. There is in this matter no hard and fast rule, of course. On the one hand, the approved methods of corporation finance may in some measure be resorted to by a private firm, without formal conversion of the concern into the corporate form; and on the other hand, an incorporated company may continue to carry on its business after the manner usual with privately owned concerns. But taken by and large, it will be found that with the assumption of the corporate form is associated a more modern method of capitalization and a freer use of credit. The advantages which the corporate form offers in these respects are commonly not neglected. The more archaic forms of organization and business management, in which recourse is commonly not had to the characteristic methods of corporation finance, prevail chiefly in those "backward" lines of industry in which monopoly or other differential [142] advantages of an intangible nature are not readily attainable; such, e.g., as farming, fishing, local merchandising, and the minor mechanical trades and occupations. In this range of industries large (corporate) organization has hitherto been virtually impracticable, and here at the same time differential advantages, of the nature of good-will (as indicated above), are relatively scant and precarious. Where extensive differential advantages of this kind come in, the corporate form of organization is also likely to come in.

The cases are also frequent where a corporation starts out full-fledged from the beginning, without derivation from a previously existing private firm. Where this happens, the start is commonly made with some substantial body of immaterial goods on which to build up the capitalization; it may be a franchise, as in the case of a railway, telegraph, telephone, street-car, gas, or water company; or it may be the control of peculiar sources of material, as in the case of an oil or natural gas company, or a salt, coal, iron, or lumber company; or it may be a special industrial process, patented or secret; or it may be several of these. When a corporation begins its life history without such a body of immaterial differential advantages, the endeavors of its management are early directed to working up a basis of good-will in the way of trade-marks, clientele, and trade connections which will place it in [143] something of a monopoly position, locally or generally.[8] Should the management not succeed in these endeavors to gain an assured footing on some such "immaterial" ground, its chances of success among rival corporations are precarious, its standing is insecure, and its managers have not accomplished what is looked for at their hands. The substantial foundation of the industrial corporation is its immaterial assets.

The typical modern industrial corporation is a concern of sufficient magnitude to be of something more than barely local consequence, and extends its trade relations beyond the range of the personal contact of its directive

---

8 See Chapter III [in Veblen, *The Theory of Business Enterprise*. Chapter not included in this
  volume. – Eds.].

officials. Its properties and its debts are also commonly owned, in part at least, by persons who stand in no direct personal relation to the board of managers. In an up-to-date corporation of this character the typical make-up of the corporate capital, or capitalization, is somewhat as follows: The common stock approximately covers the immaterial properties of the concern, unless these immaterial properties are disproportionately large and valuable; in case of a relatively small and local corporation the common stock will ordinarily somewhat more than cover the value of the immaterial property and comprise something of the plant; in case of the larger concerns the converse is likely to be true, so that here [144] the immaterial property, intangible assets, is made to serve in some measure as a basis for other securities as well as for the common stock. The common stock, typically, represents intangible assets and is accounted for by valuable trade-marks, patents, processes, franchises, etc. Whatever material properties, tangible assets, are in hand or to be acquired are covered by preferred stock or other debentures. The various forms of debentures account for the material equipment and the working capital (the latter item corresponding roughly to the economists' categories of raw materials, wages fund, and the like). Of these debentures the preferred stock is the most characteristic modern development. It is, *de jure*, counted as a constituent of the concern's capital and the principal is not repayable; in this (legal) respect it is not an evidence of debt or a credit instrument.[9] But it has little voice in the direction of the concern's business policy.[10] In practice the management rests chiefly on the holdings of common stock. This is due in part to the fact that the preferred bears a stated rate of dividends and is therefore taken up by scattered purchasers as an investment security to a greater extent than the common. In [145] this (practical) respect it amounts to a debenture. Its practical character as a debenture is shown by the stated rate of dividends, and where it is "cumulative" that feature adds a further step of assimilation to the ordinary class of debentures. Indeed, in point of practical effect preferred stock is in some respects commonly a more pronounced credit instrument than the ordinary mortgage; it alienates the control of the property which it represents more effectually than the ordinary bond or mortgage loan, in that it may practically be a debt which, by its own terms, cannot be collected, so that by its own terms it may convey a credit extension from the holder to the issuing corporation in perpetuity. Its effect is to convey the discretionary control of the material properties which it is held to represent into the hands of the holders of the common stock of the concern. The discretionary management of the corporate capital is, by this device, quite as

9 On the books of the corporation it is, of course, carried as an item of liability; as is the common stock; but that is a technical expedient of accountancy, and does not touch the substantial question.
10 See testimony of various witnesses on "Capitalization" before the [United States] Industrial Commission, vols. I., IX., XIII.

effectually as by the use of ordinary credit instruments, vested in the common stock, which is held to represent the corporation's good-will. The discretionary disposal of the entire capital vests in securities representing the intangible assets. In this sense, then, the nucleus of the modern corporate capitalization is the immaterial goods covered by the common stock.[11] [146]

This method of capitalization, therefore, effects a somewhat thoroughgoing separation between the management and the ownership of the industrial equipment. Roughly speaking, under corporate organization the owners of the industrial material have no voice in its management, and where preferred stock is a large constituent of the capital this alienation of control on the parts of the owners may be, by so much, irrevocable. Preferred stock is, practically, a device for placing the property it represents in perpetual trust with the holders of the common stock, and, with certain qualifications, these trustees are not answerable for the administration of the property to their trustors. The property relation of the owners to their property is at this point attenuated to an extreme degree. For most business purposes, it should be added, the capital covered by other forms of debentures is in [147] much the same position as that covered by the preferred stock.[12] [148]

---

11 As one of many illustrative cases, the Rubber Goods Manufacturing Company may be taken as a typical instance of a corporation [146] organized in a conservative but up-to-date manner for permanent success and stable value. Its authorized issue of stock is $25,000,000 7 per cent, cumulative preferred, and $25,000,000 common. The actual issue in 1901 was about $8,000,000 preferred and $17,000,000 common, of which the preferred was presumed to cover the value of the tangible assets. Another coalition organized by the same promoter (Mr. C. R. Flint), the American Chicle Company, illustrates the same general feature. The preferred stock of this company ($3,000,000) "in round numbers was three times the amount of tangible assets," while the common stock ($6,000,000) represents no tangible assets. The aggregate capitalization is about nine times the tangible assets. The witness says that this corporation has been proved by events to be "on a conservative basis from the fact that the company has paid 8 per cent. on its common stock," which has been selling at 80. [United States Industrial Commission,] *Report of the Industrial Commission*, vol. XIII. pp. 47, 50.

12 It may be argued that this identification of the common stock with the intangible assets holds true in theory only, in the sense that this is the view held by the business men who occupy themselves with such matters; while in point of fact no distinction of this nature between common and preferred stock is or can practically be maintained after the stock has once found its way into the market. It might seem, in other words, that when the stock has once passed the stage of organization and gone into the hands of the purchasers, each share represents nothing but an undivided interest in the aggregate capitalization of the concern, so that the particular item of wealth represented by a given share or given form of security can no longer be identified.

On the face of the situation such appears to be the case, but there are facts which argue for the view set out above. It is, e.g., well known that whenever circumstances arise which immediately affect the value of the good-will of a corporation, it is the quotations of the common stock that first and most decidedly are affected. If the good-will of the concern makes a great and rapid gain, e.g. through manoeuvres which put it in a position of monopoly or through changes in the goods market which greatly increase the demand for the concern's product, and the like, it is the quotation of the common stock that measures and registers the

The various descriptions of securities which in this way represent corporate capital are quotable on the market and are subject to market fluctuations; whereby it comes about that the aggregate effective magnitude of the corporate capital varies with the tone of the market, with the manoeuvres of the business men to whom is delegated the management of the companies, and with the accidents of the seasons and the chances of peace and war. Accordingly, the amount of the business capital of a given concern, or of the business community as a whole, varies in magnitude in great measure independently of the mechanical facts of industry, as was noted above in speaking of loan credit.[13] The market fluctuations in the amount [149] of capital proceed on variations of confidence on the part of the investors, on current belief as to the probable policy or tactics of the business men in control, on forecasts as to the seasons and the tactics of the guild of politicians, and on the indeterminable, largely instinctive, shifting movements of public sentiment and apprehension. So that under modern conditions the magnitude of the business capital and its mutations from day to day are in great measure a question of folk psychology rather than of material fact.

---

advantage which thereby accrues to the concern, and the market fluctuation of the common stock is likewise the instrument by means of which manipulations are carried through that affect these intangible assets. At the same time this rule does not hold hard and fast, as is seen in case of a liquidation when the capital of the concern may have shrunk to such dimensions that the entire capital, including the intangible assets, will no more than satisfy the claims represented by the debentures. Still, in point of practical fact, the (theoretical) preconception of businessmen that the common stock in some intelligible sense covers the intangible assets is fairly borne out by everyday experience, taken by and large.

A curious parallel might be traced between the current endeavors of the business community to organize and manage the industrial equipment on the basis of immaterial assets and the medieval business perplexities and actions relative to loans on interest. In both cases the business community has had to face untried exigencies together with a popular, traditional prejudice that discountenances the expedients by which these exigencies are to be met. The mediaeval presumption was that the management of productive goods and the [148] profits accruing from their use must go to their users. (Cf. Ashley, *Economic History*, vol. I. ch. III, vol. II. ch. VI.; Endemann, *Die nationalökonomischen Grundsätze der kanonistischen Lehre.*) The modern presumption is that the management of the equipment and the gains from such management must vest in the owner. The modern exigencies decide that the equipment must be managed by others than the owners and that profits must largely accrue to those who financially manage the concern. The expedient by which this result is sought to be reached is the fiction of intangible assets and the impersonal, irrevocable credit extension covered by the preferred stock. The effect is to dissociate ownership from management. This is the necessary outcome of a "credit economy" consistently and fully carried through. The management of the material equipment of industry is thrown into the hands of those who own the immaterial wealth; that is to say, those who own the claim to manage the equipment. The current prejudice which insists on management by the owners is set aside by feigning that this claim has an industrial value, and so capitalizing it on the basis of the differential advantage which accrues to its holders.

13 See also a discussion by E. S. Meade, *Quarterly Journal of Economics*, February 1902, pp. 217 et seq., of how "good-will" may [149] vary in magnitude, or even disappear, when a concern enters a larger coalition; also, on the same general head, W.F. Willoughby, "Integration of Industry in the United States," *ibid.*, November 1902.

But in this uncertain and shifting relation of the business capital to the material equipment there are one or two points which may be set down as fairly secure. Since the credit instruments involved in modern capitalization may be used as collateral for a further credit extension, as noted in the chapter on loan credit,[14] the aggregate nominal capital in hand at a given time is, normally, larger by an appreciable amount than the aggregate value of the material properties involved;[15] and at the same time the current value of these material properties is also greater than it would be in the absence of that credit [150] financiering for which corporate capitalization affords a basis.[16]

German writers have familiarized economic readers with the terms "credit economy," "money economy" (*Geldwirtschaft*), and "natural economy" (*Naturalwirtschaft*), the later-modern scheme of economic life being characterized as a "credit economy." What characterizes the early-modern scheme, the "money economy," and sets it off in contrast with the natural economy (distribution in kind) that went before it in West-European culture, is the ubiquitous resort to the market as a vent for products and a source of supply of goods. The characteristic feature of this money economy is the goods market [151]. About the goods market business and industrial interests turn in early modern times; and to this early-modern system of industrial life the current doctrines of political economy are adapted, as indicated above.

The credit economy – the scheme of economic life of the immediate past and the present – has made an advance over the money economy in the respect which chiefly distinguishes the latter. The goods market, of course, in absolute terms is still as powerful an economic factor as ever, but it is no longer the dominant factor in business and industrial traffic, as it once was. The capital market has taken the first place in this respect. The capital market is the modern economic feature which makes and identifies the higher "credit

---

14 [See Chapter V in Veblen, *The Theory of Business Enterprise*. Chapter not included in this volume. – Eds.].

15 cap′ = cap + cap/n > cap, in which cap′ is the nominal capital, as increased by the credit element cap/n.

16 mat′ = mat + (1/n)(cap/n) > mat, in which mat′ is the current value of the material equipment, as increased (over mat) by the competitive demand for equipment due to the credit element cap/n. One of the substantial secondary benefits to be noted as flowing from these modern business expedients is the effect of corporation finance upon the aggregate nominal wealth of the community. A given community, possessed of a given complement of material wealth, is richer in capital if a large proportion of its industrial equipment is capitalized and managed by corporation methods, quite apart from any increase in the material items of which the community is possessed. (Cf. [United States Census Office,] *Twelfth Census of the United States*, "Manufactures," pt. I. p. xcvi). Wealth may in this way be increased (about twofold on an average), inexpensively, by the simple expedient of incorporating the community's business concerns in the form of joint-stock companies. The more highly involved and the more widely extended the corporation financiering is, the richer, in statistical terms of capital, is the community, other things equal. Among these other things are the material facts of the case.

economy" as such. In this credit economy resort is habitually had to the market as a vent for accumulated money values and a source of supply of capital.[17]

Trading under the old régime was a traffic in goods; under the new régime there is added, as the dominant and characteristic trait, trading in capital. Both in the capital and in the goods market there are professional traders, as well as [152] buyers and sellers who resort to the market to dispose of their holdings and to supply their needs of what the market affords. In either class of trading the ends sought by those engaged in the business are generically the same. The endeavors of those who are in the business of trading, who buy in order to sell and sell in order to buy, are directed to the pecuniary gain that is to be got through an advantageous discrepancy between the price paid and the price obtained; but on the part of those who resort to the market to supply their needs the end sought is not the same in the two cases. The last buyer of goods buys for consumption, but the last negotiator of capital buys for the sake of the ulterior profit; in substance he buys in order to sell again at an advance. The advance which he has in view is to come out of the pro-spective earnings of the capital for which he negotiates. What he has in view as his ulterior end in the transaction is the conversion of the values for which he negotiates into a larger outcome of money values, – whatever process of production and the like may intervene between the inception and the goal of his traffic.[18]

The value of any given block of capital, therefore, turns on its earning-capacity; or, as the mathematical expression has it, the value of capital is a function [153] of its earning-capacity,[19] not of its prime cost or of its mechanical efficiency. It is only more remotely, and through the mediation of the earning-capacity, that these last-named factors sensibly affect the value of the capital. This earning-capacity of capital depends in its turn, not so much on the mechanical efficiency of the valuable items bought and sold in the capital market, as on the tension of the market for goods. To recur to an expression already employed in a similar connection, the question of earning-capacity of capital relates primarily to its effectiveness for purposes of

---

17 The commodities bought and sold in the goods market are the outcome of a process of production and are useful for a material purpose; those bought and sold in the capital market are the outcome of a process of valuation and are useful for purposes of pecuniary gain.

18 Cf. Marx, *Das Kapital* (4th ed.) bk. I., ch. IV.

19 Effective capital = current market value of nominal capital = presumptive earning capacity x purchase period, neglecting fortuitous and incalculable items which may affect any given case.

If nominal capital = cap, effective capital = cap$'$, presumed annual earnings = ea$'$, and the purchase period of capitalized property (years' purchase) = yp = 1/(interest rate per annum), we have cap $\lessgtr$ cap$'$ = ea$'$ × yp = ea$'$/int.

This equation between cap$'$ and ea$'$ is disturbed by the presence in any given case of variable factors which cannot be included in the equation, but it remains true after all qualification has been made that cap$'$ = f(ea$'$/int).

vendibility, and only at the second remove to its effectiveness in the way of material serviceability. But the earning-capacity which in this way affords ground for the valuation of marketable capital (or for the market capitalization of the securities bought and sold) is not its past or actual earning-capacity, but its presumptive future earning-capacity; so that the [154] fluctuations in the capital market – the varying market capitalization of securities – turn about imagined future events. The forecast in the case may be more or less sagacious, but, however sagacious, it retains the character of a forecast based on other grounds besides the computation of past results.

All capital which is put on the market is in this way subjected to an interminable process of valuation and revaluation – i.e. a capitalization and recapitalization – on the basis of its presumptive earning-capacity, whereby it all assumes more or less of a character of intangibility. But the most elusive and intangible items of this marketable capital are, of course, those items which consist of capitalized good-will, since these are intangible goods from start to finish. It is upon this factor of good-will in capital that a change in presumptive earning-capacity falls most immediately, and this factor shows the widest and freest market fluctuations. The variations in the capitalized value of merchantable good-will are relatively wide and unstable, as is shown by the quotations of common stock.

In the capital market the commodity in which trading is done, then, is the capitalized putative earning-capacity of the property covered by the securities bought and sold. This property is in part tangible, in part intangible, the two categories [155] being seldom clearly distinguishable. The items bought and sold are put into merchantable form by being standardized in terms of money and subdivided into convenient imaginary shares, which greatly facilitates the traffic. The earning-capacity on which the market capitalization runs and about which the traffic in merchantable capital turns is a putative earning-capacity. It follows that this putative earning-capacity of a given block of capital, as it takes shape in the surmises of outside investors, may differ appreciably from the actual earning-capacity of the capital as known to its managers; and it may readily be to the latter's interest that such a discrepancy between actual and imputed earning-capacity should arise.[20] When, e.g., the putative earning capacity of the capital covered by a given line of securities, as shown by the market quotations, rises appreciably above what is known to its managers to be its actual earning-capacity, the latter may find their advantage in selling out, or even in selling short; while in the converse case they will be inclined to buy. Moreover, putative

---

20 Something of this kind is the usual ground of the obstinate resistance which most business men oppose to publicity of accounts. In lines of business, as, e.g. railroading, in which accounts are readily and effectually sophisticated ("doctored"), the objections to publicity are commonly less strenuous.

earning-capacity is the outcome of many surmises with respect to prospective earnings and the like; and these surmises [156] will vary from one man to the next, since they proceed on an imperfect, largely conjectural, knowledge of present earning-capacity and on the still more imperfectly known future course of the goods market and of corporate policy. Hence sales of securities are frequent, both because outsiders vary in their estimates and forecasts, and because the information of the outsiders does not coincide with that of the insiders. The consequence is that a given block of capital, representing, e.g., a controlling interest in a given industrial enterprise, may, and in practice it commonly will, change owners much more frequently than a given industrial plant was wont to change owners under the old régime, before the fully developed corporation finance came to occupy the field of industrial business.[21]

It follows, further, that under these circumstances the men who have the management of such an industrial enterprise, capitalized and quotable on the market, will be able to induce a discrepancy between the putative and the actual earning-capacity, by expedients well known and approved for the purpose. Partial information, as well as misinformation, sagaciously given out at a critical juncture, will go far toward producing a favorable temporary discrepancy of this kind, and so enabling the managers to buy or sell the securities of the [157] concern with advantage to themselves. If they are shrewd business men, as they commonly are, they will aim to manage the affairs of the concern with a view to an advantageous purchase and sale of its capital rather than with a view to the future prosperity of the concern, or to the continued advantageous sale of the output of goods or services produced by the industrial use of this capital.

That is to say, the interest of the managers of a modern corporation need not coincide with the permanent interest of the corporation as a going concern; neither does it coincide with the interest which the community at large has in the efficient management of the concern as an industrial enterprise. It is to the interest of the community at large that the enterprise should be so managed as to give the best and largest possible output of goods or services; whereas the interest of the corporation as a going concern is that it be managed with a view to maintaining its efficiency and selling as large an output as may be at the best prices obtainable in the long run; but the interest of the managers, and of the owners for the time being, is to so manage the enterprise as to enable them to buy it up or to sell out as expeditiously and as advantageously as may be. The interest of the community at large demands industrial efficiency and serviceability of the product; while the business interest of the concern as such demands vendibility [158] of the product; and the interest of those men who have the final discretion in the management of these corporate enterprises demands

---

21 Cf., e.g., Eberstadt, *Deutsche Kapitalsmarkt.*

vendibility of the corporate capital. The community's interest demands that there should be a favorable difference between the material cost and the material serviceability of the output; the corporation's interest demands a favorable pecuniary difference between expenses and receipts, cost and sale price of the output; the corporation directorate's interest is that there should be a discrepancy, favorable for purchase or for sale as the case may be, between the actual and the putative earning-capacity of the corporation's capital.

It has been noted in an earlier chapter that there unavoidably results a discrepancy, not uncommonly a divergence, between the industrial needs of the community and the business needs of the corporations. Under the régime of the old-fashioned "money economy," with partnership methods and private ownership of industrial enterprises, the discretionary control of the industrial processes is in the hands of men whose interest in the industry is removed by one degree from the interests of the community at large. But under the régime of the more adequately developed "credit economy," with vendible corporate capital,[22] the interest of the men [159] who hold the discretion in industrial affairs is removed by one degree from that of the concerns under their management, and by two degrees from the interests of the community at large.

The business interest of the managers demands, not serviceability of the output, nor even vendibility of the output, but an advantageous discrepancy in the price of the capital which they manage. The ready vendibility of corporate capital has in great measure dissociated the business interest of the directorate from that of the corporation whose affairs they direct and whose business policy they dictate, and has led them to centre their endeavors upon the discrepancy between the actual and the putative earning-capacity rather than upon the permanent efficiency of the concern. Their connection with the concern is essentially transient; it can be terminated speedily and silently whenever their private fortune demands its severance. Instances are abundant, more particularly in railway management, where this discrepancy between the business interest of the concern and the private business interest of the managers for the time being has led to very picturesque developments, such as could not occur if the interests of the management [160] were bound up with those of the corporation in the manner and degree that once prevailed. The fact is significant that the more frequent and striking instances of such management of corporate

---

22 The capital of any industrial concern under the "money economy" is, of course, also vendible, but with relative difficulty; while [159] the readier vendibility of modern corporate capital is so characteristic and consequential a factor in business and contrasts so broadly with the old-fashioned business methods that it may fairly be spoken of as vendibility par excellence. The "holding company" is the mature development of this traffic in vendible capital in industrial business.

affairs for private ends have hitherto occurred in railroading, at the same time that the methods and expedients of modern corporation finance have also first and most widely reached a fair degree of maturity in railroading. It holds out a suggestion as to what may fairly be looked for when corporation finance shall have made itself more thoroughly at home in the "industrials" proper. Indeed, the field of the "industrials" is by no means barren of instances comparable with the maturer and more sagacious railroad financiering.[23]

The stock market interest of those men who have the management of industrial corporations is a wide and multifarious one. It is not confined [161] to the profitable purchase and sale of properties whose management they may have in hand. They are also interested in making or marring various movements of coalition or reorganization, and to this ulterior end it is incumbent on them to "manipulate" securities with a view to buying and selling in such a manner as to gain control of certain lines of securities.[24] Hence it is a rule of this class of business traffic to cultivate appearance, – to avoid, or sometimes to court, the appearance of sin. So that under this leadership the course of industrial affairs is, in great measure, if not altogether, guided with a view to a plausible appearance of prosperity or of adversity, as the case may be. Under given circumstances it may as well become the aim of men in control to make an adverse showing as a favorable one. The higher exigencies of the captain of industry's personal fortunes, as distinct from those of the corporation controlled by him, may from time to time be best served by an apparent, if not an actual, mismanagement of industrial affairs. A convincing appearance of decline or disaster will lower the putative earning-capacity of the concern below its real earning-capacity and so will afford an advantageous opportunity for buying with a view to future advance or with a view to strategic control. Various other expedients looking to the like outcome are well known to [162] the craft, besides bona fide mismanagement. A given line of securities may be temporarily depressed by less heroic tactics; but the point in question here is the fact that under this system of corporation

23 It may be noted, by the way, that the question of the turnover (spoken of [in Chapter V in Veblen, *The Theory of Business Enterprise*]) becomes, under the circumstances of the modern corporation finance, in great part a question of the interval between the purchase and sale of the capital engaged in industry on the one hand, and of the magnitude of the discrepancy between actual and putative earning-capacity on the other hand, rather than a question of the period of the industrial process and the magnitude of the output and its price. The formula there shown becomes:- turnover = (capital/time) (actual earning capacity/n = putative earning capacity – actual earning capacity), in which capital is the amount of the operator's investment in the concern's securities, the time is the interval between purchase and sale of the securities, and the putative earning capacity is taken to exceed the actual earning capacity by an indeterminate fraction of the latter.

24 Cf. Chapter III [in Veblen, *The Theory of Business Enterprise*. Chapter not included in this volume. – Eds.].

finance the affairs of the corporation are in good part managed for tactical ends which are of interest to the manager rather than to the corporation as a going concern.

What was said in speaking of credit extension without a determinate time interval[25] applies to this class of business, with a slight change of phrase. In this higher development of corporation finance, in the manipulations of vendible capital, the interval of the turnover spoken of above becomes an indeterminate factor. The gains of the business come to have but an uncertain and shifty relation to the lapse of time and cannot well be calculated per cent, per time-unit. There is, therefore, on these higher levels of business management, properly speaking no ascertainable ordinary rate of earnings. The capital which may be distinctively regarded as operative in the business of manipulation, the valuable items specifically employed in the traffic in vendible corporate capital, is made up of the operator's good-will and his financial solvency. Solvency on a large scale is requisite to carrying on traffic of this class, but the collateral on which this extensive solvency constructively rests is to [163] but a partial extent drawn into the business as a basis for an actual credit extension. What counts in the case is the solvency of the operator rather than an outright resort to the credit extension which this solvency might afford. The working capital involved in these transactions is accordingly of a peculiarly elusive character, and the time element in the use of this capital is hard to determine, if such a time element can properly be said to enter into the case at all.

More in detail, the business man in pursuit of gain along this line must, in the ordinary case, be possessed of large holdings of property, this being the basis of the solvency necessary to the business. These holdings are commonly in the form of securities in the concern whose vendible capital is the subject of his traffic, as well as in other corporations. These securities represent capital, tangible and intangible, which is already employed in the ordinary business of the concern by which they have been issued; the capital, therefore, is already in use to the full extent and is presumably yielding the ordinary rate of earnings. But the solvency for which the ownership of this capital affords a basis may further be useful in enabling the owner to carry on a traffic in vendible corporate capital without withdrawing any appreciable portion of his holdings from the lucrative investments in which they have been placed. In other words, [164] he is able, under modern circumstances, to make a secondary use of his investments for the purpose of trading in vendible corporate capital; but this secondary use of investments bears no hard and fast quantitative relation to the investments in question, nor does it in any determinate way interfere with the ordinary employment of this invested capital in the commonplace conduct of the corporations' business traffic. The capital employed, as well as

---

25 Cf. Chapter V [in Veblen, *The Theory of Business Enterprise*. Chapter not included in this volume. – Eds.].

the potential credit extension which it affords for the purposes of this higher business traffic, is therefore in a peculiar degree intangible, and, in respect of its amount, highly elusive.

Much the same is true of the good-will employed in this traffic. It is also in good part good-will which already serves the purposes of the commonplace business traffic of the corporations on whose securities the business man in question rests his solvency. So that in this higher business traffic the good-will engaged is also here turned to a secondary use. The business economies which are in this way made practicable by a reduplication of uses and made to inure to the greater business men's profit are of great magnitude; but the magnificent additions which are in this way made to the business community's capitalizable forces need scarcely be dwelt on here.

The elusive and flexuous character of the elements of wealth engaged, as well as the absence of [165] an ascertainable ordinary rate of earnings in this line of business, has led economists to speak of this traffic in vendible capital as a "speculative" business.[26] The mere buying and selling of stocks by outsiders for a rise or a decline is of course a speculative business; it is a typical form of speculative business. But in so far as such buying and selling is carried on by the managers of the corporations whose securities are the subject of the traffic, and especially where the securities are bought and sold with a view to the control of the corporations in question and their management for private, tactical ends, a characterization of the business as "speculative" is inadequate and beside the point. This higher reach of corporation financiering has little if any more of a speculative character than what belongs to the commonplace business management of any industrial enterprise. In all business enterprise that stands in relations with the market and depends on vendibility of its output there is more or less uncertainty as to the outcome.[27] In this sense all industrial business, as well as commercial business, has something of a speculative character. But it is little to the purpose on that account to lump industrial enterprises and [166] corporation financiering together as "speculative business" and deal with them as if this were their most salient and consequential bearing. What speculative risk there is in these lines of business is incidental, and it neither affords the incentive to engaging in these pursuits nor does it bound the scope of their bearing upon economic affairs. The speculative risk involved is no greater, relatively to the magnitude of the interests involved, in this larger traffic that deals in vendible capital than it is in the ordinary lines of business traffic that deal in vendible products. In both cases there may be speculation, but in both

---

26 Cf. Emery, "Place of the Speculator in the Theory of Distribution," Proceedings of the Twelfth Annual Meeting of the American Economic Association; also "Discussion" following Mr. Emery's paper.

27 Well shown in Mr. Emery's paper cited above [in note 26 in this Selection].

cases it is a side issue. Indeed, as near as one may confidently hold an opinion on so dark a question, the certainty of gain, though perhaps not the relative amount of it, seems rather more assured in the large-scale manipulation of vendible capital than in business management with a view to a vendible product.

What may obscure the question is the fact that the manipulations involved in this traffic in vendible capital commonly impose increased risks upon the business concerns engaged in industry – the corporations whose capital is involved, as well as other firms. The everyday business of the corporations whose securities are involved, as well as of other business concerns engaged in rival or related lines of industry, is rendered more hazardous than it might be in the absence of this financiering [167] traffic in vendible capital. The manipulations carry risk, not so much to the manipulators as such, as to the corporations whose properties are the subject of manipulation; but since the manipulators commonly own but a relatively small proportion of the properties involved or touched by their manipulations, the risks which arise do not fall chiefly on them. To this is to be added, as of prime importance for the whole question, that the manipulators have the advantage of being able, in great part, to foresee the nature, magnitude, and incidence of the risks which they create. Rightly seen, this, of course, goes to say that the increased speculative risk due to the traffic in vendible capital does not fall on that traffic, but on the business enterprise engaged about the output of vendible goods. The traffic in vendible capital is not without its speculative risks, but the risks which it creates fall with relatively greater weight upon the business men who are not immediately concerned in this traffic. Indeed, so secure and lucrative is this class of business, that it is chiefly out of gains accruing, directly and indirectly, from such traffic in vendible capital that the great modern fortunes are being accumulated; and both the rate and the magnitude of these accumulations, whether taken absolutely or relatively to the total increase of wealth, surpass all recorded phenomena of their kind. Nothing so effective for the accumulation [168] of private wealth is known to the history of human culture.

The aim and substantial significance of the "manipulations" of vendible capital here spoken of is an ever recurring recapitalization of the properties involved, whereby the effective capitalization of the corporations whose securities are the subject of the traffic is increased and decreased from time to time. The fluctuations, or pulsations, of this effective capitalization are shown by the market quotations of the securities, as noted above.[28] It is out of these variations in capitalization that the gains of the traffic arise, and it is also through the means of these variations of capitalization that the business men engaged in this higher finance are enabled to control the fortunes of the corporations and to effect their strategic work of coalition and

28 [p. 344 in this Selection.]

reorganization of business enterprises. Hence this traffic in vendible capital is the pivotal and dominant factor in the modern situation of business and industry.[29] [169]

29 As is true of good-will and credit extensions generally, so with respect to the good-will and credit strength of these greater business men; it affords a differential advantage and gives a differential gain. In the traffic of corporation finance this differential gain is thrown immediately into the form of capital and so is added to the nominal capitalized wealth of the community. What it gives to its holders in this capitalized form is a claim to a proportionate share in the existing wealth. If other things are supposed to remain the same (which may not be the case), the claim so enforced by the great financiers on the basis of good-will and credit extension deducts that much from the wealth held by the rest, the previous holders, as counted in terms of material wealth; as counted in [169] terms of money value, of course, the holdings of previous holders do (or need) not suffer, since the new claims take the form of an addition to the number of capitalized value units, although the increased aggregate number of value units constitutes a claim on the same aggregate mass of wealth as before. The pro rata reduction of the material magnitude of the several shares of wealth is not felt as an impoverishment, because it does not take the form of a reduction of the nominal value of the shares.

This capitalization of the gains arising from a differential advantage results in a large "saving" and increase of capital. The wealth so drawn in by the financiers (entrepreneurs) is nearly all held as capital, very little of it being consumed in current expenses of living. It has been cogently argued that the profits of the undertakers is the chief and normal source of capitalized savings in the modern situation, and the method here indicated seems to be the method by which such saving is chiefly effected. An extremely suggestive discussion of the undertaker's gains in this connection occurs in a paper by L. V. Birck ("Driftsherrens Gevinst"), read before the Danish Economic Association, December 1901. More immediately to the point still is V. Schou's discussion of Mr. Birck's paper. (See *Nationalökonomisk Tidsskrift*, January–February 1902, pp. 76, 78–80.) J. B. Clark, in lectures hitherto unprinted, follows a line of analysis somewhat closely parallel with Schou, though not carried to quite the same length.

This process of combined recapitalization and saving may be stated formally as follows: The initial value of the properties submitted for coalition and recapitalization, cap, is in the normal case augmented by the increment Δ, making the effective value of the properties = cap $+\Delta$, in effective units, U_e. This augmented effective value of the properties = U_e(cap $+\Delta$) is capitalized at a nominal value of cap' = U_n(cap $+\Delta$), in nominal units, U_n, nominally equivalent to U_e. In the recapitalization the number of units of capitalization is increased by an element of intangible assets assigned the owners on account of a presumed increase of earning-capacity due to the coalition. This element of good-will due to coalition may be called co. Further there is added the bonus of the promoter, taken as a block of stock in the new capitalization, pro. Hence U_n(cap') ⇌ U_n(cap $+\Delta$) ⇌ U_n(cap + co + pro). U_n(pro) ⇌ U_n(cap' – cap – co) ⇌ $U_n(\Delta$ – co) is evidently a secure gain to the promoter of $U_e(\Delta$ – co), which is a fraction of the effective value U_e(cap + Δ). This is saved by him in the capitalized form. The account of the former owners of the properties will then stand as follows: [170] U_e(cap + Δ – pro) ≷ U_e(cap) according as $U_e\Delta$ ≷ U_e(pro). The nominal gain of the owners, co, may or may not be a real gain according as the event may prove that the promoter's bonus has not or has absorbed the entire effective augmentation of value, Δ, due to the coalition; it is therefore a problematical gain, which may or may not, in the event, prove to be an effective element of capitalized savings.

The constitution of Δ will decide what is the ultimate source of the savings effected by this transaction. If Δ consists entirely of economies of production, the capitalized savings held by the promoter and former owners as a result of the transaction represent new values added to, or saved to, the aggregate wealth of the community. If Δ consists entirely of good-will in the shape of monopoly advantage, the saving is effected at the cost of the community and for the benefit of the

It has been noted above that what may be called the working capital on which this higher corporation [170] finance proceeds is made up, chiefly, of two elements: the solvency (and consequent potential credit) of the men engaged, and the "good-will" of these men. Both of these elements are of a somewhat intangible and elusive character, resting, as they do, somewhat indirectly and shiftily on elements already elsewhere engaged in business enterprise. The solvency in question rests in large part on the capital of the corporations whose capitalization is subject to the fluctuations induced by the traffic in vendible capital. It is therefore necessarily a some-what indeterminate and unstable magnitude. To this is to be added the "floating [171] capital" and banking capital at the disposal of these men. If a common-sense view be taken of the business, the good-will engaged must also be added to the assets. There is involved a very considerable and very valuable body of good-will, appertaining to the financiers engaged and to the financing firms associated with them.[30] This good-will and this solvency is capital, for the purpose in hand, as effectually as the good-will and securities incorporated in the capitalization of any corporation engaged in industrial business.

But hitherto this particular category of good-will has not been formally capitalized. There may be peculiar difficulties in the way of reducing this good-will to the form of a fund, expressing it in terms of a standard unit, and so converting it into quotable common stock, as has been done with the corresponding good-will of incorporated industrial enterprises. So also as regards the body of solvency engaged, – the potential credit, or credit capa-city, of the promoters and financiers. Perhaps this latter had best also be treated as an element [172] of good-will; it is difficult to handle under any other, more tangible, conception. It may be difficult to standardize, fund, and capitalize these unstable but highly efficient factors of business enterprise; but the successful capitalization of good-will and credit extensions in the case of the modern industrial corporations argues that this difficulty should not be insurmountable in case an urgent need, – that is to say, the prospect of

---

promoter and owners; it is then an involuntary or subconscious saving on the part of the community, whereby a part of the community's wealth at large passes into the hands of the recapitalized corporation. Where Δ is made up of these two constituents together, the result, as regards the present point, should be plain without discussion. If, on the other hand, $\Delta = 0$, so that cap$'$ = cap, then the promoter's savings, pro, are secured at the cost of the former owners; $U_e(\text{cap}' - \text{pro}) = U_e(\text{cap} + (\Delta = 0) - \text{pro}) \lessgtr U_e(\text{cap} - \text{pro})$. Whereas if $U_e(\text{pro}) = U_e(\Delta)$, $U_e(\text{co}) = 0$, leaving the owners without effective profit or loss in spite of any nominal increase of the capitalization.

30 "Good-will" in this field of enterprise most frequently takes the form of a large ability to help or hinder other financiers and financing houses in any similar manoeuvres in which they may be engaged, or an ability to put them in the way of lucrative financing transactions. The guild of financiers is commonly split up into more or less well-defined factions, each comprising an extensive ramification of financing houses and financiers furthering one another's endeavors under more or less settled working arrangements. These working arrangements are a large part of the financiers' "good-will."

a profitably vendible result, – should press for a formal capitalization of these peculiar elements of business wealth. There can be no question, e.g., but that the good-will and large solvency belonging to such a firm as J. P. Morgan and Company for the purposes of this class of business enterprise are an extremely valuable and substantial asset, as is also, and more unequivocally, the good-will of the head of that firm. These intangible assets, immaterial goods, should, in all consistency, be reduced to standard units, funded, issued as common stock, and so added to the statistical aggregate of the country's capitalized wealth.

It is safe to affirm that this good-will of the great reorganizer has in some measure entered in capitalized form into the common stock of the United States Steel Corporation, as also into that of some of the other great combinations that have latterly been effected. The "good-will" of Mr. Carnegie and his lieutenants, as well as of many [173] other large business men connected with the steel industry, has also no doubt gone to swell the capitalization of the great corporation. But good-will on this higher level of business enterprise has a certain character of inexhaustibility, so that its use and capitalization in one corporation need not, and indeed does not, hinder or diminish the extent to which it may be used and capitalized in any other corporation.[31] The case is analogous, though scarcely similar, to that of the workmanlike or artistic skill of a handicraftsman, or an artist, which may be embodied in a given product without abating the degree of skill possessed by the workman. Like other good-will, though perhaps in a higher degree of sublimation, it is of a spiritual nature, such that, by virtue of the ubiquity proper to spiritual bodies, the whole of it may undividedly be present in every part of the various structures which it has created. Indeed, the fact of such good-will having been incorporated in capitalized form in the stock of any given corporation seems rather to augment than to diminish the amount at which it may advantageously be capitalized in the stock of the next corporation into which it enters. It has also the correlative spiritual attribute that it may imperceptibly and inscrutably [174] withdraw its animating force from any one of its creatures without thereby altering the material circumstances of the corporation which suffers such an intangible shrinkage of its forces.

There can be no question but that the good-will of the various great organizers and their financiering houses has repeatedly been capitalized, probably to its full amount, in the common stock of the various corporations which they have created; but taken in the sense of an asset belonging to the financing house as a corporation, it is not known that this item of immaterial wealth has yet been formally capitalized and offered in

---

31 This category of good-will stands in a relation to the creation of vendible capital similar to that which the corporate good-will of an industrial business concern bears to the creation of vendible products.

quotable shares on the market or included in the schedules of personal property.[32]

The sublimation of business capital that has been going forward in recent times has grave consequences for the owners of property as well as for the conduct of industry. In so far as invested property is managed by the methods of modern corporation finance, it is evident that the management is separated from the ownership of [175] the property, more and more widely as the scope of corporation finance widens. The discretion, the management, lies in the hands of the holders of the intangible forms of property; and with the extension of corporation methods it is increasingly true that this management, again, centres in the hands of those greater business men who hold large blocks of these intangible assets. The reach of a business man's discretionary control, under corporation methods, is not proportioned simply to the amount of his holdings. If his holdings are relatively small, they give him virtually no discretion. Whereas if they are relatively large, they may give him a business discretion of much more than a proportionate reach. The effective reach of a business man's discretion might be said to increase as the square of his holdings; although this is to be taken as a suggestive characterization rather than as an exact formula.

Among the holdings of industrial property that count in this way toward control of the business situation, the intangible assets (represented by common stock, good-will, and the like) are chiefly of consequence. Hence follow these two results: the fortunes of property owners are in large measure dependent on the discretion of others – the owners of intangible property; and the management of the industrial equipment tends strongly to centre in the hands of men who do not own the [176] industrial equipment, and who have only a remote interest in the efficient working of this equipment. The property of those who own less, or who own only material goods, is administered by those who own more, especially of immaterial goods; and the material processes of industry are under the control of men whose interest centres on an increased value of the immaterial assets.[33]

32 Parenthetically it may be remarked that the failure to capitalize such items of good-will is likely to involve a virtual evasion of the tax on personal property, and may, therefore, be questionable on moral grounds.

  The case of J. P. Morgan and Company is, of course, not here cited as being a unique or peculiar instance, but simply as a typical and striking illustration of what happens and of what might be accomplished in a number of large and very consequential cases of the same class.

33 This dissociation of the business control from workmanlike efficiency and from immediate contact with or ownership of the industrial plant gives the existing situation a superficial resemblance to the feudal system, in so far as touches the immateriality of the captain's connections with the everyday life and interests of the community of whose affairs he is master. It gives a certain plausibility to the attempted interpretation of latter-day economic developments in feudalistic terms. – See Ghent, *Our Benevolent Feudalism.*

Selection 30

The place of science in modern civilization

Source: *American Journal of Sociology*, March 1906
(vol. 11, pp. 585–609).

Veblen (1906a)

It is commonly held that modern Christendom is superior to any and all other systems of civilized life. Other ages and other cultural regions are by contrast spoken of as lower, or more archaic, or less mature. The claim is that the modern culture is superior on the whole, not that it is the best or highest in all respects and at every point. It has, in fact, not an all-around superiority, but a superiority within a closely limited range of intellectual activities, while outside this range many other civilizations surpass that of the modern occidental peoples. But the peculiar excellence of the modern culture is of such a nature as to give it a decisive practical advantage over all other cultural schemes that have gone before or that have come into competition with it. It has proved itself fit to survive in a struggle for existence as against those civilizations which differ from it in respect of its distinctive traits.

Modern civilization is peculiarly matter-of-fact. It contains many elements that are not of this character, but these other elements do not belong exclusively or characteristically to it. The modern civilized peoples are in a peculiar degree capable of an impersonal, dispassionate insight into the material facts with which mankind has to deal. The apex of cultural growth is at this point. Compared with this trait the rest of what is comprised [586] in the cultural scheme is adventitious, or at the best it is a by-product of this hard-headed apprehension of facts. This quality may be a matter of habit or of racial endowment, or it may be an outcome of both; but whatever be the explanation of its prevalence, the immediate consequence is much the same for the growth of civilization. A civilization which is dominated by this matter-of-fact insight must prevail against any cultural scheme that lacks this element. This characteristic of western civilization comes to a head in modern science, and it finds its highest material expression in the technology of the machine industry. In these things modern culture is creative and self-sufficient; and these being given, the rest of what may seem characteristic in western civilization follows by easy consequence. The cultural structure clusters about this body of matter-of-fact knowledge as its substantial core. Whatever is not consonant with these opaque creations of science is an intrusive feature in the modern scheme, borrowed or standing over from the barbarian past.

Other ages and other peoples excel in other things and are known by other virtues. In creative art, as well as in critical taste, the faltering talent of Christendom can at the best follow the lead of the ancient Greeks and the Japanese. In deft workmanship the handicraftsmen of the middle Orient, as well as of the Far East, stand on a level securely above the highest European achievement, old or new. In myth-making, folklore, and occult symbolism many of the lower barbarians have achieved things beyond what the latter-day priests and poets know how to propose. In metaphysical insight and dialectical versatility many orientals, as well as the Schoolmen of the Middle Ages, easily surpass the highest reaches of the New Thought and the Higher Criticism. In a shrewd sense of the religious verities, as well as in an unsparing faith in devout observances, the people of India or Thibet, or even the mediaeval Christians, are past-masters in comparison even with the select of the faith of modern times. In political finesse, as well as in unreasoning, brute loyalty, more than one of the ancient peoples give evidence of a capacity to which no modern civilized nation may aspire. In [587] warlike malevolence and abandon, the hosts of Islam, the Sioux Indian, and the "heathen of the northern sea" have set the mark above the reach of the most strenuous civilized warlord.

To modern civilized men, especially in their intervals of sober reflection, all these things that distinguish the barbarian civilization seem of dubious value and are required to show cause why they should not be slighted. It is not so with the knowledge of facts. The making of states and dynasties, the founding of families, the prosecution of feuds, the propagation of creeds and the creation of sects, the accumulation of fortunes, the consumption of superfluities – these have all in their time been felt to justify themselves as an end of endeavor; but in the eyes of modern civilized men all these things seem futile in comparison with the achievements of science. They dwindle in men's esteem as time passes, while the achievements of science are held higher as time passes. This is the one secure holding-ground of latter-day conviction, that "the increase and diffusion of knowledge among men" is indefeasibly right and good. When seen in such perspective as will clear it of the trivial perplexities of workday life, this proposition is not questioned within the horizon of the western culture, and no other cultural ideal holds a similar unquestioned place in the convictions of civilized mankind.

On any large question which is to be disposed of for good and all the final appeal is by common consent taken to the scientist. The solution offered in the name of science is decisive so long as it is not set aside by a still more searching scientific inquiry. This state of things may not be altogether fortunate, but such is the fact. There are other, older grounds of finality that may conceivably be better, nobler, worthier, more profound, more beautiful. It might conceivably be preferable, as a matter of cultural ideals, to leave the last word with the lawyer, the duelist, the priest, the moralist, or the college of heraldry. In past times people have been content to leave their weightiest questions to the decision of some one or other of these tribunals, and, it cannot be denied, with very happy results in those respects that were then looked to with the greatest solicitude. But whatever the common-sense of earlier generations may have held in this [588] respect, modern common-sense holds that the scientist's answer is the only ultimately true one. In the last resort enlightened common-sense sticks by the opaque truth and refuses to go behind the returns given by the tangible facts.

Quasi lignum vitae in paradiso Dei, et quasi lucerna fulgoris in domo Domini,[1] such is the place of science in modern civilization. This latter-day faith in matter-of-fact knowledge may be well grounded or it may not. It has come about that men assign it this high place, perhaps idolatrously, perhaps to the detriment of the best and most intimate interests of the race. There is room for much more than a vague doubt that this cult of science is not altogether a wholesome growth – that the unmitigated quest of knowledge, of this matter-of-fact kind, makes for race-deterioration and discomfort on the whole, both in its immediate effects upon the spiritual life of mankind, and in the material consequences that follow from a great advance in matter-of-fact knowledge.

But we are not here concerned with the merits of the case. The question here is: How has this cult of science arisen? What are its cultural antecedents? How far is it in consonance with hereditary human nature? and, What is the nature of its hold on the convictions of civilized men?

In dealing with pedagogical problems and the theory of education, current psychology is nearly at one in saying that all learning is of a "pragmatic" character; that knowledge is inchoate action inchoately directed to an end; that all knowledge is "functional;" that it is of the nature of use. This, of course, is only a corollary under the main postulate of the latter-day psychologists, whose catchword is that The Idea is essentially active. There is no need of quarreling with this "pragmatic" school of psychologists. Their aphorism may not contain the whole truth, perhaps, but at least it goes nearer to the heart of the epistemological problem than any earlier formulation. It may confidently be said to do so because, for one thing, its argument meets the requirements of modern science. It is such a concept as matter of-fact science can make effective use of; it is drawn in terms [589] which are, in the last analysis, of an impersonal, not to say tropismatic, character; such as is demanded by science, with its insistence on opaque cause and effect. While knowledge is construed in teleological terms, in terms of personal interest and attention, this

---

1 [*As the tree of life in God's paradise, and as the lamp of light in the house of the Lord.* This is the second appearance of this Latin quotation in one of Veblen's publications. In lengthier form, the quotation also appears in Veblen's translation, six years earlier, of Ferdinand Lassalle's *Science and the Workingmen.* Its context is a passage where Lassalle cites Pope Alexander IV, in 1255, as he likens the place of the tree in paradise and of the lamp in God's house to the place of the Church in the world of learning (Lassalle [1863] 1900, p. 16). – Eds.].

teleological aptitude is itself reducible to a product of unteleological natural selection. The teleological bent of intelligence is a hereditary trait settled upon the race by the selective action of forces that look to no end. The foundations of pragmatic intelligence are not pragmatic, nor even personal or sensible.

This impersonal character of intelligence is, of course, most evident on the lower levels of life. If we follow Mr. Loeb, e.g., in his inquiries into the psychology of that life that lies below the threshold of intelligence, what we meet with is an aimless but unwavering motor response to stimulus.[2] The response is of the nature of motor impulse, and in so far it is "pragmatic," if that term may fairly be applied to so rudimentary a phase of sensibility. The responding organism may be called an "agent" in so far. It is only by a figure of speech that these terms are made to apply to tropismatic reactions. Higher in the scale of sensibility and nervous complication instincts work to a somewhat similar outcome. On the human plane, intelligence (the selective effect of inhibitive complication) may throw the response into the form of a reasoned line of conduct looking to an outcome that shall be expedient for the agent. This is naive pragmatism of the developed kind. There is no longer a question but that the responding organism is an "agent," and that his intelligent response to stimulus is of a teleological character. But that is not all. The inhibitive nervous complication may also detach another chain of response to the given stimulus, which does not spend itself in a line of motor conduct and does not fall into a system of uses. Pragmatically speaking, this outlying chain of response is unintended and irrelevant. Except in urgent cases, such an idle response seems commonly to be present as a subsidiary phenomenon. If credence is given to the view [590] that intelligence is, in its elements, of the nature of an inhibitive selection, it seems necessary to assume some such chain of idle and irrelevant response to account for the further course of the elements eliminated in giving the motor response the character of a reasoned line of conduct. So that associated with the pragmatic attention there is found more or less of an irrelevant attention, or idle curiosity. This is more particularly the case where a higher range of intelligence is present. This idle curiosity is, perhaps, closely related to the aptitude for play, observed both in man and in the lower animals.[3] The aptitude for play, as well as the functioning of idle curiosity, seems peculiarly lively in the young, whose aptitude for sustained pragmatism is at the same time relatively vague and unreliable.

This idle curiosity formulates its response to stimulus, not in terms of an expedient line of conduct, nor even necessarily in a chain of motor activity, but in terms of the sequence of activities going on in the observed phenomena. The "interpretation" of the facts under the guidance of this idle curiosity may take the form of anthropomorphic or animistic explanations of the

2 Jacques Loeb, *Heliotropismus der Thiere* and *Comparative Psychology and Physiology of the Brain*.
3 Cf. Groos, *Spiele der Thiere*, chap. 3 (esp. pp. 65–76), and chap. 5; *The Play of Man*, Part III, sec. 3; Spencer, *Principles of Psychology*, secs. 533–35.

"conduct" of the objects observed. The interpretation of the facts takes a dramatic form. The facts are conceived in an animistic way, and a pragmatic animus is imputed to them. Their behavior is construed as a reasoned procedure on their part looking to the advantage of these animistically conceived objects, or looking to the achievement of some end which these objects are conceived to have at heart for reasons of their own.

Among the savage and lower barbarian peoples there is commonly current a large body of knowledge organized in this way into myths and legends, which need have no pragmatic value for the learner of them and no intended bearing on his conduct of practical affairs. They may come to have a practical value imputed to them as a ground of superstitious observances, but they may also not.[4] All students of the lower cultures are aware of [591] the dramatic character of the myths current among these peoples, and they are also aware that, particularly among the peaceable communities, the great body of mythical lore is of an idle kind, as having very little intended bearing on the practical conduct of those who believe in these myth-dramas. The myths on the one hand, and the workday knowledge of uses, materials, appliances, and expedients on the other hand, may be nearly independent of one another. Such is the case in an especial degree among those peoples who are prevailingly of a peaceable habit of life, among whom the myths have not in any great measure been canonized into precedents of divine malevolence.

The lower barbarian's knowledge of the phenomena of nature, in so far as they are made the subject of deliberate speculation and are organized into a consistent body, is of the nature of life-histories. This body of knowledge is in the main organized under the guidance of an idle curiosity. In so far as it is systematized under the canons of curiosity rather than of expediency, the test of truth applied throughout this body of barbarian knowledge is the test of dramatic consistency. In addition to their dramatic cosmology and folk legends, it is needless to say, these peoples have also a considerable body of worldly wisdom in a more or less systematic form. In this the test of validity is usefulness.[5]

4 The myths and legendary lore of the Eskimo, the Pueblo Indians, and some tribes of the northwest coast afford good instances of such idle creations. Cf. various Reports of the Bureau of American Ethnology; also, e. g., Tylor, *Primitive Culture*, esp. the chapters on "Mythology" and "Animism."

5 "Pragmatic" is here used in a more restricted sense than the distinctively pragmatic school of modern psychologists would commonly assign the term. "Pragmatic," "teleological" and the like terms have been extended to cover imputation of purpose as well as conversion to use. It is not intended to criticise this ambiguous use of terms, nor to correct it; but the terms are here used only in the latter sense, which alone belongs to them by force of early usage and etymology. "Pragmatic" knowledge, therefore, is such as is designed to serve an expedient end for the knower, and is here contrasted with the imputation of expedient conduct to the facts observed. The reason for preserving this distinction is simply the present need of a simple term by which to mark the distinction between worldly wisdom and idle learning.

The pragmatic knowledge of the early days differs scarcely at all in character from that of the maturest phases of culture. Its highest achievements in the direction of systematic formulation consist of didactic exhortations to thrift, prudence, equanimity, and shrewd management – a body of maxims of expedient conduct. [592] In this field there is scarcely a degree of advance from Confucius to Samuel Smiles. Under the guidance of the idle curiosity, on the other hand, there has been a continued advance toward a more and more comprehensive system of knowledge. With the advance in intelligence and experience there come closer observation and more detailed analysis of facts.[6] The dramatization of the sequence of phenomena may then fall into somewhat less personal, less anthropomorphic formulations of the processes observed; but at no stage of its growth – at least at no stage hitherto reached – does the output of this work of the idle curiosity lose its dramatic character. Comprehensive generalizations are made and cosmologies are built up, but always in dramatic form. General principles of explanation are settled on, which in the earlier days of theoretical speculation seem invariably to run back to the broad vital principle of generation. Procreation, birth, growth, and decay constitute the cycle of postulates within which the dramatized processes of natural phenomena run their course. Creation is procreation in these archaic theoretical systems, and causation is gestation and birth. The archaic cosmological schemes of Greece, India, Japan, China, Polynesia, and America, all run to the same general effect on this head.[7]

Throughout this biological speculation there is present, obscurely in the background, the tacit recognition of a material causation, such as conditions the vulgar operations of workday life from hour to hour. But this causal relation between vulgar work and product is vaguely taken for granted and not made a principle for comprehensive generalizations. It is overlooked as a trivial matter of course. The higher generalizations take their color from the broader features of the current scheme of life. The habits of thought that rule in the working-out of a system of knowledge are such as are fostered by the more impressive affairs of life, by the institutional structure under which the community lives. So long as the ruling institutions are those of blood-relationship, descent, and clannish discrimination, so long the canons of knowledge are of the same complexion. [593]

When presently a transformation is made in the scheme of culture from peaceable life with sporadic predation to a settled scheme of predaceous life, involving mastery and servitude, gradations of privilege and honor, coercion and personal dependence, then the scheme of knowledge undergoes an analogous change. The predaceous, or higher barbarian, culture is, for the present purpose, peculiar in that it is ruled by an accentuated pragmatism. The institutions of this cultural phase are conventionalized relations of force and

6 Cf. Ward, *Pure Sociology*, esp. pp. 437–48.
7 Cf., e. g., Tylor, *Primitive Culture*, chap. 8.

fraud. The questions of life are questions of expedient conduct as carried on under the current relations of mastery and subservience. The habitual distinctions are distinctions of personal force, advantage, precedence, and authority. A shrewd adaptation to this system of graded dignity and servitude becomes a matter of life and death, and men learn to think in these terms as ultimate and definitive. The system of knowledge, even in so far as its motives are of a dispassionate or idle kind, falls into the like terms, because such are the habits of thought and the standards of discrimination enforced by daily life.[8]

The theoretical work of such a cultural era, as, for instance, the Middle Ages, still takes the general shape of dramatization, but the postulates of the dramaturgic theories and the tests of theoretic validity are no longer the same as before the scheme of graded servitude came to occupy the field. The canons which guide the work of the idle curiosity are no longer those of generation, blood-relationship, and homely life, but rather those of graded dignity, authenticity, and dependence. The higher generalizations take on a new complexion, it may be without formally discarding the older articles of belief. The cosmologies of these higher barbarians are cast in terms of a feudalistic hierarchy of agents and elements, and the causal nexus between phenomena is conceived animistically after the manner of sympathetic magic. The laws that are sought to be discovered in the natural universe are sought in terms of authoritative enactment. The relation in which the deity, or deities, are conceived to stand to facts is no longer the relation of progenitor, so much as that [594] of suzerainty. Natural laws are corollaries under the arbitrary rules of status imposed on the natural universe by an all-powerful Providence with a view to the maintenance of his own prestige. The science that grows in such a spiritual environment is of the class represented by alchemy and astrology, in which the imputed degree of nobility and prepotency of the objects and the symbolic force of their names are looked to for an explanation of what takes place.

The theoretical output of the Schoolmen has necessarily an accentuated pragmatic complexion, since the whole cultural scheme under which they lived and worked was of a strenuously pragmatic character. The current concepts of things were then drawn in terms of expediency, personal force, exploit, prescriptive authority, and the like, and this range of concepts was by force of habit employed in the correlation of facts for purposes of knowledge even where no immediate practical use of the knowledge so gained was had in view. At the same time a very large proportion of the scholastic researches and speculations aimed directly at rules of expedient conduct, whether it took the form of a philosophy of life under temporal law and custom, or of a scheme of salvation under the decrees of an autocratic Providence. A naive apprehension of the dictum that all knowledge is pragmatic would find more

---

8 Cf. James, *[Principles of] Psychology*, chap. 9, esp. sec. 5.

satisfactory corroboration in the intellectual output of scholasticism than in any system of knowledge of an older or a later date.

With the advent of modern times a change comes over the nature of the inquiries and formulations worked out under the guidance of the idle curiosity – which from this epoch is often spoken of as the scientific spirit. The change in question is closely correlated with an analogous change in institutions and habits of life, particularly with the changes which the modern era brings in industry and in the economic organization of society. It is doubtful whether the characteristic intellectual interests and teachings of the new era can properly be spoken of as less "pragmatic," as that term is sometimes understood, than those of the scholastic times; but they are of another kind, being conditioned [595] by a different cultural and industrial situation.[9] In the life of the new era conceptions of authentic rank and differential dignity have grown weaker in practical affairs, and notions of preferential reality and authentic tradition similarly count for less in the new science. The forces at work in the external world are conceived in a less animistic manner, although anthropomorphism still prevails, at least to the degree required in order to give a dramatic interpretation of the sequence of phenomena.

The changes in the cultural situation which seem to have had the most serious consequences for the methods and animus of scientific inquiry are those changes that took place in the field of industry. Industry in early modern times is a fact of relatively greater preponderance, more of a tone-giving factor, than it was under the regime of feudal status. It is the characteristic trait of the modern culture, very much as exploit and fealty were the characteristic cultural traits of the earlier times. This early-modern industry is, in an obvious and convincing degree, a matter of workmanship. The same has not been true in the same degree either before or since. The workman, more or less skilled and with more or less specialized efficiency, was the central figure in the cultural situation of the time; and so the concepts of the scientists came to be drawn in the image of the workman. The dramatizations of the sequence of external phenomena worked out under the impulse of the idle curiosity were then conceived in terms of workmanship. Workmanship gradually supplanted differential dignity as the authoritative canon of scientific truth, even on the higher levels of speculation and research. This, of course, amounts to saying in other words that the law of cause and effect was given the first place, as contrasted with dialectical consistency and authentic tradition. But this early-modern law of cause and effect – the law of efficient causes – is of an anthropomorphic kind. "Like causes produce like effects," in

9 As currently employed, the term "pragmatic" is made to cover both conduct looking to the agent's preferential advantage, expedient conduct, and workmanship directed to the production of things that may or may not be of advantage to the agent. If the term be taken in the latter meaning, the culture of modern times ist no less "pragmatic" than that of the Middle Ages. It is here intended to be used in the former sense.

much the [596] same sense as the skilled workman's product is like the workman; "nothing is found in the effect that was not contained in the cause," in much the same manner.

These dicta are, of course, older than modern science, but it is only in the early days of modern science that they come to rule the field with an unquestioned sway and to push the higher grounds of dialectical validity to one side. They invade even the highest and most recondite fields of speculation, so that at the approach to the transition from the early-modern to the late-modern period, in the eighteenth century they determine the outcome even in the counsels of the theologians. The deity, from having been in mediaeval times primarily a suzerain concerned with the maintenance of his own prestige, becomes primarily a creator engaged in the workmanlike occupation of making things useful for man. His relation to man and the natural universe is no longer primarily that of a progenitor, as it is in the lower barbarian culture, but rather that of a talented mechanic. The "natural laws" which the scientists of that era make so much of are no longer decrees of a preternatural legislative authority, but rather details of the workshop specifications handed down by the master-craftsman for the guidance of handicraftsmen working out his designs. In the eighteenth-century science these natural laws are laws specifying the sequence of cause and effect, and will bear characterization as a dramatic interpretation of the activity of the causes at work, and these causes are conceived in a quasi-personal manner. In later modern times the formulations of causal sequence grow more impersonal and more objective, more matter-of-fact; but the imputation of activity to the observed objects never ceases, and even in the latest and maturest formulations of scientific research the dramatic tone is not wholly lost. The causes at work are conceived in a highly impersonal way, but hitherto no science (except ostensibly mathematics) has been content to do its theoretical work in terms of inert magnitude alone. Activity continues to be imputed to the phenomena with which science deals; and activity is, of course, not a fact of observation, but is imputed to the phenomena by the observer.[10] This is, also [597] of course, denied by those who insist on a purely mathematical formulation of scientific theories, but the denial is maintained only at the cost of consistency. Those eminent authorities who speak for a colorless mathematical formulation invariably and necessarily fall back on the (essentially metaphysical) preconception of causation as soon as they go into the actual work of scientific inquiry.[11]

10 Epistemologically speaking, activity is imputed to phenomena for the purpose of organizing them into a dramatically consistent system.

11 Cf., e. g., Karl Pearson, *Grammar of Science*, and compare his ideal of inert magnitudes as set forth in his exposition with his actual work as shown in chaps. 9, 10, and 12, and more particularly in his discussions of "Mother Right" and related topics in *The Chances of Death*.

Since the machine technology has made great advances, during the nineteenth century, and has become a cultural force of wide-reaching consequence, the formulations of science have made another move in the direction of impersonal matter-of-fact. The machine process has displaced the workman as the archetype in whose image causation is conceived by the scientific investigators. The dramatic interpretation of natural phenomena has thereby become less anthropomorphic; it no longer constructs the life-history of a cause working to produce a given effect – after the manner of a skilled workman producing a piece of wrought goods – but it constructs the life-history of a process in which the distinction between cause and effect need scarcely be observed in an itemized and specific way, but in which the run of causation unfolds itself in an unbroken sequence of cumulative change. By contrast with the pragmatic formulations of worldly wisdom these latter-day theories of the scientists appear highly opaque, impersonal, and matter-of-fact; but taken by themselves they must be admitted still to show the constraint of the dramatic prepossessions that once guided the savage myth-makers.

In so far as touches the aims and the animus of scientific inquiry, as seen from the point of view of the scientist, it is a wholly fortuitous and insubstantial coincidence that much of the knowledge gained under machine-made canons of research can be turned to practical account. Much of this knowledge is useful, or may be made so, by applying it to the control of the processes in which natural forces are engaged. This employment of scientific [598] knowledge for useful ends in technology, in the broad sense in which the term includes, besides the machine industry proper, such branches of practice as engineering, agriculture, medicine, sanitation, and economic reforms. The reason why scientific theories can be turned to account for these practical ends is not that these ends are included in the scope of scientific inquiry. These useful purposes lie outside the scientist's interest. It is not that he aims, or can aim, at technological improvements. His inquiry is as "idle" as that of the Pueblo myth-maker. But the canons of validity under whose guidance he works are those imposed by the modern technology, through habituation to its requirements; and therefore his results are available for the technological purpose. His canons of validity are made for him by the cultural situation; they are habits of thought imposed on him by the scheme of life current in the community in which he lives; and under modern conditions this scheme of life is largely machine-made. In the modern culture, industry, industrial processes, and industrial products have progressively gained upon humanity, until these creations of man's ingenuity have latterly come to take the dominant place in the cultural scheme; and it is not too much to say that they have become the chief force in shaping men's daily life, and therefore the chief factor in shaping men's habits of thought. Hence men have learned to think in the terms in which the technological processes act. This is particularly true of those men who by virtue of a peculiarly strong susceptibility in this direction become addicted to that habit of matter-of-fact inquiry that constitutes scientific research.

Modern technology makes use of the same range of concepts, thinks in the same terms, and applies the same tests of validity as modern science. In both, the terms of standardization, validity, and finality are always terms of impersonal sequence, not terms of human nature or of preternatural agencies. Hence the easy copartnership between the two. Science and technology play into one another's hands. The processes of nature with which science deals and which technology turns to account, the sequence of changes in the external world, animate and inanimate, run in terms of brute causation, as do the theories of science. These [599] processes take no thought of human expediency or inexpediency. To make use of them they must be taken as they are, opaque and unsympathetic. Technology, therefore, has come to proceed on an interpretation of these phenomena in mechanical terms, not in terms of imputed personality nor even of workmanship. Modern science, deriving its concepts from the same source, carries on its inquiries and states its conclusions in terms of the same objective character as those employed by the mechanical engineer.

So it has come about, through the progressive change of the ruling habits of thought in the community, that the theories of science have progressively diverged from the formulations of pragmatism, ever since the modern era set in. From an organization of knowledge on the basis of imputed personal or animistic propensity the theory has changed its base to an imputation of brute activity only, and this latter is conceived in an increasingly matter-of-fact manner; until, latterly, the pragmatic range of knowledge and the scientific are more widely out of touch than ever, differing not only in aim, but in matter as well. In both domains knowledge runs in terms of activity, but it is on the one hand knowledge of what had best be done, and on the other hand knowledge of what takes place; on the one hand knowledge of ways and means, on the other hand knowledge without any ulterior purpose. The latter range of knowledge may serve the ends of the former, but the converse does not hold true.

These two divergent ranges of inquiry are to be found together in all phases of human culture. What distinguishes the present phase is that the discrepancy between the two is now wider than ever before. The present is nowise distinguished above other cultural eras by any exceptional urgency or acumen in the search for pragmatic expedients. Neither is it safe to assert that the present excels all other civilizations in the volume or the workmanship of that body of knowledge that is to be credited to the idle curiosity. What distinguishes the present in these premises is (1) that the primacy in the cultural scheme has passed from pragmatism to a disinterested inquiry whose motive is idle curiosity, and (2) that in the domain of the latter the making of [600] myths and legends in terms of imputed personality, as well as the construction of dialectical systems in terms of differential reality, has yielded the first place to the making of theories in terms of matter-of-fact sequence.[12]

---

12 Cf. James, *[Principles of] Psychology*, Vol. II, chap. 28, pp. 633–71, esp. p. 640 note.

Pragmatism creates nothing but maxims of expedient conduct. Science creates nothing but theories.[13] It knows nothing of policy or utility, of better or worse. None of all that is comprised in what is today accounted scientific knowledge. Wisdom and proficiency of the pragmatic sort does not contribute to the advance of a knowledge of fact. It has only an incidental bearing on scientific research, and its bearing is chiefly that of inhibition and misdirection. Wherever canons of expediency are intruded into or are attempted to be incorporated in the inquiry, the consequence is an unhappy one for science, however happy it may be for some other purpose extraneous to science. The mental attitude of worldly wisdom is at cross-purposes with the disinterested scientific spirit, and the pursuit of it induces an intellectual bias that is incompatible with scientific insight. Its intellectual output is a body of shrewd rules of conduct, in great part designed to take advantage of human infirmity. Its habitual terms of standardization and validity are terms of human nature, of human preference, prejudice, aspiration, endeavor, and disability, and the habit of mind that goes with it is such as is consonant with these terms. No doubt, the all-pervading pragmatic animus of the older and non-European civilizations has had more than anything else to do with their relatively slight and slow advance in scientific knowledge. In the modern scheme of knowledge it holds true, in a similar manner and with analogous effect, that training in divinity, in law, and in the related branches of diplomacy, business tactics, military affairs, and political theory, is alien to the skeptical scientific spirit and subversive of it.

The modern scheme of culture comprises a large body of worldly wisdom, as well as of science. This pragmatic lore stands over against science with something of a jealous reserve. The pragmatists value themselves somewhat on being useful as [601] well as being efficient for good and evil. They feel the inherent antagonism between themselves and the scientists, and look with some doubt on the latter as being merely decorative triflers, although they sometimes borrow the prestige of the name of science – as is only good and well, since it is of the essence of worldly wisdom to borrow anything that can be turned to account. The reasoning in these fields turns about questions of personal advantage of one kind or another, and the merits of the claims canvassed in these discussions are decided on grounds of authenticity. Personal claims make up the subject of the inquiry, and these claims are construed and decided in terms of precedent and choice, use and wont, prescriptive authority, and the like. The higher reaches of generalization in these pragmatic inquiries are of the nature of deductions from authentic tradition, and the training in this class of reasoning gives discrimination in respect of authenticity and expediency. The resulting habit of mind is a bias for substituting dialectical distinctions and decisions *de jure* in the place of explanations

---

13 Cf. Ward, *Principles of Psychology*, pp. 439–43. [Citation to this source cannot be traced; possibly a reference to James, *Principles of Psychology*, vol.1, pp. 439–45. – Eds.].

de facto. The so-called "sciences" associated with these pragmatic disciplines, such as jurisprudence, political science, and the like, is a taxonomy of credenda. Of this character was the greater part of the "science" cultivated by the Schoolmen, and large remnants of the same kind of authentic convictions are, of course, still found among the tenets of the scientists, particularly in the social sciences, and no small solicitude is still given to their cultivation. Substantially the same value as that of the temporal pragmatic inquiries belongs also, of course, to the "science" of divinity. Here the questions to which an answer is sought, as well as the aim and method of inquiry, are of the same pragmatic character, although the argument runs on a higher plane of personality, and seeks a solution in terms of a remoter and more metaphysical expediency.

In the light of what has been said above, the questions recur: How far is the scientific quest of matter-of-fact knowledge consonant with the inherited intellectual aptitudes and propensities of the normal man? and, What foothold has science in the modern culture? The former is a question of the temperamental heritage [602] of civilized mankind, and therefore it is in large part a question of the circumstances which have in the past selectively shaped the human nature of civilized mankind. Under the barbarian culture, as well as on the lower levels of what is currently called civilized life, the dominant note has been that of competitive expediency for the individual or the group, great or small, in an avowed struggle for the means of life. Such is still the ideal of the politician and business man, as well as of other classes whose habits of life lead them to cling to the inherited barbarian traditions. The upper-barbarian and lower-civilized culture, as has already been indicated, is pragmatic, with a thoroughness that nearly bars out any non-pragmatic ideal of life or of knowledge. Where this tradition is strong there is but a precarious chance for any consistent effort to formulate knowledge in other terms than those drawn from the prevalent relations of personal mastery and subservience and the ideals of personal gain.

During the Dark and Middle Ages, for instance, it is true in the main that any movement of thought not controlled by considerations of expediency and conventions of status are to be found only in the obscure depths of vulgar life, among those neglected elements of the population that lived below the reach of the active class struggle. What there is surviving of this vulgar, non-pragmatic intellectual output takes the form of legends and folk-tales, often embroidered on the authentic documents of the Faith. These are less alien to the latest and highest culture of Christendom than are the dogmatic, dialectical, and chivalric productions that occupied the attention of the upper classes in mediaeval times. It may seem a curious paradox that the latest and most perfect flower of the western civilization is more nearly akin to the spiritual life of the serfs and villeins than it is to that of the grange or the abbey. The courtly life and the chivalric habits of thought of that past phase of culture have left as nearly no trace in the cultural scheme of later modern times as could well be. Even the romancers who ostensibly rehearse the phenomena of chivalry, unavoidably make their knights and ladies speak the language and the sentiments of the slums of that time, tempered with certain schematized modern reflections and speculations. [603] The gallantries, the genteel inanities and devout imbecilities of mediaeval high-life would be insufferable even to the meanest and most romantic modern intelligence. So that in a later, less barbarian age the precarious remnants of folklore that have come down through that vulgar channel – half savage and more than half pagan – are treasured as containing the largest spiritual gains which the barbarian ages of Europe have to offer.

The sway of barbarian pragmatism has, everywhere in the western world, been relatively brief and relatively light; the only exceptions would be found in certain parts of the Mediterranean seaboard. But wherever the barbarian culture has been sufficiently long-lived and unmitigated to work out a thoroughly selective effect in the human material subjected to it, there the pragmatic animus may be expected to have become supreme and to inhibit all movement in the direction of scientific inquiry and eliminate all effective aptitude for other than worldly wisdom. What the selective consequences of such a protracted regime of pragmatism would be for the temper of the race may be seen in the human flotsam left by the great civilizations of antiquity, such as Egypt, India, and Persia. Science is not at home among these leavings of barbarism. In these instances of its long and unmitigated dominion the barbarian culture has selectively worked out a temperamental bias and a scheme of life from which objective, matter-of-fact knowledge is virtually excluded in favor of pragmatism, secular and religious. But for the greater part of the race, at least for the greater part of civilized mankind, the regime of the mature barbarian culture has been of relatively short duration, and has had a correspondingly superficial and transient selective effect. It has not had force and time to eliminate certain elements of human nature handed down from an earlier phase of life, which are not in full consonance with the barbarian animus or with the demands of the pragmatic scheme of thought. The barbarian-pragmatic habit of mind, therefore, is not properly speaking a temperamental trait of the civilized peoples, except possibly within certain class limits (as, e.g., the German nobility). It is rather a tradition, and it does not constitute so tenacious a bias as to make head against the [604] strongly materialistic drift of modern conditions and set aside that increasingly urgent resort to matter-of-fact conceptions that makes for the primacy of science. Civilized mankind does not in any great measure take back atavistically to the upper-barbarian habit of mind. Barbarism covers too small a segment of the life-history of the race to have given an enduring temperamental result. The unmitigated discipline of the higher barbarism in Europe fell on a relatively small proportion of the population, and in the course of time this select element of the population was crossed and blended with the blood of the lower elements whose life always continued to run in the ruts of savagery rather than in those of the high-strung, finished barbarian culture that gave rise to the chivalric scheme of life.

Of the several phases of human culture the most protracted, and the one which has counted for most in shaping the abiding traits of the race, is unquestionably that of savagery. With savagery, for the purpose in hand, is to be classed that lower, relatively peaceable barbarism that is not characterized by wide and sharp class discrepancies or by an unremitting endeavor of one individual or group to get the better of another. Even under the full-grown barbarian culture – as, for instance, during the Middle Ages – the habits of life and the spiritual interests of the great body of the population continue in large measure to bear the character of savagery. The savage phase of culture accounts for by far the greater portion of the life-history of mankind, particularly if the lower barbarism and the vulgar life of later barbarism be counted in with savagery, as in a measure they properly should. This is particularly true of those racial elements that have entered into the composition of the leading peoples of Christendom.

The savage culture is characterized by the relative absence of pragmatism from the higher generalizations of its knowledge and beliefs. As has been noted above, its theoretical creations are chiefly of the nature of mythology shading off into folklore. This genial spinning of apocryphal yarns is, at its best, an amiably inefficient formulation of experiences and observations in terms of something like a life-history of the phenomena observed. [605] It has, on the one hand, little value, and little purpose, in the way of pragmatic expediency, and so it is not closely akin to the pragmatic-barbarian scheme of life; while, on the other hand, it is also ineffectual as a systematic knowledge of matter-of-fact. It is a quest of knowledge, perhaps of systematic knowledge, and it is carried on under the incentive of the idle curiosity. In this respect it falls in the same class with the civilized man's science; but it seeks knowledge not in terms of opaque matter-of-fact, but in terms of some sort of a spiritual life imputed to the facts. It is romantic and Hegelian rather than realistic and Darwinian. The logical necessities of its scheme of thought are necessities of spiritual consistency rather than of quantitative equivalence. It is like science in that it has no ulterior motive beyond the idle craving for a systematic correlation of data; but it is unlike science in that its standardization and correlation of data run in terms of the free play of imputed personal initiative rather than in terms of the constraint of objective cause and effect.

By force of the protracted selective discipline of this past phase of culture, the human nature of civilized mankind is still substantially the human nature of savage man. The ancient equipment of congenital aptitudes and propensities stands over substantially unchanged, though overlaid with barbarian traditions and conventionalities and readjusted by habituation to the exigencies of civilized life. In a measure, therefore, but by no means altogether, scientific inquiry is native to civilized man with his savage heritage, since scientific inquiry proceeds on the same general motive of idle curiosity as guided the savage myth-makers, though it makes use of concepts and standards in great measure alien to the myth-makers' habit of mind. The ancient human predilection for discovering a dramatic play of passion and intrigue in the phenomena of nature still asserts itself. In the most advanced communities, and even among the adepts of modern science, there comes up persistently the revulsion of the native savage against the inhumanly dispassionate sweep of the scientific quest, as well as against the inhumanly ruthless fabric of technological processes that have come out of this [606] search for matter-of-fact knowledge. Very often the savage need of a spiritual interpretation (dramatization) of phenomena breaks through the crust of acquired materialistic habits of thought, to find such refuge as may be had in articles of faith seized on and held by sheer force of instinctive conviction. Science and its creations are more or less uncanny, more or less alien, to that fashion of craving for knowledge that by ancient inheritance animates mankind. Furtively or by an overt breach of consistency, men still seek comfort in marvelous articles of savage-born lore, which contradict the truths of that modern science whose dominion they dare not question, but whose findings at the same time go beyond the breaking point of their jungle-fed spiritual sensibilities.

The ancient ruts of savage thought and conviction are smooth and easy; but however sweet and indispensable the archaic ways of thinking may be to the civilized man's peace of mind, yet such is the binding force of matter-of-fact analysis and inference under modern conditions that the findings of science are not questioned on the whole. The name of science is after all a word to conjure with. So much so that the name and the mannerisms, at least, if nothing more of science, have invaded all fields of learning and have even overrun territory that belongs to the enemy. So there are "sciences" of theology, law, and medicine, as has already been noted above. And there are such things as Christian Science, and "scientific" astrology, palmistry, and the like. But within the field of learning proper there is a similar predilection for an air of scientific acumen and precision where science does not belong. So that even that large range of knowledge that has to do with general information rather than with theory – what is loosely termed scholarship – tends strongly to take on the name and forms of theoretical statement. However decided the contrast between these branches of knowledge on the one hand, and science properly so called on the other hand, yet even the classical learning, and the humanities generally, fall in with this predilection more and more with each succeeding generation of students. The students of literature, for instance, are more and more prone to substitute critical [607] analysis and linguistic speculation, as the end of their endeavors, in the place of that discipline of taste and that cultivated sense of literary form and literary feeling that must always remain the chief end of literary training, as distinct from philology and the social sciences. There is, of course, no intention to question the legitimacy of a science of philology or of the analytical study of literature as a fact in cultural history, but these things do not constitute training in literary taste, nor can they take the place of it. The effect of this straining after scientific formulations in a field alien to the scientific spirit is as curious as it is wasteful. Scientifically speaking, the quasi-scientific inquiries necessarily begin nowhere and end in the same place; while in point of cultural gain they commonly come to nothing better than spiritual abnegation. But these blindfold endeavors to conform to the canons of science serve to show how wide and unmitigated the sway of science is in the modern community.

Scholarship – that is to say an intimate and systematic familiarity with past cultural achievements – still holds its place in the scheme of learning, in spite of the unadvised efforts of the short-sighted to blend it with the work of science, for it affords play for the ancient genial propensities that ruled men's quest of knowledge before the coming of science or of the outspoken pragmatic barbarism. Its place may not be so large in proportion to the entire field of learning as it was before the scientific era got fully under way. But there is no intrinsic antagonism between science and scholarship, as there is between pragmatic training and scientific inquiry. Modern scholarship shares with modern science the quality of not being pragmatic in its aim. Like science it has no ulterior end. It may be difficult here and there to draw the line between science and scholarship, and it may even more be unnecessary to draw such a line; yet while the two ranges of discipline belong together in many ways, and while there are many points of contact and sympathy between the two; while the two together make up the modern scheme of learning; yet there is no need of confounding the one with the other, nor can the one do the work of the other. The scheme of learning has changed in such manner [608] as to give science the more commanding place, but the scholar's domain has not thereby been invaded, nor has it suffered contraction at the hands of science, whatever may be said of the weak-kneed abnegation of some whose place, if they have one, is in the field of scholarship rather than of science.

All that has been said above has of course nothing to say as to the intrinsic merits of this quest of matter-of-fact knowledge. In point of fact, science gives its tone to modern culture. One may approve or one may deprecate the fact that this opaque, materialistic interpretation of things pervades modern thinking. That is a question of taste, about which there is no disputing. The prevalence of this matter-of-fact inquiry is a feature of modern culture, and the attitude which critics take toward this phenomenon is chiefly significant as indicating how far their own habit of mind coincides with the enlightened common-sense of civilized mankind. It shows in what degree they are abreast of the advance of culture. Those in whom the savage predilection or the barbarian tradition is stronger than their habituation to civilized life will find that this dominant factor of modern life is perverse, if not calamitous; those whose habits of thought have been fully shaped by the machine process and scientific inquiry are likely to find it good. The modern western culture, with its core of matter-of-fact knowledge, may be better or worse than some other cultural scheme, such as the classic Greek, the mediaeval Christian, the Hindu, or the Pueblo Indian. Seen in certain lights, tested by certain standards, it is doubtless better; by other standards, worse. But the fact remains that the current cultural scheme, in its maturest growth, is of that complexion; its characteristic force lies in this matter-of-fact insight; its highest discipline and its maturest aspirations are these.

In point of fact, the sober common-sense of civilized mankind accepts no other end of endeavor as self-sufficient and ultimate. That such is the case seems to be due chiefly to the ubiquitous presence of the machine technology and its creations in the life of modern communities. And so long as the machine process continues to hold its dominant place as a disciplinary [609] factor in modern culture, so long must the spiritual and intellectual life of this cultural era maintain the character which the machine process gives it.

But while the scientist's spirit and his achievements stir an unqualified admiration in modern men, and while his discoveries carry conviction as nothing else does, it does not follow that the manner of man which this quest of knowledge produces or requires comes near answering to the current ideal of manhood, or that his conclusions are felt to be as good and beautiful as they are true. The ideal man, and the ideal of human life, even in the apprehension of those who most rejoice in the advances of science, is neither the finikin skeptic in the laboratory nor the animated slide-rule. The quest of science is relatively new. It is a cultural factor not comprised, in anything like its modern force, among those circumstances whose selective action in the far past has given to the race the human nature which it now has. The race reached the human plane with little of this searching knowledge of facts; and throughout the greater part of its life-history on the human plane it has been accustomed to make its higher generalizations and to formulate its larger principles of life in other terms than those of passionless matter-of-fact. This manner of knowledge has occupied an increasing share of men's attention in the past, since it bears in a decisive way upon the minor affairs of workday life; but it has never until now been put in the first place, as the dominant note of human culture. The normal man, such as his inheritance has made him, has therefore good cause to be restive under its dominion.

Selection 31

The socialist economics of Karl Marx and his followers[1]

Source: *Quarterly Journal of Economics*, August 1906 (vol. 20, pp. 575–95) and February 1907 (vol. 21, pp. 299–322).

Veblen (1906b, 1907a)

Part I. The theories of Karl Marx

The system of doctrines worked out by Marx is characterized by a certain boldness of conception and a great logical consistency. Taken in detail, the constituent elements of the system are neither novel nor iconoclastic, nor does Marx at any point claim to have discovered previously hidden facts or to have invented recondite formulations of facts already known; but the system as a whole has an air of originality and initiative such as is rarely met with among the sciences that deal with any phase of human culture. How much of this distinctive character the Marxian system owes to the personal traits of its creator is not easy to say, but what marks it off from all other systems of economic theory is not a matter of personal idiosyncrasy. It differs characteristically from all systems of theory that had preceded it, both in its premises and in its aims. The (hostile) critics of Marx have not sufficiently appreciated the radical character of his departure in both of these respects, and have, therefore, commonly lost themselves in a tangled scrutiny of supposedly abstruse details; whereas those writers who have been in sympathy with his teachings have too commonly been disciples bent on exegesis and on confirming their fellow-disciples in the faith.

Except as a whole and except in the light of its postulates and aims, the Marxian system is not only not tenable, but it is not even intelligible. A discussion of a given isolated [576] feature of the system (such as the theory of value) from the point of view of classical economics (such as that offered by Böhm-Bawerk) is as futile as a discussion of solids in terms of two dimensions.

Neither as regards his postulates and preconceptions nor as regards the aim of his inquiry is Marx's position an altogether single-minded one. In neither respect does his position come of a single line of antecedents. He is of no single school

1 The substance of lectures before students in Harvard University in April, 1906.

of philosophy, nor are his ideals those of any single group of speculators living before his time. For this reason he takes his place as an originator of a school of thought as well as the leader of a movement looking to a practical end.

As to the motives which drive him and the aspirations which guide him, in destructive criticism and in creative speculation alike, he is primarily a theoretician busied with the analysis of economic phenomena and their organization into a consistent and faithful system of scientific knowledge; but he is, at the same time, consistently and tenaciously alert to the bearing which each step in the progress of his theoretical work has upon the propaganda. His work has, therefore, an air of bias, such as belongs to an advocate's argument; but it is not, therefore, to be assumed, nor indeed to be credited, that his propagandist aims have in any substantial way deflected his inquiry or his speculations from the faithful pursuit of scientific truth. His socialistic bias may color his polemics, but his logical grasp is too neat and firm to admit of any bias, other than that of his metaphysical preconceptions, affecting his theoretical work.

There is no system of economic theory more logical than that of Marx. No member of the system, no single article of doctrine, is fairly to be understood, criticised, or defended except as an articulate member of the whole and in the light of the preconceptions and postulates which afford [577] the point of departure and the controlling norm of the whole. As regards these preconceptions and postulates, Marx draws on two distinct lines of antecedents, – the Materialistic Hegelianism and the English system of Natural Rights. By his earlier training he is an adept in the Hegelian method of speculation and inoculated with the metaphysics of development underlying the Hegelian system. By his later training he is an expert in the system of Natural Rights and Natural Liberty, ingrained in his ideals of life and held inviolate throughout. He does not take a critical attitude toward the underlying principles of Natural Rights. Even his Hegelian preconceptions of development never carry him the length of questioning the fundamental principles of that system. He is only more ruthlessly consistent in working out their content than his natural-rights antagonists in the liberal-classical school. His polemics run against the specific tenets of the liberal school, but they run wholly on the ground afforded by the premises of that school. The ideals of his propaganda are natural-rights ideals, but his theory of the working out of these ideals in the course of history rests on the Hegelian metaphysics of development, and his method of speculation and construction of theory is given by the Hegelian dialectic.

What first and most vividly centred interest on Marx and his speculations was his relation to the revolutionary socialistic movement; and it is those features of his doctrines which bear immediately on the propaganda that still continue to hold the attention of the greater number of his critics. Chief among these doctrines, in the apprehension of his critics, is the theory of value, with its corollaries: (a) the doctrines of the exploitation of labor by capital; and (b) the laborer's claim to the whole product of his labor. Avowedly, Marx traces his doctrine of labor [578] value to Ricardo, and through him to the classical economists.[2] The laborer's claim to the whole product of labor, which is pretty constantly implied, though not frequently avowed by Marx, he has in all probability taken from English writers of the early nineteenth century,[3] more particularly from William Thompson. These doctrines are, on their face, nothing but a development of the conceptions of natural rights which then pervaded English speculation and afforded the metaphysical ground of the liberal movement. The more formidable critics of the Marxian socialism have made much of these doctrinal elements that further the propaganda, and have, by laying the stress on these, diverted attention from other elements that are of more vital consequence to the system as a body of theory. Their exclusive interest in this side of "scientific socialism" has even led them to deny the Marxian system all substantial originality, and make it a (doubtfully legitimate) offshoot of English Liberalism and natural rights.[4] But this is one-sided criticism. It may hold as against certain tenets of the so-called "scientific socialism," but it is not altogether to the point as regards the Marxian system of theory. Even the Marxian theory of value, surplus value, and exploitation, is not simply the doctrine of William Thompson, transcribed and sophisticated in a forbidding terminology, however great the superficial resemblance and however large Marx's unacknowledged debt to Thompson may be on these heads. For many details and for much of his animus Marx may be indebted to the Utilitarians; but, after all, his system of theory, taken as a whole, lies within the frontiers of neo-Hegelianism, and [579] even the details are worked out in accord with the preconceptions of that school of thought and have taken on the complexion that would properly belong to them on that ground. It is, therefore, not by an itemized scrutiny of the details of doctrine and by tracing their pedigree in detail that a fair conception of Marx and his contribution to economics may be reached, but rather by following him from his own point of departure out into the ramifications of his theory, and so overlooking the whole in the perspective which the lapse of time now affords us, but which he could not himself attain, since he was too near to his own work to see why he went about it as he did.

The comprehensive system of Marxism is comprised within the scheme of the Materialistic Conception of History.[5] This materialistic conception is essentially Hegelian,[6] although it belongs with the Hegelian Left, and its

2 Cf. [*A Contribution to the*] *Critique of Political Economy*, chap. i, "Notes on the History of the Theory of Commodities," pp. 56–73 (English translation, New York, 1904).
3 See Menger, *Right to the Whole Produce of Labor*, sections iii–v and viii–ix, and Foxwell's admirable Introduction to Menger.
4 See Menger and Foxwell, as above [in note 3 in this Selection], and Schaeffle, *Quintessence of Socialism*, and *The Impossibility or Social Democracy*.
5 See Engels, *The Development of Socialism from Utopia to Science*, especially section ii. and the opening paragraphs of section iii.; also [Marx,] preface of *Zur Kritik der politischen Oekonomie*.
6 See Engels, as above [in note 5 in this Selection], and also his *Feuerbach: The Roots of Socialist Philosophy* (translation, Chicago, Kerr & Co., 1903).

immediate affiliation is with Feuerbach, not with the direct line of Hegelian orthodoxy. The chief point of interest here, in identifying the materialistic conception with Hegelianism, is that this identification throws it immediately and uncompromisingly into contrast with Darwinism and the post-Darwinian conceptions of evolution. Even if a plausible English pedigree should be worked out for this Materialistic Conception, or "Scientific Socialism," as has been attempted, it remains none the less true that the conception with which Marx went to his work was a transmuted framework of Hegelian dialectic.[7]

Roughly, Hegelian materialism differs from Hegelian orthodoxy by inverting the main logical sequence, not by [580] discarding the logic or resorting to new tests of truth or finality. One might say, though perhaps with excessive crudity, that, where Hegel pronounces his dictum, *Das Denken ist das Sein*, the materialists, particularly Marx and Engels, would say *Das Sein macht das Denken*.[8] But in both cases some sort of a creative primacy is assigned to one or the other members of the complex, and in neither case is the relation between the two members a causal relation. In the materialistic conception man's spiritual life – what man thinks – is a reflex of what he is in the material respect, very much in the same fashion as the orthodox Hegelian would make the material world a reflex of the spirit. In both the dominant norm of speculation and formulation of theory is the conception of movement, development, evolution, progress; and in both the movement is contrived necessarily to take place by the method of conflict or struggle. The movement is of the nature of progress, – gradual advance towards a goal, toward the realization in explicit form of all that is implicit in the substantial activity involved in the movement. The movement is, further, self-conditioned and self-acting: it is an unfolding by inner necessity. The struggle which constitutes the method of movement or evolution is, in the Hegelian system proper, the struggle of the spirit for self-realization by the process of the well-known three-phase dialectic. In the materialistic conception of history this dialectical movement becomes the class struggle of the Marxian system.

The class struggle is conceived to be "material," but the term "material" is in this connection used in a metaphorical sense. It does not mean mechanical or physical, or even physiological, but economic. It is material in the sense that it is a struggle between classes for the material means of life. "The materialistic conception of history proceeds on the principle that production and, next to [581] production, the exchange of its products is the groundwork of every social order."[9] The social order takes its form through the class struggle, and the character of the class struggle at any given phase of the unfolding development of society is determined by "the prevailing mode of economic production and exchange." The dialectic of the movement of social

---

7 See, e.g., Seligman, *The Economic Interpretation of History*, Part I.
8 [Thinking is Being . . . Being causes thinking. – Eds.].
9 Engels, *Development of Socialism*, beginning of section iii.

progress, therefore, moves on the spiritual plane of human desire and passion, not on the (literally) material plane of mechanical and physiological stress, on which the developmental process of brute creation unfolds itself. It is a sublimated materialism; sublimated by the dominating presence of the conscious human spirit; but it is conditioned by the material facts of the production of the means of life.[10] The ultimately active forces involved in the process of unfolding social life are (apparently) the material agencies engaged in the mechanics of production; but the dialectic of the process – the class struggle – runs its course only among and in terms of the secondary (epigenetic) forces of human consciousness engaged in the valuation of the material products of industry. A consistently materialistic conception, consistently adhering to a materialistic interpretation of the process of development as well as of the facts involved in the process, could scarcely avoid making its putative dialectic struggle a mere unconscious and irrelevant conflict of the brute material forces. This would have amounted to an interpretation in terms of opaque cause and effect, without recourse to the concept of a conscious class struggle, and it might have led to a concept of evolution similar to the unteleological Darwinian concept of natural selection. It could scarcely have led to the Marxian notion of a [582] conscious class struggle as the one necessary method of social progress, though it might conceivably, by the aid of empirical generalization, have led to a scheme of social process in which a class struggle would be included as an incidental though perhaps highly efficient factor.[11] It would have led, as Darwinism has, to a concept of a process of cumulative change in social structure and function; but this process, being essentially a cumulative sequence of causation, opaque and unteleological, could not, without an infusion of pious fancy by the speculator, be asserted to involve progress as distinct from retrogression or to tend to a "realization" or "self-realization" of the human spirit or of anything else. Neither could it conceivably be asserted to lead up to a final term, a goal to which all lines of the process should converge and beyond which the process would not go, such as the assumed goal of the Marxian process of class struggle which is conceived to cease in the classless economic structure of the socialistic final term. In Darwinianism there is no such final or perfect term, and no definitive equilibrium.

The disparity between Marxism and Darwinism, as well as the disparity within the Marxian system between the range of material facts that are conceived to be the fundamental forces of the process, on the one hand, and the range of spiritual facts within which the dialectic movement proceeds, – this disparity is shown in the character assigned the class struggle by Marx and Engels. The

---

10 Cf., on this point, Max Adler, "Kausalitat und Teleologie im Streite um die Wissenschaft" (included in *Marx – Studien*, edited by Adler and Hilferding, vol. i), particularly section xi.; cf. also Ludwig Stein, *Die soziale Frage im Lichte der Philosophie*, whom Adler criticizes and claims to have refuted.

11 Cf., Adler as above [in note 10 in this Selection].

struggle is asserted to be a conscious one, and proceeds on a recognition by the competing classes of their mutually incompatible interests with regard to the material means of life. The class struggle proceeds on motives of interest, and a recognition of class interest can, of course, be reached only by reflection on the facts of the case. There is, therefore, not even a direct causal connection between the material forces in the case and the choice of a given interested [583] line of conduct. The attitude of the interested party does not result from the material forces so immediately as to place it within the relation of direct cause and effect, nor even with such a degree of intimacy as to admit of its being classed as a tropismatic, or even instinctive, response to the impact of the material force in question. The sequence of reflection, and the consequent choice of sides to a quarrel, run entirely alongside of the range of material facts concerned.

A further characteristic of the doctrine of class struggle requires mention. While the concept is not Darwinian, it is also not legitimately Hegelian, whether of the Right or the Left. It is of a utilitarian origin and of English pedigree, and it belongs to Marx by virtue of his having borrowed its elements from the system of self-interest. It is in fact a piece of hedonism, and is related to Bentham rather than to Hegel. It proceeds on the grounds of the hedonistic calculus, which is equally foreign to the Hegelian notion of an unfolding process and to the post-Darwinian notions of cumulative causation. As regards the tenability of the doctrine, apart from the question of its derivation and its compatibility with the neo-Hegelian postulates, it is to be added that it is quite out of harmony with the later results of psychological inquiry, just as is true of the use made of the hedonistic calculus by the classical (Austrian) economics.

Within the domain covered by the materialistic conception, that is to say within the domain of unfolding human culture, which is the field of Marxian speculation at large, Marx has more particularly devoted his efforts to an analysis and theoretical formulation of the present situation, – the current phase of the process, the capitalistic system. And, since the prevailing mode of the production of goods determines the institutional, intellectual, and spiritual life [584] of the epoch, by determining the form and method of the current class struggle, the discussion necessarily begins with the theory of "capitalistic production," or production as carried on under the capitalistic system.[12]

---

12 It may be noted, by way of caution to readers familiar with the terms only as employed by the classical (English and Austrian) economists, that in Marxian usage "capitalistic production" means production of goods for the market by hired labor under the direction of employers who own (or control) the means of production and are engaged in industry for the sake of profit. "Capital" is wealth (primarily funds) so employed. In these and other related points of terminological usage Marx is, of course, much more in touch with colloquial usage than those economists of the classical line who make capital signify "the products of past industry used as aids to further production." With Marx "Capitalism" implies certain relations of ownership, no less than the "productive use" which is alone insisted on by so many later economists in defining the term.

Under the capitalistic system, that is to say under the system of modern business traffic, production is a production of commodities, merchantable goods, with a view to the price to be obtained for them in the market. The great fact on which all industry under this system hinges is the price of marketable goods. Therefore it is at this point that Marx strikes into the system of capitalistic production, and therefore the theory of value becomes the dominant feature of his economics and the point of departure for the whole analysis, in all its voluminous ramifications.[13]

It is scarcely worth while to question what serves as the beginning of wisdom in the current criticisms of Marx; namely, that he offers no adequate proof of his labor-value theory.[14] It is even safe to go further, and say that [585] he offers no proof of it. The feint which occupies the opening paragraphs of the *Kapital* and the corresponding passages of *Zur Kritik*, etc., is not to be taken seriously as an attempt to prove his position on this head by the ordinary recourse to argument. It is rather a self-satisfied superior's playful mystification of those readers (critics) whose limited powers do not enable them to see that his proposition is self-evident. Taken on the Hegelian (neo-Hegelian) ground, and seen in the light of the general materialistic conception, the proposition that value = labor-cost is self-evident, not to say tautological. Seen in any other light, it has no particular force.

In the Hegelian scheme of things the only substantial reality is the unfolding life of the spirit. In the neo-Hegelian scheme, as embodied in the materialistic conception, this reality is translated into terms of the unfolding (material) life of man in society.[15] In so far as the goods are products of industry, they are the output of this unfolding life of man, a material residue embodying a given fraction of this forceful life process. In this life process lies all substantial reality, and all finally valid relations of quantivalence between the products of this life process must run in its terms. The life

---

13 In the sense that the theory of value affords the point of departure and the fundamental concepts out of which the further theory of the workings of capitalism is constructed, – in this sense, and in this sense only, is the theory of value the central doctrine and the critical tenet of Marxism. It does not follow that Marxist doctrine of an irresistible drift towards a socialistic consummation hangs on the defensibility of the labor-value theory, nor even that the general structure of the Marxist economics would collapse if translated into other terms than those of this doctrine of labor value. Cf. Böhm-Bawerk, *Karl Marx and the Close of his System*; and, on the other hand, Franz Oppenheimer, *Das Grundgesetz der Marx'schen Gesellschaftslehre*, and Rudolf Goldscheid, *Verelendungs- oder Meliorationstheorie*.

14 Cf., e.g., Böhm-Bawerk, as above [in note 13 in this Selection]; Georg Adler, *Grundlagen der Karl Marx'schen Kritik*.

15 In much the same way, and with an analogous effect on their theoretical work, in the preconceptions of the classical (including the Austrian) economists, the balance of pleasure and pain is taken to be the ultimate reality in terms of which all economic theory must be stated and to terms of which all phenomena should finally be reduced in any definitive analysis of economic life. It is not the present purpose to inquire whether the one of these uncritical assumptions is in any degree more meritorious or more serviceable than the other.

process, which, when it takes the specific form of an expenditure of labor power, goes to produce goods, is a process of material forces, the spiritual or mental features of the life process and of labor being only its insubstantial reflex. It is consequently only in the material changes wrought by this expenditure of labor power that the metaphysical substance of life – labor power – can be embodied; but in these changes of material [586] fact it cannot but be embodied, since these are the end to which it is directed.

This balance between goods in respect of their magnitude as output of human labor holds good indefeasibly, in point of the metaphysical reality of the life process, whatever superficial (phenomenal) variations from this norm may occur in men's dealings with the goods under the stress of the strategy of self-interest. Such is the value of the goods in reality; they are equivalents of one another in the proportion in which they partake of this substantial quality, although their true ratio of equivalence may never come to an adequate expression in the transactions involved in the distribution of the goods. This real or true value of the goods is a fact of production, and holds true under all systems and methods of production, whereas the exchange value (the "phenomenal form" of the real value) is a fact of distribution, and expresses the real value more or less adequately according as the scheme of distribution force at the given time conforms more or less closely to the equities given by production. If the output of industry were distributed to the productive agents strictly in proportion to their shares in production, the exchange value of the goods would be presumed to conform to their real value. But, under the current, capitalistic system, distribution is not in any sensible degree based on the equities of production, and the exchange value of goods under this system can therefore express their real value only with a very rough, and in the main fortuitous, approximation. Under a socialistic régime, where the laborer would get the full product of his labor, or where the whole system of ownership, and consequently the system of distribution, would lapse, values would reach a true expression, if any.

Under the capitalistic system the determination of exchange value is a matter of competitive profit-making, and [587] exchange values therefore depart erratically and incontinently from the proportions that would legitimately be given them by the real values whose only expression they are. Marx's critics commonly identify the concept of "value" with that of "exchange value,"[16] and show that the theory of "value" does not square with the run of the facts of price under the existing system of distribution, piously hoping thereby to have refuted the Marxian doctrine; whereas, of course, they have for the most part not touched it. The misapprehension of the critics may be due to a (possibly intentional) oracular obscurity on the part of Marx. Whether by his fault or their own, their refutations have hitherto been quite

16 Böhm-Bawerk, *Capital and Interest*, Book VI, chap. iii; also *Karl Marx and the Close of his System*, particularly chap. iv; Adler, *Grundlagen*, chaps. ii and iii.

inconclusive. Marx's severest stricture on the iniquities of the capitalistic system is that contained by implication in his development of the manner in which actual exchange value of goods systematically diverges from their real (labor-cost) value. Herein, indeed, lies not only the inherent iniquity of the existing system, but also its fateful infirmity, according to Marx.

The theory of value, then, is *contained* in the main postulates of the Marxian system rather than derived from them. Marx identifies this doctrine, in its elements, with the labor-value theory of Ricardo,[17] but the relationship between the two is that of a superficial coincidence in their main propositions rather than a substantial identity of theoretic contents. In Ricardo's theory the source and measure of value is sought in the effort and sacrifice undergone by the producer, consistently, on the whole, with the Benthamite-utilitarian position to which Ricardo somewhat [588] loosely and uncritically adhered. The decisive fact about labor, that quality by virtue of which it is assumed to be the final term in the theory of production, is its irksomeness. Such is of course not the case in the labor-value theory of Marx, to whom the question of the irksomeness of labor is quite irrelevant, so far as regards the relation between labor and production. The substantial diversity or incompatibility of the two theories shows itself directly when each is employed by its creator in the further analysis of economic phenomena. Since with Ricardo the crucial point is the degree of irksomeness of labor, which serves as a measure both of the labor expended and the value produced, and since in Ricardo's utilitarian philosophy there is no more vital fact underlying this irksomeness, therefore no surplus-value theory follows from the main position. The productiveness of labor is not cumulative in its own working; and the Ricardian economics goes on to seek the cumulative productiveness of industry in the functioning of the products of labor when employed in further production and in the irksomeness of the capitalist's abstinence. From which duly follows the general position of classical economics on the theory of production.

With Marx, on the other hand, the labor power expended in production being itself a product and having a substantial value corresponding to its own labor cost, the value of the labor power expended and the value of the product created by its expenditure need not be the same. They are not the same, by supposition, as they would be in any hedonistic interpretation of the facts. Hence a discrepancy arises between the value of the labor power expended in production and the value of the product created, and this discrepancy is covered by the concept of surplus value. Under the capitalistic system, wages being the value (price) of the labor

---

17 Cf. *Das Kapital*, vol. i, chap. xv, p. 486 (4th ed.). See also notes 9 and 16 to chap. i of the same volume, where Marx discusses the labor-value doctrines of Adam Smith and an earlier (anonymous) English writer and compares them with his own. Similar comparisons with the early – Classical – value theories recur from time to time in the later portions of *Das Kapital*.

power consumed in industry, it follows that [589] the surplus product of their labor cannot go to the laborers, but becomes the profits of capital and the source of its accumulation and increase. From the fact that wages are measured by the value of labor power rather than by the (greater) value of the product of labor, it follows also that the laborers are unable to buy the whole product of their labor, and so that the capitalists are unable to sell the whole product of industry continuously at its full value, whence arise difficulties of the gravest nature in the capitalistic system, in the way of overproduction and the like.

But the gravest outcome of this systematic discrepancy between the value of labor power and the value of its product is the accumulation of capital out of unpaid labor and the effect of this accumulation on the laboring population. The law of accumulation, with its corollary, the doctrine of the industrial reserve army, is the final term and the objective point of Marx's theory of capitalist production, just as the theory of labor value is his point of departure.[18] While the theory of value and surplus value are Marx's explanation of the possibility of existence of the capitalistic system, the law of the accumulation of capital is his exposition of the causes which must lead to the collapse of that system and of the manner in which the collapse will come. And since Marx is, always and everywhere, a socialist agitator as well as a theoretical economist, it may be said without hesitation that the law of accumulation is the climax of his great work, from whatever point of view it is looked at, whether as an economic theorem or as a tenet of socialistic doctrine.

The law of capitalistic accumulation may be paraphrased [590] as follows:[19] Wages being the (approximately exact) value of the labor power bought in the wage contract; the price of the product being the (similarly approximate) value of the goods produced; and since the value of the product exceeds that of the labor power by a given amount (surplus value), which by force of the wage contract passes into the possession of the capitalist and is by him in part laid by as savings and added to the capital already in hand, it follows (a) that, other things equal, the larger the surplus value, the more rapid the increase of capital; and also (b), that the greater the increase of capital relatively to the labor force employed, the more productive the labor employed and the larger the surplus product available for accumulation. The process of accumulation, therefore, is evidently a cumulative one; and, also evidently, the increase

18 Oppenheimer (*Das Grundgesetz der Marx'schen Gesellschaftslehre*) is right in making the theory of accumulation the central element in the doctrines of Marxist socialism, but it does not follow, as Oppenheimer contends, that this doctrine is the keystone of Marx's economic theories. It follows logically from the theory of surplus value, as indicated above, and rests on that theory in such a way that it would fail (in the form in which it is held by Marx) with the failure of the doctrine of surplus value.

19 See *Das Kapital*, vol. i, chap. xxiii.

added to capital is an unearned increment drawn from the unpaid surplus product of labor.

But with an appreciable increase of the aggregate capital a change takes place in its technological composition, whereby the "constant" capital (equipment and raw materials) increases disproportionately as compared with the "variable" capital (wages fund). "Labor-saving devices" are used to a greater extent than before, and labor is saved. A larger proportion of the expenses of production goes for the purchase of equipment and raw materials, and a smaller proportion – though perhaps an absolutely increased amount – goes for the purchase of labor power. Less labor is needed relatively to the aggregate capital employed as well as relatively to the quantity of goods produced. Hence some portion of the increasing labor supply will not be wanted, and an "industrial reserve army," a "surplus labor population," an army of unemployed, comes into existence. This reserve [591] grows relatively larger as the accumulation of capital proceeds and as technological improvements consequently gain ground; so that there result two divergent cumulative changes in the situation, – antagonistic, but due to the same set of forces and, therefore, inseparable: capital increases, and the number of unemployed laborers (relatively) increases also.

This divergence between the amount of capital and output, on the one hand, and the amount received by laborers as wages, on the other hand, has an incidental consequence of some importance. The purchasing power of the laborers, represented by their wages, being the largest part of the demand for consumable goods, and being at the same time, in the nature of the case, progressively less adequate for the purchase of the product, represented by the price of the goods produced, it follows that the market is progressively more subject to glut from overproduction, and hence to commercial crises and depression. It has been argued, as if it were a direct inference from Marx's position, that this maladjustment between production and markets, due to the laborer not getting the full product of his labor, leads directly to the breakdown of the capitalistic system, and so by its own force will bring on the socialistic consummation. Such is not Marx's position, however, although crises and depression play an important part in the course of development that is to lead up to socialism. In Marx's theory, socialism is to come by way of a conscious class movement on the part of the propertyless laborers, who will act advisedly on their own interest and force the revolutionary movement for their own gain. But crises and depression will have a large share in bringing the laborers to a frame of mind suitable for such a move.

Given a growing aggregate capital, as indicated above, and a concomitant reserve of unemployed laborers growing [592] at a still higher rate, as is involved in Marx's position, this body of unemployed labor can be, and will be, used by the capitalists to depress wages, in order to increase profits. Logically, it follows that, the farther and faster capital accumulates, the larger will be the reserve of unemployed, both absolutely and relatively to the work to be done, and the more severe will be the pressure acting to reduce wages and lower the standard of living, and the deeper will be the degradation and misery of the working class and the more precipitately will their condition decline to a still lower depth. Every period of depression, with its increased body of unemployed labor seeking work, will act to hasten and accentuate the depression of wages, until there is no warrant even for holding that wages will, on an average, be kept up to the subsistence minimum.[20] Marx, indeed, is explicit to the effect that such will be the case, that wages will decline below the subsistence minimum; and he cites English conditions of child labor, misery, and degeneration to substantiate his views.[21] When this has gone far enough, when capitalist production comes near enough to occupying the whole field of industry and has depressed the condition of its laborers sufficiently to make them an effective majority of the community with nothing to lose, then, having taken advice together, they will move, by legal or extra-legal means, by absorbing the state or by subverting it, to establish the social revolution.

Socialism is to come through class antagonism due to the absence of all property interests from the laboring class, coupled with a generally prevalent misery so profound as to involve some degree of physical degeneration. This misery is to be brought about by the heightened productivity [593] of labor due to an increased accumulation of capital and large improvements in the industrial arts; which in turn is caused by the fact that under a system of private enterprise with hired labor the laborer does not get the whole product of his labor; which, again, is only saying in other words that private ownership of capital goods enables the capitalist to appropriate and accumulate the surplus product of labor. As to what the régime is to be which the social revolution will bring in, Marx has nothing particular to say beyond the general thesis that there will be no private ownership, at least not of the means of production.

Such are the outlines of the Marxian system of socialism. In all that has been said so far no recourse is had to the second and third volumes of *Kapital*. Nor is it necessary to resort to these two volumes for the general theory of socialism. They add nothing essential, although many of the details of the processes concerned in the working out of the capitalist scheme are treated with greater fulness, and the analysis is carried out with great consistency and with admirable results. For economic theory at large these further two volumes are important enough, but an inquiry into their contents in that connection is not called for here.

---

20 The "subsistence minimum" is here taken in the sense used by Marx and the classical economists, as meaning what is necessary to keep up the supply of labor at its current rate of efficiency.

21 See *Das Kapital*, vol. i, chap. xxiii, sections 4 and 5.

Nothing much need be said as to the tenability of this theory. In its essentials, or at least in its characteristic elements, it has for the most part been given up by latter-day socialist writers. The number of those who hold to it without essential deviation is growing gradually smaller. Such is necessarily the case, and for more than one reason. The facts are not bearing it out on certain critical points, such as the doctrine of increasing misery; and the Hegelian philosophical postulates, without which the Marxism of Marx is groundless, are for the most part forgotten by [594] the dogmatists of to-day. Darwinism has largely supplanted Hegelianism in their habits of thought.

The particular point at which the theory is most fragile, considered simply as a theory of social growth, is its implied doctrine of population, implied in the doctrine of a growing reserve of unemployed workmen. The doctrine of the reserve of unemployed labor involves as a postulate that population will increase anyway, without reference to current or prospective means of life. The empirical facts give at least a very persuasive apparent support to the view expressed by Marx, that misery is, or has hitherto been, no hindrance to the propagation of the race; but they afford no conclusive evidence in support of a thesis to the effect that the number of laborers must increase independently of an increase of the means of life. No one since Darwin would have the hardihood to say that the increase of the human species is not conditioned by the means of living.

But all that does not really touch Marx's position. To Marx, the neo-Hegelian history, including the economic development, is the life-history of the human species; and the main fact in this life-history, particularly in the economic aspect of it, is the growing volume of human life. This, in a manner of speaking, is the base-line of the whole analysis of the process of economic life, including the phase of capitalist production with the rest. The growth of population is the first principle, the most substantial, most material factor in this process of economic life, so long as it is a process of growth, of unfolding, of exfoliation, and not a phase of decrepitude and decay. Had Marx found that his analysis led him to a view adverse to this position, he would logically have held that the capitalist system is the mortal agony of the race and the manner of its taking off. Such a conclusion is precluded by his Hegelian point of departure, according to which the goal of the life-history of the race in a large way controls the course of that life-history in all its phases, including the phase of capitalism. This goal or end, which controls the process of human development, is the complete realization of life in all its fulness, and the realization is to be reached by a process analogous to the three-phase dialectic, of thesis, antithesis, and synthesis, into which scheme the capitalist system, with its overflowing measure of misery and degradation, fits as the last and most dreadful phase of antithesis. Marx, as a Hegelian, – that is to say, a romantic philosopher, – is necessarily an optimist, and the evil (antithetical element) in life is to him a logically necessary evil, as the antithesis is a necessary phase of the dialectic; and it is a means to the consummation, as the antithesis is a means to the synthesis.

Part II. The later Marxism

Marx worked out his system of theory in the main during the third quarter of the nineteenth century. He came to the work from the standpoint given him by his early training in German thought, such as the most advanced and aggressive German thinking was through the middle period of the century, and he added to this German standpoint the further premises given him by an exceptionally close contact with and alert observation of the English situation. The result is that he brings to his theoretical work a twofold line of premises, or rather of preconceptions. By early training he is a neo-Hegelian, and from this German source he derives his peculiar formulation of the Materialistic Theory of History. By later experience he acquired the point of view of that Liberal-Utilitarian school which dominated English thought through the greater part of his active life. To this experience he owes (probably) the somewhat pronounced individualistic preconceptions on which the doctrines of the Full Product of Labor and the Exploitation of Labor are based. These two not altogether compatible lines of doctrine found their way together into the tenets of scientific[22] socialism, and give its characteristic Marxian features to the body of socialist economics.

The socialism that inspires hopes and fears to-day is of [300] the school of Marx. No one is seriously apprehensive of any other so-called socialistic movement, and no one is seriously concerned to criticise or refute the doctrines set forth by any other school of "socialists." It may be that the socialists of Marxist observance are not always or at all points in consonance with the best accepted body of Marxist doctrine. Those who make up the body of the movement may not always be familiar with the details – perhaps not even with the general features – of the Marxian scheme of economics; but with such consistency as may fairly be looked for in any popular movements the socialists of all countries gravitate toward the theoretical position of the avowed Marxism. In proportion as the movement in any given community grows in mass, maturity, and conscious purpose, it unavoidably takes on a more consistently Marxian complexion. It is not the Marxism of Marx, but the materialism of Darwin, which the socialists of today have adopted. The Marxist socialists of Germany have the lead, and the socialists of other countries largely take their cue from the German leaders.

The authentic spokesmen of the current international socialism are avowed Marxists. Exceptions to that rule are very few. On the whole, the substantial truth of the Marxist doctrines is not seriously questioned within the lines of the socialists, though there may be some appreciable divergence as to what the true Marxist position is on one point and another. Much and eager controversy circles about questions of that class.

---

22 "Scientific" is here used in the half technical sense which by usage it often has in this connection, designating the theories of Marx and his followers.

The keepers of the socialist doctrines are passably agreed as to the main position and the general principles. Indeed, so secure is this current agreement on the general principles that a very lively controversy on matters of detail may go on without risk of disturbing the general position. This general position is avowedly Marxism. [301] But it is not precisely the position held by Karl Marx. It has been modernized, adapted, tilled out, in response to exigencies of a later date than those which conditioned the original formulation of the theories. It is, of course, not admitted by the followers of Marx that any substantial change or departure from the original position has taken place. They are somewhat jealously orthodox, and are impatient of any suggested "improvements" on the Marxist position, as witness the heat engendered in the "revisionist" controversy of a few years back. But the jealous protests of the followers of Marx do not alter the fact that Marxism has undergone some substantial change since it left the hands of its creator. Now and then a more or less consistent disciple of Marx will avow a need of adapting the received doctrines to circumstances that have arisen later than the formulation of the doctrines; and amendments, qualifications, and extensions, with this need in view, have been offered from time to time. But more pervasive though unavowed changes have come in the teachings of Marxism by way of interpretation and an unintended shifting of the point of view. Virtually, the whole of the younger generation of socialist writers shows such a growth. A citation of personal instances would be quite futile.

It is the testimony of his friends as well as of his writings that the theoretical position of Marx, both as regards his standpoint and as regards his main tenets, fell into a definitive shape relatively early, and that his later work was substantially a working out of what was contained in the position taken at the outset of his career.[23] By the [302] latter half of the forties, if not by the middle of the forties, Marx and Engels had found the outlook on human life which came to serve as the point of departure and the guide for their subsequent development of theory. Such is the view of the matter expressed by Engels during the later years of his life.[24] The position taken by the two

23 There is, indeed, a remarkable consistency, amounting substantially to an invariability of position, in Marx's writing, from the *Manifesto of the Communist Party* to the last volume of the *Capital*. The only portion of the great *Manifesto* which became antiquated, in the apprehension of its creators, is the polemics addressed to the "Philosophical" socialists of the forties and the illustrative material taken from [302] contemporary politics. The main position and the more important articles of theory, the materialistic conception, the doctrine of class struggle, the theory of value and surplus value, of increasing distress, of the reserve army, of the capitalistic collapse are to be found in *Zur Kritik der politischen Oekonomie* (1859) and much of them in the *Misère de la Philosophie* (1847), together with the masterful method of analysis and construction which he employed throughout his theoretical work.
24 Cf. Engels, *Feuerbach* (English translation, Chicago, 1903), especially Part IV., various papers published in the *Neue Zeit*; also the "Preface" to the *Manifesto of the Communist Party* written in 1888; also the "Preface" to volume II of *Capital*, where Engels argues the question of Marx's priority in connection with the leading theoretical principles of his system.

greater leaders, and held by them substantially intact, was a variant of neo-Hegelianism, as has been indicated in an earlier section of this paper.[25] But neo-Hegelianism was short-lived, particularly considered as a standpoint for scientific theory. The whole romantic school of thought, comprising neo-Hegelianism with the rest, began to go to pieces very soon after it had reached an approach to maturity, and its disintegration proceeded with exceptional speed, so that the close of the third quarter of the century saw the virtual end of it as a vital factor in the development of human knowledge. In the realm of theory, primarily of course in the material sciences, the new era belongs not to romantic philosophy, but to the evolutionists of the school of Darwin. Some few great figures, of course, stood over from the earlier days, but it turns out in the sequel that they have served mainly to mark the rate and degree in which the method of scientific knowledge has left them behind. Such were Virchow and Max Müller, and such, in economic science, were [303] the great figures of the Historical School, and such, in a degree, were also Marx and Engels. The later generation of socialists, the spokesmen and adherents of Marxism during the closing quarter of the century, belong to the new generation, and see the phenomena of human life under the new light. The materialistic conception in their handling of it takes on the color of the time in which they lived, even while they retain the phraseology of the generation that went before them.[26]

The difference between the romantic school of thought, to which Marx belonged, and the school of the evolutionists into whose hands the system has fallen, – or perhaps, better, is falling, – is great and pervading, though it may not show a staring superficial difference at any one point, – at least not yet. The discrepancy between the two is likely to appear more palpable and more sweeping when the new method of knowledge has been applied with fuller realization of its reach and its requirements in that domain of knowledge that once belonged to the neo-Hegelian Marxism. The supplanting of the one by the other has been taking place slowly, gently, in large measure unavowedly, by a sort of precession of the point of view from which men size up the facts and reduce them to intelligible order.

---

25 Cf. [Engels], *Feuerbach*, as above [in note 24 in this Selection]; *The Development of Socialism from Utopia to Science*, especially sections II and III.

26 Such a socialist as Anton Menger, e.g., comes into the neo-Marxian school from without, from the field of modern scientific inquiry, and shows, at least virtually, no Hegelian color, whether in the scope of his inquiry, in his method, or in the theoretical work which he puts forth. It should be added that his *Neue Staatslehre* and *Neue Sittenlehre* are the first socialistic constructive work of substantial value as a contribution to knowledge, outside of economic theory proper, that has appeared since Lassalle. The efforts of Engels (*Ursprung der Familie*) and Bebel (*Die Frau*) would scarcely be taken seriously as scientific monographs even by hot-headed socialists if it were not for the lack of anything better. Menger's work is not Marxism, whereas Engels' and Bebel's work of this class is practically without value or originality. The unfitness of the Marxian postulates and methods for the purposes of modern science shows itself in the sweeping barrenness of socialistic literature all along that line of inquiry into the evolution of institutions for the promotion of which the materialistic dialectic was invented.

The neo-Hegelian, romantic, Marxian standpoint was [304] wholly personal, whereas the evolutionistic – it may be called Darwinian – standpoint is wholly impersonal. The continuity sought in the facts of observation and imputed to them by the earlier school of theory was a continuity of a personal kind, – a continuity of reason and consequently of logic. The facts were construed to take such a course as could be established by an appeal to reason between intelligent and fair-minded men. They were supposed to fall into a sequence of logical consistency. The romantic (Marxian) sequence of theory is essentially an intellectual sequence, and it is therefore of a teleological character. The logical trend of it can be argued out. That is to say, it tends to a goal. It must eventuate in a consummation, a final term. On the other hand, in the Darwinian scheme of thought, the continuity sought in and imputed to the facts is a continuity of cause and effect. It is a scheme of blindly cumulative causation, in which there is no trend, no final term, no consummation. The sequence is controlled by nothing but the *vis a tergo*[27] of brute causation, and is essentially mechanical. The neo-Hegelian (Marxian) scheme of development is drawn in the image of the struggling ambitious human spirit: that of Darwinian evolution is of the nature of a mechanical process.[28]

What difference, now, does it make if the materialistic conception is translated from the romantic concepts of Marx into the mechanical concepts of Darwinism? It distorts every feature of the system in some degree, and throws a shadow of doubt on every conclusion that once [305] seemed secure.[29] The first principle of the Marxian scheme is the concept covered by the term "Materialistic," to the effect that the exigencies of the material means of life control the conduct of men in society throughout, and thereby indefeasibly guide the growth of institutions and shape every shifting trait of human culture. This control of the life of society by the material exigencies takes effect through men's taking thought of material (economic) advantages and disadvantages, and choosing that which will yield the inner material measure of life. When the materialistic conception passes under the Darwinian norm,

---

27 [Force acting from behind. – Eds.].

28 This contrast holds between the original Marxism of Marx and the scope and method of modern science; but it does not, therefore, hold between the latter-day Marxists – who are largely imbued with post-Darwinian concepts – and the non-Marxian scientists. Even Engels, in his latter-day formulation of Marxism, is strongly affected with the notions of post-Darwinian science, and reads Darwinism into Hegel and Marx with a good deal of naivete. (See his *Feuerbach*, especially pp. 93–98 of the English translation.) So, also, the serious but scarcely quite consistent qualification of the materialistic conception offered by Engels in the letters printed in the *Sozialistische Akademiker*, 1895.

29 The fact that the theoretical structures of Marx collapse when their elements are converted into the terms of modern science should of itself be sufficient proof that those structures were not built by their maker out of such elements as modern science habitually makes use of. Marx was neither ignorant, imbecile, nor disingenuous, and his work must be construed from such a point of view and in terms of such elements as will enable his results to stand substantially sound and convincing.

of cumulative causation, it happens, first, that this initial principle itself is reduced to the rank of a habit of thought induced in the speculator who depends on its light by the circumstances of his life, in the way of hereditary bent, occupation, tradition, education, climate, food supply, and the like. But under the Darwinian norm the question of whether and how far material exigencies control human conduct and cultural growth becomes a question of the share which these material exigencies have in shaping men's habits of thought; i.e., their ideals and aspirations, their sense of the true, the beautiful, and the good. Whether and how far these traits of human culture and the institutional structure built out of them are the outgrowth of material (economic) exigencies becomes a question of what kind and degree of efficiency belongs to the economic exigencies among the complex of circumstances that conduce to the formation of habits. It is no longer a question of whether material exigencies rationally should guide men's conduct, but whether, as a [306] matter of brute causation, they do induce such habits of thought in men as the economic interpretation presumes, and whether in the last analysis economic exigencies alone are, directly or indirectly, effective in shaping human habits of thought.

Tentatively and by way of approximation some such formulation as that outlined in the last paragraph is apparently what Bernstein and others of the "revisionists" have been seeking in certain of their speculations,[30] and, sitting

---

30 Cf. *Voraussetzungen des Sozialismus*, especially the first two (critical) chapters. Bernstein's reverent attitude toward Marx and Engels, as well as his somewhat old-fashioned conception of the scope and method of science, gives his discussion an air of much greater consonance with the orthodox Marxism than it really has. In his latter expressions this consonance and conciliatory animus show up more strongly rather than otherwise. (See *Socialism and Science*, including the special preface written for the French edition.) That which was to Marx and Engels the point of departure and the guiding norm – the Hegelian dialectic – is to Bernstein a mistake from which scientific socialism must free itself. He says, e.g. (*Voraussetzungen*, end of ch. iv.), "The great things achieved by Marx and Engels they have achieved not by the help of the Hegelian dialectic, but in spite of it."

The number of the "revisionists" is very considerable, and they are plainly gaining ground as against the Marxists of the older line of orthodoxy. They are by no means agreed among themselves as to details, but they belong together by virtue of their endeavor to so construe (and amend) the Marxian system as to bring it into consonance with the current scientific point of view. One should rather say points of view, since the revisionist endevors are not all directed to bringing the received views in under a single point of view. There are two main directions of movement among the revisionists: (a) those who, like Bernstein, Conrad Schmidt, Tugan-Baronowski, Labriola, Ferri, aim to bring Marxism abreast of the standpoint of modern science, essentially Darwinists; and (b) those who aim to return to some footing on the level of romantic philosophy. The best type and the strongest of the latter class are the neo-Kantians, embodying that spirit of revulsion to romantic norms of theory that makes up the philosophical side of the reactionary movement fostered by the discipline of German imperialism. (See K. Vorländer, *Die neukantische Bewegung im Sozialismus.*)

Except that he is not officially inscribed in the socialist calendar, Sombart might be cited as a particularly effective revisionist, so far as concerns the point of modernizing Marxism and putting the modernized materialistic conception to work.

austere and sufficient on a dry shoal up stream, Kautsky has uncomprehendingly been addressing them advice and admonition which they do not understand.[31] The more intelligent and enterprising among the idealist wing – where intellectual enterprise is not a particularly [307] obvious trait – have been struggling to speak for the view that the forces of the environment may effectually reach men's spiritual life through other avenues than the calculus of the main chance, and so may give rise to habitual ideals and aspirations independent of, and possibly alien to, that calculus.[32]

So, again, as to the doctrine of the class struggle. In the Marxian scheme of dialectical evolution the development which is in this way held to be controlled by the material exigencies must, it is held, proceed by the method of the class struggle. This class struggle is held to be inevitable, and is held inevitably to lead at each revolutionary epoch to a more efficient adjustment of human industry to human uses, because when a large proportion of the community find themselves ill served by the current economic arrangements, they take thought, band together, and enforce a readjustment more equitable and more advantageous to them. So long as differences of economic advantage prevail, there will be a divergence of interests between those more advantageously placed and those less advantageously placed. The members of society will take sides as this line of cleavage indicated by their several economic interests may decide. Class solidarity will arise on the basis of this class interest, and a struggle between the two classes so marked off against each other will set in, – a struggle which, in the logic of the situation, can end only when the previously less fortunate class gains the ascendency, – and so must the class struggle proceed until [308] it shall have put an end to that diversity of economic interest on which the class struggle rests. All this is logically consistent and convincing, but it proceeds on the ground of reasoned conduct, calculus of advantage, not on the ground of cause and effect. The class struggle so conceived should always and everywhere tend unremittingly toward the socialistic consummation, and should reach that consummation in the end, whatever obstructions or diversions might retard the sequence of development along the way. Such is the notion of it embodied in the system of Marx. Such, however, is not the showing of history. Not all nations or civilizations have advanced unremittingly toward a socialistic consummation, in

---

31 Cf. the files of the *Neue Zeit*, particularly during the controversy with Bernstein, and [Karl Kautsky,] *Bernstein und das Sozialdemokratische Programm.*

32 The "idealist" socialists are even more in evidence outside of Germany. They may fairly be said to be in the ascendant in France, and they are a very strong and free-spoken contingent of the socialist movement of America. They do not commonly speak the language either of science or of philosophy, but, so far as their contentions may be construed from the standpoint of modern science, their drift seems to be something of the kind indicated above. At the same time the spokesmen of this scattering and shifting group stand for a variety of opinions and aspirations that cannot be classified under Marxism, Darwinism, or any other system of theory. At the margin they shade off into theology and the creeds.

which all divergence of economic interest has lapsed or would lapse. Those nations and civilizations which have decayed and failed, as nearly all known nations and civilizations have done, illustrate the point that, however reasonable and logical the advance by means of the class struggle may be, it is by no means inevitable. Under the Darwinian norm it must be held that men's reasoning is largely controlled by other than logical, intellectual forces; that the conclusion reached by public or class opinion is as much, or more, a matter of sentiment than of logical inference; and that the sentiment which animates men, singly or collectively, is as much, or more, an outcome of habit and native propensity as of calculated material interest. There is, for instance, no warrant in the Darwinian scheme of things for asserting a priori that the class interest of the working class will bring them to take a stand against the propertied class. It may as well be that their training in subservience to their employers will bring them again to realize the equity and excellence of the established system of subjection and unequal distribution of wealth. Again, no one, for instance, can tell to-day what will be the outcome of the present situation [309] in Europe and America. It may be that the working classes will go forward along the line of the socialistic ideals and enforce a new deal, in which there shall be no economic class discrepancies, no international animosity, no dynastic politics. But then it may also, so far as can be foreseen, equally well happen that the working class, with the rest of the community in Germany, England, or America, will be led by the habit of loyalty and by their sportsmanlike propensities to lend themselves enthusiastically to the game of dynastic politics which alone their sportsmanlike rulers consider worth while. It is quite impossible on Darwinian ground to foretell whether the "proletariat" will go on to establish the socialistic revolution or turn aside again, and sink their force in the broad sands of patriotism. It is a question of habit and native propensity and of the range of stimuli to which the proletariat are exposed and are to be exposed, and what may be the outcome is not a matter of logical consistency, but of response to stimulus.

So, then, since Darwinian concepts have begun to dominate the thinking of the Marxists, doubts have now and again come to assert themselves both as to the inevitableness of the irrepressible class struggle and to its sole efficacy. Anything like a violent class struggle, a seizure of power by force, is more and more consistently deprecated. For resort to force, it is felt, brings in its train coercive control with all its apparatus of prerogative, mastery, and subservience.[33]

33 Throughout the revisionist literature in Germany there is visible a softening of the traits of the doctrine of the class struggle, and the like shows itself in the programs of the party. Outside of Germany the doctrinaire insistence on this tenet is weakening even more decidedly. The opportunist politicians, with strong aspirations, but with relatively few and ill-defined theoretical preconceptions, are gaining ground.

So, again, the Marxian doctrine of progressive proletarian distress, the so-called *Verelendungstheorie*,[34] which [310] stands pat on the romantic ground of the original Marxism, has fallen into abeyance, if not into disrepute, since the Darwinian conceptions have come to prevail. As a matter of reasoned procedure, on the ground of enlightened material interest alone, it should be a tenable position that increasing misery, increasing in degree and in volume, should be the outcome of the present system of ownership; and should at the same time result in a well-advised and well-consolidated working-class movement that would replace the present system by a scheme more advantageous to the majority. But so soon as the question is approached on the Darwinian ground of cause and effect, and is analyzed in terms of habit and of response to stimulus, the doctrine that progressive misery must effect a socialistic revolution becomes dubious, and very shortly untenable. Experience, the experience of history, teaches that abject misery carries with it deterioration and abject subjection. The theory of progressive distress fits convincingly into the scheme of the Hegelian three-phase dialectic. It stands for the antithesis that is to be merged in the ulterior synthesis; but it has no particular force on the ground of an argument from cause to effect.[35]

It fares not much better with the Marxian theory of value and its corollaries and dependent doctrines when Darwinian concepts are brought in to replace the romantic elements out of which it is built up. Its foundation is the meta-physical equality between the volume of human life force productively spent in the making of goods and the magnitude of these goods considered as human products. The question of such an equality has no meaning in terms of cause and effect, nor does it bear in any intelligible [311] way upon the Darwinian question of the fitness of any given system of production or distribution. In any evo-lutionary system of economics the central question touching the efficiency and fitness of any given system of production is necessarily the question as to the excess of serviceability in the product over the cost of production.[36]

It is in such an excess of serviceability over cost that the chance of survival lies for any system of production, in so far as the question of survival is a

---

34 [Theory of immiseration. – Eds.]

35 Cf. Bernstein, *Die heutige Sozialdemokratie in Theorie und Praxis*, an answer to Brunhuber, *Die heutige Sozialdemokratie*, which should be consulted in the same connection; Goldscheid, *Verelendungs-oder Meliorationstheorie*; also Sombart, *Sozialismus und soziale Bewegung*, 5th edition, pp. 86–89.

36 Accordingly, in later Marxian handling of the questions of exploitation and accumulation, the attention is centred on the "surplus product" rather than on the "surplus value." It is also currently held that the doctrines and practical consequences which Marx derived from the theory of surplus value would remain substantially well founded, even if the theory of surplus value were given up. These secondary doctrines could be saved – at the cost of orthodoxy – by putting a theory of surplus product in the place of the theory of surplus value, as in effect is done by Bernstein (*Sozialdemokratie in Theorie und Praxis*, sec. 5. Also various essays included in *Zur Geschichte und Theorie des Sozialismus*).

question of production, and this matter comes into the speculation of Marx only indirectly or incidentally, and leads to nothing in his argument.

And, as bearing on the Marxian doctrines of exploitation, there is on Darwinian ground no place for a natural right to the full product of labor. What can be argued in that connection on the ground of cause and effect simply is the question as to what scheme of distribution will help or hinder the survival of a given people or a given civilization.[37]

But these questions of abstruse theory need not be pursued, since they count, after all, but relatively little among the working tenets of the movement. Little need be done by the Marxists to work out or to adapt the Marxian system of value theory, since it has but slight [312] bearing on the main question, – the question of the trend towards socialism and of its chances of success. It is conceivable that a competent theory of value dealing with the excess of serviceability over cost, on the one hand, and with the discrepancy between price and serviceability, on the other hand, would have a substantial bearing upon the advisability of the present as against the socialistic régime, and would go far to clear up the notions of both socialists and conservatives as to the nature of the points in dispute between them. But the socialists have not moved in the direction of this problem, and they have the excuse that their critics have suggested neither a question nor a solution to a question along any such line. None of the value theorists have so far offered anything that could be called good, bad, or indifferent in this connection, and the socialists are as innocent as the rest. Economics, indeed, has not at this point yet begun to take on a modern tone, unless the current neglect of value theory by the socialists be taken as a negative symptom of advance, indicating that they at least recognize the futility of the received problems and solutions, even if they are not ready to make a positive move.

The shifting of the current point of view, from romantic philosophy to matter-of-fact, has affected the attitude of the Marxists towards the several articles of theory more than it has induced an avowed alteration or a substitution of new elements of theory for the old. It is always possible to make one's peace with a new standpoint by new interpretations and a shrewd use of figures of speech, so far as the theoretical formulation is concerned, and something of this kind has taken place in the case of Marxism; but when, as in the case of Marxism, the formulations of theory are drafted into practical use, substantial changes of appreciable magnitude are apt to show themselves in [313]

---

37 The "right to the full product of labor" and the Marxian theory of exploitation associated with that principle has fallen into the background, except as a campaign designed to stir the emotions of the working class. Even as a campaign it has not the prominence, nor apparently the efficacy, which it once had. The tenet is better preserved, in fact, among the "idealists," who draw for their antecedents on the French Revolution and the English philosophy of natural rights, than among the latter-day Marxists.

a changed attitude towards practical questions. The Marxists have had to face certain practical problems, especially problems of party tactics, and the substantial changes wrought in their theoretical outlook have come into evidence here. The real gravity of the changes that have overtaken Marxism would scarcely be seen by a scrutiny of the formal professions of the Marxists alone. But the exigencies of a changing situation have provoked readjustments of the received doctrinal position, and the shifting of the philosophical standpoint and postulates has come into evidence as marking the limits of change in their professions which the socialistic doctrinaires could allow themselves.

The changes comprised in the cultural movement that lies between the middle and the close of the nineteenth century are great and grave, at least as seen from so near a standpoint as the present day, and it is safe to say that, in whatever historical perspective they may be seen, they must, in some respects, always assert themselves as unprecedented. So far as concerns the present topic, there are three main lines of change that have converged upon the Marxist system of doctrines, and have led to its latter-day modification and growth. One of these – the change in the postulates of knowledge, in the metaphysical foundations of theory – has been spoken of already, and its bearing on the growth of socialist theory has been indicated in certain of its general features. But, among the circumstances that have conditioned the growth of the system, the most obvious is the fact that since Marx's time his doctrines have come to serve as the platform of a political movement, and so have been exposed to the stress of practical party politics dealing with a new and changing situation. At the same time the industrial (economic) situation to which the doctrines are held to apply – of which they are the theoretical formulation – has also in important respects [314] changed its character from what it was when Marx first formulated his views. These several lines of cultural change affecting the growth of Marxism cannot be held apart in so distinct a manner as to appraise the work of each separately. They belong inextricably together, as do the effects wrought by them in the system.

In practical politics the Social Democrats have had to make up their account with the labor movement, the agricultural population, and the imperialistic policy. On each of these heads the preconceived program of Marxism has come in conflict with the run of events, and on each head it has been necessary to deal shrewdly and adapt the principles to the facts of the time. The adaptation to circumstances has not been altogether of the nature of the compromise, although here and there the spirit of compromise and conciliation is visible enough. A conciliatory party policy may, of course, impose an adaptation of form and color upon the party principles, whether thereby seriously affecting the substance of the principles themselves; but the need of a conciliatory policy may, even more, provoke a substantial change of attitude toward practical questions in a case where a shifting of the theoretical point of view makes room for a substantial change.

Apart from all merely tactical expedients, the experience of the past thirty years has led the German Marxists to see the facts of the labor situation in a new light, and has induced them to attach an altered meaning to the accepted formulations of doctrine. The facts have not freely lent themselves to the scheme of the Marxist system, but the scheme has taken on such a new meaning as would be consistent with the facts. The untroubled Marxian economics, such as it finds expression in the *Kapital* and earlier documents of the theory, has no place and no use for a trade-union movement, or, indeed, for any similar non-political organization among the working class, and [315] the attitude of the Social-Democratic leaders of opinion in the early days of the party's history was accordingly hostile to any such movement,[38] – as much so, indeed, as the loyal adherents of the classical political economy. That was before the modern industrial era had got under way in Germany, and therefore before the German socialistic doctrinaires had learned by experience what the development of industry was to bring with it. It was also before the modern scientific postulates had begun to disintegrate the neo-Hegelian preconceptions as to the logical sequence in the development of institutions.

In Germany, as elsewhere, the growth of the capitalistic system presently brought on trade-unionism; that is to say, it brought on an organized attempt on the part of the workmen to deal with the questions of capitalistic production and distribution by business methods, to settle the problems of working-class employment and livelihood by a system of nonpolitical, businesslike bargains. But the great point of all socialist aspiration and endeavor is the abolition of all business and all bargaining, and, accordingly, the Social Democrats were heartily out of sympathy with the unions and their endeavors to make business terms with the capitalist system, and make life tolerable for the workmen under that system. But the union movement grew to be so serious a feature of the situation that the socialists found themselves obliged to deal with unions, since they could not deal with the [316] workmen over the heads of the unions. The Social Democrats, and therefore the Marxian theorists, had to deal with a situation which included the union movement, and this movement was bent on improving the workman's conditions of life from day to day. Therefore it was necessary to figure out how the union movement could and must further the socialistic advance; to work into the body of doctrines a theory of how the unions belong in the course of

---

38 It is, of course, well known that even in the transactions and pronunciamentos of the International a good word is repeatedly said for the trade-unions, and both the Gotha and the Erfurt programs speak in favor of labor organizations, and put forth demands designed to further the trade-union endeavors. But it is equally well known that these expressions were in good part perfunctory, and that the substantial motive behind them was the politic wish of the socialists to conciliate the unionists, and make use of the unions for the propaganda. The early expressions of sympathy with the unionist cause were made for an ulterior purpose. Later on, in the nineties, there comes a change in the attitude of the socialist leaders toward the unions.

economic development that leads up to socialism, and to reconcile the unionist efforts at improvement with the ends of Social Democracy. Not only were the unions seeking improvement by unsocialistic methods, but the level of comfort among the working classes was in some respects advancing, apparently as a result of these union efforts. Both the huckstering animus of the workmen in their unionist policy and the possible amelioration of working-class conditions had to be incorporated into the socialistic platform and into the Marxist theory of economic development. The Marxist theory of progressive misery and degradation has, accordingly, fallen into the background, and a large proportion of the Marxists have already come to see the whole question of working-class deterioration in some such apologetic light as is shed upon it by Goldscheid in his *Verelendungs- oder Meliorationstheorie*. It is now not an unusual thing for orthodox Marxists to hold that the improvement of the conditions of the working classes is a necessary condition to the advance of the socialistic cause, and that the unionist efforts at amelioration must be furthered as a means toward the socialistic consummation. It is recognized that the socialistic revolution must be carried through not by an anaemic working class under the pressure of abject privation, but by a body of full-blooded workingmen gradually gaining strength from improved conditions of life. Instead of the revolution being worked out by the leverage of desperate [317] misery, every improvement in working-class conditions is to be counted as a gain for the revolutionary forces. This is a good Darwinism, but it does not belong in the neo-Hegelian Marxism.

Perhaps the sorest experience of the Marxist doctrinaires has been with the agricultural population. Notoriously, the people of the open country have not taken kindly to socialism. No propaganda and no changes in the economic situation have won the sympathy of the peasant farmers for the socialistic revolution. Notoriously, too, the large-scale industry has not invaded the agricultural field, or expropriated the small proprietors, in anything like the degree expected by the Marxist doctrinaires of a generation ago. It is contained in the theoretical system of Marx that, as modern industrial and business methods gain ground, the small proprietor farmers will be reduced to the ranks of the wage-proletariat, and that, as this process of conversion goes on, in the course of time the class interest of the agricultural population will throw them into the movement side by side with the other wage-workmen.[39] But at this point the facts have hitherto not come out in consonance with the Marxist theory. And the efforts of the Social Democrats to convert the peasant population to socialism have been practically unrewarded. So it has come about that the political leaders and the keepers of the doctrines have, tardily and reluctantly, come to see the facts of the agrarian situation in a new light, and to give a new phrasing to the articles of Marxian theory that touch

39 Cf. *Das Kapital*, vol. i. ch. xiii., sect. 10.

on the fortunes of the peasant farmer. It is no longer held that either the small properties of the peasant farmer must be absorbed into larger properties, and then taken over by the State, or that they must be taken over by the State directly, when the socialistic revolution is established. On the contrary, it is now coming [318] to be held that the peasant proprietors will not be disturbed in their holdings by the great change. The great change is to deal with capitalistic enterprise, and the peasant farming is not properly "capitalistic." It is a system of production in which the producer normally gets only the product of his own labor. Indeed, under the current régime of markets and credit relations, the small agricultural producer, it is held, gets less than the product of his own labor, since the capitalistic business enterprises with which he has to deal are always able to take advantage of him. So it has become part of the overt doctrine of socialists that as regards the peasant farmer it will be the consistent aim of the movement to secure him in the untroubled enjoyment of his holding, and free him from the vexatious exactions of his creditors and the ruinous business traffic in which he is now perforce involved. According to the revised code, made possible by recourse to Darwinian concepts of evolution instead of the Hegelian three-phase dialectic, therefore, and contrary to the earlier prognostications of Marx, it is no longer held that agricultural industry must go through the capitalistic mill, and it is hoped that under the revised code it may be possible to enlist the interest and sympathy of this obstinately conservative element for the revolutionary cause. The change in the official socialist position on the agricultural question has come about only lately, and is scarcely yet complete, and there is no knowing what degree of success it may meet with either as a matter of party tactics or as a feature of the socialistic theory of economic development. All discussions of party policy, and of theory so far as bears on policy, take up the question; and nearly all authoritative spokesmen of socialism have modified their views in the course of time on this point.

The socialism of Karl Marx is characteristically inclined [319] to peaceable measures and disinclined to a coercive government and belligerent politics. It is, or at least it was, strongly averse to international jealousy and patriotic animosity, and has taken a stand against armaments, wars, and dynastic aggrandizement. At the time of the French–Prussian war the official organization of Marxism, the International, went so far in its advocacy of peace as to urge the soldiery on both sides to refuse to fight. After the campaign had warmed the blood of the two nations, this advocacy of peace made the International odious in the eyes of both French and Germans. War begets patriotism, and the socialists fell under the reproach of not being sufficiently patriotic. After the conclusion of the war, the Socialistic Workingmen's Party of Germany sinned against the German patriotic sentiment in a similar way and with similarly grave results. Since the foundation of the empire and of the Social-Democratic party, the socialists and their doctrines have passed through a further experience of a similar kind, but on a larger scale and more protracted. The government has gradually strengthened its autocratic position at home, increased its warlike equipment, and enlarged its pretensions in international politics, until what would have seemed absurdly impossible a generation ago is now submitted to by the German people, not only with a good grace, but with enthusiasm. During all this time that part of the population that has adhered to the socialist ideals has also grown gradually more patriotic and more loyal, and the leaders and keepers of socialist opinion have shared in the growth of chauvinism with the rest of the German people. But at no time have the socialists been able to keep abreast of the general upward movement in this respect. They have not attained the pitch of reckless loyalty that animates the conservative German patriots, although it is probably safe to say that the Social Democrats of to-day are as [320] good and headlong patriots as the conservative Germans were a generation ago. During all this period of the new era of German political life the socialists have been freely accused of disloyalty to the national ambition, of placing their international aspirations above the ambition of imperial aggrandizement.

The socialist spokesmen have been continually on the defensive. They set out with a round opposition to any considerable military establishment, and have more and more apologetically continued to oppose any "undue" extension of the warlike establishments and the warlike policy. But with the passage of time and the habituation to warlike politics and military discipline, the infection of jingoism has gradually permeated the body of Social Democrats, until they have now reached such a pitch of enthusiastic loyalty as they would not patiently hear a truthful characterization of. The spokesmen now are concerned to show that, while they still stand for international socialism, consonant with their ancient position, they stand for national aggrandizement first and for international comity second. The relative importance of the national and the international ideals in German socialist professions has been reversed since the seventies.[40] The leaders are busy with interpretation of their earlier formulations. They have come to excite themselves over nebulous distinctions between patriotism and jingoism. The Social Democrats have come to be German patriots first and socialists second, which comes to saying that they are a political party working for the maintenance of the existing order, with modifications. They are no longer a party of revolution, but of reform, though the measure of reform which they demand greatly exceeds the Hohenzollern limit of tolerance. They are now as much, if not [321] more, in touch with the ideas of English liberalism than with those of revolutionary Marxism.

The material and tactical exigencies that have grown out of changes in the industrial system and in the political situation, then, have brought on far-reaching changes of adaptation in the position of the socialists. The change may not be extremely large at any one point, so far as regards the specific articles of the program, but, taken as a whole, the resulting modification of the socialistic position is a very substantial one. The process of change is, of

---

40 Cf. Kautsky, *Erfurter Programm*, ch. v., sect. 13; Bernstein, *Voraussetzungen*, ch. iv., sect. e.

course, not yet completed, – whether or not it ever will be, but it is already evident that what is taking place is not so much a change in amount or degree of conviction on certain given points as a change in kind, – a change in the current socialistic habit of mind.

The factional discrepancies of theory that have occupied the socialists of Germany for some years past are evidence that the conclusion, even a provisional conclusion, of the shifting of their standpoint has not been reached. It is even hazardous to guess which way the drift is setting. It is only evident that the past standpoint, the standpoint of neo-Hegelian Marxism, cannot be regained, – it is a forgotten standpoint. For the immediate present the drift of sentiment, at least among the educated, seems to set toward a position resembling that of the National Socials and the Rev. Mr. Naumann; that is to say, imperialistic liberalism. Should the conditions, political, social, and economic, which to-day are chiefly effective in shaping the habits of thought among the German people, continue substantially unchanged and continue to be the chief determining causes, it need surprise no one to find German socialism gradually changing into a somewhat characterless imperialistic democracy. The imperial policy seems in a fair way to get the better of revolutionary socialism, not by repressing it, but by force of the discipline [322] in imperialistic ways of thinking to which it subjects all classes of the population. How far a similar process of sterilization is under way, or is likely to overtake the socialist movement in other countries, is an obscure question to which the German object-lesson affords no certain answer.

Introduction to Part IV

1907–1914: the penultimate period

The writings collected here in the fourth part of this volume cover the period from Veblen's installation at Stanford University in August 1906 to the publication of *The Instinct of Workmanship* – his third book – in 1914. His Stanford appointment allowed him ample time for research and he was able to continue his momentum of high productivity and creativity that he had sustained from the late 1890s. In particular, from 1906 to 1909 he developed his enduring critique of what he had described in 1900 as "neo-classical" economics (Veblen 1900a, pp. 239, 241, 243 [in this volume]; Aspromourgos 1986; Fayazmanesh 1998), including its predilection for equilibria, its concept of capital and its theory of distribution. Also by 1909 he had drafted parts of *The Instinct of Workmanship*.

Selections 32, 33, 35 and 36 below (all published in the two years 1908–09) constitute much of Part IV and contain Veblen's mature and powerful critique of neoclassical theory. Identifying John Bates Clark as one of the leading American neoclassical economists, Veblen in Selection 32 identifies in this genre a "readiness to reduce all phenomena to terms of a 'normal,' or natural,' scheme of life constructed on the basis of this hedonistic calculus" (p. 411). He then proceeds to analyze the theory of capital that lies at the foundation of Clark's theory of distribution and neoclassical economics as a whole.

As noted in the General Introduction, Veblen identifies defects in the neoclassical theory of capital in terms of its confusion of pecuniary and physical assets, its neglect of the role of knowledge and other intangible assets, and its failure to understand that many of these intangibles have value only when they are deployed within groups. A theory of capital and distribution based on individual ownership and individual marginal products is thus fatally flawed. These points retain their resonance today.

While some of Veblen's (pp. 428–32) technical criticisms of Clark carry less force, particularly in the light of later rigorous formulations of neoclassical theory, Veblen (pp. 437–39) makes an incisive observation when he points out that the appropriate equilibrium (especially at the point of contract) is not of "pain-cost" and "pleasure-gain" but of "pain-cost" and "pleasure-gain anticipated." Given a tendency to overestimate future gains, consumers are likely to be disappointed. Instead of a consumer surplus there could be a "net hedonistic deficit" (p. 439).

Overall, the balance sheet is still very much in Veblen's favor. His criticisms of neoclassical economics in general and neoclassical capital theory in particular have enduring relevance and force.

Selection 33 is a two-part analysis of the "Nature of Capital." Veblen starts with the observation that humankind is a social and cultural species. Consequently, no individual "can maintain its life in isolation ... this is the characteristic trait of humanity that separates mankind from the other animals" (pp. 441–42). The history of humanity is "a life-history of human communities, of more or less considerable size, with more or less of group solidarity, and with more or less of cultural continuity over successive generations" (p. 442). For Veblen, economics is not the abstract study of individual choice – where the individual can be anything from a bacterium to a pigeon – but a science that reflects the socio-cultural nature of human existence.

Veblen's next step is to establish that this solidarity and cultural continuity is not primarily a matter of material goods but is "a matter of knowledge, usage, habits of life and habits of thought" (p. 442). He also emphasizes the role of "technological knowledge, – knowledge serviceable and requisite to the quest of a livelihood" (p. 442). He argues that it is the retention and transmission of this knowledge in a group that is vital to human productivity and survival. For Veblen there is "matter-of-fact" knowledge relevant for production "beyond what any one individual has learned or can learn by his own experience alone" (p. 442). This information and proficiency is a by-product of "the group at large" and "can also be maintained and retained only by the community at large" (p. 442).

This is the foundation of Veblen's critique of neoclassical capital theory, which he develops in several of his essays. For Veblen (pp. 445–47) private ownership of the means of production arises when the complexity, scale, and physical location of production provide extensive opportunities for specialization and local monopolies of technique. While large-scale industry undermined the possibility that knowledge and control of its processes could rest with one person, economic theory still treats ownership and management as if they matters of "natural" individual liberty (pp. 450–51).

Veblen (pp. 474–75) argues that the power and income of the capitalist, by "force of the ownership of the material equipment," draws out an "excess of the product above the industrial community's livelihood" through "the conjunctures of advantageous purchase and sale" and "his constant endeavor to create or gain for himself some peculiar degree of advantage in the market, in the way of monopoly, good-will, legalized privilege, and the like, – something in the way of intangible assets."

There is some resemblance to Marx's theory of surplus value, although Veblen avoids that term and refrains from making any such connection. But where for Marx the surplus had its origin in the process of production – whereby the authority of the capitalist and his agents is used to draw out labor from the workforce – for Veblen the origin of this "excess of product" comes through "bargaining" and obtaining "advantage in the market." A problem in this part of Veblen's argument is that he ignores the potential power of competition to drive down the capacity of the capitalist to seek rents and other monopoly advantages. It is thus weakened in the face of criticism from the perspective of neoclassical "perfect competition." By contrast, Marx starts by assuming competition and a lack of monopoly in order to show that exploitation will still occur in such extreme circumstances. Veblen's argument would come into its own if Veblen were able to show that oligopoly or monopoly were an inevitable and unavoidable part of the capitalist system. He hints at this – and some later institutionalists followed this lead – but Veblen himself does not establish this point.

Selection 34 is on another theme that is prominent in Veblen's writing in the early years of the twentieth century (Veblen 1904b, ch. 9, as well as Selection 30 in this volume). He is concerned to explain the origins of modern science and its institutions. Veblen's innovation is to apply the canons of Darwinism to the evolution of science itself, redolent of modern authors (Hull 1988, Kitcher 1993). In emphasizing the appearance and disappearance of habits of thought, he gives the ideas and institutions of the scientific community a psychological grounding.

Another interesting feature of this selection is Veblen's discussion of causality. Veblen acknowledges the necessity of adopting "metaphysical" assumptions, in particular of causal relations. Generally, all science involves such particular ontological commitments.

Veblen sees technology as impinging upon science: "modern science comes into the field under the cloak of technology," prompted by "workmanlike initiative and efficiency" (p. 488). But modern science retains the preconceptions of an earlier era. Hence notions of "natural laws" and "natural rights" are retained within the scientific culture and "evolution" is mistakenly conceived "to mean amelioration or 'improvement'" (pp. 489–91).

Selection 35 consists of lengthy critiques of two connected books by Irving Fisher (1906, 1908), who was an American neoclassical economist of some prominence. The two books under review are devoted to definitions of key concepts, and only partly to explanations. Veblen regrets this confinement to taxonomy but accepts the need for clear definitions. He argues that these must be broadly in line with prevailing habits of thought and "consensus of usage," and notes that Fisher's definition of capital departs from conventional practice (p. 493). As one of the originators of the "human capital" concept, Fisher regards persons as well as goods as capital. Veblen responds (p. 495):

> A serviceable definition of capital, one that shall answer to the concept as it is found in practice in the habits of thought of business men, will

not include persons. ... And as for a business man's capitalizing other persons, the law does not allow it, even in the form of peonage.

Veblen thus suggests that the term "capital" should not be applied to individual or groups of individuals.[1] But while including persons, Fisher's definition excludes intangible assets. Veblen roots these definitional deficiencies in the hedonistic and utilitarian conception of valuation and income adopted by Fisher. The Benthamite calculus forces the theorist to adopt strange and inadequate definitions. By contrast, for Veblen: "The logic of economic life in a modern community runs in terms of pecuniary, not of hedonistic magnitudes" (p. 499). An appreciation of intangible assets is vital to understand capitalization, speculation, and the role of credit in crises.

The principal point made by Veblen in his review of Fisher's *Rate of Interest* (1908) is that interest is "eminently a pecuniary phenomenon, and its rate is a question of business adjustments" (p. 508). Contrary to Fisher, it is not explained by the apparently universal preference for present over future consumption. This marginal-utility point of view misleads Fisher and others into regarding interest as universal, rather than an historically specific outcome of particular economic institutions. Veblen argues that the phenomenon of interest emerges "only during a relatively brief phase of civilization that has been preceded by thousands of years of cultural growth during which the existence of such a thing as interest was never suspected" (p. 509).

By contrast, Fisher and other devotees of the marginal-utility approach are obliged to trace the source of interest not in cultural and institutional specificities but in presumed eternal universalities of human nature. But "if men universally acted not on the conventional grounds and values afforded by the fabric of institutions, but solely and directly on the grounds and values afforded by the unconventionalized propensities and aptitudes of hereditary human nature, then there would be no institutions and no culture" (p. 509). For Veblen, these vital cultural and institutional factors are irreducible to human nature alone.

Having stripped away the vital cultural and institutional underpinnings, the marginal-utility theorists simply end up placing the phenomena in their conceptual schemes, rather than explaining their nature and causal origins. As Veblen puts it: "Mr. Fisher's theory of the rate of interest suffers from the same oversight of this difference between explaining facts and explaining them away, as do the common run of marginal-utility doctrines" (p. 510).

Selection 36 consists of one of Veblen's most important and powerful essays: "The Limitations of Marginal Utility." Its barbed criticisms of

---

1 See also Fetter (1930) and Hodgson (2008) among others.

utilitarianism and neoclassical economics are quoted frequently. But its underlying philosophical themes are less widely discussed. Some of these, particularly concerning teleology, causality and ontological commitments, are raised in the General Introduction to this volume, where several quotations from this "Limitations" essay appear.

Veblen (pp. 513–14) argues that marginal-utility economics is primarily concerned with the distribution or allocation of goods, rather than their production or consumption. In addition, this type of analysis is static rather than dynamic because "as to the causes of change or the unfolding sequence of the phenomena of economic life they have had nothing to say hitherto ... since their theory is not drawn in causal terms but in terms of teleology" (p. 513). Veblen emphasizes "the phenomena of growth and change" and points to technological factors as having a bearing on their explanation. To the deficient treatment of technology in the marginal-utility school, Veblen adds the criticism that it takes institutions and culture as given.

Veblen also suggests that the proper "subject of inquiry" of economics "is the conduct of man in his dealings with the material means of life" (p. 518). This broad definition was consonant with most other mainstream economists at the time.[2] It was later that economics was redefined as the "science of choice" assuming given preferences (Robbins 1932, Samuelson 1948, Backhouse and Medema 2009).

Because marginal-utility economics builds principally on the presumed universals of human nature, it cannot explain the "growth of culture" and the evolution of institutions. Because it abstracts from cultural and institutional change it ends up being largely static. Furthermore, by focusing on the individual, and excluding the ensemble of institutional relations, marginal-utility economics cannot capture the detailed institutional and cultural changes that are behind economic transformations. As noted in the General Introduction, Veblen was neither a methodological individualist nor a methodological collectivist, as a passage in this essay makes clear (pp. 519–20).

In particular marginal-utility economics abstracts from the pecuniary and possessive institutions of modern society. As Veblen puts it, "All pecuniary notions arising from ownership are treated simply as expedients of computation which mediate between the pain-cost and the pleasure-gain of hedonistic choice, without lag, leak, or friction; they are conceived simply as the immutably correct, God-given notation of the hedonistic

---

2 For example Marshall (1890, p. 1) wrote in his *Principles:* "Political Economy or Economics is the study of mankind in the ordinary business of life; it examines that part of individual and social action which is most closely connected with the attainment and with the use of the material requisites of wellbeing." In a once influential text, Cannan (1888, p. 1) wrote: "The aim of Political Economy is the explanation of the general causes on which the wealth or material welfare of human beings depends."

calculus" (p. 521). In other words, by reducing explanations universally to the utilitarian calculus, marginal-utility theory fails to acknowledge the historically specific features of such institutions as property.

Instead, for Veblen, pecuniary institutions "induce pecuniary habits of thought which affect men's discrimination outside of pecuniary matters ... the price system visibly dominates the modern community's thinking in matters that lie outside the economic interest" (p. 522). Money, in particular, is more than "a convenient method by which to procure the pleasurable sensations of consumption" (p. 522). Particularly in business, money is an end in itself, and this gives rise to the whole machinery of credit and speculation. If, by contrast, utility is the centerpiece of the analysis of human motivation, important historically specific institutional factors are neglected, particularly property, money and modern business institutions.

Neoclassical theory treats money as "an expedient of computation" (p. 523). This defect is not remedied, even with later developments in neoclassical theory, including general equilibrium analysis.[3] Veblen further observes that a similar reduction of monetary phenomena – such as investment, borrowing, and credit – to the utilitarian calculus overlooks "the run of the facts in modern business" (p. 523). The whole money economy is treated as if it were equivalent to a "refined system of barter." Instead, Veblen argues, "a theoretical account of the phenomena of this life must be drawn in these terms in which the phenomena occur": they must incorporate the real institutions of a money-driven economy (p. 524).

Selection 37 is one of a few essays that Veblen wrote in his lifetime on biological anthropology and the evolution of human races. (See also Veblen 1913b, 1934a.) In the past these have been ignored or even dismissed as "racist." This accusation is rebutted in a footnote in the General Introduction to this volume. And it should be pointed out that Veblen (1934a) has a brilliant and witty attack on eugenics. The Veblen (1913b) essay is reprinted in *The Place of Science* collection (Veblen 1919j).

Part of the interest in Selection 37 is that it shows that Veblen (at least until the First World War) kept up to date with developments in biology. In 1901 the Dutch biologist Hugo De Vries published *Die Mutationstheorie* in German (De Vries 1901, 1909). He noted the forgotten genetic discoveries of Gregor Mendel and proposed his own "mutation theory." This work caused a big stir, and was welcomed with enthusiasm by Veblen's Chicago colleague, Jacques Loeb. The rediscovery of Mendelian genetics eventually led to the modern neo-Darwinian synthesis in biology and the victory of the Darwinians over the Lamarckians. But this did not occur until the 1940s,

---

3 As Frank Hahn (1988, p. 972) put it: "monetary theory cannot simply be grafted on to Walrasian theory with minor modifications." And as Stephen Horwitz (1992, p. 15) remarked: "the properties of real-world moneys throw a monkey wrench into the neoclassical theory of economic exchange."

long after Veblen's death. Three years after De Vries, Veblen (1904b, p. 342 [in this volume]) first mentioned the concept of mutation. He was to use the term, and refer to Mendel, several times in his later works.[4] In 1910 – a year after the publication of the English translation of De Vries's book – Veblen started work on this paper that explicitly incorporated some of De Vries's ideas (Dorfman 1934, p. 295). For these reasons alone, Selection 37 is worthy of consideration.

Like most biologists of his time – but unlike few biologists today – Veblen regards the Mendelian theory and Darwinism as "incompatible" or "incongruous" explanations in the biological sphere (p. 525). But Veblen ducks this issue by focusing on the matter of cultural evolution. Although he regards (what came to be called as) genetic evolution as important, Veblen insists that "questions of cultural origins and relationship are necessarily drawn into the inquiry" (p. 526).

Veblen (pp. 527–30) emphasizes the climatic changes, and the advances and retreats of ice, that played a part in the evolution of European races since the previous interglacial period. Many of the details of Veblen's account, including the classification of races and the migrations involved, are now challenged by modern scholarship based on DNA, linguistic, archaeological, and other evidence (Cavalli-Sforza 2000, Wells 2002, Dunbar 2004, Oppenheimer 2004, Klein 2009). But in a sentence of enormous prescience, Veblen writes (p. 528):

> A considerable climatic change, such as would seriously alter the conditions of life either directly or through its effect on the food supply, might be conceived to bring on a mutating state in the race; or the like effect might be induced by a profound cultural change, particularly any such change in the industrial arts as would radically affect the material conditions of life.

Veblen thus argues that climate change has driven cultural and technological evolution. The idea that climate change is a major factor in human cultural evolution has re-emerged in recent years (Potts 1996, Richerson *et al.*, 2001, Calvin 2002). Veblen's argument is similar to these latter-day theorists: rapid climate change gave the advantage to cultures that were more flexible and adaptable.

---

4 Veblen (1913a, pp. 525, 527, 532, 535 [in this volume]; 1914, pp. 544–45, 548–49 [in this volume]; 1915a, pp. 277–78; 1925, p. 51) repeatedly referred to Mendelian theory. The word "mutation" appears in Veblen (1904b, p. 342 [in this volume]; 1908d, 484 [in this volume]; 1909c, pp. 518–19 [in this volume]; 1910, p. 171; 1913a, pp. 525–31; 1914, 545, 547–48 [in this volume]; 1919b, pp. 5, 40, 57). Although several of the Veblen (1913a) references refer to genetic mutations, in almost all other cases "mutation" is used to refer to changes in habits, institutions or technology.

By referring to De Vries, Veblen (pp. 530–36) also considers mutations that we would today describe as genetic. Veblen's conjecture is that human intermixing and hybridization has proved more conducive to survival than racial purity. Hence Veblen strongly counters eugenic and other injunctions concerning racial purity that were tragically gaining ground at that time.

But a defect of this essay is Veblen's failure to distinguish clearly between the processes of evolution at the biological and cultural levels, and thereby consider how evolution at one level may influence evolution on another. He applies the term "mutation" to both levels, without always making his meaning clear. His treatment of these issues is much more satisfactory in the book from which the following selection is taken.

Selection 38 consists of the preface, the first chapter, and part of the second chapter of one of Veblen's most important books. His *Instinct of Workmanship* was planned as early as 1900, and five of its seven long chapters were probably drafted by 1911 (Dorfman 1934, p. 197, Jorgensen and Jorgensen 1999, pp. 140, 207).

Veblen states in the preface that the aim of the book is to analyze the "correlation … between industrial use and wont and those other institutional facts that go to make up any given phase of civilisation." While upholding that technology is "fundamental and definitive" in the "growth of culture," the causality is not unidirectional because institutions and conventions "in their turn react on the state of the industrial arts" (p. 537).

But the achievement of the book goes beyond this. It is by far the most important statement by Veblen of his views on human psychology. Influenced by the psychology of William James (1890) and others, Veblen retains the term "instinct" in the title of this work. By this, both James and Veblen mean a biologically inherited behavioral disposition. But Veblen is aware that the concept had come under attack and was declining in popularity. It was not until the 1960s and 1970s that the concept was rehabilitated (Degler 1991). Veblen wryly notes that skepticism of instinct involved less consideration of any "innate propensity or predisposition" and more of the psychological "elements" of "behavior" (p. 538). He thus warns of the rise of behaviorism, and its focus on behavior rather than dispositions.[5] When the concept of instinct is no longer defined as a disposition and misleadingly treated as an element of behavior, immense definitional and other problems arise, including the conceptual separation of cultural and genetic influences. But when we return to the question of innate, biologically inherited propensities or predispositions, the original Jamesian concept of instinct returns to its effective role.

---

5 Behaviorism had its first manifesto in Watson's (1914) work. By 1919 it "took on the dimensions of an intellectual revolution" (Kallen 1930, p. 497). This radical shift of opinion among psychologists led most institutionalists to abandon Veblen's Jamesian legacy by the 1930s (Hodgson 2004).

For Veblen, the two most important instincts are the "instinct of work-manship" and the "parental bent." His primary focus in this volume is clearly the former. Veblen (1914, pp. 85–86) also refers to "idle curiosity" as an instinct. He distinguishes instincts from tropisms, by emphasizing the intelligent and purposeful character of instinct. He argues that instincts are translated into behavior through the medium of habits, which are prompted by instincts but modified by contingent cultural and institutional circumstances. In this way the instincts become "contaminated." Accordingly, for example, a society with strong religious institutions and coercive government "will have its industrial organisation and its industrial arts fashioned to meet the demands and the logic of these institutions" (p. 559). Veblen takes us through a number of examples of such "contamination."

Selection 32

Professor Clark's economics

Source: *Quarterly Journal of Economics*, February 1908
(vol. 22, pp. 147–95).

Veblen (1908a)

Summary

Professor Clark's commanding position, 410–12. – Harmless misinformation as to primitive man, 412–14. – Significance of the accumulated experience of mankind overlooked, 414–16. – The classical school and Clark are alike hedonistic, utilitarian, taxonomic, 416–18. – His doctrine as to capital and capital goods, 419–22. – Natural distribution, final productivity, and effective utility, 422–26. – The supposition of consumer's surplus vitiates that of reward according to productivity, 426–28. – Consistently, monopolists also must be admitted to get rewards based on effective utility and so on "natural" law, 428–32. – The legislation proposed by Clark as to monopoly not related to his theoretic principles, 432–34. – How far any surplus of utility over disutility can be consistently reasoned out, 434–36. – Consumer's surplus and producer's surplus vanish on close examination, 437–39. – Conclusion, 439–40.

For some time past economists have been looking with lively anticipation for such a comprehensive statement of Mr. Clark's doctrines as is now offered. The leading purpose of the present volume[1] is "to offer a brief and provi- [148] sional statement of the more general laws of progress": although it also comprises a more abridged restatement of the laws of "Economic Statics" already set forth in fuller form in his *Distribution of Wealth*. Though brief, this treatise is to be taken as systematically complete, as including in due correlation all the "essentials" of Mr. Clark's theoretical system. As such, its publication is an event of unusual interest and consequence.

   Mr. Clark's position among this generation of economists is a notable and commanding one. No serious student of economic theory will, or can afford to, forego a pretty full acquaintance with his development of doctrines. Nor will any such student avoid being greatly influenced by the position which Mr. Clark takes on any point of theory on which he may speak, and many

---

1 *The Essentials of Economic Theory, as Applied to Modern Problems of Industry and Public Policy.* By John Bates Clark. New York: The Macmillan Company, 1907.

look confidently to him for guidance where it is most needed. Very few of those interested in modern theory are under no obligations to him. He has, at the same time, in a singular degree the gift of engaging the affections as well as the attention of students in his field. Yet the critic is required to speak impersonally of Mr. Clark's work as a phase of current economic theory.

In more than one respect Mr. Clark's position among economists recalls the great figures in the science a hundred years ago. There is the same rigid grasp of the principles, the "essentials," out of which the broad theorems of the system follow in due sequence and correlation; and like the leaders of the classical era, while Mr. Clark is always a theoretician, never to be diverted into an inconsistent makeshift, he is moved by an alert and sympathetic interest in current practical problems. While his aim is a theoretical one, it is always with a view to the theory of current affairs; and his speculations are animated with a large sympathy and an aggressive interest in the amelioration of the lot of man. [149]

His relation to the ancient adepts of the science, however, is something more substantial than a resemblance only. He is, by spiritual consanguinity, a representative of that classical school of thought that dominated the science through the better part of the nineteenth century. This is peculiarly true of Mr. Clark, as contrasted with many of those contemporaries who have fought for the marginal-utility doctrines. Unlike these spokesmen of the Austrian wing, he has had the insight and courage to see the continuity between the classical position and his own, even where he advocates drastic changes in the classical body of doctrines. And although his system of theory embodies substantially all that the consensus of theorists approves in the Austrian contributions to the science, yet he has arrived at his position on these heads not under the guidance of the Austrian school, but, avowedly, by an unbroken development out of the position given by the older generation of economists.[2] Again, in the matter of the psychological postulates of the science, he accepts a hedonism as simple, unaffected, and uncritical as that of Jevons or of James Mill. In this respect his work is as true to the canons of the classical school as the best work of the theoreticians of the Austrian observance. There is the like unhesitating appeal to the calculus of pleasure and pain as the indefeasible ground of action and solvent of perplexities, and there is the like readiness to reduce all phenomena to terms of a "normal," or "natural," scheme of life constructed on the basis of this hedonistic calculus. Even in the ready recourse to "conjectural history," to use Steuart's phrase, Mr. Clark's work is at one with both the early classical and the late (Jevons–Austrian) marginal-utility school. It has the virtues of both, coupled with the graver shortcomings of both. But, as his view exceeds theirs in breadth and generosity, [150] so his system of theory is a more competent expression of current economic science than what is offered by the spokesmen of the

2 Cf., e.g., [John Bates Clark,] *Distribution of Wealth*, p. 376, note.

Jevons–Austrian wing. It is as such, as a competent and consistent system of current economic theory, that it is here intended to discuss Mr. Clark's work, not as a body of doctrines peculiar to Mr. Clark or divergent from the main current.

Since hedonism came to rule economic science, the science has been in the main a theory of distribution, – distribution of ownership and of income. This is true both of the classical school and of those theorists who have taken an attitude of ostensible antagonism to the classical school. The exceptions to the rule are late and comparatively few, and they are not found among the economists who accept the hedonistic postulate as their point of departure. And, consistently with the spirit of hedonism, this theory of distribution has centered about a doctrine of exchange value (or price) and has worked out its scheme of (normal) distribution in terms of (normal) price. The normal economic community, upon which theoretical interest has converged, is a business community, which centers about the market, and whose scheme of life is a scheme of profit and loss. Even when some considerable attention is ostensibly devoted to theories of consumption and production, in these systems of doctrine the theories are constructed in terms of ownership, price, and acquisition, and so reduce themselves in substance to doctrines of distributive acquisition.[3] In this respect Mr. Clark's work is true to the received canons. The "Essentials of Economic Theory" are the essentials of the hedonistic theory of distribution, with sundry reflections on related topics. The scope of Mr. Clark's economics, indeed, is [151] even more closely limited by concepts of distribution than many others, since he persistently analyses production in terms of value, and value is a concept of distribution.

As Mr. Clark justly observes (p. 4), "The primitive and general facts concerning industry ... need to be known before the social facts can profitably be studied." In these early pages of the treatise, as in other works of its class, there is repeated reference to that more primitive and simple scheme of economic life out of which the modern complex scheme has developed, and it is repeatedly indicated that in order to an understanding of the play of forces in the more advanced stages of economic development and complication, it is necessary to apprehend these forces in their unsophisticated form as they work out in the simple scheme prevalent on the plane of primitive life. Indeed, to a reader not well acquainted with Mr. Clark's scope and method of economic theorizing, these early pages would suggest that he is preparing for something in the way of a genetic study, – a study of economic institutions approached from the side of their origins. It looks as if the intended line of

---

3 See, e.g., J. S. Mill, *Political Economy*, Book I; Marshall, *Principles of Economics*, Vol. I, Books II–V.

approach to the modern situation might be such as an evolutionist would choose, who would set out with showing what forces are at work in the primitive economic community, and then trace the cumulative growth and complication of these factors as they presently take form in the institutions of a later phase of the development. Such, however, is not Mr. Clark's intention. The effect of his recourse to "primitive life" is simply to throw into the foreground, in a highly unreal perspective, those features which lend themselves to interpretation in terms of the normalized competitive system. The best excuse that can be offered for these excursions into "primitive life" is that they have substantially nothing to do with the main argument [152] of the book, being of the nature of harmless and graceful misinformation.

In the primitive economic situation – that is to say, in savagery and the lower barbarism – there is, of course, no "solitary hunter," living either in a cave or otherwise, and there is no man who "makes by his own labor all the goods that he uses," etc. It is, in effect, a highly meretricious misrepresentation to speak in this connection of "the economy of a man who works only for himself," and say that "the inherent productive power of labor and capital is of vital concern to him," because such a presentation of the matter overlooks the main facts in the case in order to put the emphasis on a feature which is of negligible consequence. There is no reasonable doubt but that, at least since mankind reached the human plane, the economic unit has been not a "solitary hunter," but a community of some kind; in which, by the way, women seem in the early stages to have been the most consequential factor instead of the man who works for himself. The "capital" possessed by such a community – as, *e.g.*, a band of California "Digger" Indians – was a negligible quantity, more valuable to a collector of curios than to any one else, and the loss of which to the "Digger" squaws would mean very little. What was of "vital concern" to them, indeed, what the life of the group depended on absolutely, was the accumulated wisdom of the squaws, the technology of their economic situation.[4] The loss of the basket, digging-stick, and mortar, simply as physical objects, would have signified little, but the conceivable loss of the squaw's knowledge of the soil and seasons, of food and fiber plants, and of mechanical expedients, would have meant the present dispersal and starvation of the community.

This may seem like taking Mr. Clark to task for an [153] inconsequential gap in his general information on Digger Indians, Eskimos, and paleolithic society at large. But the point raised is not of negligible consequence for economic theory, particularly not for any theory of "economic dynamics" that turns in great part about questions of capital and its uses at different stages of economic development. In the primitive culture the quantity and the value of mechanical appliances is relatively slight; and whether the group is actually possessed of more or less of such appliances at a given time is not a question of first-rate importance. The loss of these objects – tangible assets – would

4 Cf., e.g., such an account as Barrows, *Ethno-botany of the Coahuilla Indians.*

entail a transient inconvenience. But the accumulated, habitual knowledge of the ways and means involved in the production and use of these appliances is the outcome of long experience and experimentation; and, given this body of commonplace technological information, the acquisition and employment of the suitable apparatus is easily arranged. The great body of commonplace knowledge made use of in industry is the product and heritage of the group. In its essentials it is known by common notoriety, and the "capital goods" needed for putting this commonplace technological knowledge to use are a slight matter, – practically within the reach of every one. Under these circumstances the ownership of "capital-goods" has no great significance, and, as a practical fact, interest and wages are unknown, and the "earning power of capital" is not seen to be "governed by a specific power of productivity which resides in capital-goods." But the situation changes, presently, by what is called an advance "in the industrial arts." The "capital" required to put the commonplace knowledge to effect grows larger, and so its acquisition becomes an increasingly difficult matter. Through "difficulty of attainment" in adequate quantities, the apparatus and its ownership become a matter of consequence; increasingly so, until [154] presently the equipment required for an effective pursuit of industry comes to be greater than the common man can hope to acquire in a lifetime. The commonplace knowledge of ways and means, the accumulated experience of mankind, is still transmitted in and by the body of the community at large; but, for practical purposes, the advanced "state of the industrial arts" has enabled the owners of goods to corner the wisdom of the ancients and the accumulated experience of the race. Hence "capital," as it stands at that phase of the institution's growth contemplated by Mr. Clark.

The "natural" system of free competition, or, as it was once called, "the obvious and simple system of natural liberty," is accordingly a phase of the development of the institution of capital; and its claim to immutable dominion is evidently as good as the like claim of any other phase of cultural growth. The equity, or "natural justice," claimed for it is evidently just and equitable only in so far as the conventions of ownership on which it rests continue to be a secure integral part of the institutional furniture of the community; that is to say, so long as these conventions are part and parcel of the habits of thought of the community; that is to say, so long as these things are currently held to be just and equitable. This normalized present, or "natural," state of Mr. Clark, is, as near as may be, Senior's "Natural State of Man," – the hypothetically perfect competitive system; and economic theory consists in the definition and classification of the phenomena of economic life in terms of this hypothetical competitive system.

Taken by itself, Mr. Clark's dealing with the past development might be passed over with slight comment, except for its negative significance, since it has no theoretical connection with the present, or even with the "natural" state in which the phenomena of economic life [155] are assumed to arrange themselves in a stable, normal scheme. But his dealings with the future, and with the present in so far as the present situation is conceived to comprise "dynamic" factors, is of substantially the same kind. With Senior's "natural state of man" as the baseline of normality in things economic, questions of present and future development are treated as questions of departure from the normal, aberrations and excesses which the theory does not aim even to account for. What is offered in place of theoretical inquiry when these "positive perversions of the natural forces themselves" are taken up (*e.g.*, in chapters xxii.–xxix.) is an exposition of the corrections that must be made to bring the situation back to the normal static state, and solicitous advice as to what measures are to be taken with a view to this beneficent end. The problem presented to Mr. Clark by the current phenomena of economic development is: how can it be stopped? or, failing that, how can it be guided and minimized? Nowhere is there a sustained inquiry into the dynamic character of the changes that have brought the present (deplorable) situation to pass, nor into the nature and trend of the forces at work in the development that is going forward in this situation. None of this is covered by Mr. Clark's use of the word "dynamic." All that it covers in the way of theory (chapters xii.–xxi.) is a speculative inquiry as to how the equilibrium re-established itself when one or more of the quantities involved increases or decreases. Other than quantitative changes are not noticed, except as provocations to homiletic discourse. Not even the causes and the scope of the quantitative changes that may take place in the variables are allowed to fall within the scope of the theory of economic dynamics.

So much of the volume, then, and of the system of doctrines of which the volume is an exposition, as is [156] comprised in the later eight chapters (pp. 372–554), is an exposition of grievances and remedies, with only sporadic intrusions of theoretical matter, and does not properly constitute a part of the theory, whether static or dynamic. There is no intention here to take exception to Mr. Clark's outspoken attitude of disapproval toward certain features of the current business situation or to quarrel with the remedial measures which he thinks proper and necessary. This phase of his work is spoken of here rather to call attention to the temperate but uncompromising tone of Mr. Clark's writings as a spokesman for the competitive system, considered as an element in the Order of Nature, and to note the fact that this is not economic theory.[5]

---

5 What would be the scientific rating of the work of a botanist who should spend his energy in devising ways and means to neutralize the ecological variability of plants, or of a physiologist who conceived it the end of his scientific endeavors to rehabilitate the vermiform appendix or the pineal eye, or to denounce and penalize the imitative coloring of the Viceroy butterfly? What scientific interest would attach to the matter if Mr. Loeb, *e.g.*, should devote a few score pages to canvassing the moral responsibilities incurred by him in his parental relation to his parthenogenetically developed sea-urchin eggs?

Those phenomena which Mr. Clark characterizes as "positive perversions" may be distasteful and troublesome, perhaps, but "the economic necessity of doing what is legally difficult" is not of the "essentials of theory."

The theoretical section specifically scheduled as Economic Dynamics (chapters xii.–xxi.), on the other hand, is properly to be included under the caption of Statics. As already remarked above, it presents a theory of equilibrium between variables. Mr. Clark is, indeed, barred out by his premises from any but a statical development of theory. To realize the substantially statical character of his Dynamics, it is only necessary to turn to his chapter xii. (Economic Dynamics). "A highly dynamic condition, then, is one in which the economic organism changes rapidly and yet, at any time in the course of its changes, is relatively near to a certain static model" (p. 196). "The actual shape of society at any one time is not the static model of that time; but it tends to conform to it; and in a very dynamic society is more nearly like it [157] than it would be in one in which the forces of change are less active" (p. 197). The more "dynamic" the society, the nearer it is to the static model; until in an ideally dynamic society, with a frictionless competitive system, to use Mr. Clark's figure, the static state would be attained, except for an increase in size, – that is to say, the ideally perfect "dynamic" state would coincide with the "static" state. Mr. Clark's conception of a dynamic state reduces itself to a conception of an imperfectly static state, but in such a sense that the more highly and truly "dynamic" condition is thereby the nearer to a static condition. Neither the static nor the dynamic state, in Mr. Clark's view, it should be remarked, is a state of quiescence. Both are states of more or less intense activity, the essential difference being that in the static state the activity goes on in perfection, without lag, leak, or friction; the movement of parts being so perfect as not to disturb the equilibrium. The static state is the more "dynamic" of the two. The "dynamic" condition is essentially a deranged static condition: whereas the static state is the absolute perfect, "natural" taxonomic norm of competitive life. This dynamic-static state may vary in respect of the magnitude of the several factors which hold one another in equilibrium, but these are none other than quantitative variations. The changes which Mr. Clark discusses under the head of dynamics are all of this character, – changes in absolute or relative magnitude of the several factors comprised in the equation.

But, not to quarrel with Mr. Clark's use of the term "static" and "dynamic," it is in place to inquire into the merits of this class of economic science apart from any adventitious shortcomings. For such an inquiry Mr. Clark's work offers peculiar advantages. It is lucid, concise, and unequivocal, with no temporizing euphemisms [158] and no politic affectations of sentiment. Mr. Clark's premises, and therewith the aim of his inquiry, are the standard ones of the classical English school (including the Jevons–Austrian wing). This school of economics stands on the pre-evolutionary ground of normality and "natural law," which the great body of theoretical science occupied in the early nineteenth century. It is like the other theoretical sciences that grew out of the rationalistic and humanitarian conceptions of the eighteenth century in that its theoretical aim is taxonomy – definition and classification – with the purpose of subsuming its data under a rational scheme of categories which are presumed to make up the Order of Nature. This Order of Nature, or realm of Natural Law, is not the actual run of material facts, but the facts so interpreted as to meet the needs of the taxonomist in point of taste, logical consistency, and sense of justice. The question of the truth and adequacy of the categories is a question as to the consensus of taste and predilection among the taxonomists; *i.e.*, they are an expression of trained human nature touching the matter of what ought to be. The facts so interpreted make up the "normal," or "natural," scheme of things, with which the theorist has to do. His task is to bring facts within the framework of this scheme of "natural" categories. Coupled with this scientific purpose of the taxonomic economist is the pragmatic purpose of finding and advocating the expedient course of policy. On this latter head, again, Mr. Clark is true to the animus of the school.

The classical school, including Mr. Clark and his contemporary associates in the science, is hedonistic and utilitarian – hedonistic in its theory and utilitarian in its pragmatic ideals and endeavors. The hedonistic postulates on which this line of economic theory is built up are of a statical scope and character, and nothing but [159] statical theory (taxonomy) comes out of their development.[6] These postulates, and the theorems drawn from them, take account of none but quantitative variations, and quantitative variation alone does not give rise to cumulative change, which proceeds on changes in kind.

Economics of the line represented at its best by Mr. Clark has never entered this field of cumulative change. It does not approach questions of the class which occupy the modern sciences, – that is to say, questions of genesis, growth, variation, process (in short, questions of a dynamic import), – but confines its interest to the definition and classification of a mechanically limited range of phenomena. Like other taxonomic sciences, hedonistic economics does not, and cannot, deal with phenomena of growth except so far as growth is taken in the quantitative sense of a variation in magnitude, bulk, mass, number, frequency. In its work of taxonomy this economics has consistently bound itself, as Mr. Clark does, by distinctions of a mechanical, statistical nature, and has drawn its categories of classification on those grounds. Concretely, it is confined, in substance, to the determination of and refinements upon the concepts of land, labor, and capital, as handed down by the great economists of the classical era, and the correlate concepts of rent,

6 It is a notable fact that even the genius of Herbert Spencer could extract nothing but taxonomy from his hedonistic postulates; *e.g.*, his *Social Statics*. Spencer is both evolutionist and hedonist, but it is only by recourse to other factors, alien to the rational hedonistic scheme, such as habit, delusions, use and disuse, sporadic variation, environmental forces, that he is able to achieve anything in the way of genetic science, since it is only by this recourse that he is enabled to enter the field of cumulative change within which the modern post-Darwinian sciences live and move and have their being.

wages, interest and profits. Solicitously, with a painfully meticulous circumspection, the normal, mechanical metes and bounds of these several concepts are worked out, the touchstone of the absolute truth aimed at being the hedonistic calculus. The facts of use and wont are not of the essence of this mechanical refinement. These several categories [160] are mutually exclusive categories, mechanically speaking. The circumstance that the phenomena covered by them are not mechanical facts is not allowed to disturb the pursuit of mechanical distinctions among them. They nowhere overlap, and at the same time between them they cover all the facts with which this economic taxonomy is concerned. Indeed, they are in logical consistency, required to cover them. They are hedonistically "natural" categories of such taxonomic force that their elemental lines of cleavage run through the facts of any given economic situation, regardless of use and wont, even where the situation does not permit these lines of cleavage to be seen by men and recognized by use and wont; so that, *e.g.*, a gang of Aleutian Islanders slushing about in the wrack and surf with rakes and magical incantations for the capture of shell-fish are held, in point of taxonomic reality, to be engaged on a feat of hedonistic equilibration in rent, wages, and interest. And that is all there is to it. Indeed, for economic theory of this kind, that is all there is to any economic situation. The hedonistic magnitudes vary from one situation to another, but, except for variations in the arithmetical details of the hedonistic balance, all situations are, in point of economic theory, substantially alike.[7]

Taking this unfaltering taxonomy on its own recognizances, let us follow the trail somewhat more into the arithmetical details, as it leads along the narrow ridge of rational calculation, above the tree-tops, on the levels of clear sunlight and moonshine. For the purpose in [161] hand – to bring out the character of this current economic science as a working theory of current facts, and more particularly "as applied to modern problems of industry and public policy" (title-page) – the sequence to be observed in questioning the several sections into which the theoretical structure falls is not essential. The structure of classical theory is familiar to all students, and – Mr. Clark's redaction offers no serious departure from the conventional lines. Such divergence from conventional lines as may occur is a matter of details, commonly of improvements in detail; and the revisions of detail do not stand in such an organic relation to one another, nor do they support and strengthen one another in such a manner, as to suggest anything like a revolutionary trend or a breaking away from the conventional lines.

7 "The capital-goods have to be taken unit by unit if their value for productive purposes is to be rightly gauged. A part of a supply of potatoes is traceable to the hoes that dig them. ... We endeavor simply to ascertain how badly the loss of one hoe would affect us or how much good the restoration of it would do us. This truth, like the foregoing ones, has a universal application in economics; for primitive men as well as civilized ones must estimate the specific productivity of the tools that they use," etc., [*The Essentials of Economic Theory*], p. 43.

So as regards Mr. Clark's doctrine of Capital. It does not differ substantially from the doctrines which are gaining currency at the hands of such writers as Mr. Fisher or Mr. Fetter; although there are certain formal distinctions peculiar to Mr. Clark's exposition of the "Capital Concept." But these peculiarities are peculiarities of the method of arriving at the concept rather than peculiarities substantial to the concept itself. The main discussion of the nature of capital is contained in chapter ii. (Varieties of Economic Goods). The conception of capital here set forth is of fundamental consequence to the system, partly because of the important place assigned capital in this system of theory, partly because of the importance which the conception of capital must have in any theory that is to deal with problems of the current (capitalistic) situation. Several classes of capital-goods are enumerated, but it appears that in Mr. Clark's apprehension – at variance with Mr. Fisher's view – persons are not to be included among the items of capital. It is also clear from the run of the argument, [162] though not explicitly stated, that only material, tangible, mechanically definable articles of wealth go to make up capital. In current usage, in the business community, "capital" is a pecuniary concept, of course, and is not definable in mechanical terms; but Mr. Clark, true to the hedonistic taxonomy, sticks by the test of mechanical demarcation and draws the lines of his category on physical grounds; whereby it happens that any pecuniary conception of capital is out of the question. Intangible assets, or immaterial wealth, have no place in the theory; and Mr. Clark is exceptionally subtle and consistent in avoiding such modern notions. One gets the impression that such a notion as intangible assets is conceived to be too chimerical to merit attention, even by way of protest or refutation.

Here, as elsewhere in Mr. Clark's writings, much is made of the doctrine that the two facts of "capital" and "capital-goods" are conceptually distinct, though substantially identical. The two terms cover virtually the same facts as would be covered by the terms "pecuniary capital" and "industrial equipment." They are for all ordinary purposes coincident with Mr. Fisher's terms, "capital value" and "capital," although Mr. Clark might enter a technical protest against identifying his categories with those employed by Mr. Fisher.[8] "Capital is this permanent fund of productive goods, the identity of whose component elements is forever changing. Capital-goods are the shifting component parts of this permanent aggregate" (p. 29). Mr. Clark admits (pp. 29–33) that capital is colloquially spoken and thought of in terms of value, but he insists that in point of substantial fact the working concept of capital is (should be) that of "a fund of productive goods," considered as an "abiding entity." The phrase itself, "a fund of productive goods," is a [163] curiously confusing mixture of pecuniary and mechanical terms, though the

8 Cf. a criticism of Mr. Fisher's conception in the *Political Science Quarterly* for February, 1908. [Selection 35 in this volume.]

pecuniary expression, "a fund," is probably to be taken in this connection as a permissible metaphor.

This conception of capital, as a physically "abiding entity" constituted by the succession of productive goods that make up the industrial equipment, breaks down in Mr. Clark's own use of it when he comes (pp. 37–38) to speak of the mobility of capital; that is to say, so soon as he makes use of it. A single illustration of this will have to suffice, though there are several points in his argument where the frailty of the conception is patent enough. "The transfer of capital from one industry to another is a dynamic phenomenon which is later to be considered. What is here important is the fact that it is in the main accomplished without entailing transfers of capital-goods. An instrument wears itself out in one industry, and instead of being succeeded by a like instrument in the same industry, it is succeeded by one of a different kind which is used in a different branch of production" (p. 38), – illustrated on the preceding page by a shifting of investment from a whaling-ship to a cotton-mill. In all this it is plain that the "transfer of capital" contemplated is a shifting of investment, and that it is, as indeed Mr. Clark indicates, not a matter of the mechanical shifting of physical bodies from one industry to the other. To speak of a transfer of "capital" which does not involve a transfer of "capital-goods" is a contradiction of the main position, that capital is made up of "capital-goods." The continuum in which the "abiding entity" of capital resides is a continuity of ownership, not a physical fact. The continuity, in fact, is of an immaterial nature, a matter of legal rights, of contract, of purchase and sale. Just why this patent state of the case is overlooked, as it somewhat elaborately is, is not easily seen. But it is plain that, if the concept [164] of capital were elaborated from observation of current business practice, it would be found that "capital" is a pecuniary fact, not a mechanical one; that it is an outcome of a valuation, depending immediately on the state of mind of the valuers; and that the specific marks of capital, by which it is distinguishable from other facts, are of an immaterial character. This would, of course, lead, directly, to the admission of intangible assets; and this, in turn, would upset the law of the "natural" remuneration of labor and capital to which Mr. Clark's argument looks forward from the start. It would also bring in the "unnatural" phenomena of monopoly as a normal outgrowth of business enterprise.

There is a further logical discrepancy avoided by resorting to the alleged facts of primitive industry, when there was no capital, for the elements out of which to construct a capital concept, instead of going to the current business situation. In a hedonistic-utilitarian scheme of economic doctrine, such as Mr. Clark's, only physically productive agencies can be admitted as efficient factors in production or as legitimate claimants to a share in distribution. Hence capital, one of the prime factors in production and the central claimant in the current scheme of distribution, must be defined in physical terms and delimited by mechanical distinctions. This is necessary for reasons which appear in the succeeding chapter, on The Measure of Consumers' Wealth.

On the same page (38), and elsewhere, it is remarked that "business disasters" destroy capital in part. The destruction in question is a matter of values; that is to say, a lowering of valuation, not in any appreciable degree a destruction of material goods. Taken as a physical aggregate, capital does not appreciably decrease through business disasters, but, taken as a fact of ownership and counted in standard units of value, it decreases; there is [165] a destruction of values and a shifting of ownership, a loss of ownership perhaps; but these are pecuniary phenomena, of an immaterial character, and so do not directly affect the material aggregate of the industrial equipment. Similarly, the discussion (pp. 301–14) of how changes of method, as, *e.g.*, labor-saving devices, "liberate capital," and at times "destroy" capital, is intelligible only on the admission that "capital" here is a matter of values owned by investors and is not employed as a synonym for industrial appliances. The appliances in question are neither liberated nor destroyed in the changes contemplated. And it will not do to say that the aggregate of "productive goods" suffers a diminution by a substitution of devices which increases its aggregate productiveness, as is implied, *e.g.*, by the passage on page 307,[9] if Mr. Clark's definition of capital is strictly adhered to. This very singular passage (pp. 306–11, under the captions, Hardships entailed on Capitalists by Progress, and the Offset for Capital destroyed by Changes of Method) implies that the aggregate of appliances of production is decreased by a change which increases the aggregate of these articles in that respect (productivity) by virtue of which they are counted in the aggregate. The argument will hold good if "productive goods" are rated by bulk, weight, number, or some such irrelevant test, instead of by their productivity or by their consequent capitalized value. On such a showing it should be proper to say that the polishing of plowshares before they are sent out from the factory diminishes the amount of capital embodied in plowshares by as much as the weight or bulk [166] of the waste material removed from the shares in polishing them.

Several things may be said of the facts discussed in this passage. There is, presumably, a decrease, in bulk, weight, or number, of the appliances that make up the industrial equipment at the time when such a technological change as is contemplated takes place. This change, presumably, increases the productive efficiency of the equipment as a whole, and so may be said without hesitation to increase the equipment as a factor of production, while it may decrease it, considered as a mechanical magnitude. The owners of the obsolete or obsolescent appliances presumably suffer a diminution of their capital,

---

9 "The machine itself is often a hopeless specialist. It can do one minute thing and that only, and when a new and better device appears for doing that one thing, the machine has to go, and not to some new employment, but to the junk heap. There is thus taking place a considerable waste of capital in consequence of mechanical and other progress." "Indeed, a quick throwing away of instruments which have barely begun to do their work is often the secret of the success of an enterprising manager, but it entails a destruction of capital."

whether they discard the obsolete appliances or not. The owners of the new appliances, or rather those who own and are able to capitalize the new technological expedients, presumably gain a corresponding advantage, which may take the form of an increase of the effective capitalization of their outfit, as would then be shown by an increased market value of their plant. The largest theoretical outcome of the supposed changes, for an economist not bound by Mr. Clark's conception of capital, should be the generalization that industrial capital – capital considered as a productive agent – is substantially a capitalization of technological expedients, and that a given capital invested in industrial equipment is measured by the portion of technological expedients whose usufruct the investment appropriates. It would accordingly appear that the substantial core of all capital is immaterial wealth, and that the material objects which are formally the subject of the capitalist's ownership are, by comparison, a transient and adventitious matter. But if such a view were accepted, even with extreme reservations, Mr. Clark's scheme of the "natural" distribution of incomes between capital and labor would "go up in the air," as the colloquial [167] phrase has it. It would be extremely difficult to determine what share of the value of the joint product of capital and labor should, under a rule of "natural" equity, go to the capitalist as an equitable return for his monopolization of a given portion of the intangible assets of the community at large.[10] The returns actually accruing to him under competitive conditions would be a measure of the differential advantage held by him by virtue of his having become legally seized of the material contrivances by which the technological achievements of the community are put into effect.

Yet, if in this way capital were apprehended as "an historical category," as Rodbertus would say, there is at least the comfort in it all that it should leave a free field for Mr. Clark's measures of repression as applied to the discretionary management of capital by the makers of trusts. And yet, again, this comforting reflection is coupled with the ugly accompaniment that by the same move the field would be left equally free of moral obstructions to the extreme proposals of the socialists. A safe and sane course for the quietist in these premises should apparently be to discard the equivocal doctrines of the passage (pp. 306–11) from which this train of questions arises, and hold fast to the received dogma, however unworkable, that "capital" is a congeries of physical objects with no ramifications or complications of an immaterial kind, and to avoid all recourse to the concept of value, or price, in discussing matters of modern business.

The center of interest and of theoretical force and validity in Mr. Clark's work is his law of "natural" distribution. Upon this law hangs very much of the

---

10 The position of the laborer and his wages, in this light, would not be substantially different from that of the capitalist and his interest. Labor is no more possible, as a fact of industry, without the community's accumulated technological knowledge than is the use of "productive goods."

rest, if not substantially [168] the whole structure of theory. To this law of distribution the earlier portions of the theoretical development look forward, and this the succeeding portions of the treatise take as their point of departure. The law of "natural" distribution says that any productive agent "naturally" gets what it produces. Under ideally free competitive conditions – such as prevail in the "static" state, and to which the current situation approximates – each unit of each productive factor unavoidably gets the amount of wealth which it creates, – its "virtual product," as it is sometimes expressed. This law rests, for its theoretical validity, on the doctrine of "final productivity," set forth in full in *The Distribution of Wealth*, and more concisely in *The Essentials*[11] – "one of those universal principles which govern economic life in all its stages of evolution."[12]

In combination with a given amount of capital, it is held, each succeeding unit of added labor adds a less than proportionate increment to the product. The total product created by the labor so engaged is at the same time the distributive share received by such labor as wages; and it equals the increment of product added by the "final" unit of labor, multiplied by the number of such units engaged. The law of "natural" interest is the same as this law of wages, with a change of terms. The product of each unit of labor or capital being measured by the product of the "final" unit, each gets the amount of its own product.

In all of this the argument runs in terms of value; but it is Mr. Clark's view, backed by an elaborate exposition of the grounds of his contention,[13] that the use of these terms of value is merely a matter of convenience for the argument, and that the conclusions so reached – the equality so established between productivity and remuneration [169] – may be converted to terms of goods, or "effective utility," without abating their validity.

Without recourse to some such common denominator as value the outcome of the argument would, as Mr. Clark indicates, be something resembling the Ricardian law of differential rent instead of a law drawn in homogeneous terms of "final productivity"; and the law of "natural" distribution would then, at the best, fall short of a general formula. But the recourse to terms of value does not, as Mr. Clark recognizes, dispose of the question without more ado. It smooths the way for the argument, but, unaided, it leaves it nugatory. According to Hudibras, "The value of a thing is just as much as it will bring," and the later refinements on the theory of value have not set aside this dictum of the ancient authority. It answers no pertinent question of equity to say that the wages paid for labor are as much as it will bring. And Mr. Clark's chapter (xxiv) on "The Unit for Measuring Industrial Agents and their Products" is designed to show how this tautological statement in terms of market value converts itself, under competitive conditions, into a competent formula of

---

11 Cf. *Distribution of Wealth*, chaps. xii, xiii, vii, viii; *Essentials*, chaps. v–x.
12 *Essentials*, p. 158.
13 *Distribution*, chap. xxiv.

distributive justice. It does not conduce to intelligibility to say that the wages of labor are just and fair because they are all that is paid to labor as wages. What further value Mr. Clark's extended discussion of this matter may have will lie in his exposition of how competition converts the proposition that the value of a thing is just as much as it will bring "into the proposition that" the market rate of wages (or interest) gives to labor (or capital) the full product of labor (or capital).

In following up the theory at this critical point, it is necessary to resort to the fuller statement of *The Distribution of Wealth*,[14] the point being not so adequately covered in *The Essentials*. Consistently hedonistic, Mr. Clark recognizes that his law of natural justice must be reduced [170] to elementary hedonistic terms, if it is to make good its claim to stand as a fundamental principle of theory. In hedonistic theory, production of course means the production of utilities, and utility is of course utility to the consumer.[15] A product is such by virtue of and to the amount of the utility which it has for a consumer. This utility of the goods is measured, as value, by the sacrifice (disutility) which the consumer is willing to undergo in order to get the utility which the consumption of the goods yields him. The unit and measure of productive labor is in the last analysis also a unit of disutility; but it is disutility to the productive laborer, not to the consumer. The balance which establishes itself under competitive conditions is a compound balance, being a balance between the utility of the goods to the consumer and the disutility (cost) which he is willing to undergo for it, on the one hand, and, on the other hand, a balance between the disutility of the unit of labor and the utility for which the laborer is willing to undergo this disutility. It is evident, and admitted, that there can be no balance, and no commensurability, between the laborer's disutility (pain) in producing the goods and the consumer's utility (pleasure) in consuming them, inasmuch as these two hedonistic phenomena lie each within the consciousness of a distinct person. There is, in fact, no continuity of nervous tissue over the interval between consumer and producer, and a direct comparison, equilibrium, equality, or discrepancy in respect of pleasure and pain can, of course, not be sought except within each self-balanced individual complex of nervous tissue.[16] The wages of [171] labor (i.e., the utility of the goods received by the laborer) is not equal to the disutility undergone by him, except in the sense that he is competitively willing to accept it; nor are these wages equal to the utility got by the consumer of the

---

14 Chap. xxiv.

15 *Essentials*, p. 40.

16 Among modern economic hedonists, including Mr. Clark, there stands over from the better days of the order of nature a presumption, disavowed, but often decisive, that the sensational response to the like mechanical impact of the stimulating body is the same in different individuals. But, while this presumption stands ever in the background, and helps to many important conclusions, as in the case under discussion, few modern hedonists would question the statement in the text.

goods, except in the sense that he is competitively willing to pay them. This point is covered by the current diagrammatic arguments of marginal-utility theory as to the determination of competitive prices.

But, while the wages are not equal to or directly comparable with the disutility of the productive labor engaged, they are, in Mr. Clark's view, equal to the "productive efficiency" of that labor.[17] "Efficiency in a worker is, in reality, power to draw out labor on the part of society. It is capacity to offer that for which society will work in return." By the mediation of market price, under competitive conditions, it is held, the laborer gets, in his wages, a valid claim on the labor of other men (society) as large as they are competitively willing to allow him for the services for which he is paid his wages. The equitable balance between work and pay contemplated by the "natural" law is a balance between wages and "efficiency," as above defined; that is to say, between the wages of labor and the capacity of labor to get wages. So far, the whole matter might evidently have been left as Bastiat left it. It amounts to saying that the laborer gets what he is willing to accept and the consumers give what they are willing to pay. And this is true, of course, whether competition prevails or not.

What makes this arrangement just and right under competitive conditions, in Mr. Clark's view, lies in his further doctrine that under such conditions of unobstructed competition the prices of goods, and therefore the wages of labor, are determined, within the scope of the given market, by a quasi-consensus of all the parties in interest. [172] There is of course no formal consensus, but what there is of the kind is implied in the fact that bargains are made, and this is taken as an appraisement by "society" at large. The (quasi-) consensus of buyers is held to embody the righteous (quasi-) appraisement of society in the premises, and the resulting rate of wages is therefore a (quasi-) just return to the laborer.[18] "Each man accordingly is paid an amount that equals the total product that he personally creates."[19] If competitive conditions are in any degree disturbed, the equitable balance of prices and wages is disturbed by that much. All this holds true for the interest of capital, with a change of terms.

The equity and binding force of this finding is evidently bound up with that common-sense presumption on which it rests; namely, that it is right and good that all men should get what they can without force or fraud and without disturbing existing property relations. It springs from this presumption, and, whether in point of equity or of expediency, it rises no higher than its

17 *Distribution*. p. 394.
18 In Mr. Clark's discussion, elsewhere, the "quasi"-character of the productive share of the laborer is indicated by saying that it is the product "imputed" or "imputable" to him.
19 *Essentials*, p. 92. *Et si sensus deficit, ad firmandum cor sincerum sola fides sufficit.* [And if senses fail to see, faith alone the true heart waketh to behold the mystery. Verse of St. Thomas Aquinas's hymn *Pange Lingua*; Gerald Manley Hopkins translation. – Eds.]

source. It does not touch questions of equity beyond this, nor does it touch questions of the expediency or probable advent of any contemplated change in the existing conventions as to rights of ownership and initiative. It affords a basis for those who believe in the old order – without which belief this whole structure of opinions collapses – to argue questions of wages and profits in a manner convincing to themselves, and to confirm in the faith those who already believe in the old order. But it is not easy to see that some hundreds of pages of apparatus should be required to find one's way back to these time-worn commonplaces of Manchester. [173]

In effect, this law of "natural" distribution says that whatever men acquire without force or fraud under competitive conditions is their equitable due, no more and no less, assuming that the competitive system, with its underlying institution of ownership, is equitable and "natural." In point of economic theory the law appears on examination to be of slight consequence, but it merits further attention for the gravity of its purport. It is offered as a definitive law of equitable distribution comprised in a system of hedonistic economics which is in the main a theory of distributive acquisition only. It is worth while to compare the law with its setting, with a view to seeing how its broad declaration of economic justice shows up in contrast with the elements out of which it is constructed and among which it lies.

Among the notable chapters of *The Essentials* is one (vi.) on Value and its Relation to Different Incomes, which is not only a very substantial section of Mr. Clark's economic theory, but at the same time a type of the achievements of the latter-day hedonistic school. Certain features of this chapter alone can be taken up here. The rest may be equally worthy the student's attention, but it is the intention here not to go into the general substance of the theory of marginal utility and value, to which the chapter is devoted, but to confine attention to such elements of it as bear somewhat directly on the question of equitable distribution already spoken of. Among these latter is the doctrine of the "consumer's surplus," – virtually the same as what is spoken of by other writers as "consumer's rent."[20] "Consumer's surplus" is the surplus of utility (pleasure) derived by the consumer of goods above the (pain) cost of the goods to him. This is held to be a very generally prevalent phenomenon. Indeed, it is held to be all but universally present in the [174] field of consumption. It might, in fact, be effectively argued that even Mr. Clark's admitted exception[21] is very doubtfully to be allowed, on his own showing. Correlated with this element of utility on the consumer's side is a similar volume of disutility on the producer's side, which may be called "producer's abatement," or "producer's rent": it is the amount of disutility by which the disutility-cost of a given article to any given producer (laborer) falls short of (or conceivably exceeds) the disutility

---

20 See [*Essentials,*] pp. 102–13; also p, 172, note.
21 "The cheapest and poorest grades of articles." [*Essentials,*] p.113.

incurred by the marginal producer. Marginal buyers or consumers and marginal sellers or producers are relatively few: the great body on both sides come in for something in the way of a "surplus" "of utility or disutility."

All this bears on the law of "natural" wages and interest as follows, taking that law of just remuneration at Mr. Clark's rating of it. The law works out through the mediation of price. Price is determined, competitively, by marginal producers or sellers and marginal consumers or purchasers: the latter alone on the one side get the precise price-equivalent of the disutility incurred by them, and the latter alone on the other side pay the full price-equivalent of the utilities derived by them from the goods purchased.[22] Hence the competitive price – covering competitive wages and interest – does not reflect the consensus of all parties concerned as to the "effective utility" of the goods, on the one hand, or as to their effective (disutility) cost, on the other hand. It reflects instead, if anything of this kind, the valuations which the marginal unfortunates on each side concede under stress of competition; and it leaves on each side of the bargain relation an uncovered "surplus," which marks the (variable) interval by which price fails to cover "effective [175] utility." The excess utility – and the conceivable excess cost – does not appear in the market transactions that mediate between consumer and producer.[23] In the balance, therefore, which establishes itself in terms of value between the social utility of the product and the remuneration of the producer's "efficiency," the margin of utility represented by the aggregate "consumer's surplus" and like elements is not accounted for. It follows, when the argument is in this way reduced to its hedonistic elements, that no man "is paid an amount that equals the amount of the total product that he personally creates."

Supposing the marginal-utility (final-utility) theories of objective value to be true, there is no consensus, actual or constructive, as to the "effective utility" of the goods produced: there is no "social" decision in the case beyond what may be implied in the readiness of buyers to profit as much as may be by the necessities of the marginal buyer and seller. It appears that there is warrant, within these premises, for the formula: Remuneration $\gtreqless$ than Product. Only by an infinitesimal chance would it hold true in any given case that, hedonistically, Remuneration = Product; and, if it should ever happen to be true, there would be no finding it out.

The (hedonistic) discrepancy which so appears between remuneration and product affects both wages and interest in the same manner, but there is some (hedonistic) ground in Mr. Clark's doctrines for holding that the discrepancy does not strike both in the same degree. There is indeed no

---

22 See [*Essentials*,] p. 113.

23 The disappearance, and the method of disappearance, of such elements of differential utility and disutility occupies a very important place in all marginal-utility ("final-utility") theories of market value, or "objective value."

warrant for holding that there is anything like an equable distribution of this discrepancy among the several industries or the several industrial [176] concerns; but there appears to be some warrant, on Mr. Clark's argument, for thinking that the discrepancy is perhaps slighter in those branches of industry which produce the prime necessaries of life.[24] This point of doctrine throws also a faint (metaphysical) light on a, possibly generic, discrepancy between the remuneration of capitalists and that of laborers: the latter are, relatively, more addicted to consuming the necessaries of life, and it may be that they thereby gain less in the way of a consumer's surplus.

All the analysis and reasoning here set forth has an air of undue tenuity; but in extenuation of this fault it should be noted that this reasoning is made up of such matter as goes to make up the theory under review, and the fault, therefore, is not to be charged to the critic. The manner of argument required to meet this theory of the "natural law of final productivity" on its own ground is itself a sufficiently tedious proof of the futility of the whole matter in dispute. Yet it seems necessary to beg further indulgence for more of the same kind. As a needed excuse, it may be added that what immediately follows bears on Mr. Clark's application of the law of "natural distribution" to modern problems of industry and public policy, in the matter of curbing monopolies.

Accepting, again, Mr. Clark's general postulates – the postulates of current hedonistic economics – and applying the fundamental concepts, instead of their corollaries, to his scheme of final productivity, it can be shown to fail on grounds even more tenuous and hedonistically more fundamental than those already passed in review. In all final-utility (marginal-utility) theory it is of the essence of the scheme of things that successive increments [177] of a "good" have progressively less than proportionate utility. In fact, the coefficient of decrease of utility is greater than the coefficient of increase of the stock of goods. The solitary "first loaf" is exorbitantly useful. As more loaves are successively added to the stock, the utility of each grows small by degrees and incontinently less, until, in the end, the state of the "marginal" or "final" loaf is, in respect of utility, shameful to relate. So, with a change of phrase, it fares with successive increments of a given productive factor – labor or capital – in Mr. Clark's scheme of final productivity. And so, of course, it also fares with the utility of successive increments of product created by successively adding unit after unit to the complement of a given productive factor engaged in the case. If we attend to this matter of final productivity in consistently hedonistic terms, a curious result appears.

A larger complement of the productive agent, counted by weight and tale, will, it is commonly held, create a larger output of goods, counted by weight

---

24 Only the simplest and cheapest things that are sold in the market at all bring just what they are worth to the buyers, [*Essentials,*] p. 113.

and tale;[25] but these are not hedonistic terms and should not be allowed to cloud the argument. In the hedonistic scheme the magnitude of goods, in all the dimensions to be taken account of, is measured in terms of utility, which is a different matter from weight and tale. It is by virtue of their utility that they are "goods," not by virtue of their physical dimensions, number and the like; and utility is a matter of the production of pleasure and the prevention of pain. Hedonistically speaking, the amount of the goods, the magnitude of the output, is the quantity [178] of utility derivable from their consumption; and the utility per unit decreases faster than the number of units increases.[26] It follows that in the typical or undifferentiated case an increase of the number of units beyond a certain critical point entails a decrease of the "total effective utility" of the supply.[27] This critical point seems ordinarily to be very near the point of departure of the curve of declining utility, perhaps it frequently coincides with the latter. On the curve of declining final utility, at any point whose tangent cuts the axis of ordinates at an angle of less than 45 degrees, an increase of the number of units entails a decrease of the "total effective utility of the supply,"[28] so that a gain in physical productivity is a loss as counted in "total effective utility." Hedonistically, therefore, the productivity in such a case diminishes, not only relatively to the (physical) magnitude of the productive agents, but absolutely. This critical point, of maximum "total effective utility," is, if the practice of shrewd business men is at all significant, commonly somewhat short of the point of maximum physical productivity, at least in modern industry and in a modern community.

25 It is, *e.g.*, open to serious question whether Mr. Clark's curves of final productivity ([*Essentials,*] pp. 139, 148), showing a declining output per unit in response to an increase of one of the complementary agents of production, will fit the common run of industry in case the output be counted by weight and tale. In many cases they will, no doubt; in many other cases they will not. But this is no criticism of the curves in question, since they do not, or at least should not, purport to represent the product in such terms, but in terms of utility.

26 To resort to an approximation after the manner of Malthus, if the supply of goods be supposed to increase by arithmetical progression, their final utility may be said concomitantly to decrease by geometrical progression.

27 Cf. *Essentials,* chap. iii, especially pp. 40–41.

28 The current marginal-utility diagrams are not of much use in this connection, because the angle of the tangent with the axis of ordinates, at any point, is largely a matter of the draftsman's taste. The abscissa and the ordinate do not measure commensurable units. The units on the abscissa are units of frequency, while those on the ordinate are units of amplitude; and the greater or less segment of line allowed per unit on either axis is a matter of independently arbitrary choice. Yet the proposition in the text remains true, – as true as hedonistic propositions commonly are. The magnitude of the angle of the tangent with the axis of ordinates decides whether the total (hedonistic) productivity at a given point in the curve increases or decreases with a (mechanical) increase of the productive agent, – no student at all familiar with marginal-utility arguments will question that patent fact. But the angle of the tangent depends on the fancy of the draftsman, – no one possessed of the elemental mathematical notions will question that equally patent fact.

The "total effective utility" may commonly be increased [179] by decreasing the output of goods. The "total effective utility" of wages may often be increased by decreasing the amount (value) of the wages per man, particularly if such a decrease is accompanied by a rise in the price of articles to be bought with the wages. Hedonistically speaking, it is evident that the point of maximum net productivity is the point at which a perfectly shrewd business management of a perfect monopoly would limit the supply; and the point of maximum (hedonistic) remuneration (wages and interest) is the point which such a management would fix on in dealing with a wholly free, perfectly competitive supply of labor and capital.

Such a monopolistic state of things, it is true, would not answer to Mr. Clark's ideal. Each man would not be "paid an amount that equals the amount of the total product that he personally creates," but he would commonly be paid an amount that (hedonistically, in point of "effective utility") exceeds what he personally creates, because of the high final utility of what he receives. This is easily proven. Under the monopolistic conditions supposed, the laborers would, it is safe to assume, not be fully employed all the time; that is to say, they would be willing to work some more in order to get some more articles of consumption; that is to say, the articles of consumption which their wages offer them have so high a utility as to afford them a consumer's surplus, – the articles are worth more than they cost:[29] Q. E. D.

The initiated may fairly doubt the soundness of the chain of argument by which these heterodox theoretical results are derived from Mr. Clark's hedonistic postulates, more particularly since the adepts of the school, including Mr. Clark, are not accustomed to draw conclusions to this effect from these premises. Yet the argument proceeds according to the rules of marginal-utility permutations. [180] In view of this scarcely avoidable doubt, it may be permitted, even at the risk of some tedium, to show how the facts of every-day life bear out this unexpected turn of the law of natural distribution, as briefly traced above. The principle involved is well and widely accepted. The familiar practical maxim of "charging what the traffic will bear" rests on a principle of this kind, and affords one of the readiest practical illustrations of the working of the hedonistic calculus. The principle involved is that a larger aggregate return (value) may be had by raising the return per unit to such a point as to somewhat curtail the demand. In practice it is recognized, in other words, that there is a critical point at which the value obtainable per unit, multiplied by the number of units that will be taken off at that price, will give the largest net aggregate result (in value to the seller) obtainable under the given conditions. A calculus involving the same principle is, of course, the guiding consideration in all monopolistic buying and selling; but a moment's reflection will show that it is, in fact, the ruling principle in all commercial transactions

---

29 A similar line of argument has been followed up by Mr. Clark for capital and interest, in a different connection. See *Essentials*, pp. 340–45, 356.

and, indeed, in all business. The maxim of "charging what the traffic will bear" is only a special formulation of the generic principle of business enterprise. Business initiative, the function of the entrepreneur (business man) is comprehended under this principle taken in its most general sense.[30] In business the buyer, it is held by the theorists, bids up to the point of greatest obtainable advantage to himself under the conditions prevailing, and the seller similarly bids down to the point of greatest obtainable net aggregate gain. For the trader (business man, entrepreneur) doing business in the open (competitive) market or for the business concern with a partial or limited monopoly, the critical point above referred to is, of course, reached at a lower [181] point on the curve of price than would be the case under a perfect and unlimited monopoly, such as was supposed above; but the principle of charging what the traffic will bear remains intact, although the traffic will not bear the same in the one case as in the other.

Now, in the theories based on marginal (or "final") utility, value is an expression or measure of "effective utility" – or whatever equivalent term may be preferred. In operating on values, therefore, under the rule of charging what the traffic will bear, the sellers of a monopolized supply, *e.g.*, must operate through the valuations of the buyers; that is to say, they must influence the final utility of the goods or services to such effect that the "total effective utility" of the limited supply to the consumers will be greater than would be the "total effective utility" of a larger supply, which is the point in question. The emphasis falls still more strongly on this illustration of the hedonistic calculus, if it is called to mind that in the common run of such limitations of supply by a monopolistic business management the management would be able to increase the supply at a progressively declining cost beyond the critical point by virtue of the well-known principle of increasing returns from industry. It is also to be added that, since the monopolistic business gets its enhanced return from the margin by which the "total effective utility" of the limited supply exceeds that of a supply not so limited, and since there is to be deducted from this margin the costs of monopolistic management in addition to other costs, therefore the enhancement of the "total effective utility" of the goods to the consumer in the case must be appreciably larger than the resulting net gains to the monopoly.

By a bold metaphor – a metaphor sufficiently bold to take it out of the region of legitimate figures of speech – the gains that come to enterprising business concerns [182] by such monopolistic enhancement of the "total effective utility" of their products are spoken of as "robbery," extortion, "plunder"; but the theoretical complexion of the case should not be overlooked by the hedonistic theorist in the heat of outraged sentiment. The monopolist is only pushing the principle of all business enterprise (free competition) to its logical conclusion; and, in point of hedonistic theory, such monopolistic gains are to be accounted

---

30 Cf. *Essentials*, pp. 83–90, 118–20.

the "natural" remuneration of the monopolist for his "productive" service to the community in enhancing their enjoyment per unit of consumable goods to such point as to swell their net aggregate enjoyment to a maximum.

This intricate web of hedonistic calculations might be pursued further, with the result of showing that, while the consumers of the monopolized supply of goods are gainers by virtue of the enhanced "total effective utility" of the goods, the monopolists who bring about this result do so in great part at their own cost, counting cost in terms of a reduction of "total effective utility." By injudiciously increasing their own share of goods, they lower the marginal and effective utility of their wealth to such a point as, probably, to entail a considerable (hedonistic) privation in the shrinkage of their enjoyment per unit. But it is not the custom of economists, nor does Mr. Clark depart from this custom, to dwell on the hardships of the monopolists. This much may be added, however, that this hedonistically consistent exposition of the "natural law of final productivity" shows it to be "one of those universal principles which govern economic life in all its stages of evolution," even when that evolution enters the phase of monopolistic business enterprise, – granting always the sufficiency of the hedonistic postulates from which the law is derived. Further, the considerations reviewed above go to show that, on two counts, [183] Mr. Clark's crusade against monopoly in the later portion of his treatise is out of touch with the larger theoretical speculations of the earlier portions: (a) it runs counter to the hedonistic law of "natural" distribution; and (b) the monopolistic business against which Mr. Clark speaks is but the higher and more perfect development of that competitive business enterprise which he wishes to reinstate, – competitive business, so called, being incipiently monopolistic enterprise.

Apart from this theoretical hearing, the measures which Mr. Clark advocates for the repression of monopoly, under the head of applications "to modern problems of industry and public policy," may be good economic policy or they may not, – they are the expression of a sound common sense, an unvitiated solicitude for the welfare of mankind, and a wide information as to the facts of the situation. The merits of this policy of repression, as such, cannot be discussed here. On the other hand, the relation of this policy to the theoretical groundwork of the treatise needs also not be discussed here, inasmuch as it has substantially no relation to the theory. In this later portion of the volume Mr. Clark does not lean on doctrines of "final utility," "final productivity," or, indeed, on hedonistic economics at large. He speaks eloquently for the material and cultural interests of the community, and the references to his law of "natural distribution" might be cut bodily out of the discussion without lessening the cogency of his appeal or exposing any weakness in his position. Indeed, it is by no means certain that such an excision would not strengthen his appeal to men's sense of justice by eliminating irrelevant matter.

Certain points in this later portion of the volume, however, where the argument is at variance with specific articles of theory professed by

Mr. Clark, may be taken up, [184] mainly to elucidate the weakness of his theoretical position at the points in question. He recognizes with more than the current degree of freedom that the growth and practicability of monopolies under modern conditions is chiefly due to the negotiability of securities representing capital, coupled with the joint-stock character of modern business concerns.[31] These features of the modern (capitalistic) business situation enable a sufficiently few men to control a section of the community sufficiently large to make an effective monopoly. The most effective known form of organization for purposes of monopoly, according to Mr. Clark, is that of the holding company, and the ordinary corporation follows it closely in effectiveness in this respect. The monopolistic control is effected by means of the vendible securities covering the capital engaged. To meet the specifications of Mr. Clark's theory of capital, these vendible securities – as, *e.g.*, the securities (common stock) of a holding company – should be simply the formal evidence of the ownership of certain productive goods and the like. Yet, by his own showing, the ownership of a share of productive goods proportionate to the face value, or the market value, of the securities is by no means the chief consequence of such an issue of securities.[32] One of the consequences, and for the purposes of Mr. Clark's argument the gravest consequence, of the employment of such securities, is the dissociation of ownership from the control of the industrial equipment, whereby the owners of certain securities, which stand in certain immaterial, technical relations to certain other securities, are enabled arbitrarily to control the use of the industrial equipment covered by the latter. These are facts of the modern organization of capital, affecting the productivity of the industrial equipment and its serviceability both to its owners and to the community. [185] They are facts, though not physically tangible objects; and they have an effect on the serviceability of industry no less decisive than the effect which any group of physically tangible objects of equal market value have. They are, moreover, facts which are bought and sold in the purchase and sale of these securities, as, *e.g.*, the common stock of a holding company. They have a value, and therefore they have a "total effective utility."

In short, these facts are intangible assets, which are the most consequential element in modern capital, but which have no existence in the theory of capital by which Mr. Clark aims to deal with "modern problems of industry." Yet, when he comes to deal with these problems, it is, of necessity, these intangible assets that immediately engage his attention. These intangible assets are an outgrowth of the freedom of contract under the conditions imposed by the machine industry; yet Mr. Clark proposes to suppress this category of intangible assets without prejudice to freedom of contract or to the machine industry, apparently without having taken thought of the lesson

31 Cf. [*Essentials*] chap. xxii, especially pp. 378–92.
32 Cf. [*Essentials*,] p. 391.

which he rehearses (pp. 390–390) from the introduction of the holding company, with its "sinister perfection," to take the place of the (less efficient) "trust" when the latter was dealt with somewhat as it is now proposed to deal with the holding company. One is tempted to remark that a more naive apprehension of the facts of modern capital would have afforded a more competent realization of the problems of monopoly.

It appears from what has just been said of Mr. Clark's "natural" distribution and of his dealing with the problems of modern industry that the logic of hedonism is of no avail for the theory of business affairs. Yet it is held, perhaps justly, that the hedonistic interpretation may be of great avail in analyzing the industrial functions of the [186] community, in their broad, generic character, even if it should not serve so well for the intricate details of the modern business situation. It may be at least a serviceable hypothesis for the outlines of economic theory, for the first approximations to the "economic laws" sought by taxonomists. To be serviceable for this purpose, the hypothesis need perhaps not be true to fact, at least not in the final details of the community's life or without material qualification;[33] but it must at least have that ghost of actuality that is implied in consistency with its own corollaries and ramifications.

As has been suggested in an earlier paragraph, it is characteristic of hedonistic economics that the large and central element in its theoretical structure is the doctrine of distribution. Consumption being taken for granted as a quantitative matter simply, – essentially a matter of an insatiable appetite, – economics becomes a theory of acquisition; production is, theoretically, a process of acquisition, and distribution a process of distributive acquisition. The theory of production is drawn in terms of the gains to be acquired by production; and under competitive conditions this means necessarily the acquisition of a distributive share of what is available. The rest of what the facts of productive industry include, as, *e.g.*, the facts of workmanship or the "state of the industrial arts," gets but a scant and perfunctory attention. Those matters are not of the theoretical essence of the scheme. Mr. Clark's general theory of production does not differ substantially from that commonly professed by the marginal-utility school. It is a theory of competitive acquisition. An inquiry into the principles of his doctrine, therefore, as they appear, *e.g.*, in the early chapters of *The Essentials*, is, in effect, an inquiry into the competence of the main theorems of modern hedonistic economics. [187]

"All men seek to get as much net service from material wealth as they can." "Some of the benefit received is neutralized by the sacrifice incurred; but there is a net surplus of gains not thus canceled by sacrifices, and the generic motive which may properly be called economic is the desire to make this

33 Cf. *Essentials*, p. 39.

surplus large."[34] It is of the essence of the scheme that the acquisitive activities of mankind afford a net balance of pleasure. It is out of this net balance, presumably, that "the consumer's surpluses" arise, or it is in this that they merge. This optimistic conviction is a matter of presumption, of course; but it is universally held to be true by hedonistic economists, particularly by those who cultivate the doctrines of marginal utility. It is not questioned and not proven. It seems to be a surviving remnant of the eighteenth-century faith in a benevolent Order of Nature; that is to say, it is a rationalistic metaphysical postulate. It may be true or not, as matter of fact; but it is a postulate of the school, and its optimistic bias runs like a red thread through all the web of argument that envelops the "normal" competitive system. A surplus of gain is normal to the theoretical scheme.

The next great theorem of this theory of acquisition is at cross-purposes with this one. Men get useful goods only at the cost of producing them, and production is irksome, painful, as has been recounted above. They go on producing utilities until, at the margin, the last increment of utility in the product is balanced by the concomitant increment of disutility in the way of irksome productive effort, – labor or abstinence. At the margin, pleasure-gain is balanced by pain-cost. But the "effective utility" of the total product is measured by that of the final unit; the effective utility of the whole is given by the number of units of product multiplied by the [188] effective utility of the final unit; while the effective disutility (pain-cost) of the whole is similarly measured by the pain-cost of the final unit. The "total effective utility" of the producer's product equals the "total effective disutility" of his pains of acquisition. Hence there is no net surplus of utility in the outcome.

The corrective objection is ready to hand,[35] that, while the balance of utility and disutility holds at the margin, it does not hold for the earlier units of the product, these earlier units having a larger utility and a lower cost, and so leaving a large net surplus of utility, which gradually declines as the margin is approached. But this attempted correction evades the hedonistic test. It shifts the ground from the calculus to the objects which provoke the calculation. Utility is a psychological matter, a matter of pleasurable appreciation, just as disutility, conversely, is a matter of painful appreciation. The individual who is held to count the costs and the gain in this hedonistic calculus is, by supposition, a highly reasonable person. He counts the cost to him as an individual against the gain to him as an individual. He looks before and after, and sizes the whole thing up in a reasonable course of conduct. The "absolute utility" would exceed the "effective utility" only on the supposition that the "producer" is an unreflecting sensory apparatus, such as the beasts of the field are supposed to be, devoid of that gift of appraisement and calculation which is the hypothetical hedonist's only human trait. There might on such a

34 *Essentials*, p. 39.
35 Cf. *Essentials*, chap. iii, especially pp. 51–56.

supposition – if the producer were an intelligent sensitive organism simply – emerge an excess of total pleasure over total pain, but there could then be no talk of utility or of disutility, since these terms imply intelligent reflection, and they are employed because they do so. The hedonistic producer looks to his own cost and gain, as an [189] intelligent pleasure-seeker whose consciousness compasses the contrasted elements as wholes. He does not contrast the balance of pain and pleasure in the morning with the balance of pain and pleasure in the afternoon, and say that there is so much to the good because he was not so tired in the morning. Indeed, by hypothesis, the pleasure to be derived from the consumption of the product is a future, or expected, pleasure, and can be said to be present, at the point of time at which a given unit of pain-cost is incurred, only in anticipation; and it cannot be said that the anticipated pleasure attaching to a unit of product which emerges from the effort of the producer during the relatively painless first hour's work exceeds the anticipated pleasure attaching to a similar unit emerging from the second hour's work. Mr. Clark has, in effect, explained this matter in substantially the same way in another connection (*e.g.*, p. 42), where he shows that the magnitude on which the question of utility and cost hinges is the "total effective utility," and that the "total absolute utility" is a matter not of what hedonistically is, in respect of utility as an outcome of production, but of what might have been under different circumstances.

An equally unprofitable result may be reached from the same point of departure along a different line of argument. Granting that increments of product should be measured, in respect of utility, by comparison with the disutility of the concomitant increment of cost, then the diagrammatic arguments commonly employed are inadequate, in that the diagrams are necessarily drawn in two dimensions only, – length and breadth: whereas they should be drawn in three dimensions, so as to take account of the intensity of application as well as of its duration.[36] [190] Apparently, the exigencies of graphic representation, fortified by the presumption that there always emerges a surplus of utility, have led marginal-utility theorists, in effect, to overlook this matter of intensity of application.

When this element is brought in with the same freedom as the other two dimensions engaged, the argument will, in hedonistic consistency, run somewhat as follows, – the run of the facts being what it may. The producer, setting out on this irksome business, and beginning with the production of the exorbitantly useful initial unit of product, will, by hedonistic necessity, apply himself to the task with a correspondingly extravagant intensity, the irksomeness (disutility) of which necessarily rises to such a pitch as to leave no

36 This difficulty is recognized by the current marginal-utility arguments, and an allowance for intensity is made or presumed. But the allowance admitted is invariably insufficient. It might be said to be insufficient by hypothesis, since it is by hypothesis too small to offset the factor which it is admitted to modify.

excess of utility in this initial unit of product above the concomitant disutility of the initial unit of productive effort.[37] As the utility of subsequent units of product progressively declines, so will the producer's intensity of irksome application concomitantly decline, maintaining a nice balance between utility and disutility throughout. There is, therefore, no excess of "absolute utility" above "effective utility" at any point on the curve, and no excess of "total absolute utility" above "total effective utility" of the product as a whole, nor above the "total absolute disutility" or the "total effective disutility" of the pain-cost.

A transient evasion of this outcome may perhaps be sought by saying that the producer will act wisely, as a good hedonist should, and save his energies during the earlier moments of the productive period in order to get the best aggregate result from his day's labor, instead [191] of spending himself in ill-advised excesses at the outset. Such seems to be the fact of the matter, so far as the facts wear a hedonistic complexion; but this correction simply throws the argument back on the previous position and concedes the force of what was there claimed. It amounts to saying that, instead of appreciating each successive unit of product in isolated contrast with its concomitant unit of irksome productive effort, the producer, being human, wisely looks forward to his total product and rates it by contrast with his total pain-cost. Whereupon, as before, no net surplus of utility emerges, under the rule which says that irksome production of utilities goes on until utility and disutility balance.

But this revision of "final productivity" has further consequences for the optimistic doctrines of hedonism. Evidently, by a somewhat similar line of argument the "consumer's surplus" will be made to disappear, even as this that may be called the "producer's surplus" has disappeared. Production being acquisition, and the consumer's cost being cost of acquisition, the argument above should apply to the consumer's case without abatement. On considering this matter in terms of the hedonistically responsive individual concerned, with a view to determining whether there is, in his calculus of utilities and costs, any margin of uncovered utilities left over after he has incurred all the disutilities that are worth while to him, – instead of proceeding on a comparison between the pleasure-giving capacity of a given article and the market price of the article, all such alleged differential advantages within the scope of a single sensory are seen to be nothing better than an illusory diffractive effect due to a faulty instrument.

---

37 The limit to which the intensity rises is a margin of the same kind as that which limits the duration. This supposition, that the intensity of application necessarily rises to such a pitch that its disutility overtakes and offsets the utility of the product, may be objected to as a bit of puerile absurdity; but it is a long time since puerility or absurdity has been a bar to any supposition in arguments on marginal utility.

But the trouble does not end here. The equality: pain-cost = pleasure-gain, is not a competent formula. It should be: pain-cost incurred = pleasure-gain anticipated. [192] And between these two formulas lies the old adage, "there's many a slip 'twixt the cup and the lip." In an appreciable proportion of ventures, endeavors, and enterprises, men's expectations of pleasure-gain are in some degree disappointed, – through miscalculation, through disserviceable secondary effects of their productive efforts, by "the act of God," by fire, flood, and pestilence. In the nature of things these discrepancies fall out on the side of loss more frequently than on that of gain. After all allowance has been made for what may be called serviceable errors, there remains a margin of disserviceable error, so that pain-cost > eventual pleasure-gain = anticipated pleasure-gain – n. Hence, in general, pain-cost > pleasure-gain. Hence it appears that, in the nature of things, men's pains of production are underpaid by that much; although it may, of course, be held that the nature of things at this point is not "natural" or "normal."

To this it may be objected that the risk is discounted. Insurance is a practical discounting of risk; but insurance is resorted to only to cover risk that is appreciated by the person exposed to it, and it is such risks as are not appreciated by those who incur them that are chiefly in question here. And it may be added that insurance has hitherto not availed to equalize and distribute the chances of success and failure. Business gains – entrepreneur's gains, the rewards of initiative and enterprise – come out of this uncovered margin of adventure, and the losses of initiative and enterprise are to be set down to the same account. In some measure this element of initiative and enterprise enters into all economic endeavor. And it is not unusual for economists to remark that the volume of unsuccessful or only partly successful enterprise is very large. There are some lines of enterprise that are, as one might say, extra hazardous, in which the average falls out habitually on the wrong side of the account. [193] Typical of this class is the production of the precious metals, particularly as conducted under that régime of free competition for which Mr. Clark speaks. It has been the opinion, quite advisedly, of such economists of the classic age of competition as J. S. Mill and Cairnes, *e.g.*, that the world's supply of the precious metals has been got at an average or total cost exceeding their value by several fold. The producers, under free competition at least, are over-sanguine of results.

But, in strict consistency, the hedonistic theory of human conduct does not allow men to be guided in their calculation of cost and gain, when they have to do with the precious metals, by different norms from those which rule their conduct in the general quest of gain. The visible difference in this respect between the production of the precious metals and production generally should be due to the larger proportions and greater notoriety of the risks in this field rather than to a difference in the manner of response to the stimulus of expected gain. The canons of hedonistic calculus permit none but a quantitative difference in the response. What happens in the production of the precious metals is typical of what happens in a measure and more obscurely throughout the field of productive effort.

Instead of a surplus of utility of product above the disutility of acquisition, therefore, there emerges an average or aggregate net hedonistic deficit. On a consistent marginal-utility theory, all production is a losing game. The fact that Nature keeps the bank, it appears, does not take the hedonistic game of production out of the general category known of old to that class of sanguine hedonistic calculators whose day-dreams are filled with safe and sane schemes for breaking the bank. "Hope springs eternal in the human breast." Men are congenitally over-sanguine, it appears; and the production [194] of utilities is, mathematically speaking, a function of the pig-headed optimism of mankind. It turns out that the laws of (human) nature malevolently grind out vexation for men instead of benevolently furthering the greatest happiness of the greatest number. The sooner the whole traffic ceases, the better, – the smaller will be the net balance of pain. The great hedonistic Law of Nature turns out to be simply the curse of Adam, backed by the even more sinister curse of Eve.

The remark was made in an earlier paragraph that Mr. Clark's theories have substantially no relation to his practical proposals. This broad declaration requires an equally broad qualification. While the positions reached in his theoretical development count for nothing in making or fortifying the positions taken on "problems of modern industry and public policy," the two phases of the discussion – the theoretical and the pragmatic – are the outgrowth of the same range of preconceptions and run back to the same metaphysical ground. The present canvass of items in the doctrinal system has already far overpassed reasonable limits, and it is out of the question here to pursue the exfoliation of ideas through Mr. Clark's discussion of public questions, even in the fragmentary fashion in which scattered items of the theoretical portion of his treatise have been passed in review. But a broad and rudely drawn characterization may yet be permissible. This latter portion of the volume has the general complexion of a Bill of Rights. This is said, of course, with no intention of imputing a fault. It implies that the scope and method of the discussion is governed by the preconception that there is one right and beautiful definitive scheme of economic life, "to which the whole creation tends." Whenever and in so far as current phenomena depart or diverge [195] from this definitive "natural" scheme or from the straight and narrow path that leads to its consummation, there is a grievance to be remedied by putting the wheels back into the rut. The future, such as it ought to be the only normally possible, natural future scheme of life, – is known by the light of this preconception; and men have an indefeasible right to the installation and maintenance of those specific economic relations, expedients, institutions, which this "natural" scheme comprises, and to no others. The consummation is presumed to dominate the course of things which is presumed to lead up to the consummation. The measures of redress whereby the economic Order of Nature is to renew its youth are simple, direct, and short-sighted, as becomes the proposals of pre-Darwinian hedonism, which is not troubled about the exuberant uncertainties of cumulative change. No doubt presents itself but that the community's code of right and equity in economic matters will remain unchanged under changing conditions of economic life.

Selection 33

On the nature of capital

Source: *Quarterly Journal of Economics*, August 1908
(vol. 22, pp. 517–42) and November 1908 (vol. 23, pp. 104–36).

Veblen (1908c, 1908e)

Part I: The productivity of capital goods[1]

Summary

The knowledge of ways and means is a communal product, 441. – Access to
the common stock of technological knowledge is necessary to the production
of a livelihood, 445. – With the advance of the industrial arts the possession
of material equipment has become a requisite to the effective use of this
common stock of knowledge and skill, 447. – Hence the grant advantage of
owning capital goods, 449; and hence the dominant position of the owner-
employer in modern economic life, 453. – Summary conclusion, 456.

It has been usual in expositions of economic theory to speak of capital as an
array of "productive goods." What is immediately had in mind in this
expression, as well as in the equivalent "capital goods," is the industrial
equipment, primarily the mechanical appliances employed in the processes of
industry. When the productive efficiency of these and of other, subsidiary
classes of capital goods is subjected to further analysis, it is not unusual to
trace it back to the productive labor of the workmen, the labor of the individual workman being the ultimate productive factor in the commonly accepted
systems of theory. The current theories of production, as also those of distribution, are drawn in individualistic terms, particularly when these theories
are based on hedonistic premises, as they commonly are.

   Now, whatever may or may not be true for human conduct in some other
bearing, in the economic respect man has never lived an isolated, self-sufficient life as an individual, either actually or potentially. Humanly speaking,
such a thing is impossible. Neither an individual person nor a single household, nor a single line of descent, can maintain its life in isolation. Economically speaking, [518] this is the characteristic trait of humanity that separates

---

1 [Inadvertently omitted when Part I was first published, this title for Part I is given in Veblen's first
   footnote to the publication of Part II. See note 14 in this Selection. – Eds.]

mankind from the other animals. The life-history of the race has been a life-history of human communities, of more or less considerable size, with more or less of group solidarity, and with more or less of cultural continuity over successive generations. The phenomena of human life occur only in this form.

This continuity, congruity, or coherence of the group, is of an immaterial character. It is a matter of knowledge, usage, habits of life and habits of thought, not a matter of mechanical continuity or contact, or even of consanguinity. Wherever a human community is met with, as, e.g., among any of the peoples of the lower cultures, it is found in possession of something in the way of a body of technological knowledge, – knowledge serviceable and requisite to the quest of a livelihood, comprising at least such elementary acquirements as language, the use of fire, of a cutting edge, of a pointed stick, of some tool for piercing, of some form of cord, thong, or fibre, together with some skill in the making of knots and lashings. Co-ordinate with this knowledge of ways and means, there is also uniformly present some matter-of-fact knowledge of the physical behavior of the materials with which men have to deal in the quest of a livelihood, beyond what any one individual has learned or can learn by his own experience alone. This information and proficiency in the ways and means of life vests in the group at large; and, apart from accretions borrowed from other groups, it is the product of the given group, though not produced by any single generation. It may be called the immaterial equipment, or, by a license of speech, the intangible assets[2] of the community; [519] and, in the early days at least, this is far and away the most important and consequential category of the community's assets or equipment. Without access to such a common stock of immaterial equipment no individual and no fraction of the community can make a living, much less make an advance. Such a stock of knowledge and practice is perhaps held loosely and informally; but it is held as a common stock, pervasively, by the group as a body, in its corporate capacity, as one might say; and it is transmitted and augmented in and by the group, however loose and haphazard the transmission may be conceived to be, not by individuals and in single lines of inheritance.

The requisite knowledge and proficiency of ways and means is a product, perhaps a by-product, of the life of the community at large; and it can also be maintained and retained only by the community at large. Whatever may be true for the unsearchable prehistoric phases of the life-history of the race, it appears to be true for the most primitive human groups and phases of which

---

2 "Assets" is, of course, not to be taken literally in this connection. The term properly covers a pecuniary concept, not an industrial (technological) one, and it connotes ownership as well as value; and it will be used in this literal sense when in a later article [Part II of this Selection] ownership and investment come into the discussion. In the present connection it is used figuratively, for want of a better term, to convey the connotation of value and serviceability without thereby implying ownership.

there is available information that the mass of technological knowledge possessed by any community, and necessary to its maintenance and to the
maintenance of each of its members or subgroups, is too large a burden for
any one individual or any single line of descent to carry. This holds true, of
course, all the more rigorously and consistently, the more advanced the "state
of the industrial arts" may be. But it seems to hold true with a generality that
is fairly startling that whenever a given cultural community is broken up or
suffers a serious diminution of members, its technological heritage deterio-
rates and dwindles, even though it may have been apparently meagre enough
before. On the other hand, it seems to hold true with a similar uniformity
that, when an individual member or a fraction of a community on what we
call a lower stage [520] of economic development is drawn away and trained
and instructed in the ways of a larger and more efficient technology, and is
then thrown back into his home community, such an individual or fraction
proves unable to make head against the technological bent of the community
at large or even to create a serious diversion. Slight, perhaps transient, and
gradually effective technological consequences may result from such an
experiment; but they become effective by diffusion and assimilation through
the body of the community, not in any marked degree in the way of an
exceptional efficiency on the part of the individual or fraction which has been
subjected to exceptional training. And inheritance in technological matters
runs not in the channels of consanguinity, but in those of tradition and habituation, which are necessarily as wide as the scheme of life of the community.
Even in a relatively small and primitive community the mass of detail comprised in its knowledge and practice of ways and means is large, – too large
for any one individual or household to become competently expert in it all;
and its ramifications are extensive and diverse at the same time that all these
ramifications bear, directly or indirectly, on the life and work of each member
of the community. Neither the standard and routine of living nor the daily
work of any individual in the community would remain the same after the
introduction of an appreciable change, for good or ill, in any branch of the
community's equipment of technological expedients. If the community grows
larger, to the dimensions of a modern civilized people, and this immaterial
equipment grows proportionately great and various, then it will become
increasingly difficult to trace the connection between any given change in
technological detail and the fortunes of any given obscure member of the
community. But it is at least safe to say that an increase in the volume and
complexity of the body of technological [521] knowledge and practise does
not progressively emancipate the life and work of the individual from its
dominion.

The complement of technological knowledge so held, used, and transmitted
in the life of the community is, of course, made up out of the experience of
individuals. Experience, experimentation, habit, knowledge, initiative, are
phenomena of individual life, and it is necessarily from this source that the
community's common stock is all derived. The possibility of its growth lies in

the feasibility of accumulating knowledge gained by individual experience and initiative, and therefore it lies in the feasibility of one individual's learning from the experience of another. But the initiative and technological enterprise of individuals, such, e.g., as shows itself in inventions and discoveries of more and better ways and means, proceeds on and enlarges the accumulated wisdom of the past. Individual initiative has no chance except on the ground afforded by the common stock, and the achievements of such initiative are of no effect except as accretions to the common stock. And the invention or discovery so achieved always embodies so much of what is already given that the creative contribution of the inventor or discoverer is trivial by comparison.

In any known phase of culture this common stock of intangible, technological equipment is relatively large and complex, – i.e., relatively to the capacity of any individual member to create or to use it; and the history of its growth and use is the history of the development of material civilization. It is a knowledge of ways and means, and is embodied in the material contrivances and processes by means of which the members of the community make their living. Only by such means does technological efficiency go into effect. These "material contrivances" ("capital goods," material equipment) are such things as tools, vessels, vehicles, raw materials, [522] buildings, ditches, and the like, including the land in use; but they include also, and through the greater part of the early development chiefly, the useful minerals, plants, and animals. To say that these minerals, plants, and animals are useful – in other words, that they are economic goods – means that they have been brought within the sweep of the community's knowledge of ways and means.

In the relatively early stages of primitive culture the useful plants and minerals are, no doubt, made use of in a wild state, as, e.g., fish and timber have continued to be used. Yet in so far as they are useful they are unmistakably to be counted in among the material equipment ("tangible assets") of the community. The case is well illustrated by the relation of the Plains Indians to the buffalo, and by the north-west coast Indians to the salmon, on the one hand, and by the use of a wild flora by such communities as the Coahuila Indians, the Australian blacks, or the Andamanese, on the other hand.

But with the current of time, experience, and initiative, domesticated (that is to say improved) plants and animals come to take the first place. We have then such "technological expedients" in the first rank as the many species and varieties of domestic animals, and more particularly still the various grains, fruits, root crops, and the like, virtually all of which were created by man for human use; or perhaps a more scrupulously veracious account would say that they were in the main created by the women through long ages of workmanlike selection and cultivation. These things, of course, are useful because men have learned their use, and their use, so far as it has been learned, has been learned by protracted and voluminous experience and experimentation, proceeding at each step on the accumulated achievements of the past. Other things, which may in time, come to exceed these in [523] usefulness are still useless, economically non-existent, on the early levels of culture, because of what men in that time have not yet learned.

While this immaterial equipment of industry, the intangible assets of the community, have apparently always been relatively very considerable and are always mainly in the keeping of the community at large, the material equipment, the tangible assets, on the other hand, have, in the early stages (say the earlier 90 per cent.) of the life-history of human culture, been relatively slight, and have apparently been held somewhat loosely by individuals or household groups. This material equipment is relatively very slight in the earlier phases of technological development, and the tenure by which it is held is apparently vague and uncertain. At a relatively primitive phase of the development, and under ordinary conditions of climate and surroundings, the possession of the concrete articles ("capital goods") needed to turn the commonplace knowledge of ways and means to account is a matter of slight consequence, – contrary to the view commonly spoken for by the economists of the classical line. Given the commonplace technological knowledge and the commonplace training, – and these are given by common notoriety and the habituation of daily life, – the acquisition, construction, or usufruct of the slender material equipment needed arranges itself almost as a matter of course, more particularly where this material equipment does not include a stock of domestic animals or a plantation of domesticated trees and vegetables. Under given circumstances a relatively primitive technological scheme may involve some large items of material equipment, as the buffalo pens (*piskun*) of the Black-foot Indians or the salmon weirs of the river Indians of the north-west coast. Such items of material equipment [524] are then likely to be held and worked collectively, either by the community at large or by subgroups of a considerable size. Under ordinary, more generally prevalent conditions it appears that even after a relatively great advance has been made in the cultivation of crops the requisite industrial equipment is not a matter for serious concern, particularly so aside from the tilled ground and the cultivated trees, as is indicated by the singularly loose and inconsequential notions of ownership prevalent among peoples occupying such a stage of culture. A primitive stage of communism is not known.

But, as the common stock of technological knowledge increases in volume, range, and efficiency, the material equipment whereby this knowledge of ways and means is put into effect grows greater, more considerable relatively to the capacity of the individual. And so soon, or in so far, as the technological development falls into such shape as to require a relatively large unit of material equipment for the effective pursuit of industry, or such as otherwise to make the possession of the requisite material equipment a matter of consequence, so as seriously to handicap the individuals who are without these material means, and to place the current possessors of such equipment at a marked advantage, then the strong arm intervenes, property rights apparently begin to fall into definite shape, the principles of ownership gather force and consistency, and men begin to accumulate capital goods and take measures to make them secure.

An appreciable advance in the industrial arts is commonly followed or accompanied by an increase of population. The difficulty of procuring a livelihood may be no greater after such an increase: it may even be less; but there results a relative curtailment of the available area and raw materials, and commonly also an increased accessibility of the several portions of the community. A wide-reaching [525] control becomes easier. At the same, time a larger unit of material equipment is needed for the effective pursuit of industry. As this situation develops, it becomes worth while – that is to say, it becomes feasible – for the individual with the strong arm to engross, or "corner," the usufruct of the commonplace knowledge of ways and means by taking over such of the requisite material as may be relatively scarce and relatively indispensable for procuring a livelihood under the current state of the industrial arts.[3] Circumstances of space and numbers prevent escape from the new technological situation. The commonplace knowledge of ways and means cannot be turned to account, under the new conditions, without a material equipment adapted to the then current state of the industrial arts; and such a suitable material equipment is no longer a slight matter to be compassed by workmanlike initiative and application. *Beati possidentes.*[4]

The emphasis of the technological situation, as one might say, may fall now on one line of material items, now on another, according as the exigencies of climate, topography, flora and fauna, density of population, and the like, may decide. So also, under the rule of the game exigencies, the early growth of property rights and of the principles (habits of thought) of ownership may settle on one or another line of material items, according as one or another affords the strategic advantage for engrossing the current technological efficiency of the community.

Should the technological situation, the state of the industrial arts, be such as to throw the strategic emphasis on manual labor, on workmanlike skill and application, and [526] if at the same time the growth of population has made land relatively scarce, or hostile contact with other communities has made it impracticable for members of the community to range freely over outlying tracts, then it would be expected that the growth of ownership should take the direction primarily of slavery, or of some equivalent form of servitude, so effecting a naive and direct monopolistic control of the current knowledge of

---

3 Motives of exploit and emulation, no doubt, play a serious part in bringing on the practise of ownership and in establishing the principles on which it rests; but this play of motives and the concomitant growth of institutions cannot be taken up here. Cf. [Veblen,] *Theory of the Leisure Class*, chaps. i, ii, iii.

4 [Blessed are those who possess. – Eds.]

ways and means.[5] Whereas if the development has taken such a turn, and the community is so placed as to make the quest of a livelihood a matter of the natural increase of flocks and herds, then it should reasonably be expected that these items of equipment will be the chief and primary subject of property rights. In point of fact, it appears that a pastoral culture commonly involves also some degree of servitude, along with the ownership of flocks and herds.

Under different circumstances the mechanical appliances of industry, or the tillable land, might come into the position of strategic advantage, and might come in for the foremost place in men's consideration as objects of ownership. The evidence afforded by the known (relatively) primitive cultures and communities seems to indicate that slaves and cattle have in this way come into the primacy as objects of ownership at an earlier period in the growth of material civilization than land or the mechanical appliances. And it seems similarly evident – more so, indeed – that land has on the whole preceded the mechanical equipment as the stronghold of ownership and the means of engrossing the community's industrial efficiency.

It is not until a late period in the life-history of material civilization that ownership of the industrial equipment, in the narrower sense in which that phrase is commonly [527] employed, comes to be the dominant and typical method of engrossing the immaterial equipment. Indeed, it is a consummation which has been reached only a very few times even partially, and only once with such a degree of finality as to leave the fact indisputable. If it may be said, loosely, that mastery through the ownership of slaves, cattle, or land comes on in force only after the economic development has run through some nine-tenths of its course hitherto, then it may be said likewise that some ninety-nine one-hundredths of this course of development had been completed before the ownership of the mechanical equipment came into undisputed primacy as the basis of pecuniary dominion. So late an innovation, indeed, is this modern institution of "capitalism," – the predominant ownership of industrial capital as we know it, – and yet so intimate a fact is it in our familiar scheme of life, that we have some difficulty in seeing it in perspective at all, and we find ourselves hesitating between denying its existence, on the one hand, and affirming it to be a fact of nature antecedent to all human institutions, on the other hand.

In so speaking of the ownership of industrial equipment as being an institution for cornering the community's intangible assets, there is conveyed an unavoidably implied, tho unintended, note of condemnation. Such an implication of merit or demerit is an untoward circumstance in any theoretical inquiry. Any sentimental bias, whether of approval or disapproval, aroused by such an implied censure, must unavoidably hamper the dispassionate pursuit of the argument. To mitigate the effect of this jarring note as far as may be, therefore, it will be expedient to turn back for a moment to other more

---

5 Cf. H. Nieboer, *Slavery as an Industrial System*, chap. iv., sect. 12.

primitive and remoter forms of the institution, – as slavery and landed wealth, – and so reach the modern facts of industrial capital by a roundabout and gradual approach. [528]

These ancient institutions of ownership, slavery and landed wealth, are matters of history. Considered as dominant factors in the community's scheme of life, their record is completed; and it needs no argument to enforce the proposition that it is a record of economic dominion by the owners of the slaves or the land, as the case may be. The effect of slavery in its best day, and of landed wealth in mediaeval and early modern times, was to make the community's industrial efficiency serve the needs of the slave-owners in the one case and of the land-owners in the other. The effect of these institutions in this respect is not questioned now, except in such sporadic and apologetical fashion as need not detain the argument.

But the fact that such was the direct and immediate effect of these institutions of ownership in their time by no means involves the instant condemnation of the institutions in question. It is quite possible to argue that slavery and landed wealth, each in its due time and due cultural setting, have served the amelioration of the lot of man and the advance of human culture. What these arguments may be that aim to show the merits of slavery and landed wealth as a means of cultural advance does not concern the present inquiry, neither do the merits of the case in which the arguments are offered. The matter is referred to here to call to mind that any similar theoretical outcome of an analysis of the productivity of "capital goods" need not be admitted to touch the merits of the case in controversy between the socialistic critics of capitalism and the spokesmen of law and order.

The nature of landed wealth, in point of economic theory, especially as regards its productivity, has been sifted with the most jealous precautions and the most tenacious logic during the past century; and any economic student can easily review the course of the argument whereby that line of economic theory has been run to earth. It is only [529] necessary here to shift the point of view slightly to bring the whole argument concerning the rent of land to bear on the present question. Rent is of the nature of a differential gain, resting on a differential advantage in point of productivity of the industry employed upon or about it. This differential advantage attaching to a given parcel of land may be a differential as against another parcel or as against industry applied apart from land. The differential advantage attaching to agricultural land – e.g., as against industry at large – rests on certain broad peculiarities of the technological situation. Among them are such peculiarities as these: the human species, or the fraction of it concerned in the case, is numerous, relatively to the extent of its habitat; the methods of getting a living, as hitherto elaborated, the ways and means of life, make use of certain crop plants and certain domestic animals. Apart from such conditions, taken for granted in arguments concerning agricultural rent, there could manifestly be no differential advantage attaching to land and no production of rent. With increased command of methods of transportation, the agricultural lands of England, e.g., and of Europe at large, declined in value, not because these lands became less fertile, but because an equivalent result could more advantageously be got by a new method. So, again, the flint- and amber-bearing regions that are now Danish and Swedish territory about the waters at the entrance to the Baltic were in the neolithic culture of northern Europe the most favored and valuable lands within that cultural region. But, with the coming of the metals and the relative decline of the amber trade, they began to fall behind in the scale of productivity and preference. So also in later time, with the rise of "industry" and the growth of the technology of communication, urban property has gained, as contrasted with rural property, and land placed in an advantageous position relatively to [530] shipping and railroads has acquired a value and a "productiveness" which could not be claimed for it apart from these modern technological expedients.

The argument of the single-tax advocates and other economists as to the "unearned increment" is sufficiently familiar, but its ulterior implications have not commonly been recognized. The unearned increment, it is held, is produced by the growth of the community in numbers and in the industrial arts. The contention seems to be sound, and is commonly accepted; but it has commonly been overlooked that the argument involves the ulterior conclusion that all land values and land productivity, including the "original and indestructible powers of the soil," are a function of the "state of the industrial arts." It is only within the given technological situation, the current scheme of ways and means, that any parcel of land has such productive powers as it has. It is, in other words, useful only because, and in so far, and in such manner, as men have learned to make use of it. This is what brings it into the category of "land," economically speaking. And the preferential position of the landlord as a claimant of the "net product" consists in his legal right to decide whether, how far, and on what terms men shall put this technological scheme into effect in those features of it which involve the use of his parcel of land.

All this argument concerning the unearned increment may be carried over, with scarcely a change of phrase, to the case of "capital goods." The Danish flint supply was of first-rate economic consequence, for a thousand years or so, during the stone age; and the polished-flint utensils of that time were then "capital goods" of inestimable importance to civilization, and were possessed of a "productivity" so serious that the life of mankind in that world may be said to have been balanced on the [531] fine-ground edge of those magnificent polished-flint axes. All that lasted through its technological era. The flint supply and the mechanical expedients and "capital goods," whereby it was turned to account, were valuable and productive then, but neither before nor after that time. Under a changed technological situation the capital goods of that time have become museum exhibits, and their place in human economy has been taken by technological expedients which embody another "state of the industrial arts," the outcome of later and different phases of human experience. Like the polished-flint axe, the metal utensils which gradually displaced it and its like in the economy of the Occidental culture were the product of long experience and the gradual learning of ways and means. The steel axe, as well as the flint axe, embodies the same ancient technological expedient of a cutting edge, as well as the use of a helve and the efficiency due to the weight of the tool. And in the case of the one or the other, when seen in historical perspective and looked at from the point of view of the community at large, the knowledge of ways and means embodied in the utensils was the serious and consequential matter. The construction or acquisition of the concrete "capital goods" was simply an easy consequence. It "cost nothing but labor," as Thomas Mun would say.[6]

Yet it might be argued that each concrete article of "capital goods" was the product of some one man's labor, and, as such, its productivity, when put to use, was but the indirect, ulterior, deferred productiveness of the maker's labor. But the maker's productivity in the case was but a function of the immaterial technological equipment at his command, and that in its turn was the slow spiritual distillate of the community's time-long experience and initiative. To the individual producer or owner, to whom the community's accumulated stock of [532] immaterial equipment was open by common notoriety, the cost of the concrete material goods would be the effort involved in making or getting them and in making good his claim to them. To his neighbor who had made or acquired no such parcel of "productive goods," but to whom the resources of the community, material and immaterial, were open on the same easy terms, the matter would look very much the same. He would have no grievance, nor would he have occasion to seek one. Yet, as a resource in the maintenance of the community's life and a factor in the advance of material civilization, the whole matter would have a different meaning.

So long, or rather in so far, as the "capital goods" required to meet the technological demands of the time were slight enough to be compassed by the common man with reasonable diligence and proficiency, so long the draft upon the common stock of immaterial assets by any one would be no hindrance to any other, and no differential advantage or disadvantage would emerge. The economic situation would answer passably to the classical theory of a free competitive system, – "the simple and obvious system of natural liberty,"[7] which rests on the presumption of equal opportunity. In a roughly approximate way, such a situation supervened in the industrial life of western Europe on the transition from mediaeval to modern times, when handicraft and "industrial" enterprise superseded landed wealth as the chief economic factor. Within the "industrial system," as distinct from the privileged non-industrial classes, a man with a modicum of diligence, initiative, and thrift

---

6 [Veblen here quotes a phrase from *England's Treasure by Forraign Trade. or The Ballance of our Forraign Trade is The Rule of our Treasure* (1664) by Thomas Mun, an early mercantilist theorist. – Eds.]

7 [A famous quotation from Book IV of Adam Smith's *Wealth of Nations*. – Eds.]

might make his way in a tolerable fashion without special advantages in the way of prescriptive right or accumulated means. The principle of equal opportunity was, no doubt, met only in a very rough and dubious fashion; but so favorable became the conditions in this respect that men came to persuade [533] themselves in the course of the eighteenth century that a substantially equitable allotment of opportunities would result from the abrogation of all prerogatives other than the ownership of goods. But so precarious and transient was this approximation to a technologically feasible system of equal opportunity that, while the liberal movement which converged upon this great economic reform was still gathering head, the technological situation was already outgrowing the possibility of such a scheme of reform. After the Industrial Revolution came on, it was no longer true, even in the roughly approximate way in which it might have been true some time earlier, that equality before the law, barring property rights, would mean equal opportunity. In the leading, aggressive industries which were beginning to set the pace for all that economic system that centred about the market, the unit of industrial equipment, as required by the new technological era, was larger than one man could compass by his own efforts with the free use of the commonplace knowledge of ways and means. And the growth of business enterprise progressively made the position of the small, old-fashioned producer more precarious. But the speculative theoreticians of that time still saw the phenomena of current economic life in the light of the handicraft traditions and of the preconceptions of natural rights associated with that system, and still looked to the ideal of "natural liberty" as the goal of economic development and the end of economic reform. They were ruled by the principles (habits of thought) which had arisen out of an earlier situation, so effectually as not to see that the rule of equal opportunity which they aimed to establish was already technologically obsolete.[8]

During the hundred years and more of this ascendency [534] of the natural-rights theories in economic science, the growth of technological knowledge has unremittingly gone forward, and concomitantly the large-scale industry has grown great and progressively dominated the field. This large-scale, industrial régime is what the socialists, and some others, call "capitalism." "Capitalism," as so used, is not a neat and rigid technical term, but it is definite enough to be useful for many purposes. On its technological side the characteristic trait of this capitalism is that the current pursuit of industry requires a larger unit of material equipment than one individual can compass by his own labor, and larger than one person can make use of alone.

So soon as the capitalist régime, in this sense, comes in, it ceases to be true that the owner of the industrial equipment (or the controller of it) in any

---

8 For a more extended discussion of this point see [Veblen,] *Quarterly Journal of Economics*, July, 1899, "The Preconceptions of Economic Science" [Part II of Selection 19 in this volume]; also [Veblen,] *The Theory of Business Enterprise*, chap. iv. especially pp. 70–82.

given case is or may be the producer of it, in any naive sense of "production." He is under the necessity of acquiring its ownership or control by some other expedient than that of industrially productive work. The pursuit of industry requires an accumulation of wealth, and, barring force, fraud, and inheritance, the method of acquiring such an accumulation of wealth is necessarily some form of bargaining; that is to say, some form of business enterprise. Wealth is accumulated, within the industrial field, from the gains of business; that is to say, from the gains of advantageous bargaining.[9] Taking the situation by and large, looking to the body of business enterprise as a whole, the advantageous bargaining from which gains accrue and from which, therefore, accumulations of capital are derived, is necessarily, in the last analysis, a bargaining between [535] those who own (or control) industrial wealth and those whose work turns this wealth to account in productive industry. This bargaining for hire – commonly a wage agreement – is conducted under the rule of free contract, and is concluded according to the play of demand and supply, as has been well set forth by many writers.

On this technological view of capital, as here spoken for, the relations between the two parties to the bargain, the capitalist-employer and the working class, stand as follows. More or less rigorously, the technological situation enforces a certain scale and method in the various lines of industry.[10] The industry can, in effect, be carried on only by recourse to the technologically requisite scale and method, and this requires a material equipment of a certain (large) magnitude; while material equipment of this required magnitude is held exclusively by the capitalist-employer, and is *de facto* beyond the reach of the common man.

A corresponding body of immaterial equipment – knowledge and practice of ways and means – is likewise requisite, under the rule of the same technological exigencies. This immaterial equipment is in part drawn on in the making of the material equipment held by the capitalist-employers, in part in the use to be made of this material equipment in the further processes of industry. This body of immaterial equipment so drawn on in any line of industry is, relatively, still larger, being, on any exhaustive analysis, virtually the whole body of industrial experience accumulated by the community up to

---

9 Marx holds that the "primitive accumulation" from which capitalism takes its rise is a matter of force and fraud (*Capital*, Book I., chap. xxiv.). Sombart holds the source to have been landed wealth (*Moderne Kapitalismus*, Book II., Part II., especially chap. xii.). Ehrenberg and other critics of Sombart incline to the view that the most important source was usury and the petty trade (*Zeitalter der Fugger*, chaps. i., ii.).

10 The phrase "more or less" covers a certain margin of tolerance in respect of scale and method, which may be very appreciably wider in some lines of industry than in others, and which, cannot be more adequately defined or described here within such space as could reasonably be allowed. The requirement of scale and method is enforced by competition. The force and reach of this competitive adjustment can also not be dealt with here, but the familiar current acceptance of the fact will dispense with details.

date. A free draft on this common stock of technological wisdom [536] must be had both in the construction and in the subsequent use of the material equipment; although no one person can master, or himself employ, more than an inconsiderable fraction of the immaterial equipment so drawn on for the installation or operation of any given block of the material equipment.

The owner of the material equipment, the capitalist-employer, is, in the typical case, not possessed of any appreciable fraction of the immaterial equipment necessarily drawn on in the construction and subsequent use of the material equipment owned (controlled) by him. His knowledge and training, so far as it enters into the question, is a knowledge of business, not of industry.[11] The slight technological proficiency which he has or needs for his business ends is of a general character, wholly superficial and impracticable in point of workman-like efficiency; nor is it turned to account in actual workmanship. He there-fore "needs in his business" the service of persons who have a competent working mastery of this immaterial technological equipment, and it is with such persons that his bargains for hire are made. By and large, the measure of their serviceability for his ends is the measure of their technological compe-tency. No workman not possessed of some fractional mastery of the techno-logical requirements is employed, – imbeciles are useless in proportion to their imbecility; and even unskilled and "unintelligent" workmen, so called, are of relatively little use, although they may be possessed of a proficiency in the commonplace industrial details such as would bulk large in absolute magnitude. The "common laborer" is, in fact, a highly trained and widely proficient workman when contrasted with the conceivable human blank supposed to have drawn on the community for nothing but his physique. [537]

In the hands of these workmen – the industrial community, the bearers of the immaterial, technological equipment – the capital goods owned by the capitalist become a "means of production." Without them, or in the hands of men who do not know their use, the goods in question would be simply raw materials, somewhat deranged and impaired through having been given the form which now makes them "capital goods." The more proficient the work-men in their mastery of the technological expedients involved, and the greater the facility with which they are able to put these expedients into effect, the more productive will be the processes in which the workmen turn the employer's capital goods to account. So, also, the more competent the work of "superintendence," the foremanlike oversight and correlation of the work in respect of kind, speed, volume, the more will it count in the aggregate of productive efficiency. But this work of correlation is a function of the fore-man's mastery of the technological situation at large and his facility in pro-portioning one process of industry to the requirements and effects of another. Without this due and sagacious correlation of the processes of industry, and their current adaptation to the demands of the industrial situation at large,

11 Cf. [Veblen,] *Theory of Business Enterprise*, chap. III.

the material equipment engaged would have but slight efficiency and would count for but little in the way of capital goods. The efficiency of the control exercised by the master-workman, engineer, superintendent, or whatever term may be used to designate the technological expert who controls and correlates the productive processes, – this workmanlike efficiency determines how far the given material equipment is effectually to be rated as "capital goods."

Through all this functioning of the workman and the foreman the capitalist's business ends are ever in the background, and the degree of success that attends his business [538] endeavors depends, other things equal, on the efficiency with which these technologists carry on the processes of industry in which he has invested. His working arrangements with these workmen, the bearers of the immaterial equipment engaged, enables the capitalist to turn the processes for which his capital goods are adapted to account for his own profit, but at the cost of such a deduction from the aggregate product of these processes as the workmen may be able to demand in return for their work. The amount of this deduction is determined by the competitive bidding of other capitalists who may have use for the same lines of technological efficiency, in the manner set forth by writers on wages.

With the conceivable consolidation of all material assets under one business management, so as to eliminate competitive bidding between employers, it is plain that the resulting business concern would command the undivided forces of the technological situation, with such deduction as is involved in the livelihood of the working population. This livelihood would in such a case be reduced to the most economical footing, as seen from the standpoint of the employer. And the employer (capitalist) would be the *de facto* owner of the community's aggregate knowledge of ways and means, except so far as this body of immaterial equipment serves also the housekeeping routine of the working population. How nearly the current economic situation may approach to this finished state is a matter of opinion. There is also place for a broad question whether the conditions are more or less favorable to the working population under the existing business régime, involving competitive bidding between the several business concerns, than they would be in case a comprehensive business consolidation had eliminated competition and placed the ownership of the material assets on a footing of unqualified monopoly. Nothing but vague [539] surmises can apparently be offered in answer to these questions.

But as bearing on the question of monopoly and the use of the community's immaterial equipment it is to be kept in mind that the technological situation as it stands to-day does not admit of a complete monopolization of the community's technological expedients, even if a complete monopolization of the existing aggregate of material property were effected. There is still current a large body of industrial processes to which the large-scale methods do not apply and which do not presume such a large unit of material equipment or involve such rigorous correlation with the large-scale industry as to take them out of the range of discretionary use by persons not possessed of appreciable material wealth. Typical of such lines of work, hitherto not amenable to monopolization, are the details of housekeeping routine alluded to above. It is, in fact, still possible for an appreciable fraction of the population to "pick up a living," more or less precarious, without recourse to the large-scale processes that are controlled by the owners of the material assets. This somewhat precarious margin of free recourse to the commonplace knowledge of ways and means appears to be what stands in the way of a neater adjustment of wages to the "minimum of subsistence" and the virtual ownership of the immaterial equipment by the owners of the material equipment.

It follows from what has been said that all tangible[12] assets owe their productivity and their value to the immaterial industrial expedients which they embody or which their ownership enables their owner to engross. These immaterial industrial expedients are necessarily a product of the community, the immaterial residue of the community's [540] experience, past and present, which has no existence apart from the community's life, and can be transmitted only in the keeping of the community at large. It may be objected by those who make much of the productivity of capital that tangible capital goods on hand are themselves of value and have a specific productive efficiency, if not apart from the industrial processes in which they serve, then at least as a prerequisite to these processes, and therefore a material condition-precedent standing in a causal relation to the industrial product. But these material goods are themselves a product of the past exercise of technological knowledge, and so back to the beginning. What there is involved in the material equipment, which is not of this immaterial, spiritual nature, and so what is not an immaterial residue of the community's experience, is the raw material out of which the industrial appliances are constructed, with the stress falling wholly on the "raw."

The point is illustrated by what happens to a mechanical contrivance which goes out of date because of a technological advance and is displaced by a new contrivance embodying a new process. Such a contrivance "goes to the junkheap," as the phrase has it. The specific technological expedient which it embodies ceases to be effective in industry, in competition with "improved methods." It ceases to be an immaterial asset. When it is in this way eliminated, the material repository of it ceases to have value as capital. It ceases to be a material asset. "The original and indestructible powers"[13] of the material constituents of capital goods, to adapt Ricardo's phrase, do not make these constituents capital goods; nor, indeed, do these original and indestructible powers of themselves bring the objects in question into the category of economic goods at all. The raw materials – land, minerals, and the like – may, of course, be valuable property, [541] and may be counted among the assets of a business. But the value which they so have is a function of the anticipated use

---

12 "Tangible assets" is here taken to signify serviceable capital goods considered as valuable possessions yielding income to their owner.

13 [This phrase is taken from David Ricardo's *Principles of Political Economy and Taxation*. Ricardo's reference is to land, and the quote is part of his explanation of rent. – Eds.]

to which they may be put, and that is a function of the technological situation under which it is anticipated that they will be useful.

All this may seem to undervalue or perhaps to overlook the physical facts of industry and the physical nature of commodities. There is, of course, no call to understate the importance of material goods or of manual labor. The goods about which this inquiry turns are the products of trained labor working on the available materials; but the labor has to be trained, in the large sense, in order to be labor, and the materials have to be available in order to be materials of industry. And both the trained efficiency of the labor and the availability of the material objects engaged are a function of the "state of the industrial arts."

Yet the state of the industrial arts is dependent on the traits of human nature, physical, intellectual, and spiritual, and on the character of the material environment. It is out of these elements that the human technology is made up; and this technology is efficient only as it meets with the suitable material conditions and is worked out, practically, in the material forces required. The brute forces of the human animal are an indispensable factor in industry, as are likewise the physical characteristics of the material objects with which industry deals. And it seems bootless to ask how much of the products of industry or of its productivity is to be imputed to these brute forces, human and non-human, as contrasted with the specifically human factors that make technological efficiency. Nor is it necessary to go into questions of that import here, since the inquiry here turns on the productive relation of capital to industry; that is to say, the relation [542] of the material equipment and its ownership to men's dealings with the physical environment in which the race is placed. The question of capital goods (including that of their ownership and therefore including the question of investment) is a question of how mankind as a species of intelligent animals deals with the brute force at its disposal. It is a question of how the human agent deals with his means of life, not of how the forces of the environment deal with man. Questions of the latter class belong under the head of ecology, a branch of the biological sciences dealing with the adaptive variability of plants and animals. Economic inquiry would belong under that category if the human response to the forces of the environment were instinctive and variational only, including nothing in the way of a technology. But in that case there would be no question of capital goods, or of capital, or of labor. Such questions do not arise in relation to the non-human animals.

In an inquiry into the productivity of labor some perplexity might be met with as to the share or the place of the brute forces of the human organism in the theory of production; but in relation to capital that question does not arise, except so far as these forces are involved in the production of the capital goods. As a parenthesis, more or less germane to the present inquiry into capital, it may be remarked that an analysis of the productive powers of labor would apparently take account of the brute energies of mankind (nervous and muscular energies) as material forces placed at the disposal of man by circumstances largely beyond human control, and in great part not theoretically dissimilar to the like nervous and muscular forces afforded by the domestic animals.

Part II: Investment, intangible assets, and the pecuniary magnate

Summary

Introductory summary, 457. – Certain effects of investment and the price system, 458. – Intangible assets, their nature, derivation, and basis, 461. – Summary of analysis of assets, 464. – Tangible and intangible assets distinct, but mutually convertible, 464. – Dependence of all assets on industrial production, 468. – Non-capitalizable income from assets, 470. – Place and function of the "Pecuniary Magnate," 470. – "Timeless" gains from the use of (large) capital, 473. – Source of such "timeless" gains, 474. – Consequences for ordinary business men and ordinary profits, 476.

What has been said in the earlier section of this paper[14] applies to "capital goods," so called, and it is intended to apply to these in their character of "productive goods" rather than in their character of "capital"; that is to say, what is had in mind is the industrial, or technological, efficiency and subservience of the material means of production rather than the pecuniary use and effect of invested wealth. The inquiry has dealt with the industrial equipment as "plant" rather than as "assets." In the course of this inquiry it has appeared that out of the profitable engrossing of the community's industrial efficiency through control of the material equipment there arises the practise of investment, which has further consequences that merit more detailed attention.

Investment is a pecuniary transaction, and its aim is pecuniary gain, – gain in terms of value and ownership. Invested wealth is capital, a pecuniary magnitude, measured [105] in terms of value and determined in respect of its magnitude by a valuation which proceeds on an appraisement of the gain expected from the ownership of this invested wealth. In modern business practise, capital is distinguished into two co-ordinate categories of assets, tangible and intangible. "Tangible assets" is here taken to designate pecuniarily serviceable capital goods, considered as a valuable possession yielding an income to their owner. Such goods, material items of wealth, are "assets" to the amount of their capitalizable value, which may be more or less closely related to their industrial serviceability as productive goods. "Intangible assets" are immaterial items of wealth, immaterial facts owned, valued, and capitalized on an appraisement of the gain to be derived from their possession. These are also assets to the amount of their capitalizable value, which

---

14 See this journal [*Quarterly Journal of Economics*] for August 1908 [Part I of this Selection]. By an oversight the subtitle of the earlier section was omitted. It should have read "The Productivity of Capital Goods."

has commonly little, if any, relation to the industrial serviceability of these items of wealth considered as factors of production.

Before going into the matter of intangible assets, it is necessary to speak further of the consequences which investment – and hence capitalization – has for the use and serviceability of (material) capital goods. It has commonly been assumed by economists, without much scrutiny, that the gains which accrue from invested wealth are derived from and (roughly) measured by the productivity of the industrial process in which the items of wealth so invested are employed, productivity being counted in some terms of material serviceability to the community, conduciveness to the livelihood, comfort, or consumptive needs of the community. In the course of the present inquiry it has appeared that the gainfulness of such invested wealth (tangible assets) is due to a more or less extensive engrossing of the community's industrial efficiency. The aggregate gains of the aggregate material [106] capital accrue from the community's industrial activity, and bear some relation to the productive capacity of the industrial traffic so engrossed. But it will be noted that there is no warrant in the analysis of these phenomena as here set forth for alleging that the gains of investment bear a relation of equality or proportion to the material serviceability of the capital goods, as rated in terms of effectual usefulness to the community. Given capital goods, tangible assets, may owe their pecuniary serviceability to their owner, and so their value, to other things than their serviceability to the community; although the gains of investment in the aggregate are drawn from the aggregate material productivity of the community's industry.

The ownership of the material equipment gives the owner not only the right of use over the community's immaterial equipment, but also the right of abuse and of neglect or inhibition. This power of inhibition may be made to afford an income, as well as the power to serve; and whatever will yield an income may be capitalized and become an item of wealth to its possessor. Under modern conditions of investment it happens not infrequently that it becomes pecuniarily expedient for the owner of the material equipment to curtail or retard the processes of industry, – "restraint of trade." The motive in all such cases of retardation is the pecuniary expediency of the measure for the owner (controller) of capital, – expediency in terms of income from investment, not expediency in terms of serviceability to the community at large or to any fraction of the community except the owner (manager). Except for the exigencies of investment, i.e., exigencies of pecuniary gain to the investor, phenomena of this character would have no place in the industrial system. They invariably come of the endeavors of business men to secure a pecuniary gain or to avoid a pecuniary loss. More frequently, perhaps, manoeuvres of inhibition [107] – advised idleness of plant – in industry aim to effect a saving or avoid a waste than to procure an increase of gain; but the saving to be effected and the waste to be avoided are always pecuniary saving to the owner and pecuniary waste in the matter of ownership, not a saving of goods to the community or a prevention of wasteful consumption or wasteful expenditure of effort and resources on the part of the community. Pecuniary – that is to say, differential – advantage to the capitalist-manager has, under the régime of investment, taken precedence of economic advantage to the community; or rather, the differential advantage of ownership is alone regarded in the conduct of industry under this system.

Business practises which inhibit industrial efficiency and curtail the industrial output are too well known to need particular enumeration. Nor is it necessary to cite evidence to show that such inhibition and curtailment are resorted to from motives of pecuniary expediency. But an illustrative example or two will make the theoretical point clearer, and perhaps more plainly bring out the wholly pecuniary grounds of such business procedure. The most comprehensive principle involved in this class of business management is that of raising prices, and so increasing the net gains of business, by limiting the supply, or "charging what the traffic will bear." Of a similar effect, for the point here in question, are the obstructive tactics designed to hinder the full efficiency of a business rival. These phenomena lie along the line of division between tangible and intangible assets. Successful strategy of this kind may, by force of custom, legislation, or the "freezing-out" of rival concerns, pass into settled conditions of differential advantage for the given business concern, which so may be capitalized as an item of intangible assets and take their place in the business community as articles of invested wealth. [108]

But, aside from such capitalization of inefficiency, it is at least an equally consequential fact that the processes of productive industry are governed in detail by the exigencies of investment, and therefore by the quest of gain as counted in terms of price, which leads to the dependence of production on the course of prices. So that, under the régime of capital, the community is unable to turn its knowledge of ways and means to account for a livelihood except at such seasons and in so far as the course of prices affords a differential advantage to the owners of the material equipment. The question of advantageous – which commonly means rising – prices for the owners (managers) of the capital goods is made to decide the question of livelihood for the rest of the community. The recurrence of hard times, unemployment, and the rest of that familiar range of phenomena, goes to show how effectual is the inhibition of industry exercised by the ownership of capital under the price system.[15]

So also as regards the discretionary abuse of the community's industrial efficiency vested in the owner of the material equipment. Disserviceability may be capitalized as readily as serviceability, and the ownership of the capital goods affords a discretionary power of misdirecting the industrial processes and perverting[16] industrial efficiency, as well as of inhibiting or curtailing industrial processes and their output, while the outcome may still

15 For the connection between prices and prosperity, hard times, unemployment, etc, see [Veblen,] *The Theory of Business Enterprise*, chap. vii (pp. 185–252, especially, 196–212).
16 By "perversion" is here meant such disposition of the industrial forces as entails a net waste or detriment to the community's livelihood.

be profitable to the owner of the capital goods. There is a large volume of capital goods whose value lies in their turning the technological inheritance to the injury of mankind. Such are, e.g., naval and military establishments, together with the docks, arsenals, schools, and manufactories [109] of arms, ammunition, and naval and military stores, that supplement and supply such establishments. These armaments and the like are, of course, public and quasi-public enterprises, under the current régime, with somewhat disputable relations to the system of current business enterprise. But it is no far-fetched interpretation to say that they are, in great part, a material equipment for the maintenance of law and order, and so enable the owners of capital goods with immunity to inhibit or pervert the industrial processes when the exigencies of business profits make it expedient; that they are, further, a means – more or less ineffectual, it is true – for extending and protecting trade, and so serve the differential advantage of business men at the cost of the community; and that they are also in large part a material equipment set apart for the diversion of a livelihood from the community at large to the military, naval, diplomatic, and other official classes. These establishments may in any case be taken as illustrating how items of material equipment may be devoted to and may be valued for the use of the technological expedients for the damage and discomfort of mankind, without sensible offset or abatement.

Typical of a class of investments which derive profits from capital goods devoted to uses that are altogether dubious, with a large presumption of net detriment, are such establishments as race-tracks, saloons, gambling-houses, and houses of prostitution.[17] Some spokesmen of [110] the "non-Christian tribes" might wish to include churches under the same category, but the consensus of opinion in modern communities inclines to look on churches as serviceable, on the whole; and it may be as well not to attempt to assign them a specific place in the scheme of serviceable and disserviceable use of invested wealth.

There is, further, a large field of business, employing much capital goods and many technological processes, whose profits come from products in which serviceability and disserviceability are mingled with waste in the most varying

17 Should the connection at this point with the main argument of the paper as set forth in the earlier section seem doubtful or obscure, it may be called to mind that these dubious enterprises in dissipation are cases of investment for a profit, and that the "capital goods" engaged are invested wealth yielding an income, but that they yield an income only on the fulfilment of two conditions (a) the possession and employment of these capital goods enables their holder to turn to account the common stock of technological proficiency, in those bearings in which it may be of use in his enterprise; and (b) the limited amount of wealth available for the purpose enables their holder to "engross" the usufruct of such a fraction of the common stock of technological proficiency, in the degree determined by this limitation of the amount available. In so far, these enterprises are like any other industrial enterprise, but beyond this they have the peculiarity that they do not, or need not, even ostensibly, turn the current knowledge and use of ways and means to "productive" account for the community at large, but simply take their stand on the (institutionally sacred) "accomplished fact" of invested wealth. They have less of the fog of apology about them than the common run of business enterprise.

proportion. Such are the production of goods of fashion, disingenuous proprietary articles, sophisticated household supplies, newspapers and advertising enterprise. In the degree in which business of this class draws its profits from wasteful practises, spurious goods, illusions and delusions, skilled mendacity, and the like, the capital goods engaged must be said to owe their capitalizable value to a perverse use of the technological expedients employed.

These wasteful or disserviceable uses of capital goods have been cited, not as implying that the technological proficiency embodied in these goods or brought into effect in their use, intrinsically has a disserviceable bearing, nor that investment in these things, and business enterprise in the management of them, need aim at disserviceability, but only to bring out certain minor points of theory, obvious but commonly overlooked: (a) technological proficiency is not of itself and intrinsically serviceable or disserviceable to mankind, – it is only a means of efficiency for good or ill; (b) the enterprising use of capital goods by their businesslike owner aims not at [111] serviceability to the community, but only at serviceability to the owner; (c) under the price system – under the rule of pecuniary standards and management – circumstances make it advisable for the business man at times to mismanage the processes of industry, in the sense that it is expedient for his pecuniary gain to inhibit, curtail, or misdirect industry, and so turn the community's technological proficiency to the community's detriment. These somewhat commonplace points of theory are of no great weight in themselves, but they are of consequence for any theory of business or of life under the rules of the price system, and they have an immediate bearing here on the question of intangible assets.

At the risk of some tedium it is necessary to the theory of intangible assets to pursue this analysis and piecing together of commonplaces somewhat farther. As has already been remarked, "assets" is a pecuniary concept, not a technological one; a concept of business, not of industry. Assets are capital, and tangible assets are items of material equipment and the like, considered as available for capitalization. The tangibility of tangible assets is a matter of the materiality of the items of wealth of which they are made up, while they are assets to the amount of their value. Capital goods, which typically make up the category of tangible assets, are capital goods by virtue of their technological serviceability, but they are capital in the measure, not of their technological serviceability, but in the measure of the income which they may yield to their owner. The like is, of course, true of intangible assets, which are likewise capital, or assets, in the measure of their income-yielding capacity. Their intangibility is a matter of the immateriality of the item of wealth – objects of ownership – of which they are made up, but their character and magnitude as assets is a matter [112] of the gainfulness to their owner of the processes which their ownership enables him to engross. The facts so engrossed, in the case of intangible assets, are not of a technological or industrial character; and herein lies the substantial disparity between tangible and intangible assets.

Mankind has other dealings with the material means of life, besides those covered by the community's technological proficiency. These other dealings have to do with the use, distribution, and consumption of the goods procured by the employment of the community's technological proficiency, and are carried out under working arrangements of an institutional character, – use and wont, law and custom. The principles and practise of the distribution of wealth vary with the changes in technology and with the other cultural changes that are going forward; but it is probably safe to assume that the principles of apportionment, – that is to say, the consensus of habitual opinion as to what is right and good in the distribution of the product, – these principles and the concomitant methods of carrying them out in practise have always been such as to give one person or group or class something of a settled preference above another. Something of this kind, something in the way of a conventionally arranged differential advantage in the apportionment of the common livelihood, is to be found in all cultures and communities that have been observed at all carefully; and it is perhaps needless to remark that in the higher cultures such economic preferences, privileges, prerogatives, differential advantages and disadvantages, are numerous and varied, and that they make up an intricate fabric of economic institutions. Indeed, peculiarities of class difference in some such respect are among the most striking and decisive features that distinguish one cultural era from another. In all phases of material civilization these preferential advantages are sought and valued. Classes or groups which [113] are in a position to make good a claim to such differential advantages commonly come, in due course, to put forward such claims; as, e.g., the priesthood, the princely and ruling class, the men as contrasted with the women, the adults as against minors, the able-bodied as against the infirm. Principles (habits of thought) countenancing some form of class or personal preference in the distribution of income are to be found incorporated in the moral code of all known civilizations and embodied in some form of institution. Such items of immaterial wealth are of a differential character, in that the advantage of those who secure the preference is the disadvantage of those who do not; and it may be mentioned in passing, that such a differential advantage inuring to any one class or person commonly carries a more than equal disadvantage to some other class or person or to the community at large.[18]

When property rights fall into definite shape and the price system comes in, and more particularly when the practise of investment arises and business enterprise comes into vogue, such differential advantages take on something

---

18 This statement may not seem clear without indicating in a more concrete manner some terms in which to measure the relative differential advantage and disadvantage which so emerge in such a case of prerogative or privilege. Where, as in the earlier non-pecuniary phases of culture, no price test is applicable, the statement in the text may be taken to mean that the differential disadvantage at the cost of which the differential benefit in question is gained is greater than the beneficiary would be willing to undergo in order to procure this benefit.

of the character of intangible assets. They come to have a pecuniary value and rating, whether they are transferable or not; and if they are transferable, if they can be sold and delivered, they become assets in a fairly clear and full sense of that term. Such immaterial wealth, preferential benefits of the nature of intangible assets, may be a matter of usage simply, as the vogue of a given public house, or of a given tradesman, or of a given brand of consumable goods; or may be a matter of arrogation, as the King's Customs in early times, or [114] the once notorious Sound Dues,[19] or the closing of public highways by large land-owners; or of contractual concession, as the freedom of a city or a gild, or a franchise in the Hanseatic League or in the Associated Press; or of government concession, whether on the basis of a bargain or otherwise, as the many trade monopolies of early modern times, or a corporation charter, or a railway franchise, or letters of marque, or letters patent; or of statutory creation, as trade protection by import, export, or excise duties or navigation laws; or of conventionalized superstitious punctilio, as the creation of a demand for wax by the devoutly obligatory consumption of consecrated tapers, or the similar devout consumption of and demand for fish during Lent.

Under the régime of investment and business enterprise these and the like differential benefits may turn to the business advantage of a given class, group, or concern, and in such an event the resulting differential business advantage in the pursuit of gain becomes an asset, capitalized on the basis of its income-yielding capacity, and possibly vendible under the cover of a corporation security (as, e.g., common stock), or even under the usual form of private sale (as, e.g., the appraised good-will of a business concern).

But the régime of business enterprise has not only taken over various forms of institutional privileges and prerogatives out of the past: it also gives rise to new kinds of differential advantage and capitalizes them into intangible assets. These are all (or virtually all) of one kind, in that their common aim and common basis of value and capitalization is a preferentially advantageous sale. Naturally so, since the end of all business endeavor, in the last analysis, is an advantageous sale. The commonest and typical kind of such intangible assets is "good-will," so called, – a term which has come to cover a great variety [115] of differential business advantages, but which in the original business usage of it meant the customary resort of a clientèle to the concern so possessed of the good-will. It seems originally to have implied a kindly sentiment of trust and esteem on the part of a customer, but as the term is now used it has lost this sentimental content. In the broad and loose sense in which it is now currently employed it is extended to cover such special advantages as inure to a monopoly or a combination of business

19 [The Sound Dues applied to the straits between Denmark and Sweden, and constituted much of Denmark's state income from the fifteenth to the nineteenth centuries. If a ship refused to pay the toll, cannons in both Helsingør and Helsingborg could open fire and sink it. – Eds.]

concerns through its power to limit or engross the supply of a given line of goods or services. So long as such a special advantage is not specifically protected by special legislation or by a due legal instrument, – as in the case of a franchise or a patent right, – it is likely to be spoken of loosely as "good-will."

The results of the analysis may be summed up to show the degree of coincidence and the distinctions between the two categories of assets: (a) the value (that is to say, the amount) of given assets, whether tangible or intangible, is the capitalized (or capitalizable) value of the given articles of wealth, rated on the basis of their income-yielding capacity to their owner; (b) in the case of tangible assets there is a presumption that the objects of wealth involved have some (at least potential) serviceability at large, since they serve a materially productive work, and there is therefore a presumption, more or less well founded, that their value represents, tho it by no means measures, an item of serviceability at large; (c) in the ease of intangible assets there is no presumption that the objects of wealth involved have any serviceability at large, since they serve no materially productive work, but only a differential advantage to the owner in the distribution of the industrial product;[20] (d) given tangible assets may [116] be disserviceable to the community, – a given material equipment may owe its value as capital to a disserviceable use, tho in the aggregate or on an average the body of tangible assets are (presumptively) serviceable; (e) given intangible assets may be indifferent in respect of serviceability at large, tho in the aggregate, or on an average, intangible assets are (presumably) disserviceable to the community.

On this showing it would appear that the substantial difference between tangible and intangible assets lies in the different character of the immaterial facts which are turned to pecuniary account in the one case and in the other. The former, in effect, capitalize such fraction of the technological proficiency

20 A doubt has been offered as to the applicability of this characterization to such intangible assets as a patent right and other items of the same class. The doubt seems to arise from a misapprehension of the analysis and of its intention. It should be remarked that there is no intention to condemn or disapprove any of the items here spoken of as intangible assets. The patent right may be justifiable or it may not – there is no call to discuss that question here. Other intangible assets are in the same case in this respect.

Further, as to the character of a patent right considered as an asset. The invention or innovation covered by the patent right is a contribution to the common stock of technological proficiency. It may be (immediately) serviceable to the community at large, or it may not; – e.g., a cash register, a bank-check punch, a street-car fare register, a burglar-proof safe and the like are of no immediate service to the community at large, but serve only a pecuniary use to their users. But, whether the innovation is useful or not, the patent right, as an asset, has no (immediate) usefulness at large, since its essence is the restriction of the usufruct of the innovation to the patentee. Immediately and directly the patent right must be considered a detriment to the community at large, since its purport is to prevent the community from making use of the patented innovation, whatever may be its ulterior beneficial effects or its ethical justification.

of the community as the ownership of the capital goods involved enables the owner to engross. The latter capitalize such habits of life, of a non-technological character, – settled by usage, convention, arrogation, legislative action, or what not, – as will effect a differential advantage to the concern to which the assets in question appertain. The former owe their existence and magnitude to the usufruct of technological expedients involved in the industrial process proper; while the latter are in like manner due to the usufruct of what may be called the interstitial correlations and adjustments [117] both within the industrial system and between industry proper and the market, in so far as these relations are of a pecuniary rather than a technological character. Much the same distinction may be put in other words, so as to bring the expression nearer the current popular apprehension of the matter, by saying that tangible assets, commonly so called, capitalize the processes of production, while intangible assets, so called, capitalize certain expedients and processes of acquisition, not productive of wealth, but affecting only its distribution. Formulated in either way, the distinction seems not to be an altogether hard-and-fast one, as will immediately appear if it is called to mind that intangible assets may be converted into tangible assets, and conversely, as the exigencies of business may decide. Yet, while the two categories of assets stand in such close relation to one another as this state of things presumes, it is still evident from the same state of things that they are not to be confounded with one another.

Taking "good-will" as typical of the category of "intangible assets," as being the most widely prevalent and at the same time the farthest removed in its characteristics from the range of "tangible assets," some slight further discussion of it may serve to bring out the difference between the two categories of assets and at the same time to enforce their essential congruity as assets as well as the substantial connection between them. In the earlier days of the concept, in the period of growth to which it owes its name, when good-will was coming into recognition as a factor affecting assets, it was apparently looked on habitually as an adventitious differential advantage accruing spontaneously to the business concern to which it appertained; an immaterial by-product of the concern's conduct of business, – commonly presumed to be an adventitious blessing incident to an upright and [118] humane course of business life. Poor Richard would express this sense of the matter in the saying that "honesty is the best policy." But presently, no doubt, some thought would be taken of the acquirement of good-will and some effort would be expended by the wise business man in that behalf. Goods would be given a more elegant finish for the sake of a readier sale, beyond what would conduce to their brute serviceability simply; smooth-spoken and obsequious salesmen and solicitors, gifted with a tactful effrontery, have come to be preferred to others, who, without these merits, may be possessed of all the diligence, dexterity, and muscular force required in their trade; something is expended on convincing, not to say vain-glorious, show-windows that shall promise something more than one would like to commit one's self to in words;

itinerant agents, and the like, are employed at some expense to secure a clientèle; much thought and substance is spent on advertising of many kinds.

This last-named item may be taken as typical of the present stage of growth in the production or generation of good-will, and therefore in the creation of intangible assets. Advertising has come to be an important branch of business enterprise by itself, and it employs a large and varied array of material appliances and processes (tangible assets). Investment is made in certain material items (productive goods), such as printed matter, signboards, and the like, with a view to creating a certain body of good-will. The precise magnitude of the product may not be foreseen, but, if sagaciously made, such investment rarely fails of the effect aimed at – unless a business rival with even greater sagacity should outmanoeuvre and offset these endeavors with a superior array of appliances (productive goods) and workmen for the generation of good-will. The product aimed at, commonly with effect, is good-will, – an intangible asset, – which [119] may be considered to have been generated by converting certain tangible assets into this intangible; or it may be considered as an industrial product, the output of certain industrial processes in which the given items of material equipment are employed and give effect to the requisite technological proficiency. Whichever view be taken of the causal relation between the material equipment and processes employed, on the one hand, and the output of good-will, on the other hand, the result is substantially the same for the purpose in hand.

The ulterior end of the advertising is, it may be said, the sale of an increased quantity of the advertised articles, at an increased net gain; which would mean an increased value of the material items offered for sale; which, in turn, is the same as saying an increase of tangible assets. It may be assumed without debate that the end of business endeavor is a gain in final terms of tangible values. But this ulterior end is, in the case of advertising enterprise, to be gained only by the intermediate step of a production of an immaterial item of good-will, an intangible asset.

So the case in illustration shows not only the conversion of tangible assets (material capital goods, such as printed matter) into intangible wealth, or, if that formula be preferred, the production of immaterial wealth by the productive use of material wealth, but also, conversely, in the second step of the process, it shows the conversion of intangible assets into tangible wealth (enhanced value of vendible goods), or, if the expression seems preferable, the production of tangible assets by the use of intangible wealth.

This creation of tangible wealth out of intangible assets is seen perhaps at its neatest in the enhancement of land values by the endeavors of interested parties. Real estate is, of course, a tangible asset of the most authentic tangibility, and it is an asset to the amount of its value, which is determined, say, by the figures at which the real estate [120] in question is currently bought and sold. This is the current value of the real estate, and therefore its current actual magnitude as a tangible asset. The value of the real estate might also be computed by capitalizing its rental value; but, where the current market value does not coincide with the capitalized rental value, the former must, according to business conceptions, be accepted as the actual value. In many parts of this country, perhaps in most, but particularly in the Western States and in the neighborhood of flourishing towns, these two methods of rating the pecuniary magnitude of real estate will habitually not coincide. Due allowance, often very considerable, being made, the capitalized rental value of the land may be taken as measuring its current serviceability as an item of material equipment; while the amount by which the market value of the land exceeds its capitalized rental value may be taken as the product, the tangible residue, of an intangible asset of the nature of good-will, turned to account, or "productively employed," in behalf of this parcel of land.[21]

Some of the lands of California may be taken as a very good, though perhaps not an extreme, example of such a creation of real estate by spiritual instrumentalities. It is probably well within the mark to say that some of these lands owe not more than one-half their current market value to their current serviceability as an instrument of production or use. The excess may be attributable to illusions touching the chances of future sale, to anticipation of a prospective enhanced usefulness, and the like; but all these are immaterial factors, of the nature of good-will. [121] Like other assets, these lands are capitalized on the basis of the anticipated income from them, part of which income is anticipated from profitable sales to persons who, it is hoped, will be persuaded to take a very sanguine view of the land situation, while part of it may be due to over-sanguine anticipations of usefulness generated by the advertising matter and the efforts of the land agents directed to what is called "developing the country."

To any one preoccupied with the conceit that "capital" means "capital goods" such a conversion of intangible into tangible goods, or such a generation of intangible assets by the productive use of tangible assets, might be something of a puzzle. If "assets" were a physical concept, covering a range of physical things, instead of a pecuniary concept, such conversion of tangible into intangible assets, and conversely, would be a case of transubstantiation. But there is nothing miraculous in the matter. "Assets" are a pecuniary magnitude, and belong among the facts of investment. Except in relation to investment the items of wealth involved are not assets. In other words, assets are a matter of capitalization, which is a special case of valuation; and the question of tangibility or intangibility as regards a given parcel of assets is a question what article or class of articles the valuation shall attach to or be

---

21 Neither as a physical magnitude ("land") nor as a pecuniary magnitude ("real estate") is the capitalized land in question an item of "good-will"; but its value as real estate – i.e., its magnitude as an asset – is in part a product of the "good-will" (illusions and the like) worked up in its behalf and turned to account, by the land agent. The real estate is a tangible asset, an item of material wealth, while the "good-will" to which in part it owes its magnitude as an item of wealth is an intangible asset, an item of immaterial wealth.

imputed to. If, e.g., the fact to which value is imputed in the valuation is the habitual demand for a given article of merchandise, or the habitual resort of a given group of customers to a particular shop or merchant, or a monopolistic control or limitation of price and supply, then the resulting item of assets will be "intangible," since the object to which the capitalized value in question is imputed is an immaterial object. If the fact which is by imputation made the bearer of the capitalized value is a material object, as, e.g., the merchantable goods of which the supply is arbitrarily limited or the price arbitrarily fixed, [122] or if it is the material means of supplying such goods, then the capitalized value in question is a case of tangible assets. The value involved is, like all value, a matter of imputation, and as assets it is a matter of capitalization; but capitalization is an appraisement of a pecuniary "income-stream" in terms of the vendible objects to the ownership of which the income is assumed to inure. To what object the capitalized value of the "income-stream" shall be imputed is a question of what object of ownership secures to the owner an effectual claim on this "income-stream"; that is to say, it is a question of what object of ownership the strategic advantage is assumed to attach to, which is a question of the play of business exigencies in the given case.

The "income-stream" in question is a pecuniary income stream, and is in the last resort traceable to transactions of sale. Within the confines of business – and therefore within the scope of capital, investments, assets, and the like business concepts – transactions of purchase and sale are the final terms of any analysis. But beyond these confines, comprehending and conditioning the business system, lie the material facts of the community's work and livelihood. In the final transaction of sale the merchantable goods are valued by the consumer, not as assets, but as livelihood;[22] and in the last analysis and long run it is to some such transaction that all business imputations of value and capitalistic appraisement of assets must have regard and by which they must finally be checked. Dissociated from the facts of work and livelihood, therefore, assets cease to be assets; but this does not preclude their relation to these facts of work and livelihood being at times somewhat remote and loose. [123]

Without recourse, immediately or remotely, to certain material facts of industrial process and equipment, assets would not yield earnings; that is to say, wholly disjoined from these material facts, they would in effect not be assets. This is true for both tangible and intangible assets, although the relation of the assets to the material facts of industry is not the same in the two cases. The case of tangible assets needs no argument. Intangible assets, such as patent right or monopolistic control, are likewise of no effect except in effectual contact with industrial facts. The patent right becomes effective for the purpose only in the material working of the innovation covered by it; and

---

22 "Livelihood" is, of course, here taken in a loose sense, not as denoting the means of subsistence simply or even the means of physical comfort, but as signifying that the purchases in question are made with a view to the consumptive use of the goods rather than with a view to their use for a profit.

monopolistic control is a source of gain only in so far as it effectually modifies or divides the supply of goods.

In the light of these considerations it seems feasible to indicate both the congruence and the distinction between the two categories of assets a little more narrowly than was done above. Both are assets, – that is to say, both are values determined by a capitalization of anticipated income-yielding capacity; both depend for their income-yielding capacity on the preferential use of certain immaterial factors; both depend for their efficiency on the use of certain material objects; both may increase or decrease, as assets, apart from any increase or decrease of the material objects involved. The tangible assets capitalize the preferential use of technological, industrial expedients, – expedients of production, dealing with the facts of brute nature under the laws of physical cause and effect, – this preferential use being secured by the ownership of material articles employed in the processes in which these expedients are put into effect. The intangible assets capitalize the preferential use of certain facts of human nature – habits, propensities, beliefs, aspirations, necessities – to be dealt with under the psychological laws of human motivation; this preferential use being secured by [124] custom, as in the case of old-fashioned good-will, by legal assignment, as in patent or copyright, by ownership of the instruments of production, as in the case of industrial monopolies.[23]

Intangible assets are capital as well as tangible assets; that is to say, they are items of capitalized wealth. Both categories of assets, therefore, represent expected "income-streams" which are of such definite character as to admit of their being rated in set terms per cent. per time unit; although the expected income need not therefore be anticipated to come in an even flow or to be distributed in any equable manner over a period of time. The income-streams to be so rated and capitalized are associated in such a manner with some external fact (impersonal to their claimant), whether material or immaterial, as to permit their being traced or attributed to an income-yielding capacity on the part of this external fact, to which their valuation as a whole may be imputed and which may then be capitalized as an item of wealth yielding this income-stream. Income-streams which do not meet these requirements do not give rise to assets, and so do not swell the volume of capitalized wealth.

There are income-streams which do not meet the necessary specifications of capitalizable wealth; and in modern business traffic, particularly, there are large and secure sources of income that are in this way not capitalizable and yet yield a legitimate business income. Such are, indeed, to be rated among

---

23 The instruments of production so monopolized are, of course, tangible assets, but the ownership of such means of production in amount sufficient to enable the owner to monopolize or control the market, whether for purchase (as of materials or labor) or for sale (as of marketable goods or services), gives rise to a differential business advantage which is to be classed as intangible assets.

the most consequential factors in the current business situation. Under the guidance of traditions carried over from a more primitive business [125] situation, it has been usual to speak of income-streams derived in such a manner as "wages of superintendence," or "undertaker's wages," or "entrepreneur's profits," or, latterly, as "profits" simply and specifically. Such phenomena of this class as are of consequence in business are commonly accounted for, theoretically, under this head; and the effort so to account for them is to be taken as, at least, a laudable endeavor to avoid an undue multiplication of technical terms and categories.[24] Yet the most striking phenomena of this class, and the most consequential for modern business and industry, both in respect of their magnitude and in respect of the pecuniary dominion and discretion which they represent, cannot well be accounted undertaker's gains, in the ordinary sense of that term. The great gains of the great industrial financiers or of the great "interests," e.g., do not answer the description of undertaker's gains, in that they do not accrue to the captain of industry on the basis of his "managerial ability" alone, apart from his wealth or out of relation to his wealth; and yet it is not safe to say that such gains (which are over and above ordinary returns on his investments) accrue on the ground of the requisite amount of wealth alone, apart from the exercise of a large business discretion on the part of the owner of such wealth or on the part of his agent to whom discretion has been delegated. Administrative, or strategic, discretion and activity must necessarily be present in the case: otherwise, the income in question would rightly be rated as income from capital simply.

The captain of industry, the pecuniary magnate, is normally in receipt of income in excess of the ordinary [126] rate per cent. on investment; but apart from his large holdings he is not in a position to get those large gains. Dissociated from his large holdings, he is not a large captain of industry; but it is not the size of his holdings alone that determines what the gains of the pecuniary magnate in modern industry shall be. Gains of the kind and magnitude that currently come to this class of business men come only on condition that the owner (or his agent) shall exercise a similarly large discretion and control in the affairs of the business community; but the magnitude of the gains, as well as of the discretion and control exercised, is somewhat definitely conditioned by the magnitude of the wealth which gives effect to this discretion.

The disposition of pecuniary forces in such matters may be well seen in the work and remuneration of any coalition of "interests," such as the modern business community has become familiar with. The "interests" in such a case are of a personal character, – they are "interested parties," – and the sagacity, experience, and animus of these various interested parties counts in the outcome, both as

24 One writer even goes so far in the endeavor to bring the facts within the scope of the staple concepts of theory at this point as to rate the persons concerned in such a case as "capital," after having satisfied himself that such income-streams are traceable to a personal source – see Fisher, *Nature of Capital and Income*, chap. v.

regards the aggregate gains of the coalition and as regards the distribution of these gains among the several parties in interest; but the weight of any given "interest" in a coalition or "system" is more nearly proportioned to the wealth controlled by the given "interest," and to the strategic position of such wealth, than to any personal talents or proficiency of the "interested party." The talents and proficiency involved are not the main facts. Indeed, the movements of such a "system," and of the several component "interests," are largely a matter of artless routine, in which the greatest ingenuity and initiative engaged in the premises are commonly exercised by the legal counsel working for a fee.

A dispassionate student of the current business traffic, who is not overawed by round numbers, will be more impressed [127] by the ease and simplicity of the manoeuvres that lead to large pecuniary results in the higher business finance than by any evidence of pre-eminent sagacity and initiative among the pecuniary magnates. One need only call to mind the simple and obvious way in which the promoters of the Steel Corporation were magnificently checkmated by the financiers of the Carnegie "interest," when that great and reluctant corporation was floated, or the pettyfogging tactics of Standard Oil in its later career. In extenuation of their visible lack of initiative and insight it may not be ungraceful to call to mind that many of the discretionary heads of the great "interests" are men of advanced years, and that in the nature of the case the pecuniary magnates of the present generation must commonly be men of a somewhat advanced age; and it is only during the present generation that the existing situation has arisen, with its characteristic opportunities and demands. To take their present foremost rank in the new business finance which is here under inquiry, they have had to accumulate the great wealth on which alone their discretionary control of business affairs rests, and their best vigor has been spent in this work of preparation; so that they have commonly attained the requisite strategic position only after they had outlived their "years of discretion."

But there is no intention here to depreciate the work of the pecuniary magnates or the spokesmen of the great "interests." The matter has been referred to only as it bears on this category of capitalistic income which accrues on other ground than the "earning-capacity" of the assets involved, and which still cannot be imputed to the "earning-capacity" of these business men apart from these assets. The case is evidently not one of "wages of superintendence" or "undertaker's profits"; but it is as evidently not a case of the earning-capacity of the [128] assets. The proof of the latter point is quite as easy as of the former. If the gains of the "system" or of its constituent "interests" and magnates were imputable to the earning-capacity of the assets involved, – in any accepted sense of "earnings," – then it would immediately follow that those assets would be recapitalized on the basis of these extra-ordinary earnings, and that the income derived in this class of traffic should reappear as interest or dividends on the capital so increased to correspond with the increased earnings. But such recapitalization takes place only to a relatively very limited extent, and the question then bears on the income which is not so accounted for in the recapitalization.

The gains of this class of traffic are, of course, themselves capitalized, – for the most part they accrue in the capitalized form, as issues of securities and the like; but the sources of this income are not capitalized as such. The (large) accumulated wealth, or assets, which gives weight to the movements of the "interests" and magnates in question, and which affords the ground for the discretionary control of business affairs exercised by them, are, for the most part at least, invested in ordinary business ventures, in the form of corporation securities and the like, and are there earning dividends or interest at current rates; and these assets are valued in the market (and thereby capitalized) on the basis of their current earnings in the various enterprises in which they are so invested. But their being so invested in profitable business enterprises does not in the least hinder their usefulness in the hands of the magnates as a basis or means of carrying on the large and highly profitable transactions of the higher industrial finance. To impute these gains to those assets as "earnings," therefore, would be to count the assets twice as capital, or rather to count them over and over. [129]

An additional perplexity in endeavoring to handle gains of this class theoretically as earnings, in the ordinary sense, arises from the fact that they stand in no definable time relation to their underlying assets. They have no definable "time-shape," as Mr. Fisher might put it.[25] Such gains are timeless, in the sense that the time relation does not count in any substantial manner or in any sensible degree in their determination.[26]

In a more painstaking statement of this point of theory it would be necessary to note that these gains are "timeless," in the sense indicated, in so far as the enterprise from which they accrue is dissociated from the technological circumstances and processes of industry, and only in so far. Technological (industrial) procedure, being of the nature of physical causation, is subject to the time relation under which causal sequence runs. This is the basis of such discussions of capital and interest as those of Böhm-Bawerk, and of Fisher. But business traffic, as distinguished from the processes of industry, being not immediately concerned with the technological process, is also not immediately or uniformly subject to the time relation involved in the causal sequence of the technological process. Business traffic is subject to the time relation because and in so far as it depends upon and follows up the processes of production. The commonplace or old-fashioned business enterprise, the competitive system of investment in industrial business simply, commonly rests pretty directly on the due sequence of the industrial processes in which the investments of such enterprise are placed. Such enterprise, as conceived by

25 Cf. Fisher, *Rate of Interest*, chap. vi.
26 This conclusion is reached, e.g., by Mr. G. P. Watkins (*The Growth of Large Fortunes*, chap. iii, sec. 10), although, through a curious etymological misapprehension, he rejects the term "timeless" as not available.

the current theories of capital, does business at first hand [130] in the industrial efficiency of the community, which is conditioned by the time relation of the causal sequence, and which is, indeed, in great measure a function of the time consumed in the technological processes. Therefore, the gains, as well as the transactions, of such enterprise are also commonly somewhat closely conditioned by the like time relation, and they typically emerge under the form of a per cent. per time unit; that is to say, as a function of the lapse of time. Yet the business transactions themselves are not a matter of the lapse of time. Time is not of the essence of the case. The magnitude of a pecuniary transaction is not a function of the time consumed in concluding it, nor are the gains which accrue from the transaction. In business enterprise on the higher plane, which is here under inquiry, the relation of the transactions, and of their gains, to the consecution of the technological processes remotely underlying them is distant, loose, and uncertain, so that the time element here does not obtrude itself: rather, it somewhat obviously falls into abeyance, marking the degree of its remoteness. Yet this phase of business enterprise, like any other, of course takes place in time; and, it is also to be remarked, the volume of the traffic and the gains derived from it are, no doubt, somewhat closely conditioned in the long run by the time relation which dominates that technological (industrial) efficiency on which this enterprise, too, ultimately and indirectly rests and from which in the last resort its gains are finally drawn, however remotely and indirectly.

An analysis of these phenomena on lines similar to those which have been followed in the discussion of assets above is not without difficulty, nor can it fairly be expected to yield any but tentative and provisional results. The matter has received so little attention from economic theoreticians that even significant mistakes in this connection [131] are of very rare occurrence.[27] The cause of this scant attention to these matters lies, no doubt, in the relative novelty of the facts in question. The facts may be roughly drawn together under the caption "Traffic in Vendible Capital"; although that term serves rather as a comprehensive designation of the class of business enterprise from which these gains accrue than as an adequate characterization of the play of forces involved.[28] Traffic in vendible capital has not been unknown in the past, but it is only recently that it has come into the foreground as the most important line of business enterprise. Such it now is, in that it is in this traffic that the ultimate initiative and discretion in business are now to be found. It is at the same time the most gainful of business enterprise, not only in absolute terms, but relatively to the magnitude of the assets involved as well. One

---

27 Even Mr. Watkins (as cited above [in note 26 in this Selection]), e.g., is led by a superficial generalization to class these gains as "speculative," and so to excuse himself from a closer acquaintance with their character and with the bearings of the class of business enterprise out of which they arise.

28 Cf. [Veblen,] *Theory of Business Enterprise*, chap v., pp. 119–30; chap. vi, pp. 162–74.

reason for this superior gainfulness is the fact that the assets involved in this traffic are at the same time engaged as assets to their full extent in ordinary business, so that the peculiar gains of this traffic are of the nature of a bonus above the earnings of the invested wealth. "It is like finding money."

As was said above, the method, or the ways and means, characteristic of this superior business enterprise is a traffic in vendible capital. The wealth gained in this field is commonly in the capitalized form, and constitutes, in each transaction or "deal," a deduction or abstraction from the capitalized wealth of the business commonly in favor of the magnates or "interests" to whom the gains accrue. Its proximate aim is a transfer of capitalized [132] wealth from other capitalists to those who so gain. This transfer or abstraction of capitalized wealth from the former owners is commonly effected by all augmentation of the nominal capital, based on a (transient) advantage inuring to the particular concerns whose capitalization is so augmented.[29] Any such increase of the community's aggregate capitalization, without a corresponding increase of the material wealth on which the capitalization is based, involves, of course, in effect a redistribution of the aggregate capitalized wealth; and in this redistribution the great financiers are in a position to gain. The gains in question, it will be seen, come out of the business community, out of invested wealth, and only remotely and indirectly out of the community at large from which the business community draws its income. These gains, therefore, are a tax on commonplace business enterprise, in much the same manner and with much the like effect as the gains of commonplace business (ordinary profits and interest) are a tax on industry.[30]

In a manner analogous to the old-fashioned capitalist-employer's engrossing of the industrial community's technological efficiency does the modern pecuniary magnate engross the business community's capitalistic efficiency. This capitalistic efficiency lies in the capitalist-employer's ability – by force of the ownership of the material equipment – to induce the industrial community, through suitable bargaining, to turn over to the owner of the material equipment the excess of the product above the industrial [133] community's livelihood. The fortunes of the capitalist-employer are closely dependent on the run of the market, – the conjunctures of advantageous purchase and sale; and it is his constant endeavor to create or gain for himself some peculiar degree of advantage in the market, in the way of monopoly, good-will, legalized privilege, and the like, – something in the way of intangible assets. But the pecuniary magnate, in the measure in which he truly answers to the concept, is superior to the market

---

29 Cf. [Veblen,] *Theory of Business Enterprise*, footnote on pp. 169–70.

30 As should be evident from the run of the argument in the earlier portions of this paper, the use of the words "tax," "deduction," "abstraction," in this connection, is not to be taken as implying approval or disapproval of the phenomena, so characterized. The words are used for want of better terms to indicate the source of business gains, and objectively to characterize the relation of give-and-take between industry and ordinary capitalistic business, on the one hand, and between ordinary business and this business enterprise on the higher plane, on the other hand.

on which the capitalist-employer depends, and can make or mar its conjunctures of advantageous purchase and sale of goods; that is to say, he is in a position to make or mar any peculiar advantage possessed by the given capitalist-employer who comes in his way. He does this by force of his large holdings of capital at large, the weight of which he can shift from one point of investment to another as the relative efficiency – earning-capacity – of one and another line of investment may make it expedient; and at each move of this kind, in so far as it is effective for his ends, he cuts into and assimilates a fraction of the invested wealth involved, in that he cuts into and sequesters a fraction of the capital's earning-capacity in the given line. That is to say, in the measure in which he is a pecuniary magnate, and not simply a capitalist-employer, he engrosses the capitalistic efficiency of invested wealth; he turns to his own account the capitalist-employer's effectual engrossing of the community's industrial efficiency. He engrosses the community's pecuniary initiative and proficiency. In the measure, therefore, in which this relatively new-found serviceability of extraordinarily large wealth is effective for its peculiar business function, the old-fashioned capitalist-employer loses his discretionary initiative and becomes a mediator, an instrumentality of extraction and transmission, a collector and conveyer of revenue from the community at large to the pecuniary [134] magnate, who, in the ideal case, should leave him only such an allowance out of the gross earnings collected and transmitted as will induce him to continue in business.

To the community at large, whose industrial efficiency is already virtually engrossed by the capitalist-employer's ownership and control of the material equipment, this later step in the evolution of the economic situation should apparently not be a matter of substantial consequence or a matter for sentimental disturbance. On the face of it, it should appear to have little more than a speculative interest for those classes of the community who do not derive an income from investments; particularly not for the working classes, who own nothing to speak of and whose only dependence is their technological efficiency, which has virtually ceased to be their own. But such is not the current state of sentiment. This inchoate new phase of capitalism, this business enterprise on the higher plane, is in fact viewed with the most lively apprehension. In a maze of consternation and solicitude the boldest, wisest, most public-spirited, most illustrious gentlemen of our time are spending their manhood in an endeavor to make the hen continue sitting on the nest after the chickens are out of the shell. The modern community is imbued with business principles – of the old dispensation. By precept and example, men have learned that the business interests (of the authentic superannuated scale and kind) are the palladium of our civilization, as Mr. Dooley[31] would say; and it is felt that any disturbance

31 [Mr. Dooley is a fictional character created by the Chicago satirist Finley Peter Dunne in *Mr. Dooley in Peace and War* (1898) and seven further volumes including *Observations by Mr. Dooley* (1902). The phrase "palajeems iv our liberties" appears in the latter. – Eds.]

of the existing pecuniary dominion of the capitalist-employer – as contrasted with the pecuniary magnate – would involve the well-being of the community in one common agony of desolation.

The merits of this perturbation, or of the remedies proposed for saving the pecuniary life of the old-fashioned capitalist-employer, of course do not concern the present [135] inquiry; but the matter has been referred to here as evidence that the pecuniary magnate's work, and the dominion which his extraordinarily large wealth gives him, are, in effect, substantially a new phase of the economic development, and that these phenomena are distastefully unfamiliar and are felt to be consequential enough to threaten the received institutional structure. That is to say, it is felt to be a new phase of business enterprise, – distasteful to those who stand to lose by it.

The basis of this business enterprise on the higher plane is capital-at-large, as distinguished from capital invested in a given line of industrial enterprise, and it becomes effective when wealth has accumulated in holdings sufficiently large to give the holder (or combination of holders, the "system") a controlling weight in any group or ramification of business interests into which he may throw his weight by judicious investment (or by underwriting and the like). The pecuniary magnate must be able effectually to engross the pecuniary initiative and the business opportunities on which such a section or ramification of the business community depends for its ordinary gains. How large a proportion of the business community's capital is needed for such an effectual engrossing of its capitalistic efficiency, in any given bearing, is a question that cannot be answered in anything like absolute terms, or even in relative terms of a satisfactorily definite kind. It is, of course, evident that a relatively large disposable body of capital is needed for such a purpose; and it is also evident, from the current facts of business, that the body of capital so disposed of need not amount to a majority, or anything near a majority, of the investments involved, – at least not at the present relatively inchoate phase of this larger business enterprise. The larger the holdings of the magnate, the more effectual and expeditious will be his work of absorbing the holdings of the smaller [136] capitalist-employer, and the more precipitately will the latter yield his assets to the new claimant.

Evidently, this work of the pecuniary magnate bears a great resemblance to the creation of intangible assets under the ordinary competitive system. This is, no doubt, the point of its nearest relation to the current capitalistic enterprise. But, as has already been indicated above, it cannot be said that the magnate's peculiar work is the creation of intangible, or other assets, although there is commonly some recapitalization involved in his manoeuvres, and although his gains commonly come as assets, i.e., in the capitalized form. Nor can it, as has also been indicated above, be said that the wealth which serves him as the means of his peculiar enterprise stands in the relation of assets to this enterprise or to the gains in question, since this wealth already stands in an exhaustive relation as assets to some corporate enterprise in ordinary business and to the corresponding items of interest and dividends. It may, of course, be contended that the present state of things on this higher plane of enterprise is transient and transitional only, and that in the settled condition which may conceivably supervene the magnate's relation to business at large will be capitalized in some form of intangible assets, after the manner in which the monopoly advantage of an ordinary "trust" is now capitalized. But this is at the best only a surmise, guided by inapplicable generalizations drawn from a past situation in which this higher enterprise has not engrossed the pecuniary initiative and played the ruling part.

Selection 34

The evolution of the scientific point of view

Source: *University of California Chronicle*, October 1908
(vol. 10, pp. 395–416).

Veblen (1908d)

A discussion of the scientific point of view which avowedly proceeds from this point of view itself has necessarily the appearance of an argument in a circle; and such in great part is the character of what here follows.[1] It is in large part an attempt to explain the scientific point of view in terms of itself, but not altogether. This inquiry does not presume to deal with the origin or the legitimation of the postulates of science, but only with the growth of the habitual use of these postulates, and the manner of using them. The point of inquiry is the changes which have taken place in the secondary postulates involved in the scientific point of view – in great part a question of the progressive redistribution of emphasis among the preconceptions under whose guidance successive generations of scientists have gone to their work.

The sciences which are in any peculiar sense modern take as an (unavowed) postulate the fact of consecutive change. Their inquiry always centers upon some manner of process. This notion of process about which the researches of modern science cluster, is a notion of a sequence, or complex, of consecutive change in which the *nexus* of the sequence, that by [396] virtue of which the change inquired into is consecutive, is the relation of cause and effect. The consecution, moreover, runs in terms of persistence of quantity or of force. In so far as the science is of a modern complexion, in so far as it is not of the nature of taxonomy simply, the inquiry converges upon a matter of process; and it comes to rest, provisionally, when it has disposed of its facts in terms of process. But modern scientific inquiry in any case comes to rest only provisionally; because its prime postulate is that of consecutive change, and consecutive change can, of course, not come to rest except provisionally. By its own nature the inquiry cannot reach a final term in any direction. So it is something of a homiletical commonplace to say that the outcome of any serious research can only be to make two questions grow where one question grew before. Such is necessarily the case because the postulate of the scientist

---

1 Read before the Kosmos Club, at the University of California, May 4, 1908.

is that things change consecutively. It is an unproven and unprovable postulate – that is to say, it is a metaphysical preconception – but it gives the outcome that every goal of research is necessarily a point of departure; every term is transitional.[2] [397]

2 It is by no means unusual for modern scientists to deny the truth of this characterization, so far as regards this alleged recourse to the concept of causation. They deny that such a concept – of efficiency, activity, and the like – enters, or can legitimately enter, into their work, whether as an instrument of research or as a means or guide to theoretical formulation. They even deny the substantial continuity of the sequence of changes that excite their scientific attention. This attitude seems particularly to commend itself to those who by preference attend to the mathematical formulations of theory and who are chiefly occupied with proving up and working out details of the system of theory which have previously been left unsettled or uncovered. The concept of causation is recognized to be a metaphysical postulate, a matter of imputation, not of observation; whereas it is claimed that scientific inquiry neither does nor can legitimately, nor, indeed, currently, make use of a postulate more metaphysical than the concept of an idle concomitance of variation, such as is adequately expressed in terms of mathematical function.

The contention seems sound, to the extent that the materials – essentially statistical materials – with which scientific inquiry is occupied are of this non-committal character, and that the mathematical formulations of theory include no further element than that of idle variation. [397] Such is necessarily the case because causation is a fact of imputation, not of observation, and so cannot be included among the data; and because nothing further than non-committal variation can be expressed in mathematical terms. A bare notation of quantity can convey nothing further.

If it were the intention to claim only that the conclusions of the scientists are, or should be, as a matter of conservative caution, overtly stated in terms of function alone, then the contention might well be allowed. Causal sequence, efficiency or continuity is, of course, a matter of metaphysical imputation. It is not a fact of observation, and cannot be asserted of the facts of observation except as a trait imputed to them. It is so imputed, by scientists and others, as a matter of logical necessity, as a basis of a systematic knowledge of the facts of observation.

Beyond this, in their exercise of scientific initiative, as well as in the norms which guide the systematization of scientific results, the contention will not be made good – at least not for the current phase of scientific knowledge. The claim, indeed, carries its own refutation. In making such a claim, both in rejecting the imputation of metaphysical postulates and in defending their position against their critics, the arguments put forward by the scientists run in causal terms. For the polemical purposes, where their antagonists are to be scientifically confuted, the defenders of the non-committal postulate of concomitance find that postulate inadequate. They are not content, in this precarious conjuncture, simply to attest a relation of idle quantitative concomitance (mathematical function) between the allegations of their critics, on the one hand, and their own controversial exposition of these matters on the other hand. They argue that they do not "make use of" such a postulate as "efficiency," whereas they claim to "make use of" the concept of function. But "make use of" is not a notion of functional variation but of causal efficiency in a somewhat gross and highly anthropomorphic form. The relation between their own thinking and the "principles" which they "apply" or the experiments and calculations which they "institute" in their "search" for facts, is not held to be of this non-committal kind. It will not be claimed that the shrewd insight and the bold initiative of a man eminent in the empirical sciences bear no more efficient or consequential a relation than that of mathematical function to the ingenious experiments by which he tests his hypotheses and extends the secure bounds of human knowledge. Least of all is the masterly experimentalist himself in a position to deny that his intelligence counts for something more efficient [398] than idle concomitance in such a case. The connection between his premises, hypotheses, and experiments, on the one hand, and his

A hundred years ago, or even fifty years ago, scientific men were not in the habit of looking at the matter in this way. At least it did not then seem a matter of course, lying in the nature of things, that scientific inquiry could not reach a final term in any direction. To-day it is a matter of course, and will be so avowed without argument. Stated in the broadest terms, this is the substantial outcome of that [398] nineteenth-century movement in science with which the name of Darwin is associated as a catch-word.

This use of Darwin's name does not imply that this epoch of science is mainly Darwin's work. What merit may belong to Darwin, specifically, in these premises, is a question which need not detain the argument. He may, by way of creative initiative, have had more or less to do with shaping the course of things scientific. Or, if you choose, [399] his voice may even be taken as only one of the noises which the wheels of civilization make when they go round. But by scientifically colloquial usage we have come to speak of pre-Darwinian and post-Darwinian science, and to appreciate that there is a significant difference in the point of view between the scientific era which preceded and that which followed the epoch to which his name belongs.

Before that epoch the animus of a science was, on the whole, the animus of taxonomy; the consistent end of scientific inquiry was definition and classification, – as it still continues to be in such fields of science as have not

---

theoretical results, on the other hand, is not felt to be of the nature of mathematical function. Consistently adhered to, the principle of "function" or concomitant variation precludes recourse to experiment, hypotheses or inquiry – indeed, it precludes "recourse" to anything whatever. Its notation does not comprise anything so anthropomorphic.

The case is illustrated by the latter-day history of theoretical physics. Of the sciences which affect a non-committal attitude in respect of the concept of efficiency and which claim to get along with the notion of mathematical function alone, physics is the most outspoken and the one in which the claim has the best *prima facie* validity. At the same time, latter-day physicists, for a hundred years or more, have been much occupied with explaining how phenomena which to all appearance involve action at a distance do not involve action at a distance at all. The greater theoretical achievements of physics during the past century lie within the sweep of this (metaphysical) principle that action at a distance does not take place, that apparent action at a distance must be explained by effective contact, through a continuum, or by a material transference. But this principle is nothing better than an unreasoning repugnance on the part of the physicists to admitting action at a distance. The requirement of a continuum involves a gross form of the concept of efficient causation. The "functional" concept, concomitant variation, requires no contact and no continuum. Concomitance at a distance is quite as simple and convincing a notion as concomitance within contact or by the intervention of a continuum, if not more so. What stands in the way of its acceptance is the irrepressible anthropomorphism of the physicists. And yet the great achievements of physics are due to the initiative of men animated with this anthropomorphic repugnance to the notion of concomitant variation at a distance. All the generalizations on undulatory motion and translation belong here. The latter-day researches in light, electrical transmission, the theory of ions, together with what is known of the obscure and late-found radiations and emanations, are to be credited to the same metaphysical preconception, which is never absent in any "scientific" inquiry in the field of physical science. It is only the "occult" and "Christian" "Sciences" that can dispense with this metaphysical postulate and take recourse to "absent treatment."

been affected by the modern notion of consecutive change. The scientists of that era looked to a final term, a consummation of the changes which provoked their inquiry, as well as to a first beginning of the matters with which their researches were concerned. The questions of science were directed to the problem, essentially classificatory, of how things had been in the presumed primordial stable equilibrium out of which they, putatively, had come, and how they should be in the definitive state of settlement into which things were to fall as the outcome of the play of forces which intervened between this primordial and the definitive stable equilibrium. To the pre-Darwinian taxonomists the center of interest and attention, to which all scientific inquiry must legitimately converge, was the body of natural laws governing phenomena under the rule of causation. These natural laws were of the nature of rules of the game of causation. They formulated the immutable relations in which things "naturally" stood to one another before causal disturbance took place between them, the orderly unfolding of the complement of causes involved in the transition over this interval of transient activity, and the settled relations that would supervene when the disturbance had passed and the transition from cause to effect had been consummated, – the emphasis falling on the consummation.

The characteristic feature by which post-Darwinian [400] science is contrasted with what went before is a new distribution of emphasis, whereby the process of causation, the interval of instability and transition between initial cause and definitive effect, has come to take the first place in the inquiry; instead of that consummation in which causal effect was once presumed to come to rest. This change of the point of view was, of course, not abrupt or catastrophic. But it has latterly gone so far that modern science is becoming substantially a theory of the process of consecutive change, which is taken as a sequence of cumulative change, realized to be self-continuing or self-propagating and to have no final term. Questions of a primordial beginning and a definitive outcome have fallen into abeyance within the modern sciences, and such questions are in a fair way to lose all claim to consideration at the hands of the scientists. Modern science is ceasing to occupy itself with the natural laws – the codified rules of the game of causation – and is concerning itself wholly with what has taken place and what is taking place.

Rightly seen from this ultra-modern point of view, this modern science and this point of view which it affects are, of course, a feature of the current cultural situation, – of the process of life as it runs along under our eyes. So also, when seen from this scientific point of view, it is a matter of course that any marked cultural era will have its own characteristic attitude and animus toward matters of knowledge, will bring under inquiry such questions of knowledge as lie within its peculiar range of interest, and will seek answers to these questions only in terms that are consonant with the habits of thought current at the time. That is to say, science and the scientific point of view will vary characteristically in response to those variations in the prevalent habits of thought which constitute the sequence of cultural development; the current science and the current scientific point of view, the knowledge sought and the manner of [401] seeking it, are a product of the cultural growth. Perhaps it would all be better characterized as a by-product of the cultured growth.

This question of a scientific point of view, of a particular attitude and animus in matters of knowledge, is a question of the formation of habits of thought; and habits of thought are an outcome of habits of life. A scientific point of view is a consensus of habits of thought current in the community, and the scientist is constrained to believe that this consensus is formed in response to a more or less consistent discipline of habituation to which the community is subjected, and that the consensus can extend only so far and maintain its force only so long as the discipline of habituation exercised by the circum- stances of life enforces it and backs it up. The scheme of life, within which lies the scheme of knowledge, is a consensus of habits in the individuals which make up the community. The individual subjected to habituation is each a single individual agent, and whatever affects him in any one line of activity, therefore, necessarily affects him in some degree in all his various activities. The cultural scheme of any community is a complex of the habits of life and of thought prevalent among the members of the community. It makes up a more or less congruous and balanced whole, and carries within it a more or less consistent habitual attitude toward matters of knowledge – more or less consistent according as the community's cultural scheme is more or less con- gruous throughout the body of the population; and this in its turn is in the main a question of how nearly uniform or consonant are the circumstances of experience and tradition to which the several classes and members of the community are subject.

So, then, the change which has come over the scientific point of view between pre-Darwinian and post-Darwinian times is to be explained, at least in great part, by the changing circumstances of life, and therefore of habi- tuation, [402] among the people of Christendom during the life-history of modern science. But the growth of a scientific point of view begins farther back than modern Christendom, and a record of its growth would be a record of the growth of human culture. Modern science demands a genetic account of the phenomena with which it deals, and a genetic inquiry into the scientific point of view necessarily will have to make up its account with the earlier phases of cultural growth. A life-history of human culture is a large topic, not to be attempted here even in the sketchiest outline. The most that can be attempted is a hasty review of certain scattered questions and salient points in this life-history.

In what manner and with what effect the idle curiosity of mankind first began to tame the facts thrown in its way, far back in the night of time, and to break them in under a scheme of habitual interpretation, what may have been the earliest norms of systematic knowledge, such as would serve the curiosity of the earliest generations of men in a way analogous to the service rendered the curiosity of later generations by scientific inquiry – all that is, of course, a matter of long-range conjecture, more or less wild, which cannot be gone into here. But among such peoples of the lower cultures as have been consistently observed, norms of knowledge and schemes for its systematization are always found. These norms and systems of knowledge are naive and crude, perhaps, but there is fair ground for presuming that out of the like norms and systems in the remoter ages of our own antecedents have grown up the systems of knowledge cultivated by the peoples of history and by their representatives now living.

It is not unusual to say that the primitive systems of knowledge are constructed on animistic lines; that animistic sequence is the rule to which the facts are broken in. This seems to be true, if "animism" be construed in a sufficiently naive and inchoate sense. But this is not the whole case. [403] In their higher generalizations, in what Powell calls their "sophiology,"[3] it appears that the primitive peoples are guided by animistic norms; they make up their cosmological schemes, and the like, in terms of personal or quasi-personal activity, and the whole is thrown into something of a dramatic form. Through the early cosmological lore runs a dramatic consistency which imputes something in the way of initiative and propensity to the phenomena that are to be accounted for. But this dramatization of the facts, the accounting for phenomena in terms of spiritual or quasi-spiritual initiative, is by no means the whole case of primitive men's systematic knowledge of facts. Their theories are not all of the nature of dramatic legend, myth, or animistic life-history, although the broader and more picturesque generalizations may take that form. There always runs along by the side of these dramaturgic life-histories, and underlying them, an obscure system of generalizations in terms of matter-of-fact. The system of matter-of-fact generalizations, or theories, is obscurer than the dramatic generalizations only in the sense that it is left in the background as being less picturesque and of less vital interest, not in the sense of being less familiar, less adequately apprehended, or less secure. The peoples of the lower cultures "know" that the broad scheme of things is to be explained in terms of creation, perhaps of procreation, gestation, birth, growth, life and initiative; and these matters engross the attention and stimulate speculation. But they know equally well the matter of fact that water will run down hill, that two stones are heavier than one of them, that an edge-tool will cut softer substances, that two things may be tied together with a string, that a pointed stick may be stuck in the ground, and the like. There is no range of knowledge that is held more securely by any people than such matters of fact; and these are generalizations from experience; they are theoretical knowledge, and they are a matter of course. They underlie the dramatical generalizations of

---

3 [Veblen here refers to Powell (1901) who defines "sophiology" as "the science of activities designed to give instruction." – Eds.]

the broad [404] scheme of things, and are so employed in the speculations of the myth-makers and the learned.

It may be that the exceptional efficiency of a given edge-tool, e.g., will be accounted for on animistic or quasi-personal grounds, – grounds of magical efficacy; but it is the exceptional behavior of such a tool that calls for explanation on the higher ground of animistic potency, not its work-day performance of common work. So also if an edge-tool should fail to do what is expected of it as a matter of course, its failure may require an explanation in other terms than matter-of-fact. But all that only serves to bring into evidence the fact that a scheme of generalizations in terms of matter-of-fact is securely held and is made use of as a sufficient and ultimate explanation of the more familiar phenomena of experience. These commonplace matter-of-fact generalizations are not questioned and do not clash with the higher scheme of things.

All this may seem like taking pains about trivialities. But the data with which any scientific inquiry has to do are trivialities in some other bearing than that one in which they are of account.

In all succeeding phases of culture, developmentally subsequent to the primitive phase supposed above, there is found a similar or analogous division of knowledge between a higher range of theoretical explanations of phenomena, an ornate scheme of things, on the one hand, and such an obscure range of matter-of-fact generalizations as is here spoken of, on the other hand. And the evolution of the scientific point of view is a matter of the shifting fortunes which have in the course of cultural growth overtaken the one and the other of these two divergent methods of apprehending and systematizing the facts of experience.

The historians of human culture have, no doubt justly, commonly dealt with the mutations that have occurred on the higher levels of intellectual enterprise, in the more ambitious, more picturesque, and less secure of these two [405] contrasted ranges of theoretical knowledge; while the lower range of generalizations, which has to do with work-day experience, has in great part been passed over with scant ceremony as lying outside the current of ideas, and as belonging rather among the things which engage the attention than among the modes, expedients and creations of this attention itself. There is good reason for this relative neglect of the work-day matters of fact. It is on the higher levels of speculative generalization that the impressive mutations in the development of thought have taken place, and that the shifting of points of view and the clashing of convictions have drawn men into controversy and analysis of their ideas and have given rise to schools of thought. The matter-of-fact generalizations have met with relatively few adventures and have afforded little scope for intellectual initiative and profoundly picturesque speculation. On the higher levels speculation is freer, the creative spirit has some scope, because its excursions are not so immediately and harshly checked by material facts.

In these speculative ranges of knowledge it is possible to form and to maintain habits of thought which shall be consistent with themselves and with the habit of mind and run of tradition prevalent in the community at the time, though not thereby consistent with the material actualities of life in the community. Yet this range of speculative generalization, which makes up the higher learning of the barbarian culture, is also controlled, checked, and guided by the community's habits of life; it, too, is an integral part of the scheme of life and is an outcome of the habituation enforced by experience. But it does not rest immediately on men's dealings with the refractory phenomena of brute creation, nor is it guided, undisguised and directly, by the habitual material (industrial) occupations. The fabric of institutions intervenes between the material exigencies of life and the speculative scheme of things.

The higher theoretical knowledge, that body of tenets [406] which rises to the dignity of a philosophical or scientific system, in the early culture, is a complex of habits of thought which reflect the habits of life embodied in the institutional structure of society; while the lower, matter-of-fact generalizations of work-day efficiency – the trivial matters of course – reflect the workmanlike habits of life enforced by the commonplace material exigencies under which men live. The distinction is analogous, and indeed, closely related, to the distinction between "intangible" and "tangible" assets. And the institutions are more flexible, they involve or admit a larger margin of error, or of tolerance, than the material exigencies. The latter are systematized into what economists have called "the state of the industrial arts," which enforce a somewhat rigorous standardization of whatever knowledge falls within their scope; whereas the institutional scheme is a matter of law and custom, politics and religion, taste and morals, on all of which matters men have opinions and convictions, and on which all men "have a right to their own opinions." The scheme of institutions is also not necessarily uniform throughout the several classes of society; and the same institution (as, e.g., slavery, ownership, or royalty) does not impinge with the same effect on all parties touched by it. The discipline of any institution of servitude, e.g., is not the same for the master as for the serf, etc. if there is a considerable institutional discrepancy between an upper and a lower class in the community, leading to divergent lines of habitual interest or discipline; if by force of the cultural scheme the institutions of society are chiefly in the keeping of one class, whose attention is then largely engrossed with the maintenance of the scheme of law and order; while the workmanlike activities are chiefly in the hands of another class, in whose apprehension the maintenance of law and order is at the best a wearisome tribulation, there is likely to be a similarly considerable divergence or discrepancy between the speculative knowledge, cultivated primarily by [407] the upper class, and the work-day knowledge which is primarily in the keeping of the lower class. Such, in particular, will be the case if the community is organized on a coercive plan, with well-marked ruling and subject classes. The important and interesting institutions in such a case, those institutions which fill a large angle in men's vision and carry a great force of authenticity, are the institutions of coercive control, differential authority and subjection, personal dignity and consequence; and the speculative generalizations, the institutions of the realm of knowledge, are created in the image of these social institutions of status and personal force, and fall into a scheme drawn after the plan of the code of honor. The work-day generalizations, which emerge from the state of the industrial arts, concomitantly fall into a deeper obscurity, answering to the depth of indignity to which workmanlike efficiency sinks under such a cultural scheme; and they can touch and check the current speculative knowledge only remotely and incidentally. Under such a bifurcate scheme of culture, with its concomitant two-cleft systematization of knowledge, "reality" is likely to be widely dissociated from fact – that is to say, the realities and verities which are accepted as authentic and convincing on the plane of speculative generalization; while science has no show – that is to say, science in that modern sense of the term which implies a close contact, if not a coincidence, of reality with fact.

Whereas, if the institutional fabric, the community's scheme of life, changes in such a manner as to throw the work-day experience into the foreground of attention and to center the habitual interest of the people on the immediate material relations of men to the brute actualities, then the interval between the speculative realm of knowledge, on the one hand, and the work-day generalizations of fact, on the other hand, is likely to lessen, and the two ranges of knowledge are likely to converge more or less effectually upon a common ground. When the growth of culture falls into [408] such lines, these two methods and norms of theoretical formulation may presently come to further and fortify one another, and something in the way of science has at least a chance to arise.

On this view there is a degree of interdependence between the cultural situation and the state of theoretical inquiry. To illustrate this interdependence, or the concomitance between the cultural scheme and the character of theoretical speculation, it may be in place to call to mind certain concomitant variations of a general character which occur in the lower cultures between the scheme of life and the scheme of knowledge. In this tentative and fragmentary presentation of evidence there is nothing novel to be brought forward; still less is there anything to be offered which carries the weight of authority.

On the lower levels of culture, even more decidedly than on the higher, the speculative systematization of knowledge is prone to take the form of theology (mythology) and cosmology. This theological and cosmological lore serves the savage and barbaric peoples as a theoretical account of the scheme of things, and its characteristic traits vary in response to the variations of the institutional scheme under which the community lives. In a prevailingly peaceable agricultural community, such, e.g., as the more peaceable Pueblo Indians or the more settled Indians of the Middle West, there is little coercive authority, few and slight class distinctions involving superiority and inferiority; property rights are few, slight and unstable; relationship is likely to be counted in the female line. In such a culture the cosmological lore is likely to offer explanations of the scheme of things in terms of generation or germination and growth. Creation by fiat is not obtrusively or characteristically present. The laws of nature bear the character of an habitual behavior of things, rather than that of an authoritative code of ordinances imposed by an overruling providence. [409] The theology is likely to be polytheistic in an extreme degree and in an extremely loose sense of the term, embodying relatively little of the suzerainty of God. The relation of the deities to mankind is likely to be that of consanguinity, and as if to emphasize the peaceable, non-coercive character of the divine order of things, the deities are, in the main, very apt to be females. The matters of interest dealt with in the cosmological theories are chiefly matters of the livelihood of the people, the growth and care of the crops, and the promotion of industrial ways and means.

With these phenomena of the peaceable culture may be contrasted the order of things found among a predatory pastoral people – and pastoral peoples tend strongly to take on a predatory cultural scheme. Such a people will adopt male deities, in the main, and will impute to them a coercive, imperious, arbitrary animus and a degree of princely dignity. They will also tend strongly to a monotheistic, patriarchal scheme of divine government; to explain things in terms of creative fiat; and to a belief in the control of the natural universe by rules imposed by divine ordinance. The matters of prime consequence in this theology are matters of the servile relation of man to God, rather than the details of the quest of a livelihood. The emphasis falls on the glory of God rather than on the good of man. The Hebrew scriptures, particularly the Jahvistic elements, show such a scheme of pastoral cultural and predatory theoretical generalizations.

The learning cultivated on the lower levels of culture might be gone into at some length if space and time permitted, but even what has been said may serve to show, in the most general way, what are the characteristic marks of this savage and barbarian lore. A similarly summary characterization of a cultural situation nearer home will bear more directly on the immediate topic of inquiry. The learning of mediaeval Christendom shows such a concomitance between the scheme of knowledge and the scheme of institutions, [410] somewhat analogous to the barbaric Hebrew situation. The mediaeval scheme of institutions was of a coercive, authoritative character, essentially a scheme of graded mastery and graded servitude, in which a code of honor and a bill of differential dignity held the most important place. The theology of that time was of a like character. It was a monotheistic, or rather a monarchical system, and of a despotic complexion. The cosmological scheme was drawn in terms of fiat: and the natural philosophy was occupied, in the main and in its most solemn endeavors, with the corollaries to be subsumed under the divine fiat. When the philosophical speculation dealt with facts it aimed to interpret them into systematic consistency with the glory of God and the divine purpose. The "realities" of the scholastic lore were spiritual, quasi-personal, intangible, and fell into a scale of differential dignity and pre-potency. Matter-of-fact knowledge and work-day information were not then fit topics of dignified inquiry. The interval, or discrepancy, between reality and actuality was fairly wide. Throughout that era, of course, work-day knowledge also continually increased in volume and consistency; technological proficiency was gaining; the effective control of natural processes was growing larger and more secure; showing that matter-of-fact theories drawn from experience were being extended and were made increasing use of. But all this went on in the field of industry; the matter-of-fact theories were accepted as substantial and ultimate only for the purposes of industry, only as technological maxims, and were beneath the dignity of science.

With the transition to modern times industry comes into the foreground in the west-European scheme of life, and the institutions of European civilization fall into a more intimate relation with the exigencies of industry and technology. The technological range of habituation progressively counts for more in the cultural complex, and the discrepancy between the technological discipline and the discipline of [411] law and order under the institutions then in force grows progressively less. The institutions of law and order take on a more impersonal, less coercive character. Differential dignity and invidious discriminations between classes gradually lose force.

The industry which so comes into the foreground and so affects the scheme of institutions is peculiar in that its most obvious and characteristic trait is the workmanlike initiative and efficiency of the individual handicraftsman and the individual enterprise of the petty trader. The technology which embodies the theoretical substance of this industry is a technology of workmanship, in which the salient factors are personal skill, force and diligence. Such a technology, running as it does in great part on personal initiative, capacity, and application, approaches nearer to the commonplace features of the institutional fabric than many another technological system might; and its disciplinary effects in some considerable measure blend with those of the institutional discipline. The two lines of habituation, in the great era of handicraft and petty trade, even came to coalesce and fortify one another; as in the organization of the craft gilds and of the industrial towns. Industrial life and usage came to intrude creatively into the cultural scheme on the one hand and into the scheme of authentic knowledge on the other hand. So the body of matter-of-fact knowledge, in modern times, is more and more drawn into the compass of theoretical inquiry; and theoretical inquiry takes on more and more of the animus and method of technological generalization. But the matter-of-fact elements so drawn in are construed in terms of workmanlike initiative and efficiency, as required by the technological preconceptions of the era of handicraft.

In this way, it may be conceived, modern science comes into the field under the cloak of technology and gradually encroaches on the domain of authentic theory previously held by other, higher, nobler, more profound, more spiritual, [412] more intangible conceptions and systems of knowledge. In this early phase of modern science its central norm and universal solvent is the concept of workmanlike initiative and efficiency. This is the new organon. Whatever is to be explained must be reduced to this notation and explained in these terms; otherwise the inquiry does not come to rest. But when the requirements of this notation in terms of workmanship have been duly fulfilled the inquiry does come to rest.

By the early decades of the nineteenth century, with a passable degree of thoroughness, other grounds of validity and other interpretations of phenomena, other vouchers for truth and reality, had been eliminated from the quest of authentic knowledge and from the terms in which theoretical results were conceived or expressed. The new organon had made good its pretensions. In this movement to establish the hegemony of workmanlike efficiency – under the style and title of the "law of causation," or of "efficient cause" – in the realm of knowledge, the English-speaking communities took the lead after the earlier scientific onset of the south-European communities had gone up in the smoke of war, politics and religion during the great era of state-making. The ground of this British lead in science is apparently the same as that of the British lead in technology which came to a head in the Industrial Revolution; and these two associated episodes of European civilization are apparently both traceable to the relatively peaceable run of life, and so of habituation, in the English-speaking communities, as contrasted with the communities of the continent.[4] [413]

Along with the habits of thought peculiar to the technology of handicraft, modern science also took over and assimilated much of the institutional preconceptions of the era of handicraft and petty trade. The "natural laws," with the formulation of which this early modern science is occupied, are the rules governing natural "uniformities of sequence"; and they punctiliously formulate the due procedure of any given cause creatively working out the achievement of a given effect, very much as the craft rules sagaciously

---

4 A broad exception may perhaps be taken at this point, to the effect that this sketch of the growth of the scientific animus overlooks the science of the Ancients. The scientific achievements of classical antiquity are a less obscure topic to-day than ever before during modern times, and the more there is known of them the larger is the credit given them. But it is to be noted that, (a) the relatively large and free growth of scientific inquiry in classical antiquity is to be found in the relatively peaceable and industrial Greek communities (with an industrial [413] culture of unknown pre-Hellenic antiquity), and (b) that the sciences best and chiefly cultivated were those which rest on a mathematical basis, if not mathematical sciences in the simpler sense of the term. Now, mathematics occupies a singular place among the sciences, in that it is, in its pure form, a logical discipline simply; its subject matter being the logic of quantity, and its researches being of the nature of an analysis of the intellect's modes of dealing with matters of quantity. Its generalizations are generalizations of logical procedure, which are tested and verified by immediate self-observation. Such a science is in a peculiar degree, but only in a peculiar degree, independent of the detail-discipline of daily life, whether technological or institutional, and, given the propensity – the intellectual enterprises, or "idle curiosity" – to go into speculation in such a field, the results can scarcely vary in a manner to make the variants inconsistent among themselves; nor need the state of institutions or the state of the industrial arts seriously color or distort such analytical work in such a field. Mathematics is peculiarly independent of cultural circumstances, since it deals analytically with mankind's native gifts of logic, not with the ephemeral traits acquired by habituation.

specified the due routine for turning out a staple article of merchantable goods. But these "natural laws" of science are also felt to have something of that integrity and prescriptive moral force that belongs to the principles of the system of "natural rights" which the era of handicraft has contributed to the institutional scheme of later times. The natural laws were not only held to be true to fact, but they were also felt to be right and good. They were looked upon as intrinsically meritorious and beneficent, and were held to carry a sanction of their own. This habit of uncritically imputing merit and equity to the "natural laws" of science continued in force through much of the nineteenth century; very much as the habitual acceptance [414] of the principles of "natural rights" has held on by force of tradition long after the exigencies of experience out of which these "rights" sprang ceased to shape men's habits of life.[5] This traditional attitude of submissive approval toward the "natural laws" of science has not yet been wholly lost, even among the scientists of the passing generation, many of whom have uncritically invested these "laws" with a prescriptive rectitude and excellence; but so far, at least, has this animus progressed toward disuse that it is now chiefly a matter for expatiation in the pulpit, the accredited vent for the exudation of effete matter from the cultural organism.

The traditions of the handicraft technology lasted over as a commonplace habit of thought in science long after that technology had ceased to be the decisive element in the industrial situation: while a new technology, with its inculcation of new habits of thought, new preconceptions, gradually made its way among the remnants of the old, altering them, blending with them, and little by little superseding them. The new technological departure, which made its first great epoch in the so-called industrial revolution, in the technological ascendancy of the machine-process, brought a new and characteristic discipline into the cultural situation. The beginnings of the machine-era lie far back, no doubt; but it is only of late, during the past century at the most, that the machine-process can be said to have come into the dominant place in the technological scheme; and it is only later still that its discipline has, even in great [415] part, remodeled the current preconceptions as to the substantial nature of what goes on in the current of phenomena whose changes excite the scientific curiosity. It is only relatively very lately, whether in technological work or in scientific inquiry, that men have fallen into the habit of thinking in terms of process rather than in terms of the workmanlike efficiency of a given cause working to a given effect.

---

5 "Natural laws," which are held to be not only correct formulations of the sequence of cause and effect in a given situation but also meritoriously right and equitable rules governing the run of events, necessarily impute to the facts and events in question a tendency to a good and equitable, if not beneficent, consummation; since it is necessarily the consummation, the effect considered as an accomplished outcome, that is to be adjudged good and equitable, if anything. Hence these "natural laws," as traditionally conceived, are laws governing the accomplishment of an end – that is to say, laws as to how a sequence of cause and effect comes to rest in a final term.

These machine-made preconceptions of modern science, being habits of thought induced by the machine technology in industry and in daily life, have of course first and most consistently affected the character of those sciences whose subject matter lies nearest to the technological field of the machine-process; and in these material sciences the shifting to the machine-made point of view has been relatively very consistent, giving a highly impersonal interpretation of phenomena in terms of consecutive change, and leaving little of the ancient preconceptions of differential reality or creative causation. In such a science as physics or chemistry, e.g., we are threatened with the disappearance or dissipation of all stable and efficient substances; their place being supplied, or their phenomena being theoretically explained, by appeal to unremitting processes of inconceivably high-pitched consecutive change.

In the sciences which lie farther afield from the technological domain, and which, therefore, in point of habituation, are remoter from the center of disturbance, the effect of the machine discipline may even yet be scarcely appreciable. In such lore as ethics, e.g., or political theory, or even economics, much of the norms of the régime of handicraft still stands over; and very much of the institutional preconceptions of natural rights, associated with the régime of handicraft in point of genesis, growth and content, is not only still intact in this field of inquiry, but it can scarcely even be claimed that there is ground for serious apprehension of its prospective obsolescence. Indeed, something [416] even more ancient than handicraft and natural rights may be found surviving in good vigor in this "moral" field of inquiry, where tests of authenticity and reality are still sought and found by those who cultivate these lines of inquiry that lie beyond the immediate sweep of the machine's discipline. Even the evolutionary process of cumulative causation as conceived by the adepts of these sciences is infused with a preternatural, beneficent trend; so that "evolution" is conceived to mean amelioration or "improvement." The metaphysics of the machine technology has not yet wholly, perhaps not mainly, superseded the metaphysics of the code of honor in those lines of inquiry that have to do with human initiative and aspiration. Whether such a shifting of the point of view in these sciences shall ever be effected is still an open question. Here there still are spiritual verities which transcend the sweep of consecutive change. That is to say, there are still current habits of thought which definitively predispose their bearers to bring their inquiries to rest on grounds of differential reality and invidious merit.

Selection 35

Fisher's *Capital and Income*

Source: *Political Science Quarterly*, March 1908
(vol. 23, pp. 112–28).

and

Fisher's *Rate of Interest*

Source: *Political Science Quarterly*, June 1909
(vol. 24, pp. 296–303).

Veblen (1908b, 1909a)

Fisher's *Capital and Income*

The Nature of Capital and Income is of that class of books that have kept the gild of theoretical economists content to do nothing toward "the increase and diffusion of knowledge" during the past quarter of a century.[1] Of this class Mr. Fisher's work is of the best – thoughtful, painstaking, sagacious, exhaustive, lucid, and tenaciously logical. What it lacks is the breath of life; and this lack it shares with the many theoretical productions of the Austrian diversion as well as of the economists of more strictly classical antecedents. Not that Mr. Fisher's work falls short of the mark set by those many able men who have preceded him in this field. No reader of Mr. Fisher can justly feel disappointed in his performance of the difficult task which he sets himself. The work performs what it promises and does it in compliance with all the rules of the craft. But it does not set out substantially to extend the theory or to contribute to the sum of knowledge, either by bringing hitherto refractory phenomena into the organized structure of the science, or by affording farther or more comprehensive insight into the already familiar processes of modern economic life. Consistently with its aim, it is a work of taxonomy, of definition and classification; and it is carried through wholly within the limits imposed by this its taxonomic aim. There are many shrewd observations on the phenomena of current business, and much evidence of an extensive and

---

1 *The Nature of Capital and Income*, by Irving Fisher, New York, The Macmillan Company, 1906, pp. xxi+427

intimate acquaintance with such facts of modern culture as are still awaiting scientific treatment at the hands of the economists (e.g., in chapters v and vi, "Capital Accounts" and "Capital Summation," as also in chapters viii, ix, xiii, xiv, "Income Accounts," "Income Summation," "Value of Capital," "Earnings and Income," "The Risk Element"). But the facts of observation so drawn into the discussion are chiefly drawn in to illustrate or fortify an argument, somewhat polemical, not as material calling for theoretical explanation. As affects the development of the theory, these observations and this information run along on the side and are not allowed to disturb the argument in its secure march toward its taxonomic goal.

There is no intention here to decry taxonomy, of course. Definition and classification are as much needed in economics as they are in [113] those other sciences which have already left the exclusively taxonomic standpoint behind. The point of criticism, on this head, is that this class of economic theory differs from the modern sciences in being substantially nothing but definition and classification. Taxonomy for taxonomy's sake, definition and classification for the sake of definition and classification, meets no need of modern science. Work of this class has no value and no claims to consideration except so far as it is of use to the science in its endeavor to know and explain the processes of life. This test of usefulness applies even more broadly in economics and similar sciences of human conduct than in the natural sciences, commonly so-called. It is on this head, as regards the serviceability of his taxonomic results, that Mr. Fisher's work falls short. A modern science has to do with the facts as they come to hand, not with putative phenomena warily led out from a primordial metaphysical postulate, such as the "hedonic principle." To meet the needs of science, therefore, such modern concepts as "capital" and "income" must be defined by observation rather than by ratiocination. Observation will not yield such a hard-and-fast definition of the term as is sought by Mr. Fisher and his co-disputants, a definition which shall mark off a pecuniary concept by physical distinctions, which shall be good for all times and places and all economic situations, ancient and modern, whether there is investment of capital or not.

"Capital" is a concept much employed by modern men of affairs. If it were not for the use of the concept in economic affairs – its growing use for a century past – the science would not be concerned about the meaning of the term today. It is this use of the concept in the conduct of affairs that obtrudes it upon the attention of economists; and it is, primarily at least, for a better knowledge of these pecuniary affairs, in which the concept of capital plays so large a part, that a better knowledge of the concept itself is sought. As it plays its part in these affairs of business, the concept of capital is, substantially, a habit of thought of the men engaged in business, more or less closely defined in practice by the consensus of usage in the business community. A serviceable definition of it therefore, for the use of modern science, can be got only by observation of the current habits of thought of business men. This painfully longwinded declaration of what must appear to be a patent truism so soon as it is put in words may seem a gratuitous insistence on a stale commonplace. But it is an even more painfully tedious fact that the current polemics about "the capital concept" goes on year after year without recognition of this patent truism. [114]

What may help to cover, rather than to excuse, the failure of many economists to resort to observation for a knowledge of what the term "capital" means is the fact, adverted to by the way in various writers, that business usage of the term is not uniform and stable; it does not remain the same from generation to generation; and it cannot, at least as regards present usage, be identified and defined by physical marks. The specific marks of the concept – the characteristics of the category – in the common usage are not physical marks, and the categories with which it is, in usage, related and contrasted are not categories that admit of definition in material terms; because it is, in usage, a pecuniary concept and stands in pecuniary relations and contrasts with other categories. It is a pecuniary term, primarily a term of investment, and as such, as a habit of thought of the men who have to do with pecuniary affairs, it necessarily changes in response to the changes going forward in the pecuniary situation and in the methods of conducting pecuniary affairs. "Capital," is the usage of current business, undoubtedly has not precisely the same meaning as it had in the corresponding usage of half a century ago; and it is safe to say that it will not retain its present meaning, unimpaired and unimproved, in the usage of ten years hence; nor does it cover just the same details in one connection as in another. Yet business men know what the term means to them. With all its shifting ambiguities, they know it securely enough for their use. The concept has sufficient stability and precision to serve their needs; and, if the economist is to deal with the phenomena of modern life in which this concept serves a use of first-rate importance, he must take the term and the concept as he finds them. It is idle fatigue to endeavor to normalize them into a formula which may suit his prepossessions but which is not true to life. The mountain will not come to Mahomet.

It is not for its idiosyncrasies that Mr. Fisher's analysis and formulation of the "capital concept" merits particular attention, but because it is the most elaborate outcome of classificatory economics to this date. Except for certain minor features – important, no doubt, within the school – his definition of capital is by no means a wide departure. It is only worked out more consistently, painstakingly, and circumspectly than has hitherto been done. Some of these special features peculiar to Mr. Fisher's position have been carefully and very ably discussed by Mr. Fetter.[2] The merits of the discussion of these [115] matters between the critic and his author, with the incidental balancing of accounts, need not detain the present argument. Nor need particular

---

2 [Frank A. Fetter,] *Journal of Political Economy*, March, 1907, "The Nature of Capital and Income." See also Mr. Fisher's reply in the same journal, July, 1907 – "Professor Fetter on Capital and Income."

attention here be given to the points in dispute so far as regards their consistency with the general body of theory upheld by Mr. Fisher and other economists who cultivate the classificatory science. But there are some details of the "nature of capital" as set forth by Mr. Fisher – and in large part assented to by Mr. Fetter and others of the like way of thinking – that require particular attention as regards their adequacy for other purposes than that of a science of classification.

(1) In the general definition of "capital" (e.g., pp. 51–53, 66–68, 324), the concept is made to comprise all wealth (in its relation to future income); and "wealth" has, in the same as well as in earlier pages, been defined "to signify material objects owned by human beings," which, in turn, includes all persons, as well as other material objects. As an aggregate, therefore, as an outcome of a comprehensive "capital summation," "capital" comprises the material universe in so far as the material universe may be turned to use by man (see p. 328). This general definition includes too much and too little. A serviceable definition of capital, one that shall answer to the concept as it is found in practice in the habits of thought of business men, will not include persons. Hitherto, there is no question, the distinction between the capitalist and his capital is not disregarded by practical men, except possibly by way of an occasional affectation of speech; and it is highly improbable that, at any point in the calculable future, business men can come habitually to confuse these two disparate concepts. Modern business proceeds on the distinction. It is only in pulpit oratory that a man's person is legitimately spoken of as an item of his assets. And as for a business man's capitalizing other persons, the law does not allow it, even in the form of peonage. There are also other material objects "under the dominion of man" which are not currently thought of as items of capital.

There are apparently two main perplexities of the mechanical classification which constrain Mr. Fisher to include the person of the owner among the owner's assets as capital: (a) Contrary to business usage, he is required by his premises to exclude immaterial wealth because it is not amenable to classification by mechanical tests, and it is therefore necessary to find some roundabout line of approach to such elements as good will, and the like;[3] and (b) persons are conceived to yield [116] income (in the sense of Mr. Fisher's definition of "income" presently to be noted), and since capital is held to be anything which yields "income" – indeed "capital" is such by virtue of its yielding "income" – persons are included under "capital" by force of logic, though contrary to fact.

(2) As has already been indicated in passing, "immaterial wealth," or "intangible assets," is excluded from "capital" in Mr. Fisher's analysis. Indeed, the existence of intangible assets is denied. The phrase is held to be an untoward misnomer for certain classes of property rights in material

---

3 See [Fisher, *The Nature of Capital and Income*], chapter ii, section 6, pp. 24–31; also section 10.

objects which are not wholly owned by the individual to whom these property rights inure. An important part of these incomplete property rights are rights of quasi-ownership in other persons, or claims to services performed by such persons. This denial of immaterial wealth Mr. Fisher intends as a salutary correction of current business usage (see p. 39); and he takes pains to show how, by a cumbersome ratiocination (see chapter ii, sections 6–10), the term "intangible assets" may be avoided without landing the theory in the instant confusion which a simple denial of the concept would bring about. As a correction of current usage the attempted exclusion of intangible assets from "capital" does not seem a wise innovation. It cripples the definition for the purposes which alone would make a definition worth while. The concept of intangible assets is present in current usage on no such doubtful or precarious tenure as could be canceled by a bit of good advice. Its vogue is growing and its use is becoming more secure and more definite. The habit and the necessity of taking account, under one name or another, of the various immaterial items of wealth classed as intangible assets counts for more and more in the conduct of affairs; and any theory that aims to deal with the actualities of modern business will have to make its peace with the term or terms by which these elements of capital are called, however wrong-headed a habit it may be conceived to be. The men of affairs find the concept serviceable, or rather they find it forced upon them, and the theorist of affairs cannot afford to dispense with a concept which is so large a constituent in the substance of affairs.

But the fault of the definition at this point is more serious than the mere exclusion of a serviceable general term which might be avoided by a circumlocution. "Intangible assets" is not simply a convenient general term covering certain more or less fluctuating property rights in certain material items of wealth. The elements of capital so designated are chiefly of the nature of differential advantages of a given business man, or a given concern, as against another. But they are [117] capitalized in the same way as tangible items of wealth are capitalized, and in large part they are covered by negotiable securities, indistinguishable, and in most cases inseparable from, securities representing tangible assets. So, being blended in the process of capitalization with the tangible assets, the securities based on the intangible assets create claims of ownership co-ordinate with those based on the material items and enter, in practice, into "capital summation" on the same footing as other items of wealth. Hence they become a basis of credit extensions, serving to increase the aggregate claims of creditors beyond what the hypothecable material wealth of the debtors would satisfy. Hence, in a period of general liquidation, when the differential advantages of the various concerns greatly contract, the legitimate claims of creditors come greatly to exceed the paying capacity of debtors, and the collapse of the credit system follows. The failure of classical theory to give an intelligent account of credit and crises is in great part due to the habitual refusal of economists to recognize intangible assets, and Mr. Fisher's argument is, in effect, an accentuation of this ancient infirmity of the classical theory.

It may be added that differential competitive advantages cannot be added together to make an aggregate even apart from the tangible items of "capital wealth," since the advantage of one concern is the disadvantage of another. These assets come forth, grow great, and decay, according to the advance or decline of the strategic advantage achieved by given individuals or business concerns. Their "summation" is a spurious summation, in the main, since they represent competitive advantages, in the main; and their capitalization adds a spurious volume to the aggregate property rights of the community. So that it follows from the capitalization of these items of differential wealth, particularly when they are covered by vendible securities, that the aggregate property rights of the community come to exceed the aggregate wealth of the community.[4] This is, of course, a sufficiently grave trait of the modern business situation, but the effect of Mr. Fisher's contention is to deny its existence by the turn of a phrase and to put economic theory back where it stood before the modern situation had arisen. There are other turns in modern business affairs traceable to the vogue of this concept of "intangible assets," but this illustration of its grave consequences should be a sufficient caution to any taxonomist who endeavors to simplify his scheme of definition by denying inconvenient facts. [118]

The point is perhaps sufficiently plain from what has been said, but it will bear specific mention that the apparent success of Mr. Fisher's analysis of intangible assets (pp. 32–40, 96–97) is due to his not going beyond the first move. So soon as the actualities of business complication and the cumulative effects of capitalization are taken into account, it is evident that, with the best intentions, Mr. Fisher's explanation of intangible assets as a roundabout claim to certain concrete (tangible) items of wealth will not serve. The treatment of credit suffers from a like unwillingness to accept the facts of observation or to look farther than the first move in an analysis. This shortsightedness of the taxonomic economist is a logical consequence of the hedonistic postulates of the school, not a personal peculiarity of the present or any other author.

As to Mr. Fisher's definition and handling of the second concept with which the book is occupied – income – much the same is true as of the discussion of capital. Income is re-defined with a close adherence to the logic of that hedonistic-taxonomic system of theory for which he speaks. The concept of income here offered is more tenaciously consistent with the logical run of current classificatory economics, perhaps, than any that has been offered before. It is the perfect flower of economic taxonomy, and it shows, as no previous exposition of the kind has shown, the inherent futility of this class of work for other than purely taxonomic ends.

---

4 Contrary to Mr. Fisher's elaborate doctrine of property rights as defined by mechanical limits [Fisher, *The Nature of Capital and Income*], Chapter ii.

The concept of income, like that of capital, is well at home in current business usage; and professedly, it is the concept of income as it plays its part in the affairs of business that occupies the author's attention. But here, again, as before, the definition – "the nature of income" – is not worked out from observation of current facts, with an endeavor to make the demarcation of the concept square with the habitual apprehension of the phenomena of income in the business community. Taken at its current import, as the concept is taken in the run of business and in the economic affair of any community of men dominated by the animus of business enterprise, there can be no question but that "income" is a pecuniary concept; it is money income, or is as an element which is convertible into terms of money income and amenable to the pecuniary scheme of accountancy. As a business proposition, nothing that cannot be rated in terms of money income is to be accounted income at all; which is the same as saying that no definition which goes beyond or behind the pecuniary concept can be a serviceable definition of income for modern use. There may be something beyond or behind this pecuniary concept which it may be [119] desirable to reach and discuss for some other purpose more or less germane to the affairs of modern life; but such a something, whatever its nature, cannot be called "income" in the same sense in which that term is employed in modern business usage. When the term is applied to such an extra-pecuniary or praetor-pecuniary concept, such an extension of the term is a rhetorical license; it is a figure of speech which is bound to work confusion in any argument or analysis that deals with the two inconvertible concepts. "Income" in modern usage, is a business concept; "psychic income" is not; and, as Mr. Fisher is in an eminently good position to admit, the two are incommensurable, or rather disparate, magnitudes. The one cannot be reduced to terms of the other. This state of the case may be deprecated, but it cannot be denied; and it is no service to the science of modern economic life to confuse this distinction by running the two under one technical term.

Chapter xiv ("Earnings and Income"), and more particularly the latter sections of the chapter, illustrate how far from facts one may be led by a consistent adherence to Mr. Fisher's hedonistic working-out of the concept of income. "To regard 'savings' as income is essentially to regard an increase of capital as income" (pp. 254–253). Now, apart from the hedonistic prepossession, there is, of course, no reason for not regarding such an increase of capital as income. The two ideas – "income" and "increase of capital" – are by no means mutually exclusive in the current usage; and ordinarily, so long as the terms are taken in their current (pecuniary) meaning, such an increase of capital would unhesitatingly be rated as income to the owner. The need of making "income" and "increase of capital" mutually exclusive categories is a need incident to a mechanically drawn scheme of classification, and it disappears so soon as classification for classification's sake is given up. It is traceable to a postulated (hedonistic) principle presumed to rule men and things, not to observation of the run of facts in modern life. Indeed, even in Mr. Fisher's analysis the distinction goes into abeyance for a while where, in the doctrine of "capital value" (chapter xiii, especially section 11, and chapter xvlii, section 2) the facts will absolutely not tolerate its being kept up. The hedonistic taxonomy breaks down at this juncture. And the fact is significant that this point of doctrine – viz., that capital considered as a magnitude of value "is the discounted value of the expected income" – is the latest and most highly prized advance in economic theory to whose initiation Mr. Fisher's writings give him a defensible claim.[5] [120]

The day when Bentham's conception of economic life was serviceable for the purposes of contemporary science lies about one hundred years back, and Mr. Fisher's reduction of "income" to "psychic income" is late by that much. The absolute merits of the hedonistic conception of economic theory need not be argued here. It was a far-reaching conception, and its length of life has made it a grand conception. But great as may be the due of courtesy to that conception for the long season of placid content which economic theory has spent beneath its spreading chestnut tree, yet the fact is not to be over-looked that its scheme of accountancy is not that of the modern business community. The logic of economic life in a modern community runs in terms of pecuniary, not of hedonistic magnitudes.

Mr. Fisher's farthest advance, his definition and handling of "capital value," involves the breaking down of the classical hedonistic taxonomy; and the breakdown is typical of the best work done by the school. This move of the classifiers is, of course, nothing sudden; nor is it an accident. It means, in substance, only that the modern facts have increasingly shown themselves incompatible with the mechanical scheme of classical definitions, and that this discrepancy between the facts and the received categories has finally forced a breaking away from the old categories. The whole voluminous discussion of the capital concept, for the past twenty years or so, has, indeed, turned about this discrepancy between business practice and the hedonistic classification by means of which economists have tried to deal with this business practice. All expedients of classification, definition, refinement, and interpretation of tech-nical phrases have been tried, except the surrender of the main position – that economic conduct must be read in terms of the hedonistic calculus.[6]

Under the stress of this controversy of interpretation, the hedonistic con-cept of capital as a congeries of "productive goods" has gradually and reluc-tantly, but hitherto not wholly, been replaced by something more serviceable. But this gain in serviceability has been won – in so far as the achievement may be spoken of in the past tense – at some cost to the hedonistic point of view. Such serviceability as the newly achieved interpretation of the capital concept has, it has because, and only so far as, it substitutes a pecuniary for a

---

5 Cf. *Journal of Political Economy*, papers cited above [in note 2 of this Selection].
6 The argument will return to the hedonistic calculus presently to show how the logic of this calculus has forced the theory at certain points.

hedonistic construction of the phenomena of capitalization. Among those who speak for the new (pecuniary) construction is Mr. Fisher, although he is not by any [121] means the freest of those who are breaking away. His position is, no doubt, deprecated by many taxonomic economists as being an irreverently, brutally iconoclastic innovation, quite indefensible on taxonomic grounds; but, after all, as Mr. Fetter has shown in more courteous words,[7] it is an equivocal, or perhaps rather an irresolute position at the best.

"Capital," in the classical definition, was, as required by the hedonistic point of view, a congeries of what has latterly been named "productive goods." From such a concept of capital, which is hopelessly and increasingly out of touch with business usage, the theorists have been straining away; and Mr. Fisher has borne a large part in the speculations that are leading up to the emancipation of theorists from the chore work required by that white elephant. But he is not content formally to give up the heirloom; although, as Mr. Fetter indicates, he now makes little use of it except for parade. He offers two correlate definitions of capital: "capital wealth," i.e., productive goods, and "capital value," i.e., pecuniary capital.[8] The former of these, the authentic hedonistic concept, shortly drops out of the discussion, although it does not drop out so tracelessly as Mr. Fetter's criticism may suggest. The argument then proceeds, almost throughout, on the concept of "capital value."[9] But there is a recurrent, and, one is tempted to say, dutiful, reminder that this "capital value," or capitalization of values, is to be taken as the value of a congeries of tangible objects (productive goods); whereby a degree of taxonomic consistency with the authentic past and with the hedonistic postulate is formally maintained, and whereby also, dutifully and authentically, intangible assets are excluded from the capital concept, as already indicated above. Capital value is "simply the present worth of the future income from the specified capital"[10] (p. 202); but this capital value, it is held, is always the value of tangible items (including persons?).

It is the uncanny office of the critic to deal impersonally with his author's work as an historical phenomenon. Under cover of this [122] license it may be pardonable to speak badly and broadly of the logic of this retention of the authentic postulate that physically productive goods (including persons) alone are to be included in the capitalization out of which capital value emerges. And what is here said in this connection is not to be taken as a presumptuous

---

7 *Journal of Political Economy*, [vol. 15,] pp. 143–44 [as cited above in note 2 of this Selection].

8 [Fisher, *The Nature of Capital and Income*], pp. 66–67, 327, and elsewhere.

9 Mr. Fetter, in advance of Mr. Fisher in the position taken if not in priority of departure, advocates discarding the older (authentic hedonistic) concept, in form as well as in fact.

10 In this and similar passages Mr. Fisher appears to be in search of a more competent phrase, which has been used, but which he apparently has not met with – "putative earning-capacity." Certain infirmities of such a definition, whether under one phrase or another, for the taxonomic purpose, will be indicated presently.

make-believe of reproducing the sequence of ideas by which Mr. Fisher has arrived to trace the logical sequence between the main hedonistic body of theory and the historical outcome of its development at this point.

In the classical-Austrian scheme of theory the center and circumference of economic life is the production of what a writer on ethics has called "pleasant feeling." Pleasant feeling is produced only by tangible, physical objects (including persons), acting somehow upon the sensory. The inflow of pleasant feeling is "income" – "psychic income" net and positive. The purpose of capital is to serve this end – the increase of pleasant feeling – and things are capital, in the authentic hedonistic scheme, by as much as they serve this end. Capital, therefore, must be tangible, material goods, since only tangible goods will stimulate the human sensory pleasantly. Intangible assets, being not physical, do not impinge upon the sensory; therefore they are not capital. Since they unavoidably are thrown prominently on the screen in the show of modern life, they must, consistently with the hedonistic conception, be explained away by construing them in terms of some authentic category of tangible items.

There is a second line of approach to the same conclusion comprised in the logical scheme of hedonistic economics, more cogent on practical grounds than that sketched above and perhaps of equally convincing metaphysical force. The hedonistic (classical-Austrian) economics is a system of taxonomic science – a science of normalities. Its office is the definition and classification of "normal" phenomena, or, perhaps better, phenomena as they occur in the normal case. And in this normal case, when and so far as the laws of nature work out their ends unvitiated, nature does all things well. This is also according to the ancient and authentic canons of taxonomic science. In the hedonistically normal scheme of life wasteful, disserviceable, or futile acts have no place.[11] The current competitive, capitalistic business scheme of life is normal, when rightly seen in the hedonistic light. There is not (normally) in it anything of a wasteful, disserviceable, or futile [123] character. Whatever phenomena do not fit into the scheme of normal economic life, as tested by the hedonistic postulate, are to be taken account of by way of exception. If there are discrepancies, in the way of waste, disserviceability, or futility, e.g., they are not inherent in the normal scheme and they do not call for incorporation in the theory of the situation in which they occur, except for interpretative elimination and correction. In this course the hedonistic economics, with its undoubting faith that whatever (normally) is is right, simply follows the rule of all authentic taxonomic science.

As indicated above, the normal end of capital, as of all the multifarious phenomena of economic life, is the production of pleasure and the prevention of pain; and in the Benthamite system of theory – which includes the classical-Austrian economics – the normal end of the life of man in society,

11 Cf., e.g., Clark, *Essentials of Economic Theory,* passim. – "Each man who gets in a normal way, any income at all performs one or more productive functions" etc. – p. 92.

economic and otherwise, is the greatest happiness of the greatest number. Such may not be the outcome in any given actual situation, but in so far as such is not the outcome the situation departs from the normal; and such departures from the normal do not properly concern the (hedonistic) "science" of economics, but fall authentically to the care of the "art" of economics, whose concern it is to find correctives for these, essentially sporadic, aberrations. Under the rule of normal serviceability nothing can be included in the theoretically right "capital summation" which does not go to swell the aggregate of hedonistic "services" to man – nothing which is not "productive," in the sense of increasing the well-being of mankind at large. Persons may, indeed they "normally" should always, be productive in this sense, and persons, therefore, should properly be included in the capital summation.[12] [124]

In this normalized scheme of economic life all claims represented by negotiable instruments, e.g., must be led back, as is done by Mr. Fisher,[13] to tangible items of serviceable goods; and in its application to the concrete case, the actual situation, if follows from this rule that all such instruments are, normally, evidences of the ownership of such tangible items as serve the

---

12 What is to be done, theoretically, with persons leading disserviceable or futile lives, "undesirable citizens," does not clearly appear. They are undesirable, but they are of the human breed and so are presumably to be included in the normal human aggregate whose "greatest number" are elected for the "greatest happiness" by the (normally) benevolent laws of nature. The suggestion is, of course, obvious that they should be deducted from the gross aggregate of items – i.e., algebraically added in as negative magnitudes – so as to leave a net algebraic sum of positively serviceable capital goods, including persons. The like might apparently be done with impersonal material items which are wastefully or noxiously employed.

But the converse suggestion is at least equally cogent, that such disserviceable items, personal and impersonal, are simply abnormal, aberrant, exceptional, and that therefore they simply drop tracelessly out of the theoretical scheme, so as to the theoretically correct "summation" as large as it would be had these disserviceable negative times items not been present. That is to say, the theoretically correct net aggregate serviceability is the same as the gross serviceability; since the negative quantities [124] actually present among the aggregate of items are not normally present, and are, therefore, theoretically non-existent.

There is a third alternative. The abnormal disserviceable items being indubitably present in fact, and some part of them being present with the hedonistically sacred stamp of the human breed, it may be that, in the apprehension of the adepts, should this problem of taxonomy present itself to them, at least so much of the disserviceable productive goods as are human beings should be counted in; but, since they are persons, and since it is the normal estate of man to be serviceable to his fellows, they should be theoretically counted as normally serviceable, and therefore included in the net aggregate of serviceability at the magnitude of serviceability normally imputable to them. What rule should guide in fixing the true magnitude of imputed normal serviceability for such disserviceable persons in such a case is a further problem of taxonomy which would take the present argument too far afield. This much seems clear, however, that under this third alternative the net aggregate serviceability to be imputed to the sum of capital goods (including persons) should exceed the actual aggregate serviceability by the addition of an amount approximately equal to the disservice rendered by the disserviceable persons in question.

13 [*The Nature of Capital and Income*], Chapter ii, especially sections 4–9, and pp. 93–96.

material needs of mankind at large. It follows also that there are, normally, no items of differential serviceability included among the property rights covered by negotiable instruments; that in the hedonistic theory of business there are no differential advantages and no differential or competitive gains; that the gain of each business man is, at the most, simply the sum of his own contributions to the aggregate of services that maintain the life and happiness of the community. This optimistic light shed on the business situation by the hedonistic postulate is one of the most valued, and for the wise quietist assuredly the most valuable, of the theoretical results following from the hedonistic taxonomy. And this optimistic light will fail with the surrender of the authentic position that capital is a congeries of physically productive goods. But while this light lasts the hedonistic economist is able to say that, although the scheme of economic life contemplated by him as normal is a competitive system, yet the gains of the competitors are in no degree of a competitive character; no one (normally) gains at the cost of another or at the cost of the community at large; nor does any one (normally) turn any part of his equipment of capital goods to use for a competitive or differential advantage. In this light, the competitive struggle is seen to work out as, in effect, a [125] friendly rivalry in the service of mankind at large, with an eye single to the greatest happiness of the greatest number. If intangible assets are recognized by the theory this comforting outlook on the business situation fails, because intangible assets are, in the main, of a differential effect only. Hence they are excluded by the logic of the hedonistic taxonomy.

Returning to a point left uncovered above (p. 120), it may be in place to look more narrowly into the definition of capital as "capital value" arrived at by Mr. Fisher, ably spoken for by Mr. Fetter, and apparently in train to be accepted by many economists interested in questions of theory.[14] On its face this formulation seems definite, tangible, and stable enough. Such a concept appears to serve the needs of business traffic. But it is a more delicate question, and more to the present purpose, whether the definition has the requisite stability and mechanical precision for the purposes of a taxonomy such as Mr. Fisher's, which seeks to set up mutually exclusive categories of things distinguished from one another by statistically determined lines of demarcation. The question obtrudes itself, as regards this putative value of expected income: Whose imputation of value is to be accepted? Value, of course, is a

---

14 [Fisher, *The Nature of Capital and Income*:] The value of capital is the discounted value of the expected income (p. 328). "It is found by discounting (or 'capitalizing') the value of the income expected from the wealth of property." (p. 330). "Capital today may be defined as economical wealth expressed in terms of the general unit of value." [See also:] Fetter, *Principles of Economics* (p. 115) ... "every good becoming capital when it is capitalized, that is, when the totality of its uses is expressed as a present sum of values." (Ibid. p. 116) It has elsewhere been characterized as "capitalization of putative earning capacity." The latter is perhaps the more serviceable definition, being nearer to the concept of capital current in the business community.

fact of imputation; and it may seem a ready solution to say that the decision in this question of appraisement is rendered by a consensus of imputation between or among the parties concerned in the capitalization. This consensus would be shown concretely by market quotations of securities, and it would be shown in generalized form by the familiar diagrams offered by all taxonomists of the marginal-utility school. But, concretely, there is not always a consensus of imputations as to the expected value of a given flow of income; in the case of unlisted securities, as well as of other capitalizable property in like case, the appeal to a consensus fails. And, in point of taxonomic theory, the marginal-utility curves apply to the case in hand only when and in so far as the property in question is the subject of a bargain; and, further, the diagrams of intersections and the [126] like are of no avail for the cases, frequent enough in practice, where bargains are struck at the same time for different lots of the same line of goods at different heights on the ordinate. It is only by virtue of broad and untenable generalizations concerning the higgling of the market that the diagrams appear to cover a general proposition as to the actual value of property. The upshot of the matter is that a given block of capital need not, in practice it frequently does not, have one particular value at a given time; no more than a given expected flow of income need have one particular value alone imputed to it by all, or by a consensus of, the various parties in interest.

A summary review of an actual case taken from current business traffic may illustrate some of the difficulties of arriving, in detail, at such a definite and stable determination of capital value as will serve the needs of "capital summation" as expounded by Mr. Fisher.

A relatively small and inconspicuous corporation managed by two men, A and B, had for a series of years been doing a successful, conservative business in one of the necessaries of life, and had achieved an enviable reputation for efficiency and reliability; that is to say, it had accumulated a large and valuable body of "good will." The only form of securities outstanding was common stock, unlisted, and held by relatively few stockholders. During the late winter and spring of the present year (1907), the managers of the company gathered from the course of the market that business in their line would probably slacken off appreciably in the immediate future, with small chance of a prompt recovery. They determined to sell out and withdraw to another line of business, not similarly dependent on prices. To this end they set about buying in all the stock of their company, A–B, with a view to selling out the going concern to another corporation, C–D, whose appraisement of the future (imputation of value) was apparently more sanguine than their own. The outstanding shares of stock were bought in, during a period of some six weeks, by A and B bargaining separately with the several stockholders as opportunity offered, at prices ranging from about 105 to about 125. Meantime, negotiation had been going forward with company C–D for the sale of the concern as a whole on the basis of an inventory of the plant, including the stock of goods on hand. Both the plant and the stock of goods were somewhat extensive and scattered. With the inventory as a basis the concern was sold at an aggregate price which included a fair allowance for the intangible assets (good will) of the going concern. The inventory was taken on the basis of the last previous monthly price-current, and the transfer to C–D took place on that basis. As counted on by A–B, and as apparently [127] not counted on by C–D, the next succeeding monthly price-current showed a decline in the market value of the stock of goods on hand of some nine or ten percent; and the subsequent course of the market, as well as of the volume of traffic in this line of business, has been of the same complexion. The transfer of the concern, all told, from A–B to C–D took place at figures which aggregated an advance of some 25 percent over the cost to A and B, counting the stock of the corporation at an average of the prices paid by them for such shares of stock as they bought in from other stockholders, which was rather more than one-half of all the outstanding stock.

The question now is: What, for purposes of "capital summation," should be taken as the basis of the capital value of corporation A–B last spring, say, at the date of the transfer to C–D, or at any date during the buying in of the outstanding stock? During all this time the "capital value" must have been something over 100 percent of the nominal capital, since none of the stock was bought at less than 105. But the shares of stocks were bought in, scatteringly, from 105 to 125, with an average in the neighborhood of 115; while the aggregate price of the going concern at the same time seems to have been in the neighborhood of 140 percent of the nominal capitalization. Should the last transaction in the purchase of stock from day to day, running uncertainly between 105 and 125, be construed to revise the "capital value" of the concern to that date? This would make the "capital value" skip capriciously back and forth within the 20 points of the margin, in attendance upon the last previous "consensus of imputation" between a given seller and one or the other of the two buyers. The final average of, say, 115, had not at that time been established, so that that figure could not be taken as a basis during the interval. Or should the stipulated price of the going concern rule the case, in the face of these transactions taking place at figures incompatible with it? Again, at the date of the transfer to C–D, was the "capital value" immediately before the transfer the (indefinite) rating given by the then owners, A and B; and was it, the next minute, to be counted at the price paid by C–D; or, at the nominal capitalization; or, at the (indefinite) figure at which C–D might have been willing to sell? What further serves to muddle the whole question is the fact that the transfer price of the going concern had been agreed upon between A–B and C–D before the whole amount of the outstanding stock had been bought in by A–B.

This case, which is after all sufficiently commonplace, offers a chance for further refinements of confusion, but what has been said may serve [128] to illustrate the point in question. The difficulty, it will be noticed, is a difficulty of classification, not of business procedure. There are no difficulties of mutual intelligibility among the various parties engaged in the transactions. The difficulties arise when it is attempted to define the phenomena for some (taxonomic) purpose not germane to the transactions in question, and to draw lines of demarcation that are of no effect in the business affairs in which these phenomena arise. The resulting confusion marks a taxonomic infirmity in the proposed capital concept, due to an endeavor to reach a definition from a metaphysical postulate (of hedonism) not comprised among the postulates on which business traffic proceeds.

This fable teaches that it is a wise hedonist who keeps his capital concept clear of all entanglement with "capital value," and, more particularly, with the live business notion of capitalized earning-capacity.

Fisher's *Rate of Interest*

There is less novelty, either in the course of the argument or in the results achieved, in *The Rate of Interest*[15] than in Mr. Fisher's earlier volume on *The Nature of Capital and Income*. Substantially the whole of it lies within the accustomed lines of that marginal-utility school of economics for which its author has so often and so convincingly spoken. It is true to the canons of the school, even to the point of making the usual error of logic in the usual place. But while it makes no material innovation, beyond a new distribution of emphasis among the factors held by the school to determine the rate of interest, it carries out the analysis of these determinants with unexampled thoroughness and circumspection, such, indeed, it may fairly be hoped, as will close the argument, on the main heads of the theory at least, within the school. There is all the breadth and facility of command over materials, which Mr. Fisher's readers have learned to expect, such as to make the book notable even among a group of writers to whom such facility seems native. If fault is to be found with this exposition of the marginal-utility doctrines it is scarcely to be sought in details of fact or unauthorized discrepancies of logic. Exception may be taken to the argument as a whole, but scarcely from the accepted ground of the marginal-utility school. Nor should that remnant of the classical school which has not yet given its adherence to the marginal-utility doctrines readily find fault with an exposition which finds its foundations in so good and authentic a utilitarian theorist as John Rae.

The theory of interest arrived at is the so-called "agio" or discount theory, already familiar to Mr. Fisher's readers and substantially in accord with the like theory spoken for by Böhm-Bawerk. Mr. Fisher takes issue with Böhm-Bawerk on the one grave and far-famed point of doctrine concerning the "Roundabout Process." And on this head, I apprehend, it will be conceded that the later writer occupies the stronger and more consistent position, whatever exceptions may be taken to his line of argument in refutation of the doctrine in dispute. [297] In his critical survey of competing and inadequate

15 *The Rate of Interest: Its Nature, Determination and Relation to Economic Phenomena.* By Irving Fisher, New York, Macmillan Company, 1908. – pp. xxii+442.

interest theories, occupying the first four chapters of the volume, this doctrine of the roundabout process comes in for more serious attention than all the rest; and justly so, since it is an alien in the school – a heresy which has been brought in by oversight. Leaving on one side for the moment all question as to the merits of this doctrine, it may readily be shown not to belong in the same explanation of interest with the agio theory, at least not as a proposition correlative with the theorem about the differential preference for present over future income. Interest and the rate of interest is a matter of value, therefore to be explained in terms of valuation, and so in terms of marginal utility. Within the scheme of value theory for which Mr. Fisher and Böhm-Bawerk are spokesmen no analysis of a value phenomenon can be brought to a conclusion until it is stated in terms of marginal utility. All fundamental propositions, all theorems of the first order in this theoretical scheme must be stated in these terms, since these terms alone are ultimate. Facts of a different order bear on any question of value, in this scheme, only as they bear on the process of valuation, which is matter to be stated in terms of marginal utility. This scheme of theory is a branch of applied psychology – of that school of psychology which was in vogue in the early nineteenth century; whereas the roundabout process is not a psychological phenomenon – at least not of the same class with the doctrines of marginal utility. It is a technological matter. The roundabout process has a bearing on the rate of interest, therefore, only as it bears on the main theorem concerning the preference for present over future income; that is to say, the doctrine of the greater productivity of the roundabout process is, at the best, a secondary proposition, subsidiary to the main theorem. The valuations out of which the rate of interest emerges take account of various circumstances affecting the desirability of present as contrasted with future goods; among these circumstances may be the greater productivity of the roundabout process; but this is as near to the core of the problem as that phenomenon can be brought. The problem of the rate of interest in the marginal-utility system is a problem of applied psychology, more precisely a problem of the hedonistic calculus; whereas the alleged greater productivity of the roundabout process is a technological phenomenon, an empirical generalization concerning the mechanical efficiency of given industrial ways and means. As an explanation of interest the doctrine of the roundabout process belongs among the productivity theories, as Mr. Fisher has indicated: and as such it cannot be admitted as a competent, or indeed a relevant, [298] explanation of interest in a system of theory whose purpose is to formulate a scheme of economic conduct in terms of the hedonistic calculus.

It is quite conceivable that in some other system of economic theory, worked out for some other purpose than the hedonistic explanation of value, the roundabout process might be brought into the central place in a doctrine of interest; but such a doctrine would have as its theoretical core, upon which the theorist's attention should be concentrated, the physical production of that increment of wealth that is presumed to go to interest, rather than the pecuniary determination of the rate of interest through which this increment is distributed among its claimants. Such a doctrine would belong in a theory of production, or of industry, not in a theory of distribution, or of business. But the marginal-utility system is primarily a theoretical scheme of production; and, therefore, in so far as it is or aims to be primarily a theory of business traffic, not of the processes of industry, particularly not of technological efficiency or of technological changes. This is well shown, e.g., in Mr. Fisher's discussion of invention (ch. x, ch. xi, sec. 4, ch. xvii, sec. 6).

Apart from all question of consistency or conclusiveness within the premises of the marginal-utility school, the test to which Mr. Fisher's theory of interest must finally be brought is the question of its adequacy as an explanation of interest in modern business. Mr. Fisher has recognized this, and the most painstaking and most admirable portions of the volume are those which discuss interest as involved in current business transactions (e.g., ch. xii–xvi). In modern life distribution takes place almost wholly in pecuniary terms and by means of business transactions. In so far as it does not, e.g., in the distribution of consumable goods within the household or in the distributive use of public utilities, it does not bear sensibly on any question of interest, particularly does it not bear immediately as a determinant on the rate of interest. Interest, as demanding the attention of the modern economist, is eminently a pecuniary phenomenon, and its rate is a question of business adjustments. It is in the business community and under the guidance and incitement of business exigencies that the rate is determined. The rate of interest in any other bearing in modern life is wholly subordinate and subsidiary. It is therefore an inversion of the logical sequence when Mr. Fisher, with others of the school, explains pecuniary interest and its rate by appeal to non-pecuniary factors. But such are the traditions of the school, and such a line of analysis is imposed by their premises. [299]

As has been remarked above, Mr. Fisher's development of the doctrine of interest is true to these premises and traditions to a degree of nicety never excelled by any of the adepts. These premises or postulates on which the marginal-utility scheme rests are derived from the English classical economists, and through them from the hedonistic philosophy of the earlier decades of the last century. According to the hedonistic postulates the end and incentive is necessarily the pleasurable sensations to be derived from the consumption of goods, what Mr. Fisher calls "enjoyable income" or "psychic income" (see Glossary, pp. 339–40), and for reasons set forth in his analysis (ch. vi), it is held that, on the whole, men prefer present to future consumption. This is the beginning of economic (marginal-utility) wisdom; but it is also the end of the wisdom of marginal utility. To these elemental terms it has been incumbent on all marginal-utility theorists to reduce their formulations of economic phenomena. And from the acceptance of these limitations follow several characteristic excrescences and incongruities in Mr. Fisher's theory, presently to be spoken of.

To save argument it may be conceded that the hedonistic interpretation of human conduct is fundamentally sound. It is not requisite for the purpose in hand to discard that postulate, however frail it might prove on closer scrutiny.

But if it be granted that the elemental motive force of economic life is the hedonistic calculus it does not follow that the same elemental calculus of preference for present over future sensations of consumption is to be directly appealed to in explanation of a phenomenon so far from elementary as the rate of interest. In point of historical fact anything like a consistent rate of interest emerges into the consciousness of mankind only after business traffic has reached some appreciable degree of development; and this development of business enterprise has taken place only on the basis and within the lines of the so-called "money economy," and virtually only on that higher stage of the money economy specifically called a "credit economy." Indeed interest is, strictly, a phenomenon of credit transactions alone. But a money economy and the consequent credit transactions which give rise to the phenomena of interest can emerge only on the basis afforded by the mature development of the institution of property. The whole matter lies within the range of a definite institutional situation which is to be found only during a relatively brief phase of civilization that has been preceded by thousands of years of cultural growth during which the existence of such a thing as interest was never suspected. In short, interest is a business proposition and is to be explained only in terms of business, not in terms [300] of livelihood, as Mr. Fisher aims to do. Business may be intimately concerned with livelihood, it may even be that in modern life business activity is the sole or chief method of getting a livelihood, but the two are not convertible terms, as Mr. Fisher's argument would require; neither are business gains convertible with the sensations of consumption, as his argument would also require.

The reason why these terms are not convertible, and therefore the reason why an argument proceeding on their convertibility or equivalence must reach a fallacious outcome, is that a growth of institutions intervenes between the two – granting that the hedonistic calculus is the primary incentive and guide of economic activity. In economic life, as in other lines of human conduct, habitual modes of activity and relations have grown up and have by convention settled into a fabric of institutions. These institutions, and the usual concepts involved in them, have a prescriptive, habitual force of their own, although it is not necessary at every move to ravel out and verify the intricate web of precedents, accidents, compromises, indiscretions, and appetites, out of which in the course of centuries the current cultural situation has arisen. If the contrary were true, if men universally acted not on the conventional grounds and values afforded by the fabric of institutions, but solely and directly on the grounds and values afforded by the unconventionalized propensities and aptitudes of hereditary human nature, then there would be no institutions and no culture. But the institutional structure of society subsists and men live within its lines, with more or less questioning, it is true, but with more acquiescence than dissent.

Business proceeds on the ground afforded by the institution of property, more particularly of property as rated in terms of money values. The rate of interest is one of the phenomena involved in this business traffic, and its theoretical explanation must run in terms of business, and so in terms of money. When the question is removed from this institutional basis and is pushed back to the grounds on which property and money are conceived to rest, it ceases to be a question of interest and becomes a detail of the analysis of the phenomena of value. But value, as understood by living economists, has no existence apart from the institution of property – since it is concerned with the exchange of property. Interest is a pecuniary concept having no validity (except by force of an ambiguity) outside of the pecuniary relations of the business community, and to construe it in other, presumably more elementary, terms is to explain it away by dissolving it into the elements out of which it is remotely derived, or [301] rather to which it is presumed to be remotely related. The phenomena of modern business, including the rate of interest, can no more be handled in non-pecuniary terms than human physiology can be handled in terms of the amphioxus. The difference is that between explaining current facts and endeavoring to explain them away.

There is (probably) no science except economics in which such an endeavor to explain the phenomena of an institution in terms of one class of the rudiments which have afforded the point of departure for the growth of the institution would be listened to with any degree of civility. The philologists, for example, have various infirmities of their own, but they would have little patience with a textual critic who should endeavor to reduce the Homeric hymns to terms of those onomatopoetic sounds out of which it is presumed that human speech has grown. What fortune would have overtaken E. B. Tylor's [*Primitive Culture:*] *Researches into the Development of Mythology, Philosophy, Religion, Language, Art and Custom*, if he had set out to explain away the facts and show these institutions are of no effect because he knows something about the remote sources from which they have come? Scientific vagaries of that heroic stature are not unknown among ethnologists, but it is to be noted to the credit of the craft that they are known as vagaries.

Mr. Fisher's theory of the rate of interest suffers from the same oversight of this difference between explaining facts and explaining them away, as do the common run of marginal-utility doctrines. So, since interest is to be formulated in terms of consumptive hedonism, instead of in business concepts, and since price is to be formulated in the same terms, there arises an unavoidable confusion between the two, as appears in the discussion of "Appreciation and Interest" (ch. v, and elsewhere). In the main, this discussion belongs properly in a theory of prices. Appreciation and depreciation of the standard of payments may of course – so far as they are foreseen – affect the rate of interest; but they are, after all, phenomena of price. Business transactions run in terms of money. Interest is rated in money and paid with a view to money gain. Many contingencies bear on the changes of such gain, and changes of price are notoriously among those contingencies. Speculative buying and selling look to this contingency chiefly, and may look to such a change in the price of the goods bought or sold as shall offset the interest on the funds tied up in the speculation, but the rate of interest does not thereby come to be conceived or stated in terms of the advance or decline of the price of goods. Appreciation and depreciation, if foreseen, are circumstances to be taken into account by lender and borrower very much as the productivity of [302] the roundabout process (if that doctrine be allowed) will be taken into account in making the rate of interest. But this state of the case does not make either of these phenomena a rate of interest; nor does it reduce interest to a technological matter on the one hand or to a variation of prices on the other hand.

Now and again, especially in ch. xiv (pp. 276–85), Mr. Fisher cites facts showing that neither investment nor interest are counted in terms of livelihood or in the sensations of consumption, and showing also that questions of livelihood touch these phenomena only uncertainly and incidentally. He well shows (a) that business men habitually do not (adequately) appreciate variations in the commodity-value of money, and (b) that with rising prices they simply do business at a high money profit and are content to pay a high rate of interest without suspecting that all this has any connection with the "commodity interest" of Mr. Fisher. (Cf. the passages cited from Baxter and from Jevons). But his hedonistic preconceptions lead him to take note of this state of things as exceptional and anomalous, whereas, of course, it is the rule. It is not only the rule, but there is no avoiding it so long as business is done in terms of money, and in the absence of a foregone conclusion these facts should persuade any observer that money value has an institutional force in the counsels of business men.

This chapter (xiv), and in good part the succeeding one, explain interest without support from or reference to Mr. Fisher's "agio" theory, although they are offered as an "inductive verification" of that theory. Except for the author's recurrent intimations, nothing in this inductive verification bears on, or leans on, the doctrine of a preference for present over future income. Not only so, but chapter xiv, incidentally helped out by various passages elsewhere, goes far to disprove that the rate of interest is a matter of the preference for present over future income, taking "income" in Mr. Fisher's sense of the term. There is a strikingly ingenuous passage in ch. xv, (p. 315): "For him [the farmer] the lowest ebb is in the fall, when gathering and marketing his crops cause him a sudden expenditure of labor or of money for the labor of others. To tide him over this period he may need to borrow. ... The rate of interest tends upward." The farmer, in other words, bids up the rate of interest when his crops are in hand or are coming in; particularly just after he has secured them, when he is required to meet certain pecuniary obligations. But the farmer's crops are his "income" in the case assumed, and when his income has come in, at this springtide of his income stream, his preference for present over future goods should logically be at its lowest, and, indeed, there need [303] be little question but such is the case. There is also no doubt that the farmer is willing to bid high for funds at this period; and the reason seems to be that then the fresh access of income enables him to bid high, at the same time that he needs the funds to meet pecuniary obligations. His need of borrowing is due to the necessity of marketing his crops and so "realizing" on them; that is to say, it is a business or pecuniary need, not a matter of smoothing out the income stream. Farming is a business venture in modern times, and the end of business is gain in terms of money. The cycle of business enterprise closes with a sale, a conversion of "income" into money values, not conversely, and the farmer is under more or less pecuniary pressure to bring this pecuniary cycle to a close.

Selection 36

The limitations of marginal utility

Source: *Journal of Political Economy*, November 1909
(vol. 17, pp. 620–36).

Veblen (1909c)

The limitations of the marginal-utility economics are sharp and characteristic.
It is from first to last a doctrine of value, and in point of form and method it
is a theory of valuation. The whole system, therefore, lies within the theoretical field of distribution, and it has but a secondary bearing on any other
economic phenomena than those of distribution – the term being taken in its
accepted sense of pecuniary distribution, or distribution in point of ownership. Now and again an attempt is made to extend the use of the principle of
marginal utility beyond this range, so as to apply it to questions of production, but hitherto without sensible effect, and necessarily so. The most
ingenious and the most promising of such attempts have been those of
Mr. Clark, whose work marks the extreme range of endeavor and the extreme
degree of success in so seeking to turn a postulate of distribution to account
for a theory of production. But the outcome has been a doctrine of the
production of values, and value, in Mr. Clark's as in other utility systems, is a
matter of valuation; which throws the whole excursion back into the field of
distribution. Similarly, as regards attempts to make use of this principle in an
analysis of the phenomena of consumption, the best results arrived at are
some formulation of the pecuniary distribution of consumption goods.

Within this limited range marginal utility theory is of a wholly statical
character. It offers no theory of a movement of any kind, being occupied with
the adjustment of values to a given situation. Of this, again, no more convincing illustration need be had than is afforded by the work of Mr. Clark,
which is not excelled in point of earnestness, perseverance, or insight. For all
their use of the term "dynamic," neither Mr. Clark nor any of his associates
in this line of research have yet contributed anything at all appreciable to a
theory of genesis, growth, sequence, change, process, or the like, in economic
life. They have had something to say as to the bearing which given economic
[621] changes, accepted as premises, may have on economic valuation, and so
on distribution; but as to the causes of change or the unfolding sequence of
the phenomena of economic life they have had nothing to say hitherto; nor
can they, since their theory is not drawn in causal terms but in terms of
teleology.

In all this the marginal utility school is substantially at one with the classical economics of the nineteenth century, the difference between the two being that the former is confined within narrower limits and sticks more consistently to its teleological premises. Both are teleological, and neither can consistently admit arguments from cause to effect in the formulation of their main articles of theory. Neither can deal theoretically with phenomena of change, but at the most only with rational adjustment to change which may be supposed to have supervened.

To the modern scientist the phenomena of growth and change are the most obtrusive and most consequential facts observable in economic life. For an understanding of modern economic life the technological advance of the past two centuries – e.g., the growth of the industrial arts – is of the first importance; but marginal utility theory does not bear on this matter, nor does this matter bear on marginal utility theory. As a means of theoretically accounting for this technological movement in the past or in the present, or even as a means of formally, technically stating it as an element in the current economic situation, that doctrine and all its works are altogether idle. The like is true for the sequence of change that is going forward in the pecuniary relations of modern life; the hedonistic postulate and its propositions of differential utility neither have served nor can serve an inquiry into these phenomena of growth, although the whole body of marginal utility economics lies within the range of these pecuniary phenomena. It has nothing to say to the growth of business usages and expedients or to the concomitant changes in the principles of conduct which govern the pecuniary relations of men, which condition and are conditioned by these altered relations of business life or which bring them to pass.

It is characteristic of the school that wherever an element of the cultural fabric, an institution or any institutional phenomenon, [622] is involved in the facts with which the theory is occupied, such institutional facts are taken for granted, denied, or explained away. If it is a question of price, there is offered an explanation of how exchanges may take place with such effect as to leave money and price out of the account. If it is a question of credit, the effect of credit extension on business traffic is left on one side and there is an explanation of how the borrower and lender cooperate to smooth out their respective income streams of consumable goods or sensations of consumption. The failure of the school in this respect is consistent and comprehensive. And yet these economists are lacking neither in intelligence nor in information. They are, indeed, to be credited, commonly, with a wide range of information and an exact control of materials, as well as with a very alert interest in what is going on; and apart from their theoretical pronouncements the members of the school habitually profess the sanest and most intelligent views of current practical questions, even when these questions touch matters of institutional growth and decay.

The infirmity of this theoretical scheme lies in its postulates which confine the inquiry to generalizations of the teleological or "deductive" order. These postulates, together with the point of view and logical method that follow from them, the marginal utility school shares with other economists of the classical line – for this school is but a branch or derivative of the English classical economists of the nineteenth century. The substantial difference between this school and the generality of classical economists lies mainly in the fact that in the marginal utility economics the common postulates are more consistently adhered to at the same time that they are more neatly defined and their limitations are more adequately realized. Both the classical school in general and its specialized variant, the marginal utility school, in particular, take as their common point of departure the traditional psychology of the early nineteenth-century hedonists, which is accepted as a matter of course or of common notoriety and is held quite uncritically. The central and well defined tenet so held is that of the hedonistic calculus. Under the guidance of this tenet and of the other psychological conceptions associated and consonant [623] with it, human conduct is conceived of and interpreted as a rational response to the exigencies of the situation in which mankind is placed; as regards economic conduct it is such a rational and unprejudiced response to the stimulus of anticipated pleasure and pain – being, typically and in the main, a response to the promptings of anticipated pleasure, for the hedonists of the nineteenth century and of the marginal utility school are in the main of an optimistic temper.[1] Mankind is, on the whole and normally, (conceived to be) clearsighted and farsighted in its appreciation of future sensuous gains and losses, although there may be some (inconsiderable) difference between men in this respect. Men's activities differ, therefore, (inconsiderably) in respect of the alertness of the response and the nicety of adjustment of irksome pain cost to apprehended future sensuous gain; but, on the whole, no other ground or line or guidance of conduct than this rationalistic calculus falls properly within the cognizance of the economic hedonists. Such a theory can take account of conduct only in so far as it is rational conduct, guided by deliberate and exhaustively intelligent choice – wise adaption to the demands of the main chance.

The external circumstances which condition conduct are variable, of course, and so they will have a varying effect upon conduct; but their variation is, in effect, construed to be of such a character only as to vary the degree of strain to which the human agent is subject by contact with these external circumstances. The cultural elements involved in the theoretical scheme, elements

---

1 The conduct of mankind differs from that of the brutes in being determined by anticipated sensations of pleasure and pain, instead of actual sensations. Hereby, in so far, human conduct is taken out of the sequence of cause and effect and falls instead under the rule of sufficient reason. By virtue of this rational faculty in man the connection between stimulus and response is teleological instead of causal.

The reason for assigning the first and decisive place to pleasure,rather than pain, in the determination of human conduct, appears to be the (tacit) acceptance of that optimistic doctrine of a beneficent order of nature which the nineteenth century inherited from the eighteenth.

that are of the nature of institutions, human relations governed by use and wont in whatever kind and connection, are not subject to inquiry but are taken from granted as pre-existing [624] in a finished, typical form and as making up a normal and definite economic situation, under which and in terms of which human intercourse is necessarily carried on. This cultural situation comprises a few large and simple articles of institutional furniture, together with their logical implications or corollaries; but it includes nothing of the consequences or effects caused by these institutional elements. The cultural elements so tacitly postulated as immutable conditions precedent to economic life are ownership and free contract, together with such other features of the scheme of natural rights as are implied in the exercise of these. These cultural products are, for the purpose of the theory, conceived to be given a priori in unmitigated force. They are part of the nature of things; so that there is no need of accounting for them or inquiring into them, as to how they have come to be such as they are, or how and why they have changed and are changing, or what effect all this may have on the relations of men who live by or under this cultural situation.

Evidently the acceptance of these immutable premises, tacitly, because uncritically and as a matter of course, by hedonistic economics gives the science a distinctive character and places it in contrast with other sciences whose premises are of a different order. As has already been indicated, the premises in question, so far as they are peculiar to the hedonistic economics, are (a) a certain institutional situation, the substantial feature of which is the natural right of ownership, and (b) the hedonistic calculus. The distinctive character given to this system of theory by these postulates and by the point of view resulting from their acceptance may be summed up broadly and concisely in saying that the theory is confined to the ground of sufficient reason instead of proceeding on the ground of efficient cause. The contrary is true of modern science, generally (except mathematics), particularly of such sciences as have to do with the phenomena of life and growth. The difference may seem trivial. It is serious only in its consequences. The two methods of inference – from sufficient reason and from efficient cause – are out of touch with one another and there is no transition from one to the other; no method of converting the procedure or the results of the one into [625] those of the other. The immediate consequence is that the resulting economic theory is of a teleological character – "deductive" or "a priori" as it is often called – instead of being drawn in terms of cause and effect. The relation sought by this theory among the facts with which it is occupied is the control exercised by future (apprehended) events over present conduct. Current phenomena are dealt with as conditioned by their future consequences; and in strict marginal-utility theory they can be dealt with only in respect of their control of the present by consideration of the future. Such a (logical) relation of control or guidance between the future and the present of course involves an exercise of intelligence, a taking thought, and hence an intelligent agent through whose discriminating forethought the apprehended future may affect the current course of events; unless, indeed, one were to admit something in the way of a providential order of nature or some occult line of stress of the nature of sympathetic magic. Barring magical and providential elements, the relation of sufficient reason runs by way of the interested discrimination, the forethought, of an agent who takes thought of the future and guides his present activity by regard for this future. The relation of sufficient reason runs only from the (apprehended) future into the present, and it is solely of an intellectual, subjective, personal, teleological character and force; while the relation of cause and effect runs only in the contrary direction, and it is solely of an objective, impersonal materialistic character and force. The modern scheme of knowledge, on the whole, rests, for its definitive ground, on the relation of cause and effect; the relation of sufficient reason being admitted only provisionally and as a proximate factor in the analysis, always with the unambiguous reservation that the analysis must ultimately come to rest in terms of cause and effect. The merits of this scientific animus, of course, do not concern the present argument.

Now, it happens that the relation of sufficient reason enters very substantially into human conduct. It is this element of discriminating forethought that distinguishes human conduct from brute behavior. And since the economist's subject of inquiry is this human conduct, that relation necessarily comes in for a large [626] share of his attention in any theoretical formulation of economic phenomena, whether hedonistic or otherwise. But while modern science at large has made the causal relation the sole ultimate ground of theoretical formulation; and while the other sciences that deal with human life admit the relation of sufficient reason as a proximate, supplementary, or intermediate ground, subsidiary, and subservient to the argument from cause and effect; economics has had the misfortune – as seen from the scientific point of view – to let the former supplant the latter. It is, of course, true that human conduct is distinguished from other natural phenomena by the human faculty for taking thought, and any science that has to do with human conduct must face the patent fact that the details of such conduct consequently fall into the teleological form; but it is the peculiarity of the hedonistic economics that by force of its postulates its attention is confined to this teleological bearing of conduct alone. It deals with this conduct only in so far as it may be construed in rationalistic, teleological terms of calculation and choice. But it is at the same time no less true that human conduct, economic or otherwise, is subject to the sequence of cause and effect, by force of such elements as habituation and conventional requirements. But facts of this order, which are to modern science of graver interest than the teleological details of conduct, necessarily fall outside the attention of the hedonistic economist, because they cannot be construed in terms of sufficient reason, such as his postulates demand, or be fitted into a scheme of teleological doctrines.

There is, therefore, no call to impugn these premises of the marginal-utility economics within their field. They commend themselves to all serious and uncritical persons at first glance. They are principles of action which underlie the current, business-like scheme of economic life, and as such, as practical grounds of conduct, they are not to be called in question without questioning the existing law and order. As a matter of course, men order their lives by these principles and, practically, entertain no question of their stability and finality. That is what is meant by calling them institutions; they are settled habits of thought common to the generality of men. But it would be mere absent-mindedness [627] in any student of civilization therefore to admit that these or any other human institutions have this stability which is currently imputed to them or that they are in this way intrinsic to the nature of things. The acceptance by the economists of these or other institutional elements as given and immutable limits their inquiry in a particular and decisive way. It shuts off the inquiry at the point where the modern scientific interest sets in. The institutions in question are no doubt good for their purpose as institutions, but they are not good as premises for a scientific inquiry into the nature, origin, growth, and effects of these institutions and of the mutations which they undergo and which they bring to pass in the community's scheme of life.

To any modern scientist interested in economic phenomena, the chain of cause and effect in which any given phase of human culture is involved, as well as the cumulative changes wrought in the fabric of human conduct itself by the habitual activity of mankind, are matters of more engrossing and more abiding interest than the method of inference by which an individual is presumed invariably to balance pleasure and pain under given conditions that are presumed to be normal and invariable. The former are questions of the life-history of the race or the community, questions of cultural growth and of the fortunes of generations; while the latter is a question of individual casuistry in the face of a given situation that may arise in the course of this cultural growth. The former bear on the continuity and mutations of that scheme of conduct whereby mankind deals with its material means of life; the latter, if it is conceived in hedonistic terms, concerns a disconnected episode in the sensuous experience of an individual member of such a community.

In so far as modern science inquires into the phenomena of life, whether inanimate, brute, or human, it is occupied about questions of genesis and cumulative change, and it converges upon a theoretical formulation in the shape of a life-history drawn in causal terms. In so far as it is a science in the current sense of the term, any science, such as economics, which has to do with human conduct, becomes a genetic inquiry into the human scheme of life; and where, as in economics, the subject of inquiry is the [628] conduct of man in his dealings with the material means of life, the science is necessarily an inquiry into the life-history of material civilization, on a more or less extended or restricted plan. Not that the economist's inquiry isolates material civilization from all other phases and bearings of human culture, and so studies the motions of an abstractly conceived "economic man." On the contrary, no theoretical inquiry into this material civilization that shall be at all adequate to any scientific purpose can be carried out without taking this material civilization in its causal, that is to say, its genetic, relations to other phases and bearings of the cultural complex; without studying it as it is wrought upon by other lines of cultural growth and as working its effects in these other lines. But in so far as the inquiry is economic science, specifically, the attention will converge upon the scheme of material life and will take in other phases of civilization only in their correlation with the scheme of material civilization.

Like all human culture this material civilization is a scheme of institutions – institutional fabric and institutional growth. But institutions are an outgrowth of habit. The growth of culture is a cumulative sequence of habituation, and the ways and means of it are the habitual response of human nature to exigencies that vary incontinently, cumulatively, but with something of a consistent sequence in the cumulative variations that so go forward, – incontinently, because each new move creates a new situation which induces a further new variation in the habitual manner of response; cumulatively, because each new situation is a variation of what has gone before it and embodies as causal factors all that has been effected by what went before; consistently, because the underlying traits of human nature (propensities, aptitudes, and what not) by force of which the response takes place, and on the ground of which the habituation takes effect, remain substantially unchanged.

Evidently an economic inquiry which occupies itself exclusively with the movements of this consistent, elemental human nature under given, stable institutional conditions – such as is the case with the current hedonistic economics – can reach statical [629] results alone; since it makes abstraction from those elements that make for anything but a statical result. On the other hand an adequate theory of economic conduct, even for statical purposes, cannot be drawn in terms of the individual simply – as is the case in the marginal-utility economics – because it cannot be drawn in terms of the underlying traits of human nature simply; since the response that goes to make up human conduct takes place under institutional norms and only under stimuli that have an institutional bearing; for the situation that provokes and inhibits action in any given case is itself in great part of institutional, cultural derivation. Then, too, the phenomena of human life occur only as phenomena of the life of a group or community; only under stimuli due to contact with the group and only under the (habitual) control exercised by canons of conduct imposed by the group's scheme of life. Not only is the individual's conduct hedged about and directed by his habitual relations to his fellows in the group, but these relations, being of an institutional character, vary as the institutional scheme varies. The wants and desires, the end and aim, the ways and means, the amplitude and drift of the individual's conduct are functions of an institutional variable that is of a highly complex and wholly unstable character.

The growth and mutations of the institutional fabric are an outcome of the conduct of the individual members of the group, since it is out of the experience of the individuals, through the habituation of individuals, that institutions arise; and it is in this same experience that these institutions act to direct and define the aims and end of conduct. It is, of course, on individuals that the system of institutions imposes those conventional standards, ideals, and canons of conduct that make up the community's scheme of life. Scientific inquiry in this field, therefore, must deal with individual conduct and must formulate its theoretical results in terms of individual conduct. But such an inquiry can serve the purposes of a genetic theory only if and in so far as this individual conduct is attended to in those respects in [630] which it counts toward habituation, and so toward change (or stability) of the institutional fabric, on the one hand, and in those respects in which it is prompted and guided by the received institutional conceptions and ideals on the other hand. The postulates of marginal utility, and the hedonistic preconceptions generally, fail at this point in that they confine the attention to such bearings of economic conduct as are conceived not to be conditioned by habitual standards and ideals and to have no effect in the way of habituation. They disregard or abstract from the causal sequence of propensity and habituation in economic life and exclude from theoretical inquiry all such interest in the facts of cultural growth, in order to attend to those features of the case that are conceived to be idle in this respect. All such facts of institutional force and growth are put on one side as not being germane to pure theory; they are to be taken account of, if at all, by afterthought, by a more or less vague and general allowance for inconsequential disturbances due to occasional human infirmity. Certain institutional phenomena, it is true, are comprised among the premises of the hedonists, as has been noted above; but they are included as postulates a priori. So the institution of ownership is taken into the inquiry not as a factor of growth or an element subject to change, but as one of the primordial and immutable facts of the order of nature, underlying the hedonistic calculus. Property, ownership, is presumed as the basis of hedonistic discrimination and it is conceived to be given in its finished (nineteenth-century) scope and force. There is no thought either of a conceivable growth of this definitive nineteenth-century institution out of a cruder past or of any conceivable cumulative change in the scope and force of ownership in the present or future. Nor is it conceived that the presence of this institutional element in men's economic relations in any degree affects or disguises the hedonistic calculus, or that its pecuniary conceptions and standards in any degree standardize, color, mitigate, or divert the hedonistic calculator from the direct and unhampered quest of the net sensuous gain. While the institution of property is included in this way among the postulates of the theory, and is even presumed to be ever-present in the economic situation, it is allowed to have no force in shaping economic conduct, which is conceived to run its course to its hedonistic outcome as if no such [631] institutional factor intervened between the impulse and its realization. The institution of property, together with all the range of pecuniary conceptions that belong under it and that cluster about it, are presumed to give rise to no habitual or conventional canons of conduct or standards of valuation, no proximate ends, ideals, or aspirations. All pecuniary notions arising from ownership are treated simply as expedients of computation which mediate between the pain-cost and the pleasure-gain of hedonistic choice, without lag, leak, or friction; they are conceived simply as the immutably correct, God-given notation of the hedonistic calculus.

The modern economic situation is a business situation, in that economic activity of all kinds is commonly controlled by business considerations. The exigencies of modern life are commonly pecuniary exigencies. That is to say they are exigencies of the ownership of property. Productive efficiency and distributive gain are both rated in terms of price. Business considerations are considerations of price, and pecuniary exigencies of whatever kind in the modern communities are exigencies of price. The current economic situation is a price system. Economic institutions in the modern civilized scheme of life are (prevailing) institutions of the price system. The accountancy to which all phenomena of modern economic life are amenable is an accountancy in terms of price; and by the current convention there is no other recognized scheme of accountancy, no other rating, either in law or in fact, to which the facts of modern life are held amenable. Indeed, so great and pervading a force has this habit (institution) of pecuniary accountancy become that it extends, often as a matter of course, to many facts which properly have no pecuniary bearing and no pecuniary magnitude, as, e.g., works of art, science, scholarship, and religion. More or less freely and fully, the price system dominates the current common sense in its appreciation and rating of these non-pecuniary ramifications of modern culture; and this in spite of the fact that, on reflection, all men of normal intelligence will freely admit that these matters lie outside the scope of pecuniary valuation.

Current popular taste and the popular sense of merit and [632] demerit are notoriously affected in some degree by pecuniary considerations. It is a matter of common notoriety, not to be denied or explained away, that pecuniary ("commercial") tests and standards are habitually made use of outside of commercial interests proper. Precious stones, it is admitted, even by hedonistic economists, are more esteemed than they would be if they were more plentiful and cheaper. A wealthy person meets with more consideration and enjoys a larger measure of good repute than would fall to the share of the same person with the same habit of mind and body and the same record of good and evil deeds if he were poorer. It may well be that this current "commercialization" of taste and appreciation has been overstated by superficial and hasty critics of contemporary life, but it will not be denied that there is a modicum of truth in the allegation. Whatever substance it has, much or little, is due to carrying over into other fields of interest the habitual conceptions induced by dealing with and thinking of pecuniary matters. These "commercial" conceptions of merit and demerit are derived from business experience. The pecuniary tests and standards so applied outside of business transactions and relations are not reducible to sensuous terms of pleasure and pain. Indeed, it may, e.g., be true, as is commonly believed, that the contemplation of a wealthy neighbor's pecuniary superiority yields painful rather than pleasurable sensations as an immediate result; but it is equally true that such a wealthy neighbor is, on the whole, more highly regarded and more considerately treated than another neighbor who differs from the former only in being less enviable in respect of wealth.

It is the institution of property that gives rise to these habitual grounds of discrimination, and in modern times, when wealth is counted in terms of money, it is in terms of money value that these tests and standards of pecuniary excellence are applied. This much will be admitted. Pecuniary institutions induce pecuniary habits of thought which affect men's discrimination outside of pecuniary matters; but the hedonistic interpretation alleges that such pecuniary habits of thought do not affect men's discrimination in pecuniary matters. Although the institutional [633] scheme of the price system visibly dominates the modern community's thinking in matters that lie outside the economic interest, the hedonistic economists insist, in effect, that this institutional scheme must be accounted of no effect within that range of activity to which it owes its genesis, growth, and persistence. The phenomena of business, which are peculiarly and uniformly phenomena of price, are in the scheme of the hedonistic theory reduced to non-pecuniary hedonistic terms and the theoretical formulation is carried out as if pecuniary conceptions had no force within the traffic in which such conceptions originate. It is admitted that preoccupation with commercial interests has "commercialized" the rest of modern life, but the "commercialization" of commerce is not admitted. Business transactions and computations in pecuniary terms, such as loans, discounts, and capitalization, are without hesitation or abatement converted into terms of hedonistic utility, and conversely.

It may be needless to take exception to such conversion from pecuniary into sensuous terms, for the theoretical purpose for which it is habitually made; although, if need were, it might not be excessively difficult to show that the whole hedonistic basis of such a conversion is a psychological misconception. But it is to the remoter theoretical consequences of such a conversion that exception is to be taken. In making the conversion abstraction is made from whatever elements do not lend themselves to its terms; which amounts to abstracting from precisely those elements of business that have an institutional force and that therefore would lend themselves to scientific inquiry of the modern kind – those (institutional) elements whose analysis might contribute to an understanding of modern business and of the life of the modern business community as contrasted with the assumed primordial hedonistic calculus.

The point may perhaps be made clearer. Money and the habitual resort to its use are conceived to be simply the ways and means by which consumable goods are acquired, and therefore simply a convenient method by which to procure the pleasurable sensations of consumption; these latter being in hedonistic theory the sole and overt end of all economic endeavor. Money values [634] have therefore no other significance than that of purchasing power over consumable goods, and money is simply an expedient of computation. Investment, credit extensions, loans of all kinds and degrees, with payment of interest and the rest, are likewise taken simply as intermediate steps between the pleasurable sensations of consumption and the efforts induced by the anticipation of these sensations, other bearings of the case being disregarded. The balance being kept in terms of the hedonistic consumption, no disturbance arises in this pecuniary traffic so long as the extreme terms of this extended hedonistic equation – pain-cost and pleasure-gain – are not altered, what lies between these extreme terms being merely algebraic notation employed for convenience of accountancy. But such is not the run of the facts in modern business. Variations of capitalization, e.g., occur without its being practicable to refer them to visibly equivalent variations either in the state of the industrial arts or in the sensations of consumption. Credit extensions tend to inflation of credit, rising prices, overstocking of markets, etc., likewise without a visible or securely traceable correlation in the state of the industrial arts or in the pleasures of consumption; that is to say, without a visible basis in those material elements to which the hedonistic theory reduces all economic phenomena. Hence the run of the facts, in so far, must be thrown out of the theoretical formulation. The hedonistically presumed final purchase of consumable goods is habitually not contemplated in the pursuit of business enterprise. Business men habitually aspire to accumulate wealth in excess of the limits of practicable consumption, and the wealth so accumulated is not intended to be converted by a final transaction of purchase into consumable goods or sensations of consumption. Such commonplace facts as these, together with the endless web of business detail of a like pecuniary character, do not in hedonistic theory raise a question as to how these conventional aims, ideals, aspirations, and standards have come into force or how they affect the scheme of life in business or outside of it; they do not raise the questions because such questions cannot be answered in the terms which the hedonistic economists are content to use, or, indeed, which their premises permit them to use. The question [635] which arises is how to explain the facts away; how theoretically to neutralize them so that they will not have to appear in the theory, which can then be drawn in direct and unambiguous terms of rational hedonistic calculation. They are explained away as being aberrations due to oversight or lapse of memory on the part of business men, or to some failure of logic or insight. Or they are construed and interpreted into the rationalistic terms of the hedonistic calculus by resort to an ambiguous use of the hedonistic concepts. So that the whole "money economy," with all the machinery of credit and the rest, disappears in a tissue of metaphors to reappear theoretically expurgated, sterilized, and simplified into a "refined system of barter," culminating in a net aggregate maximum of pleasurable sensations of consumption.

But since it is in just this unhedonistic, unrationalistic pecuniary traffic that the tissue of business life consists, since it is this peculiar conventionalism of aims and standards that differentiates the life of the modern business community from any conceivable earlier or cruder phase of economic life; since it is in this tissue of pecuniary intercourse and pecuniary concepts, ideals, expedients, and aspirations that the conjunctures of business life arise and run their course of felicity and devastation; since it is here that those institutional changes take place which distinguish one phase or era of the business community's life from any other; since the growth and change of these habitual, conventional elements make the growth and character of any business era or business community; any theory of business which sets these elements aside or explains them away misses the main facts which it has gone out to seek. Life and its conjunctures and institutions being of this complexion, however much that state of the case may be depreciated, a theoretical account of the phenomena of this life must be drawn in these terms in which the phenomena occur. It is not simply that the hedonistic interpretation of modern economic phenomena is inadequate or misleading; if the phenomena are subjected to the hedonistic interpretation in the theoretical analysis they disappear from the theory; and if they would bear the interpretation in fact they would disappear in fact. If, in fact, all the conventional relations and principles of [636] pecuniary intercourse were subject to such a perpetual rationalized, calculating revision, so that each article of usage, appreciation, or procedure must approve itself *de novo* on hedonistic grounds of sensuous expediency to all concerned at every move, it is not conceivable that the institutional fabric would last over night.

Selection 37

The mutation theory and the blond race

Source: *Journal of Race Development*, April 1913
(vol. 3, pp. 491–507).

Veblen (1913a)

The theories of racial development by mutation, associated with the name of Mendel, when they come to be freely applied to man, must greatly change the complexion of many currently debated questions of race – as to origins, migrations, dispersion, chronology, cultural derivation and sequence. In some respects the new theories should simplify current problems of ethnology, and they may even dispense with many analyses and speculations that have seemed of great moment in the past.

The main postulate of the Mendelian theories – the stability of type – has already done much service in anthropological science, being commonly assumed as a matter of course in arguments dealing with the derivation and dispersion of races and peoples. It is only by force of this assumption that ethnologists are able to identify any given racial stock over intervals of space or time, and so to trace the racial affinities of any given people. Question has been entertained from time to time as to the racial fixity of given physical traits – as, e.g., stature, the cephalic indices, or hair and eye color – but on the whole these and other standard marks of race are still accepted as secure grounds of identification.[1] Indeed, without some such assumption any ethnological inquiry must degenerate into mere wool-gathering.

But along with this, essentially Mendelian, postulate of the stability of types, ethnologists have at the same time habitually accepted the incompatible Darwinian doctrine that racial types vary incontinently after a progressive fashion, arising through insensible cumulative variations and passing into new specific forms by the same method, [492] under the Darwinian rule of the selective survival of slight and unstable (non-typical) variations. The effect of these two incongruous premises has been to leave discussions of race derivation somewhat at loose ends wherever the two postulates cross one another.

If it be assumed, or granted, that racial types are stable, it follows as a matter of course that these types or races have not arisen by the cumulative acquirement of unstable non-specific traits, but must have originated by

---

1 Cf., however, W. Ridgeway, "The Application of Zoölogical Laws to Man," *Report [of the Seventy-eighth Meeting of the] British Association for Advancement of Science.*

mutation or by some analogous method, and this view must then find its way into anthropology as into the other biological sciences. When such a step is taken an extensive revision of questions of race will be unavoidable, and an appreciable divergence may then be looked for among speculations on the mutational affinities of the several races and cultures.

Among matters so awaiting revision are certain broad questions of derivation and ethnography touching the blond race or races of Europe. Much attention, and indeed much sentiment, has been spent on this general topic. The questions involved are many and diverse, and many of them have been subject of animated controversy, without definitive conclusions.

The mutation theories, of course, have immediately to do with the facts of biological derivation alone, but when the facts are reviewed in the light of these theories it will be found that questions of cultural origins and relationship are necessarily drawn into the inquiry. In particular, an inquiry into the derivation and distribution of the blond stock will so intimately involve questions of the Aryan speech and institutions as to be left incomplete without a somewhat detailed attention to this latter range of questions. So much so that an inquiry into the advent and early fortunes of the blond stock in Europe will fall, by convenience, under two distinct but closely related captions: The Origin of the Blond Type, and The Derivation of the Aryan Culture.

(a) It is held, on the one hand, that there is but a single blond race, type or stock (Keane, Lapouge, Sergi), and on the other hand that there are several such races or types, more or less distinct but presumably related (Deniker, [493] Beddoe, and other, especially British, ethnologists). (b) There is no good body of evidence going to establish a great antiquity for the blond stock, and there are indications, though perhaps inconclusive, that the blond strain, including all the blond types, is of relatively late date – unless a Berber (Kabyle) blond race is to be accepted in a more unequivocal manner than hitherto. (c) Neither is there anything like convincing evidence that this blond strain has come from outside of Europe – except, again, for the equivocal Kabyle – or that any blond race has ever been widely or permanently distributed outside of its present European habitat. (d) The blond race is not found unmixed. In point of pedigree all individuals showing the blond traits are hybrids, and the greater number of them show their mixed blood in their physical traits. (e) There is no community, large or small, made up exclusively of blonds, or nearly so, and there is no good evidence available that such an all-blond or virtually all-blond community ever has existed, either in historic or prehistoric times. The race appears never to have lived in isolation. (f) It occurs in several (perhaps hybrid) variants – unless these variants are to be taken (with Deniker) as several distinct races. (g) Counting the dolicho-blond as the original type of the race, its nearest apparent relative among the races of mankind is the Mediterranean (of Sergi), at least in point of physical traits. At the same time the blond race, or at least the dolicho-blond type, has never since neolithic times, so far as known, extensively and permanently lived in contact with the Mediterranean. (h) The various (national) ramifications of the blond stock – or rather the various racial mixtures into which an appreciable blond element enters – are all, and to all appearance have always been, of Aryan ("Indo-European," "Indo-Germanic") speech – with the equivocal exception of the Kabyle. (i) Yet far the greater number and variety (national and linguistic) of men who use the Aryan speech are not prevailingly blond, or even appreciably mixed with blond. (j) The blond race, or the peoples with an appreciable blond admixture, and particularly the communities [494] in which the dolicho-blond element prevails, show little or none of the peculiarly Aryan institutions – understanding by that phrase not the known institutions of the ancient Germanic peoples, but that range of institutions said by competent philologists to be reflected in the primitive Aryan speech. (k) These considerations raise the presumption that the blond race was not originally of Aryan speech or of Aryan culture, and they also suggest (l) that the Mediterranean, the nearest apparent relative of the dolicho-blond, was likewise not originally Aryan.

Accepting the mutation theory, then, for the purpose in hand, and leaving any questions of Aryanism on one side for the present, a canvass of the situation so outlined may be offered in such bold, crude and summary terms as should be admissible in an analysis which aims to be tentative and provisional only. It may be conceived that the dolichocephalic blond originated as a mutant of the Mediterranean type (which it greatly resembles in its scheme of biometric measurements[2]) probably some time after that race had effected a permanent lodgment on the continent of Europe. The Mediterranean stock may be held (Sergi and Keane) to have come into Europe from Africa,[3] whatever its remoter derivation may have been. It is, of course, not impossible that the mutation which gave rise to the dolicho-blond may have occurred before the parent stock left Africa, or rather before it was shut out of Africa by the submergence of the land connection across Sicily, but the probabilities seem to be against such a view. The conditions would appear to have been less favorable to a mutation of this kind in the African habitat of the parent stock than in Europe, and less favorable in Europe during earlier quaternary time than toward the close of the glacial period.

The causes which give rise to a variation of type have always been sufficiently obscure, whether the origin of species be conceived after the Darwinian or the Mendelian fashion, and the mutation theories have hitherto afforded [495] little light on that question. Yet the Mendelian postulate that the type is stable except for such a mutation as shall establish a new type raises at least the presumption that such a mutation will take place only under exceptional circumstances, that is to stay, under circumstances so substantially

2 Cf. Sergi, *The Mediterranean Race*, ch. xi, xiii.
3 Sergi, *Arii e Italici*; Keane, *Man Past and Present*, ch. xii.

different from what the type is best adapted to as to subject it to some degree of physiological strain. It is to be presumed that no mutation will supervene so long as the conditions of life do not vary materially from what they have been during the previous uneventful life-history of the type. Such is the presumption apparently involved in the theory and such is also the suggestion afforded by the few experimental cases of observed mutation, as, e.g., those studied by De Vries.

A considerable climatic change, such as would seriously alter the conditions of life either directly or through its effect on the food supply, might be conceived to bring on a mutating state in the race; or the like effect might be induced by a profound cultural change, particularly any such change in the industrial arts as would radically affect the material conditions of life. These considerations, mainly speculative it is true, suggest that the dolicho-blond mutant could presumably have emerged only at a time when the parent stock was exposed to notably novel conditions of life, such as would be presumed (with De Vries) to tend to throw the stock into a specifically unstable (mutating) state; at the same time these novel conditions of life must also have been specifically of such a nature as to favor the survival and multiplication of this particular human type. The climatic tolerance of the dolicho-blond, e.g., is known to be exceptionally narrow. Now, it is not known, indeed there is no reason to presume, that the Mediterranean race was exposed to such variations of climate or of culture before it entered Europe as might be expected to induce a mutating state in the stock, and at the same time a mutant gifted with the peculiar climatic intolerance of the dolicho-blond would scarcely have survived under the conditions offered by northern Africa in late quaternary time. But the required conditions are had later on in Europe, after the Mediterranean was securely at home in that continent. [496]

The whole episode may be conceived to have run off somewhat in the following manner. The Mediterranean race is held to have entered Europe in force during quaternary time, presumably after the quaternary period was well advanced, most likely during the last genial, interglacial period. This race then brought the neolithic culture, but without the domestic animals (or plants?) that are a characteristic feature of the later neolithic age, and it encountered at least the remnants of an older, palaeolithic population. This older European population was made up of several racial stocks, some of which still persist as obscure and minor elements in the later peoples of Europe. The (geologic) date to be assigned this intrusion of the Mediterranean race into Europe is of course not, and can perhaps never be, determined with any degree of nicety or confidence. But there is a probability that it coincides with the recession of the ice-sheet, following one or another of the severer periods of glaciations, that occurred before the submergence of the land connection between Europe and Africa, over Gibraltar, Sicily, and perhaps Crete. How late in quaternary time the final submergence of the Mediterranean basin occurred is still a matter of surmise; the intrusion of the Mediterranean race into Europe appears, on archaeological evidence, to have occurred in late quaternary time, and in the end this archaeological evidence may help to decide the geologic date of the severance of Europe from Africa.

The Mediterranean race seems to have spread easily over the habitable surface of Europe and shortly to have grown numerous and taken rank as the chief racial element in the neolithic population; which argues that no very considerable older population occupied the European continent at the time of the Mediterranean invasion; which in turn implies that the fairly large (Magdalenian) population of the close of the palaeolithic age was in great part destroyed or expelled by the climatic changes that coincided with or immediately preceded the advent of the Mediterranean race. The known characteristics of the Magdalenian culture indicate a technology, a situation and perhaps a race, somewhat closely [497] paralleled by the Eskimo;[4] which argues that the climatic situation before which this Magdalenian race and culture gave way would have been that of a genial interglacial period rather than a period of glaciation.

During this genial (perhaps sub-tropical) interglacial period immediately preceding the last great glaciation the Magdalenian stock would presumably find Europe climatically untenable, judging by analogy with the Eskimo; whereas the Mediterranean stock should have found it an eminently favorable habitat, for this race has always succeeded best in a warm-temperate climate. Both the extensive northward range of the early neolithic (Mediterranean) settlements and the total disappearance of the Magdalenian culture from the European continent point to a climatic situation in Europe more favorable to the former race and more unwholesome for the latter than the conditions known to have prevailed at any time since the last interglacial period, especially in the higher latitudes. The indications would seem to be that the whole of Europe, even the Baltic and Arctic seaboards, became climatically so fully impossible for the Magdalenian race during this interglacial period as to result in its extinction or definitive expulsion; for when, in recent times, climatically suitable conditions return, on the Arctic seaboard, the culture which takes the place that should have been occupied by the Magdalenian is the Finnic (Lapp) – a culture unrelated to the Magdalenian either in race or technology, although of much the same cultural level and dealing with a material environment of much the same character. And this genial interval that was fatal to the Magdalenian was, by just so much, favorable to the Mediterranean race.

But glacial conditions presently returned, though with less severity than the next preceding glacial period; and roughly coincident with the close of the genial interval in Europe the land connection with Africa was cut off by submergence, shutting off retreat to the south. How far communication with

---

4 Cf. W. J. Sollas, "Palaeolithic Races and their Modern Representatives," *Science Progress*, vol. iv, 1909.

Asia may have been interrupted during [498] the subsequent cold period, by the local glaciation of the Caucasus, Elburz and Armenian highlands, is for the present apparently not to be determined, although it is to be presumed that the outlet to the east would at least be seriously obstructed during the glaciation. There would then be left available for occupation, mainly by the Mediterranean race, central and southern Europe together with the islands, notably Sicily and Crete, left over as remnants of the earlier continuous land between Europe and Africa. The southern extensions of the mainland, and more particularly the islands, would still afford a favorable place for the Mediterranean race and its cultural growth. So that the early phases of the great Cretan (Aegean) civilization are presumably to be assigned to this period that is covered by the last advance of the ice in northern Europe. But the greater portion of the land area so left accessible to the Mediterranean race, in central or even in southern Europe, would have been under glacial or subglacial climatic conditions. For this race, essentially native to a warm climate, this situation on the European mainland would be sufficiently novel and trying, particularly throughout that ice-fringed range of country where they would be exposed to such cold and damp as this race has never easily tolerated.

The situation so outlined would afford such a condition of physiological strain as might be conceived to throw the stock into a specifically unstable state and so bring on a phase of mutation. At the same time this situation, climatic and technological, would be notably favorable to the survival and propagation of a type gifted with all the peculiar capacities and limitations of the dolicho-blond; so that any mutant showing the traits characteristic of that type would then have had an eminently favorable chance of survival. Indeed, it is doubtful, in the present state of the available evidence, whether such a type of man could have survived in Europe from or over any period of quaternary time prior to the last period of glaciation. The last preceding interglacial period appears to have been of a sufficiently genial (perhaps subtropical) character throughout Europe to have definitively eliminated the Magdalenian race [499] and culture, and a variation of climate in the genial sense sufficiently pronounced to make Europe absolutely untenable for the Magdalenian – presumed to be something of a counterpart to the Eskimo both in race and culture – should probably have reached the limit of tolerance for the dolicho-blond as well. The latter is doubtless not as intolerant of a genial – warm temperate – climate as the former, but the dolicho-blond after all stands much nearer to the Eskimo in this matter of climatic tolerance than to either of the two chief European stocks with which it is associated. Apparently no racial stock with a climatic tolerance approximately like that of the Eskimo, the Magdalenian, or the current races of the Arctic seaboard, survived over the last interglacial period; and if the dolicho-blond is conceived to have lived through that period it would appear to have been by a precariously narrow margin. So that, on one ground and another, the mutation out of which the dolicho-blond has arisen is presumably to be assigned to the latest period of glaciation in Europe, and with some probability to the time when the latest glaciation was at its maximum, and to the region where glacial and seaboard influences combined to give that racial type a differential advantage over all others.

This dolicho-blond mutation may, of course, have occurred only once, in a single individual, but it should seem more probable, in the light of De Vries' experiments, that the mutation will have been repeated in the same specific form in several individuals in the same general locality and in the same general period of time. Indeed, it would seem highly probable that several typically distinct mutations will have occurred, repeatedly, at roughly the same period and in the same region, giving rise to several new types, some of which, including the dolicho-blond, will have survived. Many, presumably the greater number, of these mutant types will have disappeared, selectively, being unfit to survive under those subglacial seaboard conditions that were eminently favorable to the dolicho-blond; while other mutants arising out of the same mutating period and adapted [500] to climatic conditions of a more continental character, suitable to more of a continental habitat, less humid, at a higher altitude and with a wider seasonal variation of temperature, may have survived in the regions farther inland, particularly eastward of the selectively defined habitat of the dolicho-blond. These latter may have given rise to several blond races, such as are spoken for by Deniker[5] and certain British ethnologists.

The same period of mutation may well have given rise also to one or more brunet types, some of which may have survived. But if any new brunet type has come up within a period so recent as this implies, the fact has not been noted or surmised hitherto – unless the brunet races spoken for by Deniker are to be accepted as typically distinct and referred to such an origin. The evidence for the brunet stocks has not been canvassed with a question of this kind in view. These stocks have not been subject of such eager controversy as the dolicho-blond, and the attention given them has been correspondingly less. The case of the blond is unique in respect of the attention spent on questions of its derivation and prehistory, and it is also singular in respect of the facility with which it can be isolated for the purposes of such an inquiry. This large and persistent attention, from all sorts of ethnologists, has brought the evidence bearing on the dolicho-blond into such shape as to permit more confident generalizations regarding that race than any other.

In any case the number of mutant individuals, whether of one or of several specific types, will have been very few as compared with the numbers of the parent stock from which they diverged, even if they may have been somewhat numerous as counted absolutely, and the survivors whose offspring produced a permanent effect on the European peoples will have been fewer still. It results that these surviving mutants will not have been isolated from the parent stock, and so could not breed in isolation, but must forthwith be crossed on the parent stock and could therefore [501] yield none but hybrid

5 *The Races of Mankind* [1900] and "Les six races composant la population de l'Europe," *Journal Anth. Inst.*, 1904.

offspring. From the outset, therefore, the community or communities in which the blond mutants were propagated would be made up of a mixture of blond and brunet, with the brunet greatly preponderating. It may be added that in all probability there were also present in this community from the start one or more minor brunet elements besides the predominant Mediterranean, and that at least shortly after the close of the glacial period the new brachyce-phalic brunet (Alpine) race comes into the case; so that the chances favor an early and persistent crossing of the dolicho-blond with more than one brunet type, and hence they favor complications and confusion of types from the start. It follows that, in point of pedigree, according to this view there neither is nor ever has been a pure-bred dolicho-blond individual since the putative original mutant with which the type came in. But under the Mendelian rule of hybrids it is none the less to be expected that, in the course of time and of climatically selective breeding, individuals (perhaps in appreciable numbers) will have come up from time to time showing the type characters unmixed and unweakened, and effectively pure-bred in point of heredity. Indeed, such individuals, effectively pure-bred or tending to the establishment of a pure line, will probably have emerged somewhat frequently under conditions favorable to the pure type. The selective action of the conditions of life in the habitat most favorable to the propagation of the dolicho-blond has worked in a rough and uncertain way toward the establishment, in parts of the Baltic and North Sea region, of communities made up prevailingly of blonds. Yet none of these communities most favorably placed for a selective breeding in the direction of a pure dolicho-blond population have gone far enough in that direction to allow it safely to be said that the composite population of any such given locality is more than half blond.

Placed as it is in a community of nations made up of a hybrid mixture of several racial stocks there is probably no way at present of reaching a convincing demonstration of the typical originality of this dolicho-bland mutant, as contrasted with the other blond types with which it is associated [502] in the European population; but certain general considerations go decidedly, perhaps decisively, to enforce such a view: (a) This type shows such a pervasive resemblance to a single one of the known older and more widely distributed types of man (the Mediterranean) as to suggest descent by mutation from this one rather than derivation by crossing of any two or more known types. The like can not be said of the other blond types, all and several of which may plausibly be explained as hybrids of known types. They have the appearance of blends, or rather of biometrical compromises, between two or more existing varieties of man. Whereas it does not seem feasible to explain the dolicho-blond as such a blend or compromise between any known racial types. (b) The dolicho-blond occurs, in a way, centrally to the other blond types, giving them a suggestive look of being ramifications of the blond stock, by hybridization, into regions not wholly suited to the typical blond. The like can scarcely be said for any of the other European types or races. The most plausible exception would be Deniker's East-European or

Oriental race, Beddoe's Saxon, which stands in a somewhat analogous spacial relation to the other blond types. But this brachycephalic blond is not subject to the same sharp climatic limitations that hedge about the dolicho-blond; it occurs apparently with equally secure viability within the littoral home area of the dolicho-blond and in continental situations where conditions of altitude and genial climate would bar the latter from permanent settlement. The ancient and conventionally accepted center of diffusion of blondness in Europe lies within the seaboard region bordering on the south Baltic, the North Sea and the narrow waters of the Scandinavian peninsulas. Probably, if this broad central area of diffusion were to be narrowed down to a particular spot, the consensus of opinion as to where the narrower area of characteristic blondness is to be looked for, would converge on the lands immediately about the narrow Scandinavian waters. This would seem to hold true for historic and for prehistoric times alike. This region is at the same time, by common consent, the peculiar home of the dolicho-blond, rather than of any other blond type. (c) The well known but little discussed climatic limitation of the blond race applies particularly to the dolicho-blond, [503] and only in a pronouncedly slighter degree to the other blond types. The dolicho-blond is subject to a strict regional limitation, the other blond types to a much less definite and wider limitation of the same kind. Hence these others are distributed somewhat widely, over regions often remote and climatically different from the home area of the dolicho-blond, giving them the appearance of being dispersed outward from this home area as hybrid extensions of the central and typical blond stock. A further and equally characteristic feature of this selective localization of the dolicho-blond race is the fact that while this race does not succeed permanently outside the seaboard region of the south Baltic and North Sea, there is no similar selective bar against other races intruding into this region. Although the dolicho-blond perhaps succeeds better within its home area than any other competing stock or type, yet several other types of man succeed so well within the same region as to hold it, and apparently always to have held it, in joint tenancy with the dolicho-blond.

A close relationship, amounting to varietal identity, of the Kabyle with the dolicho-blond has been spoken for by Keane and by other ethnologists. But the very different climatic tolerance of the two races should put such an identity out of the question. The Kabyle lives and thrives best, where his permanent home area has always been, in a high and dry country, sufficiently remote from the sea to make it a continental rather than a littoral habitat. The dolicho-blond, according to all available evidence, can live in the long run only in a seaboard habitat, damp and cool, at a high latitude and low altitude. There is no known instance of this race having gone out from its home area on the northern seaboard into such a region as that inhabited by the Kabyle and having survived for an appreciable number of generations. That this type of man should have come from Mauritania, where it could apparently not live under the conditions known to have prevailed there in the [504] recent or the remoter past, would seem to be a biologic impossibility. Hitherto, when the dolicho-blond has migrated into such or a similar habitat it has not adapted itself to the new climatic requirements but has presently disappeared off the face of the land. Indeed, the experiment has been tried in Mauritanian territory. If the Kabyle blond is to be correlated with those of Europe, it will in all probability have to be assigned an independent origin, to be derived from an earlier mutation of the same Mediterranean stock to which the dolicho-blond is to be traced.

Questions of race in Europe are greatly obscured by the prevalence of hybrid types having more or less fixity and being more or less distinctly localized. The existing European peoples are hybrid mixtures of two or more racial stocks. The further fact is sufficiently obvious, though it has received less critical attention than might be, that these several hybrid populations have in the course of time given rise to a number of distinct national and local types, differing characteristically from one another and having acquired a degree of permanence, such as to simulate racial characters and show well marked national and local traits in point of physiognomy and temperament. Presumably, these national and local types of physique and temperament are hybrid types that have been selectively bred into these characteristic forms in adaptation to the peculiar circumstances of environment and culture under which each particular local population is required to live, and that have been so fixed (provisionally) by selective breeding of the hybrid material subject to such locally uniform conditions – except so far as the local characters in question are of the nature of habits and are themselves therefore to be classed as an institutional element rather than as characteristics of race.

It is evident that under the Mendelian law of hybridization the range of favorable, or viable, variations in any hybrid population must be very large – much larger than the range of fluctuating (non-typical) variations obtainable under any circumstances in a pure-bred race. It also follows from these same laws of hybridization that by virtue of the [505] mutual exclusiveness of allelomorphic characters or groups of characters it is possible selectively to obtain an effectually "pure line" of hybrids combining characters drawn from each of the two or more parent stocks engaged, and that such a composite pure line may selectively be brought to a provisional fixity[6] in any such hybrid population. And under conditions favorable to a type endowed with any given hybrid combination of characters so worked out the given hybrid type (composite pure line) may function in the racial mixture in which it is so placed very much as an actual racial type would behave under analogous circumstances; so that, e.g., under continued intercrossing such a hybrid population would tend cumulatively to breed true to this provisionally stable hybrid type, rather than to the actual racial type represented by any one of the parent stocks of which the hybrid population is ultimately made up,

---

6 Illustrated by the various pure breeds or "races" of domestic animals.

unless the local conditions should selectively favor one or another of these ultimate racial types. Evidently, too, the number of such provisionally stable composite pure lines that may be drawn from any hybrid mixture of two or more parent stocks must be very considerable – indeed virtually unlimited; so that on this ground there should be room for any conceivable number of provisionally stable national or local types of physique and temperament, limited only by the number of characteristically distinguishable local environments or situations that might each selectively act to characterize and establish a locally characteristic composite pure line; each answering to the selective exigencies of the habitat and cultural environment in which it is placed, and each responding to these exigencies in much the same fashion as would an actual racial type – provided only that this provisionally stable composite pure line is not crossed on pure-bred individuals of either of the parent stocks from which it is drawn, pure-bred in respect of the allelomorphic characters which give the hybrid type its typical traits.

When the hybrid type is so crossed back on one or other of its parent stocks it should be expected to break down; [506] but in so slow-breeding a species as man, with so large a complement of unit characters (some 4000 it has been estimated), it will be difficult to decide empirically which of the two lines – the hybrid or the parent stock – proves itself in the offspring effectively to be a racial type; that is to say, which of the two (or more) proves to be an ultimately stable type arisen by a Mendelian mutation, and which is a provisionally stable composite pure line selectively derived from a cross. The inquiry at this point, therefore, will apparently have to content itself with arguments of probability drawn from the varying behavior of the existing hybrid types under diverse conditions of life.

Such general consideration of the behavior of the blond types of Europe, other than the dolicho-blond, and more particularly consideration of their viability under divergent climatic conditions, should apparently incline to the view that they are hybrid types, of the nature of provisionally stable composite pure lines.

So far, therefore, as the evidence has yet been canvassed, it seems probable on the whole that the dolicho-blond is the only survivor from among the several mutants that may have arisen out of this presumed mutating period; that the other existing blond types, as well as certain brunets, are derivatives of the hybrid offspring of the dolicho-blond crossed on the parent Mediterranean stock or on other brunet stocks with which the race has been in contact early or late; and that several of these hybrid lines have in the course of time selectively been established as provisionally stable types (composite pure lines), breakable only by a fresh cross with one or other of the parent types from which the hybrid line sprang, according to the Mendelian rule.[7]

7 Mr. R. B. Bean's discussion of Deniker's "Six Races," e.g., goes far to show that such is probably the standing of the blond types, other than the dolicho-blond, among these six races of Europe; although such is not the conclusion to which Mr. Bean comes. *Philippine Journal of Science*, September, 1909.

All these considerations may not be convincing, but they are at least suggestive to the effect that if originality is to [507] be claimed for any one of the blond types or stocks it can best be claimed for the dolicho-blond, while the other blond types may better be accounted for as the outcome of the crossing of this stock on one or another of the brunet stocks of Europe.

Selection 38

The Instinct of Workmanship and the State of the Industrial Arts

Source: Preface, Chapter I, and Chapter II, pp. li–lii, 1–73.
New York: Macmillan, 1914.

Veblen (1914)

Preface

The following essay attempts an analysis of such correlation as is visible between industrial use and wont and those other institutional facts that go to make up any given phase of civilisation. It is assumed that in the growth of culture, as in its current maintenance, the facts of technological use and wont are fundamental and definitive, in the sense that they underlie and condition the scope and method of civilisation in other than the technological respect, but not in such a sense as to preclude or overlook the degree in which these other conventions of any given civilisation in their turn react on the state of the industrial arts.

As should appear from its slight bulk, the essay is of the nature of a cursory survey rather than an exhaustive inquiry with full documentation. The few references given and the authorities cited in the course of the argument are accordingly not to be taken as an inclusive [lii] presentation of the materials on which the inquiry rests. It will also be remarked that where authoritative documents are cited the citation is general and extensive rather than specific and detailed. Wherever detailed references are given they will be found to bear on specific facts brought into the argument by way of illustrative detail.

I. Introductory

For mankind as for the other higher animals, the life of the species is conditioned by the complement of instinctive proclivities and tropismatic aptitudes with which the species is typically endowed. Not only is the continued life of the race dependent on the adequacy of its instinctive proclivities in this way, but the routine and details of its life are also, in the last resort, determined by these instincts. These are the prime movers in human behaviour, as in the behaviour of all those animals that show self-direction or discretion. Human activity, in so far as it can be spoken of as conduct, can never exceed the scope of these instinctive dispositions, by initiative of which man takes action. Nothing falls within the human scheme of things desirable to be done except what answers to these native proclivities of man. These native proclivities alone make anything worth while, and out of their working emerge not only the purpose and efficiency of life, but its substantial pleasures and pains as well.

Latterly the words "instinct" and "instinctive" are no longer well seen among students of those biological [2] sciences where they once had a great vogue. Students who occupy themselves with the psychology of animal behaviour are cautiously avoiding these expressions, and in this caution they are doubtless well advised. For such use the word appears no longer to be serviceable as a technical term. It has lost the requisite sharp definition and consistency of connotation, apparently through disintegration under a more searching analysis than the phenomena comprised under this concept had previously been subjected to. In these biological sciences interest is centering not on the question of what activities may be set down to innate propensity or predisposition at large, but rather on the determination of the irreducible psychological – and, indeed, physiological – elements that go to make up animal behaviour. For this purpose "instinct" is a concept of too lax and shifty a definition to meet the demands of exact biological science.

For the sciences that deal with the psychology of human conduct a similarly searching analysis of the elementary facts of behaviour is doubtless similarly desirable; and under such closer scrutiny of these facts it will doubtless appear that here, too, the broad term "instinct" is of too unprecise a character to serve the needs of an exhaustive psychological analysis. But the needs of an inquiry into the nature and causes of the growth of institutions are not precisely the same as those of such an exhaustive psychological analysis. A genetic inquiry into institutions will address itself to the growth of habits and conventions, as conditioned by the material environment and by the innate and persistent propensities of human nature; and for these propensities, as they take effect in the give and take of cultural growth, [3] no better designation than the time-worn "instinct" is available.

In the light of recent inquiries and speculations it is scarcely to be questioned that each of these distinguishable propensities may be analysed into simpler constituent elements, of a quasi-tropismatic or physiological nature;[1] but in the light of every-day experience and common notoriety it is at the same time not to be questioned that these simple and irreducible

1 Cf. Jacques Loeb, *Comparative Physiology of the Brain and Comparative Psychology*, ch. i.

psychological elements of human behaviour fall into composite functional groups, and so make up specific and determinate propensities, proclivities, aptitudes that are, within the purview of the social sciences, to be handled as irreducible traits of human nature. Indeed, it would appear that it is in the particular grouping and concatenation of these ultimate psychological elements into characteristic lines of interest and propensity that the nature of man is finally to be distinguished from that of the lower animals.

These various native proclivities that are so classed together as "instincts" have the characteristic in common that they all and several, more or less imperatively, propose an objective end of endeavour. On the other hand what distinguishes one instinct from another is that each sets up a characteristic purpose, aim, or object to be attained, different from the objective end of any other instinct. Instinctive action is teleological, consciously so, and the teleological scope and aim of each instinctive propensity differs characteristically from all the rest. The several instincts are teleological categories, [4] and are, in colloquial usage, distinguished and classed on the ground of their teleological content. As the term is here used, therefore, and indeed as it is currently understood, the instincts are to be defined or described neither in mechanical terms of those anatomical or physiological aptitudes that causally underlie them or that come into action in the functioning of any given instinct, nor in terms of the movements of orientation or taxis involved in the functioning of each. The distinctive feature by the mark of which any given instinct is identified is to be found in the particular character of the purpose to which it drives.[2] "Instinct," as contra-distinguished from tropismatic action, involves consciousness and adaptation to an end aimed at.

It is, of course, not hereby intended to set up or to prescribe a definition of "instinct" at large, but only to indicate as closely as may be what sense is attached to the term as here used. At the same time it is believed that this definition of the concept does violence neither to colloquial usage nor to the usage of such students as have employed the term in scientific discussion, particularly in discussion of the instinctive proclivities of mankind. But it is not to be overlooked that this definition of the term may be found inapplicable, or at least of doubtful service, when applied to those simpler and more immediate impulses that are sometimes by tradition spoken of as "instinctive," even in human behaviour, – impulses that might with better effect be designated [5] "tropismatic." In animal behaviour, for instance, as well as in such direct and immediate impulsive human action as is fairly to be classed with animal behaviour, it is often a matter of some perplexity to draw a line between tropismatic activity and instinct. Notoriously, the activities

---

2 Cf. W. James, *Principles of Psychology*, ch. xxiv and xxv, where, however, the difference between tropism and instinct is not kept well in hand, – the tropisms having at that date not been subjected to inquiry and definition as has been true since then; William McDougall, *Introduction to Social Psychology*, ch. i.

commonly recognised as instinctive differ widely among themselves in respect of the degree of directness or immediacy with which the given response to stimulus takes place. They range in this respect all the way from such reactions as are doubtfully to be distinguished from simple reflex action on the one hand, to such as are doubtfully recognised as instinctive because of the extent to which reflection and deliberation enter into their execution on the other hand. By insensible gradation the lower (less complex and deliberate) instinctive activities merge into the class of unmistakable tropismatic sensibilities, without its being practicable to determine by any secure test where the one category should be declared to end and the other to begin.[3] Such quasi-tropismatic activities may be rated as purposeful by an observer, in the sense that they are seen to further the life of the individual agent or of the species, while there is no consciousness of purpose on the part of the agent under observation; whereas "instinct," in the narrower and special sense to which it seems desirable to restrict the term for present use, denotes the conscious pursuit of an objective end which the instinct in question makes worth while.

The ends of life, then, the purposes to be achieved, are assigned by man's instinctive proclivities; but the ways [6] and means of accomplishing those things which the instinctive proclivities so make worth while are a matter of intelligence. It is a distinctive mark of mankind that the working-out of the instinctive proclivities of the race is guided by intelligence to a degree not approached by the other animals. But the dependence of the race on its endowment of instincts is no less absolute for this intervention of intelligence; since it is only by the prompting of instinct that reflection and deliberation come to be so employed, and since instinct also governs the scope and method of intelligence in all this employment of it. Men take thought, but the human spirit, that is to say the racial endowment of instinctive proclivities, decides what they shall take thought of, and how and to what effect.

Yet the dependence of the scheme of life on the complement of instinctive proclivities hereby becomes less immediate, since a more or less extended logic of ways and means comes to intervene between the instinctively given end and its realisation; and the lines of relation between any given instinctive proclivity and any particular feature of human conduct are by so much the more devious and round-about and the more difficult to trace. The higher the degree of intelligence and the larger the available body of knowledge current in any given community, the more extensive and elaborate will be the logic of ways and means interposed between these impulses and their realisation, and the more multifarious and complicated will be the apparatus of expedients and resources employed to compass those ends that are instinctively worth while.

This apparatus of ways and means available for the [7] pursuit of whatever may be worth seeking is, substantially all, a matter of tradition out of the

---

3 Loeb, *Comparative Physiology of the Brain*, pp. 177–78.

past, a legacy of habits of thought accumulated through the experience of past generations. So that the manner, and in a great degree the measure, in which the instinctive ends of life are worked out under any given cultural situation is somewhat closely conditioned by these elements of habit, which so fall into shape as an accepted scheme of life. The instinctive proclivities are essentially simple and look directly to the attainment of some concrete objective end; but in detail the ends so sought are many and diverse, and the ways and means by which they may be sought are similarly diverse and various, involving endless recourse to expedients, adaptations, and concessive adjustment between several proclivities that are all sufficiently urgent.

Under the discipline of habituation this logic and apparatus of ways and means falls into conventional lines, acquires the consistency of custom and prescription, and so takes on an institutional character and force. The accustomed ways of doing and thinking not only become an habitual matter of course, easy and obvious, but they come likewise to be sanctioned by social convention, and so become right and proper and give rise to principles of conduct. By use and wont they are incorporated into the current scheme of common sense. As elements of the approved scheme of conduct and pursuit these conventional ways and means take their place as proximate ends of endeavour. Whence, in the further course of unremitting habituation, as the attention is habitually focussed on these proximate ends, they occupy the interest to such an extent as commonly to throw their [8] own ulterior purpose into the background and often let it be lost sight of; as may happen, for instance, in the acquisition and use of money. It follows that in much of human conduct these proximate ends alone are present in consciousness as the object of interest and the goal of endeavour, and certain conventionally accepted ways and means come to be set up as definitive principles of what is right and good; while the ulterior purpose of it all is only called to mind occasionally, if at all, as an afterthought, by an effort of reflection.[4]

Among psychologists who have busied themselves with these questions there has hitherto been no large measure of agreement as to the number of specific instinctive proclivities that so are native to man; nor is there any agreement as to the precise functional range and content ascribed to each. In a loose way it is apparently taken for granted that these instincts are to be conceived as discrete and specific elements in human nature, each working out its own determinate functional content without greatly blending with or being diverted by the working of its neighbours in that spiritual complex into which they all enter as constituent elements.[5] For the purposes of an exhaustive psychological analysis it is doubtless expedient to make the most of such discreteness as is

4 Cf. Graham Wallas, *Human Nature in Politics*, especially ch. i.
5 Cf., e.g., James, *Principles of Psychology*, ch. xxiv; William McDougall, *Introduction to Social Psychology*, ch. iii.

observable among the instinctive proclivities. But for an inquiry into the scope and method of their working-out in the growth of institutions it is perhaps even more to the purpose to take note of how and with [9] what effect the several instinctive proclivities cross, blend, overlap, neutralise or reënforce one another.

The most convincing genetic view of these phenomena throws the instinctive proclivities into close relation with the tropismatic sensibilities and brings them, in the physiological respect, into the same general class with the latter.[6] If taken uncritically and in general terms this view would seem to carry the implication that the instincts should be discrete and discontinuous among themselves somewhat after the same fashion as the tropismatic sensibilities with which they are in great measure bound up; but on closer scrutiny such a genetic theory of the instincts does not appear to enforce the view that they are to be conceived as effectually discontinuous or mutually exclusive, though it may also not involve the contrary, – that they make a continuous or ambiguously segmented body of spiritual elements. The recognised tropisms stand out, to all appearance, as sharply defined physiological traits, transmissible by inheritance intact and unmodified, separable and unblended, in a manner suggestively like the "unit characters" spoken of in latter day theories of heredity.[7] [10]

While the instinctive sensibilities may not be explained as derivatives of the tropisms, there is enough of similarity in the working of the two to suggest that the two classes of phenomena must both be accounted for on somewhat similar physiological grounds. The simple and more narrowly defined instinctive dispositions, which have much of the appearance of immediate reflex nervous action and automatically defined response, lend themselves passably to such an interpretation, – as, for example, the gregarious instinct, or the instinct of repulsion with its accompanying emotion of disgust. Such as these are shared by mankind with the other higher animals on a fairly even footing; and these are relatively simple, immediate, and not easily sophisticated or offset by habit. These seem patently to be of much the same nature as the tropismatic sensibilities; though even in these simpler instinctive dispositions the characteristic quasi-tropismatic sensibility distinctive of each appears to be complicated with obscure stimulations of the nerve centres arising out of

---

6 Loeb, *Comparative Physiology of the Brain*, especially ch. xiii.

7 It is of course only as physiological traits that the tropisms are conceived not to overlap, blend or interfere, and it is likewise only in respect of their physiological discontinuity that the like argument would bear on the instincts. In respect of their expression, in the way of orientation, movement, growth, secretion, and the like, the tropismatic response to dissimilar stimuli is often so apparently identical that expert investigators have at times been at a loss to decide to which one of two or several recognised tropismatic sensibilities a given motor response should be ascribed. But in respect of their ultimate physiological character, the intimate physiological process by which the given sensibility takes effect, the response due to different tropismatic sensibilities appears in each case to be distinctive and not to blend with any other response to a different stimulus, with which it may happen to synchronise.

the functioning of one or another of the viscera. And what is true of the simpler instincts in this respect should apply to the vaguer and more complex instincts also, but with a larger allowance for a more extensive complication of visceral and organic stimuli.

Whether these subconscious stimulations of the nerve centres through the functioning of the viscera are to be conceived in terms of tropismatic reaction is a difficult question which has had little attention hitherto. But in any case, whatever the expert students of these phenomena may have to say of this matter, the visceral or organic [11] stimuli engaged in any one of the instinctive sensibilities are apparently always more than one and are usually somewhat complex. Indeed, while it seems superficially an easy matter to refer any one of the simple instincts directly to some certain one of the viscera as the main or primary source from which its appropriate stimulation comes to the nerve centres, it is by no means easy to decide what one or more of the viscera, or of the other organs that are not commonly classed as viscera, will have no part in the matter.

It results that, on physiological grounds, the common run of human instincts are not to be conceived as severally discrete and elementary proclivities. The same physiological processes enter in some measure, though in varying proportions, into the functioning of each. In instinctive action the individual acts as a whole, and in the conduct which emerges under the driving force of these instinctive dispositions the part which each several instinct plays is a matter of more or less, not of exclusive direction. They must therefore incontinently touch, blend, overlap and interfere, and can not be conceived as acting each and several in sheer isolation and independence of one another. The relations of give and take among the several instinctive dispositions, therefore – of inosculation, "contamination" and cross purposes – are presumably slighter and of less consequence for the simpler and more apparently tropismatic impulses while on the other hand the less specific and vaguer instinctive predispositions, such as the parental bent or the proclivity to construction or acquisition, will be so comprehensively and intricately bound in a web of correlation and interdependence – will so unremittingly contaminate, [12] offset or fortify one another, and have each so large and yet so shifting a margin of common ground with all the rest – that hard and fast lines of demarcation can scarcely be drawn between them. The best that can practically be had in the way of a secure definition will be a descriptive characterisation of each distinguishable propensity, together with an indication of the more salient and consequential ramifications by which each contaminates or is contaminated by the working of other propensities that go to make up that complex of instinctive dispositions that constitutes the spiritual nature of the race. So that the schemes of definition that have hitherto been worked out are in great part to be taken as arrangements of convenience, serviceable apparatus for present use, rather than distinctions enforced at all points by an equally sharp substantial discreteness of the facts.[8]

8 Cf., e.g., McDougall, *Introduction to Social Psychology*, ch. i–iii.

This fact, that in some measure the several instincts spring from a common ground of sentient life, that they each engage the individual as a whole, has serious consequences in the domain of habit, and therefore it counts for much in the growth of civilisation and in the everyday conduct of affairs. The physiological apparatus engaged in the functioning of any given instinct enters in part, though in varying measure, into the working of some or of any other instinct; whereby, even on physiological grounds alone, the habituation that touches the functioning of any given instinct must, in a less degree but pervasively, affect the habitual conduct of the same agent when driven by any other instinct. So that on this view the scope of habit, in so far as it bears on the [13] instinctive activities, is necessarily wider than the particular concrete line of conduct to which the habituation in question is due.

The instincts are hereditary traits. In the current theories of heredity they would presumably be counted as secondary characteristics of the species, as being in a sense by-products of the physiological activities that give the species its specific character; since these theories in the last resort run in physiological terms. So the instinctive dispositions would scarcely be accounted unit characters, in the Mendelian sense, but would rather count as spiritual traits emerging from a certain concurrence of physiological unit characters and varying somewhat according to variations in the complement of unit characters to which the species or the individual may owe his constitution. Hence would arise variations of individuality among the members of the race, resting in some such manner as has just been suggested on the varying endowment of instincts, and running back through these finally to recondite differences of physiological function. Some such account of the instinctive dispositions and their relation to the physical individual seems necessary as a means of apprehending them and their work without assuming a sheer break between the physical and the immaterial phenomena of life.

Characteristic of the race is a degree of vagueness or generality, an absence of automatically determinate response, a lack of concrete eventuality as it might be called, in the common run of human instincts. This vague and shifty character of the instincts, or perhaps [14] rather of the habitual response to their incitement, is to be taken in connection with the breadth and variability of their physiological ground as spoken of above. For the long-term success of the race it is manifestly of the highest value, since it leaves a wide and facile margin of experimentation, habituation, invention and accommodation open to the sense of workmanship. At the same time and by the same circumstance the scope and range of conventionalisation and sophistication are similarly flexible, wide and consequential. No doubt the several racial stocks differ very appreciably in this respect.

The complement of instinctive dispositions, comprising under that term both the native propensity and its appropriate sentiment, makes up what would be called the "spiritual nature" of man – often spoken of more simply as "human nature." Without allowing it to imply anything like a dualism or dichotomy between material and immaterial phenomena, the term "spiritual" may conveniently be so used in its colloquial sense. So employed it commits the discussion to no attitude on the question of man's single or dual constitution, but simply uses the conventional expression to designate that complement of functions which it has by current usage been employed to designate.

The human complement of instincts fluctuates from one individual to another in an apparently endless diversity, varying both in the relative force of the several instinctive proclivities and in the scheme of co-ordination, coalescence or interference that prevails among them. This diversity of native character is noticeable among all peoples, though some of the peoples of the lower cultures show a notable approach to uniformity of type, [15] both physical and spiritual. The diversity is particularly marked among the civilised peoples, and perhaps in a peculiar degree among the peoples of Europe and her colonies. The extreme diversity of native character, both physical and spiritual, noticeable in these communities is in all probability due to their being made up of a mixture of racial stocks. In point of pedigree, all individuals in the peoples of the Western culture are hybrids, and the greater number of individuals are a mixture of more than two racial stocks. The proportions in which the several transmissible traits that go to make up the racial type enter into the composition of these hybrid individuals will accordingly vary endlessly. The number of possible permutations will therefore be extremely large; so that the resulting range of variation in the hybrids that so result from the crossing of these different racial stocks will be sufficiently large, even when it plays within such limits as to leave the generic human type intact. From time to time the variation may even exceed these limits of human normality and give a variant in which the relative emphasis on the several constituent instinctive elements is distributed after a scheme so far from the generically human type as to throw the given variant out of touch with the common run of humanity and mark him as of unsound mind or as disserviceable for the purposes of the community in which he occurs, or even as disserviceable for life in any society.

Yet, even through these hybrid populations there runs a generically human type of spiritual endowment prevalent as a general average of human nature throughout, and suitable to the continued life of mankind in [16] society. Disserviceably wide departures from this generically human and serviceable type of spiritual endowment will tend constantly to be selectively eliminated from the race, even where the variation arises from hybridism. The like will hold true in a more radical fashion as applied to any variants that may arise through a Mendelian mutation.

So that the numerous racial types now existing represent only such mutants as lie within the limits of tolerance imposed by the situation under which any given mutant type has emerged and survived. A surviving mutant type is necessarily suited more or less closely to the circumstances under which it emerged and first made good its survival, and it is presumably less suited to any other situation. With a change in the situation, therefore, such as may come with the migration of a given racial stock from one habitat to another, or with an equivalent shifting growth of culture or change of climate, the requirements of survival are likely to change. Indeed, so grave are the alterations that may in this way supervene in the current requirements for survival, that any given racial stock may dwindle and decay for no other reason than that the growth of its culture has come to subject the stock to methods of life widely different from those under which its type of man originated and made good its fitness to survive. So, in the mixture of races that make up the population of the Western nations a competitive struggle for survival has apparently always been going on among the several racial stocks that enter into the hybrid mass, with varying fortunes according as the shifting cultural demands and opportunities have favoured now one, now another type of man. These cultural [17] conditions of survival in the racial struggle for existence have varied in the course of centuries, and with grave consequences for the life-history of the race and of its culture; and they are perhaps changing more substantially and rapidly in the immediate present than at any previous time within the historical period. So that, for instance, the continued biological success of any given one of these stocks in the European racial mixture has within a moderate period of time shifted from the ground of fighting capacity, and even in a measure from the ground of climatic fitness, to that of spiritual fitness to survive under the conditions imposed by a new cultural situation, by a scheme of institutions that is insensibly but incessantly changing as it runs.[9]

These unremitting changes and adaptations that go forward in the scheme of institutions, legal and customary, unremittingly induce new habits of work and of thought in the community, and so they continually instil new principles of conduct; with the outcome that the same range of instinctive dispositions innate in the population will work out to a different effect as regards the demands of race survival. To all appearance, what counts first in this connection toward the selective survival of the several European racial stocks is their relative fitness to meet the material requirements of life, – their economic fitness to live under the new cultural limitations and with the new training which this altered cultural situation gives. But the fortunes of the Western [18] civilisation as a cultural scheme, apart from the biological survival or success of any given racial constituent in the Western peoples, is likewise bound up with the viability of European mankind under these institutional changes, and dependent on the spiritual fitness of inherited human nature successfully and enduringly to carry on the altered scheme of life so imposed on these peoples by the growth of their own culture. Such limitations

---

9 Cf., e.g., Otto Ammon, *Die Gesellschaftsordnung*; G. Vacher de Lapouge, *Les sélections sociales*, and *Race et milieu social*, especially "Lois fondamentales de l'Anthroposociologie."

imposed on cultural growth by native proclivities ill suited to civilised life are sufficiently visible in several directions and in all the nations of Christendom.

What is known of heredity goes to say that the various racial types of man are stable; so that during the life-history of any given racial stock, it is held, no heritable modification of its typical make-up, whether spiritual or physical, is to be looked for. The typical human endowment of instincts, as well as the typical make-up of the race in the physical respect, has according to this current view been transmitted intact from the beginning of humanity, – that is to say from whatever point in the mutational development of the race it is seen fit to date humanity, – except so far as subsequent mutations have given rise to new racial stocks, to and by which this human endowment of native proclivities has been transmitted in a typically modified form. On the other hand the habitual elements of human life change unremittingly and cumulatively, resulting in a continued proliferous growth of institutions. Changes in the institutional structure are continually taking place in response to the altered discipline of life under changing cultural conditions, but human nature remains specifically the same. [19]

The ways and means, material and immaterial, by which the native pro- clivities work out their ends, therefore, are forever in process of change, being conditioned by the changes cumulatively going forward in the institutional fabric of habitual elements that governs the scheme of life. But there is no warrant for assuming that each or any of these successive changes in the scheme of institutions affords successively readier, surer or more facile ways and means for the instinctive proclivities to work out their ends, or that the phase of habituation in force at any given point in this sequence of change is more suitable to the untroubled functioning of these instincts than any phase that has gone before. Indeed, the presumption is the other way. On grounds of selective survival it is reasonably to be presumed that any given racial type that has endured the test of selective elimination, including the complement of instinctive dispositions by virtue of which it has endured the test, will on its first emergence have been passably suited to the circumstances, material and cultural, under which the type emerged as a mutant and made good its sur- vival; and in so far as the subsequent growth of institutions has altered the available scope and method of instinctive action it is therefore to be presumed that any such subsequent change in the scheme of institutions will in some degree hinder or divert the free play of its instinctive proclivities and will thereby hinder the direct and unsophisticated working-out of the instinctive dispositions native to this given racial type.

What is known of the earlier phases of culture in the life-history of the existing races and peoples goes to say that the initial phase in the life of any given racial type, [20] the phase of culture which prevailed in its environment when it emerged, and under which the stock first proved its fitness to survive, was presumably some form of savagery. Therefore the fitness of any given type of human nature for life after the manner and under the conditions imposed by any later phase in the growth of culture is a matter of less and less secure presumption the farther the sequence of institutional change has departed from that form of savagery which marked the initial stage in the life-history of the given racial stock. Also, presumably, though by no means assuredly, the younger stocks, those which have emerged from later mutations of type, have therefore initially fallen into and made good their survival under the conditions of a relatively advanced phase of savagery, – these younger races should therefore conform with greater facility and better effect to the requirements imposed by a still farther advance in that cumulative complication of institutions and intricacy of ways and means that is involved in cultural growth. The older or more primitive stocks, those which arose out of earlier mutations of type and made good their survival under a more elementary scheme of savage culture, are presumably less capable of adaptation to an advanced cultural scheme.

But at the same time it is on the same grounds to be expected that in all races and peoples there should always persist an ineradicable sentimental disposition to take back to something like that scheme of savagery for which their particular type of human nature once proved its fitness during the initial phase of its life-history. This seems to be what is commonly intended in the cry, "Back to Nature!" The older known racial stocks, [21] the offspring of earlier mutational departures from the initially generic human type, will have been selectively adapted to more archaic forms of savagery, and these show an appreciably more refractory penchant for elementary savage modes of life, and conform to the demands and opportunities of a "higher" civilisation only with a relatively slight facility, amounting in extreme cases to a practical unfitness for civilised life. Hence the "White Man's burden" and the many perplexities of the missionaries.

Under the Mendelian theories of heredity some qualification of these broad generalisations is called for. As has already been noted above, the peoples of Europe, each and several, are hybrid mixtures made up of several racial stocks. The like is true in some degree of most of the peoples outside of Europe; particularly of the more important and better known nationalities. These various peoples show more or less distinct and recognisable national types of physique – or perhaps rather of physiognomy – and temperament, and the lines of differentiation between these national types incontinently traverse the lines that divide the racial stocks. At the same time these national types have some degree of permanence; so much so that they are colloquially spoken of as types of race. While no modern anthropologist would confuse nationality with race, it is not to be overlooked that these national hybrid types are frequently so marked and characteristic as to simulate racial characters and perplex the student of race who is intent on identifying the racial stocks out of which any one of these hybrid populations has been compounded. Presumably these [22] national and local types of physiognomy and temperament are to be rated as hybrid types that have been fixed by selective breeding, and for an explanation of this phenomenon recourse is to be taken to the latterday theories of heredity.

To any student familiar with the simpler phenomena of hybridism it will be evident that under the Mendelian rules of hybridisation the number of biologically successful – viable – hybrid forms arising from any cross between two or more forms may diverge very widely from one another and from either of the parent types. The variation must be extreme both in the number of hybrid types so constructed and in the range over which the variation extends, – much greater in both respects than the range of fluctuating (non-typical) variations obtainable under any circumstances in a pure-bred race, particularly in the remoter filial generations. It is also well known, by experiment, that by selective breeding from among such hybrid forms it is possible to construct a composite type that will breed true in respect of the characters upon which the selection is directed, and that such a "pure line" may be maintained indefinitely, in spite of its hybrid origin, so long as it is not crossed back on one or other of the parent stocks, or on a hybrid stock that is not pure-bred in respect of the selected characters.

So, if the conditions of life in any community consistently favour a given type of hybrid, whether the favouring conditions are of a cultural or of a material nature, something of a selective trend will take effect in such a community and set toward a hybrid type which shall meet these conditions. The result will be the establishment of a composite pure line showing the advantageous [23] traits of physique and temperament, combined with a varying complement of other characters that have no such selective value. Traits that have no selective value in the given case will occur with fortuitous freedom, combining in unconstrained diversity with the selectively decisive traits, and so will mark the hybrid derivation of this provisionally established composite pure line. With continued intercrossing within itself any given population of such hybrid origin as the European peoples, would tend cumulatively to breed true to such a selectively favourable hybrid type, rather than to any one of the ultimate racial types represented by the parent stocks out of which the hybrid population is ultimately made up. So would emerge a national or local type, which would show the selectively decisive traits with a great degree of consistency but would vary indefinitely in respect of the selectively idle traits comprised in the composite heredity of the population. Such a composite pure line would be provisionally stable only; it should break down when crossed back on either of the parent stocks. This "provisionally stable composite pure line" should disappear when crossed on pure-bred individuals of one or other of the parent stocks from which it is drawn, – pure-bred in respect of the allelomorphic characters which give the hybrid type its typical traits.

But whatever the degree of stability possessed by these hybrid national or local types, the outcome for the present purpose is much the same; the hybrid populations afford a greater scope and range of variation in their human nature than could be had within the limits of any pure-bred race. Yet, for all the multifarious diversity of racial and national types, early and late, and [24] for all the wide divergence of hybrid variants, there is no difficulty about recognising a generical human type of spiritual endowment, just as the zoölogists have no difficulty in referring the various races of mankind to a single species on the ground of their physical characters. The distribution of emphasis among the several instinctive dispositions may vary appreciably from one race to another, but the complement of instincts native to the several races is after all of much the same kind, comprising substantially the same ends. Taken simply in their first incidence, the racial variations of human nature are commonly not considerable; but a slight bias of this kind, distinctive of any given race, may come to have decisive weight when it works out cumulatively through a system of institutions, for such a system embodies the cumulative sophistications of untold generations during which the life of the community has been dominated by the same slight bias.[10]

Racial differences in respect of these hereditary spiritual traits count for much in the outcome, because in the last resort any race is at the mercy of its instincts. In the course of cultural growth most of those civilisations or peoples that have had a long history have from time to time been brought up against an imperative call to revise their scheme of institutions in the light of their native instincts, on pain of collapse or decay; and they have chosen variously, and for the most part blindly, to live or not to live, according as their instinctive bias [25] has driven them. In the cases where it has happened that those instincts which make directly for the material welfare of the community, such as the parental bent and the sense of workmanship, have been present in such potent force, or where the institutional elements at variance with the continued life-interests of the community or the civilisation in question have been in a sufficiently infirm state, there the bonds of custom, prescription, principles, precedent, have been broken – or loosened or shifted so as to let the current of life and cultural growth go on, with or without substantial retardation. But history records more frequent and more spectacular instances of the triumph of imbecile institutions over life and culture than of peoples who have by force of instinctive insight saved themselves alive out of a desperately precarious institutional situation, such as now (1913) faces the peoples of Christendom.

Chief among those instinctive dispositions that conduce directly to the material well-being of the race, and therefore to its biological success, is perhaps the instinctive bias here spoken of as the sense of workmanship. The only other instinctive factor of human nature that could with any likelihood dispute this primacy would be the parental bent. Indeed, the two have much in common. They spend themselves on much the same concrete objective ends,

---

10 The all-pervading modern institution of private property appears to have been of such an origin, having cumulatively grown out of the self-regarding bias of men in their oversight of the community's material interests.

and the mutual furtherance of each by the other is indeed so broad and intimate as often to leave it a matter of extreme difficulty to draw a line between
them. Any discussion of either, therefore, must unavoidably draw the other
into the inquiry to a greater or less extent, and a characterisation [26] of the
one will involve some dealing with the other.

As the expression is here understood, the "Parental Bent" is an instinctive
disposition of much larger scope than a mere proclivity to the achievement of
children.[11] This latter is doubtless to be taken as a large and perhaps as a
primary element in the practical working of the parental solicitude; although,
even so, it is in no degree to be confused with the quasi-tropismatic impulse to
the procreation of offspring. The parental solicitude in mankind has a much
wider bearing than simply the welfare of one's own children. This wider
bearing is particularly evident in those lower cultures where the scheme of
consanguinity and inheritance is not drawn on the same close family lines as
among civilised peoples, but it is also to be seen in good vigour in any civilised community. So, for instance, what the phrase-makers have called "race-
suicide" meets the instinctive and unsolicited reprobation of all men, even of
those who would not conceivably go the length of contributing in their own
person to the incoming generation. So also, virtually all thoughtful persons, –
that is to say all persons who hold an opinion in these premises, – will agree
that it is a despicably inhuman thing for the current generation wilfully to
make the way of life harder for the next generation, whether through neglect
of due provision for their subsistence and proper training or through wasting
their heritage of resources and opportunity by improvident greed and indolence.
Providence is a virtue only so far as its aim is provision for posterity.

It is difficult or impossible to say how far the current [27] solicitude for the
welfare of the race at large is to be credited to the parental bent, but it is
beyond question that this instinctive disposition has a large part in the sentimental concern entertained by nearly all persons for the life and comfort of
the community at large, and particularly for the community's future welfare.
Doubtless this parental bent in its wider bearing greatly reënforces that sentimental approval of economy and efficiency for the common good and disapproval of wasteful and useless living that prevails so generally throughout
both the highest and the lowest cultures, unless it should rather be said that
this animus for economy and efficiency is a simple expression of the parental
disposition itself. It might on the other hand be maintained that such an
animus of economy is an essential function of the instinct of workmanship,
which would then be held to be strongly sustained at this point by a parental
solicitude for the common good.

In making use of the expression, "instinct of workmanship" or "sense of
workmanship," it is not here intended to assume or to argue that the proclivity so designated is in the psychological respect a simple or irreducible

---

11 Cf. McDougall, *Social Psychology*, ch. x.

element; still less, of course, is there any intention to allege that it is to be traced back in the physiological respect to some one isolable tropismatic sensibility or some single enzymotic or visceral stimulus. All that is matter for the attention of those whom it may concern. The expression may as well be taken to signify a concurrence of several instinctive aptitudes, each of which might or might not prove simple or irreducible when subjected to psychological or physiological analysis. For the present inquiry it is enough to note that in human [28] behaviour this disposition is effective in such consistent, ubiquitous and resilient fashion that students of human culture will have to count with it as one of the integral hereditary traits of mankind.[12]

As has already appeared, neither this nor any other instinctive disposition works out its functional content in isolation from the instinctive endowment at large. [29] The instincts, all and several, though perhaps in varying degrees, are so intimately engaged in a play of give and take that the work of any one has its consequences for all the rest, though presumably not for all equally. It is this endless[13] complication and contamination of instinctive elements in human conduct, taken in conjunction with the pervading and cumulative effects of habit in this domain, that makes most of the difficulty and much of the interest attaching to this line of inquiry.

12 Latterly the question of instincts has been a subject of somewhat extensive discussion among students of animal behaviour, and throughout this discussion the argument has commonly been conducted on neurological, or at the most on physiological ground. This line of argument is well and lucidly presented in a volume recently published (*The Science of Human Behavior*, New York, 1913) by Mr. Maurice Parmalee. The book offers an incisive critical discussion of the Nature of Instinct (ch. xi) with a specific reference to the instinct of workmanship (p. 252). The discussion runs, faithfully and competently, on neurological ground and reaches the outcome to be expected in an endeavour to reduce instinct to neurological (or physiological) terms. As has commonly been true of similar endeavours, the outcome is essentially negative, in that "instinct" is not so much explained as explained away. The reason of this outcome is sufficiently evident; "instinct," being not a neurological or physiological concept, is not statable in neurological or physiological terms. The instinct of workmanship no more than any other instinctive proclivity is an isolable, discrete neural function; which, however, does not touch the question of its status as a psychological element. The effect of such an analysis as is offered by Mr. Parmalee is not to give terminological precision to the concept of "instinct" in the sense assigned it in current usage, but to dispense with it; which is an untoward move in that it deprives the student of the free use of this familiar term in its familiar sense and therefore constrains him to bring the indispensable concept of instinct in again surreptitiously under cover of some unfamiliar term or some terminological circumlocution. The current mechanistic analyses of animal behaviour are of great and undoubted value to any inquiry into human conduct, but their value does not lie in an attempt to make them supersede those psychological phenomena which it is their purpose to explain. That such supersession of psychological phenomena by the mechanistic formulations need nowise follow and need not be entertained appears, e.g., in such work as that of Mr. Loeb, referred to above, *Comparative Physiology of the Brain and Comparative Psychology.*

13 Endless in the sense that the effects of such concatenation do not run to a final term in any direction.

There are few lines of instinctive proclivity that are not crossed and coloured by some ramification of the instinct of workmanship. No doubt, response to the direct call of such half-tropismatic, half-instinctive impulses as hunger, anger, or the promptings of sex, is little if at all troubled with any sentimental suffusion of workmanship; but in the more complex and deliberate activities, particularly where habit exerts an appreciable effect, the impulse and sentiment of workmanship comes in for a large share in the outcome. So much so, indeed, that, for instance, in the arts, where the sense of beauty is the prime mover, habitual attention to technique will often put the original, and only ostensible, motive in the background. So, again, in the life of religious faith and observance it may happen now and again that theological niceties and ritual elaboration will successfully, and in great measure satisfactorily, substitute themselves for spiritual communion; while in the courts of law a tenacious following out of legal technicalities will not infrequently defeat the ends of justice. [30]

As the expression is here understood, all instinctive action is intelligent in some degree; though the degree in which intelligence is engaged may vary widely from one instinctive disposition to another, and it may even fall into an extremely automatic shape in the case of some of the simpler instincts, whose functional content is of a patently physiological character. Such approach to automatism is even more evident in some of the lower animals, where, as for instance in the case of some insects, the response to the appropriate stimuli is so far uniform and mechanically determinate as to leave it doubtful whether the behaviour of the animal might not best be construed as tropismatic action simply.[14] Such tropismatic directness of instinctive response is less characteristic of man even in the case of the simpler instinctive proclivities; and the indirection which so characterises instinctive action in general, and the higher instincts of man in particular, and which marks off the [31] instinctive dispositions from the tropisms, is the indirection of intelligence. It enters more largely in the discharge of some proclivities than of others; but all

---

14 Many students of animal behaviour are still, as psychologists generally once were, inclined to contrast instinct with intelligence, and to confine the term typically to such automatically determinate action as takes effect without deliberation or intelligent oversight. This view would appear to be a remnant of an earlier theoretical position, according to which all the functions of intelligence were referred to a distinct immaterial entity, entelechy, associated in symbiosis with the physical organism. If all such preconceptions of a substantial dichotomy between physiological and psychological activity be abandoned it becomes a matter of course that intellectual functions themselves take effect only on the initiative of the instinctive dispositions and under their surveillance, and the antithesis between instinct and intelligence will consequently fall away. What expedients of terminology and discrimination may then be resorted to in the study of those animal instincts that involve a minimum of intellect is of course a question for the comparative psychologists. Cf., for instance, C. Lloyd Morgan, *Introduction to Comparative Psychology* (2nd edition, 1906) ch. xii, especially pp. 206–9, and *Habit and Instinct*, ch. i and vi.

instinctive action is intelligent in some degree. This is what marks it off from the tropisms and takes it out of the category of automatism.[15]

Hence all instinctive action is teleological. It involves holding to a purpose. It aims to achieve some end and involves some degree of intelligent faculty to compass the instinctively given purpose, under surveillance of the instinctive proclivity that prompts the action. And it is in this surveillance and direction of the intellectual processes to the appointed end that the instinctive dispositions control and condition human conduct; and in this work of direction the several instinctive proclivities may come to conflict and offset, or to concur and reënforce one another's action.

The position of the instinct of workmanship in this complex of teleological activities is somewhat peculiar, in that its functional content is serviceability for the ends of life, whatever these ends may be; whereas these ends to be subserved are, at least in the main, appointed and made worth while by the various other instinctive dispositions. So that this instinct may in some sense be said to be auxiliary to all the rest, to be concerned with the ways and means of life rather than with any one given ulterior end. It has essentially to do with proximate rather than ulterior ends. Yet workmanship is none the less an object of attention and sentiment in its own right. Efficient use of the means at hand and adequate management of the resources available for the purposes of life [32] is itself an end of endeavour, and accomplishment of this kind is a source of gratification.

All instinctive action is intelligent and teleological. The generality of instinctive dispositions prompt simply to the direct and unambiguous attainment of their specific ends, and in his dealings under their immediate guidance the agent goes as directly as may be to the end sought, – he is occupied with the objective end, not with the choice of means to the end sought; whereas under the impulse of workmanship the agent's interest and endeavour are taken up with the contriving of ways and means to the end sought.

The point of contrast may be unfamiliar, and an illustration may be pertinent. So, in the instinct of pugnacity and its attendant sentiment of anger[16] the primary impulse is doubtless to a direct frontal attack, assault and battery pure and simple; and the more highly charged the agent is with the combative impulse, and the higher the pitch of animation to which he has been wrought up, the less is he inclined or able to take thought of how he may shrewdly bring mechanical devices to bear on the object of his sentiment and compass his end with the largest result per unit of force expended. It is only the well-trained fighter that will take without reflection to workmanlike ways and means at such a juncture; and in case of extreme exasperation and urgency even such a one, it is said, may forget his workmanship in the premises and throw himself into the middle of things instead of resorting to the indirections

15 Cf. H. S. Jennings, *Behavior of the Lower Animals*, ch. xii, xx, xxi.
16 See McDougall, *Introduction to Social Psychology*, ch. iii and x.

and leverages to which his workmanlike training in the art of fighting has habituated him. So, again, the immediate promptings [33] of the parental bent urge to direct personal intervention and service in behalf of the object of solicitude. In persons highly gifted in this respect the impulse asserts itself to succor the helpless with one's own hands, to do for them in one's own person not what might on reflection approve itself as the most expedient line of conduct in the premises, but what will throw the agent most personally into action in the case. Notoriously, it is easier to move well-meaning people to unreflecting charity on an immediate and concrete appeal than it is to secure a sagacious, well sustained and well organised concert of endeavour for the amelioration of the lot of the unfortunate. Indeed, refinements of workman-like calculation of causes and effects in such a case are instinctively felt to be out of touch with the spirit of the thing. They are distasteful; not only are they not part and parcel of the functional content of the generous impulse, but an undue injection of these elements of workmanship into the case may even induce a revulsion of feeling and defeat its own intention.

The instinct of workmanship, on the other hand, occupies the interest with practical expedients, ways and means, devices and contrivances of efficiency and economy, proficiency, creative work and technological mastery of facts. Much of the functional content of the instinct of workmanship is a proclivity for taking pains. The best or most finished outcome of this disposition is not had under stress of great excitement or under extreme urgency from any of the instinctive propensities with which its work is associated or whose ends it serves. It shows at its best, both in the individual workman's technological efficiency and in the growth of technological [34] proficiency and insight in the community at large, under circumstances of moderate exigence, where there is work in hand and more of it in sight, since it is initially a disposition to do the next thing and do it as well as may be; whereas when interest falls off unduly through failure of provocation from the instinctive dispositions that afford an end to which to work, the stimulus to workmanship is likely to fail, and the outcome is as likely to be an endless fabrication of meaningless details and much ado about nothing. On the other hand, in seasons of great stress, when the call to any one or more of the instinctive lines of conduct is urgent beyond measure, there is likely to result a crudity of technique and presently a loss of proficiency and technological mastery.

It is, further, pertinent to note in this connection that the instinct of work-manship will commonly not run to passionate excesses; that it does not, under pressure, tenaciously hold its place as a main interest in competition with the other, more elemental instinctive proclivities; but that it rather yields ground somewhat readily, suffers repression and falls into abeyance, only to reassert itself when the pressure of other, urgent interests is relieved. What was said above as to the paramount significance of the instinct of workmanship for the life of the race will of course suffer no abatement in so recognising its characteristically temperate urgency. The grave importance that attaches to it is a matter of its ubiquitous subservience to the ends of life, and not a matter of vehemence.

The sense of workmanship is also peculiarly subject to bias. It does not commonly, or normally, work to an independent, creative end of its own, but is rather concerned [35] with the ways and means whereby instinctively given purposes are to be accomplished. According, therefore, as one or another of the instinctive dispositions is predominant in the community's scheme of life or in the individual's every-day interest, the habitual trend of the sense of workmanship will be bent to one or another line of proficiency and technological mastery. By cumulative habituation a bias of this character may come to have very substantial consequences for the range and scope of technological knowledge, the state of the industrial arts, and for the rate and direction of growth in workmanlike ideals.

Changes are going forward constantly and incontinently in the institutional apparatus, the habitual scheme of rules and principles that regulate the community's life, and not least in the technological ways and means by which the life of the race and its state of culture are maintained; but changes come rarely – in effect not at all – in the endowment of instincts whereby mankind is enabled to employ these means and to live under the institutions which its habits of life have cumulatively created. In the case of hybrid populations, such as the peoples of Christendom, some appreciable adaptation of this spiritual endowment to meet the changing requirements of civilisation may be counted on, through the establishment of composite pure lines of a hybrid type more nearly answering to the later phases of culture than any one of the original racial types out of which the hybrid population is made up. But in so slow-breeding a species as man, and with changes in the conditions of life going forward at a visibly rapid pace, the chance of [36] an adequate adaptation of hybrid human nature to new conditions seems doubtful at the best. It is also to be noted that the vague character of many of the human instincts, and their consequent pliability under habituation, affords an appreciable margin of adaptation within which human nature may adjust itself to new conditions of life. But after all has been said it remains true that the margin within which the instinctive nature of the race can be effectively adapted to changing circumstances is relatively narrow – narrow as contrasted with the range of variation in institutions – and the limits of such adaptation are somewhat rigid. As the matter stands, the race is required to meet changing conditions of life to which its relatively unchanging endowment of instincts is presumably not wholly adapted, and to meet these conditions by the use of technological ways and means widely different from those that were at the disposal of the race from the outset. In the initial phases of the life-history of the race, or of any given racial stock, the exigencies to which its spiritual (instinctive) nature was selectively required to conform were those of the savage culture, as has been indicated above, – presumably in all cases a somewhat "low" or elementary form of savagery. This savage mode of life, which was, and is, in a sense, native to man, would be characterised by a considerable group solidarity within a relatively small group, living very near the soil, and unremittingly dependent for their daily life on the workmanlike efficiency of all the members of the group. The prime requisite for survival under these conditions would be a propensity unselfishly and impersonally to make the most of the material means at hand and a penchant for turning all [37] resources of knowledge and material to account to sustain the life of the group.

At the outset, therefore, as it first comes into the life-history of any one or all of the racial stocks with which modern inquiry concerns itself, this instinctive disposition will have borne directly on workmanlike efficiency in the simple and obvious sense of the word. By virtue of the stability of the racial type, such is still its character, primarily and substantially, apart from its sophistication by habit and tradition. The instinct of workmanship brought the life of mankind from the brute to the human plane, and in all the later growth of culture it has never ceased to pervade the works of man. But the extensive complication of circumstances and the altered outlook of succeeding generations, brought on by the growth of institutions and the accumulation of knowledge, have led to an extension of its scope and of its canons and logic to activities and conjunctures that have little traceable bearing on the means of subsistence. [38]

II. Contamination of instincts in primitive technology

All instinctive behaviour is subject to development and hence to modification by habit.[17] Such impulsive action as is in no degree intelligent, and so suffers no adaptation through habitual use, is not properly to be called instinctive; it is rather to be classed as tropismatic. In human conduct the effects of habit in this respect are particularly far-reaching. In man the instincts appoint less of a determinate sequence of action, and so leave a more open field for adaptation of behaviour to the circumstances of the case. When instinct enjoins little else than the end of endeavour, leaving the sequence of acts by which this end is to be approached somewhat a matter of open alternatives, the share of reflection, discretion and deliberate adaptation will be correspondingly large. The range and diversity of habituation is also correspondingly enlarged.

In man, too, by the same fact, habit takes on more of a cumulative character, in that the habitual acquirements of the race are handed on from one generation to the next, by tradition, training, education, or whatever general term may best designate that discipline of habituation [39] by which the young acquire what the old have learned. By similar means the like elements of habitual conduct are carried over from one community or one culture to another, leading to further complications. Cumulatively, therefore, habit creates usages, customs, conventions, preconceptions, composite principles of conduct that run back only indirectly to the native predispositions of the race,

---

17 Cf. M. F. Washburn, *The Animal Mind*, ch. x, xi, where the simpler facts of habituation are suggestively presented in conformity with current views of empirical psychology.

but that may affect the working-out of any given line of endeavour in much the same way as if these habitual elements were of the nature of a native bias.

Along with this body of derivative standards and canons of conduct, and handed on by the same discipline of habituation, goes a cumulative body of knowledge, made up in part of matter-of-fact acquaintance with phenomena and in greater part of conventional wisdom embodying certain acquired predilections and preconceptions current in the community. Workmanship proceeds on the accumulated knowledge so received and current, and turns it to account in dealing with the material means of life. Whatever passes current in this way as knowledge of facts is turned to account as far as may be, and so it is worked into a customary scheme of ways and means, a system of technology, into which new elements of information or acquaintance with the nature and use of things are incorporated, assimilated as they come.

The scheme of technology so worked out and carried along in the routine of getting a living will be serviceable for current use and have a substantial value for a further advance in technological efficiency somewhat in proportion as the knowledge so embodied in technological practice [40] is effectually of the nature of matter-of-fact. Much of the information derived from experience in industry is likely to be of this matter-of-fact nature; but much of the knowledge made use of for the technological purpose is also of the nature of convention, inference and authentic opinion, arrived at on quite other grounds than workmanlike experience. This alien body of information, or pseudo-information, goes into the grand total of human knowledge quite as freely as any matter of fact, and it is therefore also necessarily taken up and assimilated in that technological equipment of knowledge and proficiency by use of which the work in hand is to be done.

But the experience which yields this useful and pseudo-useful knowledge is got under the impulsion and guidance of one and another of the instincts with which man is endowed, and takes the shape and color given it by the instinctive bias in whose service it is acquired. At the same time, whatever its derivation, the knowledge acquired goes into the aggregate of information drawn on for the ways and means of workmanship. Therefore the habits formed in any line of experience, under the guidance of any given instinctive disposition, will have their effect on the conduct and aims of the workman in all his work and play; so that progress in technological matters is by no means an outcome of the sense of workmanship alone.

It follows that in all their working the human instincts are in this way incessantly subject to mutual "contamination," whereby the working of any one is incidentally affected by the bias and proclivities inherent in all the rest; and in so far as these current habits and customs in [41] this way come to reënforce the predispositions comprised under any one instinct or any given group of instincts, the bias so accentuated comes to pervade the habits of thought of all the members of the community and gives a corresponding obliquity to the technological groundwork of the community. So, for instance, addiction to magical, superstitious or religious conceptions will necessarily have its effect on the conceptions and logic employed in technological theory and practice, and will impair its efficiency by that much. A people much given to punctilios of rank and respect of persons will in some degree carry these habitual predilections over into the field of workmanship and will allow considerations of authenticity, of personal weight and consequence, to decide questions of technological expediency; so that ideas which have none but a putative efficiency may in this way come in for a large share in the state of the industrial arts. A people whose culture has for any reason taken on a pronounced coercive (predatory) character, with rigorous class distinctions, an arbitrary governmental control, formidable gods and an authoritative priesthood, will have its industrial organisation and its industrial arts fashioned to meet the demands and the logic of these institutions. Such an institutional situation exerts a great and pervasive constraint on the technological scheme in which workmanship takes effect under its rule, both directly by prescribing the things to do and the time, place and circumstance of doing them, and indirectly through the habits of thought induced in the working population living under its rule. Innovation, the utilisation of newly acquired technological insight, is greatly hindered by such institutional [42] requirements that are enforced by other impulses than the sense of workmanship.

In the known lower cultures such institutional complications as might be expected greatly to hinder or deflect the sense of workmanship are commonly neither large, rigorous nor obvious. Something of the kind there apparently always is, in the way, for instance, of the customary prerogatives and perquisites of the older men, as well as their tutelary oversight of the younger generation and of the common interests of the group.[18] When this rule of seniority is elaborated into such set forms as the men's (secret) societies, with exacting initiatory ceremonies and class tabus,[19] its effect on workday life is often very considerable, even though the community may show little that can fairly be classed as autocracy, chieftainship, or even aristocratic government. In many or all of these naive and early developments of authority, and perhaps especially in those cultures where the control takes this inchoate form of a customary "gerontocracy,"[20] its immediate effect is that an abiding sense of authenticity comes to pervade the routine of daily life, such as effectually to obstruct all innovation, whether in the ways and means of work or in the conduct of life more at large. Control by a gerontocracy appears to reach its best development and to run with the fullest consistency and effect in communities where an appreciable degree of predatory exploit is habitual, and the inference is ready, and at least plausible, that this institution is substantially [43] of a predatory origin, that the principles (habits of thought) on which it

18 Cf., e.g., Spencer and Gillen, *Native Tribes of Central Australia*; Seligmann [and Seligmann], *The Veddas.*
19 Hutton Webster, *Primitive Secret Societies*, especially ch. iii and iv.
20 J. G. Frazer, *Early History of the Kingship*, ch. iv, p. 107.

rests are an outgrowth of pugnacity, self-aggrandisement and fear. Under favouring conditions of friction and jealousy between groups these propensities will settle into institutional habits of authority and deference, and so long as the resultant exercise of control is vested by custom in the class of elders the direct consequence is a marked abatement of initiative throughout the community and a consequent appearance of conservatism and stagnation in its technological scheme as well as in the customary usages under whose guidance the community lives.[21] So these instinctive propensities which have no primary significance in the way of workmanship may come to count very materially in shaping the group's technological equipment of ideas and in deflecting the sense of workmanship from the naive pursuit of material efficiency.

The rule of the elders appears to have been extremely prevalent in the earlier phases of culture. So much so that it may even be set down as the most characteristic trait of the upper savagery and of the lower barbarism; whether it takes the elaborately institutionalised form of a settled gerontocracy, as among the Australian blacks, with sharply defined class divisions and perquisites and a consistent subjection of women and children; or the looser customary rule of the Elders, with a degree of deference and circumspection on the part of the younger generation and an uncertain conventional inferiority of women and children, as seen among the pagans of the [44] Malay peninsula,[22] the Eskimo of the Arctic seaboard,[23] the Mincopies of the Andamans,[24] or, on a somewhat higher level, the Pueblo Indians of the American Southwest.[25] Illustrative instances of such an inchoate organisation of authority are very widely distributed, but the communities that follow such a naive scheme of life are commonly neither large, powerful, wealthy, nor much in the public eye. The presumption is that the sense of authenticity which pervades these and similar cultures, amounting to a degree of tabu on innovation, has had much to do with the notably slow advance of technology among savage peoples. Such appears presumably to have been the prevalent run of the facts throughout the stone age in all quarters of the Earth.

It is not altogether plain just what are the innate predispositions chiefly involved in this primitive social control which at its untroubled best develops into a "gerontocracy." There can apparently be little question but that its prime motive force is the parental bent, expressing itself in a naive impulsive surveillance of the common interests of the group and a tutelage of the

---

21 E.g., some native tribes of Australia; cf. Spencer and Gillen, *The Native Tribes of Central Australia*, especially ch. i.

22 Skeat and Blagden, *Pagan Races of the Malay Peninsula.*

23 Murdoch, "The Point Barrow Eskimo," *Report of the Bureau of American Ethnology, 1887–'88*; F. Boas, "The Central Eskimo," Ibid, *1884–'85*.

24 E. H. Man, "On the Aboriginal Inhabitants of the Andaman Islands," *Journal Anth. Inst.*, vol. xii.

25 [*Annual*] *Reports [of the] Bureau of American Ethnology,* numerous papers by different writers, perhaps especially Mrs. Stevenson, "The Sia," *Report of the Bureau of American Ethnology, 1889–'90*.

incoming generation. But here as in other social relations the self-regarding sentiments unavoidably come into play; so that (a) the tutelage of the elders takes [45] something of an authoritative tone and blends self-aggrandisement with their quasi-parental solicitude, giving an institutional outcome which makes the young generation subservient to the elders, ostensibly for the mutual and collective good of both parties to the relation; (b) if predatory or warlike exploit in any degree becomes habitual to the community the sentiment of self-aggrandisement gets the upper hand, and subservience to the able-bodied elders becomes the dominant note in this relation of tutelage, and their parental interest in the welfare of the incoming generation in a corresponding degree goes into abeyance under the pressure of the appropriate sentiments of pugnacity and self-seeking, giving rise to a coercive régime of a more or less ruthless character; (c) correlatively, along with unwearying insistence on their own prerogatives and collective discretion, on the part of the elders, there goes, on the part of the community at large, a correspondingly habitual acceptance of their findings and the precedents they have established, resulting in a universal addiction to the broad principles of unmitigated authenticity, with no power anywhere capable of breaking across the accumulated precedents and tabus. Even the ruling class of elders, being an unwieldy deliberative body or executive committee, is held by parliamentary inertia, as well as by a circumspect regard for their prescriptive rights, to a due observance of the customary law. The force of precedent is notoriously strong on the lower levels of culture. Under the rule of the elders deference to precedent grows into an inveterate habit in the young, and when presently these come to take their turn as discretionary elders the habit of deference to the precedents [46] established by those who have gone before still binds them, and the life and thought of the community never escape the dead hand of the parent.

When worked out into an institution of control in this way, and crossed with the other instinctive propensities that go to make governmental authority, it is apparently unavoidable that the parental bent should suffer this curious inversion. In the simplest and unsophisticated terms, its functional content appears to be an unselfish solicitude for the well-being of the incoming generation – a bias for the highest efficiency and fullest volume of life in the group, with a particular drift to the future; so that, under its rule, contrary to the dictum of the economic theorists, future goods are preferred to present goods[26] and the

---

26 Current economic theory commonly proceeds on the "hedonistic calculus," so called, (cf. Jeremy Bentham, *Introduction to the Principles of Morals and Legislation*) or the "hedonic principle", as it has also been called, (cf. Pantaleoni, *Pure Economics*, ch. i). This "principle" affords the major premise of current theory. It postulates that individual self-seeking is the prime mover of all economic conduct. There is some uncertainty and disagreement among latterday economists as to the precise terms proper to be employed to designate this principle of conduct and its working-out; in the apprehension of later speculators Bentham's "pleasure and pain" has seemed too bald and materialistic, and they have had recourse to such less precise and definable terms as "gratification," "satisfactions," "sacrifice," "utility" and "disutility,"

filial generation is given the [47] preference over the parental generation in all that touches their material welfare. But where the self-regarding sentiments, self-complacency and self-abasement, come largely into play, as they are bound to do in any culture that partakes appreciably of a predatory or coercive character, the prerogatives of the ruling class and the principles of authentic usage become canons of truth and right living and presently take precedence of workmanlike efficiency and the fullness of life of the group. It results that conventional tests of validity presently accumulate and increasingly deflect and obstruct the [48] naive pursuit of workmanlike efficiency, in large part by obscuring those matters of fact that lend themselves to technological insight.

But like other innate predispositions the parental bent continually reasserts itself in its native and untaught character, as an ever resilient solicitude for the welfare of the young and the prospective fortunes of the group. As such it constantly comes in to reënforce the instinct of workmanship and sustain interest in the direct pursuit of efficiency in the ways and means of life. So closely in touch and so concurrent are the parental bent and the sense of workmanship in this quest of efficiency that it is commonly difficult to guess which of the two proclivities is to be credited with the larger or the leading part in any given line of conduct; although taken by and large the two are after all fairly distinct in respect of their functional content. This thorough

---

"psychic income," etc., but hitherto without any conclusive revision of the terminology. These differences and suggested innovations do not touch the substance of the ancient postulate. Proceeding on this postulate the theoreticians have laid down the broad proposition that "present goods are preferred to future goods"; from which arise many meticulous difficulties of theory, particularly in any attempt to make the deliverances of theory square with workday facts. The modicum of truth contained in this Proposition would appear to be better expressed in the formula: "Prospective security is preferred to prospective risk," which seems to [47] be nearly all that is required either as a generalisation of the human motives in the case or as a premise for the theoretical refinements aimed at, whereas the dictum that "present goods are preferred to future goods" must, on reflection, commend itself as substantially false. By and large, of course, goods are not wanted except for prospective use – beyond the measure of that urgent current consumption that plays no part in the theoretical refinements for which the dictum is invoked. It will immediately be apparent on reflection that even for the individual's own advantage "present goods are preferred to future goods" only where and in so far as property rights are secure, and then only for future use. It is for productive use in the future, or more particularly for the sake of prospective revenue to be drawn from wealth so held, by lending or investing it, that such a preference becomes effective. Apart from this pecuniary advantage that attaches to property held over from the present to the future there appears to be no such preference even as a matter of individual self-seeking, and where such pecuniary considerations are not-dominant there is no such preference for "present goods." It is present "wealth," not present "goods," that is the object of desire; and present wealth is desired mainly for its prospective advantage. It is well known that in communities where there are habitually no businesslike credit extensions or investments for profit, savings take the form of hoarding, that is, accumulation for future use in preference to present consumption. There might be some division of opinion as to the character of the prospective use for which goods are sought, but there can be little question that much, if not most, of this prospective use is not of a self-regarding character and is not sought from motives of sensuous gain.

and far-going concurrence of the two may perhaps be taken to mean that the instinct of workmanship is in the main a propensity to work out the ends which the parental bent makes worth while.

It seems to be these two predispositions in conjunction that have exercised the largest and most consistent control over that growth of custom and conventional principles that has standardised the life of mankind in society and so given rise to a system of institutions. This control bears selectively on the whole range of institutions created by habitual response to the call of the other instincts and has the effect of a "common-sense" surveillance which prevents the scheme of life from running into an insufferable tangle of grotesque extravagances. That their surveillance has not always been decisive [49] need scarcely be specifically called to mind; human culture in all ages presents too many imbecile usages and principles of conduct to let anyone overlook the fact that disserviceable institutions easily arise and continue to hold their place in spite of the disapproval of native common sense. The selective control exercised over custom and usage by these instincts of serviceability is neither too close nor too insistent. Wide, even extravagant, departures from the simple dictates of this native common sense occur even within the narrow range of the domestic and minor civil institutions, where these two common-sense predispositions should concur to create a prescriptive usage looking directly to the continuation and welfare of the race. Considerations, or perhaps rather conventional preconceptions, running on other grounds, as, for instance, on grounds of superstition or religion, of propriety and gentility, of pecuniary or political expediency, have come in for a large share in ordering the institutions of family and neighbourhood life. Yet doubtless it is the parental bent and the sense of workmanship in concurrence that have been the primary and persistent factors in (selectively) shaping the household organisation among all peoples, however great may have been the force of other factors, instinctive and habitual, that have gone to diversify the variegated outcome.

It appears, then, that so long as the parental solicitude and the sense of workmanship do not lead men to take thought and correct the otherwise unguarded drift of things, the growth of institutions – usage, customs, canons of conduct, principles of right and propriety, the course of cumulative habituation as it goes forward under the [50] driving force of the several instincts native to man, – will commonly run at cross purposes with serviceability and the sense of workmanship.[27]

---

27 Traditionally a theoretical presumption has been held to the contrary. It has been taken for granted that the institutional outcome of men's native dispositions will be sound and salutary; but this presumption overlooks the effects of complication and deflection among instincts, due to cumulative habit. The tradition has come down as an article of uncritical faith from the historic belief in a beneficent Order of Nature; which in turn runs back to the early-modern religious conception of a Providential Order instituted by a shrewd and benevolent Creator; which rests on an anthropomorphic imputation of parental solicitude and workmanship to an assumed metaphysical substratum of things. This traditional view therefore is substantially

That such should be the case lies in the nature of things, as will readily appear on reflection. Under given circumstances and under the impulsion of a given instinctive propensity a given line of behaviour becomes habitual and so is installed by use and wont as a principle of conduct. The principle or canon of conduct so gained takes its place among the habitual verities of life in the community and is handed on by tradition. Under further impulsion of the same and other instinctive propensities, and under altered circumstances, conduct in other, unrelated lines will be referred to this received principle as a bench-mark by which its goodness is appraised and to which all conduct is accommodated, giving a result which is related to the exigencies of the case only at the second remove and by channels of habit which have only a conventional relevancy to the case. The farther this manner of crossing and grafting of habitual elements proceeds in the elaboration of principles and usage, the [51] larger will be the mass and the graver will be the complication of materially irrelevant considerations present in any given line of conduct, the more extensive and fantastic will be the fabric of conventionalities which come to condition the response to any one of the innate human propensities, and the more "irrelevant, incompetent and impertinent" will be the line of conduct prescribed by use and wont. Except by recourse to the sense of workmanship there is no evading this complication of ineptitudes and irrelevancies, and such recourse is not easily had. For the bias of settled habit goes to sustain the institutional fabric of received sophistications, and these sophistications are bound in such a network of give and take that a disturbance of the fabric at any point will involve more or less of a derangement throughout.

This body of habitual principles and preconceptions is at the same time the medium through which experience receives those elements of information and insight on which workmanship is able to draw in contriving ways and means and turning them to account for the uses of life. And the conventional verities count in this connexion almost wholly as obstructions to workmanlike efficiency. Worldly wisdom, insight into the proprieties and expediencies of human intercourse, the scheme of tabus, consanguinities, and magical efficacies, yields very little that can effectually be turned to account for technological ends. The experience gained by habituation under the stress of these other proclivities and their derivative principles is necessarily made use of in workmanship, and so enters into the texture of the technological system, but a large part of it is of very doubtful value [52] for the purpose. Much of this experience runs at cross purposes with workmanship, not only in that the putative information which this experience brings home to men has none but a putative serviceability, but also in that the habit of mind induced by its discipline obscures that insight into matter of fact that is indispensable to workmanlike efficiency.

---

theological and has that degree of validity that may be derived from the putative characteristics of any anthropomorphic divinity.

But the most obstructive derangement that besets workmanship is what may be called the self-contamination of the sense of workmanship itself. This applies in a peculiar degree to the earlier or more elementary phases of culture, but it holds true only with lessening force throughout the later growth of civilisation. The hindrance to technological efficiency from this source will often rise to large proportions even in advanced communities, particularly where magical, religious or other anthropomorphic habits of thought are prevalent. The difficulty has been spoken of as anthropomorphism, or animism, – which is only a more archaic anthropomorphism. The essential trait of anthropomorphic conceptions, so far as bears on the present argument, is that conduct, more or less fully after the human fashion of conduct, is imputed to external objects; whether these external objects are facts of observation or creatures of mythological fancy. Such anthropomorphism commonly means an interpretation of phenomena in terms of workmanship, though it may also involve much more than this, particularly in the higher reaches of myth-making. But the simpler anthropomorphic or animistic beliefs that pervade men's every-day thinking commonly amount to little if anything more than the naive imputation [53] of a workmanlike propensity in the observed facts. External objects are believed to do things; or rather it is believed that they are seen to do things.

The reason of this imputation of conduct to external things is simple, obvious, and intimate in all men's apprehension; so much so, indeed, as not readily to permit its being seen in perspective and appreciated at anything like its effectual force. All facts of observation are necessarily seen in the light of the observer's habits of thought, and the most intimate and inveterate of his habits of thought is the experience of his own initiative and endeavours. It is to this "apperception mass" that objects of apperception are finally referred, and it is in terms of this experience that their measure is finally taken. No psychological phenomenon is more familiar than this ubiquitous "personal equation" in men's apprehension of whatever facts come within their observation.

The sense of workmanship is like all human instincts in the respect that when the occasion offers, the agent moved by its impulse not only runs through a sequence of actions suitable to the instinctive end, but he is also given to dwelling, more or less sentimentally, on the objects and activities about which his attention is engaged by the promptings of this instinctive propensity. In so far as he is moved by the instinct of workmanship man contemplates the objects with which he comes in contact from the point of view of their relevancy to ulterior results, their aptitude for taking effect in a consequential outcome. Habitual occupation with workmanlike conceptions, – and in the lower cultures all men and women are habitually so occupied, since there is no considerable class or season not engaged in the quest of a [54] livelihood, – this occupation with workmanlike interests, leaving the attention alert in the direction towards workmanlike phenomena, carries with it habitual thinking in the terms in which the logic of workmanship runs. The facts of observation are conceived as facts of workmanship, and the logic of workmanship becomes the logic of events. Their apprehension in these terms is easy, since it draws into action the faculties of apperception and reflection that are already alert and facile through habitual use, and it assimilates the facts in an apperceptive system of relationships that is likewise ready and satisfactory, convincing through habitual service and by native proclivity to this line of systematisation. By instinct and habit observed phenomena are apprehended from this (teleological) point of view, and they are construed, by way of systematisation, in terms of such an instinctive pursuit of some work-manlike end. In latterday psychological jargon, human knowledge is of a "pragmatic" character.

As all men habitually act under the guidance of instincts, and therefore by force of sentiment instinctively look to some end in all activity, so the objects with which the primitive workman has to do are also conceived as acting under impulse of an instinctive kind, and a bent, a teleological or pragmatic nature, is in some degree imputed to them and comes as a matter of course to be accepted as a constituent element in their apprehended make-up. A puta-tive pragmatic bent innate in external things comes in this way to pass current as observed matter of fact. By force of the sense of workmanship external objects are in great part apperceived in respect of what they will do; and their most substantial characteristic [55] therefore, their intimate individual nature, in so far as they are conceived as individual entities, is that they will do things.

In the workmanlike apprehension of them the nature of things is twofold: (a) what can be done with them as raw material for use under the creative hand of the workman who makes things, and (b) what they will do as entities acting in their own right and working out their own ends. The former is matter of fact, the latter matter of imputation; but both alike, and in the naive apprehension of uncritical men both equally, are facts of observation and elements of objective knowledge. The two are, of course, of very unequal value for the purposes of workmanship. It should seem, at least on first con-tact with the distinction, that the former category alone can have effectually conduced or contributed to workmanlike efficiency, and so it should be the only substantial factor in the growth of technological insight and proficiency: while the latter category of knowledge should presumably have always been an unmitigated hindrance to effective work and to technological advance. But such does not appear on closer scrutiny to have been the case in the past: whether such sheer discrimination against the technological serviceability of all these putative facts would hold good in latter-day civilisation is a question which may perhaps best be left to the parties in interest in "pragmatic" and theological controversy.

These two categories of knowledge, or of *cognoscenda*, are incongruous, of course, and they seem incompatible when applied to the same phenomena, the same external objects. But such incongruity does not disturb anyone who is at all content to take facts at their face value, – [56] for both ways of apprehending the facts are equally given in the face value of the facts apprehended. And on the known lower levels of culture it appears that in the workman's apprehension of the facts with which he has to do there is no evident strain due to this twofold nature and twofold interpretation of the objects of knowledge. So, the Pueblo potter (woman) may (putatively) be aware of certain inherent, quasi-spiritual, pragmatic qualities, claims and proclivities personal to the day beds from which her raw material is drawn: different clay beds have, no doubt, a somewhat different quasi-personality, which has, among other things, to do with the goodness of the raw material they afford. Even the clay in hand will have its pragmatic peculiarities and idiosyncracies which are duly to be respected; and, notably, the finished pot is an entity with a life-history of its own and with temperament, fortunes and fatalities that make up the substance of good and evil in its world.[28] But all that does not perceptibly affect the technology of the Pueblo potter's art, beyond carrying a sequence of ceremonial observance that may run along by the side of the technological process; nor does it manifestly affect the workmanlike use of the pot during its lifetime, except that the pragmatic nature of the given pot will decide, on grounds of ceremonial competency, to what use it may be put.[29] [57]

Matter of fact and matter of imputation run along side by side in inextricable contact but with slight apparent mutual interference across the line. The potter digs her clay as best she has learned how, and it is a matter of workmanlike efficiency, in which empirical knowledge of the mechanical qualities of the material is very efficiently combined with the potter's trained proficiency in the discretionary use of her tools; the tools, of course, also have their (putative) temperamental idiosyncracies, but they are employed in her hands in uncritical conformity with such matter-of-fact laws of physics as she has learned. The clay is washed, kneaded and tempered with the same circumspect regard to the opaque facts known about clay through long handling of it. What and how much tempering material may best be used, and how it is to be worked in, may all have a recondite explanation in the subtler imputed traits of the clay; a certain clay may have a putative quasi-spiritual affinity for certain tempering material; but the work of selection and mixing is carried out with a watchful regard to the mechanical character of the materials and without doubt that the given materials will respond in definite, empirically ascertained ways to the pressure brought on them by the potter's hands, and without questioning the matter of fact that such and so much of manipulation will mix such and so much of tempering material with the given lot of clay.

---

28 Cf., e.g., F. H. Cushing, "A Study of Pueblo Pottery as illustrative of Zuni Culture Growth," *Report of the Bureau of American Ethnology, 1882–'83* (vol. iv); J. W. Fewkes, "Archeological Expedition to Arizona in 1895," sections on Pottery and Paleography of the Pottery, ibid, *1895–'96* (vol. xvii; [part 2]); W. H. Holmes, "The Ancient Art of Chiriqui," ibid, *1884–'85* (vol. vi).

29 The restrictions in this respect are mainly those which devote the [57] "sacred" vessels, distinguished by peculiar shapes and decorations, to particular ceremonial uses.

The clay is "as wax in her hands;" what comes of it is the product of her insight and proficiency. Still the pragmatic nature of all these materials viewed as distinct entities is never to be denied, and in those [58] respects in which she does not creatively design, manipulate and construct the work of her hands, its putative self-sufficiency of existence, meaning and propensity goes on its own recognisances unshorn and inalienable.

Technological efficiency rests on matter-of-fact knowledge, as contrasted with knowledge of the traits imputed to external objects in making acquaintance with them. Therefore every substantial advance in technological mastery necessarily adds something to this body of opaque fact, and with every such advance proportionably less of the behaviour of inanimate things will come to be construed in terms of an imputed workmanlike or teleological bent. At the same time the imputation of a teleological meaning or workmanlike bent to the external facts that are made use of is likely to take a more circumspect, ingenious and idealised form. Under the circumstances that condition an increasing technological mastery there is an ever-growing necessity to avoid conflict between the imputed traits of external objects and those facts of their behaviour that are constantly in evidence in their technological use. In so far, therefore, as a simple and immediate imputation of workmanlike self-direction is seen manifestly to traverse the facts of daily use its place will be supplied by more shadowy anthropomorphic agencies that are assumed to carry on their life and work in some degree of detachment from the material objects in question, and to these anthropomorphic agencies which so lie obscurely in the background of the observed facts will be assigned a larger and larger share of the required initiative and self-direction. For so alien to mankind, with its instinctive sense of workmanship, is the mutilation of brute creation into [59] mere opaque matter-of-fact, and so indefeasibly does the "consciousness of kind" assert itself, that each successive renunciation of such an imputed bias of workmanship in concrete objects is sought to be redeemed by pushing the imputation farther into the background of observed phenomena and running their putative workmanlike bias in more consummately anthropomorphic terms. So an animistic conception[30] of things comes presently to supplement, and in part supplant, the more naive and immediate imputation of workmanship, leading up to farther and more elaborate myth-making; until in the course of elaboration and refinement there may emerge a monotheistic and providential Creator seated in an infinitely remote but ubiquitous space of four dimensions.

This imputation of bias and initiative has doubtless lost ground among civilised communities, as contrasted with the matter-of-fact apprehension of things, so that where it once was the main body of knowledge it now is believed to live and move only within that margin of things not yet overtaken by matter-of-fact information, – at least so it is held in the vainglorious

30 Cf. E. B. Tylor, *Primitive Culture*, especially ch. xvii.

scepticism of the Western culture. Meantime it is to be noted that the proclivity to impute a workmanlike bias to external facts has not been lost, nor
has it become inoperative even among the adepts of Occidental scepticism. On the
one hand it still enables the modern scientist to generalise his observations
in terms of causation,[31] and on the other hand it has preserved the life of God
the Father unto this day. It is as the creative workman, the [60] Great Artificer,
that he has taken his last stand against the powers of spiritual twilight.

Out of the simpler workday familiarity with the raw materials and processes employed in industry, in the lower cultures, there emerges no system of
knowledge avowed as such; although in all known instances of such lower
cultures the industrial arts have taken on a systematic character, such as often
to give rise to definite, extensive and elaborate technological processes as well
as to manual and other technological training; both of which will necessarily
involve something like an elementary theory of mechanics systematised on
grounds of matter-of-fact, as well as a practical routine of empirical ways and
means. In the lower cultures the growth of this body of opaque facts and of its
systematic coherence is simply the habitual growth of technological procedure. Considered as a knowledge of things it is prosy and unattractive; it does
not greatly appeal to men's curiosity, being scarcely interesting in itself, but
only for the use to be made of it. Its facts are not lighted up with that spiritual fire of pragmatic initiative and propensity which animates the same phenomena when seen in the light of an imputed workmanlike behaviour and so
construed in terms of conduct. On the other hand, when the phenomena are
interpreted anthropomorphically they are indued with a "human interest,"
such as will draw the attention of all men in all ages, as witness the worldwide
penchant for myth-making.

Such animistic imputation of end and endeavour to the facts of observation
will in no case cover the whole of men's apprehension of the facts. It is a
matter of imputation, not of direct observation; and there is always a [61]
fringe of opaque matter-of-fact bound up with even the most animistically
conceived object. Such is unavoidably the case. The animistic conception
imputes to its subject a workmanlike propensity to do things, and such an
imputation necessarily implies that, as agent, the object in question engages
in something like a technological process, a workmanlike manipulation
wherein he has his will with the raw materials upon which his workmanlike
force and proficiency spends itself. Workmanship involves raw material, and
in the respect in which this raw material is passively shaped to his purposes by
the workman's manipulation it is not conceived to be actively seeking its own
ends on its own initiative. So that by force of the logic of workmanship the
imputation of a workmanlike (animistic) propensity to brute facts, itself
involves the assumption of crude inanimate matter as a correlate of the putative

31 Cf. [Veblen,] "The Evolution of the Scientific Point of View," *University of California Chronicle*,
Oct., 1908. [Selection 34 in this volume.]

workmanlike agent. The anthropomorphic fancy of the primitive workman, therefore, can never carry the teleological interpretation of phenomena to such a finality but that there will always in his apprehension be an inert residue of matter-of-fact left over. The material facts never cease to be, within reasonable limits, raw material; though the limits may be somewhat vague and shifting. And this residue of crude matter-of-fact grows and gathers consistency with experience and always remains ready to the hand of the workman for what it is worth, unmagnified and unbeautified by anthropomorphic interpretation.

The animistic, or better the anthropomorphic, elements so comprised by imputation in the common-sense apprehension of things will pass in the main for facts of observation. With the current of time and experience this [62] may under favourable conditions grow into a developed animistic system and come to the dignity of myth, and ultimately of theology. But as it plays its part in the cruder uses of technology its common and most obstructive form is the inchoate animism or anthropomorphic bias spoken of above. In its bearing on technological efficiency, it commonly vitiates the available facts in a greater or less degree. Matter-of-fact knowledge alone will serve the uses of workmanship, since workmanship is effective only in so far as its outcome is matter-of-fact work. Any higher and more subtle potencies found in or imputed to the facts about which the artificer is engaged can only serve to divert and defeat his efforts, in that they lead him into methods and expedients that have only a putative effect.

This obstructive force of the anthropomorphic interpretation of phenomena is by no means the same in all lines of activity. The difficulty, at least in the earlier days, seems to be greatest along those lines of craft where the workman has to do with the mechanical, inanimate forces – the simplest in point of brute concreteness and the least amenable to a consistent interpretation in animistic terms. While man is conventionally distinguished from brute creation as a "tool-using animal," his early progress in the devising and use of efficient tools, taking the word in its native sense, seems to have gone forward very slowly, both absolutely and as contrasted with those lines of workmanship in which he could carry his point by manual dexterity unaided by cunningly devised implements and mechanical contrivances;[32] and [63] still more striking is the contrast between the incredibly slow and blindfold advance of the savage culture shown in the sequence of those typical stone implements which serve conventionally as land-marks of the early technology, on the one hand, and the concomitant achievements of the same stone-age peoples in the domestication and use of plants and animals on the other hand.

---

32 So, e.g., the proficiency of Bushmen, Veddas, Australians, American [63] Indians, and other peoples of a low technological plane, in tracking game has been remarked on with great admiration by all observers; and the efficiency of these and others of their like is no less admirable as regards swimming, boating, riding, climbing, stalking, etc.

No man can offer a confident conjecture as to how long a time and what a volume of experience was taken up in the growth of technological insight and proficiency up to the point when the neolithic period begins in European prehistory. In point of duration it has been found convenient to count it up roughly in units of geologic time, where a thousand years are as a day. Attempts to reduce it to such units as centuries or millennia have hitherto not come to anything appreciable. In the present state of information on this head it is doubtless a safe conjecture that the interval between the beginning of the human era and the close of palaeolithic time, say in Europe or within the cultural sequence in which Europe belongs, is to be taken as some multiple of the interval that has elapsed from the beginning of the neolithic culture in Europe to the present;[33] and the neolithic period itself was in its turn no doubt of longer duration than the history of Europe since the bronze first came in.[34] [64]

The series of stone implements recovered from palaeolithic deposits show the utmost reach of palaeolithic technology on its mechanical side, in the way of workmanlike mastery of brute matter simply; for these implements are the tools of the tool-makers of that technological era. They indicate the ultimate terms of the technological situation on the mechanical side, for the craftsman working in more perishable materials could go no farther than these primary elements of the technological equipment would carry him.

The strict limitation imposed on the technology of any culture, on its mechanical side, by the "state of the industrial arts" in respect of the primary tools and materials available, whether availability is a question of knowledge or of material environment, is illustrated, for instance, by the case of the Eskimo, the North-west Coast Indians, or some of the islands of the South Sea. In each of these cultures, perhaps especially in that of the Eskimo, technological mastery had been carried as far as the circumstances of the case would permit, and in each case the decisive circumstances that limit the scope and range of workmanship are the character of the primary tools of the tool-maker and the limits of his knowledge of the mechanical properties of the materials at his disposal for such use. The Eskimo culture, for instance, is complete after its kind, worked out to the last degree of workmanlike mastery possible with the Eskimo's knowledge of those materials on which he depended for his primary tools and on which he was able to draw for the raw materials of his industry. At the same time the Eskimo shows how considerable a superstructure of the secondary mechanic arts may be erected [65] on a scant groundwork of the primary mechanical resources.[35]

---

33 Cf. G. and A. de Mortillet, *Le Préhistorique*, especially the chapter "Données chronologiques," pp. 662–64; W. G. Sollas, *Ancient Hunters*, ch. i and xiv.

34 Cf. Sophus Müller, *L'Europe Préhistorique*.

35 Cf., e.g., *Report of the Bureau of American Ethnology, 1884-'85*; Franz Boas, "The Central Eskimo;" ibid, *1887-'88*; John Murdoch, "The Point Barrow Eskimo" [ibid., *1887-'88*].

In the light of such a familiar instance as the Eskimo or the Polynesian culture it is evident that very much must be allowed, in the case, e.g., of the European stone age, for work in perishable materials that have disappeared; but after all allowance of this kind, the showing for palaeolithic man is not remarkable, considering the ample time allowed him, and considering also that, in Europe at least, he was by native gift nowise inferior to some of the racial elements that still survive in the existing population and that are not notoriously ill furnished either in the physical or the intellectual respect. And what is true of palaeolithic times as regards the native character of this population is true in a more pronounced degree for later prehistoric times.[36]

The very moderate pace of the technological advance in early times in the mechanic arts stands out more strikingly when it is contrasted with what was accomplished [66] in those arts, or rather in those occupations, that have to do immediately with living matter. Some of the crop plants, for instance, and presently some of the domestic animals, make their appearance in Denmark late in the period of the kitchen middens; which falls in the early stone age of the Danish chronology, that is to say in the early part of the neolithic period as counted in terms of the European chronology at large. These, then, are improved breeds of plants and animals, very appreciably different from their wild ancestors, arguing not only a shrewd insight and consistent management in the breeding of these domesticated races but also a long continued and intelligent use of these items of technological equipment, during which the nature and uses of the plants and animals taken into domestication must have been sufficiently understood and taken advantage of, at the same time that a workmanlike selection and propagation of favourable variations was carried out. Some slight reflection on what is implied in the successful maintenance, use and improvement of several races of crop plants and domestic animals will throw that side of the material achievements of the kitchen-midden peoples into sufficiently high contrast with their chipped flint implements and the degree of mechanical insight and proficiency which these implements indicate.

To this Danish illustrative case it may of course be objected, and with some apparent reason, that these plants and animals which begin to come in evidence in a state of domestication in the kitchen middens, and which presently afforded the chief means of life to the later stone-age population, were

---

36 What is assumed here is what is commonly held, viz. that the racial stocks that made up the late palaeolithic population of Europe are still represented in a moderate way in the racial mixture that fills Europe today, and that these older racial types not only recur sporadically in the European population at large but are also present locally in sufficient force to give a particular character to the population of given localities. (See G. de Mortillet, *Formation de la nation française*, 4me partie, and Conclusions, pp. 275–329.) Great changes took place in the racial complexion of Europe in the beginning and early phases of the neolithic period, but since then no intrusion of new stocks has seriously disturbed the mixture of races, except in isolated areas, of secondary consequence to the cultural situation at large. See also W. G. Sollas, *Ancient Hunters and their Modern Representatives*.

introduced in a domestic state from outside; and that this technological gain was [67] the product of another and higher culture than that into which they were thus intruded. The objection will have what force it may; the facts are no doubt substantially as set forth. However, the domestication and use of these races of plants and animals embodied no less considerable a workmanlike mastery of its technological problem wherever it was worked out, whether in Denmark – as is at least highly improbable – or in Turkestan, as may well have been the case. And the successful introduction of tillage and cattle-breeding among the kitchen-midden peoples from a higher culture, without the concomitant introduction of a corresponding gain in the mechanic arts from the same source, leaves the force of the argument about as it would be in the absence of this objection. The comparative difficulty of acquiring the mechanic arts, as compared with the arts of husbandry, would appear in much the same light whether it were shown in the relatively slow acquirement of these arts through a home growth of technological mastery or in the relatively tardy and inept borrowing of them from outside. So far as bears on the present question, much the same habits of mind take effect in the acquirement of such a technological gain whether it takes place by home growth or by borrowing from without. In either case the point is that the peoples of the kitchen-middens appear to have been less able to learn the use of serviceable mechanical expedients than to acquire the technology of tillage and cattle-breeding. The appearance of tillage and cattle-breeding ("mixed farming") at this period of Danish prehistory, without the concomitant appearance of anything like a similar technological gain in the mechanic arts, argues either (a) that in the culture [68] from which husbandry was ultimately borrowed and in which the domestication was achieved there was no similarly substantial gain made in the mechanic arts at the same time, so that this culture from which the crop plants and animals originally came into the North of Europe had no corresponding mechanical gain to offer along with husbandry; or (b) that the kitchen-midden peoples, and the other peoples through whose hands the arts of husbandry passed on their way to the North, were unable to profit in a like degree by what was offered them in the primary mechanic arts. The known evidence seems to say that the visible retardation in the mechanic arts, as compared with husbandry, in prehistoric Denmark was due partly to the one, partly to the other of these difficulties.

To avoid confusion and misconception it may be pertinent to recall that, taken absolutely, the rate and magnitude of advance in the primary mechanic arts in Denmark at this time was very considerable; so much so indeed that the visible absolute gain in this respect has so profoundly touched the imagination of the students of that culture as to let them overlook the disparity, in point of the rate of gain, between the mechanic arts and husbandry. In the same connection it is also to be remarked that the entire neolithic culture of the kitchen-middens, as well as their husbandry, was introduced from outside of Europe, having been worked out in its early rudiments before the kitchen-midden peoples reached the Baltic seaboard. At the same time the raw materials for the mechanic arts of the neolithic culture were available to the kitchen-midden technologist in abundant quantity and unsurpassed quality; while the [69] raw material of husbandry, the crop plants and domestic animals, were exotics. Further, in point of race, and therefore presumably in point of native endowment, the peoples of the Baltic seaboard at that time were substantially the same mixture of stocks that has in modern times carried the technology of the mechanic arts in western Europe and its colonies to a pitch of mastery never approached before or elsewhere. And the retardation in the mechanic arts as contrasted with husbandry is no greater, probably less, in neolithic Denmark than in any other culture on the same general level of efficiency.

Wherever the move may have been made, in one or in several places, and whatever may have been the particular circumstances attending the domestication and early use of crop plants and animals, the case sums up to about the same result. Through long ages of work and play men (perhaps primarily women) learned the difficult and delicate crafts of husbandry and carried their mastery of these pursuits to such a degree of proficiency, and followed out the lead given by these callings with such effect, that by the (geologic) date of early neolithic times in Europe virtually all the species of domesticable animals in three continents had been brought in and had been bred into improved races.[37] At the same time the leading crop plants of the old world, those on whose yield the life of the Western peoples depends today, had [70] been brought under cultivation, improved and specialised with such effect that all the advance that has been made in these respects since the early neolithic period is greatly less than what had been accomplished up to that time. By early neolithic times as counted in West Europe, or by the early bronze age as counted in western Asia, the leading domestic animals had been distributed, in domesticated and improved breeds, throughout central and western Asia and the inhabited regions of Europe and North Africa. The like is true for the main crop plants that now feed the occidental peoples, except that these, in domesticated and specialised breeds, were distributed through this entire cultural region at an appreciably earlier date, – earlier by some thousands of years.[38] In [71] late modern times there have been added to the civilised

37 These improved races are commonly, if not always, a product of hybridisation, though it is conceivable that such a race might arise as a "sport," a Mendelian mutant. To establish such a race or "composite pure line" of hybrids and to propagate and improve it in the course of further breeding demands a degree of patient attention and consistent aim.

38 The late neolithic, or "aeneolithic," culture brought to light by Pumpelly at Anau in Transcaspia shows the synchronism of advance between the technology of the mechanic arts on the one hand and of tillage and cattle-breeding on the other hand in a remarkably lucid way. The site is held to date back to some 8000 B.C. or earlier and shows continuous occupation through a period of several thousand years. The settlers at Anau brought cereals (barley and wheat) when the settlement was made; so that the cultivation of these grains must date back some considerable distance farther into the stone age of Asia. In succeeding ages the people of

world's complement of crop plants a very large and important contingent whose domestication and development was worked out in America and the regions of the Pacific; though most of these belong in the low latitudes and are on that account less available to the Western culture than what has come down from the Prehistoric cultures of the old world. These are also the work of the stone age, in large part no doubt dating back to palaeolithic times.

America, with the Polynesian and Indonesian cultural regions, shows the correlation and the systematic discrepancy in time between the rate, range and magnitude of the advance in tillage on the one hand and of the primary mechanic arts on the other hand. When this culture was interrupted it had, in the mechanical respect, reached an advanced neolithic phase at its best; but its achievements in the crop plants are perhaps to be rated as unsurpassed by all that has been done elsewhere in all time.[39] In the primary mechanic arts this cultural region had in the same time reached a stage of perfection comparable at its best with pre-dynastic Egypt, or neolithic Denmark, or pre-Minoan Crete. The really great advance achieved was in the selection, improvement, use and cultivation of the crop plants; and not in any appreciable degree even in the mechanical appliances employed in the cultivation and consumption of these crops; though something considerable is to be noted in this latter respect in such inventions as the mandioca [72] squeezer and the metate; and great things were done in the way of irrigation and road building.[40] But the contrast, for instance, between the metate and the contrivances for making paper bread on the one side, and the technologically consummate corn-plant (maize) on the other, should be decisive for the point here in question. The mechanic appliances of corn cultivation had not advanced beyond the digging stick, a rude hoe and a rudimentary spade, though here as well as in other similar connections the local use of well-devised irrigation works, terraced fields,[41] and graneries is not to be overlooked; but the corn itself had been brought from its grass-like ancestral form to the maize of the present corn crop. Like most of the American crop plants the maize under

---

Anau made some further advance in the use of crop plants; whether by improvement and innovation at home or by borrowing has not been determined. Presently, in the course of the next few thousand years, they brought into domestication and adapted to domestic use by selective breeding the greater number of those species of animals that have since made up the complement of live stock in the Western culture. In the mechanic arts the visible advance is slight as compared with the work in cattle-breeding, though it cannot be called insignificant taken by itself. The more notable improvements in this direction are believed to be due to borrowing. Perhaps the most characteristic trait of the mechanic technology at Anau is the total absence of weapons in the lower half of the deposits. – Raphael Pumpelly, *Explorations in Turkestan: Prehistoric Civilizations of Anau* (Carnegie Publication No. 73.) Washington, 1908.

39 Cf. O. F. Cook, "Food Plants of Ancient America," *Annual Report of the Smithsonian Institution, 1903*. E. J. Payne, *History of the New World Called America*, vol. i (1892), pp. 336–427.

40 Cf. E. J. Payne [as cited above in note 39 of this Selection].

41 Cf., e.g., Lumholtz, *Unknown Mexico*, vol. i, ch. vi.

selective cultivation had been carried so far from its wild form as no longer to stand a chance of survival in the wild state, and indeed so far that it is still a matter of controversy what its wild ancestor may have been.

Perhaps the races of this American-Polynesian region are gifted with some special degree of spiritual (instinctive) fitness for plant-breeding. They seem to be endowed with a particular proclivity for sympathetically identifying themselves with and patiently waiting upon the course of natural phenomena, perhaps especially the phenomena of animate nature, which never seem alien or incomprehensible to the Indian. Such at least is the consistent suggestion carried by their myths, legends and symbolism. The typical American cosmogony is a tissue of legends of fecundity and growth, even more than appears to hold true of primitive cosmogonies [73] elsewhere.[42] And yet some caution in accepting such a generalisation is necessary in view, for instance, of the mythological output along similar lines on the Mediterranean seaboard in early times. By native gift the Indian is a "nature-faker," given to unlimited anthropomorphism. Mechanical, matter-of-fact appreciation of external and material phenomena seems to be in a peculiar degree difficult, irrelevant and incongruous with the genius of the race.

But even if it should seem that this race, or group of races, is peculiarly given to such sympathetic interpretation of natural phenomena in terms of human instinct, the difference between them and the typical racial stocks of the old world in this respect is after all a difference in degree, not in kind. The like proclivity is in good evidence throughout, wherever any race of men have endeavoured to put their acquaintance with natural phenomena into systematic form. The bond of combination in the making of systems, whether cosmologic, mythic, philosophic or scientific, has been some putative human trait or traits. It may be that in their appreciation of facts and their making of systems the American races have by some peculiar native gift been inclined to an interpretation in terms of fertility, growth, nurture and life-cycles.

42 Cf., e.g., J. W. Powell, "Mythology of the North American Indians," *Report of the Bureau of American Ethnology, 1879–'80* (vol. i); F. H. Cushing, "Outlines of Zuni Creation Myths," ibid, *1891–'92*; J. O. Dorsey, "A Study of Siouan Cults," ibid, *1889–'90*.

Bibliographies

1. Complete List of Thorstein Veblen's Published Writings

This bibliography omits posthumous collections of Thorstein Veblen's work with the exception of the standard compilations listed below as Veblen 1934b, 1964b, and 1973.

(1882) "Mill's Theory of the Taxation of Land," *Johns Hopkins University Circulars*, **13**, February, p. 176. [Selection 1 in this volume.]

(1884) "Kant's Critique of Judgment," *Journal of Speculative Philosophy*, **43**, July, pp. 260–74. [Reprinted in Veblen (1934b); Selection 2 in this volume.]

(1891) "Some Neglected Points in the Theory of Socialism." *Annals of the American Academy of Political and Social Science*, **2**, November, pp. 345–62. [Reprinted in Veblen (1919j); Selection 3 in this volume.]

(1892a) "Böhm-Bawerk's Definition of Capital and the Source of Wages." *Quarterly Journal of Economics*, **6** (2), January, pp. 247–52. [Reprinted in Veblen (1934b); Selection 4 in this volume.]

(1892b) "The Overproduction Fallacy," *Quarterly Journal of Economics*, **6**(4), July, pp. 484–92. [Reprinted in Veblen (1934b).]

(1892c) "The Price of Wheat since 1867", *Journal of Political Economy*, **1**(1), December, pp. 68–103. [Reprinted in Veblen (1973).]

(1893a) Review of *A History of Socialism* by Thomas Kirkup, *Journal of Political Economy*, **1**(2), March, pp. 300–302. [Reprinted in Veblen (1973).]

(1893b) Review of *Geschichte des Socialismus und Communismus im 19. Jahrhundert* by Otto Warschauer, *Journal of Political Economy*, **1**(2), March, p. 302. [Reprinted in Veblen (1973).]

(1893c) "The Food Supply and the Price of Wheat," *Journal of Political Economy*, **1** (3), June, pp. 365–79. [Reprinted in Veblen (1973); Selection 5 in this volume.]

(1893d) Review of *The Land-Systems of British India* by B. H. Baden-Powell, *Journal of Political Economy*, **2**(1), December, pp. 112–15. [Reprinted in Veblen (1973); Selection 6 in this volume.]

(1894a) Review of *Der Parlamentarismus und die Volksgesetzgebung und die Socialdemokratie* by Karl Kautsky, *Journal of Political Economy*, **2**(2), March, pp. 312–14. [Reprinted in Veblen (1973); Selection 7 in this volume.]

(1894b) Review of *A Study of Small Holdings* by William E. Bear, *Journal of Political Economy*, **2**(2), March, pp. 325–26. [Reprinted in Veblen (1973).]

(1894c) "The Army of the Commonweal," *Journal of Political Economy*, **2**(3), June, pp. 456–61. [Reprinted in Veblen (1934b).]

(1894d) Review of *Bibliographie des Socialismus und Communismus* by Joseph Stammhammer, *Journal of Political Economy*, **2**(3), June, pp. 474–75. [Reprinted in Veblen (1973).]

(1894e) Review of *History of the English Landed Interest (Modern Period)* by M. Garnier, *Journal of Political Economy*, **2**(3), June, pp. 475–77. [Reprinted in Veblen (1973).]

(1894f) Review of *L'Agriculture aux États-Unis* by Émile Levasseur, *Journal of Political Economy*, **2**(4), September, pp. 592–96. [Reprinted in Veblen (1973).]

(1894g) "The Economic Theory of Woman's Dress," *Popular Science Monthly*, **46**(2), December, pp. 198–205. [Reprinted in Veblen (1934b); Selection 8 in this volume.]

(1895) Review of *Socialism* by Robert Flint, *Journal of Political Economy*, **3**(2), March, pp. 247–52. [Reprinted in Veblen (1973).]

(1896) Review of *Misére de la Philosophie* by Karl Marx and *Socialisme et Science Positive* by Enrico Ferri, *Journal of Political Economy*, **5**(1), December, pp. 97–103. [Reprinted in Veblen (1973); Selection 9 in this volume.]

(1897a) Review of *Einführung in den Socialismus* by Richard Calwer, *Journal of Political Economy*, **5**(2), March, pp. 270–72. [Reprinted in Veblen (1973); Selection 10 in this volume.]

(1897b) Review of *La Viriculture – Ralentissement de la Population – Dégénérescence – Causes et Remèdes* by G. de Molinari, in *Journal of Political Economy*, **5**(2), March, pp. 273–75. [Reprinted in Veblen (1973).]

(1897c) Review of *Essais sur la conception matérialiste de l'histoire* by Antonio Labriola, in *Journal of Political Economy*, **5**(3), June, pp. 390–91. [Reprinted in Veblen (1973); Selection 11 in this volume.]

(1897d) Review of *Sozialismus und soziale Bewegung im 19. Jahrhundert* by Werner Sombart, in *Journal of Political Economy*, **5**(3), June, pp. 391–92. [Reprinted in Veblen (1973).]

(1897e) Review of *Esquisses de literature politico-économique* by N. Ch. Bunge, *Journal of Political Economy*, **6**(1), December, pp. 126–28. [Reprinted in Veblen (1973).]

(1897f) Review of *Die Marxistische Socialdemokratie* by Max Lorenz, in *Journal of Political Economy*, **6**(1), December, pp. 136–37. [Reprinted in Veblen (1973); Selection 12 in this volume.]

(1898a) Review of *Über einige Grundfragen der Socialpolitik und der Volkswirtschaftslehre* by Gustav Schmoller, *Journal of Political Economy*, **6**(3), June, pp. 416–19. [Reprinted in Veblen (1973); Selection 13 in this volume.]

(1898b) Review of *Aristocracy and Evolution: A Study of the Rights, the Origins and the Social Functions of the Wealthier Classes* by William H. Mallock, in *Journal of Political Economy*, **6**(3), June, pp. 430–35. [Reprinted in Veblen (1973); Selection 14 in this volume.]

(1898c) "Why Is Economics Not an Evolutionary Science?" *Quarterly Journal of Economics*, **12**(3), July, pp. 373–97. [Reprinted in Veblen (1919j); Selection 15 in this volume.]

(1898d) "The Instinct of Workmanship and the Irksomeness of Labor," *American Journal of Sociology*, **4**(2), September, pp. 187–201. [Reprinted in Veblen (1934b); Selection 16 in this volume.]

(1898e) Review of *Reflections on the Formation and the Distribution of Riches* by A. R. J. Turgot, in *Journal of Political Economy*, **6**(4), September, pp. 575–76. [Reprinted in Veblen (1973).]

(1898f) "The Beginnings of Ownership." *American Journal of Sociology*, **4**(3), November, pp. 352–65. [Reprinted in Veblen (1934b); Selection 17 in this volume.]

(1899a) "The Barbarian Status of Women," *American Journal of Sociology*, **4**(4), January, pp. 503–14. [Reprinted in Veblen (1934b); Selection 18 in this volume.]

(1899b) "The Preconceptions of Economic Science: I," *Quarterly Journal of Economics*, **13**(2), January, pp. 121–50. [Reprinted in Veblen (1919j); Part I of Selection 19 in this volume.]

(1899c) *The Theory of the Leisure Class: An Economic Study in the Evolution of Institutions*. (New York: Macmillan). [Chapter VIII is Selection 21 in this volume.] Note: title of book changed in 1905 to *The Theory of the Leisure Class: An Economic Study of Institutions*.

(1899d) "The Preconceptions of Economic Science: II," *Quarterly Journal of Economics*, **13**(4), July, pp. 396–426. [Reprinted in Veblen (1919j); Part II of Selection 19 in this volume.]

(1899e) Review of *The Development of English Thought: A Study in the Economic Interpretation of History* by Simon N. Patten, *Annals of the American Academy of Political and Social Science*, **14**, July, pp. 125–31. [Reprinted in Veblen (1973); Selection 20 in this volume.]

(1899f) "Mr. Cummings's Strictures on *The Theory of the Leisure Class*," *Journal of Political Economy*, **8**(1), December, pp. 106–17. [Reprinted in Veblen (1934b); Selection 22 in this volume.]

(1900a) "The Preconceptions of Economic Science: III," *Quarterly Journal of Economics*, **14**(2), February, pp. 240–69. [Reprinted in Veblen (1919j); Part III of Selection 19 in this volume.]

(1900b) Review of *The Wheat Problem, Revised, with an Answer to Various Critics* by Sir William Crooks, *Journal of Political Economy*, **8**(2), March, pp. 284–86. [Reprinted in Veblen (1973).]

(1900c) Review of *Die Entstehung des socialen Problems* by Arnold Fischer, *Journal of Political Economy*, **8**(2), March, pp. 286–87. [Reprinted in Veblen (1973).]

(1900d) Review of *Pamphlets socialistes: Le droit à la pareses; La religion du capital; L'appetit vendu; Pie IX au paradis* by Paul Lafargue, *Journal of Political Economy*, **8**(2), March, pp. 287–88. [Reprinted in Veblen (1973).]

(1900e) Review of *Social Laws: An Outline of Sociology* by Gabriel Tarde (translated from the French by Howard C. Warren, with a Preface by James Mark Baldwin), *Journal of Political Economy*, **8**(4), September, pp. 562–63. [Reprinted in Veblen (1973); Selection 23 in this volume.]

(1900f) Review of *The Impending Crisis; Conditions Resulting from the Concentration of Wealth in the United States* by Basil A. Bauroff, *Journal of Political Economy*, **9**(1), December, pp. 159–60. [Reprinted in Veblen (1973).]

(1901a) "Industrial and Pecuniary Employments," *Publications of the American Economic Association*, Series 3, **2**(1), February, pp. 190–235. [Reprinted in Veblen (1919j); Selection 24 in this volume.]

(1901b) "Gustav Schmoller's Economics," *Quarterly Journal of Economics*, **16**(1), November, pp. 69–93. [Reprinted in Veblen (1919j); Selection 25 in this volume.]

(1902a) "Arts and Crafts," *Journal of Political Economy*, **11**(1), December, pp. 108–11. [Reprinted in Veblen (1934b).]

(1902b) Review of *Associations industrielles et commerciales: Fédérations – Ententes partialles – Syndicats – Cartels – Comptoirs – Affiliations – Trusts* by Jules Gernaert and Vte. De Herbais de Thun, *Journal of Political Economy*, **11**(1), December, pp. 130–31. [Reprinted in Veblen (1973).]

(1902c) Review of *Psychologie économique* by Gabriel Tarde, *Journal of Political Economy*, **11**(1), December, pp. 146–48. [Reprinted in Veblen (1973); Selection 26 in this volume.]

580   *Bibliographies*

(1903a) "The Use of Loan Credit in Modern Business," *Decennial Publications of the University of Chicago*, Series 1, **4**, March, pp. 31–50. [Reprinted in Veblen (1904b).]

(1903b) Review of *Der moderne Kapitalismus* by Werner Sombart, *Journal of Political Economy*, **11**(2), March, pp. 300–305. [Reprinted in Veblen (1973); Selection 27 in this volume.]

(1903c) Review of *Værdi – og Prillærens Historie* by T. H. Aschehoug, *Journal of Political Economy*, **11**(2), March, p. 306. [Reprinted in Veblen (1973).]

(1903d) Review of *L'Impérialisme allemand* by Maurice Lair, *Journal of Political Economy*, **11**(2), March, p. 311. [Reprinted in Veblen (1973).]

(1903e) Review of *Imperialism: a Study* by J. A. Hobson, *Journal of Political Economy*, **11**(2), March, pp. 311–14. [Reprinted in Veblen (1973).]

(1903f) Review of *The New Empire* by Brooks Adams, *Journal of Political Economy*, **11**(2), March, pp. 314–15. [Reprinted in Veblen (1973).]

(1903g) Review of *Financial Crises and Periods of Industrial and Commercial Depression* by Theodore E. Burton, *Journal of Political Economy*, **11**(2), March, pp. 324–26. [Reprinted in Veblen (1973).]

(1903h) Review of *Pure Sociology: A Treatise Concerning the Origin and Spontaneous Development of Society* by Lester F. Ward, *Journal of Political Economy*, **11**(4), September, pp. 655–56. [Reprinted in Veblen (1973); Selection 28 in this volume.]

(1903i) Review of *Bevölkerungsbewegung, Kapitalbildung und periodische Wirtschaftskrisen* by Ludwig Pohle, *Journal of Political Economy*, **11**(4), September, pp. 656–57. [Reprinted in Veblen (1973).]

(1903j) Review of *Kartell und Trust: Vergleichende Untersuchungen über dem Wesen und Bedeutung* by S. Tschievschky, *Journal of Political Economy*, **11**(4), September, pp. 657–58. [Reprinted in Veblen (1973).]

(1904a) "An Early Experiment in Trusts," *Journal of Political Economy*, **12**(2), March, pp. 270–79. [Reprinted in Veblen (1919j).]

(1904b) *The Theory of Business Enterprise* (New York: Charles Scribners). [Chapter VI is Selection 29 in this volume.]

(1904c) Review of *Zur Genesis des modernen Kapitalismus: Forschungen zur Entstehung der grossen burgerlichen Kapitalvermogen am Ausgang des Mittelalters und zu Beginn der Neuzeit, zunachst in Augsburg* by Jacob Streider, *Journal of Political Economy*, **13**(1), December, pp. 120–22. [Reprinted in Veblen (1973).]

(1904d) Review of *An Inquiry into the Nature and Causes of the Wealth of Nations* by Adam Smith, *Journal of Political Economy*, **13**(1), December, p. 136. [Reprinted in Veblen (1973).]

(1904e) Review of *Adam Smith* by Frances W. Hirst, *Journal of Political Economy*, **13**(1), December, pp. 136–37. [Reprinted in Veblen (1973).]

(1905a) Review of *The Code of Hammurabi, King of Babylon about 2250 B. C. Autographed Text, Transliteration, Translation, Glossary, Index of Subjects, Lists of Proper Names, Signs, Numerals, Corrections and Erasures, with Map, Frontispiece, and Photograph of Text* by Robert Francis Harper, *Journal of Political Economy*, **13**(2), March, pp. 319–20. [Reprinted in Veblen (1973).]

(1905b) "Credit and Prices," *Journal of Political Economy*, **13**(3), June, pp. 460–72. [Reprinted in Veblen (1934b).]

(1906a) "The Place of Science in Modern Civilization," *American Journal of Sociology*, **11**(5), March, pp. 585–609. [Reprinted in Veblen (1919j); Selection 30 in this volume.]

(1906b) "The Socialist Economics of Karl Marx and His Followers. I: The Theories of Karl Marx," *Quarterly Journal of Economics*, **20**(3), August, pp. 575–95. [Reprinted in Veblen (1919j); Part I of Selection 31 in this volume.]

(1907a) "The Socialist Economics of Karl Marx and His Followers. II: The Later Marxism," *Quarterly Journal of Economics*, **21**(1), February, pp. 299–322. [Reprinted in Veblen (1919j); Part II of Selection 31 in this volume.]

(1907b) Review of *The Cost of Competition, An Effort at the Understanding of Familiar Facts* by Sidney A. Reeve, *Yale Review*, **16**, May, pp. 92–95. [Reprinted in Veblen (1973).]

(1908a) "Professor Clark's Economics," *Quarterly Journal of Economics*, **22**(2), February, pp. 147–95. [Reprinted in Veblen (1919j); Selection 32 in this volume.]

(1908b) "Fisher's Capital and Income," *Political Science Quarterly*, **23**(1), March, pp. 112–28. [Reprinted in Veblen (1934b); first part of Selection 35 in this volume.]

(1908c) "On the Nature of Capital, *Quarterly Journal of Economics*, **22**(4), August, pp. 517–42. [Reprinted in Veblen (1919j); Part I of Selection 33 in this volume.]

(1908d) "The Evolution of the Scientific Point of View," *University of California Chronicle*, **10**(4), October, pp. 395–416. [Reprinted in Veblen (1919j); Selection 34 in this volume.]

(1908e) "On the Nature of Capital: Investment, Intangible Assets, and the Pecuniary Magnate," *Quarterly Journal of Economics*, **23**(1), November, pp. 104–36. [Reprinted in Veblen (1919j); Part II of Selection 33 in this volume.]

(1909a) "Fisher's Rate of Interest," *Political Science Quarterly*, **24**(2), June, pp. 296–303. [Reprinted in Veblen (1934b); second part of Selection 35 in this volume.]

(1909b) Review of *L'individualisme économique et social: ses origines – son évolution – ses formes contemporaines* by Albert Schatz, *Journal of Political Economy*, **17**(6), June, pp. 378–79. [Reprinted in Veblen (1973).]

(1909c) "The Limitations of Marginal Utility," *Journal of Political Economy*, **17**(9), November, pp. 620–36. [Reprinted in Veblen (1919j); Selection 36 in this volume.]

(1910) "Christian Morals and the Competitive System," *International Journal of Ethics*, **20**(2), January, pp. 168–85. [Reprinted in Veblen (1934b).]

(1913a) "The Mutation Theory and the Blond Race," *Journal of Race Development*, **3**(4), April, pp. 491–507. [Reprinted in Veblen (1919j); Selection 37 in this volume.]

(1913b) "The Blond Race and the Aryan Culture," *University of Missouri Bulletin, Science Series*, **2**(3), April, pp. 39–57. [Reprinted in Veblen (1919j).]

(1914) *The Instinct of Workmanship, and the State of the Industrial Arts* (New York: Macmillan). [The Preface, Chapter I, and excerpt from Chapter II form Selection 38 in this volume.]

(1915a) *Imperial Germany and the Industrial Revolution* (New York: Macmillan).

(1915b) "The Opportunity of Japan," *Journal of Race Development*, **6**, July, pp. 23–38. [Reprinted in Veblen (1934b).]

(1915c) Review of *Der Bourgeois: zur Geistesgeschichte des modernen Wirtschafts-menschen* by Werner Sombart, *Journal of Political Economy*, **23**(8), October, pp. 846–48. [Reprinted in Veblen (1973).]

(1916) Review of *The Ruling Caste and Frenzied Trade in Germany* by Maurice Millioud, *Journal of Political Economy*, **24**(10), December, pp. 1019–20. [Reprinted in Veblen (1973).]

(1917a) "Another German Apologist," review of *England, Its Political Organisation and Development and the War Against Germany* by Edward Meyer, *Dial*, April 19, pp. 344–45.

(1917b) *An Inquiry into the Nature of Peace and the Terms of its Perpetuation* (New York: Macmillan).

(1917c) "The Japanese Lose Hopes for Germany," letter to *New Republic*, June 30, pp. 246–47. [Reprinted in Veblen (1934b).]

(1918a) "On the General Principles of a Policy of Reconstruction," *Journal of the National Institute of Social Sciences*, **4**, April, pp. 37–46. [Reprinted in Veblen (1973).]

(1918b) "A Policy of Reconstruction," *New Republic*, April 13, pp. 318–20. [Reprinted in Veblen (1934b).]

(1918c) "Passing of National Frontiers," *Dial*, April 25, pp. 387–90. [Reprinted in Veblen (1934b).]

(1918d) "Menial Servants during the Period of the War." *Public*, May 11, pp. 595–99. [Reprinted in Veblen (1934b).]

(1918e) "Farm Labour for the Period of the War: I," *Public*, July 13, pp. 882–85. [Reprinted in Veblen (1934b).]

(1918f) "The War and Higher Learning." *Dial*, July 18, pp. 45–49. [Reprinted in Veblen (1934b).]

(1918g) *The Higher Learning in America: A Memorandum on the Conduct of Universities by Business Men* (New York: Huebsch).

(1918h) "Farm Labour for the Period of the War: II." *Public*, July 20, pp. 918–22. [Reprinted in Veblen (1934b).]

(1918i) "Farm Labour for the Period of the War: III." *Public*, July 27, pp. 947–52. [Reprinted in Veblen (1934b).]

(1918j) "Farm Labour for the Period of the War: IV." *Public*, August 3, pp. 981–85. [Reprinted in Veblen (1934b).]

(1918k) "The Modern Point of View and the New Order: I," *Dial*, October 19, pp. 289–93.

(1918l) "The Modern Point of View and the New Order: II." *Dial*, November 2, pp. 349–54.

(1918m) "The Modern Point of View and the New Order: III." *Dial*, November 16, pp. 409–14.

(1918n) "The Modern Point of View and the New Order: IV." *Dial*, November 30, pp. 482–88.

(1918o) "The Modern Point of View and the New Order: V." *Dial*, December 14, pp. 543–49.

(1918p) "The Modern Point of View and the New Order: VI." *Dial*, December 28, pp. 605–11.

(1919a) "The Modern Point of View and the New Order: VII." *Dial*, January 11, pp. 19–24.

(1919b) "The Modern Point of View and the New Order: VIII." *Dial*, January 25, pp. 75–82.

(1919c) *The Vested Interests and the State of the Industrial Arts.* (New York: Huebsch). Note: title of book changed in 1920 to *The Vested Interests and the Common Man.*

(1919d) "Bolshevism is a Menace – to Whom?" *Dial*, February 22, pp. 174–79. [Reprinted in Veblen (1934b).]

(1919e) "The Intellectual Pre-eminence of Jews in Modern Europe," *Political Science Quarterly*, **34**(1), March, pp. 33–42. [Reprinted in Veblen (1934b).]

(1919f) "On the Nature and Uses of Sabotage," *Dial*, April 5, pp. 341–46.

(1919g) "Bolshevism is a Menace to the Vested Interests," editorial, *Dial*, April 5, pp. 360–61.

(1919h) "Sabotage," editorial, *Dial*, April 5, p. 363.

(1919i) "Congressional Sabotage," editorial, *Dial*, April 5, p. 363.

(1919j) *The Place of Science in Modern Civilization and Other Essays* (New York: Huebsch).

(1919k) "Immanuel Kant on Perpetual Peace," editorial, *Dial*, May 3, p. 469. [Reprinted in Veblen (1934b).]

(1919l) "Peace," *Dial*, May 17, pp. 485–87. [Reprinted in Veblen (1934b).]

(1919m) "The Industrial Systems and the Captains of Industry," *Dial*, May 31, pp. 552–57.

(1919n) "The Captains of Finance and the Engineers," editorial, *Dial*, June 14, pp. 599–606.

(1919o) *"Panem et Circenses,"* editorial, *Dial*, June 14, p. 609. [Reprinted in Veblen (1934b).]

(1919p) "'Open Covenants Openly Arrived At' and the Elder Statesmen," editorial, *Dial*, July 12, pp. 25–26. [Reprinted in Veblen (1934b).]

(1919q) "A World Safe for the Vested Interests," editorial, *Dial*, July 12, pp. 26.

(1919r) "The Red Terror – At Last it Has Come to America," editorial, *Dial*, September 6, p. 205.

(1919s) "The Red Terror and the Vested Interests," editorial, *Dial*, September 6, pp. 206.

(1919t) "Bolshevism and the Vested Interests in America: I," *Dial*, October 4, pp. 296–301.

(1919u) "Bolshevism and the Vested Interests in America: II." *Dial*, October 18, pp. 339–46.

(1919v) "Bolshevism and the Vested Interests in America: III." *Dial*, November 1, pp. 373–80.

(1919w) "The Twilight Peace of the Armistice." editorial, *Dial*, November 15, p. 443. [Reprinted in Veblen (1934b).]

(1920) Review of *Economic Consequences of the Peace* by John Maynard Keynes, *Political Science Quarterly*, **35**(3), September, pp. 467–72. [Reprinted in Veblen (1934b).]

(1921a) *The Engineers and the Price System* (New York: Harcourt Brace and World).

(1921b) "Between Bolshevism and War." *Freeman*, May 25, pp. 248–51. [Reprinted in Veblen (1934b).]

(1922) "Dementia Præcox." *Freeman*, June 21, pp. 344–47. [Reprinted in Veblen (1934b).]

(1923a) "The Captain of Industry." *Freeman*, April 18, pp. 127–32.

(1923b) "The Timber Lands and Oil Fields: I," *Freeman*, May 23, pp. 248–50.

(1923c) "The Timber Lands and Oil Fields: II," *Freeman*, May 30, pp. 272–74.

(1923d) "The Independent Farmer," *Freeman*, June 13, pp. 321–24.

(1923e) "The Country Town: I." *Freeman*, July 11, pp. 417–20.

(1923f) "The Country Town: II," *Freeman*, July 18, pp. 440–43.

(1923g) *Absentee Ownership and Business Enterprise in Recent Times; The Case of America* (New York: Huebsch).

(1925a) "Economic Theory in the Calculable Future." *American Economic Review (Papers and Proceedings)*, **15**(1, Supplement), March, pp. 48–55. [Reprinted in Veblen (1934b).]

(1925b) Introduction to translation of the *Laxdaela Saga* (New York: Huebsch).

(1932a) "Suggestions Touching the Working Program of an Inquiry into the Prospective Terms of Peace" (memorandum submitted to U.S. Presidential Committee of Inquiry in 1917), *Political Science Quarterly*, **47**(2), June, pp. 186–89. [Reprinted in Veblen (1934b).]

(1932b) "An Outline of a Policy for the Control of the 'Economic Penetration' of Backward Countries and of Foreign Investments" (memorandum submitted to U.S. Presidential Committee of Inquiry in 1917), *Political Science Quarterly*, **47**(2), June, pp. 189–203. [Reprinted in Veblen (1934b).]

(1932c) "An Unpublished Paper on the I. W. W. by Thorstein Veblen" (memorandum for Statistical Division of the U.S. Food Administration in 1918), *Journal of Political Economy*, **46**(6), December, pp. 496–807. [Reprinted in Veblen (1934b).]

(1933a) "An Unpublished Memorandum of Thorstein Veblen on Government Regulation of the Food Supply" (memorandum for Statistical Division of the U.S. Food Administration in 1918), *Southwestern Social Science Quarterly*, **13**(4), March, pp. 372–77. [Reprinted in Veblen (1934b).]

(1933b) "As to a Proposed Inquiry into Baltic and Cretan Antiquities" (memorandum submitted to Carnegie Institution in 1910), *American Journal of Sociology*, **39**(2), September pp. 237–41. [Reprinted in Veblen (1973).]

(1933c) Report ad interim to Raymond Pearl on Trip through Prairie States on Behalf of the U.S. Food Administration (written 1918), *American Economic Review*, **23**(3), September, pp. 478–79.

(1934a) "An Experiment in Eugenics" (written 1927), first published in Veblen (1934b).

(1934b) *Essays on Our Changing Order*, ed. Leon Ardzrooni (New York: Viking Press).

(1964a) "Wire Barrage" (memorandum of 1920), first published in Veblen (1964b).

(1964b) *Essays on Our Changing Order with the Addition of a Recently Discovered Memorandum "Wire Barrage" Supplied by Joseph Dorfman*, ed. Leon Ardzrooni (New York: Viking Press).

(1973) *Essays, Reviews and Reports*, ed. with an introduction by Joseph Dorfman (New York: Augustus Kelley).

Translations by Thorstein Veblen

Anon. *Laxdaela Saga* (1925) (New York: Huebsch).

Cohn, Gustav (1895) *The Science of Finance*, translated from *System der Finanzwissenschaft* (Chicago, IL: University of Chicago Press).

Lassalle, Ferdinand (1900) *Science and the Workingman*, translated from *Die Wissenschaft und die Arbeiter* (Chicago, IL: Charles H. Kerr). Republished 1914 in *The German Classics*, vol. 10 (New York: German Publication Society).

2. List of Works Cited by Thorstein Veblen[1]

Adler, Georg (1887) *Die Grundlagen der Karl Marx'schen Kritik der bestehendenVolkswirtschaft* (Tübingen: H. Laupp).

---

1 The purpose of this bibliography is to assist readers in locating the sources that Veblen cites in the selections included in this volume. (In other works, he cites many additional sources as well.) To this end, we have sought to provide fuller bibliographic information than Veblen's own writings furnish, identifying titles, dates, editions, publishers, and places of publication as accurately as possible in the absence (in most cases) of direct evidence as to which texts Veblen himself used. In presenting this information, we have standardized it following present-day scholarly conventions, which differ from the more idiosyncratic citation practices of Veblen and his contemporaries.

Adler, Max (1904) "Kausalität und Teleologie im Streite um die Wissenschaft," *Marx-Studien*, **1**, pp. 3–241.

Ammon, Otto (1895) *Die Gesellschaftsordnung und ihre natürlichen Grundlagen* (Jena: Fischer).

Ashley, W. J (1888) *An Introduction to English Economic History and Theory* (London: Rivingtons).

Baden-Powell, B. H (1892) *The Land-Systems of British India* (Oxford: Clarendon).

Barrows, David Prescott (1900) *The Ethno-Botany of the Coahuilla Indians of Southern California* (Chicago: University of Chicago Press).

Bean, Robert Bennett (1909) "Filipino Types," *Philippine Journal of Science*, **4**, pp. 263–446.

Bebel, August (1883) *Die Frau in der Vergangenheit, Gegenwart und Zukunft* (Zurich: J. Schabelitz).

Bentham, Jeremy (1789) *Introduction to the Principles of Morals and Legislation* (London: T. Payne).

Bernstein, Eduard (1899) *Die Voraussetzungen des Sozialismus und die Aufgaben der Sozialdemokratie* (Stuttgart: J. H. W. Dietz).

——(1901) *Zur Geschichte und Theorie des Sozialismus* (Berlin : Akademie Verlag für Soziale Wissenschaft).

——(1906) *Die heutige Sozialdemokratie in Theorie und Praxis* (Munich: G. Birk & Co.).

Birck, Laurits V. (1902) "Driftsherrens Gevinst," Paper presented at meeting of the Danish National Economic Association, December 1901. *Nationaløkonomisk Tidsskrift*, **3**, pp. 72–76.

Boas, Franz (1888) "The Central Eskimo." *Sixth Annual Report of the Bureau of American Ethnology, 1884–'85* (Washington, DC: Government Printing Office).

Böhm-Bawerk, Eugen von (1889) *Positive Theorie des Kapitales* (Innsbruck: Wagner).

——(1890) *Capital and Interest* (New York: Macmillan).

——(1898) *Karl Max and the Close of His System* (New York: Macmillan).

Bonar, James (1885) *Malthus and His Work* (New York: Harper & Brothers).

——(1893) *Philosophy and Political Economy in Some of Their Historical Relations* (New York: Macmillan).

Brunhuber, Robert (1906) *Die heutige Sozialdemokratie* (Jena: Fischer).

Bücher, Karl (1896) *Arbeit und Rythmus* (Leipzig: Trübner).

——(1898) *Entstehung der Volkswirtschaft: Vorträge und Versuche*, 2nd edn (Tübingen: Laupp).

Burgess, Gelett (1895) *The Purple Cow* (San Francisco: William Doxey).

Cairnes, J. E. (1873) *Essays in Political Economy* (New York: Macmillan).

——(1874) *Some Leading Principles of Political Economy Newly Expounded* (New York: Harper & Brothers).

——(1875) *Character and Logical Method of Political Economy*, 2nd edn (New York: Macmillan).

Calwer, Richard (1896) *Einführung in den Socialismus* (Leipzig: Georg H. Wigand).

Cannan, Edwin (1898) *A History of the Theories of Production and Distribution in English Political Economy from 1776 to 1848* (London: Staples).

Clark, John Bates (1898) "The Future of Economic Theory." *Quarterly Journal of Economics*, **13**, pp. 1–14.

——(1899) *The Distribution of Wealth* (New York: Macmillan).

——(1907) *The Essentials of Economic Theory, as Applied to Modern Problems of Industry and Public Policy* (New York: Macmillan).

——(1910) "The Phenomena of Economic Dynamics—Discussion." *American Economic Association Quarterly*, **11**, pp. 122–35.

Cook, O. F. (1904) "Food Plant of Ancient America." *Annual Report of the Smithsonian Institution, 1903*, pp. 481–97.

Cummings, John (1899) "The Theory of the Leisure Class." *Journal of Political Economy*, **7**, pp. 425–55.

Cushing, Frank Hamilton (1886) "A Study of Pueblo Pottery as illustrative of Zuñi Culture Growth." *Fourth Annual Report of the Bureau of American Ethnology, 1882–'83* (Washington, DC: Government Printing Office).

——(1896) "Outlines of Zuñi Creation Myths." *Thirteenth Annual Report of the Bureau of American Ethnology, 1891–'92* (Washington, D.C.: Government Printing Office).

Deniker, Joseph (1900) *The Races of Man: An Outline of Anthropology and Ethnography* (London: Walter Scott).

——(1904) "Les Six Races Composant la Population Actuelle de l'Europe," *Journal of the Anthropological Institute of Great Britain and Ireland*, **34**, pp. 181–206.

Dorsey, J. Owen (1894) "A Study of Siouan Cults." *Eleventh Annual Report of the Bureau of American Ethnology, 1889–'90* (Washington, D.C.: Government Printing Office).

Dunne, Finley Peter (1898) *Mr. Dooley in Peace and in War* (Boston: Small, Maynard).

——(1902) *Observations by Mr. Dooley* (London: Heinemann).

Eberstadt, Rudolph (1901) *Der deutsche Kapitalmarkt* (Leipzig: Duncker & Humboldt).

Ehrenberg, Richard (1896) *Das Zeitalter der Fugger: Geldkapital und Creditverkehr im 16. Jahrhundert* (Jena: Fischer).

Emery, Henry Crosby (1900) "The Place of the Speculator in the Theory of Distribution," Paper presented at proceedings of 12th annual meeting of the American Economic Association. *Publications of the American Economic Association*, 3rd series, **1**, pp. 103–22.

Endemann, Wilhelm (1863) *Die nationalökonomischen Grundsätze der kanonistischen Lehre* (Jena: Fischer).

Engels, Friedrich (1885) "Preface." in Karl Marx, *Capital: A Critique of Political Economy*, volume 2 (Chicago: Charles H. Kerr and Co.), pp. 1–42.

——(c. 1887–1895) Various articles. *Die neue Zeit: Wochenschrift der Deutschen Sozialdemokratie.*

——(1888) "Preface to the English Edition," in Karl Marx and Frederick Engels, *Manifesto of the Communist Party* (Chicago: Charles H. Kerr and Co.), pp. 15–22.

——(1890) *Ursprung der Familie* (Stuttgart: J. H. Deitz).

——(1892) *The Development of Socialism from Utopia to Science* (New York: The "People" Educational Library).

——(1895) Letters. *Die Sozialistische Akademiker.* Issue of October 1.

——(1903) *Feuerbach: The Roots of Socialist Philosophy* (Chicago: C. H. Kerr).

Ferri, Enrico (1897) *Socialisme et Science Positive* (Paris: V. Giard & E. Briére).

Fetter, Frank A. (1900) "Recent Discussion of the Capital Concept," *Quarterly Journal of Economics*, **15**, pp. 1–45.

——(1905) *The Principles of Economics, with Applications to Practical Problems* (New York: Century).

——(1907) "The Nature of Capital and Income," *Journal of Political Economy*, **15**, pp. 129–48.

Fewkes, Jesse Walter (1898) "Archeological Expedition to Arizona in 1895," *Seventeenth Annual Report of the Bureau of American Ethnology, 1895–'96*, part 2 (Washington, D.C.: Government Printing Office).

——(1900) "Tusayan Migration Traditions." *Nineteenth Annual Report of the Bureau of American Ethnology, 1897–'98* (Washington, D.C.: Government Printing Office).

Fisher, Irving (1906) *The Nature of Capital and Income* (New York: Macmillan).

——(1907a) "Professor Fetter on Capital and Income," *Journal of Political Economy*, **15**, pp. 421–34.

——(1907b) *The Rate of Interest: Its Nature, Determination and Relation to Economic Phenomena* (New York: Macmillan).

Foxwell, H. S (1899) "Introduction," in Anton Menger, *The Right to the Whole Produce of Labour* (New York: Macmillan), pp. v–cx.

Frazer, Sir James George (1905) *Lectures on the Early History of the Kingship* (New York: Macmillan).

Ghent, William James (1902) *Our Benevolent Feudalism* (London: Macmillan).

Goldscheid, Rudolf (1906) *Verelendungs- oder Meliorationstheorie?* (Berlin: Verlag der Sozialistischen Monatshefte).

Gonner, E. C. K. (1895) "Introductory Essay," in David Ricardo, *On the Principles of Political Economy and Taxation*, ed. E. C. K. Gonner (London: Bell), pp. xxiii–lxix.

Groos, Karl (1896) *Die Spiele der Thiere* (Jena: Fischer).

——(1901) *The Play of Man* (New York: Appleton).

Hadley, Arthur Twining (1896) *Economics: An Account of the Relations between Private Property and Public Welfare* (New York: G. P. Putnam's Sons).

Hasbach, Wilhelm (1890) *Die Allgemeinen, philosophische Grundlagen der von François Quesnay und Adam Smith begründeten politischen Ökonomie* (Leipzig: Duncker & Humboldt).

Hildebrand, Richard (1896) *Recht und Sitte auf den primitiveren wirtschaftlichen Kulturstufen* (Jena: Fischer).

Holmes, William Henry (1888) "The Ancient Art of Chiriqui, Columbia," *Sixth Annual Report of the Bureau of American Ethnology, 1884–'85* (Washington, D.C.: Government Printing Office).

James, William (1890) *The Principles of Psychology*, 2 vols. (New York: Holt).

Jennings, H. S. (1906) *The Behavior of the Lower Animals* (New York: Columbia University Press).

Kant, Immanuel (1878) *Kritik der Urteilskraft*, ed. Karl Kerbach (Leipzig: Reclam).

Kautsky, Karl (1892) *Das Erfuter Programm in seinem Grundsätzlichen Theil* (Stuttgart: J. H. W. Dietz).

——(1893) *Der Parlamentarismus, die Volksgesetzgebung und die Sozialdemokratie* (Stuttgart: J. H. W. Dietz).

——(1899) *Bernstein und das Sozialdemokratische Programm* (Stuttgart: J. H. W. Dietz).

Keane, Augustus Henry (1900) *Man, Past and Present* (Cambridge: Cambridge University Press).

Keynes, John Neville (1890) *Scope and Method of Political Economy* (New York: Macmillan).

Knapp, Georg Friedrich (1897) *Grundherrschaft und Rittergut* (Leipzig: Duncker & Humboldt).

Knies, Karl (1873) *Geld und Credit* (Berlin: Weidmann).

Kőrösi, József (1900) *Die Ergebnisse der finanziellen Actiengesellschaften* (Berlin: Puttkammer & Mühlbrecht).

Labriola, Antonio (1897) *Essais sur la conception matérialiste de l'histoire* (Paris: V. Giard & E. Briére).

Lapouge, Georges Vacher de (1896) *Les Sélections sociales* (Paris: Fontemoing).

——(1897) "The Fundamental Laws of Anthropo-sociology," *Journal of Political Economy*, **6**, pp. 54–92.

——(1909) *Race et milieu social: essais d'anthroposociologie* (Paris: Marcel Rivière).

Loeb, Jacques (1890) *Der Heliotropismus der Thiere und seine Uebereinstimmung mit dem Heliotropismus der Pflanzen* (Würzburg: Hertz).

——(1900) *Comparative Physiology of the Brain and Comparative Psychology* (New York: G.P. Putman's Sons).

London Economist (1890) Issue of September 13.

Lorenz, Max (1896) *Die Marxistische Socialdemokratie* (Leipzig: Georg H. Wigand).

Lumholtz, Carl (1902) *Unknown Mexico* (New York: C. Scribners & Sons).

Mallock, William H (1898) *Aristocracy and Evolution: A Study of the Rights, the Origins and the Social Functions of the Wealthier Classes* (New York: Macmillan).

Man, E. H (1883) "On the Aboriginal Inhabitants of the Andaman Islands: I," *Journal of the Anthropological Institute of Great Britain and Ireland*, **12**, pp. 69–116.

——(1883) "On the Aboriginal Inhabitants of the Andaman Islands: II," *Journal of the Anthropological Institute of Great Britain and Ireland*, 12, pp. 117–75.

——(1883) "On the Aboriginal Inhabitants of the Andaman Islands: III," *Journal of the Anthropological Institute of Great Britain and Ireland*, **12**, pp. 327–434.

Marshall, Alfred (1891) *Principles of Economics*, 2nd edn (London: Macmillan).

——(1892) "A Reply [to William Cunningham, 'The Perversion of Economic History']," *Economic Journal*, **2**, pp. 507–19.

——(1895) *Principles of Economics*, 3rd edn (London: Macmillan).

——(1897) "The Old Generation of Economists and the New," *Quarterly Journal of Economics*, **11**, pp. 115–35.

Marx, Karl ([1847] 1896) *Misére de la philosophie*. With a preface by Friedrich Engels (Paris: V. Giard & E. Briére).

——([1859] 1897) *Zur Kritik der politischen Oekonomie* (Stuttgart: J. H. W. Deitz).

——(1890) *Capital: A Critical Analysis of Capitalist Production*, 4 volumes, ed. Friedrich Engels, trans. from 3rd German edn (New York: Humboldt).

——(1890–1894) *Das Kapital: Kritik der politischen Oekonomie*, 3 vols, ed. Friedrich Engels, 4th. edn (Hamburg: Otto Meissner).

——(1904) *A Contribution to the Critique of Political Economy* (New York: International Library Publishing Co.).

——, and Friedrich Engels (1888) *Manifesto of the Communist Party* (Chicago: Charles H. Kerr and Co.).

McDougall, William (1908) *An Introduction to Social Psychology* (London: Methuen & Co.).

Meade, Edward Sherwood (1902) "Capitalization of the United States Steel Corporation," *Quarterly Journal of Economics*, **16**, pp. 214–32.

——(1911) *Trust Finance: A Study of the Genesis, Organization, and Management of Industrial Combinations* (New York: D. Appleton and Company).

Menger, Anton (1899) *The Right to the Whole Produce of Labour* (New York: Macmillan).

——(1903) *Neue Staatslehre* (Jena: Fischer).

——(1905) *Neue Sittenlehre* (Jena: Fischer).

Mill, John Stuart (1848) *Principles of Political Economy, with Some of Their Applications to Social Philosophy.* (London: Longmans, Green and Co.).

Morgan, C. Lloyd (1894) *An Introduction to Comparative Psychology* (London: W. Scott).

——(1896) *Habit and Instinct* (London: E. Arnold).

Mortillet, Gabriel de (1883) *Le Préhistorique* (Paris: C. Reinwald).

——(1897) *Formation de la nation française* (Paris: F. Alcan).

Müller, Sophus (1907) *L'europe préhistorique. Principes d'Archéologie préhistorique* (Paris: J. Lamarre).

Mun, Thomas (1664) *England's Treasure By Forraign Trade, or. the Ballance of Our Forraign Trade Is the Rule of Our Treasure* (London: J. G. for Thomas Clark).

Murdoch, John (1892) "Ethnological Results of the Point Barrow Expedition," *Ninth Annual Report of the Bureau of American Ethnology, 1887–'88* (Washington, D.C.: Government Printing Office).

Nemours, Dupont de (1846) Correspondence avec J. B. Say, in *Collection des Principaux Économistes: Les Physiocrates*, ed. Eugène Daire (Paris: Guillaumin).

Neue Zeit, Die: Wochenschrift der Deutshcen Sozialdemokratie (1883–1906) Various issues.

Nieboer, Herman Jeremias (1900) *Slavery as an Industrial System: Ethnological Researches* (The Hague: Martinus Nijhoff).

Oppenheimer, Franz (1903) *Das Grundgesetz der Marxschen Gesellschaftslehre* (Berlin: G. Reimer).

Pantaleoni, Maffeo (1898) *Pure Economics* (London: Macmillan).

Parmalee, Maurice (1913) *The Science of Human Behavior* (New York: Macmillan).

Patten, Simon N. (1899) *The Development of English Thought: A Study in the Economic Interpretation of History* (New York: Macmillan).

Payne, Edward John (1892) *History of the New World Called America* (New York: Macmillan).

Pearson, Karl (1892) *The Grammar of Science* (New York: Charles Scribner's Sons).

——(1897) *The Chances of Death and Other Studies in Evolution* (London: Edward Arnold).

Powell, John Wesley (1881) "Sketch of the Mythology of the North American Indians," *First Annual Report of the Bureau of American Ethnology, 1879–'80* (Washington, D.C.: Government Printing Office).

——(1901) "Sophiology, or the Science of Activities Designed to Give Instruction," *American Anthropologist*, **3**, pp. 51–79.

Pumpelly, Raphael (1908) *Explorations in Turkestan: Prehistoric Civilizations of Anau* (Washington, D.C: Carnegie Institution).

Quesnay, François (1846) *Le Droit Naturel*, in *Collection des Principaux Économistes : Les Physiocrates*, ed. Eugène Daire (Paris: Guillaumin).

Ricardo, David (1817) *On the Principles of Political Economy and Taxation* (London: John Murray).

Ridgeway, William (1909) "The Application of Zoölogical Laws to Man," Presidential Address to Section H of the British Association for Advancement of Science, September 1908, *Report of the Seventy-eighth Meeting of the British Association for Advancement of Science* (London: John Murray).

Ritchie, David George (1903) *Natural Rights: A Criticism of Some Political and Ethical Conceptions* (London: Swan Sonnenschein).

Rivière, François Byssot de la (1767) *L'Ordre naturel et essentiel des sociétés politiques* (Paris: Desaint).

Roscher, Wilhelm (1843) *Grundriss zu Vorlesungen über die Staatswirthschaft nach geschichtlicher Methode* (Göttingen: Dieterichschen Buchhandlung).

Schäffle, Albert (1872) *Das gesellschaftliche System der menschlichen Wirtschaft* (Tübingen: H. Laupp Buchhandlung).

——(1889) *The Quintessence of Socialism* (London: S. Sonnenschein & Co.).

——(1892) *The Impossibility of Social Democracy* (New York: C. Scribner's Sons).

Schmoller, Gustav (1898) *Über einige Grundfragen der Socialpolitik und der Volkswirtschaftslehre* (Leipzig: Duncker & Humboldt).

——(1900) *Grundriß der allgemeinen Volkswirtschaftslehre* (Leipzig: Duncker & Humboldt).

Schou, Vilhehn (1902) "Driftsherrens Gevinst." *Nationaløkonomisk Tidsskrift*, **3**, pp. 76–80.

Seligman, Edwin R. A. (1902) *The Economic Interpretation of History* (New York: Columbia University Press).

Seligmann, C. G., and Brenda Z. Seligmann (1911) *The Veddas* (Cambridge: Cambridge University Press).

Senior, Nassau William (1872) *Political Economy* (London: C. Griffin and Co.).

Sergi, Giuseppe (1898) *Arii e Italici* (Torino: Bocca).

——(1901) *The Mediterranean Race: A Study of the Origin of European Peoples* (London: Scott).

Shirres, L. P. (1893) *An Analysis of the Ideas of Economics* (London: Longmans, Green & Co.).

Skeat, Walter William and Blagden, Charles Otto (1906) *Pagan Races of the Malay Peninsula* (London: Macmillan).

Smart, William (1895) *Studies in Economics* (New York: Macmillan).

Smith, Adam (1759) *Theory of the Moral Sentiments* (London: A. Miller, A. Kincaid & J. Bell).

——([1776] 1887) *An Inquiry into the Nature and Causes of the Wealth of Nations* (London: Henry G. Bohn).

——(1896) *Lectures on Justice, Police, Revenue and Arms*, ed. Edwin Cannan (Oxford: Clarendon).

Sollas, William Johnson (1909) "Palaeolithic Races and their Modern Representatives," *Science Progress*, **4**, pp. 16–45.

——(1911) *Ancient Hunters and their Modern Representatives* (London: Macmillan).

Sombart, Werner (1902) *Der moderne Kapitalismus* (Torino: Utet).

——(1905) *Sozialismus und soziale Bewegung*, 5th edn (Jena: Fischer).

Spencer, Baldwin and Gillen, F. J. (1899) *The Native Tribes of North Central Australia* (London: Macmillan).

Spencer, Herbert (1851) *Social Statics* (London: John Chapman).

——(1872) *Principles of Psychology*, 2nd edn (London: Williams & Norgate).

——(1891) "Introduction, From Freedom to Bondage," in Thomas MacKay (ed.), *A Plea for Liberty: An Argument against Socialism and Socialistic Legislation* (New York: D. Appleton and Co.), pp. 3–23.

Stein, Ludwig (1903) *Die soziale Frage im Licht der Philosophie* (Stuttgart: F. Enke).

Stevenson, Matilda Coxe (1894) "The Sia," *Eleventh Annual Report of the Bureau of American Ethnology, 1889–'90* (Washington, D.C.: Government Printing Office).

Tarde, Gabriel (1899) *Social Laws: An Outline of Sociology* (New York: Arno).

——(1902) *Psychologie économique* (Paris: Félix Alcan).

Torrens, Robert (1821) *An Essay on the Production of Wealth* (London: Longman).

Turgot, Anne-Robert Jacques (1766) *Réflections sur la formation et la distribution des richesses* (Paris: V. Giard & E. Briére).

Tylor, Edward (1871) *Primitive Culture: Researches into the Development of Mythology, Philosophy, Religion, Language, Art, and Custom* (London: John Murray).

United States Census Office (1901–1903) *Census Reports: Twelfth Census of the United States*, 10 vols (Washington, D.C.: United States Census Office).

United States Industrial Commission (1900–1901) *Report of the Industrial Commission*, 13 vols (Washington, D.C.: Government Printing Office).

> Note: Readers seeking to track Veblen's citations (in Selection 29) to the *Report of the Industrial Commission* should note that Veblen's main interest is in volume XIII of this multi-part report, namely in the *Report of the Industrial Commission on Trusts and Industrial Combinations* (which itself was published in two parts). However, he occasionally cites, by volume number, other reports in the series as well.

Vorländer, Karl (1902) *Die neukantische Bewegung im Sozialismus* (Berlin: Reuther & Reichard).

Wallas, Graham (1908) *Human Nature in Politics* (London: Archibald Constable & Co.).

Ward, Lester (1903) *Pure Sociology: A Treatise Concerning the Origin and Spontaneous Development of Society* (New York: Macmillan).

Washburn, Margaret F (1908) *The Animal Mind: A Text-Book of Comparative Psychology* (New York: Macmillan).

Watkins, George Pendleton (1907) *The Growth of Large Fortunes* (New York: A. M. Kelly).

Webster, Hutton (1908) *Primitive Secret Societies* (New York: Macmillan).

Wells, David Collin (1899) Review of Thorstein Veblen, *The Theory of the Leisure Class*, *Yale Review*, **8**, pp. 213–18.

Willoughby, William Franklin (1901) "Integration of Industry in the United States." *Quarterly Journal of Economics*, **16**, pp. 94–115.

Wright, Chester W (1903) "The Holyoke Water Case." *Quarterly Journal of Economics*, **17**, pp. 342–6.

Zeyss, Richard (1899) *Adam Smith und der Eigennutz* (Tübingen: Laupp).

Other Authorities Referenced

Darwin, Charles
De Vries, Hugo
Hegel, G. W. F.
Høffding, Harald
Mendel, Gregor
Mucke, Richard
Rodbertus, Karl Johann

3. References Cited by Editors

Adamson, R. (1882) Review of *Immanuel Kant's Critique of Pure Reason*, by F. Max Müller, *Mind*, **7**, pp. 277–85.

Aldrich, Howard E., Geoffrey M. Hodgson, David L. Hull, Thorbjørn Knudsen, Joel Mokyr and Viktor J. Vanberg (2008) "In Defence of Generalized Darwinism." *Journal of Evolutionary Economics*, **18**(5), October, pp. 577–96.

[Anonymous] (1881) "The Centennial of Kant's *Kritik* at Saratoga, N.Y.," *Journal of Speculative Philosophy*, **15**, pp. 293–302.

Aristotle (1956) *Metaphysics*, edited and translated by John Warrington with an introduction by W. David Ross (London: Dent).

Arrow, Kenneth J. (1994) "Methodological Individualism and Social Knowledge," *American Economic Review (Papers and Proceedings)*, **84**(2), May, pp. 1–9.

Aspromourgos, Tony (1986) 'On the Origins of the term "Neoclassical"', *Cambridge Journal of Economics*, **10**(3), September, pp. 265–70.

Atack, Jeremy, and Passell, Peter (1994) *A New Economic View of American History*, 2nd edn (New York: W.W. Norton).

Ault, Richard W. and Ekelund, Robert B., Jr (1988) "Habit in Economic Analysis: Veblen and the Neoclassicals," *History of Political Economy*, **20**(3), Fall, pp. 431–45.

Ayres, Clarence E. (1918) *The Nature of the Relationship Between Ethics and Economics* (Chicago: University of Chicago Press).

——(1921a) "Instinct and Capacity – I: The Instinct of Belief-in-Instincts," *Journal of Philosophy*, **18**(21), October 13, pp. 561–65.

——(1921b) "Instinct and Capacity – II: Homo Domesticus," *Journal of Philosophy*, **18**(22), October 27, pp. 600–606.

——(1932) *Huxley* (New York: Norton).

——(1936) "Fifty Years' Developments in Ideas of Human Nature and Motivation," *American Economic Review (Papers and Proceedings)*, **26**(1), March, pp. 224–36.

——(1942) "Economic Value and Scientific Synthesis." *American Journal of Economics and Sociology*, **1**(4), July, pp. 343–60.

——(1944) *The Theory of Economic Progress*, 1st edn (Chapel Hill University of North Carolina Press).

——(1952) *The Industrial Economy: Its Technological Basis and Institutional Destiny* (Cambridge, MA: Houghton Mifflin).

——(1958) "Veblen's Theory of Instincts Reconsidered," in Douglas F. Dowd (ed.) *Thorstein Veblen: A Critical Appraisal* (Ithaca, NY: Cornell University Press), pp. 25–37.

——(1961) *Toward a Reasonable Society: The Values of Industrial Civilization* (Austin: University of Texas Press).

——(1973) "Prolegomenon to Institutionalism." introduction to the combined reprint of Clarence E. Ayres (1927) *Science: The False Messiah*, and Clarence E. Ayres (1929) *Holier Than Thou: The Way of the Righteous* (New York: Augustus Kelley).

Backhouse, Roger E. and Medema, Stephen G. (2009) "Defining Economics: The Long Road to Acceptance of the Robbins Definition," *Economica*, **76**, October, pp. 805–20.

Baden-Powell, Baden H. (1892) *The Land-Systems of British India*, vol. 1 (Oxford: Clarendon).

Bartley, Russell H., and Bartley, Sylvia Erickson (1999a) "In the Company of T.B. Veblen: A Narrative of Biographical Recovery," *International Journal of Politics, Culture and Society*, **13**, pp. 273–331.

——(1999b) "Revising the Biography of Thorstein Veblen," *International Journal of Politics, Culture, and Society*, **13**(2), December, pp. 363–74.

——(2000) "Stigmatizing Thorstein Veblen: A Study in the Confection of Academic Reputations," *International Journal of Politics, Culture and Society*, **14**, pp. 363–400.

——(2002) "The Formal Education of Thorstein Veblen: His Carleton Years, 1874–80," paper presented at the 4th International Thorstein Veblen Association Conference.

Becker, Gary S. (1992) "Habits, Addictions and Traditions," *Kyklos*, 45, Fasc. 3, pp. 327–46.

Becker, Gary S. and Murphy, Kevin M. (1988) "A Theory of Rational Addiction," *Journal of Political Economy*, **96**(4), pp. 675–700.

Bessey, Charles E. (1893) "Evolution and Classification," *Botanical Gazette*, **18**, pp. 329–33.

Bhaskar, Roy (1975) *A Realist Theory of Science* (Leeds: Leeds Books).

Black, J. William (1893) "Savagery and Survivals," *Popular Science Monthly*, **43**, pp. 388–401.

Blair, Margaret M. (1999) "Firm-Specific Human Capital and Theories of the Firm," in Margaret M. Blair and Mark Roe (eds) (1999) *Employees and Corporate Governance* (Washington, DC: Brookings), pp. 58–89.

——(2003) "Locking in Capital: What Corporate Law Achieved for Business Organizers in the Nineteenth Century," *UCLA Law Review*, **51**(2), pp. 387–455.

Boettke, Peter J. (1989) "Evolution and Economics: Austrians as Institutionalists," *Research in the History of Economic Thought and Methodology*, **6**, pp. 73–89.

Böhm-Bawerk, Eugen von (1891) *The Positive Theory of Capital*, trans. William Smart (New York: Macmillan).

Bowles, Samuel (2004) *Microeconomics: Behavior, Institutions, and Evolution* (Princeton, NJ and New York: Princeton University Press and Russell Sage Foundation).

Boyd, Robert and Richerson, Peter J. (1985) *Culture and the Evolutionary Process* (Chicago: University of Chicago Press).

Breit, William (1967) "The Wages Fund Controversy Revisited," *Canadian Journal of Economics and Political Science*, **33**, pp. 509–28.

Broda, Philippe (1998) "Commons versus Veblen on the Place of the Individual in the Social Process," in Malcolm H. Rutherford (ed.) (1998) *The Economic Mind in America: Essays in the History of American Economics* (London and New York: Routledge), pp. 210–30.

Bromley, Daniel W. (2006) *Sufficient Reason: Volitional Pragmatism and the Meaning of Economic Institutions* (Princeton: Princeton University Press).

Bunge, Mario A. (1959) *Causality: The Place of the Causal Principle in Modern Science* (Cambridge, MA: Harvard University Press).

——(1980) *The Mind-Body Problem: A Psychobiological Approach* (Oxford: Pergamon).

Burks, Arthur W. (1996) "Peirce's Evolutionary Pragmatic Idealism," *Synthese*, **106**, pp. 232–72.

Burt, Cyril (1962) "The Concept of Consciousness," *British Journal of Psychology*, **53**, pp. 229–42.

Button, Graham (ed.) (1993) *Technology in Working Order: Studies of Work, Interaction and Technology* (London annd New York: Routledge).

Caird, Edward (1880) Review of *On the Philosophy of Kant*, by Robert Adamson, *Mind*, **5**, pp. 124–30.

Caldwell, Bruce J. (1982) *Beyond Positivism: Economic Methodology in the Twentieth Century* (London: Allen and Unwin).

Calvin, William H. (2002) *A Brain for All Seasons: Human Evolution and Abrupt Climate Change* (Chicago: University of Chicago Press).

Camic, Charles (1986) "The Matter of Habit," *American Journal of Sociology*, **91**(5), March, pp. 1039–87.

——(2011) "Schooling for Heterodoxy," in Erik S. Reinert and Francesca Lidia Viano (eds), *Thorstein Veblen: Transatlantic Social Scientist* (London: Anthem).

Cannan, Edwin (1888) *Elementary Political Economy* (Oxford: Oxford University Press).

Cashman, Sean Dennis (1993) *America in the Gilded Age: From the Death of Lincoln to the Rise of Theodore Roosevelt*, 3rd edn (New York: New York University Press).

Cavalli-Sforza, Luigi L. (2000) *Genes, People and Languages* (Berkeley: University of California Press).

Chomsky, Noam (1959) "Review of *Verbal Behavior* by B. F. Skinner," *Language*, **35**, pp. 26–58.

Clark, John Maurice (1925) "Problems of Economic Theory – Discussion," *American Economic Review (Papers and Proceedings)*, **15**(1), Supplement, March, pp. 56–58.

Coase, Ronald H. (1937) "The Nature of the Firm," *Economica*, **4**, New Series, November, pp. 386–405.

Cohn, Gustav (1889) *System der Nationalökonomie*, vol. 2, *System der Finanzwissenschaft* (Stuttgart: Ferdinand Encke Verlag).

Coleman, James S. (1988) "Social Capital in the Creation of Human Capital," *American Journal of Sociology*, **94**(supplement), pp. S95–S120.

Collard, David (1978) *Altruism and Economy: A Study in Non-Selfish Economics* (Oxford: Martin Robertson).

Collins, Harry and Kusch, Martin (eds) (1998) *The Shape of Actions – What Humans and Machines Can Do* (Cambridge, MA: MIT Press).

Commons, John R. (1924) *Legal Foundations of Capitalism* (New York: Macmillan).

——(1934) *Institutional Economics – Its Place in Political Economy* (New York: Macmillan).

Comte, Auguste (1853) *The Positive Philosophy of Auguste Comte*, 2 vols, translated by Harriet Martineau from the French volumes of 1830–42 (London: Chapman).

Cooley, Charles Horton (1902) *Human Nature and the Social Order*, 1st edn (New York: Scribner's).

Copeland, Morris A. (1931) "Economic Theory and the Natural Science Point of View." *American Economic Review*, **21**(1), March, pp. 67–79.

Cosmides, Leda and Tooby, John (1994) "Better than Rational: Evolutionary Psychology and the Invisible Hand," *American Economic Review (Papers and Proceedings)*, **84**(2), May, pp. 327–32.

Coulter, John M. (1891) "The Future of Systematic Botany," *Botanical Gazette*, **16**, pp. 243–54.

Cronon, William (1991) *Nature's Metropolis: Chicago and the Great West* (New York: W. W. Norton).

Cummings, John (1899) Review of "The Theory of the Leisure Class," *Journal of Political Economy*, **7**(4), September, pp. 425–55.

Darwin, Charles R. (1871) *The Descent of Man, and Selection in Relation to Sex*, 1st edn, 2 vols (London: Murray and New York: Hill).

Daugert, Stanley Matthew (1950) *The Philosophy of Thorstein Veblen* (New York: Columbia University Press).

Dawkins, Richard (1976) *The Selfish Gene* (Oxford: Oxford University Press).

Dawson, Hugh J. (1993) "E. B. Tylor's Theory of Survivals and Veblen's Social Criticism." *Journal of the History of Ideas*, **54**, pp. 489–504.

De Vries, Hugo (1901) *Die Mutationstheorie: Versuche und Beobachtungen über die Entstehung der Arten im Pflanzenreich*, 2 vols (Leipzig: Von Veit).

——(1909) *The Mutation Theory: Experiments and Observations on the Origin of Species in the Vegetable Kingdom*, trans. J. B. Farmer and A. D. Darbishire from the German edition of 1901, 2 vols (Chicago: Open Court).

Degler, Carl N. (1991) *In Search of Human Nature: The Decline and Revival of Darwinism in American Social Thought* (Oxford and New York: Oxford University Press).

Dewey, John (1884) "Kant and Philosophic Method." *Journal of Speculative Philosophy*, **18**, pp. 162–74.

——(1894) "Social Psychology." *Psychological Review*, **1**, pp. 400–410.

——(1896) "The Reflex Arc Concept in Psychology." *Psychological Review*, **3**, pp. 357–70.

——(1910) *The Influence of Darwin on Philosophy and Other Essays in Contemporary Philosophy* (New York: Holt).

——(1922) *Human Nature and Conduct: An Introduction to Social Psychology*, 1st edn (New York: Holt).

Dorfman, Joseph ([1934]1972) *Thorstein Veblen and His America* (New York: Viking Press).

Dosi, Giovanni (1988) "The Sources, Procedures, and Microeconomic Effects of Innovation," *Journal of Economic Literature*, **26**(3), September, pp. 1120–71.

Dugger, William M. and Sherman, Howard J. (1994) "Comparison of Marxism and Institutionalism," *Journal of Economic Issues*, **28**(1), March, pp. 101–27.

Dunbar, Robin I. M. (2004) *The Human Story* (London: Faber and Faber).

Dunning, A. (1891) Review of *A Plea for Liberty: An Argument against Socialism and Socialistic Legislation*, edited by Thomas Mackay, *Political Science Quarterly*, **6**, pp. 581–83.

Durham, William H. (1991) *Coevolution: Genes, Culture, and Human Diversity* (Stanford: Stanford University Press).

Durkheim, Émile (1984) *The Division of Labour in Society*, translated from the French edition of 1893 by W. D. Halls with an introduction by Lewis Coser (London: Macmillan).

Eaton, B. Curtis (1984) Review of *An Evolutionary Theory of Economic Change* by R. R. Nelson and S. G. Winter, *Canadian Journal of Economics*, **17**(4), November, pp. 868–71.

Eby, Clare Virginia (1999) "The Two Mrs. Veblens, among Others," *International Journal of Politics, Culture and Society*, **13**, pp. 353–61.

——(2001) "Boundaries Lost: Thorstein Veblen, *The Higher Learning in America*, and the Conspicuous Spouse," *Prospects: An Annual of American Cultural Studies*, **26**, pp. 251–93.

Edgell, Stephen (2001) *Veblen in Perspective: His Life and Thought* (Armonk, NY: M. E. Sharpe).

Elbaum, Bernard and Lazonick, William (eds) (1986) *The Decline of the British Economy* (Oxford: Oxford University Press).

Etzioni, Amitai (1988) *The Moral Dimension: Toward a New Economics* (New York: Free Press).

Fayazmanesh, Sasan (1998) 'On Veblen's Coining of the Term "Neoclassical"', in Sasan Fayazmanesh and Marc R. Tool (eds) (1998) *Institutionalist Method and Value: Essays in Honour of Paul Dale Bush*, vol. 1 (Cheltenham: Edward Elgar), pp. 74–97.

Fetter, Frank A. (1930) "Capital," in Edwin R. A. Seligman and Alvin Johnson (eds) *Encyclopaedia of the Social Sciences* (New York: Macmillan), vol. 3, pp. 187–90.

Fisher, Irving (1906) *The Nature of Capital and Income* (New York: Macmillan).

——(1908) *The Rate of Interest: Its Nature, Determination and Relation to Economic Phenomena* (New York: Macmillan).

Forster, Paul (1997) "Kant, Boole and Peirce's Early Metaphysics," *Synthese*, **113**, pp. 43–70.

Friedman, Milton (1953) "The Methodology of Positive Economics," in Milton Friedman, *Essays in Positive Economics* (Chicago: University of Chicago Press), pp. 3–43.

George, Henry (1879) *Progress and Poverty: An Inquiry Into the Cause of Industrial Depression and Increase of Want with Increase of Wealth* (London: Kegan Paul).

Gindis, David (2007) "Some Building Blocks for a Theory of the Firm as a Real Entity," in Yuri Biondi, Arnaldo Canziani and Thierry Kirat (eds) *The Firm as an Entity: Implications for Economics, Accounting and Law* (London and New York: Routledge), pp. 266–91.

——(2009) "From Fictions and Aggregates to Real Entities in the Theory of the Firm," *Journal of Institutional Economics*, **5**(1), April, pp. 25–46.

Gramsci, Antonio (1971) *Selections from the Prison Notebooks* (London: Lawrence and Wishart).

Grimmer-Solem, Erik (2003) *The Rise of Historical Economics and Social Reform in Germany, 1864–1894* (Oxford: Clarendon).

Hahn, Frank H. (1988) "On Monetary Theory." *Economic Journal*, **98**(4), December, pp. 957–73.

Hands, D. Wade (2001) *Reflection Without Rules: Economic Methodology and Contemporary Science Theory* (Cambridge and New York: Cambridge University Press).

Hansmann, Henry, Reinier Kraakman and Richard Squire (2006) "Law and the Rise of the Firm," *Harvard Law Review*, **119**(5), March, pp. 1333–1403.

Harcourt, Geoffrey C. (1972) *Some Cambridge Controversies in the Theory of Capital* (Cambridge: Cambridge University Press).

Harré, Rom and Madden, Edward H. (1975) *Causal Powers: A Theory of Natural Necessity* (Oxford: Basil Blackwell).

Harris, Abram L. (1932) "Types of Institutionalism." *Journal of Political Economy*, **40**(4), December, pp. 721–49.

Hayek, Friedrich A. (1948) *Individualism and Economic Order* (London and Chicago: George Routledge and University of Chicago Press).

——(1988) *The Fatal Conceit: The Errors of Socialism. The Collected Works of Friedrich August Hayek, Vol. I*, ed. William W. Bartley III (London: Routledge).

Haynes, John-Dylan and Rees, Geraint (2005a) "Predicting the Orientation of Invisible Stimuli from Activity in Human Primary Visual Cortex," *Nature Neuroscience*, **8**(5), May, pp. 686–91.

——(2005b) "Predicting the Stream of Consciousness from Activity in Human Visual Cortex." *Current Biology*, **15**(14), pp. 1301–7.

Haynes, John-Dylan, K. Sakai, G. Rees, S. Gilbert, C. Frith, R. Passingham (2007) "Reading Hidden Intentions in the Human Brain," *Current Biology*, **17**(4), pp. 323–28.

Hillemann, Eric (2004) "Thorstein Veblen and Carleton College, and Vice Versa," paper presented at the 5th International Thorstein Veblen Association Conference.

Hindess, Barry (1989) *Political Choice and Social Structure: An Analysis of Actors, Interests and Rationality* (Aldershot: Edward Elgar).

Hobson, John A. (1896) *The Problem of the Unemployed* (London: Methuen).
——(1902) *The Social Problem: Life and Work* (London: James Nisbet).
——(1914) *Work and Wealth: A Human Valuation* (London: Macmillan).
——(1929) *Wealth and Life: A Study in Values* (London: Macmillan).
Hodgson, Geoffrey M. (2001) *How Economics Forgot History: The Problem of Historical Specificity in Social Science* (London and New York: Routledge).
——(2003) "John R. Commons and the Foundations of Institutional Economics." *Journal of Economic Issues*, **37**(3), September, pp. 547–76.
——(2004) *The Evolution of Institutional Economics: Agency, Structure and Darwinism in American Institutionalism* (London and New York: Routledge).
——(2005) "Alfred Marshall versus the Historical School?" *Journal of Economic Studies*, **32**(4), 2005, pp. 331–48.
——(2007) "Meanings of Methodological Individualism," *Journal of Economic Methodology*, **14**(2), June, pp. 211–26.
——(2008) Editorial introduction to "Capital" by Frank A. Fetter, *Journal of Institutional Economics*, **4**(1), April 2008, pp. 127–37.
Hodgson, Geoffrey M. and Knudsen, Thorbjørn (2006) "Why We Need a Generalized Darwinism: and Why a Generalized Darwinism is Not Enough," *Journal of Economic Behavior and Organization*, **61**(1), September, pp. 1–19.
——(2010) *Darwin's Conjecture: The Search for General Principles of Social and Economic Evolution* (Chicago: University of Chicago Press).
Hofstadter, Richard (1944) *Social Darwinism in American Thought* (Boston: Beacon).
Horwitz, Steven (1992) *Monetary Evolution, Free Banking, and Economic Order* (Boulder, CO: Westview Press).
Hull, David L. (1988) *Science as a Process: An Evolutionary Account of the Social and Conceptual Development of Science* (Chicago: University of Chicago Press).
Hutchison, Terence W. (1953) *A Review of Economic Doctrines: 1870–1929* (Oxford: Oxford University Press).
Ingram, John Kells (1888) *A History of Political Economy* (New York: Macmillan).
Jaffé, William (1976) "Menger, Jevons and Walras De-Homogenized," *Economic Inquiry*, **14**(1), January, pp. 511–24.
James, William (1890) *The Principles of Psychology*, 2 vols (New York and London: Holt and Macmillan).
Joas, Hans (1993) *Pragmatism and Social Theory* (Chicago: University of Chicago Press).
——(1996) *The Creativity of Action* (Chicago: University of Chicago Press).
Johns Hopkins University Circular (1881–82).
Jones, Lamar B. (1986) "The Institutionalists and 'On the Origin of Species': A Case of Mistaken Identity," *Southern Economic Journal*, **52**(4), April, pp. 1043–55.
——(1995) "C. E. Ayres's Reliance on T. H. Huxley: Did Darwin's Bulldog Bite?" *American Journal of Economics and Sociology*, 54(4), October, pp. 413–20.
Joranger, Terje Mikael Hasle (2007) "Valdres to the Upper Midwest: The Norwegian Background of the Veblen Family and their Migration to the United States," paper presented at Conference on Thorstein Bunde Veblen (1857–1929): Transatlantic Social Scientist.
Jorgensen, Elizabeth W. and Jorgensen, Henry I. (1999) *Thorstein Veblen: Victorian Firebrand* (Armonk, NY: M. E. Sharpe).
Kant, Immanuel (1781) *Kritik der reinen Vernunft* (Riga: J. F. Hartknoch).
——(1788) *Kritik der praktischenVernunft* (Riga: J. F. Hartknoch).
——(1790) *Kritik der Urteilskraft* (Riga: J. F. Hartknoch).

Kallen, Horace M (1930) "Behaviorism," in Edwin R. A. Seligman and Alvin Johnson (eds) *Encyclopaedia of the Social Sciences* (New York: Macmillan), vol. 2, pp. 495–98.

Kerr, Charles H. (1904) "Translator Preface," in Labriola, Antonio, *Essays on the Materialistic Conception of History* (Chicago: Charles H. Kerr & Co.), pp. 3–4.

Keynes, John Maynard (1936) *The General Theory of Employment, Interest and Money* (London: Macmillan).

Khalil, Elias L. (1995) "The Socioculturalist Agenda in Economics: Critical Remarks on Thorstein Veblen's Legacy." *Journal of Socio-Economics*, **24**(4), Winter, pp. 545–69.

Kilpinen, Erkki (1998) "The Pragmatic Foundations of the Institutionalist Method: Veblen's Preconceptions and their Relation to Peirce and Dewey." in Sasan Fayazmanesh and Marc R. Tool (eds) *Institutionalist Method and Value: Essays in Honour of Paul Dale Bush, Volume 1* (Cheltenham: Edward Elgar), pp. 23–47.

——(1999) "What is Rationality? A New Reading of Veblen's Critique of Utilitarian Hedonism," *International Journal of Politics, Culture and Society*, **13**(2), pp. 187–206.

——(2000) *The Enormous Fly-Wheel of Society: Pragmatism's Habitual Conception of Action and Social Theory* (Helsinki: University of Helsinki).

Kitcher, Philip (1993) *The Advancement of Science: Science without Legend, Objectivity without Illusions* (Oxford and New York: Oxford University Press).

Klein, Richard G. (2009) *The Human Career: Human Biological and Cultural Origins*, 3rd edn (Chicago: University of Chicago Press).

Knoedler, Janet T. and Mayhew, Anne (1999) "Thorstein Veblen and the Engineers: A Reinterpretation," *History of Political Economy*, **31**(2), Summer, pp. 213–36.

Kolakowski, Leszek (1978) *Main Currents of Marxism*; vol. 2, *The Golden Age*, translated by P. S. Falla (Oxford: Oxford University Press).

Koot, Gerald M. (1987) *English Historical Economics, 1870–1926: The Rise of Economic History and Neomercantilism* (Cambridge: Cambridge University Press).

Kuhn, Thomas S. (1970) *The Structure of Scientific Revolutions*, 2nd edn (Chicago: University of Chicago Press).

Kuklick, Bruce (2001) *A History of Philosophy in America, 1720–2000* (Oxford: Clarendon).

Lassalle, Ferdinand   ([1863] 1900) *Science and the Workingmen*, ed. Eduard Bernstein, trans. Thorstein Veblen (New York: International Publishing Library).

Lawson, Tony (2003) *Reorienting Economics* (London and New York: Routledge).

Layton, Edwin (1962) "Veblen and the Engineers," *American Quarterly*, **14**(1), Spring, pp. 64–72.

Lenzer, Gertrud (ed.) (1998) *Auguste Comte and Positivism* (New Brunswick, NJ: Transaction).

Larson, Jonathan (1995) "A Restoration of Significance," *Journal of Economic Issues*, **29**, pp. 910–15.

Laughlin, J. Laurence (1894) "Economic Effects of Changes in Fashion," *The Chautauquan*, **19**, April, pp. 9–13.

——(1916) *Twenty-five Years of the Department of Political Economy, University of Chicago* (Chicago: privately printed).

Libet, Benjamin (1985) "Unconscious Cerebral Initiative and the Role of Conscious Will in Voluntary Action," *Behavioral and Brain Sciences*, **8**, pp. 529–66.

——(2004) *Mind Time: The Temporal Factor in Consciousness* (Cambridge, MA: Harvard University Press).

Libet, Benjamin, Gleason, Curtis A., Wright, Elwood W., and Pearl, Dennis K (1983) "Time of Conscious Intention to act in Relation to Onset of Cerebral Activity (Readiness-Potential): The Unconscious Initiation of a Freely Voluntary Act," *Brain*, **106**(3), pp. 623–42.

Lluch, C (1974) "Expenditures, Savings and Habit Formation," *International Economic Review*, **15**, pp. 786–97.

Lorenz, Max (1896) *Die Marxistische Socialdemokratie* (Leipzig: George M. Wigand).

Mackay, Thomas (ed.) (1891) *A Plea for Liberty: An Argument against Socialism and Socialistic Legislation* (New York: Appleton).

Mallock, W. H. (1898) *Aristocracy and Evolution: A Study of the Rights, the Origins, and the Social Functions of the Wealthier Classes* (London: Macmillan).

Margolis, Howard (1987) *Patterns, Thinking and Cognition: A Theory of Judgment* (Chicago: University of Chicago Press).

——(1994) *Paradigms and Barriers: How Habits of Mind Govern Scientific Beliefs* (Chicago: University of Chicago Press).

Marsden, Paul (2000) "Forefathers of Memetics: Gabriel Tarde and the Laws of Imitation," *Journal of Memetics – Evolutionary Models of Information Transmission*, 4, www.cpm.mmu.ac.uk/jom-emit/2000/vol4/marsden_p.html.

Marshall, Alfred (1890) *Principles of Economics: An Introductory Volume*, 1st edn (London: Macmillan).

Marx, Karl (1894) *Das Kapital: Kritik der politischen Ökonomie: Der Gesammtprocess de kapitalistischen Produktion*, vol. 3 (Hamburg: Meissner).

Mason, John W. (1980), "Political Economy and the Response to Socialism in Britain, 1870–1914," *The Historical Journal*, **23**, pp. 565–87.

McCormick, Richard L. (1997) "Public Life in Industrial America, 1877–1917," in Eric Foner (ed.) (1997) *The New American History*, rev. edn (Philadelphia: University of Pennsylvania Press), pp. 107–32.

Means, Gardiner C. (1931) "The Separation of Ownership and Control in American Industry," *Quarterly Journal of Economics*, **46**(1), December, pp. 68–100.

Melton, William C. (2004) "The Veblens in Wisconsin: A Progress Report" (Melton Research Inc.).

Menger, Carl (1883) *Untersuchungen über die Methode der Sozialwissenschaften und der politischen Ökonomie insbesondere* (Tübingen: J. C. B. Mohr). Published in English as Menger, Carl (1985) *Investigations into the Method of the Social Sciences with Special Reference to Economics*, translated by F. J. Nock from the German edition of 1883 with an 1963 introduction by Louis Schneider and a 1985 introduction by Lawrence H. White (New York: New York University Press).

Mill, John Stuart (1848) *Principles of Political Economy, With Some of Their Applications to Social Philosophy* (London: Parker).

——(1871) *Principles of Political Economy with Some of Their Applications to Social Philosophy*, 7th edn (London: Longman, Green, Reader and Dyer).

Miller, Donald L. (1996) *City of the Century: The Epic of Chicago and the Making of America* (New York: Simon & Schuster).

Mitchell, Wesley C. (1914) "Human Behavior and Economics: A Survey of Recent Literature," *Quarterly Journal of Economics*, **29**(1), November, pp. 1–47.

——(1969) *Types of Economic Theory: From Mercantilism to Institutionalism*, 2 vols, ed. J. Dorfman (New York: Augustus Kelley).

——(ed.) (1936) *What Veblen Taught* (New York: Viking).

Morgan, Lewis Henry (1877) *Ancient Society, or Researches in the Lines of Human Progress from Savagery through Barbarism to Civilization* (New York: Holt).

Morris, George S. (1882) *Kant's Critique of Pure Reason* (Chicago: Griggs).

Murphy, James Bernard (1994) "The Kinds of Order in Society," in Philip Mirowski (ed.) (1994) *Natural Images in Economic Thought: "Markets Read in Tooth and Claw"* (Cambridge and New York: Cambridge University Press), pp. 536–82.

Nelson, Richard R. and Winter, Sidney G. (1982) *An Evolutionary Theory of Economic Change* (Cambridge, MA: Harvard University Press).

O'Donnell, John M. (1985) *The Origins of Behaviorism: American Psychology, 1870–1920* (New York: New York University Press).

O'Hara, Phillip Anthony (2000) *Marx, Veblen, and Contemporary Institutional Political Economy: Principles and Unstable Dynamics of Capitalism* (Cheltenham: Edward Elgar).

Olson, Mancur, Jr. (1982) *The Rise and Decline of Nations* (New Haven: Yale University Press).

Oppenheimer, Stephen (2004) *The Real Eve* (New York: Carroll and Graf). Published in the UK as *Out of Eden* (London: Constable and Robinson).

Ouellette, Judith A. and Wood, Wendy (1998) "Habit and Intention in Everyday Life: The Multiple Processes by which Past Behavior Predicts Future Behavior," *Psychological Bulletin*, **124**, pp. 54–74.

Painter, Nell Irvin (2008) *Standing at Armageddon: A Grassroots History of the Progressive Era* (New York: W. W. Norton).

Palgrave, R. H. Inglis (ed.) (1894–99) *Dictionary of Political Economy*, 3 vols (London: Macmillan).

Papke, David Ray (1999) *The Pullman Case: The Clash of Labor and Capital in Industrial America* (Lawrence: University of Kansas Press).

Pearl, Judea (2000) *Causality: Models, Reasoning, and Inference* (Cambridge and New York: Cambridge University Press).

Pearson, Heath (2000) "*Homo Economicus* Goes Native, 1859–1945," *History of Political Economy*, **32**, pp. 933–90.

Peirce, Charles Sanders (1878) "How to Make Our Ideas Clear," *Popular Science Monthly*, **12**, January, pp. 286–302.

Philips, Louis and Spinnewyn, F. (1984) "True Indexes and Rational Habit Formation," *European Economic Review*, **24**, pp. 209–23.

Plotkin, Henry C. (1994) *Darwin Machines and the Nature of Knowledge: Concerning Adaptations, Instinct and the Evolution of Intelligence* (Harmondsworth: Penguin).

——(1997) *Evolution in Mind: An Introduction to Evolutionary Psychology* (Harmondsworth: Penguin).

Popper, Karl R. (1972) *The Logic of Scientific Discovery*, 3rd edn, translated and revised from the German edition of 1935 (London: Hutchinson).

——(1990) *A World of Propensities* (Bristol: Thoemmes).

Porter, Noah (1882) *Science and Sentiment* (New York: Scribner's).

——(1886) *Kant's Ethics* (Chicago: Griggs).

Potts, Richard (1996) *Humanity's Descent: The Consequences of Ecological Instability* (New York: William Morrow).

Powell, John Wesley (1888) "From Barbarism to Civilization," *American Anthropologist*, **1**, pp. 97–123.

——(1901) "Sophiology, or the Science of Activities Designed to Give Instruction," *American Anthropologist*, **3**(1), January-March, pp. 51–79.

Putnam, Robert D. (1995) "Tuning In, Tuning Out: The Strange Disappearance of Social Capital in America." *PS: Political Science and Politics*, **28**(4), pp. 664–83.

——(2000) *Bowling Alone: The Collapse and Revival of American Community* (New York: Simon and Schuster).

Quine, Willard van Orman (1953) *From a Logical Point of View* (Cambridge, MA: Harvard University Press).

Raines, J. Patrick and Leathers, Charles G. (1996) "Veblenian Stock Markets and the Efficient Markets Hypothesis," *Journal of Post Keynesian Economics*, **19**(1), Fall, pp. 137–51.

Richerson, Peter J. and Boyd, Robert (2004) *Not by Genes Alone: How Culture Transformed Human Evolution* (Chicago: University of Chicago Press).

Richerson, Peter J., Boyd, Robert and Bettinger, Robert L. (2001) "Was Agriculture Impossible During the Pleistocene But Mandatory During the Holocene? A Climate Change Hypothesis," *American Antiquity*, **66**, pp. 387–411.

Robbins, Lionel (1932) *An Essay on the Nature and Significance of Economic Science*, 1st edn (London: Macmillan).

Robinson, Joan (1953) "The Production Function and the Theory of Capital," *Review of Economic Studies*, **21**(1), pp. 81–106.

——(1975) *Collected Economic Papers – Volume Three*, 2nd edn (Oxford: Basil Blackwell).

——(1979) *Collected Economic Papers – Volume Five* (Oxford: Basil Blackwell).

Rodgers, Daniel T. (1998) *Atlantic Crossings: Social Politics in a Progressive Age* (Cambridge, MA: Harvard University Press).

Roscher, Wilhelm (1843) *Grundriss zu Vorlesungen über die Staatswirtschaft nach geschichtlicher Methode* (Göttingen).

Rosenberg, Nathan and Vincenti, Walter (1985) *The Britannia Bridge, the Generation and Diffusion of Technological Knowledge* (Cambridge, MA: MIT Press).

Ross, Edward Alsworth (1903) "Recent Tendencies in Sociology III," *Quarterly Journal of Economics*, **17**(3), May, pp. 438–55.

Royce, Josiah (1969) *The Basic Writings of Josiah Royce*, 2 vols, edited with an introduction by J. J. McDermott (Chicago: University of Chicago Press).

Runde, Jochen H. (1998) "Clarifying Frank Knight's Discussion of the Meaning of Risk and Uncertainty," *Cambridge Journal of Economics,* **22**(5), September, pp. 539–46.

Rutherford, Malcolm H. (1984) "Thorstein Veblen and the Processes of Institutional Change," *History of Political Economy*, **16**(3), Fall, pp. 331–48.

——(1992) "Thorstein Veblen and the Problem of the Engineers," *International Review of Sociology*, **3**, pp. 125–50.

Salmon, Wesley C. (1998) *Causality and Explanation* (Oxford: Oxford University Press).

Samuels, Warren J. (1989) "Austrian and Institutional Economics: Some Common Elements," *Research in the History of Economic Thought and Methodology*, **6**, pp. 53–71.

Samuels, Warren J., Biddle, Jeff E., and Davis, John B. (eds) (2003) *A Companion to the History of Economic Thought* (Malden, MA: Blackwell).

Samuelson, Paul A. (1948) *Economics*, 1st edn (New York: McGraw-Hill).

Sanderson, Stephen K. (1990) *Social Evolutionism: A Critical History* (Oxford: Basil Blackwell).

Schumpeter, Joseph A. (1934) *The Theory of Economic Development: An Inquiry into Profits, Capital, Credit, Interest, and the Business Cycle*, translated by Redvers Opie from the second German edition of 1926 (Cambridge, MA: Harvard University Press).

Searle, John R. (1995) *The Construction of Social Reality* (London: Allen Lane).

——(1997) *The Mystery of Consciousness* (London: Granta Books).

Sen, Amartya K. (1987) *On Ethics and Economics* (Oxford and New York: Basil Blackwell).

Simon, Herbert A. (1957) *Models of Man: Social and Rational. Mathematical Essays on Rational Human Behavior in a Social Setting* (New York: Wiley).

Sklansky, Jeffrey (2002) *The Soul's Economy: Market Society and Selfhood in America Thought, 1820–1920* (Chapel Hill: University of North Carolina Press).

Smith, Adam (1776) *An Inquiry into the Nature and Causes of the Wealth of Nations*, 2 vols (London: Strahan and Cadell).

Spencer, Herbert (1851) *Social Statics* (London: Chapman).

Sraffa, Piero (1960) *Production of Commodities by Means of Commodities: Prelude to a Critique of Economic Theory* (Cambridge: Cambridge University Press).

Star, Susan Leigh (ed.) (1995) *Ecologies of Knowledge: Work and Politics in Science and Technology* (Albany State University of New York Press).

Starr, Frederick (1891a) "Dress and Adornment; I, Deformations," *Popular Science Monthly*, **39**, pp. 488–502.

——(1891b) "Dress and Adornment; II, Dress," *Popular Science Monthly*, **39**, pp. 787–801.

——(1891c) "Dress and Adornment; III, Ornament," *Popular Science Monthly*, **40**, pp. 44–57.

——(1891d) "Dress and Adornment; IV, Religious Dress," *Popular Science Monthly*, **40**, pp. 194–206.

——(1893) "Anthropology at the World's Fair," *Popular Science Monthly*, **43**, pp. 610–21.

Stocking, George W., Jr. (1968) *Race, Culture, and Evolution* (New York: Free Press).

——(1987) *Victorian Anthropology* (New York: Free Press).

Streissler, Erich W. (1972) "To What Extent was the Austrian School Marginalist?" *History of Political Economy*, **4**(2), Fall, pp. 426–41.

Suchman, Lucy (1987) *Plans and Situated Actions: The Problem of Human-Machine Communication* (Cambridge: Cambridge University Press).

Tarde, Gabriel (1890) *Les lois de l'imitation: étude sociologique* (Paris: Alcan).

——(1899) *Social Laws: An Outline of Sociology*, translated from the French edition of 1898 by Howard C. Warren, with a Preface by James M. Baldwin (New York: Macmillan).

——(1903) *The Laws of Imitation*, translated from the French edition of 1890 by E. C. Parsons with introduction by F. H. Giddings (New York: Henry Holt).

Taussig, Frank W. (1896) *Wages and Capital: An Examination of the Wages Fund Doctrine* (New York: Appleton).

Thomas, William I. (1896) "The Scope and Method of Folk-Psychology," *American Journal of Sociology*, **1**, pp. 434–45.

——(1897) "On a Difference in the Metabolism of the Sexes," *American Journal of Sociology*, **3**, pp. 31–63.

——(1898) "The Relations of Sex to Primitive Social Control," *American Journal of Sociology*, **3**, pp. 754–76.

——(1899a) "Sex in Primitive Industry," *American Journal of Sociology*, **4**, pp. 474–88.

——(1899b) "Sex in Primitive Morality," *American Journal of Sociology*, **4**, pp. 774–87.

——(1899c) "The Psychology of Modesty and Clothing," *American Journal of Sociology*, **5**, pp. 246–62.

——(1901) "The Gaming Instinct," *American Journal of Sociology*, **6**, pp. 750–63.

Tilman, Rick (1992) *Thorstein Veblen and His Critics, 1891–1963: Conservative, Liberal, and Radical Perspectives* (Princeton NJ: Princeton University Press).

——(1996) *The Intellectual Legacy of Thorstein Veblen: Unresolved Issues* (Westport, Connecticut: Greenwood Press).

Tugan-Baranowsky, Mikhail (1901) *Studien zur Theorie und Geschichte der Handelskrisen in England* (Jena: Fischer).

Tylor, Edward B. (1871) *Primitive Culture: Researches into the Development of Mythology, Philosophy, Religion, Language, Art, and Custom.* (New York: Putnam).

Udéhn, Lars (2001) *Methodological Individualism: Background, History and Meaning* (London and New York: Routledge).

University of Chicago Annual Register (1899).

Viano, Francesca Lidia (2009) "Ithaca Transfer: Veblen and the History Profession," *History of European Ideas*, **35**, pp. 38–61.

Vincenti, Walter (1990) *What Engineers Know and How They Know It: Analytical Studies from Aeronautical History* (Baltimore: Johns Hopkins University Press).

Vining, Rutledge (1939) "Suggestions of Keynes in the Writings of Veblen," *Journal of Political Economy*, **47**(5), October, pp. 692–704.

Waller, William J., Jr. (1982) "The Evolution of the Veblenian Dichotomy: Veblen, Hamilton, Ayres, and Foster," *Journal of Economic Issues*, **16**(3), September, pp. 757–71.

——(1994) "The Veblenian Dichotomy and its Critics," in Geoffrey M. Hodgson, Warren J. Samuels. and Marc R. Tool (eds) (1994) *The Elgar Companion to Institutional and Evolutionary Economics* (Aldershot: Edward Elgar), vol. 2, pp. 368–72.

Ward, Lester Frank (1883) *Dynamic Sociology, Or Applied Social Science, as Based Upon Statical Sociology and Less Complex Sciences*, 2 vols (New York: Appleton).

——(1893) *The Psychic Factors of Civilization*, (Boston: Ginn).

——(1900) Review of *The Theory of the Leisure Class* by Thorstein Veblen, *American Journal of Sociology*, **5**(6), May, pp. 829–37.

——(1903) *Pure Sociology: A Treatise on the Origin and Spontaneous Development of Society* (New York and London: Macmillan).

——(1906) *Applied Sociology* (Boston: Ginn).

Watson, John B. (1914) *Behavior: A Textbook of Comparative Psychology* (New York: Henry Holt).

Webb, James L. (2002) "Dewey: Back to the Future," *Journal of Economic Issues*, **36**(4), December, pp. 981–1003.

Wegner, Daniel M. (2002) *The Illusion of Conscious Will* (Cambridge, MA: MIT Press).

——(2003) "The Mind's Best Trick: How We Experience Conscious Will," *Trends in Cognitive Sciences*, **7**(2), February, pp. 65–69.

Wegner, Daniel M. and Wheatley, T. (1999) "Apparent Mental Causation: Sources of the Experience of the Will," *American Psychologist*, **54**, pp. 480–92.

Wells, Spencer (2002) *The Journey of Man: A Genetic Odyssey* (London: Allen Lane).

Williamson, Oliver E. (1975) *Markets and Hierarchies: Analysis and Anti-Trust Implications: A Study in the Economics of Internal Organization* (New York: Free Press).

Wood, Wendy and Neal, David T. (2007) "A New Look at Habits and the Habit-Goal Interface," *Psychological Review*, **114**(4), October, pp. 843–63.

Wood, Wendy, Quinn, Jeffrey M. and Kashy, D. (2002) "Habits in Everyday Life: Thought, Emotion, and Action," *Journal of Personality and Social Psychology*, **83**, pp. 1281–97.

Wood, Wendy, Tam, Leona and Witt, Melissa Guerrero (2005) Changing Circumstances, Disrupting Habits, *Journal of Personality and Social Psychology*, **88**(6), pp. 918–33.

Wynarczyk, Peter (1992) "Comparing Alleged Incommensurables: Institutional and Austrian Economics as Rivals and Possible Complements?" *Review of Political Economy*, **4**(1), January, pp. 18–36.

Index

For Product Safety Concerns and Information please contact our EU representative GPSR@taylorandfrancis.com Taylor & Francis Verlag GmbH, Kaufingerstraße 24, 80331 München, Germany

T - #0047 - 230425 - C0 - 234/156/34 - PB - 9780415718714 - Gloss Lamination